ACCA

PAPER P2

CORPORATE REPORTING
(UNITED KINGDOM)

In this new syllabus first edition approved by ACCA

- We **discuss** the **best strategies** for studying for ACCA exams

- We **highlight** the **most important elements** in the syllabus and the **key skills** you will need

- We **signpost** how each chapter links to the syllabus and the study guide

- We **provide** lots of **exam focus points** demonstrating what the examiner will want you to do

- We **emphasise key points** in regular **fast forward summaries**

- We **test your knowledge** of what you've studied in **quick quizzes**

- We **examine your understanding** in our **exam question bank**

- We **reference all the important topics** in our **full index**

BPP's **i-Learn** and **i-Pass** products also support this paper.

D1581221

FOR EXAMS IN DECEMBER 2007 AND JUNE 2008

BPP
LEARNING MEDIA

First edition June 2007

ISBN 9780 7517 3301 3

British Library Cataloguing-in-Publication Data
A catalogue record for this book
is available from the British Library

Published by

BPP Learning Media Ltd
BPP House, Aldine Place
London W12 8AA

www.bpp.com/learningmedia

Printed in Great Britain by
Page Bros
Mile Cross Lane
Norwich
NR6 6SA

Your learning materials, published by BPP Learning
Media Ltd, are printed on paper sourced from
sustainable, managed forests.

We are grateful to the Association of Chartered Certified
Accountants for permission to reproduce past
examination questions. The suggested solutions in the
exam answer bank have been prepared by BPP Learning
Media Ltd, unless where otherwise stated.

Contents

Part F Evaluating current developments

Review form and free prize draw

The BPP Learning Media Effective Study Package

Distance Learning from BPP Professional Education

You can access our exam-focussed interactive e-learning materials over the **Internet**, via BPP Learn Online, hosted by BPP Professional Education.

BPP Learn Online offers **comprehensive tutor support**, **revision guidance** and **exam tips**.

Visit www.bpp.com/acca/learnonline for further details.

Learning to Learn Accountancy

BPP's ground-breaking **Learning to Learn Accountancy** book is designed to be used both at the outset of your ACCA studies and throughout the process of learning accountancy. It challenges you to consider how you study and gives you helpful hints about how to approach the various types of paper which you will encounter. It can help you **focus your studies on the subject and exam**, enabling you to **acquire knowledge**, **practise and revise efficiently and effectively**.

How the BPP ACCA-approved Study Text can help you pass

How the BPP ACCA-approved Study Text can help you pass

Tackling studying

We know that studying for a number of exams can seem daunting, particularly when you have other commitments as well.

- We therefore provide guidance on **what you need to study efficiently and effectively** – to use the limited time you have in the best way possible

- We explain the **purposes** of the **different features** in the BPP Study Text, demonstrating how they help you and improve your chances of passing

Developing exam awareness

We never forget that you're aiming to pass your exams, and our Texts are completely focused on helping you do this.

- In the section **Studying P2** we introduce the key themes of the syllabus, describe the skills you need and summarise how to succeed

- The **Introduction** to each chapter of this Study Text sets the chapter in the context of the syllabus and exam

- We provide specific tips, **Exam focus points**, on what you can expect in the exam and what to do (and not to do!) when answering questions

And our Study Text is **comprehensive**. It covers the syllabus content. No more, no less.

Using the Syllabus and Study Guide

We set out the Syllabus and Study Guide in full.

- Reading the **introduction to the Syllabus** will show you what **capabilities** (skills) you'll have to demonstrate, and how this exam links with other papers.

- The topics listed in the **Syllabus** are the **key topics** in this exam. By quickly looking through the Syllabus, you can see the breadth of the paper. Reading the Syllabus will also highlight topics to look out for when you're reading newspapers or *student accountant* magazine.

- The **Study Guide** provides the **detail**, showing you precisely what you'll be studying. Don't worry if it seems a lot when you look through it; BPP's Study Text will carefully guide you through it all.

- Remember the Study Text shows, at the start of every chapter, which areas of the Syllabus and Study Guide are covered in the chapter.

Testing what you can do

Testing yourself helps you develop the skills you need to pass the exam and also confirms that you can recall what you have learnt.

- We include **Questions** within chapters, and the **Exam Question Bank** provides lots more practice.

- Our **Quick Quizzes** test whether you have enough knowledge of the contents of each chapter.

- Question practice is particularly important if English is not your first written language. ACCA offers an **International Certificate in Financial English** promoting language skills within the international business community.

BPP
LEARNING MEDIA

Example chapter

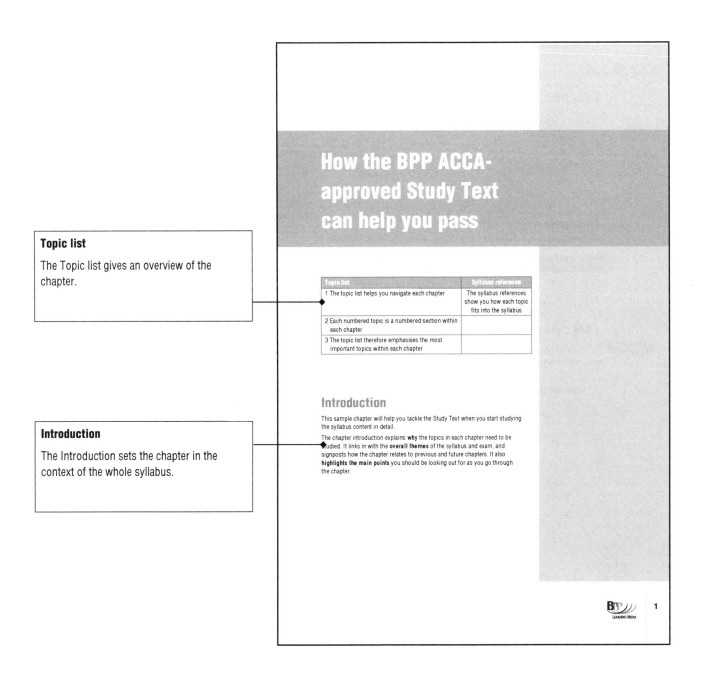

Topic list

The Topic list gives an overview of the chapter.

Introduction

The Introduction sets the chapter in the context of the whole syllabus.

How the BPP ACCA-approved Study Text can help you pass

Topic list	Syllabus reference
1 The topic list helps you navigate each chapter	The syllabus references show you how each topic fits into the syllabus
2 Each numbered topic is a numbered section within each chapter	
3 The topic list therefore emphasises the most important topics within each chapter	

Introduction

This sample chapter will help you tackle the Study Text when you start studying the syllabus content in detail.

The chapter introduction explains **why** the topics in each chapter need to be studied. It links in with the **overall themes** of the syllabus and exam, and signposts how the chapter relates to previous and future chapters. It also **highlights the main points** you should be looking out for as you go through the chapter.

BPP LEARNING MEDIA   1

Study guide

	Intellectual level
We list the topics in ACCA's Study guide that are covered in each chapter	The intellectual level indicates the depth in which the topics will be covered

Exam guide

The Exam guide highlights ways in which the main topics covered in each chapter may be examined.

Knowledge brought forward from earlier studies

Knowledge brought forward boxes summarise information and techniques that you are **assumed to know** from your earlier studies. As the exam may test your knowledge of these areas, you should **revise** your previous study material if you are unsure about them.

1 Key topic which has a section devoted to it

FAST FORWARD ▶▶ Fast forwards give you a **summary** of the content of each of the main chapter sections. They are listed together in the roundup at the end of each chapter to allow you to review each chapter quickly.

1.1 Important topic within section

The headings within chapters give you a good idea of the **importance** of the topics covered. The larger the header, the more important the topic is. The headers will help you navigate through the chapter and locate the areas that have been highlighted as important in the front pages or in the chapter introduction.

BPP LEARNING MEDIA

Study guide

The Study guide links with ACCA's own guidance.

Exam guide

The Exam guide describes the examinability of the chapter.

Knowledge brought forward

Knowledge brought forward shows you what you need to remember from previous exams.

Fast forward

Fast forwards allow you to preview and review each section easily.

Example

Examples show you how theory is put into practice.

Key term

Key terms are the core vocabulary.

Exam focus point

Exam focus points provide specific links to the exam.

Formula to learn

You must remember these formulae in the exam.

Question

Questions provide vital practice of what you've learnt.

Case Study

Case Studies link what you've learnt with the business environment.

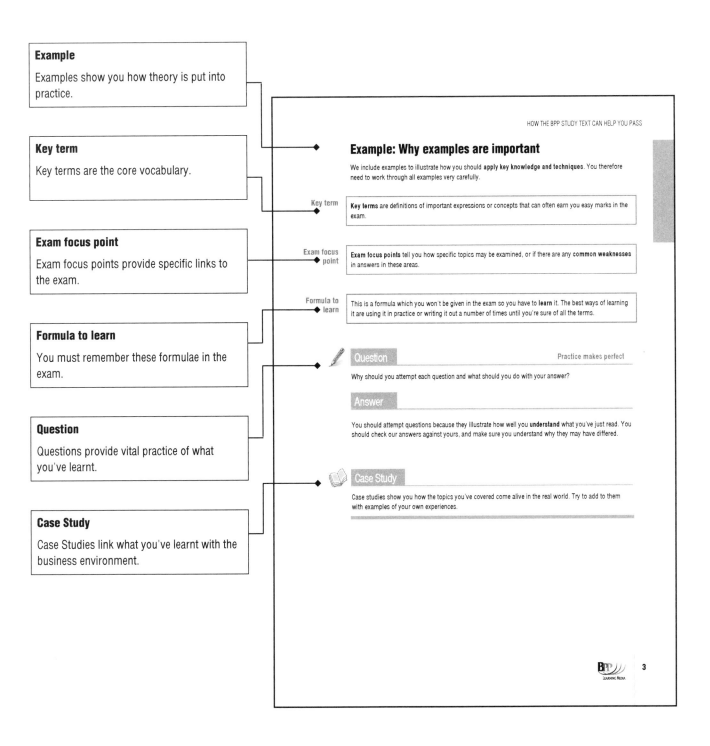

Example: Why examples are important

We include examples to illustrate how you should **apply key knowledge and techniques**. You therefore need to work through all examples very carefully.

Key term | **Key terms** are definitions of important expressions or concepts that can often earn you easy marks in the exam.

Exam focus point | **Exam focus points** tell you how specific topics may be examined, or if there are any **common weaknesses** in answers in these areas.

Formula to learn | This is a formula which you won't be given in the exam so you have to **learn** it. The best ways of learning it are using it in practice or writing it out a number of times until you're sure of all the terms.

Question — Practice makes perfect

Why should you attempt each question and what should you do with your answer?

Answer

You should attempt questions because they illustrate how well you **understand** what you've just read. You should check our answers against yours, and make sure you understand why they may have differed.

Case Study

Case studies show you how the topics you've covered come alive in the real world. Try to add to them with examples of your own experiences.

Chapter Roundup

- Fast forwards give you a **summary** of the content of each of the main chapter sections. They are listed together in the roundup at the end of each chapter to allow you to review each chapter quickly.

Quick Quiz

1   What are the main purposes of the Quick Quiz?

2   What should you do if you get Quick Quiz questions wrong?

    A   Nothing as you now know where you went wrong
    B   Note the correct answer and go on to the next chapter
    C   Practise full questions on this topic when you revise
    D   Go back and look through the topic again to ensure you know it

Answers to Quick Quiz

1   The main purposes of the Quick Quiz are to check how much you've remembered of the topics covered and to practise questions in a variety of formats.

2   D   Go back and look through the topic again to ensure that you know it.

Now try the questions below from the Exam Question Bank

Number	Level	Marks	Time
Questions that give you practice of what you've learnt in each chapter	Examination	25	45 mins

Chapter Roundup

The Chapter Roundup lists all the Fast forwards.

Quick Quiz

The Quick Quiz speedily tests your knowledge.

Exam Question Bank

Each chapter cross-references to further question practice.

4   BPP
LEARNING MEDIA

BPP
LEARNING MEDIA

Learning styles

BPP's guide to studying, *Learning to Learn Accountancy*, provides guidance on identifying how you learn and the variety of intelligencies that you have. We shall summarise some of the material in *Learning to Learn Accountancy*, as it will help you understand how to you are likely to approach the Study Text:

If you like	Then you might focus on	How the Study Text helps you
Word games, crosswords, poetry	Going through the detail in the Text	Chapter introductions, Fast forwards and Key terms help you determine the detail that's most significant
Number puzzles, Sudoku, Cluedo	Understanding the Text as a logical sequence of knowledge and ideas	Chapter introductions and headers help you follow the flow of material
Drawing, cartoons, films	Seeing how the ways material is presented show what it means and how important it is	The different features and the emphasis given by headers and emboldening help you see quickly what you have to know
Attending concerts, playing a musical instrument, dancing	Identifying patterns in the Text	The sequence of features within each chapter helps you understand what material is really crucial
Sport, craftwork, hands on experience	Learning practical skills such as preparing a set of accounts	Examples and question practice help you develop the practical skills you need

If you want to learn more about developing some or all of your intelligencies, *Learning to Learn Accountancy* shows you plenty of ways in which you can do so.

HOW THE BPP ACCA-APPROVED STUDY TEXT CAN HELP YOU PASS

Studying efficiently and effectively

What you need to study efficiently and effectively

Positive attitude

Yes there is a lot to learn. But look at the most recent ACCA pass list. See how many people have passed. They've made it; you can too. Focus on all the **benefits** that passing the exam will bring you.

Exam focus

Keep the exam firmly in your sights throughout your studies.

- Remember there's lots of **helpful guidance** about P2 in this first part of the Study Text.
- Look out for the **exam references** in the Study Text, particularly the types of question you'll be asked.

Organisation

Before you start studying you must organise yourself properly.

- We show you how to **timetable** your study so that you can ensure you have enough time to cover all of the syllabus – and revise it.
- Think carefully about the way you take **notes**. You needn't copy out too much, but if you can summarise key areas, that shows you understand them.
- Choose the notes **format** that's most helpful to you; lists, diagrams, mindmaps.
- Consider the **order** in which you tackle each chapter. If you prefer to get to grips with a theory before seeing how it's applied, you should read the explanations first. If you prefer to see how things work in practice, read the examples and questions first.

Active brain

There are various ways in which you can keep your brain active when studying and hence improve your **understanding** and **recall** of material.

- Keep asking yourself how the topic you're studying fits into the **whole picture** of this exam. If you're not sure, look back at the chapter introductions and Study Text front pages.
- Go carefully through every **example** and try every **question** in the Study Text and in the Exam Question Bank. You will be thinking deeply about the syllabus and increasing your understanding.

Review, review, review

Regularly reviewing the topics you've studied will help fix them in your memory. Your BPP Texts help you review in many ways.

- Important points are emphasised **in bold**.
- **Chapter Roundups** summarise the **Fast forward** key points in each chapter.
- **Quick Quizzes** test your grasp of the essentials.

BPP Passcards present summaries of topics in different visual formats to enhance your chances of remembering them.

Timetabling your studies

As your time is limited, it's vital that you calculate how much time you can allocate to each chapter. Following the approach below will help you do this.

Step 1   Calculate how much time you have

Work out the time you have available per week, given the following.

- The standard you have set yourself

- The time you need to set aside for work on the Practice & Revision Kit, Passcards, i-Learn and i-Pass

- The other exam(s) you are sitting

- Practical matters such as work, travel, exercise, sleep and social life

Hours

Note your time available in box A.   A ☐

Step 2   Allocate your time

- Take the time you have available per week for this Study Text shown in box A, multiply it by the number of weeks available and insert the result in box B.   B ☐

- Divide the figure in box B by the number of chapters in this Study Text and insert the result in box C.   C ☐

Remember that this is only a rough guide. Some of the chapters in this Study Text are longer and more complicated than others, and you will find some subjects easier to understand than others.

Step 3   Implement your plan

Set about studying each chapter in the time shown in box C. You'll find that once you've established a timetable, you're much more likely to study systematically.

Short of time: Skim study technique

You may find you simply do not have the time available to follow all the key study steps for each chapter, however you adapt them for your particular learning style. If this is the case, follow the **Skim study** technique below.

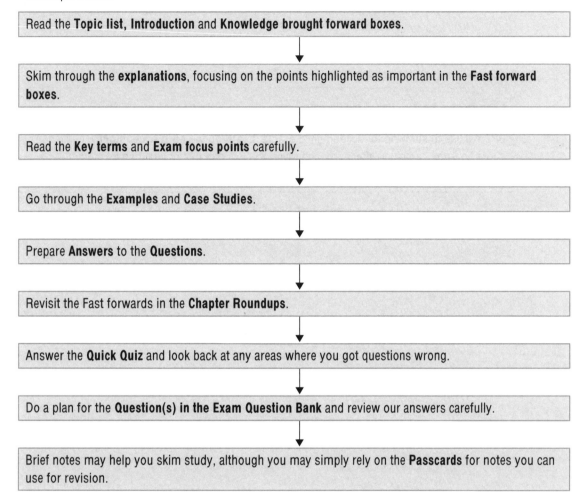

Read the **Topic list, Introduction** and **Knowledge brought forward boxes**.

Skim through the **explanations**, focusing on the points highlighted as important in the **Fast forward boxes**.

Read the **Key terms** and **Exam focus points** carefully.

Go through the **Examples** and **Case Studies**.

Prepare **Answers** to the **Questions**.

Revisit the Fast forwards in the **Chapter Roundups**.

Answer the **Quick Quiz** and look back at any areas where you got questions wrong.

Do a plan for the **Question(s) in the Exam Question Bank** and review our answers carefully.

Brief notes may help you skim study, although you may simply rely on the **Passcards** for notes you can use for revision.

Revision

When you are ready to start revising, you should still refer back to this Study Text.

- As a source of **reference** (you should find the index particularly helpful for this)

- As a way to **review** (the Fast forwards, Exam focus points, Chapter Roundups and Quick Quizzes help you here)

Remember to keep careful hold of this Study Text – you will find it invaluable in your work.

Learning to Learn Accountancy

BPP's guide to studying for accountancy exams, **Learning to Learn Accountancy**, challenges you to think about how you can study effectively and gives you lots and lots of vital tips on studying, revising and taking the exams.

Studying P2

Approaching P2

Approaching the paper

Paper P2 *Corporate Reporting* is a demanding paper, reflecting the demands that will be made upon the professional accountant in his or her working life. At the Fundamentals level, you will have studied the essentials of financial statement preparation and analysis, including those of group accounts. At the Professional level, these essentials will be assumed knowledge. You will be required to apply them, assuming the role of a professional adviser and analyst to the management as well as the shareholders and other stakeholders.

What is the paper about?

The P2 syllabus comprises eight main areas:

A   The professional and ethical duty of the accountant
B   The financial reporting framework
C   Reporting the financial performance of entities
D   Financial statements of groups of entities
E   Specialised entities
F   Implications of changes in accounting regulation on financial reporting
G   The appraisal of financial performance and position of entities
H   Current developments

There is, of course, some overlap between these areas. For example, if you are discussing current developments (H), you might be talking about the proposed changes to accounting for business combinations (D) and considering the implications of changes in accounting regulation (F) and perhaps even the ethical duty of the accountant to report those changes fairly and accurately (A).

What skills must you demonstrate?

At the Fundamentals level, or in your earlier studies, the questions would be more easily categorised into syllabus areas. However, at this level you may need to demonstrate knowledge, skills and thinking from outside the syllabus area that the question seems to be about on the surface. The examiner has stated:

> Students should be capable of relating professional issues to relevant concepts and practical situations. The evaluation of alternative accounting practices and the identification and prioritisation of issues will be a key element of the paper. Professional and ethical judgement will need to be exercised, together with the integration of technical knowledge when addressing corporate reporting issues in a business context.

So the paper is not predictable. That said, clear guidance has been given. The compulsory Section A question, worth 50 marks, will always be on group accounts. It will also deal with issues in financial reporting and will be case study based. In Section B, questions could be on any area of they syllabus, but we have been told that two questions will be scenario based and one question will be an essay. You have a choice of two from three.

Exam technique for P2

Do not be needlessly intimidated

There is no shortcut to passing this exam. It looks very difficult indeed, and many students wonder if they will ever pass. But many do. Why is this?

Easy marks

All the questions are demanding, but there are many easy marks to be gained. Suppose, for example, you had a consolidated cash flow statement with a disposal, some foreign exchange complications and an impairment calculation. There will be easy marks available simply for the basic cash flow aspects, setting out the proforma, setting up your workings, presenting your work neatly. If you recognise, as you should, that the disposal needs to be taken into account, of course you will get marks for that, even if you make a mistake in the arithmetic. If you get the foreign exchange right, so much the better, but you could pass the question comfortably omitting this altogether. If you're short of time, this is what you should do.

Be ruthless in ignoring the complications

Look at the question. Within reason, if there are complications – often only worth a few marks – that you know you will not have time or knowledge to do, cross them out. It will make you feel better. Than tackle the bits you can do. This is how people pass a seemingly impossible paper.

Be ruthless in allocating your time

At BPP, we have seen how very intelligent students do one almost perfect question, one averagely good and one sketchy. For a fifty mark question, the first twenty marks are the easiest to get. Then you have to push it up to what you think is thirty to get yourself a clear pass. For a twenty-five mark question, the first eight to ten marks are the easiest to get, and then you must try to push it up to fifteen.

Do your best question either first or second, and the compulsory question either first or second. The compulsory question, being on groups, will always have some easy marks available for consolidation techniques.

Syllabus

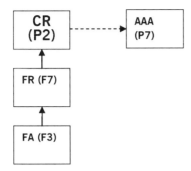

AIM

To apply knowledge, skills and exercise professional judgement in the application and evaluation of financial reporting principles and practices in a range of business contexts and situations.

MAIN CAPABILITIES

On successful completion of this paper, candidates should be able to:

A   Discuss the professional and ethical duties of the accountant

B   Evaluate the financial reporting framework

C   Advise on and report the financial performance of entities

D   Prepare the financial statements of groups of entities in accordance with relevant accounting standards

E   Explain reporting issues relating to specialised entities

F   Discuss the implications of changes in accounting regulation on financial reporting

G   Appraise the financial performance and position of entities

H   Evaluate current developments

RELATIONAL DIAGRAM OF MAIN CAPABILITIES

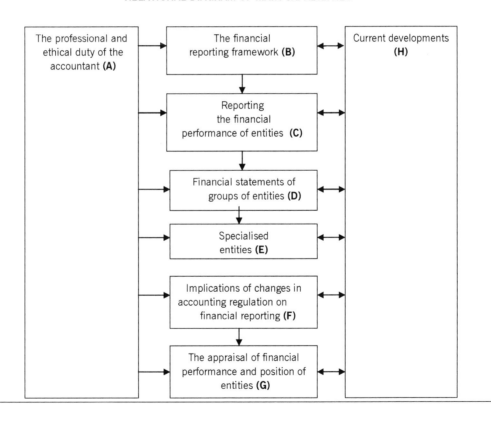

RATIONALE

The syllabus for paper P2, *Corporate Reporting*, assumes knowledge acquired at the Fundamentals level including the core technical capabilities to prepare and analyse financial reports for single and combined entities.

The Paper P2 syllabus takes the subject into greater depth and contextualises the role of the accountant as a professional steward and adviser/analyst by initially exploring the wider professional duties and responsibilities of the accountant to the stakeholders of an organisation.

The syllabus examines the financial reporting framework within which the accountant operates and examines detailed financial reporting requirements for entities leading to the preparation of group financial reports in accordance with generally accepted accounting practice and relevant standards.

The syllabus then deals with the nature of reporting for specialised entities including not-for-profit and small and medium-sized enterprises.

The final sections of the syllabus explore – in more depth – the role of the accountant as financial analyst and adviser through the assessment of financial performance and position of entities, and the accountant's role in assessing and advising on the implications of accounting regulation on corporate reporting.

Finally, the syllabus covers the evaluation of current developments and their implications for financial reporting.

DETAILED SYLLABUS

A   The professional and ethical duty of the accountant

1. Professional behaviour and compliance with accounting standards

2. Ethical requirements of corporate reporting and the consequences of unethical behaviour

3. Social responsibility

B   The financial reporting framework

1. The contribution and limitations of financial statements in meeting users' and capital markets' needs

2. The applications, strengths and weaknesses of an accounting framework

3. Critical evaluation of principles and practices

C   Reporting the financial performance of entities

1. Performance reporting

2. Fixed assets

3. Financial instruments

4. Leases

5. Segment reporting

6. Employee benefits

7. Taxation

8. Provisions, contingencies and events after the balance sheet date

9. Related parties

10. Share-based payment

D   Financial statements of groups of entities

1. Group accounting including cash flow statements

2. Continuing and discontinued interests

3. Changes in group structures

4. Foreign transactions and entities

E   Specialised entities

1. Financial reporting in specialised, not-for-profit and public sector entities

2. Reporting requirements of small and medium-sized entities (SMEs)

F Implications of changes in accounting regulation on financial reporting

1. The effect of changes in accounting standards on accounting systems

2. Proposed changes to accounting standards

G The appraisal of financial performance and position of entities

1. The creation of suitable accounting policies

2. Analysis and interpretation of financial information and measurement of performance

H Current developments

1. Environmental and social reporting

2. Convergence between national and international reporting standards

3. Comparison of national reporting requirements

4. Current reporting issues

APPROACH TO EXAMINING THE SYLLABUS

The syllabus is assessed by a three-hour paper-based examination. It examines professional competences within the corporate reporting environment.

Students will be examined on concepts, theories, and principles, and on their ability to question and comment on proposed accounting treatments.

Students should be capable of relating professional issues to relevant concepts and practical situations. The evaluation of alternative accounting practices and the identification and prioritisation of issues will be a key element of the paper. Professional and ethical judgement will need to be exercised, together with the integration of technical knowledge when addressing corporate reporting issues in a business context.

Global issues will be addressed via the current issues questions on the paper. Students will be required to adopt either a stakeholder or an external focus in answering questions and to demonstrate

personal skills such as problem solving, dealing with information and decision making.

The paper also deals with specific professional knowledge appropriate to the preparation and presentation of consolidated and other financial statements from accounting data to conform with accounting standards.

The paper will comprise two sections.

Section A Compulsory question	50 marks
Section B 2 from 3 questions of	
25 marks each	50 marks
	100 marks

Section A will consist of one scenario-based question worth 50 marks. It will deal with the preparation of consolidated financial statements including group cash flow statements and with issues in financial reporting.

Students will be required to answer two out of three questions in Section B, which will normally comprise two questions which will be scenario or case-study based and one question which will be an essay. Section B could deal with any aspects of the syllabus.

Study Guide

A THE PROFESSIONAL AND ETHICAL DUTIES OF THE ACCOUNTANT

1. Professional behaviour and compliance with accounting standards

a) Appraise and discuss the ethical and professional issues in advising on corporate reporting.[3]

b) Assess the relevance and importance of ethical and professional issues in complying with accounting standards.[3]

2. Ethical requirements of corporate reporting and the consequences of unethical behaviour

a) Appraise the potential ethical implications of professional and managerial decisions in the preparation of corporate reports.[3]

b) Assess the consequences of not upholding ethical principles in the preparation of corporate reports.[3]

3. Social Responsibility

a) Discuss the increased demand for transparency in corporate reports, and the emergence of non-financial reporting standards.[3]

b) Discuss the progress towards a framework for environmental and sustainability reporting.[3]

B THE FINANCIAL REPORTING FRAMEWORK

1. The contribution and limitations of financial statements in meeting users' and capital markets' needs

a) Evaluate the consistency and clarity of corporate reports.[3]

b) Assess the insight into financial and operational risks provided by corporate reports.[3]

c) Discuss the usefulness of corporate reports in making investment decisions.[3]

2. The applications, strengths and weaknesses of an accounting framework

a) Evaluate the "balance sheet" and "fair value" models adopted by standard setters.[3]

b) Discuss the use of an accounting framework in underpinning the production of accounting standards.[3]

c) Assess the success of such a framework in introducing rigorous and consistent accounting standards.[3]

3. Critical evaluation of principles and practices

a) Identify the relationship between accounting theory and practice.[2]

b) Critically evaluate accounting principles and practices used in corporate reporting.[3]

C REPORTING THE FINANCIAL PERFORMANCE OF ENTITIES

1. Performance reporting

a) Prepare reports relating to corporate performance for external stakeholders.[3]

b) Evaluate proposed changes to reporting financial performance.[3]

2. Fixed assets

a) Apply and discuss the timing of the recognition of fixed assets and the determination of their carrying amounts including impairments and revaluations.[3]

b) Apply and discuss the treatment of non-current assets held for sale.[3]

c) Apply and discuss the accounting treatment of investment properties including classification, recognition and measurement issues.[3]

d) Apply and discuss the accounting treatment of intangible assets including the criteria for recognition and measurement subsequent to acquisition and classification.[3]

3. **Financial Instruments**

a) Apply and discuss the recognition and de-recognition of financial assets and financial liabilities.[2]

b) Apply and discuss the classification of financial assets and financial liabilities and their measurement.[2]

c) Apply and discuss the treatment of gains and losses arising on financial assets and financial liabilities.[2]

d) Apply and discuss the treatment of impairments of financial assets.[2]

e) Account for derivative financial instruments, and simple embedded derivatives.[2]

f) Outline the principles of hedge accounting and account for fair value hedges and cash flow hedges including hedge effectiveness.[2]

4. **Leases**

a) Apply and discuss the classification of leases and accounting for leases by lessors and lessees.[3]

b) Account for and discuss sale and leaseback transactions.[3]

5. **Segment Reporting**

a) Determine business and geographical segments, and reportable segments.[3]

b) Specify and discuss the nature of segment information to be disclosed.[3]

6. **Employee Benefits**

a) Apply and discuss the accounting treatment of defined contribution and defined benefit plans.[3]

b) Account for gains and losses on settlements and curtailments.[2]

c) Report actuarial gains and losses in financial statements.[2]

7. **Taxation**

a) Apply and discuss the recognition and measurement of deferred tax liabilities and deferred tax assets.[3]

b) Determine the recognition of tax expense or income and its inclusion in the financial statements.[3]

8. **Provisions, contingencies and events after the balance sheet date**

a) Apply and discuss the recognition, derecognition and measurement of provisions, contingent liabilities and contingent assets including environmental provisions.[3]

b) Calculate and discuss restructuring provisions.[3]

c) Apply and discuss the accounting for events after the balance sheet date.[3]

d) Determine and report going concern issues arising after the balance sheet date.[3]

9. **Related parties**

a) Determine the parties considered to be related to an entity.[3]

b) Identify the implications of related party relationships and the need for disclosure.[3]

10. **Share based payment**

a) Apply and discuss the recognition and measurement criteria for share-based payment transactions.[3]

b) Account for modifications, cancellations and settlements of share based payment transactions.[2]

D FINANCIAL STATEMENTS OF GROUPS OF ENTITIES

1. Group accounting including cash flow statements

a) Apply the method of accounting for business combinations including complex group structures.[3]

b) Apply the principles in determining the cost of a business combination.[3]

c) Apply the recognition and measurement criteria for identifiable acquired assets and liabilities and goodwill including piecemeal acquisitions.[3]

d) Apply and discuss the criteria used to identify a subsidiary and an associate.[3]

e) Determine and apply appropriate procedures to be used in preparing group financial statements.[3]

f) Apply the equity method of accounting for associates.[3]

g) Outline and apply the key definitions and accounting methods which relate to interests in joint ventures.[3]

h) Prepare and discuss group cash flow statements.[3]

2. Continuing and discontinued interests

a) Prepare group financial statements where activities have been discontinued, or have been acquired or disposed of in the period.[3]

b) Apply and discuss the treatment of a subsidiary which has been acquired exclusively with a view to subsequent disposal.[3]

3. Changes in group structures

a) Discuss the reasons behind a group reorganisation.[3]

b) Evaluate and assess the principal terms of a proposed group reorganisation.[3]

4. Foreign transactions and entities

a) Outline and apply the translation of foreign currency amounts and transactions into the functional currency and the presentational currency.[3]

b) Account for the consolidation of foreign operations and their disposal.[2]

c) Describe the principal objectives of establishing a standard for enterprises reporting in the currency of a hyper inflationary economy.[1]

E SPECIALISED ENTITIES

1. Financial reporting in specialised, not-for-profit and public sector entities

a) Apply knowledge from the syllabus to straightforward transactions and events arising in specialised, not-for-profit, and public sector entities.[3]

2. Reporting requirements of small and medium entities (SMEs)

a) Outline the principal considerations in developing a set of accounting standards for SMEs.[3]

b) Discuss solutions to the problem of differential financial reporting.[3]

F IMPLICATIONS OF CHANGES IN ACCOUNTING REGULATION ON FINANCIAL REPORTING

1. The effect of changes in accounting standards on accounting systems

a) Apply and discuss the accounting implications of the first time adoption of a body of new accounting standards.[3]

b) Outline the issues in implementing a change to new accounting standards including organisational, behavioural, and procedural changes within the entity.[3]

2. Proposed changes to accounting standards

a) Identify issues and deficiencies which have led to a proposed change to an accounting standard.[2]

b) Apply and discuss the implications of a proposed change to an accounting standard on the performance and balance sheet of an entity.[2]

G THE APPRAISAL OF FINANCIAL PERFORMANCE AND POSITION OF ENTITIES

1. The creation of suitable accounting policies

a) Develop accounting policies for an entity which meet the entity's reporting requirements.[3]

b) Identify accounting treatments adopted in financial statements and assess their suitability and acceptability.[3]

2. Analysis and interpretation of financial information and measurement of performance

a) Select and calculate relevant indicators of financial and non-financial performance.[3]

b) Identify and evaluate significant features and issues in financial statements.[3]

c) Highlight inconsistencies in financial information through analysis and application of knowledge.[3]

d) Make inferences from the analysis of information taking into account the limitation of the information, the analytical methods used and the business environment in which the entity operates.[3]

H CURRENT DEVELOPMENTS

1. Environmental and social reporting

a) Appraise the impact of environmental, social, and ethical factors on performance measurement.[3]

b) Evaluate current reporting requirements in the area.[3]

c) Discuss why entities might include disclosures relating to the environment and society.[3]

2. Convergence between national and international reporting standards

a) Evaluate the implications, nationally and globally, of convergence with International Financial Reporting Standards.[3]

b) Discuss the implementation issues arising from the convergence process.[3]

3. Comparison of national reporting requirements

a) Identify the reasons for major differences in accounting practices, including culture.[2]

b) Discuss the influence of national regulators on international financial reporting.[2]

4. Current reporting issues

a) Discuss current issues in corporate reporting.[3]

READING LIST

ACCA's approved publishers:

BPP Professional Education
Contact number: +44(0)20 8740 2222
Website: www.bpp.com/acca

Kaplan Publishing Foulks Lynch
Contact number: +44(0)118 989 0629
Website: www.kaplanfoulkslynch.com

Additional reading:

Accountancy Tuition Centre (ATC) International
Contact number: +44(0)141 880 6469
Website: www.atc-global.com

'Manual of Accounting – UK GAAP 2006' –PWC
Wolters Kluwer (UK)

The exam paper

The paper will comprise two sections.

		Number of marks
Section A:	1 compulsory case study	50
Section B:	Choice of 2 from 3 questions (25 marks each)	50
		100

Section A will consist of one scenario based question worth 50 marks. It will deal with the preparation of consolidated financial statements including group cash flow statements and with issues in financial reporting.

Students will be required to answer two out of three questions in Section B, which will normally comprise two questions which will be scenario or case-study based and one question which will be an essay. Section B could deal with any aspects of the syllabus.

Analysis of pilot paper

Section A

1   Consolidated cash flow statement, criteria for consolidation; ethical behaviour

Section B

2   Substance over form; environmental provision; leasing; FRS 21; share options

3   Deferred tax

4   IFRS; proposals on business combinations

The pilot paper is reproduced in full from page 35.

Pilot paper

Paper P2

Corporate Reporting (UK)

Time allowed

Reading and planning: 15 minutes
Writing: 3 hours

This paper is divided into two sections:

Section A – This ONE question is compulsory and MUST be attempted

Section B – TWO questions ONLY to be attempted

Do NOT open this paper until instructed by the supervisor.

During reading and planning time only the question paper may be annotated. You must NOT write in your answer booklet until instructed by the supervisor.

This question paper must not be removed from the examination hall.

Warning

The pilot paper cannot cover all of the syllabus nor can it include examples of every type of question that will be included in the actual exam. You may see questions in the exam that you think are more difficult than any you see in the pilot paper.

SECTION A: This question is compulsory and MUST be attempted

Question 1

The following draft financial statements relate to Zambeze, a public limited company:

ZAMBEZE
DRAFT GROUP BALANCE SHEETS AT 30 JUNE

	20X6 £m	20X5 £m
Fixed assets		
Goodwill	30	25
Tangible assets	1,315	1,005
Investment in associate	270	290
	1,615	1,320
Current assets		
Stock	650	580
Debtors	610	530
Cash at bank and in hand	50	140
	1,310	1,250
Creditors: amounts falling due within one year	(1,581)	(1,430)
Net current liabilities	(271)	(180)
Total assets less current liabilities	1,344	1,140
Creditors: amounts falling due after more than one year	(850)	(600)
Net assets	494	540
Capital and reserves		
Called up share capital	100	85
Share premium account	30	15
Revaluation reserve	50	145
Profit and loss account	254	250
Minority interest – equity	60	45
Capital employed	494	540

ZAMBEZE
DRAFT GROUP PROFIT AND LOSS FOR THE YEAR ENDED 30 JUNE 20X6

	£m
Turnover	4,700
Cost of sales	(3,400)
Gross profit	1,300
Distribution and administrative expenses	(600)
Finance costs (interest payable)	(40)
Share of profit in associate	30
Profit before tax	690
Taxation (including tax on income from associate £10 million)	(210)
Profit after taxation	480
Minority interest	(25)
Profit attributable to members of parent company	455

ZAMBEZE
DRAFT GROUP STATEMENT OF TOTAL RECOGNISED GAINS AND LOSSES
FOR THE YEAR ENDED 30 JUNE 20X6

	£m
Profit for the financial year	455
Foreign exchange difference of associate	(5)
Impairment losses on tangible assets offset against revaluation surplus	(95)
Total recognised gains and losses for the period	355

ZAMBEZE
DRAFT RECONCILIATION OF GROUP SHAREHOLDERS' FUNDS
FOR THE YEAR ENDED 30 JUNE 20X6

	£m
Total recognised gains and losses for the period	355
Dividends paid	(446)
New shares issued	30
Total movement during the year	(61)
Shareholders' funds at 1 July 20X5	495
Shareholders' funds at 30 June 20X6	434

The following relates to Zambeze.

(i) Zambeze acquired a seventy per cent holding in Damp, a public limited company, on 1 July 20X5. The fair values of the net assets acquired were as follows:

	£m
Tangible fixed assets	70
Stock and work in progress	90
	160

The purchase consideration was £100 million in cash and £25 million (discounted value) deferred consideration which is payable on 1 July 20X6. The difference between the discounted value of the deferred consideration (£25 million) and the amount payable (£29 million) is included in 'interest payable'. Zambeze wants to set up a provision for reconstruction costs of £10 million retrospectively on the acquisition of Damp. This provision has not yet been set up.

(ii) There had been no disposals of tangible fixed assets during the year. Depreciation for the period charged in cost of sales was £60 million.

(iii) Creditors: amounts falling due within one year comprised the following items:

	20X6	20X5
	£m	£m
Trade creditors	1,341	1,200
Interest payable	50	45
Taxation	190	185
	1,581	1,430

(iv) Creditors: amounts falling due after more than one year comprised the following:

	20X6	20X5
	£m	£m
Deferred consideration – purchase of Damp	29	–
Liability for the purchase of tangible fixed assets	144	–
Loans repayable	621	555
Provision for deferred tax	30	25
Retirement benefit liability	26	20
	850	600

(v)   The retirement benefit liability comprised the following:

	£m
Movement in year	
Liability at 1 July 20X5	20
Current and past service costs charged to profit and loss	13
Contributions paid to retirement benefit scheme	(7)
Liability 30 June 20X6	26

There was no actuarial gain or loss in the year.

(vi)   Goodwill was impairment tested on 30 June 20X6 and any impairment was included in the financial statements for the year ended 30 June 20X6. Group policy is to amortise goodwill over five years but because goodwill was impairment tested on 30 June 20X6, no amortisation was charged in the year.

(vii)   The Finance Director has set up a company, River, through which Zambeze conducts its investment activities. Zambeze has paid £400 million to River during the year and this has been included in dividends paid. The money was invested in a specified portfolio of investments. Ninety five per cent of the profits and one hundred per cent of the losses in the specified portfolio of investments are transferred to Zambeze. An investment manager has charge of the company's investments and owns all of the share capital of River. An agreement between the investment manager and Zambeze sets out the operating guidelines and prohibits the investment manager from obtaining access to the investments for the manager's benefit. An annual transfer of the profit/loss will occur on 30 June annually and the capital will be returned in four years time. The transfer of £400 million cash occurred on 1 January 20X6 but no transfer of profit/loss has yet occurred. The balance sheet of River at 30 June 20X6 is as follows:

RIVER: BALANCE SHEET AT 30 JUNE 20X6

	£m
Investment at fair value through profit or loss	390
	390
Share capital	400
Retained earnings	(10)
	390

Required

(a)   Prepare a group cash flow statement for the Zambeze Group for the year ended 30 June 20X6 using the indirect method.   **(35 marks)**

(b)   Discuss the issues which would determine whether River should be consolidated by Zambeze in the group financial statements.   **(9 marks)**

(c)   Discuss briefly the importance of ethical behaviour in the preparation of financial statements and whether the creation of River could constitute unethical practice by the finance director of Zambeze.   **(6 marks)**

(Total = 50 marks)

Two marks are available for the quality of the discussion of the issue regarding the consolidation of River and the importance of ethical behaviour.

Section B: TWO questions ONLY to be attempted

Question 2

Electron, a public limited company, operates in the energy sector. The company has grown significantly over the last few years and is currently preparing its financial statements for the year ended 30 June 20X6.

Electron buys and sells oil and currently has a number of oil trading contracts. The contracts to purchase oil are treated as fixed assets and amortised over the contracts' durations. On acceptance of a contract to sell oil, fifty per cent of the contract price is recognised immediately with the balance being recognised over the remaining life of the contract. The contracts always result in the delivery of the commodity.

(4 marks)

Electron has recently constructed an ecologically efficient power station. A condition of being granted the operating licence by the government is that the power station be dismantled at the end of its life which is estimated to be 20 years. The power station cost £100 million and began production on 1 July 20X5. Depreciation is charged on the power station using the straight line method. Electron has estimated at 30 June 20X6 that it will cost £15 million (net present value) to restore the site to its original condition using a discount rate of five per cent. Ninety-five per cent of these costs relate to the removal of the power station and five per cent relates to the damage caused through generating energy. **(7 marks)**

Electron has leased another power station, which was relatively inefficient, to a rival company on 30 June 20X6. The beneficial and legal ownership remains with Electron and in the event of one of Electron's power stations being unable to produce energy, Electron can terminate the agreement. The leased power station is being treated as an operating lease with the net present value of the income of £40 million being recognised in the profit and loss account. The fair value of the power station is £70 million at 30 June 20X6. A deposit of £10 million was received on 30 June 20X6 and it is included in the net present value calculation. **(5 marks)**

The company has a good relationship with its shareholders and employees. It has adopted a strategy of gradually increasing its dividend payments over the years. On 1 August 20X6, the board proposed a dividend of 5p per share for the year ended 30 June 20X6. The shareholders will approve the dividend along with the financial statements at the general meeting on 1 September 20X6 and the dividend will be paid on 14 September 20X6. The directors feel that the dividend should be accrued in the financial statements for the year ended 30 June 20X6 as a 'valid expectation' has been created. **(3 marks)**

The company granted share options to its employees on 1 July 20X5. The fair value of the options at that date was £3 million. The options vest on 30 June 20X8. The employees have to be employed at the end of the three year period for the options to vest and the following estimates have been made:

Estimated percentage of employees leaving during vesting period at:

Grant date 1 July 20X5	5%	
30 June 20X6	6%	**(4 marks)**
Effective communication to the directors		**(2 marks)**

Required

Draft a report suitable for presentation to the director of Electron which discusses the accounting treatment of the above transactions in the financial statements for the year ended 30 June 20X6, including relevant calculations. **(Total = 25 marks)**

Question 3

The following balance sheet relates to Kesare Group, a public limited company at 30 June 20X6:

	£'000
Assets	
Fixed assets	
Tangible assets	10,000
Goodwill	6,000
Other intangible assets	5,000
Financial assets (cost)	9,000
	30,000
Debtors	7,000
Other receivables	4,600
Cash	6,700
Current assets	18,300
Trade creditors	(5,000)
Current tax liability	(3,070)
Creditors: amounts falling due within one year	(8,070)
Net current assets	10,230
Creditors: amounts falling due after more than one year	
Long term borrowings	(10,000)
Deferred tax liability	(3,600)
Employee benefit liability	(4,000)
	(17,600)
Net assets	22,630
Capital and reserves	
Share capital	9,000
Profit and loss account	9,130
Other reserves	4,500
Capital employed	22,630

The following information is relevant to the above balance sheet.

(i) The financial assets are valued at fair value through profit or loss but are shown in the above balance sheet at their cost on 1 July 20X5. The market value of the assets is £10.5 million on 30 June 20X6.Taxation is payable on the sale of the assets.

(ii) Other tangible assets comprise an asset which was purchased on 1 July 20X5 for £5 million and which qualifies for a government capital grant of £1 million. The asset has a useful life of five years. The grant has been credited to the profit and loss account and capital allowances are restricted by the amount of the grant. Assume a tax writing down allowance of 25% per annum.

(iii) The defined benefit plan had a rule change on 1 July 20X5. Kesare estimate that of the past service costs of £1 million, 40 per cent relates to vested benefits and 60 per cent relates to benefits that will vest over the next five years from that date. The past service costs have not been accounted for and the actuarial gain before accounting for the past service costs was £600,000.

(iv) The company had purchased an investment property on 1 July 20X5 at a cost of £3 million. This was included in tangible assets at this amount at 30 June 20X6. The value of the property at 30 June 20X6 was £5 million and the gain was included in the profit and loss account. The company had no intention of selling the property in the near future. The property qualifies for capital allowances at 4% per annum. No deferred taxation had been provided for on the investment property.

(v) Assume taxation is payable at 30%.

Required

(a) Discuss the main objectives of the recognition of deferred taxation and the conceptual principles upon which the timing difference approach to deferred taxation is based. **(7 marks)**

(b) Show, with suitable explanations, any adjustments that would be required to the deferred tax liabilities and balance sheet amounts as a result of items (i) – (iv) above. **(18 marks)**

(Total = 25 marks)

Two marks will be awarded for the quality of the discussion of the objectives and conceptual principles in (a).

Question 4

A significant number of entities and countries around the world have adopted International Financial Reporting Standards (IFRS) as their basis for financial reporting, often regarding these as a means to improve the quality of information on corporate performance. However, while the advantages of a common set of global reporting standards are recognised, there are a number of implementation challenges at the international and national levels if the objective of an improved and harmonised reporting system is to be achieved.

Required

(a) Discuss the implementation challenges faced by the International Accounting Standards Board (IASB) if there is to be a successful move to International Financial Reporting Standards.

(18 marks)

(b) The Accounting Standards Board recently issued FRED 36 *Business combinations* (IFRS 3) and amendments to FRS 2 *Accounting for subsidiary undertakings*. The proposals radically change the basis of reporting business combinations and transactions with minority interests.

Discuss how the above exposure draft will fundamentally affect the existing accounting practices for business combinations **(7 marks)**

(Total = 25 marks)

Two marks will be awarded for the quality of the discussion of the ideas and information.

Part A
Regulatory and ethical framework

Financial reporting framework

1

Topic list	Syllabus reference
1 Financial Reporting Standards	B1-3
2 Corporate governance	B1-3
3 Operating and Financial Review	C1
4 GAAP and conceptual framework	B2

Introduction

Welcome to the Corporate Reporting paper. We must emphasise from the start that this paper is about thinking rather than rote learning. You will have met many of the accounting standards and topics covered in your earlier studies, but at the Professional level you will be required to think critically about them and show an understanding of topical issues. Put yourself in the position of an accountant giving advice to management in the light of what you know.

In the exam you will often be called on to advise on the impact of a proposed change in financial reporting standards. Such proposals are covered in this text within the topics.

Study guide

		Intellectual level
A1	**Professional behaviour and compliance with technical accounting standards**	
(a)	Appraise the ethical and professional issues in advising on corporate reporting	3
(b)	Assess the relevance and importance of ethical and professional issues in complying with accounting standards	3
B2	**The applications, strength and weaknesses of an accounting framework**	
(a)	Evaluate the 'balance sheet' and fair value models adopted by standard setters	3
(b)	Discuss the use of the *Statement of Principles* in the production of accounting standards	3
(c)	Assess the success of the *Statement of Principles* in introducing rigorous and consistent accounting standards	3
C1	**Performance reporting**	
(a)	Prepare reports relating to corporate performance for external stakeholders	3

Exam guide

This chapter is partly background knowledge to set the scene about the reporting framework before you look at ethical issues. It also discusses briefly corporate governance and the Operating and Financial Review. Finally we revise the Conceptual Framework *(Statement of Principles)* and look at recent work in this area.

1 Financial Reporting Standards

A quick overview of regulation is given here for background as the topic will not be examined.

FAST FORWARD

You should be familiar using the **role and impact** of the following bodies.

- Accounting Standards Board
- Financial Reporting Council
- Review Panel
- Urgent Issues Task Force
- European Union/European Commission
- Company Law
- International Accounting Standards Committee

We have covered this in your earlier studies, so only a summary is given here. However, if you have any problems or if the material is unfamiliar, look back to your earlier study material.

Knowledge brought forward from earlier studies

Regulatory framework

- The reporting environment changes constantly, through new regulations, standards etc
- International influences on UK reporting are increasing, via IASC and multinational businesses

Company law

Consolidated by the Companies Act 2006. The Acts lay out the formats, contents and rules for the preparation of financial statements.

European Union law

The UK is obliged to comply with legal directives issued by the EU.

Stock Exchange rules

The Stock Exchange listing requirements (Yellow Book) must be complied with by companies on the market. The Alternative Investment Market (AIM) has less stringent requirements.

UK accounting standards

The standard-setting structure is as follows.

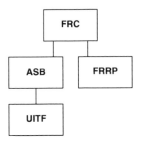

- *FRC (Financial Reporting Council)*: umbrella organisation for the standard-setting regime, responsible for financing, enforcement, appointments

- *FRRP (Financial Reporting Review Panel)*: reviews company accounts for non-compliance with accounting standards, truth and fairness, sufficient disclosure etc

- *ASB (Accounting Standards Board)*: produces FRSs from FREDs and DDs (see below)

- *UITF (Urgent Issues Task Force)*: produces 'abstracts' to tackle problem areas quickly (within one month); may be incorporated into subsequent standards

ASB and FRSs

Statement of Aims:

- *Aims*: 'to establish and improve standards of financial accounting and reporting, for the benefit of users, preparers and auditors of financial information.'

- *Achieving the aims*
    - Developing principles to provide a framework
    - Issuing new standards or amending existing ones
    - Addressing urgent issues promptly

- *Fundamental guidelines*
    1. Objectivity; represent commercial activity
    2. Clear expression; supported by analysis
    3. Inclusion of only properly researched material
    4. Due regard paid to international developments
    5. Consistency between standards and law
    6. Benefits of standards must exceed costs

1.1 Current accounting standards

The following standards are extant at the date of writing (June 2007). Most of the more recent FRSs implement International Financial Reporting Standards.

1.1.1 Accounting standards

No	Title	Issue date
	Foreword to accounting standards	Jun 93
FRS 1	Cash flow statements (revised) (see below)	Oct 96
FRS 2	Accounting for subsidiary undertakings	Jul 92
	Amendment	May 02
FRS 3	Reporting financial performance	Oct 92
FRS 4	Capital instruments (mostly superseded by FRS 26)	Dec 93
FRS 5	Reporting the substance of transactions	Apr 94
	Amendment to FRS 5: Revenue recognition	Nov 03
FRS 6	Acquisitions and mergers	Sep 94
FRS 7	Fair values in acquisition accounting	Sep 94
FRS 8	Related party disclosures	Oct 95
FRS 9	Associates and joint ventures	Nov 97
	Financial Reporting Standard for Smaller Entities	Jan 05
FRS 10	Goodwill and intangible assets	Dec 97
FRS 11	Impairment of fixed assets and goodwill	Jul 98
FRS 12	Provisions, contingent liabilities and contingent assets	Sep 98
FRS 13	Derivatives and other financial instruments: disclosure (mainly superseded by FRS 25)	Sep 98
FRS 15	Tangible fixed assets	Feb 99
FRS 16	Current tax	Dec 99
FRS 17	Retirement benefits	Nov 00
FRS 18	Accounting policies	Dec 00
FRS 19	Deferred tax	Dec 00
FRS 20	Share-based payment	Apr 04
FRS 21	Events after the balance sheet date	May 04
FRS 22	Earnings per share	Dec 04
FRS 23	The effects of changes in foreign exchange rates	Dec 04
FRS 24	Financial reporting in hyperinflationary economies	Dec 04
FRS 25	Financial instruments: disclosure and presentation	Dec 04
FRS 26	Financial instruments: measurement (amended in 2006 to include recognition)	Dec 04
FRS 27	Life assurance	Dec 04
FRS 28	Corresponding amounts	Oct 05
FRS 29	Financial instruments: disclosures	Dec 05
	Amendment to FRS 26 Financial instruments: measurement: recognition and de-recognition	Apr 06
SSAP 4	Accounting for government grants	Jul 90
SSAP 5	Accounting for value added tax	Apr 74
SSAP 9	Stocks and long-term contracts	Sep 88
SSAP 13	Accounting for research and development	Jan 89
SSAP 19	Accounting for investment properties (amended)	Nov 81
SSAP 21	Accounting for leases and hire purchase contracts	Aug 84
SSAP 25	Segmental reporting	Jun 90

1.1.2 Financial reporting exposure drafts

No	Title	Issue date
FRED 28	Inventories; Construction contracts	May 02
FRED 29	Property, plant and equipment; Borrowing costs	May 02
FRED 30	Supplement: Fair value hedge accounting for a portfolio hedge of interest rate risk	Aug 03
FRED 32	Disposal of non-current assets and presentation of discontinued operations	May 04
FRED 36	Business combinations	Jul 05
FRED 37	Intangible assets	Jul 05
FRED 38	Impairment of assets	Jul 05
FRED 39	Amendments to FRS 12	Jul 05
ED	Amendment to FRS 20 and FRS 17 Share-based payment: vesting conditions and cancellations	

1.1.3 Other documents

Accounting for the effects of changing prices: a handbook – ASC (Summary and Overview)

The Cadbury Report (1992), *The Combined Code* (1998), *The Hampel Report* (Jan 1998)

Reporting Statement: Operating and Financial Review – ASB (January 2006)

Statement of Principles for Financial Reporting – ASB (Dec 99)

ED of Policy Statement: Accounting Standard setting in a changing environment: The Role of the Accounting Standards Board

ASB Drafts for Discussion (DDs)

Title	Issue date
Segmental reporting	May 96
Discounting (working paper)	Apr 97
Leases: implementation of a new approach	Dec 99
Year end financial reports: improving communication	Feb 00
The Convergence Handbook	Dec 00
Review of the FRSSE	Feb 01
Revenue recognition	Jul 01
Statement of Principles: Proposed interpretation for public benefit entities	May 03
A 'one-stop shop' FRSSE	Mar 04
UK Accounting Standards: A Strategy for Convergence with IFRS	Mar 04

1.2 Statements of Recommended Practice (SORPs)

When the ASB took over from the old ASC, it adopted all the existing accounting standards. It did not, however, adopt the ASC's SORPs 1 and 2. As far as your syllabus is concerned, you need only be aware of the relevance of SORPs to financial reporting.

2 Corporate governance

FAST FORWARD

The impact of the **Cadbury Report** and the **Combined Code** is still being felt as some companies struggle to meet its requirements.

Your syllabus requires you to have some knowledge of topical issues relating to corporate governance. By far the most important development in this area is the report of the Cadbury Committee.

Key term

> **Corporate governance** is the system by which companies are directed and controlled.

2.1 The Combined Code

The Cadbury report was issued in 1992, and the comments in the table above show that some of the points have been addressed subsequently by the APB, particularly those in relation to fraud and going concern.

Since the Cadbury report, there have been several other committees, which all produced recommendations about various issues such as directors' remuneration. In 1998, the key guidance from all the reports was re-issued in the form of the combined code.

The Combined Code is issued as part of the Stock Exchange guidance and so generally relates to listed companies. However, this does not mean that following the guidance is not good practice for other companies also.

Provisions of the Combined code (Directors' responsibilities)	
The Board	Should **meet regularly**, and have a **formal schedule of matters** reserved to it for its decision.
	There should be clear division of responsibilities between chairman and chief executive.
	Non-executive directors should comprise at least a third of the board. Directors should submit themselves for re-election every three years.
	Directors should submit themselves for re-election at regular intervals (at least every three years).
The AGM	Companies should propose **separate resolutions** at the AGM on each substantially different issue. The chairman should ensure that members of the audit, remuneration and nomination committees are available at the AGM to **answer questions**. Notice of AGMs should be sent out at least 20 days before the meeting.
Accountability and audit	The directors should **explain** their **responsibility for preparing accounts**. They should **report that the business is a going concern**, with supporting assumptions and qualifications as necessary.
Remuneration	There should be remuneration committees composed of non-executive directors to set directors' pay, which should provide pay which attracts, retains and motivates quality directors but avoids paying more than is necessary for the purpose.
	The company's annual report should contain a statement of remuneration policy and details of the remuneration of each director.
Internal control	The directors should review the **effectiveness of internal control** systems, at least annually, and also **review the need for an internal audit function**.
Audit committee	The board **should establish an audit committee**.

Provisions of the Combined code (Auditors' responsibilities)	
Statement of responsibilities	The auditors **should include** in their report a statement of their reporting responsibilities.

2.2 Corporate governance statement

The stock exchange rules require that, as part of the **annual report**, a company must **include** a narrative **statement of how it has applied the principles set out in the combined code**. This statement must include an explanation which allows the shareholders to evaluate how the company have applied the principles.

The statement must also provide explanation of whether the company has **complied** with the principles of the combined code.

They must also provide a statement showing how they have applied the principles relating to directors' remuneration (not examined in detail here).

The auditors must review the corporate governance statement before it is published. Their duty to review it only extends to the following items:

- Board having a formal schedule of matters for their attention
- Procedure for board members to seek independent, professional advice
- Non-executive directors having specific terms of office
- Directors being subject to election and re-election by the shareholders
- The directors and auditors stating their respective responsibilities
- The directors conducting a review of internal control effectiveness
- The board establishing an audit committee

2.3 Benefits of a voluntary code

The combined code is a **voluntary code**. The Stock Exchange requires that disclosures be made as to whether it has been complied with, but there are **no statutory requirements to comply** with it.

The main benefit in having a voluntary code is that the code can be **applied flexibly**, where management believe that it is relevant. The **disclosure** requirements ensure that **shareholders** are **aware** of the position and they can make any points they want to about compliance with the code at the AGM.

It has been argued that making such a code obligatory would have **punitive effects** on some companies, due to their size or investor make up and that legislation would create a **burden of requirement** which **could be excessive in many cases**.

Critics of the view would argue:

(a) Disclosure of non-compliance is insufficient as the AGM is still not sufficient protection for shareholders.

(b) Having a voluntary code allows some companies not to comply freely, to the detriment of their shareholders.

(c) The requirement to disclose is only a Stock Exchange requirement, and there are many unlisted companies who should be encouraged to apply the codes.

The government has shown concern for this area in the past and it is believed that it **might take action in the future to regulate this area** more heavily.

However, at the moment, having a **voluntary code is a compromise** based on the points made above.

2.4 Audit committees

A major recommendation in the Cadbury Code is that **all listed companies must establish effective audit committees** if they have not already done so.

The Code takes its example from countries such as Canada where audit committees for listed companies are compulsory.

The audit committees should have formal terms of reference dealing with their membership, authority and duties. They should meet at least three times every year and membership of the committee, which should be comprised of **non-executive directors**, should be shown in the annual report.

- The committee must have the authority, resources and means of access to investigate anything within its terms of reference.

- Review of the external auditors' management letter and the company's statement on the internal control system.

The key advantage to an auditor of having an audit committee is that a committee of independent non-executive directors provides the auditor with an independent point of reference other than the executive directors of the company, in the event of disagreement arising.

Question   Voluntary codes

What are the benefits of corporate governance codes being voluntary?

Answer

- Code can be applied flexibly, as is best for the company.
- Burden of statutory requirement is not created

Exam focus point

This is background only, so you understand the professional ethics aspect.

3 Operating and Financial Review

FAST FORWARD

The **Operating and Financial Review** should be of considerable benefit to less sophisticated users. It is not a statutory requirement but is the subject of a Reporting Statement, setting out best practice.

In January 2006, the Accounting Standards Board (ASB) issued a Reporting Statement *Operating and Financial Review*.

3.1 Overview

The ASB originally issued the Statement Operating and Financial Review in 1993. The process of further developing the Statement was started in May 2004, when the UK government announced its proposals for a **statutory operating and financial review** and indicated that it intended to specify the ASB as the body to make reporting standards for the OFR.

In May 2005 Reporting Standard 1 was issued. However, in November 2005 the government announced its intention to remove the statutory requirement on quoted companies to publish an OFR. As a consequence, RS 1 was withdrawn and 'converted' into a Statement of Best Practice. The Reporting Statement recommends that directors prepare an OFR addressed to members, setting out their analysis of the business, with a forward looking orientation. It sets out principles regarded as best practice, namely that the review should both complement and supplement the financial statements, be comprehensive and understandable, balanced and neutral and comparable over time.

Amongst other key areas of business operations, the OFR sets out a framework for directors to consider and report on the **main risks** facing their company and the **measures** that are taken to **control and manage those risks**.

The Statement leaves it to directors to consider how best to structure their review, in the light of the particular circumstances of the entity. Similarly, it does not specify any specific **key performance indicators** (KPIs) that entities should disclose, nor how many, on the grounds that this is a matter for directors to decide.

The Statement is accompanied by **implementation guidance**, which the ASB believes will be useful to directors in considering what to include in their OFR. The guidance sets out some illustrations and suggestions of specific content and related KPIs that might be included in an OFR.

From a risk perspective the implementation guidance looks at ways of reporting on customer and stakeholder risks; environmental risks; employee risks and social responsibility risks.

3.1.1 Companies Act 2006 changes

The OFR is abolished from 2008, but most of its provisions will be re-introduced in an expanded business review to be contained in the directors' report.

3.2 Objective

The objective of this Reporting Statement is to specify best practice for an Operating and Financial Review, which should be a balanced and comprehensive analysis, consistent with the size and complexity of the business, of:

(a) The **development and performance** of the business of the entity during the financial year;

(b) The **position** of the entity at the end of the year;

(c) The **main trends and factors underlying the development, performance and position** of the business of the entity during the financial year

(d) The main trends and factors which are likely to affect the entity's **future development**, performance and position, prepared so as to assist members to assess the strategies adopted by the entity and the potential for those strategies to succeed.

3.3 Scope

The Reporting Statement has been written with quoted companies in mind but is also applicable to any other entities that purport to prepare on OFR.

3.4 Principles

The standard sets out the following principles.

(a) The OFR should set out the analysis of the business **through the eyes of the directors**.

(b) The OFR should focus on matters that are of **interest to members**. Other users will be interested in the information, but members' needs must be paramount.

(c) The OFR should have a **forward-looking orientation**, identifying those trends and factors relevant to the members' assessment of the current and future performance of the business and the progress towards the achievement of long-term business objectives. (The directors may warn readers to treat predictive information with caution.)

(d) The OFR should **complement as well as supplement the financial statements** in order to enhance the overall corporate disclosure.

(e)   The OFR should be **comprehensive and understandable**. For example, it must consider whether omitting information might influence users of financial statements.

(f)   It should be **balanced and neutral** dealing evenhandedly with good and bad aspects.

(g)   It should be **comparable over time**.

3.5 Disclosure framework

The key elements of the disclosure framework are set out below.

(a)   The **nature, objectives and strategies** of the business. This includes a description of the business and the external environment in which it operates, the objectives to generate and preserve value over the longer term, the directors' strategies for achieving the objectives of the business and the inclusion of other performance indicators and evidence.

(b)   The **development and performance of the business**, both in the period under review and in the future. This will focus on the business segments that are relevant to an understanding of the development and performance as a whole.

(c)   The **resources, risks and uncertainties and relationships** that may affect the entity's long-term value. It will analyse the main trends and factors likely to impact future prospects, and describe the resources available, the principle risks and uncertainties faced by the entity and significant relationships with stakeholders

(d)   **Position of the business** including a description of the capital structure, treasury policies and objectives and liquidity of the entity (particularly cash flow), both in the period under review and the future.

3.5.1 Information required for disclosures

To the extent necessary to meet the requirements set out above, the OFR should include information about:

(a)   Environmental matters (including the impact of the business of the entity on the environment)

(b)   The entity's employees

(c)   Social and community issues

(d)   Persons with whom the entity has contractual or other arrangements which are essential to the business of the entity

(e)   Receipts from, and returns to, members of the entity in respect of shares held by them

(f)   All other matters the directors consider to be relevant

For items (a) to (c) the OFR must include the policies of the entity in relation to those matters and the extent to which they have been successfully implemented.

3.6 Example: Operating and financial review

Below is the Operating and Financial Review of the InterContinental Hotels Group for the year ended 31 December 2006.

Business overview

Market and competitive environment

IHG operates in the global hotel market which has an estimated total room capacity of 18.8 million rooms. Room capacity has been growing at approximately 3% per annum over the last five years. The hotel market is geographically concentrated with 12 countries accounting for two-thirds of worldwide hotel room supply. The Group has a leadership position (top three by room numbers) in more of these markets than any other major hotel company.

The hotel market is, however, a fragmented market with the four largest companies controlling only 11% of the global hotel room supply and the 10 largest controlling less than 21%. The Group is the largest of these companies by room numbers with a 3% market share. The major competitors in this market include other large global hotel companies, smaller hotel companies and independent hotels.

Within the global market, a relatively low proportion of hotel rooms are branded (see figure 1), but there has been an increasing trend towards branded rooms. For example, Mintel, a market research company, estimates that the proportion of branded rooms in Europe has grown from 15% in 2000 to 25% in 2004. Larger branded companies are therefore gaining market share at the expense of smaller companies and independent hotels. IHG is well positioned to benefit from this trend. Hotel owners are increasingly recognising the benefits of working with a group such as IHG which can offer a portfolio of brands to suit the different real estate opportunities an owner may have. Furthermore, hotel ownership is increasingly being separated from hotel operations, encouraging hotel owners to use third parties such as IHG to manage or franchise their hotels.

Percentage of branded hotel rooms by region 2004

Source: Mintel (latest data available).

North America	65%
South America	20%
Europe	25%
Middle East	25%
East Asia	25%

Figure 1

US market data indicates a steady increase in hotel industry revenues, broadly in line with Gross Domestic Product, with growth of approximately 1-1.5% per annum in real terms since 1967, driven by a number of underlying trends:

- Change in demographics – as the population ages and becomes wealthier, increased leisure time and income encourages more travel and hotel visits;

- Increase in travel volumes as low cost airlines grow rapidly;

- Globalisation of trade and tourism;

- Increase in affluence and freedom to travel within the Chinese middle class; and

- Increase in the preference for branded hotels amongst consumers.

Potential negative trends include increased terrorism, environmental considerations and economic factors such as rising oil prices. Currently, however, there are no indications that demand is being significantly affected by these factors.

Supply growth in the industry is cyclical, averaging between zero and 5% per annum historically. The Group's profit is partly protected from supply pressure due to its model of third party ownership of hotels under IHG management and franchise contracts.

Strategy

IHG owns, operates and franchises hotels, with its brands being represented in nearly 100 countries and territories around the world. The strategy is to become the preferred hotel company for guests and owners by building the strongest operating system in the industry, focused on the largest markets and segments where scale really counts. During 2006, IHG initiated a number of research projects, the results of which will strengthen the Group's strategy with respect to brand development, franchising operations and growth opportunities.

The Group has four stated strategic priorities:

- Brand performance – to operate a portfolio of brands attractive to both owners and guests that have clear market positions in relation to competitors;

- Excellent hotel returns – to generate higher owner returns through revenue delivery and improved operating efficiency;

- Market scale and knowledge – to accelerate profitable growth in the largest markets where the Group currently has scale; and

- Aligned organisation – to create a more efficient organisation with strong core capabilities.

Executing the four strategic priorities is designed to achieve:

- Organic growth of at least 50,000 to 60,000 net rooms by the end of 2008 (starting from 537,000 in June 2005), with specific growth targets for the InterContinental brand and the key Chinese market; and

- Out-performance of total shareholder return against a competitor set.

Growth is planned to be attained predominantly from managing and franchising rather than owning hotels. Nearly 550,000 rooms operating under Group brands are managed or franchised (see figure 2). The managed and franchised model is attractive because it enables the Group to achieve its goals with limited capital investment. With a relatively fixed cost base, such growth yields high incremental margins for IHG, and is primarily how the Group has grown recently. For this reason, the Group has executed a disposal programme for most of its owned hotels, releasing capital and enabling returns of funds to shareholders.

A key characteristic of the managed and franchised business model on which the Group has focused is that it generates more cash than is required for investment in the business, with a high return on capital employed. Currently, 92% of continuing earnings before interest, tax and regional and central overheads is derived from managed and franchised operations.

The Group aims to deliver its growth targets through the strongest operating system in the industry which includes:

- A strong brand portfolio across the major markets, including two leading brands: InterContinental and Holiday Inn;

- Market coverage – a presence in nearly 100 countries and territories;

- Scale – 3,741 hotels, 556,246 rooms and 130 million guest stays per annum;

- IHG global reservation channels delivering $5.7bn of global system room revenue in 2006, $2.0bn from the internet;

- A loyalty programme, Priority Club Rewards, contributing $4.4bn of global system room revenue; and

- A strong web presence – holidayinn.com is the industry's most visited site, with around 75 million total site visits per annum.

With a clear target for rooms growth and a number of brands with market premiums offering excellent returns for owners, the Group is well placed to execute its strategy and achieve its goals.

Global room count by ownership type at 31 December 2006

■ Owned and leased   ■ Managed   Franchised

Figure 2

Business relationships

IHG maintains effective business relationships across all aspects of its operations. However, the Group's operations are not dependent upon any single customer, supplier or hotel owner due to the extent of its brands, market segments and geographical coverage. For example, the largest hotel owner controls less than 4% of the Group's total room count.

To promote effective owner relationships, the Group's management meets with owners of IHG branded hotels on a regular basis. In addition, IHG has an important relationship with the International Association of Holiday Inns (IAHI). The IAHI is an independent worldwide association for owners of the Crowne Plaza, Holiday Inn, Holiday Inn Express, Hotel Indigo, Staybridge Suites and Candlewood Suites brands. IHG and the IAHI work together to support and facilitate the continued development of IHG's brands and systems.

Many jurisdictions and countries regulate the offering of franchise agreements and recent trends indicate an increase in the number of countries adopting franchise legislation. As a significant percentage of the Group's revenues is derived from franchise fees, the Group's continued compliance with franchise legislation is important to the successful deployment of the Group's strategy.

3.7 Example: OFR key performance indicators

The following Key Performance Indicators are taken from the OFR of Cadbury Schweppes for 2005:

- Revenue
- Sales volumes
- Underlying Profit from Operations
- Underlying Operating margins
- Free Cash Flow
- Net cash from operating activities (a key component of Free Cash Flow)

4 GAAP and conceptual framework

FAST FORWARD

GAAP standards for 'Generally Accepted Accounting Practice'. It signifies all rules from whatever source, which govern accounting.

It has been said that in the past the standard setting body took a 'fire fighting' approach to developing accounting standards. The **old SSAPs** were not based on a consistent philosophy and this led to the need for a conceptual framework of accounting.

Key term

A **conceptual framework** is a constitution, a coherent system of interrelated objectives and fundamentals that can lead to consistent standards and that prescribes the nature, function and limits of financial accounting and financial statements.
Financial Accounting Standards Board (FASB)

The basic idea is to avoid the 'fire fighting' approach which characterised the development of SSAPs under the old ASC, and instead to develop an **underlying philosophy** as a basis for consistent accounting principles so that the rationale of each standard is structured into the whole framework. The process towards a conceptual framework is described briefly here.

4.1 ASC/FASB

The ASC stated in a consultative document *Setting Accounting Standards* that, whilst an agreed framework of accounting would provide a good basis on which to build accounting standards, it believed that no such framework was currently available and that conclusive results would probably not be rapidly achieved. FASB, however, began a large-scale project in 1973 to develop such a framework, with immense resources committed to the research and large volumes of material produced.

4.2 Macve Report

In the UK, a similar search for a conceptual framework was under way; a report was commissioned by the ASC from Professor Richard Macve. His report was published in 1981 and he wrote:

'the value of the current attempts to explore the conceptual framework lies, in my opinion, mainly in the discipline the process imposes of identifying the important areas where judgement is needed on questions of accounting policy, and of stimulating enquiry, with regard to users' needs and how to satisfy them.'

4.3 IASB's Framework

The IASB *Framework for the Preparation and Presentation of Financial Statements* is non-mandatory and it deals with:

    (a)   The objective of financial statements

    (b)   The qualitative characteristics that determine the usefulness of information in financial statements

    (c)   The definition, recognition and measurement of the elements from which financial statements are constructed

    (d)   Concepts of capital and capital maintenance

The IASB believes that further international harmonisation of accounting methods can best be promoted by focusing on these four topics since they will then lead to published financial statements that meet the common needs of most users.

4.4 Solomons Report

The Solomons Report, published in 1989 and entitled *Guidelines for Financial Reporting Standards*, proceeds in a similar way. Chapters deal with:

- The purpose of financial reporting
- Financial statements and their elements
- The qualitative characteristics of accounting information
- Recognition and measurement
- The choice of a general purpose accounting model

4.5 Advantages of a conceptual framework

The advantages arising from using a conceptual framework may be summarised by looking at some of the **problems** the old ASC had when developing SSAPs.

(a) SSAPs were developed on a **patchwork quilt** basis where a particular accounting problem was recognised by the ASC as having emerged, and resources were then channelled into standardising accounting practice in that area, without regard to whether that particular issue was necessarily the most important issue remaining at that time without standardisation.

(b) The development of certain SSAPs (eg SSAP 13) were subject to considerable **political interference** from interested parties. Where there is a conflict of interest between user groups on which policies to choose, policies deriving from a conceptual framework will be less open to criticism that the standard setters buckled under external pressure.

(c) Some SSAPs **concentrate** on the income statement (P&L account), some on the valuation of net assets (balance sheet).

   (i) FRS 15 ensures that depreciation is charged on a systematic basis through the P&L account to comply with the accruals concept, but the net book value figure in the balance sheet has little meaning.

   (ii) Conversely, SSAP 15 (forerunner of FRS 19) required the balance sheet provision for deferred tax to be the liability currently envisaged, but the P&L charge or credit for deferred tax has no meaning other than representing the balancing figure between a provision brought forward and carried forward in the balance sheet.

An unambiguous definition of **income** and **value** would ensure all financial statements have equal usefulness to each user group.

4.6 Disadvantages of a conceptual framework

(a) Financial statements are intended for a **variety of users**, and it is not certain that a single conceptual framework can be devised which will suit all users.

(b) Given the diversity of user requirements, there may be a need for a variety of accounting standards, each produced for a **different purpose** (and with different concepts as a basis).

(c) It is not clear that a conceptual framework will make the task of **preparing** and then **implementing** standards any easier than it is now.

The ASB has now focused its attention on developing a conceptual framework, based on both the IASB *Framework* and on the recommendations of the Solomons Report. The ASB conceptual framework is encompassed in a *Statement of Principles,* a summary of which is given below.

4.7 Generally Accepted Accounting Practice (GAAP)

This term has sprung up in recent years.

Key term

> **GAAP** signifies all the rules, from whatever source, which govern accounting. In the UK this is seen primarily as a combination of:
>
> - Company law (mainly CA 2006)
> - Accounting standards
> - Stock exchange requirements

Although those sources are the basis for UK GAAP, the concept also includes the effects of **non-mandatory sources** such as:

- International accounting standards
- Statutory requirements in other countries, particularly the US

In other words, GAAP encompasses these regulatory influences discussed in Section 1 above. In the UK, GAAP has **no statutory or regulatory authority** or definition (unlike other countries, such as the US). The term is mentioned rarely in legislation, and only then in fairly limited terms.

GAAP is in fact a **dynamic concept**: it changes constantly as circumstances alter through new legislation, standards *and* practice. This idea that GAAP is constantly changing is recognised by the ASB in its *Statement of Aims* where it states that it expects to issue new standards and amend old ones in response to:

'evolving business practices, new economic developments and deficiencies identified in current practice.'

The emphasis has shifted from 'principles' to 'practice' in UK GAAP.

The problem of what is **generally accepted** is not easy to settle, because new practices will obviously not be generally adopted yet. The criteria for a practice being 'generally accepted' will depend on factors such as whether the practice is addressed by UK accounting standards or legislation, their international equivalents, and whether other companies have adopted the practice. Most importantly, perhaps: is the practice consistent with the needs of users and the objectives of financial reporting and is it is consistent with the 'true and fair' concept?

4.8 ASB Statement of Principles

You have covered this in your earlier studies, so a summary is given here.

Knowledge brought forward from earlier studies

ASB Statement of Principles

Conceptual framework

- *Definition*: a statement of generally accepted theoretical principles which form the frame of reference for financial reporting
- The previous approach was just to tackle problems as they arose; this caused overlaps, contradictions, loopholes etc
- The IASB's *Framework* document and the *Solomons Report* have been used as a basis for the ASB's *Statement of Principles*

Statement of Principles

- Will provide the conceptual basis for UK standards
- All 8 chapters now produced together in one Statement (issued December 1999)

Chapter 1 Objective of financial statements

- To provide information about *financial position*, *performance* and *financial adaptability*, useful to assess management stewardship and to make economic decisions
- Wide range of users, with some common needs, primarily meet needs of providers of risk capital
- *Users*
  - Investors
  - Employees
  - Lenders
  - Suppliers and other creditors
  - Customers

Knowledge brought forward from earlier studies (cont'd)

- - Government and their agencies
  - The public

- Investors are the defining choice of user. They require information on
  - Financial performance
  - Financial position
  - Generation and use of cash
  - Financial adaptability

Chapter 2 The reporting entity

It is important that entities that should prepare financial statements in fact do so.

The entity must be a cohesive economic unit with a determinable boundary and it is held to account for all the things it can *control*.

Control means

- Ability to deploy the economic resources
- Ability to benefit (suffer) from their deployment

Chapter 3 Qualitative characteristics of financial information

- Qualitative characteristics that relate to content are relevance and reliability
- Qualitative characteristics that relate to presentation are comparability and understandability

Chapter 4 Elements of financial statements

- *Elements*

  - Assets
  - Liabilities
  - Ownership interest
  - Gains
  - Losses
  - Contributions from owners
  - Distributions to owners

- Any item not falling under the definition of one of these should not be included in financial statements

Chapter 5 Recognition in financial statements

There are 3 stages in the recognition of assets and liabilities.

- Initial recognition
- Subsequent remeasurement
- Derecognition

Uncertainty sometimes makes it necessary to delay the recognition process.

- Element uncertainty – does the item exist and meet the definition of elements?
- Measurement uncertainty – at what monetary amount should it be recognised?

Matching is still important, but does not *drive* the recognition process.

> Knowledge brought forward from earlier studies (continued)

Chapter 6 Measurement in financial statements

- *Initially:* record asset/liability at transaction cost = historical cost = current replacement cost

- *Remeasure:* in historical cost system

   - Write down *asset* to recoverable amount
   - Amend *liability* to monetary amount to be paid

- *Current value system* recommended

   - *Asset* current value = value to the business
   - *Liability* current value = market value = value to business

Chapter 7 Presentation of financial information

- *Components* of financial statements

   - Profit and loss account
   - Statement of total recognised gains and losses
   - Balance sheet
   - Cash flow statement

The first two are 'statements of financial performance'.

Chapter 8 Accounting for interests in other entities

This chapter deals with principles underlying consolidation, equity accounting and proportional consolidation. It focuses on the circumstances in which one business interest controls another and how to account for influence that is less than control but still significant.

4.9 Questions and answers

FAST FORWARD

There are some important debates raging in the financial reporting world at the moment on the **Statement of Principles** and on **corporate governance**.

The original November 1995 exposure draft of the *Statement of Principles* attracted a great deal of criticism, not least from the firm Ernst & Young. In an attempt to address the criticisms raised, the ASB produced a booklet to go with the revised March 1998 exposure draft, called '*Some questions answered*'. Although these have not been incorporated into the December 1999 version, they are still valid arguments and should be used if you have to comment critically on the *Statement*. Below is an outline of the topics covered.

4.9.1 Status and purpose

The points made here are as follows.

   (a)   The *Statement* is a description of the fundamental approach that should underpin the financial statements. It is intended to be:

   - Comprehensive
   - Internally consistent
   - Consistent with international approaches

   (b)   The final version is **not** an accounting standard.

   (c)   Its main influence on accounting practice will be through its influence on the standard-setting process. It is only one of the factors that will be taken into account.

4.9.2 Approach

The approach encompasses the following.

(a) There are similarities to existing practice and differences.

(b) The *Statement* is based on the International Accounting Standard Committee's framework statement and is largely consistent with the framework statements issued in Australia, Canada, New Zealand, the USA and elsewhere. This reflects the view that it will be easier to achieve harmonisation of accounting practice if standard-setters work with a common set of principles.

(c) The 'true and fair' requirement and the old SSAP 2's fundamental accounting concepts play a central role in the revised draft. The emphasis is different, however, and is reflected in FRS 18 *Accounting policies*.

(d) The *Statement's* development has not been constrained by the requirements of companies legislation because:

- It does not just apply to companies

- Legal frameworks change in response to developments in accounting thought

The use of current costs and values and current cost accounting

These points are made.

(a) The previous version of the *Statement* was criticised as heralding a move towards **current cost accounting**. However, the revised draft makes it clear that this is **not on the ASB's agenda**.

(b) The *Statement* explains that historical cost and current value are **alternative measures**. It also explains that it is envisaged that the approach now adopted by the majority of the larger UK listed companies will continue to be used. This approach involves carrying some categories of balance sheet items at historical cost and others at current value. The *Statement* then goes on to describe a framework that would guide the choice of an appropriate measurement basis for each balance sheet category.

4.9.3 The focus on assets and liabilities and the role of transactions

These points are made.

The previous version placed great emphasis on assets and liabilities and even defined the items that are to be included in the profit and loss account in terms of assets and liabilities. This approach has been retained.

(a) The approach does not mean that the P&L is unimportant. The primary source of information provided in financial statements is the transactions undertaken by the reporting entity. The primary focus of the accounting process is to allocate these transactions to accounting periods.

(b) The *Statement* regards the profit or loss for the period as the difference between the opening and closing balance sheets adjusted for capital constructions and distributions.

4.9.4 Accounting standards based on the Statement

The question was raised as to whether accounting standards published in the future and therefore based on the *Statement of Principles* will be very different from past accounting standards. The ASB's view is that they won't. Some of the principles have already played very significant roles in accounting standards and have found general acceptance. The standards include:

- FRS 2 *Accounting for subsidiary undertakings*, which uses the reporting entity concept described in Chapter 2 of the draft Statement.

- FRSs 25, 26 and 29 on *Financial instruments*. FRS 5 *Reporting the substance of transactions*, which use the definitions of assets and liabilities set out in Chapter 4.

- FRS 11 *Impairment of fixed assets and goodwill*, which uses the recoverable amount notion described in Chapter 6.

4.10 Conceptual Framework Discussion Paper

FAST FORWARD

IASB **proposals on a Conceptual Framework** are controversial and have been criticised by the ASB.

In July 2006, the IASB produced a Discussion Paper *Preliminary views on an Improved Conceptual Framework for Financial Reporting.*

4.10.1 Background

This Discussion Paper is the first in a series of publications being developed jointly by FASB and the IASB as part of a joint project to develop a common conceptual framework for financial reporting.
The aim is to provide the best common foundation for developing principles-based and converged standards.

The Paper covers the first two chapters of a proposed Conceptual Framework:

- Chapter 1: The objective of financial reporting
- Chapter 2: Qualitative characteristics of decision-useful financial reporting information.

The Discussion also includes the Draft chapters themselves.

4.10.2 Objective

The proposed objective of general purpose external financial reporting is 'to provide information that is useful to present and potential investors and creditors and others in making investment, credit, and similar resource allocation decisions'.

The focus therefore is on the capital markets.

4.10.3 Qualitative characteristics

Similar to the current Framework the proposed chapter considers the users of the financial statements, their abilities and their needs.

Proposed qualitative characteristics that make information useful and considerations in developing standards:

- **Relevance**: predictive value, confirmatory value, timeliness

- **Faithful representation**: data must be verifiable, neutral and complete (replacing 'reliability')

- **Comparability (including consistency)**

- **Understandability**: for users who have a reasonable knowledge of business and economic activities and financial accounting

- **Constraints of financial reporting**

   o   Materiality (all material information included; not cluttered with immaterial information)

   o   Benefits and costs (the benefits of financial information should justify the costs).

Exam focus point

This is a hot topic and likely to be examined in Question 4 of the paper.

4.10.4 Potential problems

The Accounting Standards Board (ASB) has highlighted a number of potential objections that may be made to the proposals.

(a) **Users.** The ASB is concerned about the proposal that the objective of financial reporting should focus only on decision-usefulness, with stewardship being subsumed within this rather than being referred to as a specific part of the objective, or a separate objective. The ASB believes that stewardship should be a separate objective. The ASB is also concerned that the shareholder user perspective is being downplayed.

(b) **Qualitative characteristics: what happens to reliability?** The Discussion Paper proposes replacing the qualitative characteristic of 'reliability' in the current *Framework* with 'faithful representation'. The ASB believes that faithful representation is a softer notion which, when combined with a lack of specific identification of substance over form as a principle, could lead to a number of problems.

(c) **Financial reporting or financial statements.** The ASB believes the boundary between financial statements and financial reporting has not been properly considered.

(d) **Limited in scope.** The Discussion Paper is limited to private enterprises, rather than, as the ASB believes it should be, encompassing the not-for profit sector.

(e) **Too theoretical.** This may alienate preparers and auditors of accounts.

Chapter Roundup

- You should be familiar using the **role and impact** of the following bodies.
  - Accounting Standards Board
  - Financial Reporting Council
  - Review Panel
  - Urgent Issues Task Force
  - European Union/European Commission
  - Company Law
  - International Accounting Standards Committee

- The impact of the **Cadbury Report** and the **Combined Code** is still being felt as some companies struggle to meet its requirements.

- The **Operating and Financial Review** should be of considerable benefit to less sophisticated users. It is not a statutory requirement, but is the subject of a Reporting Statement, setting out best practice.

- **GAAP** stands for 'Generally Accepted Accounting Practice'. It signifies all rules, from whatever source, which govern accounting.

- There are some important debates raging in the financial reporting world at the moment on the **Statement of Principles** and on **corporate governance**.

- IASB **proposals on a Conceptual Framework** are controversial and have been criticised by the ASB.

Quick Quiz

1   What is the latest FRS?

2   Name the reports that deal with corporate governance.

    ....

    ....

    ....

3   The Operating and Financial Review is compulsory/voluntary?

4   What is meant by GAAP?

5   Which of the following are chapters of the *Statement of Principles*? Circle all that apply.

    (a)   The reporting entity
    (b)   The quantitative characteristics of financial information
    (c)   Presentation of interests in other entitles
    (d)   Measurement in financial statements

6   The *Statement of Principles* is now a full accounting standard. True or false?

7   How does the *Statement* define assets?

8   Which accounting standard uses the 'recoverable amount' idea described in the *Statement of Principles*.

Answers to Quick Quiz

1   FRS 29 *Financial instruments: disclosures*

2   Cadbury
    Combined Code

3   Voluntary

4   The rules governing accounting, principally:

    •   Company law
    •   Accounting standards
    •   Stock exchange requirements

5   (a) and (d)

6   False. However, it will influence the standard-setting process.

7   Rights or other access to future economic benefits controlled by an entity as a result of past transactions or events.

8   FRS 11 *Impairment of fixed assets and goodwill.*

Professional and ethical duty of the accountant

Topic list	Syllabus reference
1 The social and ethical environment	A2
2 Ethics in organisations	A2
3 Fundamental principles and guidance on professional ethics	A2
4 Practical situations	A2
5 Examination questions: an approach	A2
6 Professional skills: guidance from the ACCA	A2

Introduction

Ethics are an important aspect of the ACCA qualification. They need to be applied in all aspects of managerial behaviour. An attempt to massage profit figures, or non-disclosure of a close relationship may amount to unethical behaviour. However, it is the nature of ethics to deny easy answers; furthermore, in the context of business, ethical prescriptions have to be practical to be of any use. This chapter focuses on the professional integrity of the accountant and director, but you will also consider ethics in the context of off balance sheet finance, covered in Chapter 11.

Study guide

		Intellectual level
A2	**Ethical requirements of reporting a true and fair view and the consequences of unethical behaviour**	
(a)	Appraise the potential ethical implications of professional and managerial decisions in the preparation of corporate reports	3
(b)	Assess the consequences of not upholding ethical principles in the preparation of corporate reports	3

Exam guide

Ethics are most likely to be considered in the context of the accountant's role as adviser to the directors. A question on the Pilot Paper asked you to explain why a deliberate misrepresentation in the financial statements was unethical. A scenario question at the end of this Study Text asks for a discussion of why directors might have acted unethically in adopting accounting policies to boost earnings.

1 The social and ethical environment   Pilot paper

FAST FORWARD

Firms have to ensure they obey the law: but they also face ethical concerns, because their reputations depend on a good image.

Key term

Ethics: a set of moral principles to guide behaviour

Whereas the political environment in which an organisation operates consists of laws, regulations and government agencies, the social environment consists of the customs, attitudes, beliefs and education of society as a whole, or of different groups in society; and the ethical environment consists of a set (or sets) of well-established rules of personal and organisational behaviour.

Social attitudes, such as a belief in the merits of education, progress through science and technology, and fair competition, are significant for the management of a business organisation. Other beliefs have either gained strength or been eroded in recent years:

(a)   There is a growing belief in preserving and improving the quality of life by reducing working hours, reversing the spread of pollution, developing leisure activities and so on. Pressures on organisations to consider the environment are particularly strong because most environmental damage is irreversible and some is fatal to humans and wildlife.

(b)   Many pressure groups have been organised in recent years to protect social minorities and under-privileged groups. Legislation has been passed in an attempt to prevent racial discrimination and discrimination against women and disabled people.

(c)   Issues relating to the environmental consequences of corporate activities are currently debated, and respect for the environment has come to be regarded as an unquestionable good.

The ethical environment refers to justice, respect for the law and a moral code. The conduct of an organisation, its management and employees will be measured against ethical standards by the customers, suppliers and other members of the public with whom they deal.

BPP
LEARNING MEDIA

1.1 Ethical problems facing managers

Managers have a duty (in most enterprises) to aim for profit. At the same time, modern ethical standards impose a duty to guard, preserve and enhance the value of the enterprise for the good of all touched by it, including the general public. Large organisations tend to be more often held to account over this than small ones.

In the area of **products and production**, managers have responsibility to ensure that the public and their own employees are protected from danger. Attempts to increase profitability by cutting costs may lead to dangerous working conditions or to inadequate safety standards in products. In the United States, product liability litigation is so common that this legal threat may be a more effective deterrent than general ethical standards. The Consumer Protection Act 1987 and EU legislation generally is beginning to ensure that ethical standards are similarly enforced in the UK.

Another ethical problem concerns **payments by companies to government or municipal officials** who have power to help or hinder the payers' operations. In *The Ethics of Corporate Conduct, Clarence Walton* refers to the fine distinctions which exist in this area.

(a) **Extortion**. Foreign officials have been known to threaten companies with the complete closure of their local operations unless suitable payments are made.

(b) **Bribery**. This refers to payments for services to which a company is not legally entitled. There are some fine distinctions to be drawn; for example, some managers regard political contributions as bribery.

(c) **Grease money**. Multinational companies are sometimes unable to obtain services to which they are legally entitled because of deliberate stalling by local officials. Cash payments to the right people may then be enough to oil the machinery of bureaucracy.

(d) **Gifts**. In some cultures (such as Japan) gifts are regarded as an essential part of civilised negotiation, even in circumstances where to Western eyes they might appear ethically dubious. Managers operating in such a culture may feel at liberty to adopt the local customs.

Business ethics are also relevant to competitive behaviour. This is because a market can only be free if competition is, in some basic respects, fair. There is a distinction between competing aggressively and competing unethically. The dispute between British Airways and Virgin centred around issues of business ethics.

1.2 Examples of social and ethical objectives

Companies are not passive in the social and ethical environment. Many organisations pursue a variety of social and ethical objectives.

Employees

(a) A minimum wage, perhaps with adequate differentials for skilled labour

(b) Job security (over and above the protection afforded to employees by government legislation)

(c) Good conditions of work (above the legal minima)

(d) Job satisfaction

Customers may be regarded as entitled to receive a produce of good quality at a reasonable price.

Suppliers may be offered regular orders and timely payment in return for reliable delivery and good service.

Society as a whole

(a) Control of pollution

(b) Provision of financial assistance to charities, sports and community activities

(c) Co-operation with government authorities in identifying and preventing health hazards in the products sold

As far as it is possible, social and ethical objectives should be expressed quantitatively, so that actual results can be monitored to ensure that the targets are achieved. This is often easier said than done – more often, they are expressed in the organisation's mission statement which can rarely be reduced to a quantified amount.

Many of the above objectives are commercial ones – for example satisfying customers is necessary to stay in business. The question as to whether it is the business of businesses to be concerned about wider issues of social responsibility *at all* is discussed shortly.

2 Ethics in organisations

Ethics is a code of moral principles that people follow with respect to what is right or wrong. Ethical principles are not necessarily enforced by law, although the law incorporates moral judgements (murder is wrong ethically, and is also punishable legally).

Companies have to follow legal standards, or else they will be subject to fines and their officers might face similar charges. Ethics in organisations relates to **social responsibility** and **business practice.**

People that work for organisations bring their own values into work with them. Organisations contain a variety of ethical systems.

(a) **Personal ethics** (eg deriving from a person's upbringing, religious or non-religious beliefs, political opinions, personality). People have different ethical viewpoints at different stages in their lives. Some will judge situations on 'gut feel'. Some will consciously or unconsciously adopt a general approach to ethical dilemmas, such as 'the end justifies the means'.

(b) **Professional ethics** (eg ACCA's ethical rules).

(c) **Organisation cultures** (eg 'customer first'). Culture, in denoting what is normal behaviour, also denotes what is the right behaviour in many cases.

(d) **Organisation systems**. Ethics might be contained in a formal code, reinforced by the overall statement of values. A problem might be that ethics does not always save money, and there is a real cost to ethical decisions. Besides, the organisation has different ethical duties to different stakeholders. Who sets priorities?

 Case Study

Organisation systems and targets do have ethical implications. The Harvard Business Review reported that the US retailer, Sears, Roebuck was deluged with complaints that customers of its car service centre were being charged for unnecessary work: apparently this was because mechanics had been given targets of the number of car spare parts they should sell.

2.1 Leadership practices and ethics

FAST FORWARD

Organisations sometimes issue codes of conduct to employees. Many employees are bound by professional codes of conduct.

The role of culture in determining the ethical climate of an organisation can be further explored by a brief reflection on the role of leaders in setting the ethical standard. A culture is partly a collection of symbols and attitudes, embodying certain truths about the organisation. Senior managers are also symbolic managers; inevitably they decide priorities; they set an example, whether they like it or not. Remember, too, that one of the roles of managers, according to Mintzberg is the **ceremonial one**.

There are four types of cultural leadership in organisations. (Note that these should *not* be confused with leadership styles.)

(a) **Creative**. The culture of an organisation often reflects its founder, and it is therefore reasonable to expect that the founding visionary should set the ethical tone. Such leaders create the ethical style.

(b) **Protective**. Such leaders sustain, or exemplify, the organisation's culture: for example a company which values customer service may have leaders who are 'heroic' in their efforts to achieve it.

(c) **Integrative**. Other leaders aim to create consensus through people, and perhaps flourish in an involvement culture. The danger is that this can turn to political manipulation; the 'consensus' created should work towards some valued cultural goal.

(d) **Adaptive**. These leaders change an existing culture or set of ethics. (When appointed to run *British Airways, Colin Marshall* changed the sign on his door from Chief Executive to his own name.) However, a leader has to send out the right signals, to ensure that competitive behaviour remains ethical, to avoid bad publicity if nothing else.

2.2 Two approaches to managing ethics

FAST FORWARD

Inside the organisation, a compliance based approach highlights conformity with the law. An integrity based approach suggests a wider remit, incorporating ethics in the organisation's values and culture.

Lynne Paine (*Harvard Business Review*, March-April 1994) suggests that ethical decisions are becoming more important as penalties, in the US at least, for companies which break the law become tougher. (This might be contrasted with UK, where a fraudster whose deception ran into millions received a sentence of community service.) Paine suggests that there are two approaches to the management of ethics in organisations.

- Compliance-based
- Integrity-based

2.3 Compliance-based approach

A compliance-based approach is primarily designed to ensure that the company acts within the letter of the law, and that violations are prevented, detected and punished. Some organisations, faced with the legal consequences of unethical behaviour take legal precautions such as those below.

- Compliance procedures
- Audits of contracts
- Systems for employees to inform superiors about criminal misconduct without fear of retribution
- Disciplinary procedures

Corporate compliance is limited in that it refers only to the law, but legal compliance is 'not an adequate means for addressing the full range of ethical issues that arise every day'. This is especially the case in the UK, where **voluntary** codes of conduct and self-regulation are perhaps more prevalent than in the US.

An example of the difference between the **legality** and **ethicality** of a practice is the sale in some countries of defective products without appropriate warnings. 'Companies engaged in international business often discover that conduct that infringes on recognised standards of human rights and decency is legally permissible in some jurisdictions.'

The compliance approach also overemphasises the threat of detection and punishment in order to channel appropriate behaviour. Arguably, some employers view compliance programmes as an insurance policy for senior management, who can cover the tracks of their arbitrary management practices. After all, some performance targets are impossible to achieve without cutting corners: managers can escape responsibility by blaming the employee for not following the compliance programme, when to do so would have meant a failure to reach target.

Furthermore, mere compliance with the law is no guide to **exemplary** behaviour.

2.4 Integrity-based programmes

'An integrity-based approach combines a concern for the law with an **emphasis on managerial responsibility** for ethical behaviour. Integrity strategies strive to define companies' guiding values, aspirations and patterns of thought and conduct. When integrated into the day-to-day operations of an organisation, such strategies can help prevent damaging ethical lapses, while tapping into powerful human impulses for moral thought and action.

It should be clear to you from this quotation that an integrity-based approach to ethics treats ethics as an issue of organisation culture.

Ethics management has several tasks.

- To define and give life to an organisation's defining values.
- To create an environment that supports ethically sound behaviour
- To instil a sense of shared accountability amongst employees.

The table below indicates some of the differences between the two main approaches.

	Compliance	Integrity
Ethos	Knuckle under to external standards	Choose ethical standards
Objective	Keep to the law	Enable legal and responsible conduct
Originators	Lawyers	Management, with lawyers, HR specialists etc
Methods (both includes education, and audits, controls, penalties)	Reduced employee discretion	Leadership, organisation systems
Behavioural assumptions	People are solitary self-interested beings	People are social beings with values
Standards	The law	Company values, aspirations (including law)
Staffing	Lawyers	Managers and lawyers

	Compliance	Integrity
Education	The law, compliance system	Values, the law, compliance systems
Activities	Develop standards, train and communicate, handle reports of misconduct, investigate, enforce, oversee compliance	Integrate values into company systems, provide guidance and consultation, identify and resolve problems, oversee compliance

In other words, an integrity-based approach **incorporates** ethics into corporate culture and systems.

 Case Study

Charles Hampden-Turner (in his book *Corporate Culture*) notes that attitudes to safety can be part of a corporate *culture*. He quotes the example of a firm called (for reasons of confidentiality) *Western Oil*.

Western Oil had a bad safety record. 'Initially, safety was totally at odds with the main cultural values of productivity (management's interests) and maintenance of a macho image (the worker's culture) ... Western Oil had a culture which put safety in conflict with other corporate values.' In particular, the problem was with its long-distance truck drivers (which in the US have a culture of solitary independence and self reliance) who drove sometimes recklessly with loads large enough to inundate a small town. The company instituted *Operation Integrity* to improve safety, in a lasting way, changing the policies and drawing on the existing features of the culture but using them in a different way.

The culture had five dilemmas.

- *Safety-first vs macho-individualism*. Truckers see themselves as 'fearless pioneers of the unconventional lifestyle ... 'Be careful boys!' is hardly a plea likely to go down well with this particular group'. Instead of trying to control the drivers, the firm recommended that they become *road safety consultants* (or design consultants). Their advice was sought on improving the system. This had the advantage that 'by making drivers critics of the system their roles as outsiders were preserved and promoted'. It tried to tap their heroism as promoters of public safety.

- *Safety everywhere vs safety specialists*. Western Oil could have hired more specialist staff. However, instead, the company promoted cross functional safety teams from existing parts of the business, for example, to help in designing depots and thinking of ways to reduce hazards.

- *Safety as cost vs productivity as benefit*. 'If the drivers raced from station to station to win their bonus, accidents were bound to occur ... . The safety engineers rarely spoke to the line manager in charge of the delivery schedules. The unreconciled dilemma between safety and productivity had been evaded at management level and passed down the hierarchy until drivers were subjected to two incompatible injunctions, work fast and work safely'. To deal with this problem, safety would be built into the reward system.

- *Long-term safety vs short-term steering*. The device of recording 'unsafe' acts in operations enabled them to be monitored by cross-functional teams, so that the causes of accidents could be identified and be reduced.

- *Personal responsibility vs collective protection*. It was felt that if 'safety' was seen as a form of management policing it would never be accepted. The habit of management 'blaming the victim' had to stop. Instead, if an employee reported another to the safety teams, the person who was reported would be free of *official* sanction. Peer presence was seen to be a better enforcer of safety than the management hierarchy.

It has also been suggested that the following institutions can be established.

- An **ethics committee** is a group of executives (perhaps including non-executive directors) appointed to oversee company ethics. It rules on misconduct. It may seek advice from specialists in business ethics.

- An **ethics ombudsperson** is a manager who acts as the corporate conscience.

Accountants can also appeal to their professional body for ethical guidance.

Whistle-blowing is the disclosure by an employee of illegal, immoral or illegitimate practices on the part of the organisation. In theory, the public ought to welcome the public trust: however, confidentiality is very important in the accountants' code of ethics. Whistle-blowing frequently involves **financial loss** for the whistleblower.

- The whistle-blower may lose his or her job.

- If the whistle-blower is a member of a professional body, he or she cannot, sadly, rely on that body to take a significant interest, or even offer a sympathetic ear. Some professional bodies have narrow interpretations of what is meant by ethical conduct. For many the duties of **commercial confidentiality** are felt to be more important.

Exam focus point

The ethics codes described above can be related to mission, culture and control strategies. A compliance-based approach suggest that bureaucratic control is necessary; an integrity based approach relies on cultural control.

3 Fundamental principles and guidance on professional ethics

FAST FORWARD

Accountants require an ethical code because they hold positions of trust, and people rely on them.

3.1 The public interest

IFAC's *Code of Ethics* gives the key reason why accountancy bodies produce ethical guidance: the public interest.

'A distinguishing mark of the accountancy profession is its acceptance of the responsibility to act in the public interest. Therefore, a professional accountant's responsibility is not exclusively to satisfy the needs of an individual client or employer.

The public interest is considered to be the collective well-being of the community of people and institutions the professional accountant serves, including clients, lenders, governments, employers, employees, investors, the business and financial community and others who rely on the work of professional accountants.'

The **key reason** that **accountants need** to have an **ethical code** is that **people rely on them and their expertise.**

Accountants deal with a range of issues on behalf of clients. They often have access to confidential and sensitive information. Auditors claim to give an independent view. It is therefore critical that accountants, and particularly auditors, are, and are seen to be, independent.

As the auditor is required to be, and seen to be, ethical in his dealings with clients, ACCA publishes guidance for its members, the *Code of Ethics and Conduct*. This guidance is given in the form of fundamental principles, guidance and explanatory notes.

IFAC also lays down fundamental principles in its *Code of Ethics*. The fundamental principles of the two associations are extremely similar.

3.2 The fundamental principles

ACCA
• **Integrity.** Members should be **straightforward** and **honest** in all professional and business relationships.
• **Objectivity.** Members **should not allow bias, conflict of interest or undue influence of others** to override professional or business judgements.
• **Professional Competence and Due Care**. Members have a continuing duty to maintain professional knowledge and skill at a level required to ensure that a client or employer receives the advantage of competent professional service based on current developments in practice, legislation and techniques. Members should act diligently and in accordance with applicable technical and professional standards when providing professional services.
• **Confidentiality**. Members should respect the confidentiality of information acquired as a result of professional or business relationships **and should not disclose** any such information to third parties without proper and specific authority **unless there is a legal or professional right or duty to disclose**. Confidential information acquired as a result of professional and business relationships should not be used for the personal advantage of the professional accountant or third parties.
• **Professional Behaviour**. Members should **comply with relevant laws and regulations and should avoid any action that discredits the profession.**

3.3 Ethical framework

The ethical guidance discussed above is in the form of a framework. It contains some rules, for example, ACCA prohibits making loans to clients, but in the main it is flexible guidance. It can be seen as being a **framework rather than a set of rules**. There are a number of advantages of a framework over a system of ethical rules. These are outlined in the table below.

Advantages of an ethical framework over a rules based system
A framework of guidance places the onus on the auditor to **actively consider** independence for every given situation, rather than just agreeing a checklist of forbidden items. It also requires him to **demonstrate** that a responsible conclusion has been reached about ethical issues.
The framework **prevents auditors interpreting legalistic requirements narrowly** to get around the ethical requirements. There is an extent to which rules engender deception, whereas principles encourage compliance.
A framework **allows for** the variations that are found in every **individual situation**. Each situation is likely to be different.
A framework can accommodate a **rapidly changing environment**, such as the one that auditors are constantly in.
However, a **framework can contain prohibitions** (as noted above) where these are necessary as safeguards are not feasible.

4 Practical situations

FAST FORWARD

Exam questions may ask you to think about what should be done if breaches of laws, regulations or ethical guidelines occur. **Close relationships** between the parties or other **conflicts of interest** are often a complication.

4.1 Examination questions

Examination questions will expect you to be able to apply your understanding of ethical issues to practical problems arising in organisations. Later in this chapter we are going to suggest an approach that you may find helpful in dealing with such questions, but first we are going to take the bare bones of a situation and see how it might be built up into the kind of scenario you will have to face.

4.2 The problem

The exam may present you with a scenario, typically containing an array of detail much of which is potentially relevant. The problem, however, will be one or other of two basic types.

(a) **A wishes B to do C which is in breach of D**

where

A	=	a situation, person, group of people, institution or the like
B	=	you/a management accountant, the person with the ethical dilemma
C	=	acting, or refraining from acting, in a certain way
D	=	an ethical principle, quite possibly one of the ACCA's fundamental principles

(b) Alternatively, the problem may be that A has done C, B has become aware of it and D requires some kind of response from B.

4.3 Example: the problem

An accountant joined a manufacturing company as its Finance Director. The company had acquired land on which it built industrial units. The Finance Director discovered that, before he had started at the company, one of the units had been sold and the selling price was significantly larger than the amount which appeared in the company's records. The difference had been siphoned off to another company – one in which his boss, the Managing Director, was a major shareholder. Furthermore, the Managing Director had kept his relationship with the second company a secret from the rest of the board.

The Finance Director confronted the Managing Director and asked him to reveal his position to the board. However, the Managing Director refused to disclose his position to anyone else. The secret profits on the sale of the unit had been used, he said, to reward the people who had secured the sale. Without their help, he added, the company would be in a worse position financially.

The Finance Director then told the Managing Director that unless he reported to the board he would have to inform the board members himself. The Managing Director still refused. The Finance Director disclosed the full position to the board.

The problem is of the **second basic type**. B is of course the easiest party to identify. Here it is the **Finance Director**. A is clear, as well: it is the **Managing Director**. C is the **MD's breach of his directorial duties** regarding related party transactions not to obtain any personal advantage from his position of director without the consent of the company for whatever gain or profit he has obtained. D is the **principle that requires B not to be a party to an illegal act**. (Note that we distinguish between ethical and legal obligations. B has legal obligations as a director of the company. He has ethical obligations not to ignore his legal obligations. In **this** case the two amount to the same thing.)

4.4 Relationships

You may have a feeling that the resolution of the problem described above is just too easy, and you would be right. This is because A, B, C and D are either people, or else situations involving people, who stand in certain relationships to each other.

- A may be B's boss, B's subordinate, B's equal in the organisational hierarchy, B's husband, B's friend.

- B may be new to the organisation, or well-established and waiting for promotion, or ignorant of some knowledge relevant to the situation that A possesses or that the people affected by C possess.

- C or D, as already indicated, may involve some person(s) with whom B or A have a relationship – for example the action may be to misrepresent something to a senior manager who controls the fate of B or A (or both) in the organisation.

Question
Relationships

Identify the relationships in the scenario above. What are the possible problems arising from these relationships?

Answer

The MD is the Finance Director's boss. He is also a member of the board and is longer established as such than B the Finance Director.

In outline the problems arising are that **by acting ethically the Finance Director will alienate the MD**. Even if the problem were to be resolved the episode would sour all future dealings between these two parties. Also, **the board may not be sympathetic to the accusations of a newcomer**. The Finance Director may find that he is ignored or even dismissed.

Relationships should never be permitted to affect ethical judgement. If you knew that your best friend at work had committed a major fraud, for example, **integrity** would demand that **in the last resort** you would have to bring it to the attention of somebody in authority. But note that this is only in the last resort. Try to imagine what you would do in practice in this situation.

Surely your **first course** would be to try to **persuade your friend** that what they had done was wrong, and that they themselves had an ethical responsibility to own up. Your **second option**, if this failed, might be to try to get **somebody** (perhaps somebody outside the organisation) that you knew could **exert pressure** on your friend to persuade him or her to own up.

There is obviously a limit to how far you can take this. The important point is that just because you are dealing with a situation that involves ethical issues, this **does not mean that all the normal principles of good human relations and good management have to be suspended**. In fact this is the time when such business principles are most important.

4.5 Consequences

Actions have consequences and the consequences themselves are quite likely to have their own ethical implications.

In the example given above, we can identify the following further issues.

(a)   The MD's secret transaction appears to have been made in order to secure the sale of an asset the proceeds of which are helping to prop up the company financially. Disclosure of the truth behind the sale may mean that the company is pursued for compensation by the buyer of the site. The **survival of the company** as a whole may be jeopardised.

(b)   If the truth behind the transaction becomes public knowledge this could be highly damaging for the company's **reputation**, even if it can show that only one black sheep was involved.

(c)   The board may simply rubber stamp the MD's actions and so the Finance Director may still find that he is expected to be party to dishonesty. (This assumes that the **company as a whole is amoral** in its approach to ethical issues. In fact the MD's refusal to disclose the matter to the board suggests otherwise.)

In the last case we are back to square one. In the first two cases, the Finance Director has to consider the ethicality or otherwise of taking action that could lead to the collapse of the company, extensive redundancies, unpaid creditors and shareholders and so on.

4.6 Actions

In spite of the difficulties, your aim will usually be to reach a satisfactory resolution to the problem. **The actions that you recommend** will often include the following.

- **Informal discussions** with the parties involved.

- **Further investigation** to establish the full facts of the matter. What extra information is needed?

- The **tightening up of controls or the introduction of new ones**, if the situation arose due to laxity in this area. This will often be the case and the principles of professional competence and due care and of technical standards will usually be relevant.

- **Attention to organisational matters** such as changes in the management structure, improving communication channels, attempting to change attitudes.

 Question   Cunning plan

Your finance director has asked you to join a team planning a takeover of one of your company's suppliers. An old school friend works as an accountant for the company concerned, the finance director knows this, and has asked you to try and find out 'anything that might help the takeover succeed, but it must remain secret'.

Answer

There are three issues here. Firstly you have a **conflict of interest** as the finance director wants you to keep the takeover a secret, but you probably feel that you should tell your friend what is happening as it may affect their job.

Second, the finance director is asking you to deceive your friend. Deception is unprofessional behaviour and will break your ethical guidelines. Therefore the situation is presenting you with **two conflicting demands**. It is worth remembering that no employer can ask you to break your ethical rules.

Finally, the request to break your own ethical guidelines constitutes **unprofessional behaviour** by the finance director. You should consider reporting him to their relevant body.

5 Examination questions: an approach

5.1 Dealing with questions

FAST FORWARD

In a situation involving ethical issues, there are **practical steps** that should be taken.

- Establish the facts of the situation by further investigation and work.
- Consider the alternative options available for action.
- Consider whether any professional guidelines have been breached.
- State the best course of action based on the steps above.

An article in a student magazine contained the following advice for candidates who wish to achieve good marks in ethics questions. (The emphasis is BPP's.)

'The precise question requirements will vary, but in general marks will be awarded for:

- **Analysis of the situation**

- **A recognition of ethical issues**

- **Explanation if appropriate of relevant part of ethical guidelines,** and **interpretation** of its relevance to the question

- Making clear, logical, and appropriate **recommendations** for action. Making inconsistent recommendations does not impress examiners

- **Justifying recommendations** in practical business terms and in ethical terms

As with all scenario based questions there is likely to be **more than one acceptable answer**, and marks will depend on how well the case is argued, rather than for getting the 'right' answer.

However, questions based on ethical issues tend to produce a range of possible solutions which are, on the one hand, consistent with the ethical guidelines and acceptable, and on the other hand, a range of clearly inadmissible answers which are clearly in breach of the ethical guidelines and possibly the law.'

5.2 Step-by-step approach

We suggest, instead, that:

(a)   **You use the question format to structure your answer**
(b)   **You bear in mind what marks are being awarded for** (see above)
(c)   **You adhere to the following list of do's and don'ts**. Be sure to read the notes following.

DO	Note	DON'T
Identify the key facts as briefly as possible (one sentence?)	1	Merely paraphrase the question
Identify the major principle(s) at issue	2	Regurgitate the entire contents of the Ethical Guidelines
Consider alternative actions and their consequences	3	List every single possible action and then explain how all the unsuitable ones can be eliminated

DO	Note	DON'T
Make a decision and recommend action as appropriate	4	Fail to make a decision or recommend action. Propose actions in breach of the *Ethical Guidelines* or the law
Justify your decision	5	Be feeble. 'This should be done because it is ethical' is not terribly convincing

Notes

1   **One sentence** is an ideal to aim for.

2   (a)   **Use the terminology of the ethical guidelines, but not *ad nauseam*.** 'Integrity' is often more clearly described as 'honesty' (although the two words are not synonymous). Don't forget the words 'fairness', 'bias', and 'influence' when discussing 'objectivity'.

    (b)   **Don't torture the case study to make it fit a fundamental principle**: if, say, 'justice' is the most persuasive word for a situation don't be afraid of using it.

    (c)   If the law is involved, don't get carried away – this is **not a law exam**. 'The director has a statutory duty to ...' is sufficient: there is no need to go into legal detail.

3   Useful ways of generating alternatives are:

    (a)   To **consider the problem from the other side of the fence**: imagine you are the guilty party

    (b)   To **consider the problem from the point of view of the organisation** and its culture and environment

4   Making a decision is often very hard, but if you cannot do this you are simply not ready to take on the responsibilities of a qualified accountant. There are usually a number of decisions that could be justified, so **don't be afraid of choosing the 'wrong' answer.**

5   This is not actually as hard as you might think.

5.3 Regurgitating the question

Possibly the most **common fault** in students' answers to questions on ethics is that they include large **amounts of unanalysed detail copied out from the question** scenarios in their answers. This earns no marks.

You can very easily avoid the temptation to merely paraphrase the question. Simply **begin your answer by stating that you are referring to 'issues'** (by which you mean all the details contained in the question) **discussed at a previous meeting, or set out in full in 'appended documents'.** If you do this you will be writing your report to someone already in possession of the same facts as you have.

5.4 Justifying your decision

The article quoted above says that **marks will be awarded for 'justifying recommendations in practical business terms and in ethical terms'.** We shall conclude by examining a passage from a model solution to a question on ethics to see how this can be done.

'Perhaps the first thing to do is to **report** the whole matter, **in confidence** and **informally**, to the chief internal auditor with suggestions that a **tactful investigation** is undertaken to **verify as many of the facts** as possible. The fact that the sales manager has already been tackled (informally) about the matter may be a positive advantage as **he/she may be recruited** to assist in the investigation. It could however be a problem as the information needed for further **investigation** may have already been removed. **Tact** is crucial as handling the matter the wrong way could adversely influence the whole situation. An understanding of who participants are and how they are implicated can be used positively to bring about change with the **minimum of disruption**.'

The key to this approach is **using the right language**, and to a large extent you cannot help doing so if you have sensible suggestions to make. The real problem that many students experience with questions of this type is lack of confidence in their own judgement. If you have sound business and managerial sense and you know the ethical guidelines there is every reason to suppose that an answer that you propose will be acceptable, so don't be shy of expressing an opinion.

<table>
<tr><td>**Exam focus point**</td><td>

In an internal company role, ethical problems could be in the following forms.

- Conflict of duties to different staff superiors

- Discovering an illegal act or fraud perpetrated by the company (ie its directors)

- Discovering a fraud or illegal act perpetrated by another employee

- Pressure from superiors to take certain viewpoints, for example towards budgets (pessimistic/optimistic etc) or not to report unfavourable findings

</td></tr>
</table>

6 Professional skills – Guidance from the ACCA

Ethics and professionalism are a key part of your ACCA qualification. Accordingly, the ACCA has stated that **marks for professional skills will be awarded at the Professional Level**. The examiner has provided specific guidance for P2 *Corporate Reporting*.

6.1 Professional skills – Basis of the award of marks

Marks will be awarded for professional skills in this paper. These skills encompass the creation, analysis, evaluation and synthesis of information, problem solving, decision making and communication skills. More specifically they will be awarded for:

(a) Developing information and ideas, and forming an opinion.

(b) Developing an understanding of the implications for the entity of the information including the entity's operating environment.

(c) Analysing information and ideas by identifying:

  (i)   The purpose of the analysis
  (ii) The limitations of given information
  (iii) Bias and underlying assumptions and their impact
  (iv) Problems of liability and inconsistency

(d) Identifying the purpose of a computation and whether it meets its purpose.

(e) Analysing information, drawing conclusions and considerable implications, and any further action required.

(f) Identifying appropriate action in response to the information/analysis including advice or amendments to the data.

(g) Considering, discussing and combining ideas and information from diverse sources to arrive at a solution or a broader understanding of the issues.

(h) Analysing the information in the context of the views and reactions of the stakeholders.

(i) Identifying solutions to problems or ranking potential solutions, or ways to manage the problem, or recommending a course of action.

(j)   Exercising good judgement and an ethical approach to providing advice in line with:

    (i)   Relevant standards

    (ii)   Stakeholders interests

    (iii)   The stated objectives

(k)   Communicating effectively and efficiently in producing required documents including:

    (i)   The intended purpose of the document

    (ii)   Its intended users and their needs

    (iii)   The appropriate type of document

    (iv)   Logical and appropriate structure/format

    (v)   Nature of background information and technical language

    (vi)   Detail required

    (vii)   Clear, concise and precise presentation

There will be **four to six marks** awarded in each paper for the above professional skills. Not all skills will be required in each paper.

Chapter Roundup

- Firms have to ensure they obey the law: but they also face ethical concerns, because their reputations depend on a good image.

- Inside the organisation, a compliance based approach highlights conformity with the law. An integrity based approach suggests a wider remit, incorporating ethics in the organisation's values and culture.

- Organisations sometimes issue codes of conduct to employees. Many employees are bound by professional codes of conduct.

- Accountants require an ethical code because they hold positions of trust, and people rely on them.

- Exam questions may ask you to think about what should be done if breaches of laws, regulations or ethical guidelines occur. **Close relationships** between the parties or other **conflicts of interest** are often a complication.

Quick Quiz

1   What ethical problems face management?

2   Why does Mintzberg say that the profit motive is not enough?

3   Describe two approaches to the management of ethics in an organisation.

4   What systems of ethics might you find in an organisation?

5   Match the fundamental principle to the characteristic.

(a)   Integrity

(b)   Objectivity

(i)   Members should be straightforward and honest in all professional and business relationships.

(ii)   Members should not allow bias, conflict or interest or undue influence of others to override professional or business judgements.

Answers to Quick Quiz

1   There is a constant tension between the need to achieve current profitability, the need to safeguard the stakeholders' long term investment and the expectations of wider society.

2   Large businesses are rarely controlled by their shareholders; they receive a lot of support from public funds; and their activities have wider consequences.

3   A compliance–based approach aims to remain within the letter of the law by establishing systems of audit and review so that transgressions may be detected and punished. An integrity-based approach tries to promote an ethical culture in which individuals will do the right thing.

4   Personal ethics, professional ethics, organisation culture, organisation systems.

5   (a)(i), (b)(ii)

Now try the questions below from the Exam Question Bank			
Number	**Level**	**Marks**	**Time**
Q1	Introduction	n/a	n/a

Environmental and social reporting

3

Topic list	Syllabus reference
1 Environmental reporting	A3, H1
2 Sustainability	A3, H1
3 Social responsibility	A3, H1
4 Human resource accounting	A3, H1

Introduction

Environmental issues are very topical. Just because these topics are discursive does not mean that you can 'waffle'. Social responsibility and ethical issues relate to many aspects of the firm: its environment, its culture and management practice.

Environmental reporting also comes under 'current developments' as this is an area that is changing.

Study guide

		Intellectual level
A3	**Social responsibility**	
(a)	Discuss the increased demand for transparency in corporate reports and the emergence of non-financial reporting standards	3
(b)	Discuss the progress towards a framework for environmental and sustainability reporting	3
H1	**Environmental and social reporting**	
(a)	Appraise the impact of environmental, social and ethical factors on performance measurement	3
(b)	Evaluate current reporting requirements in this area	3
(c)	Discuss why entities might include disclosures relating to the environment and society	3

Exam guide

This topic could be tested as a current issue, or as an aspect of the limitations of conventional financial statements, or alternatively in the context of provisions, covered in Chapter 9.

1 Environmental reporting

FAST FORWARD

> Although not compulsory, environmental reports are becoming increasingly important. You should distinguish
>
> - Items that affect the financial statements (eg FRS 12)
> - Items that affect the OFR (see Chapter 1) or environmental report

At the end of the 1980s there were perhaps only two or three companies in the world issuing environmental reports. At the time of writing (June 2007) there are around 2,000. Worldwide there are around 20 award schemes for environmental reporting, notably the ACCA's. This section looks at environmental reporting mainly under three headings:

- The effect of environmental matters on management information and accounting
- External reporting and auditing
- Possible future developments

Environmental reporting will form part of the Extended Business Review to be introduced by the Companies Act 2006 in 2008.

Let us consider the major areas of impact on (any) accountant's job caused by consideration of environmental matters.

(a) **Management accountant**

(i) Investment appraisal: evaluation of environmental costs and benefits.

(ii) Incorporating new costs, capital expenditure and so on, in to budgets and business plans.

(iii) Undertake cost/benefit analysis of any environmental improvements.

(b) **Financial accountant**

    (i)   The effect of revenue costs: site clean up costs, waste disposal or waste treatment costs and so on, which will affect the profit and loss account.

    (ii)   Gauging balance sheet impacts, particularly liabilities, contingencies, provisions *and* valuation of assets.

    (iii)   The effect of environmental matters, and particularly potential liabilities, on a company's relationship with bankers, insurers and major shareholders (institutional shareholders).

    (iv)   Environmental performance evaluation in annual reports.

(c) **Project accountant**

    (i)   Environmental audit of proposed takeovers, mergers and other planning matters.

    (ii)   Investment appraisal.

(d) **Internal auditor**: environmental audit.

(e) **Systems accountant**: effect on, and required changes to management and financial information systems.

1.1 What is environmental accounting?

The following list encompasses the major aspects of environmental accounting.

'(a)   Recognising and seeking to mitigate the negative environmental effects of conventional accounting practice.

(b)   Separately identifying environmentally related costs and revenues within the conventional accounting systems.

(c)   Devising new forms of financial and non-financial accounting systems, information systems and control systems to encourage more environmentally benign management decisions.

(d)   Developing new forms of performance measurement, reporting and appraisal for both internal and external purposes.

(e)   Identifying, examining and seeking to rectify areas in which conventional (financial) criteria and environmental criteria are in conflict.

(f)   Experimenting with ways in which, sustainability may be assessed and incorporated into organisational orthodoxy.'

Accounting for the Environment Bob Gary (with Jan Bebbington and Diane Walters)

The whole environmental agenda is **constantly changing** and businesses therefore need to monitor the situation closely. Most businesses, certainly those in the UK, have generally ignored environmental matters in the past. How long will they be able to do so?

1.2 Management information and accounting

The means of codifying a company's attitude towards the environment is often the creation of a published **environmental policy document** or charter. This may be internally generated or it may be adopted from a standard environmental charter, such as the **Valdez Principles**.

The CERES Principles

We adopt, support and will implement the principles of:

1   *Protection of the biosphere*
2   *Sustainable use of natural resources*
3   *Reduction and disposal of waste*
4   *Wise use of energy*
5   *Risk reduction*
6   *Marketing of safe products and services*
7   *Damage compensation*
8   *Disclosure*
9   *Environmental directors and managers*
10 *Assessment and annual audit*

The problem here, as with other similar principles or charters, is that the commitment required from companies is generally too high and the fear exists that the principles may have legal status which could have a severe effect on a company's liability. Other documents available which are similar to the *CERES Principles* are:

- The International Chamber of Commerce **Business Charter for Sustainable Developments**
- The Chemical Industries Association **Responsible Care Programme**
- The Confederation of British Industry **Agenda for Voluntary Action**
- Friends of the Earth Environmental **Charter for Local Government**

Adopting such a charter is one thing; implementing and monitoring it are more important and generally more difficult to achieve.

1.3 Environmental audit

Environmental auditing is exactly what it says: auditing a business to assess its impact on the environment, or as the CBI expressed it 'the systematic examination of the interactions between any business operation and its surroundings'.

The audit will cover a range of areas and will involve the performance of different types of testing. The scope of the audit must be determined and this will depend on each individual organisation. There are, however, some aspects of the approach to environmental auditing which are worth mentioning.

(a)   **Environmental Impact Assessments (EIAs)** are required, under EC directive, for all major projects which require planning permission and have a material effect on the environment. The EIA process can be incorporated into any environmental auditing strategy.

(b)   **Environmental surveys** are a good way of starting the audit process, by looking at the organisation as a whole in environmental terms. This helps to identify areas for further development, problems, potential hazards and so forth.

(c)   **Environmental SWOT analysis**. A 'strengths, weaknesses, opportunities, threats' analysis is useful as the environmental audit strategy is being developed. This can only be done later in the process, when the organisation has been examined in much more detail.

(d)   **Environmental Quality Management (EQM).** This is seen as part of TQM (Total Quality Management) and it should be built in to an environmental management system. Such a strategy has been adopted by companies such as IBM, Dow Chemicals and by the Rhone-Poulenc Environmental Index which has indices for levels of water, air and other waste products.

(e) **Eco-audit**. The European Commission has adopted a proposal for a regulation for a voluntary community environmental auditing scheme, known as the eco-audit scheme. The scheme aims to promote improvements in company environmental performance and to provide the public with information about these improvements. Once registered, a company will have to comply with certain on-going obligations involving disclosure and audit.

(f) **Eco-labelling**. Developed in Germany, this voluntary scheme will indicate those EC products which meet the highest environmental standards, probably as the result of an EQM system. It is suggested that eco-audit *must* come before an eco-label can be given.

(g) **BS 7750 Environmental Management Systems**. BS 7750 also ties in with eco-audits and eco-labelling and with the quality BSI standard BS 5750. Achieving BS 7750 is likely to be a first step in the eco-audit process.

(h) **Supplier audits**, to ensure that goods and services bought in by an organisation meet the standards applied by that organisation.

Case Study

In June 1999 BP Amoco commissioned KPMG to conduct an independent audit of its greenhouse gas emissions in the first ever environmental audit.

1.4 Financial reporting

There are **no disclosure requirements relating to environmental matters in the UK**, so any disclosures tend to be **voluntary** unless environmental matters happen to fall under standard accounting principles (eg recognising liabilities).

(a) In most cases disclosure is descriptive and unquantified.

(b) There is little motivation to produce environmental information and many reasons for not doing so, including secrecy.

(c) The main factor seems to be apathy on the part of businesses but more particularly on the part of shareholders and investors. The information is not demanded, so it is not provided.

Environmental matters may be reported in the accounts of companies in the following areas.

- Contingent liabilities
- Exceptional charges
- Operating and financial review comments
- Profit and capital expenditure forecasts

The voluntary approach contrasts with the position in the United States, where the SEC/FASB accounting standards are obligatory.

While nothing is compulsory, there are a number of **published guidelines** and **codes of practice**, including:

- The Confederation of British Industry's guideline Introducing Environmental Reporting
- The ACCA's Guide to Environment and Energy Reporting
- The Coalition of Environmentally Responsible Economies (CERES) formats for environmental reports
- The Friends of the Earth Environmental Charter for Local Government
- The Eco Management and Audit Scheme Code of Practice

1.5 Example: Environmental liabilities

You have met FRS 12 *Provisions, contingent liabilities and contingent assets* in your earlier studies. FRS 12 deals with the issue of whether environmental liabilities should be provided for. Study the example below and attempt the question which follows it.

MegaBux plc is a multinational holding company. During the year a number of situations have arisen and the board is to meet soon to determine an appropriate treatment .

Site A

This site is occupied by a small refinery. The site and some adjacent land has been contaminated by chemical spillages. The cost of remedying the contamination is £20m, but under local laws there is no requirement to clean up the site.

Site B

Similar contamination has arisen but the local government, and a neighbouring land owner, require the contamination to be remedied soon. The cost of cleaning up the site is £15m, but an extra £5m could be spent to raise the standard of the operation in line with undertakings given to the local community ten years ago.

Solution

Site A

The mere existence of contamination does not establish an obligation on the part of the company and without an obligation there is no need for a provision.

Site B

An obligation does exist which the local government and a neighbour can prove in court. At least £15m must be provided, but there may be a constructive obligation, wider than a legal obligation, to spend an extra £5m to raise the standard of rectification. Concern for its long term reputation may influence the company to honour its undertaking given to the local community.

Question Environmental liabilities

Site C

Considerable contamination needs to be remedied, but the managing director is arguing that no provision is required this year since the amount concerned cannot be estimated with accuracy.

Site D

Spillage of chemicals has reduced the value of the site from £25m, its book value, to £10m, its current realisable value. By spending £5m on rectification, the site value will be increased to £20m. The spillage has seeped into a local river and fines of £3m are now payable.

Answer

Site C

Whilst the exact amount of the expenditure may not be known with certainty, it should be possible to arrive at a realistic and prudent estimate. It is not acceptable to omit a liability on the grounds that its amount is not known with certainty – this would be a distortion.

Site D

The fines of £3m are a current cost to be charged to the profit and loss account. The spillage has impaired the value of the site, which must be written down to its new market value of £20m after rectification. The cost of the write-down (£5m) and the cost of the rectification (£5m) are charged to the profit and loss account. The site is now carried in the books at its recoverable amount.

1.6 The environmental report and the exam

You may be asked in the exam to prepare an environmental report. Your report should distinguish between:

(a) Transactions that affect the financial statements, for example provisions that need to be made under FRS 12

(b) Information to be disclosed elsewhere, for example in the operating and financial review, or in a separate environmental report.

1.7 Example: Environmental report

A good example of an environmental report is the Boots report for 1999/2000. This was published as a separate report consisting of around 20 pages. Extracts from the report are reproduced below to give you a feel for it. Note that the report is based around 'key performance indicators'. These are monitored against targets. We emphasise that this is not the only possible approach to environmental reporting.

'Environmental policy statement

We have a responsibility as a company to take proper care of the environment on behalf of our shareholders, customers, staff and the communities in which we operate. Caring for the environment is an essential part of the way we run our business.

We are committed to managing responsibly the way in which our activities affect the environment by:

- Optimising the use of energy
- Ensuring efficient use of materials
- Encouraging re-use and recycling
- Incorporating the principle of sustainable development.

By integrating environmental considerations into our everyday activities, the environment will be managed alongside other business considerations such as safety, quality and value.

Management

We will set objectives and targets for those activities which significantly affect the environment and we will measure our performance over time. Details of our progress will be published at least annually.

Environmental audits and inspections will be undertaken to monitor our progress against this policy.

Within the individual businesses there is a clear structure of responsibility devolved into each business via an appointed manager with overall environmental responsibility. At a corporate level, the Environmental Affairs team co-ordinates environmental issues for the company through the Environmental Working Party.

The company's significant impacts have been assessed and Key Performance Indicators (KPIs) have been selected to track performance over time. Data to monitor these is generated via environmental management systems that are incorporated into business systems and regularly audited.

Environmental management is integrated into everything we do from product development to the supply chain and staff training.

Key performance indicators 99/00

Energy

In 1999/2000 total company energy use decreased by 5.3 per cent, while energy efficiency improved by 10.2 per cent.

Over the last four years energy efficiency, as measured by kWh per £ thousand turnover, has improved by 12 per cent overall, maintaining a positive trend.

Transport

Commercial transport efficiency improved by 2 per cent.

Alongside the ongoing internal data verification programme, improvements to data management systems have resulted in additional transport data being reported for 1998/99. Transport efficiency over the last three years, as measured by litres of diesel consumed per £ million turnover, maintained a positive trend overall with a 2 per cent improvement recorded over the last year.

The efficiency of stock delivery, as measured by the volume of stock delivered per 1000 litres of fuel, reduced by 3.7 per cent at Boots The Chemists. This is due to a combination of factors, including new store openings and the closure of an old warehouse in an urban centre (see Progress against targets). The move to lower sulphur diesel for commercial fleets has also had a negative impact on fuel efficiency. Trials of alternative fuel vehicles have continued.

Carbon dioxide and global warming

In the last year, like-for-like CO_2 emissions decreased by 4.4 per cent.

The main greenhouse gas associated with the company's operations is CO_2 arising primarily from energy use in manufacturing and retailing, and emissions from its transport fleets. Some 84 per cent of total emissions relate to energy consumption. Similarly, around 85 per cent of transport emissions relate to commercial fleets, with around 8 per cent to company cars.

The company's modern combined heat and power (CHP) energy centre on the head office site continues to contribute to a global reduction in annual CO_2 emissions of around 44,000 tonnes compared with purchasing electricity from third party suppliers. This represents a reduction in the company's total CO_2 emissions of around 15 per cent each year. The saving is achieved through the re-use of waste heat from the electricity generation process to generate usable steam.

Waste

Around 26,000 tonnes of waste was recovered through recycling or incineration with heat recovery.

As the business is primarily retailing, the largest proportion of waste (91 per cent) is transit packaging and general office waste that is mainly non-hazardous. Other wastes arise from manufacturing processes, laboratories, garage and pharmacy operations.

Of the 54,000 tonnes of material identified as waste, some 26,000 tonnes (48 per cent) was recovered through recycling or incineration with heat recovery. The majority of the remaining 28,000 tonnes of waste (94 per cent) was disposed to landfill.

Quantifying the weight of non-hazardous waste is difficult due to small quantities of unweighed waste being collected from a large number of retail locations by multiple collection vehicles, and shopping centres amalgamating non-hazardous waste from a number of retailers for bulk collection. Because of this, although the company's data collection systems for waste have continued to improve, it is unlikely that year-on-year comparisons will be meaningful for some time to come.

Packaging

In the last year the company handled some 162,000 tonnes of packaging.

Minimising packaging is a complex business challenge where a number of considerations have to be balanced. These include evaluating the wide variety of roles performed by packaging (from improved keeping qualities for food and medical products to optimal shapes for efficient stacking and transportation) together with aspects such as design, quality, performance, cost and environment.

In addition, several factors mask the performance that can be directly attributed to packaging management. In particular, consumer and business demands in retailing require ongoing changes to the scale of product ranges and the general product mix within stores, which can produce conflicting trends in packaging use.

The issue will remain as a key performance indicator given its perceived environmental impact in the retail and manufacturing sectors, but it is unlikely that a valid, quantitative comparison of company performance will be developed in this area.

Water and effluent

In the last year Boots Contract Manufacturing reduced the effluent load per unit produced by more than 18 per cent.

Centralised monitoring of water consumption continued with substantial effort being put into the development of robust data management systems. This section relates mainly to Boots Contract Manufacturing, but from April 2000 the data available will include all business units and will be comparable across future years. The acquisition of historical water consumption data proved more difficult than expected, so the overall picture for the company is currently incomplete. Information has been included in the data section where meaningful.

Water conservation in Boots Contract Manufacturing, across all production areas, has again been an area of considerable focus. Improvements such as the elimination of 'once-through' water cooling systems have been implemented in key areas. Fitting improved temperature controls to a tempering belt reduced steam demand as well as saving cooling water.

Water use has been benchmarked across departments and factories to enable sharing of best practice in successful conservation strategies. A computerised data reporting system in the main factory on the Nottingham site allows water use profiles to be analysed. This has been a significant factor in bringing about change. For example, over the past four years water consumption in the factory over the Christmas shutdown period has been reduced from 60 per cent to less than 10 per cent of that on a normal working day. This experience has been shared and improved water metering is now being installed at the Airdrie factory.

In other areas external factors, such as the reduced use of preservatives in products and third party customer specifications that predefine equipment-cleaning procedures, resulted in some increased water use. Overall, water use per unit of production was reduced by 2.6 per cent against a target of 3 per cent.

Reducing waste discharged as effluent has been targeted in several key areas. Process changes have brought about material savings at Nottingham and, at Airdrie, a new system for cleaning pipes between product batches has reduced the amount of water required for this operation by 90 per cent. Together, all these initiatives reduced the loss of material to drain by more than 18 per cent (as measured by chemical oxygen demand and solids load per unit 'produced').'

2 Sustainability

A key environmental issue is **sustainability**. The **Global Reporting Initiative** has an important role to play.

2.1 What is sustainability

Pressure is mounting for companies to **widen** their **scope for corporate public accountability**. Many companies are responding by measuring and disclosing their social impacts.

Examples of social measures include: philanthropic donations, employee satisfaction levels and remuneration issues, community support, and stakeholder consultation information.

The next step beyond environmental and social reporting is sustainability reporting which includes the economic element of sustainability (such as wages, taxes and core financial statistics) and involves integrating environmental, social and economic performance data and measures.

2.2 The Global Reporting initiative (GRI)

The Global Reporting Initiative arose from the need to **address the failure of the current governance structures to respond to changes in the global economy**.

It is 'a long-term, multi-stakeholder, international undertaking whose mission is to develop and disseminate globally applicable Sustainability Reporting Guidelines for voluntary use by organisations reporting on the economic, environmental and social dimensions of their activities, products and services'.

2.3 GRI Guidelines

The GRI published revised Sustainability Reporting Guidelines ('G3') in 2006.

The Guidelines set out the framework of a sustainability report. It consists of five sections:

GRI Report content		Detail of GRI requirements
1	*Strategy and Analysis*	Provides a high-level, strategic view of the organisation's relationship to sustainability in order to provide context for subsequent and more detailed reporting, including a statement from the CEO.
2	*Organisational Profile*	The organisation's structure including brands, location of operations, geographical markets served and size of operations.
3	*Report Parameters*	The reporting period, materiality, report boundaries (eg countries), data measurement techniques and a GRI Content Index.
4	*Governance, Commitments and Engagement*	Governance structure of the organisation, commitments to external initiatives and how the organisation engages the stakeholders in its business.
5	*Management Approach and Performance Indicators*	Organised by economic, environmental, and social categories. Each category includes a Disclosure on Management Approach and a corresponding set of Core and Additional Performance Indicators.

2.4 Indicators in the GRI framework

GRI structures key performance indicators according to a hierarchy of category, aspect and indicator. Indicators are grouped in terms of the three dimensions of the conventional definition of sustainability – economic, environmental, and social.

CATEGORY		ASPECT
Economic	Economic	Economic performance Market presence Indirect economic impacts
Environmental	Environmental	Materials Energy Water Biodiversity Emissions, effluents, and waste Products and services Compliance Transport Overall
Social	Labour Practices and Decent Work	Employment Labour/management relations Occupational health and safety Training and education Diversity and equal opportunity
	Human Rights	Investment and procurement practices Non-discrimination Freedom of association and collective bargaining Child labour Forced and compulsory labour Security practices Indigenous rights
	Society	Community Corruption Public policy Anti-competitive behaviour Compliance
	Product Responsibility	Customer health and safety Product and service labelling Marketing communications Customer privacy Compliance

2.5 Influence of GRI

There is a trend to report on broader sustainability issues and to include **social and economic information** alongside environmental disclosures.

An increasing number of companies, including BT, Vauxhall Motors Ltd, British Airways and Shell are following the GRI guidelines to some extent in their reporting.

2.6 Example: BT

BT's Social and Environmental Report for the year ended 31 March 2004 complies with the 2002 Global Reporting Initiative Guidelines. To give an overview of the company's social and environmental performance, the report selects 11 non-financial key performance indicators. This performance relates to the 2004 financial year, compared with 2003.

(a)   Customer dissatisfaction down 22%

(b)   Broadband now available to more than 85% of all UK homes and businesses, up from 67%

(c)   People Satisfaction Index increased from 67% to 71%

(d)   Increase in the percentage of ethnic minority employees from 8.6% to 8.9% and disabled employees from 2.0% to 2.1%, though the percentage of women declined from 23.6% to 22.7%

(e)   Global Warming CO_2 emissions now 42% lower than 1996

(f)   Waste to landfill down 10,201 tonnes to 79,677 tonnes, percentage of total waste recycled up from 25% to 26%

(g)   Health & Safety significant incident rate down from 113 to 87 per 10,000 full-time employees

(h)   Percentage of suppliers stating they have a good working relationship with BT is 94%

(i)   Ethical trading risk assessment questionnaires completed by 242 suppliers and 13 on-site assessments undertaken

(j)   Awareness of our Statement of Business Practice in the UK up 1% to 84%

(k)   Direct community investment of £5.6 million plus £12.4 million in further funding and support in mind.

Question   Indicators

Compare this brief summary with the table above, ticking off performance indicators. If you have time, look for further details and developments on www.globalreporting.org.

3 Social responsibility

Not only does the environment have a significant influence on the structure and behaviour of organisations, but also organisations have some influence on their environment.

Since organisations have an effect on their environment, it is arguable that they should act in a way which shows **social awareness and responsibility**.

> 'A society, awakened and vocal with respect to the urgency of social problems, is asking the managers of all kinds of organisations, particularly those at the top, what they are doing to discharge their social responsibilities and why they are not doing more.'
>
> *Koontz, O'Donnell and Weihrich*

Social responsibility is expected from all types of organisation.

(a) **Local government** is expected to provide services to the local community, and to preserve or improve the character of that community, but at an acceptable cost to the ratepayers.

(b) **Businesses** are expected to provide goods and services, which reflect the needs of users and society as a whole. These needs may not be in harmony – arguably, the development of the Concorde aeroplane and supersonic passenger travel did not contribute to the public interest, and caused considerable inconvenience to residents near airports who suffer from excessive aircraft noise. A business should also be expected to anticipate the future needs of society; examples of socially useful products might be energy-saving devices and alternative sources of power.

(c) **Pollution control** is a particularly important example of social responsibility by industrial organisations, and some progress has been made in the development of commercial processes for re-cycling waste material. British Coal attempts to restore the environment by planting on old slag heaps.

(d) **Universities and schools** are expected to produce students whose abilities and qualifications will prove beneficial to society. A currently popular view of education is that greater emphasis should be placed on vocational training for students.

(e) In some cases, **legislation** may be required to enforce social need, for example to regulate the materials used to make crash helmets for motor cyclists, or to regulate safety standards in motor cars and furniture. Ideally, however, organisations should avoid the need for legislation by taking **earlier self-regulating action**.

3.1 Social responsibility and businesses

Arguably, institutions like hospitals, schools and so forth exist because health care and education are seen to be desirable social objectives by government at large, if they can be afforded.

However, where does this leave businesses? How far is it reasonable, or even appropriate, for businesses to exercise 'social responsibility' by giving to charities, voluntarily imposing strict environmental objectives on themselves and so forth?

One school of thought would argue that **the management of a business has only one social responsibility, which is to maximise wealth for its shareholders**. There are two reasons to support this argument.

(a) If the business is owned by the shareholders the assets of the company are, ultimately, the shareholders' property. Management has no moral right to dispose of business assets (like cash) on non-business objectives, as this has the effect of reducing the return available to shareholders. The shareholders might, for example, disagree with management's choice of beneficiary. Anyhow, it is for the shareholders to determine how their money should be spent.

(b) A second justification for this view is that management's job is to maximise wealth, as this is the best way that society can benefit from a business's activities.

(i) Maximising wealth has the effect of increasing the tax revenues available to the state to disburse on socially desirable objectives.

(ii) Maximising wealth for the few is sometimes held to have a 'trickle down' effect on the disadvantaged members of society.

(iii) Many company shares are owned by pension funds, whose ultimate beneficiaries may not be the wealthy anyway.

This argument rests on certain assumptions.

(a)   The first assumption is, in effect, the opposite of the stakeholder view. In other words, it is held that the *rights* of legal ownership are paramount over all other *interests* in a business: while other stakeholders have an interest, they have few legal or moral rights over the wealth created.

(b)   The second assumption is that a business's *only* relationship with the wider social environment is an economic one. After all, that is what businesses exist for, and any other activities are the role of the state.

(c)   The defining purpose of business organisations is the maximisation of the wealth of their owners.

Henry Mintzberg (in *Power In and Around Organisations*) suggests that simply viewing organisations as vehicles for shareholder investment is inadequate.

(a)   In practice, he says, organisations are rarely controlled effectively by shareholders. Most shareholders are passive investors.

(b)   Large corporations can manipulate markets. Social responsibility, forced or voluntary, is a way of recognising this.

(c)   Moreover, businesses do receive a lot of government support. The public pays for roads, infrastructure, education and health, all of which benefits businesses. Although businesses pay tax, the public ultimately pays, perhaps through higher prices.

(d)   Strategic decisions by businesses always have wider social consequences. In other words, says Mintzberg, the firm produces two outputs: **goods and services** and the **social consequences of its activities** (eg pollution).

3.2 Externalities

If it is accepted that businesses do not bear the total social cost of their activities, then the exercise of social responsibility is a way of compensating for this.

An example is given by the environment. Industrial pollution is injurious to health: if someone is made ill by industrial pollution, then arguably the polluter should pay the sick person, as damages or in compensation, in the same way as if the business's builders had accidentally bulldozed somebody's house.

In practice, of course, while it is relatively easy to identify statistical relationships between pollution levels and certain illnesses, mapping out the chain of cause and effect from an individual's wheezing cough to the dust particles emitted by Factory X, as opposed to Factory Y, is quite a different matter.

Of course, it could be argued that these external costs are met out of general taxation: but this has the effect of spreading the cost amongst other individuals and businesses. Moreover, the tax revenue may be spent on curing the disease, rather than stopping it at its source. Pollution control equipment may be the fairest way of dealing with this problem. Thus advocates of social responsibility in business would argue that business's responsibilities then do not rest with paying taxes.

However, is there any justification for social responsibility outside remedying the effects of a business's direct activities. For example, should businesses give to charity or sponsor the arts? There are several reasons why they should.

(a)   If the **stakeholder concept** of a business is held, then the public is a stakeholder in the business. A business only succeeds because it is part of a wider society. Giving to charity is one way of encouraging a relationship.

(b) Charitable donations and artistic sponsorship are a useful medium of **public relations** and can reflect well on the business. It can be regarded, then, as another form of promotion, which like advertising, serves to enhance consumer awareness of the business, while not encouraging the sale of a particular brand.

The arguments for and against social responsibility of business are complex ones. However, ultimately they can be traced to different assumptions about society and the relationships between the individuals and organisations within it.

Question	Social responsibility

The Heritage Carpet Company is a London-based retailer which imports carpets from Turkey, Iran and India. The company was founded by two Europeans who travelled independently through these countries in the 1970s. The company is the sole customer for carpets made in a number of villages in each of the source countries. The carpets are hand woven. Indeed, they are so finely woven that the process requires that children be used to do the weaving, thanks to their small fingers. The company believes that it is preserving a 'craft', and the directors believe that this is a justifiable social objective. Recently a UK television company has reported unfavourably on child exploitation in the carpet weaving industry. There were reports of children working twelve hour shifts in poorly lit sheds and cramped conditions, with consequent deterioration in eyesight, muscular disorders and a complete absence of education. The examples cited bear no relation to the Heritage Carpet Company's suppliers although children are used in the labour force, but there has been a spate of media attention. The regions in which the Heritage Carpet Company's supplier villages are found are soon expected to enjoy rapid economic growth.

What boundary management issues are raised for the Heritage Carpet Company?

Answer

Many. This is a case partly about boundary management and partly about enlightened self-interest and business ethics. The adverse publicity, although not about the Heritage Carpet Company's own suppliers, could rebound badly. Potential customers might be put off. Economic growth in the area may also mean that parents will prefer to send their children to school. The Heritage Carpet Company as well as promoting itself as preserving a craft could reinvest some of its profits in the villages (eg by funding a school), or by enforcing limits on the hours children worked. It could also pay a decent wage. It could advertise this in a 'code of ethics' so that customers are reassured that the children are not simply being exploited. Alternatively, it could not import child-made carpets at all. (This policy, however, would be unlikely to help communities in which child labour is an economic necessity. Children already living on the margins of subsistence might end up even more exploited, in begging or prostitution.)

4 Human resource accounting

FAST FORWARD

Human resource accounting is an approach which regards people as assets.

4.1 Introduction

Human resource accounting has at its core the principle that **employees are assets.** Competitive advantage is largely gained by **effective use of people**.

4.2 Implications of regarding people as organisational assets

(a)   **People are a resource** which needs to be carefully and efficiently managed with overriding concern for organisational objectives.

(b)   The organisation needs to **protect its investment** by retaining, safeguarding and developing its human assets.

(c)   **Deterioration in the attitudes and motivation** of employees, increases in labour turnover (followed by costs of hiring and training replacements) are **costs to the company** – even though a 'liquidation' of human assets, brought about by certain managerial styles, may produce short-term increases in profit.

(d)   A concept developed some time ago was that of **human asset accounting** (the inclusion of human assets in the financial reporting system of the organisation).

 Case Study

There are difficulties in isolating and measuring human resources, and it is also hard to forecast the time period (and area of business) over which benefits will be received from expenditure on human assets. *Texas Instruments* uses a system which identifies potential replacement costs for groups of people, taking into account the learning time required by the replacement, and the individual's salary during that period.

4.3 Intellectual assets

FAST FORWARD

There are **problems in putting a value on people** which traditional accounting has yet to overcome.

Because of the difficulties found in both theory and practice, the concept of **human assets was broadened and became intellectual assets.** Intellectual assets, or 'intellectual capital' as they are sometimes called can be divided into three main types.

(a)   **External assets.** These include the reputation of brands and franchises and the strength of customer relationships.

(b)   **Internal assets.** These include patents, trademarks and information held in customer databases.

(c)   **Competencies.** These reflect the capabilities and skills of individuals.

'Intellectual assets' thus includes 'human assets'.

The value of intellectual assets will continue to rise and will represent an increasing proportion of the value of most companies. Whether or not traditional accounting will be able to measure them, remains to be seen.

Chapter Roundup

- Although not compulsory, environmental reports are becoming increasingly important. You should distinguish

    - Items that affect the financial statements (eg FRS 12)
    - Items that affect the OFR or environmental report

- A key environmental issue is **sustainability**. The **Global Reporting Initiative** has an important role to play.

- **Human resource accounting** is an approach which regards **people as assets.**

- There are **problems in putting a value on people** which traditional accounting has yet to overcome.

Quick Quiz

1   Give an example of a recent environmental audit.

2   Name four areas of company accounts where environmental matters may be reported.

3   If a site is contaminated, a provision must be made.

    True   ☐

    False ☐

4   According to the GRI, what are the three dimensions of the definition of sustainability?

5   What objectives might a company have in relation to wider society?

6   To whom might management have responsibilities, and what are some of these responsibilities?

7   What is whistle blowing?

8   What is the basic principle of human resource accounting?

9   Give three examples of intellectual assets.

Answers to Quick Quiz

1.   In 1999 KPMG conducted an audit of the greenhouse gas emissions of BP Amoco.

2.   Contingent liabilities

    Exceptional charges

    Operating and financial review comments

    Profit and capital expenditure forecasts

3.   False. an obligation must be established.

4.   Economic, environmental and social.

5.   Protection of the environment, support for good causes, a responsible attitude to product safety.

6.   Managers of businesses are responsible to the owners for economic performance and to wider society for the externalities related to their business operations.

7.   Informing outside regulatory agencies about transgressions by one's organisation.

8.   Employees are assets.

9.   External assets

Now try the questions below from the Exam Question Bank

Number	Level	Marks	Time
Q2	Examination	25	45 mins

Part B
Accounting standards

Fixed assets: tangible assets

4

Topic list	Syllabus reference
1 Definitions and statutory requirements	C2
2 FRS 15 *Tangible fixed assets*	C2
3 Revaluation	C2
4 SSAP 19 *Accounting for investment properties*	C2
5 SSAP 4 *Accounting for government grants*	C2
6 FRED 29	C2, F2

Introduction

The main purpose of FRS 15 is to codify **best practice** on accounting for tangible fixed assets.

SSAPs 4 and 19 should be familiar to you. Try the questions and go back to your earlier studies if you have any problems.

The implications of a **proposed change** to FRS 15 is discussed in this chapter.

Study guide

		Intellectual level
C2	**Non-current assets**	
(a)	Apply and discuss the timing of the recognition of non-current assets and the determination of their carrying amounts, including impairment and revaluations	3
(c)	Apply and discuss accounting treatment of investment properties including classification, recognition and measurement issues	3
F2	**Proposed changes to accounting standards**	
(b)	Apply and discuss the implications of a proposed change to an accounting standard on the performance and balance sheet of an entity	2

Exam guide

This part of the Study Text deals with accounting standards, most of which you should already know about. However, the approach at the professional level is very different from that in our earlier studies – you will need to think critically and deal with controversial areas.

1 Definitions and statutory requirements

FAST FORWARD

Assets have been defined in various ways. The most recent definition is contained in the ASB's *Statement of Principles*, Chapter 4 *Elements of financial statements.*

Assets have been defined in many different ways and for many purposes. The definition of an asset is important because it directly affects the **treatment** of such items. A good definition will prevent abuse or error in the accounting treatment: otherwise some assets might be treated as expenses, and some expenses might be treated as assets.

Let us begin with a simple definition from the CIMA *Official Terminology*.

Key term

> An **asset** is any tangible or intangible possession which has value.

This neat, quick definition seems to cover the main points: **ownership** and **value**. An asset is so called because it is owned by someone who values it. However, this definition leaves several questions unanswered.

- What determines ownership?
- What determines value?

1.1 Accounting Standards Board (ASB)

In the ASB's *Statement of Principles*, Chapter 4 *The Elements of Financial Statements*, currently assets are defined as follows.

Key term

> **Assets** are rights or other access to future economic benefits controlled by an entity as a result of past transactions or events.
>
> *Statement of Principles*

The *Statement* goes on to discuss various aspects of this definition, and it is broadly consistent with the **IASB's** *Framework.* The *Statement* then goes further in discussing the complimentary nature of assets and liabilities.

1.2 Financial Accounting Standards Board (FASB)

The definition given by the FASB in the USA in its *Statement of Concepts* is very similar.

Key term

> **Assets** are probable future economic benefits obtained or controlled by a particular entity as a result of past transactions or events.

'Probable' is given in its general meaning merely to reflect the fact that no future outcome can be predicted with total certainty.

1.3 Comparison of definitions

It is clear from what we have seen so far that a general consensus seems to exist in the standard setting bodies as to the definition of an asset. That definition encompasses **three important characteristics**.

- (a) Future economic benefit
- (b) Control (ownership)
- (c) The transaction to acquire control has already taken place

1.4 Definition of a fixed asset

FAST FORWARD

> CA 2006 maintains **historical cost** principles, modified by the revaluations of certain assets.

Fixed assets are defined by CA 2006.

Key term

> A **fixed asset** as one intended for use on a continuing basis in the company's activities, ie it is not intended for resale.

1.5 Statutory requirements relating to fixed assets

You have already come across these in you earlier studies, besides which FRS 15 now deals much more comprehensively with the important issues from CA 2006. For completeness, a summary is given here.

Summary: statutory requirements relating to fixed assets

Initial cost

- Purchase price plus any expenses incidental to its acquisition.

- Where an asset is produced by a company for its own use, its 'production cost' must include the cost of raw materials, consumables and other attributable direct costs (such as labour). Production cost may additionally include a reasonable proportion of indirect costs, together with the interest on any capital borrowed to finance production of the asset.

Valuation: alternative accounting rules

- Historical cost is the norm, but revalued amount/current cost may be used.

- Depreciation may be provided on the basis of the new valuation.

- Where an asset is revalued, the gain or loss goes to a revaluation reserve.

- There are three alternative bases for valuation: current cost, market value and directors' valuation (for investments)

1.6 FRS 3 and revaluations

Note the effect here of FRS 3. The **statement of recognised gains and losses** (STRGL) shows the profit or loss for the period along with all other movements on reserves which reflect recognised gains and losses attributable to shareholders. It does *not* deal with the **realisation** of gains in previous periods, nor with transfers between reserves.

Important rule to learn

> The excess of the revalued amount over historical cost will *never* be recognised in the P&L account; profit or loss on disposal will be calculated as the difference between the net proceeds and the net carrying amount

This is a very important FRS 3 rule; previously, on disposal of a revalued asset, companies could transfer the surplus in the revaluation reserve which related to the asset to the P&L account. The difference between historical cost depreciation and depreciation on a revaluation will appear in the **note of historical cost profits and losses**.

1.7 UITF Abstract 5 *Transfer from current assets to fixed assets*

This abstract requires transfers from current assets to fixed assets to be made at the **lower of cost and net realisable value**, in order to prevent the practice of transfers being made at a value higher than NRV. This practice avoided charging the P&L account with any diminution in value of what were, in effect, unsold trading assets. Once transferred to fixed assets, the CA 2006 alternative accounting rules could be used to take the debit reflecting the diminution in value to a revaluation reserve. This abstract follows the *Statement of Principles*. This was triggered by a Review Panel judgement on Trafalgar House's 1991 accounts.

2 FRS 15 Tangible fixed assets

FAST FORWARD

> FRS 15 sets out **uniform principles** relating to tangible fixed assets with regard to:
> * Initial measurement
> * Valuation
> * Depreciation

FRS 15 *Tangible fixed assets* goes into a lot more detail than the Companies Act. It replaced SSAP 12 but not SSAP 19. Investment properties are still accounted for in accordance with SSAP 19 (see Section 4).

2.1 Objective

FRS 15 deals with accounting for the initial measurement, valuation and depreciation of tangible fixed assets. It also sets out the information that should be disclosed to enable readers to understand the impact of the accounting policies adopted in relation to these issues.

2.2 Initial measurement

A tangible fixed asset should **initially be measured at cost**.

Key term

> **Cost** is purchase price and any costs directly attributable to bringing the asset into working condition for its intended use.

Examples of directly attributable costs are:

- **Acquisition costs**, eg stamp duty, import duties
- Cost of **site preparation** and clearance
- Initial **delivery and handling** costs
- **Installation** costs
- **Professional fees** eg legal fees
- The estimated cost of **dismantling and removing** the asset and restoring the site, to the extent that it is recognised as a provision under FRS 12 *Provisions, contingent liabilities and contingent assets* (discussed later).

Any abnormal costs, such as those arising from design error, industrial disputes or idle capacity are not directly attributable costs and therefore should not be capitalised as part of the cost of the asset.

Question

Start-up costs

Seafood 'n' Eatitt, a trendy restaurant, opens on 1 January 20X9 with a skeleton staff. The first month is not expected to bring in many customers as it will take time to build up a reputation. Could the costs incurred in January be capitalised as start-up costs?

Answer

No. The restaurant *could* operate at normal levels immediately so the start up costs are not essential.

The above costs should only be capitalised for the period in which the activities that are necessary to get the asset ready for use are in progress.

2.2.1 Finance costs

The **capitalisation of finance costs**, including interest, is **optional**. However, if an entity does capitalise finance costs they must do so **consistently**.

All finance costs that are **directly attributable** to the construction of a tangible fixed asset should be capitalised as part of the cost of the asset.

Key term

Directly attributable finance costs are those that would have been avoided if there had been no expenditure on the asset.

If finance costs are capitalised, capitalisation should start when:

- Finance costs are being incurred
- Expenditure on the asset is being incurred
- Activities necessary to get the asset ready for use are in progress

Capitalisation of finance costs should cease when the asset is ready for use.

Sometimes construction of an asset may be completed in parts and each part is capable of being used while construction continues on other parts. An example of such an asset is a business park consisting of several units. In such cases **capitalisation of borrowing costs relating to a part should cease when substantially all the activities that are necessary to get that part ready for use are completed.**

Question   Capitalisation

Why would this not apply in the case of a steel mill?

Answer

A steel mill is an industrial plant involving several processes that are carried out **in sequence** at different parts of the plant within the same site.

Disclosures in respect of capitalisation of borrowing costs

(a)   The accounting policy adopted

(b)   The amount of borrowing costs capitalised during the period

(c)   The amount of borrowing costs recognised in the profit and loss account during the period

(d)   The capitalisation rate used to determine the amount of capitalised borrowing costs

2.2.2 Recoverable amount

The amount recognised when a tangible fixed asset is acquired or constructed should **not exceed its recoverable amount**.

It is not necessary to review tangible fixed assets for impairment when they are acquired or constructed. They need to be reviewed for impairment only if there is some indication that impairment has occurred. Such indications are specified in FRS 11 *Impairment of fixed assets and goodwill*.

2.3 Subsequent expenditure

Subsequent expenditure is repairs and maintenance expenditure which ensures that an asset maintains it originally assessed standard of performance. An example of such expenditure is the cost of servicing or overhauling plant and equipment. Without this expenditure, the depreciation expense would be increased because the useful life and perhaps the residual value of the asset would be reduced.

Rule to learn

> **Subsequent expenditure** (repairs and maintenance expenditure) should be recognised in the profit and loss account as it is incurred.

There are three exceptions to this.

(a)   It enhances the economic benefits over and above those previously estimated. An example might be modifications made to a piece of machinery that increases its capacity or useful life.

(b)   A component of an asset that has been treated separately for depreciation purposes (because it has a substantially different useful economic life from the rest of the asset) has been restored or replaced.

(c)   It relates to a major inspection or overhaul that restores economic benefits that have been consumed and reflected in the depreciation charge.

Question   Subsequent expenditure (1)

A building is repainted. How should this expenditure be treated?

Answer

It should be written off to the profit and loss account. This expenditure is too regular an occurrence to be seen as a separate 'component'.

Question   Subsequent expenditure (2)

Baldwin Ltd installs a new production process in its factory at a cost of £20,000. This enables a reduction in operating costs (as assessed when the original plant was installed) of £8,000 per year for at least the next ten years.

How should the expenditure be treated?

Answer

It should be capitalised and added to the original cost of the plant as it results in enhancement of economic benefits.

An entity often has to spend material amounts on a major refit or refurbishment every few years, in order to stay in business. For example, a furnace may require relining every few years.

Rule to learn

> Each component is depreciated over its individual useful economic life, so that the depreciation profile over the whole asset more accurately reflects the actual consumption of the asset's economic benefits.

The same approach is applied to major inspections and overhauls of tangible fixed assets.

2.4 Example: Major overhaul

An aircraft is required by law to be overhauled once every three years. Unless the overhaul is undertaken the aircraft cannot continue to be flown. The cost of the overhaul is capitalised when incurred because it restores the economic benefits of the tangible fixed asset. The carrying amount representing the cost of the benefits consumed is removed from the balance sheet.

This works in exactly the same way as when an asset is divided into separate components for depreciation. Suppose a company owns an aircraft with a useful economic life of ten years, but the aircraft needs a major overhaul every three years. The depreciation will be the estimated overhead cost written off over three years and the rest of the cost of the aircraft written off over ten years. Then in three years time, when the overhaul work is done, the cost and accumulated depreciation of the 'overhaul' portion of the asset are removed from the balance sheet and the cost of the work done is capitalised.

2.5 Valuation

FRS 15 supplements and clarifies the rules on revaluation of fixed assets which the Companies Act allows. Revaluation is discussed in the next section.

2.6 Depreciation

As noted earlier, the Companies Act 2006 requires that all fixed assets having a limited economic life should be depreciated. FRS 15 gives a useful discussion of the purpose of depreciation and supplements the statutory requirements in important ways.

Key term

> **Depreciation** is defined in FRS 15 as the measure of the cost or revalued amount of the economic benefits of the tangible fixed asset that have been consumed during the period. Consumption includes the wearing out, using up or other reduction in the useful economic life of a tangible fixed asset, whether arising from use, effluxion of time or obsolescence through either changes in technology or demand for the goods and services produced by the asset.

This definition covers the amortisation of assets with a pre-determined life, such as a leasehold, and the depletion of wasting assets such as mines.

FRS 15 contains **no detailed guidance** on the calculation of depreciation or the suitability of the various depreciation methods, merely stating the following two **general principles**.

> 'The depreciable amount of a tangible fixed asset should be allocated on a **systematic** basis over its useful economic life. The depreciation method used should reflect as fairly as possible the pattern in which the asset's economic benefits are consumed by the entity. The depreciation charge for each period should be recognised as an expense in the profit and loss account unless it is permitted to be included in the carrying amount of another asset.'

> 'A variety of methods can be used to allocate the depreciable amount of a tangible fixed asset on a systematic basis over its useful economic life. The method chosen should result in a **depreciation charge throughout the asset's useful** economic life and not just towards the end of its useful economic life or when the asset is falling in value.'

Remember!

> Systematic and throughout.
>
> Two of the most common methods – the straight line and the reducing balance method are mentioned, the former to be used where the pattern of consumption of an asset's economic benefits is uncertain.

2.7 Factors affecting depreciation

FRS 15 states that the following factors need to be considered in determining the useful economic life, residual value and depreciation method of an asset.

(a)   The **expected usage** of the asset by the entity, assessed by reference to the asset's expected capacity or physical output

(b)   The **expected physical deterioration** of the asset through use or effluxion of time; this will depend upon the repair and maintenance programme of the entity both when the asset is in use and when it is idle

(c)   **Economic or technological obsolescence**, for example arising from changes or improvements in production, or a change in the market demand for the product or service output of that asset

(d)   **Legal or similar limits** on the use of the asset, such as the expiry dates of related leases

If it becomes clear that the **original estimate** of an asset's useful life was **incorrect**, it should be **revised**. Normally, no adjustment should be made in respect of the depreciation charged in previous years; instead the remaining net book value of the asset should be depreciated over the new estimate of its remaining useful life.

FRS 15 also states that a **change from one method** of providing depreciation **to another** is permissible only on the grounds that the new method will give a **fairer presentation** of the results and of the financial position. Such a change does **not**, however, constitute a **change of accounting policy**; the carrying amount of the tangible fixed asset is depreciated using the revised method over the remaining useful economic life, beginning in the period in which the change is made.

2.7.1 Two or more components of a fixed asset

A fixed asset may comprise two or more major components with substantially different useful economic lives. In such cases each component should be accounted for separately for depreciation purposes and depreciated over its individual useful economic life. Examples include:

- Land and buildings
- The structure of a building and items within the structure, such as general fittings

Question   Components

What about the trading potential associated with a property valued as an operational entity, such as a hotel or pub? Should this be treated as a separate component?

Answer

No. The value and life of any trading potential is inherently inseparable from that of the property.

In calculating the useful economic life of an asset it is assumed that **subsequent expenditure** will be undertaken to **maintain the originally assessed standard** of performance of the asset (for example the cost of servicing or overhauling plant and equipment). Without such expenditure the depreciation expense would be increased because the useful life and/or residual value of the asset would be reduced. This type of expenditure is **recognised as an expense when incurred**.

Subsequent expenditure may be undertaken that results in a **restoration or replacement of a component** of the asset that has been depreciated or an **enhancement of economic benefits** of the asset in excess of the originally assessed standard of performance. This type of expenditure may result in an **extension of the useful economic life** of the asset.

Important!

> **Subsequent expenditure does not obviate the need to charge depreciation.** The subsequent expenditure is **capitalised as it is incurred and depreciated** over the asset's (or, where the expenditure relates to a component, the component's) useful economic life.

Tangible fixed assets other than non depreciable land, should be **reviewed for impairment** at the end of the reporting period where:

- No depreciation is charged on the grounds that it would be immaterial
- The estimated remaining useful economic life exceeds 50 years.

The review should be in accordance with FRS 11 *Impairment of fixed assets and goodwill,* discussed in the next chapter

Many companies carry fixed assets in their balance sheets at **revalued amounts**, particularly in the case of freehold buildings. When this is done, the **depreciation charge** should be calculated **on the basis of the revalued amount** (not the original cost), in spite of the alternative accounting rules in CA 2006.

Where the **residual value** is material, it should be **reviewed** at the end of each reporting period to take account of reasonably expected technological changes. A **change** in the estimated residual value should be **accounted for prospectively over the asset's remaining useful economic life**, except to the extent that the asset has been impaired at the balance sheet date.

2.8 Disclosure requirements of FRS 15

The following information should be disclosed separately in the financial statements for each class of tangible fixed assets.

(a)   The depreciation **M**ethods used

(b)   The **U**seful economic lives or the depreciation rates used

(c)   **T**otal depreciation charged for the period

(d)   Where material, the **F**inancial effect of a change during the period in either the estimate of useful economic lives or the estimate of residual values

(e)   The **C**ost or revalued amount at the beginning of the financial period and at the balance sheet date

(f)   The **C**umulative amount of provisions for depreciation or impairment at the beginning of the financial period and at the balance sheet date

(g)   A **R**econciliation of the movements, separately disclosing additions, disposals, revaluations, transfers, depreciation, impairment losses, and reversals of past impairment losses written back in the financial period

(h)   The **N**et carrying amount at the beginning of the financial period and at the balance sheet date

Remember!

> **Man United Trials in Football Can Create Raw Nerves**

2.9 Criticisms of FRS 15

FRS 15 has been largely welcomed, particularly the rules on revaluations (see below). However, some commentators have found problematic the treatment of subsequent expenditure where there is a major overhaul. The treatment has been described as 'contrived'.

2.10 UITF 24 Accounting for start up costs

The issue is whether start-up costs that cannot be included in the cost of a fixed asset may nevertheless be carried forward, for example as a prepayment, deferred expenditure or other kind of asset. FRS 15 *Tangible fixed assets* addresses the accounting for costs associated with a start-up or commissioning period. Paragraph 14 states that such costs should be included in the cost of a tangible fixed asset only where the asset is available for use but incapable of operating at normal levels without such a start-up or commissioning period.

The consensus was that **start-up costs should be accounted for on a basis consistent with the accounting treatment of similar costs incurred as part of the entity's ongoing activities**. In cases where there are no such similar costs, start-up costs that do not meet the criteria for recognition as assets under a relevant accounting standard should be recognised as an expense when they are incurred.

If start-up costs meet the definition of exceptional items they should be disclosed in accordance with FRS 3 *Reporting financial performance*. Disclosure regarding start-up costs in the Operating and Financial Review is also encouraged.

3 Revaluation

Before FRS 15, companies could pick and choose which of their assets they wished to revalue and when. This allowed companies to flatter their balance sheet figures through the inclusion of meaningless out of date valuations, thereby hindering comparability between companies from year to year. **FRS 15 puts a stop to this 'cherry picking'.**

An entity may adopt a policy of **revaluing tangible fixed assets**. Where this policy is adopted **it must be applied consistently** to all assets of the same class.

Key term

> A **class of fixed assets** is 'a category of tangible fixed assets having a similar nature, function or use in the business of an entity'. *(FRS 15)*

Where an asset is revalued its carrying amount should be its **current value** as at the balance sheet date, current value being the **lower of replacement cost and recoverable amount**.

To achieve the above, the standard states that a **full valuation** should be carried out **at least every five years** with an **interim valuation in year 3**. If it is likely that there has been a material change in value, interim valuations in years 1, 2 and 4 should also be carried out.

A full valuation should be conducted by either a **qualified external valuer** or a **qualified internal valuer**, provided that the valuation has been subject to review by a qualified external valuer. An interim valuation may be carried out by either an external or internal valuer.

For certain types of assets (other than properties) eg company cars, there may be an **active second hand market for the asset** or appropriate indices may exist, so that the directors can establish the asset's value with reasonable reliability and therefore avoid the need to use the services of a qualified valuer.

3.1 Basis

Property type	Valuation method
Specialised properties	Depreciated replacement cost
	Specialised properties are those which, due to their specialised nature, are rarely, if ever, sold on the open market for single occupation for a continuation of their existing use, except as part of a sale of the business in occupation. Eg oil refineries, chemical works, power stations, or schools, colleges and universities where there is no competing market demand from other organisations using these types of property in the locality.
Non-specialised properties	Existing use value (EUV)
Properties surplus to an entity's requirements	Open market value (OMV)

Where there is an indication of impairment, an **impairment review** should be carried out in accordance with FRS 11. The asset should be recorded at the lower of revalued amount (as above) and recoverable amount.

Tangible fixed assets other than properties should be valued using market value or, if not obtainable, depreciated replacement cost.

3.2 Reporting gains and losses on revaluation

Revaluation **gains** are recognised in the **statement of total recognised gains and losses (STRGL)** except to the extent that they reverse revaluation losses on the same assets, in which case they should be recognised in the profit and loss account.

All revaluation **losses** that are caused by a clear consumption of economic benefit (eg physical damage or a deterioration in the quality of the service provided by the asset) are recognised in the **profit and loss account**, ie the asset is clearly impaired.

Other losses are recognised in the **STRGL until the carrying amount reaches depreciated historical cost** and **thereafter in the profit and loss account**. However, if it can be demonstrated that the recoverable amount of the asset is more than its revalued amount, the loss will be recognised in the STRGL to the extent that the recoverable amount exceeds the revalued amount. This is because the difference between recoverable amount and revalued amount is not an impairment and should therefore be recognised in the STRGL as a valuation adjustment, rather than the profit and loss account.

3.3 Example: Accounting for revaluation losses

The following details are available in relation to a non specialised property.

Carrying value	£960,000
Depreciated historic cost	£800,000
Recoverable amount	£760,000
Existing use value	£700,000

How should the revaluation loss be treated?

Solution

(a) The revaluation loss on the property is £260,000 (ie carrying value of £960,000 compared with EUV of £700,000).

(b) The fall in value from carrying value (£960,000) to depreciated historic cost (£800,000) of £160,000 is recognised in the STRGL.

(c) The fall in value from depreciated historic cost (£800,000) to recoverable amount (£760,000) of £40,000 is recognised in the profit and loss account.

(d) The difference between recoverable amount (£760,000) and EUV (£700,000) is recognised in the STRGL.

3.4 Full example: revaluation

Rymachines plc is a manufacturing company with a number of separate factories scattered around England, and its head office in York. The chief accountant, Arthur Isation, is concerned about the effect on their figures for the year ending 31 December 20X7 of various transactions involving fixed assets. He has come to you with the following information.

(a) A revaluation exercise took place on 1 July 20X7. Items of plant that originally cost £80,000 on 1 January 20X5 were revalued to £97,500. The plant was, and still is, being depreciated down to zero over a ten year period from new.

(b) They are rather concerned regarding their ability to replace a specific type of machine because the price has risen so dramatically. With this in mind, Arthur would like to charge extra depreciation of £25,000 to 'retain more in the business to enable them to replace assets at the higher prices'.

(c)   The useful lives of one group of plant has been revised downwards as follows:

Plant costing £140,000 is 3 years old at the balance sheet date, and was originally to be depreciated over 7 years. The machinery is not surviving as well as hoped and it is now envisaged that it will be worthless in two years time.

(d)   The company operates a factory in Wiltshire which has suffered a decline in its volume of business since a Czech competitor company began marketing its products in England. None of the other businesses of Rymachines plc are affected.

The summarised balance sheet of this division shows:

	£'000
Goodwill	100
Tangible fixed assets	420
Other net assets (excluding tax and financing)	110
	630

The future cash flows of the division have been estimated and discounted using a risk-adjusted interest rate to give a value in use for the division as a whole of £390,000.

There is no realistic prospect of selling the business as a going concern. The fixed assets could be sold for £265,000 and the related costs would amount to £15,000. The other net assets would be expected to realise their carrying value.

Required

Draft notes in preparation for a meeting with Mr Isation explaining the accounting treatment required in respect of each of the points raised.

Solution

Notes for meeting with Arthur Isation, chief accountant of Rymachines plc on treatment of fixed assets.

(a)   *Revaluation of plant*

Depreciation charge in the profit and loss account for the period should be based on the carrying amount of the asset in the balance sheet. FRS 15 stresses the importance of the entire amount being charged through profit and loss account for the year.

Rymachines have revalued mid year, hence the appropriate depreciation charge for the year will be (assuming depreciation calculated on a monthly basis):

		£
1st 6 months	$\frac{80,000}{10} \times \frac{6}{12} =$	4,000
2nd 6 months	$\frac{97,500}{7.5} \times \frac{6}{12} =$	6,500
Charge for the year		10,500

Note that this is £2,500 higher than if no revaluation had taken place and this should be disclosed if material.

The revaluation as at 1 July 20X7 will amount to $(97,500 - (80,000 \times 7\frac{1}{2}/10)) = £37,500$, and should be credited to a revaluation reserve.

Best practice would be to transfer an amount equivalent to the excess depreciation on the revalued amount from revaluation reserve to profit and loss account as the revaluation reserve in effect becomes realised.

(b) *Supplementary depreciation*

Supplementary depreciation, namely that in excess of the depreciation based on the carrying amount of the assets, should not be charged in the profit and loss account. This does not, however, preclude the appropriation of retained profits to, for example, a reserve specially designated for replacement of fixed assets.

The additional £25,000 should not be accounted for as conventional depreciation. The depreciation charge must be based on the balance sheet carrying amount, and the additional £25,000 should merely be an intra-reserves transfer ie from profit and loss account reserve to a plant replacement reserve.

(c) *Revision of useful lives*

When, as a result of experience or of changed circumstances, it is considered that the original estimate of the useful economic life of an asset requires revision, the effect of the change in estimate on the results and financial position needs to be considered.

It would appear that the estimate of future useful life is being made at the balance sheet date, which would involve a normal £20,000 charge in respect of the year just finished (year ended 31 December 20X7), and a charge for the remaining two years of estimated useful life of

$$\frac{(140,000-60,000)}{2} = £40,000$$

(d) Under FRS 11, where there is an indication that an impairment has occurred a review must be carried out to establish whether the recoverable amount is less than the carrying value of the assets.

The recoverable amount (usually calculated for an income generating unit rather than an individual asset) is defined as the higher of

(i) net realisable value (265,000 – 15,000 +110,000)   £360,000
(ii) value in use (ie discounted future cash flows)   £390,000

Therefore the assets must be adjusted for an impairment of £240,000, allocated as follows:

£100,000 to goodwill
£140,000 to tangible fixed assets.

The total will be charged as part of operating profit and disclosed as an exceptional item. (This assumes that none of the tangible fixed assets have been revalued, otherwise the impairment of £140,000 could have been charged to the revaluation reserve until the carrying value equalled depreciated historical cost and thereafter to the profit and loss account).

4 SSAP 19 Accounting for investment properties

FAST FORWARD

SSAP 19 conflicts with the statutory requirement to depreciate all fixed assets with a limited economic life, by stating that investment properties need not ordinarily be depreciated. Companies taking advantage of this provision need to justify their departure from statute as being necessary to provide a true and fair view.

A summary of the main provisions of SSAP 19 *Accounting for investment properties* is given below, and these should be familiar to you from your earlier studies.

SSAP 19 *Accounting for investment properties*

Definition

- **Investment property:** an interest in land and/or buildings in respect of which construction work and development have been completed, and which is held for its investment potential, rental income being negotiated at arm's length.

- **Exceptions**: property owned and occupied by a company for its own purposes; and property let to and occupied by another group company (in company and group accounts). An associated company is not a group company.

Accounting treatment

- Such properties are **not depreciated**, except where a leasehold has an unexpired term of less than 20 years.

- **Revalue** each year to open market value.

- The increase in value is taken to the **IRR** (Investment Revaluation Reserve).

- For **diminutions** in value the treatment varies (this required an amendment to SSAP 19).

    - If **permanent**, it is charged to the P&L a/c.
    - If **temporary**, a temporary IRR deficit is allowed.

- **Disposals**: per FRS 3,

    - Profit/loss represents the sales proceeds less the carrying amount
    - Revaluation surplus transferred to the P&L a/c (as realised profits)

Disclosures

- Investment properties and the IRR should be **displayed prominently**.

- **Disclose**:

    - the name of the valuer;
    - whether the valuer is an employee or officer of the company; and
    - the basis of valuation used.

- **Non-compliance with CA 2006** for a true and fair view should be noted as required by UITF Abstract 7 (see below).

This chart will help to determine the application of SSAP 19.

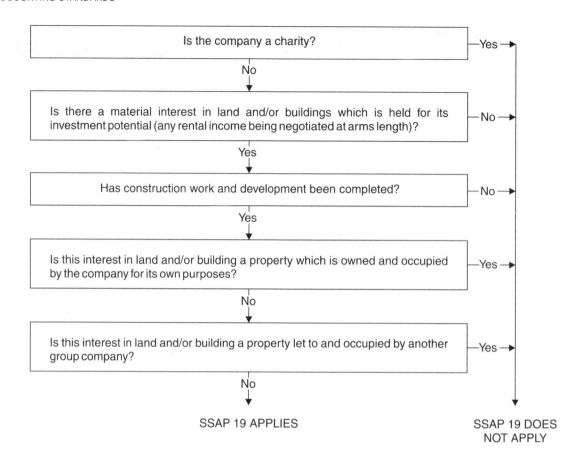

Question

The managing director of your company has always been unhappy at depreciating the company's properties because he argues that these properties are in fact appreciating in value. Recently he heard of another company which has investment properties and does not depreciate those properties.

You are required to write a report to your managing director explaining:

(a)   The consequences of not depreciating the company's existing properties
(b)   The meaning of investment properties
(c)   The accounting treatment of investment properties in published financial statements

Answer

REPORT

From: Finance Director
To: Managing Director   Date: 31 October 20X2
Subject: *Depreciation of property*

(a)   All fixed assets that have a finite economic life should be depreciated in a systematic manner over that period. While it is recognised that, generally, freehold land has an indefinite economic life, the same is not true of buildings. Even if they are properly maintained, most industrial and commercial buildings will become economically obsolete in time, even if they remain structurally sound.

The failure to provide depreciation on industrial and commercial buildings over their period of use overstates the profits of the company and this could lead to over-distribution of profit.

(b) An investment property is defined in the relevant accounting standard (SSAP 19) as one which is held for its investment potential and for which a rental is negotiated at arms length (and where construction is complete). It cannot be one which is owned and occupied by a company or its affiliated companies for its own purposes.

This means that our properties, which are used for the purposes of the company's own manufacturing, distribution and administrative activities, do not qualify for treatment as investment properties.

It also means that they could not be made to qualify as investment properties by transferring them to another group company and renting them back.

(c) Under SSAP 19 investment properties are not depreciated but are shown in the accounts at open market value. Increases in market value are credited to an investment revaluation reserve and decreases are charged to it. The open market valuation, which is related to rentals, is likely to vary considerably over time and large charges against profits could occur during periods of weakness in the property market. This could lead to greater volatility of earnings than if the properties had been depreciated, but it reflects more accurately the realities of the property market.

4.1 Problems with SSAP 19

It is likely that SSAP 19 will be amended to fit in with the new FRS 15 from which it is excluded. There are criticisms of the standard, mainly because it does give a clear definition of 'market value'. The Royal Institution of Chartered Surveyors defines **market value** as the best price at which the sale of an interest in property might reasonably be expected to have been completed unconditionally for cash consideration on the date of valuation, assuming a 'willing seller'. There is no mention of a 'willing buyer'.

There are perceived to be various difficulties with this definition.

(a) **A market transaction** cannot take place without both a seller and a buyer.

(b) The concept of **'willing seller'** (but not a willing buyer) is largely theoretical in depressed market conditions where no willing seller really exists, only unwilling and even forced sellers.

(c) This 'willing seller' concept inevitably leads to an over-emphasis on comparable evidence, forcing the valuer to look **backwards** rather than forwards.

(d) Following on from (c), such an approach cannot cope with **specialised assets**, such as large regional shopping centres, for which no ready market exits.

The deficiencies in the current definition of open market value do not become apparent **in normal market conditions** where there is a liquid market in actively traded properties. However, at the extremes of the cycle, the current definition is quite inadequate, producing over-valuation in times of boom and under-valuation in times of slump, exacerbating market cycles in an extremely damaging way.

5 SSAP 4 Accounting for government grants

SSAP 4 is summarised here as it is very straightforward and you have already studied it, look back to your previous studies if necessary.

Knowledge brought forward from earlier studies

SSAP 4 Accounting for government grants

Problems

- There is a **conflict** of the accruals concept vs the prudence concept.
- **Matching** is difficult if the expenditure is not specified to which the grant should be applied.
- It is necessary to distinguish between **revenue** and **capital grants**.

Accounting treatment

- **Government grants** should be matched in the P&L a/c with the expenditure for which they are contributed.

Knowledge brought forward from earlier studies (cont'd)

- For **fixed assets**, the grant is recognised over the useful economic life of the asset.

- The method of reducing the acquisition cost of the fixed asset by the amount of the grant and depreciating the net amount is **in conflict with CA 2006**.

- Grants are not recognised in the P&L a/c until **conditions of receipt** are complied with.

- If part or all recognition is **deferred**, treat this as deferred income.

- Any **potential liabilities** to repay should be provided for to the extent that repayment is probable.

Disclosure

- **Accounting policy note**
- Effect of **government grants** on the results for the period and/or the position at the B/S date.
- Any **potential liability** to repay grants according to FRS 12.

---

6 FRED 29

FAST FORWARD

FRED 29 *Property, plant and equipment; Borrowing costs* proposes replacing FRS 15 with the revised IASs of those names.

As part of the ASB's programme of convergence between FRS and IFRS (see Chapter 23), in May 2002 it issued FRED 29 *Property, plant and equipment; Borrowing costs.*

6.1 Main points

FRED 29 includes the text of a revised IAS 16 *Property, plant and equipment* and IAS 23 *Borrowing costs.* Like FRS 15, IAS 23 permits a **choice** between **capitalising certain borrowing costs** and treating all such costs as an **expense**.

The **principles for initial measurement and depreciation are the same** in both IAS 16 and FRS 15 *Tangible fixed assets.* Both standards allow the option of revaluing assets or keeping them at depreciated cost. But there are some significant differences, of which the most important is in relation to revaluation. Where the **UK uses a 'value to the business' model, the international standard uses a 'fair value' model.**

6.1.1 Revaluation proposals

Currently proposals on the revaluation of fixed assets are being developed by the 'Revaluation Group', which includes representatives of national standard setters from countries where revaluation is permitted (Australia, New Zealand, South Africa and the UK). The group have proposed that **assets should be stated at entry value** unless disposal would be the more economically rational course of action, in which case exit value should be used. In the absence of a market for the asset, its value would be based on an assessment of cash flows or on replacement cost.

In the light of these proposals, it is possible that **IAS 16 may undergo further revision**, with regard to its revaluation rules.

6.1.2 ASB's approach

FRED 29 proposes that the UK should replace FRS 15 with the revised IAS 16 and IAS 23, unless there are further changes to the IAS 16 requirements on revaluation.

Other changes from existing UK requirements are:

(a) There will be **no requirement for annual impairment reviews** where **no depreciation** is **charged**.

(b) **Capitalisation of interest** would be allowed on certain **inventories**.

(c) **Renewals accounting** would **not** be **allowed**.

6.2 Summary

- FRED 29 proposes two new standards which would eventually replace FRS 15.
- There would be no requirement for annual impairment reviews where no depreciation is charged.
- Renewals accounting would not be allowed.
- 'Fair value' would be used for revalued assets rather than 'value to the business'
- Capitalisation of interest would be allowed on certain inventories.

Chapter Roundup

- **Assets** have been defined in various ways. The most recent definition is contained in the ASB's *Statement of Principles*, Chapter 4 *Elements of financial statements*.

- CA 2006 maintains **historical cost** principles, modified by the revaluations of certain assets.

- **FRS 15** sets out **uniform principles** relating to tangible fixed assets with regard to:

  - Initial measurement
  - Valuation
  - Depreciation

- **SSAP 19** conflicts with the statutory requirement to depreciate all fixed assets with a limited economic life, by stating that investment properties need not ordinarily be depreciated. Companies taking advantage of this provision need to justify their departure from statute as being necessary to provide a true and fair view.

- **FRED 29** *Property, plant and equipment; Borrowing costs* proposes replacing FRS 15 with the revised IASs of those names.

Quick Quiz

1   How does the ASB's Statement of Principles define an asset?

2   Can finance costs be capitalised?

3   Can subsequent expenditure on a fixed asset be capitalised?

4   Define depreciation.

5   What accounting treatment is required if the estimated useful life of a fixed asset is revised?

6   When properties are revalued, how often, per FRS 15, is a full valuation needed?

7   Specialised properties should be valued on the basis of:

    A   Existing value in use
    B   Open market value
    C   Depreciated replacement cost
    D   Net realisable value

8   Which of the following is not a directly attributable cost associated with bringing a tangible fixed asset into working condition?

    A   Cost of site preparation and clearance
    B   Installation costs
    C   Stamp duty
    D   Design errors

9   What is the main difference between FRS 15 and FRED 29?

Answers to Quick Quiz

1   See key term.

2   Yes. This is optional. If an entity does capitalise finance costs, they must do so consistently.

3   Yes, in three cases.

    (a)   It enhances the economic benefits over and above those previously estimated.

    (b)   A component treated separately for depreciation purposes has been restored or replaced

    (c)   It relates to a major inspection or overhaul that restores economic benefits that have been consumed and reflected in the depreciation charge.

4   The measure of the cost or revalued amount of the economic benefits of the tangible fixed asset that have been consumed during the period. Consumption includes the wearing out, using up or other reduction in the economic life of a tangible fixed asset, whether arising from use, effluxion of time or obsolescence through either changes in technology or demand for the goods and services produced by the asset.

5   The net book value of the asset should be depreciated over the new estimate of its remaining useful life.

6   Every 5 years.

7   C

8   D   Abnormal costs, such as those arising from design errors, industrial disposals and idle capacity, should not be capitalised as part of the cost.

9   For revaluations, FRED 29, for now, proposes fair value, whereas FRS 15 uses 'value to the business'.

Now try the questions below from the Exam Question Bank			
Number	**Level**	**Marks**	**Time**
Q3	Introductory	n/a	n/a

Fixed assets: intangible assets

Topic list	Syllabus reference
1 FRS 10 *Goodwill and intangible assets*	C2
2 FRS 11 *Impairment of fixed assets and goodwill*	C2
3 FRED 38 *Impairment of assets*	C2, F2
4 SSAP 13 *Accounting for research and development*	C2
5 FRED 37 *Intangible assets*	C2, F2

Introduction

Probably the most important, and certainly the most contentious intangible fixed asset is **goodwill**. This is the subject of **FRS 10** *Goodwill and intangible assets* which was covered in your earlier studies.

The section on **SSAP 13** should be revision of a fairly straightforward topic, but you should make sure that you know SSAP 13's provisions.

There are proposed changes to FRS 10 and FRS 11, which you should know about.

Study guide

		Intellectual level
C2	**Non-current assets**	
(a)	Apply and discuss the timing of the recognition of non-current assets and the determination of their carrying amounts, including impairment and revaluations	3
F2	**Proposed changes to accounting standards**	
(b)	Apply and discuss the implications of a proposed change to an accounting standard on the performance and balance sheet of an entity	2

Exam guide

You may be given an unusual situation and asked to identify the issues. Is a football player an intangible asset?

1 FRS 10 Goodwill and intangible assets

FAST FORWARD

The treatment of **goodwill and intangibles** is a controversial and complex area. You must ensure that you can discuss the current thinking on the nature of fixed assets, intangible assets and goodwill and that you can discuss all the possible treatments of positive and negative goodwill in accounts and the arguments on brand accounting. You should be familiar with, and be able to explain, the ASB's requirements as set out in FRS 10 *Goodwill and intangible assets*.

You should be familiar with FRS 10 *Goodwill and intangible assets* from your earlier studies. Below is a summary of the requirements, together with one or two questions. Look back to your earlier study material if you are unsure.

Knowledge brought forward from earlier studies

FRS 10 Goodwill and intangible assets

Accounting treatment

- Under FRS 10 both purchased goodwill and intangible assets should be capitalised as assets in the B/S. Thereafter treatment depends on the nature of investment.

  - There is a rebuttable presumption that the useful economic lives (UEL) of purchased goodwill and intangible assets are limited and do not exceed 20 years from acquisition.

  - The UEL may be regarded as greater than 20 years or even indefinite, but only if the goodwill is capable of continued measurement so that annual impairment reviews can be performed

Knowledge brought forward from earlier studies

- **Positive purchased goodwill and intangible assets**
  - Where goodwill and intangible assets are regarded as having limited UEL they should be amortised
  - Where they are regarded as having indefinite UEL they should not be amortised
  - Where they are not amortised or are amortised over more than 20 years, impairment reviews should be performed each year under FRS 11

- **Negative goodwill**

  Negative goodwill should be recognised and separately disclosed on the face of the balance sheet immediately below the goodwill heading. It should be recognised in the profit and loss account in the periods in which the non monetary assets acquired are depreciated or sold

- **Internally generated goodwill**

  Internally generated goodwill should not be capitalised and internally developed intangible assets should be capitalised only where they have a readily ascertainable market value

Question

Goodwill

The circumstances where an indefinite useful economic life longer than 20 years may be legitimately presumed are limited. What factors determine the durability of goodwill?

Answer

FRS 10 mentions the following.

(a)   The nature of the business
(b)   The stability of the industry in which the acquired business operates
(c)   Typical lifespans of the products to which the goodwill attaches
(d)   The extent to which the acquisition overcomes market entry barriers that will continue to exist
(e)   The expected future impact of competition on the business

Question

Negative goodwill

Brookie plc acquired its investment in Stenders Ltd in the year ended 31 December 20X8. The goodwill on acquisition was calculated as follows.

	£'000	£'000
Cost of investment		200
Fair value of net assets acquired (remaining useful life – 7 years)		
Fixed assets	350	
Stock	50	
Net monetary assets	100	
		(500)
Negative goodwill		(300)

Required

Calculate the amount relating to negative goodwill as reflected in the profit and loss account and balance sheet for the year ended 31 December 20X8.

Answer

Amortisation in the profit and loss account for 20X8

Non-monetary assets recognised through the profit and loss account for the year ended 31 December 20X8:

	£'000
Stock	50
Depreciation (£350,000 ÷ 7)	50
	100
Proportion recognised this year	¼

This means that a credit of £75,000 (£300,000 × ¼) of the negative goodwill will be charged to the profit and loss account for the year ended 31.12.X8. The remaining £225,000 will be carried in the balance sheet as a deduction from positive goodwill as part of intangible fixed assets.

Over the next six years (the remaining useful life of the non-monetary assets originally purchased), it will be released into the profit and loss account (£37,500 a year).

1.1 Criticisms of FRS 10

Criticisms have been made of the thinking behind the standard by the firm Ernst & Young. The main criticisms are as follows.

(a) FRS 10 **still allows a choice** of accounting treatments. Companies can follow a regime that permits the goodwill to be carried as a permanent asset. This may allow some spurious assets to remain indefinitely in the balance sheet, potentially providing fuel for criticism of the profession in the next wave of accounting scandal.

(b) The **impairment review**, based on FRS 11, applies 'labyrinthine methodologies to very soft numbers'. In other words, it is **subjective**, not least in determining how the business is to be segmented. Forecasting cashflows is also problematic.

(c) The importance of **negative goodwill** has been underestimated. It is more likely to arise now that FRS 7 bans reorganisation provisions, thus raising the value of the net assets acquired.

(d) The treatment of **negative goodwill** is 'strange'. It is a **'dangling credit'** in the balance sheet and the profit and loss account treatment simply mirrors that required for depreciation without regard to the fact that this is a **credit** to the profit and loss account.

1.2 UITF Abstract 27 Revision to estimates of the useful economic life of goodwill and intangible assets

This Abstract states that a change from non-amortisation of goodwill or intangible assets, on the grounds that the life of the asset is indefinite, to amortisation over a period of 20 years or less should not be reported as a change in accounting policy. In such a circumstance, the carrying amount of the goodwill or intangible asset should be amortised over the revised remaining useful life.

2 FRS 11 Impairment of fixed assets and goodwill

FRS 11 *Impairment of fixed assets and* goodwill was introduced to ensure that

- Fixed assets and goodwill are recorded at no more than their **recoverable amount**
- Any **impairment loss** is **correctly measured**
- **Sufficient information** is disclosed

It is accepted practice that a **fixed asset** should **not be carried in the financial statements at more than its recoverable amount**, ie the higher of the amount for which it could be sold and the amount recoverable from its future use.

2.1 FRS 11 Impairment of fixed assets and goodwill

While statute provides some guidance, it provides none on how the recoverable amount should be measured and when impairment losses should be recognised. As a result, practice is inconsistent and perhaps some impairments may not be recognised on a timely basis.

Under FRS 10, where goodwill and intangible assets have a useful life in excess of twenty years or one that is indefinite, the recoverable amount of the goodwill and intangible assets has to be reviewed every year.

2.1.1 Objective of FRS 11

(a) Fixed assets and goodwill are recorded in the financial statements at no more than their **recoverable amount**.

(b) Any resulting **impairment loss** is measured and recognised on a **consistent basis**.

(c) **Sufficient information** is **disclosed** in the financial statements to enable users to understand the impact of the impairment on the financial position and performance of the reporting entity.

The FRS applies to subsidiary undertakings, associates and joint ventures but excludes fixed assets governed by FRS 13 and SSAP 19.

2.2 Indications of impairment

A **review for impairment** of a fixed asset or goodwill should be carried out if events or changes in circumstances indicate that the carrying amount of the fixed asset or goodwill may not be recoverable.

Key term

> **Impairment**: a reduction in the recoverable amount of a fixed asset or goodwill below its carrying amount.
> *(FRS 11)*

Impairment occurs due to:

- Something happening to the **fixed asset** itself
- Something occurring in the **environment** within which the asset operates.

2.2.1 Indicators of impairment

(a) There is a **current period operating loss** or **net cash outflow** from operating activities, combined with *either*:

(i) **past** operating losses or net cash outflows from operating activities; *or*

(ii)   an expectation of **continuing** operating losses or net cash outflows from operating activities.

(b)   A **fixed asset's market value has declined** significantly during the period.

(c)   Evidence is available of **obsolescence or physical damage** to the fixed asset.

(d)   There is a **significant adverse change** in any of the following.

(i)   Either the **business or the market** in which the fixed asset or goodwill is involved, such as the entrance of a major competitor.

(ii)   The **statutory or other regulatory environment** in which the business operates.

(iii)   Any **indicator of value** (eg multiples of turnover) used to measure the fair value of a fixed asset on acquisition.

(e)   A commitment by management to undertake a **significant reorganisation**.

(f)   A major loss of **key employees**.

(g)   **Market interest rates** or other market rates of return have increased significantly, and these increases are likely to affect materially the fixed asset's recoverable amount.

Where any of these occur, then an impairment review should be carried out. In the case of tangible fixed assets, if there is no cause to suspect any impairment, then **no impairment review** is necessary. Intangible assets and goodwill may, however, still require review.

Key terms

> **Intangible assets**: non-financial fixed assets that do not have physical substance but are identifiable and controlled by the entity through custody or legal rights.
>
> **Purchased goodwill**: the difference between the cost of an acquired entity and the aggregate of the fair values of that entity's identifiable assets and liabilities.
>
> **Tangible fixed assets**: assets that have physical substance and are held for use in the production or supply of goods or services, for rental to others, or for administrative purposes on a continuing basis in the reporting entity's activities.   (FRS 11)

2.3 The impairment review

The impairment review will consist of a **comparison of the carrying amount** of the fixed asset or goodwill **with its recoverable amount** (the higher of net realisable value, if known, and value in use). To the extent that the **carrying amount exceeds the recoverable amount, the fixed asset or goodwill is impaired and should be written down. The impairment loss should be recognised in the profit and loss account unless it arises on a previously revalued fixed asset.**

An impairment **loss** on a **revalued fixed asset** should be recognised in the **profit and loss account** if it is caused by a **clear consumption of economic benefits. Other impairments** of revalued fixed assets should be recognised in the **statement of total recognised gains and losses** until the carrying amount of the asset reaches its **depreciated historical cost** and **thereafter in the profit and loss account**.

Key terms

> **Net realisable value**: the amount at which an asset could be disposed of, less any direct selling costs.
>
> **Recoverable amount**: the higher of net realisable value and value in use.
>
> **Value in use**: the present value of the future cash flows obtainable as a result of an asset's continued use, including those resulting from its ultimate disposal.

Note the following **rules** here.

    (a)   If NRV *or* value in use is higher than the carrying amount, there is no impairment.

    (b)   If a reliable estimate of NRV cannot be made, the recoverable amount is its value in use.

    (c)   If NRV is less than the carrying amount, then value in use must be found to see if it is higher still. If it is higher, recoverable amount is based on value in use, not NRV.

When an impairment loss on a fixed asset or goodwill is recognised, the **remaining useful economic life** should be reviewed and revised if necessary. The revised carrying amount should be depreciated over the revised estimate of the useful economic life.

2.4 Calculation of net realisable value

The net realisable value of an asset that is **traded on an active market** will be based on **market value**. Disposal costs should include only the essential selling costs of the fixed asset and *not* any costs of reducing or reorganising the business.

2.5 Calculation of value in use

Value in use is **not always easy** to estimate.

    (a)   The value in use of a fixed asset should be estimated **individually** where reasonably practicable.

    (b)   Where it is not reasonably practicable to identify cash flows arising from an individual fixed asset, value in use should be calculated at the level of **income-generating units**.

    (c)   The **carrying amount of each income-generating unit** containing the fixed asset or goodwill under review should be compared with the **higher of the value in use and the net realisable value** (if it can be measured reliably) of the unit.

Key term

> An **income generating unit** is defined as a group of assets, liabilities and associated goodwill that generates income that is largely independent of the reporting entity's other income streams. The assets and liabilities include those already involved in generating the income and an appropriate portion of those used to generate more than one income stream.

Because it is necessary to identify only material impairments, in some cases it may be acceptable to consider a **group of income generating units together** rather than on an individual basis.

In some cases a detailed calculation of value in use will not be necessary. A **simple estimate** may be sufficient to demonstrate that either value in use is higher than carrying value, in which case there is no impairment, or value in use is lower than net realisable value, in which case impairment is measured by reference to net realisable value.

2.6 Identification of income generating units

Income generating units should be identified by **dividing the total income of the entity into as many largely independent income streams as is reasonably practicable**. Each of the entity's identifiable assets and liabilities should be attributed to, or apportioned between, one or more income generating unit(s). However, the following are **excluded**.

    •   Deferred tax balances
    •   Interest bearing debt
    •   Dividends payable
    •   Other financing items

In general terms, the income streams identified are likely to **follow** the way in which **management** monitors and makes decisions about continuing or closing the different lines of business of the entity. **Unique intangible assets**, such as brands and mastheads, are generally seen to generate income independently of each other and are usually **monitored separately**. Hence they can often be used to identify income-generating units. **Other income streams** may be identified by **reference to major products or services**.

2.7 Example: Identification of income generating units

A transport company runs a network comprising trunk routes fed by a number of supporting routes. Decisions about continuing or closing the supporting routes are not based on the returns generated by the routes in isolation but on the contribution made to the returns generated by the trunk routes.

Solution

An income-generating unit comprises a trunk route plus the supporting routes associated with it because the cash inflows generated by the trunk routes are not independent of the supporting routes.

Question   Income generating unit

Identify the income generating unit in the following cases.

(a)   A manufacturer can produce a product at a number of different sites. Not all the sites are used to full capacity and the manufacturer can choose how much to make at each site. However, there is not enough surplus capacity to enable any one site to be closed. The cash inflows generated by any one site therefore depend on the allocation of production across all sites.

(b)   A restaurant chain has a large number of restaurants across the country. The cash inflows of each restaurant can be individually monitored and sensible allocations of costs to each restaurant can be made.

Answer

(a)   The income-generating unit comprises all the sites at which the product can be made.

(b)   Each restaurant is an income-generating unit by itself. However, any impairment of individual restaurants is unlikely to be material. A material impairment is likely to occur only when a number of restaurants are affected together by the same economic factors. It may therefore be acceptable to consider groupings of restaurants affected by the same economic factors rather than each individual restaurant.

Question   Impairment loss

Ashley Ltd has an income-generating unit which has a carrying value of £4,000,000 at 31 December 20X7. This carrying value comprises £1,000,000 relating to goodwill and £3,000,000 relating to net assets. The goodwill is not being amortised as its useful life is believed to be indefinite. In 20X8, changes in the regulatory framework surrounding its business mean that the income-generating unit has a value in use of £3,200,000. As a result of losses, net assets have decreased to £2,800,000 reducing the total carrying value of the unit to £3,800,000 which has thus suffered an impairment loss of £600,000. This is charged to the profit and loss account. The carrying value of goodwill is reduced to £400,000. In 20X9 the company develops a new product with the result that the value in use of the income-generating unit is now £3,400,000. Net tangible assets have remained at £2,800,000.

Can all or any of the impairment loss be reversed?

Answer

No. Despite the value in use of the business unit now being £3,400,000 compared to its carrying value of £3,200,000, it is not possible to reverse £200,000 of the prior year's impairment loss of £600,000 since the reason for the increase in value of the business unit (the launch of the new product) is not the same as the reason for the original impairment loss (the change in the regulatory environment in which the business operates).

2.8 Central assets

Assets and liabilities that are directly involved in the production and distribution of individual products may be attributed directly to one unit. Central assets, such as group or regional head offices and working capital may have to be apportioned across the units as on a logical and systematic basis. The **sum of the carrying amounts of the units must equal the carrying amount of the net assets (excluding tax on finance) of the equity as a whole**.

It **may not be possible** to **apportion certain central assets** meaningfully **across the income generating units** to which they contribute. Such assets **may be excluded from** the **individual income generating units**.

- An additional impairment review should be performed on the excluded central assets.

- The income generating units to which the central assets contribute should be combined and their combined carrying amount (including that of the central assets) should be compared with their combined value in use.

2.9 Capitalised goodwill

This **should be attributed to income generating** units or groups of similar units.

2.10 Cash flows

The expected future cash flows of the income-generating unit, including any allocation of central overheads but excluding cash flows relating to financing and tax, should be based on **reasonable and supportable assumptions**. The cash flows should be **consistent with the most up-to-date budgets** and plans that have been formally approved by management. Cash flows for the period beyond that covered by formal budgets and plans should assume a steady or declining growth rate.

Future cash flows must be estimated for income generating units in their **current condition**, ie exclude:

(a)   Benefits expected to arise from a **future reorganisation** for which provision has not been made

(b)   **Future capital expenditure** that will improve or enhance the income generating units more than originally assessed

For the **five years** following each impairment review where the recoverable amount has been based on value in use, the **cash flows achieved should be compared with those forecast**.

(a)   If the actual cash flows are so much less than those forecast that use of the actual cash flows could have required recognition of an impairment in previous periods, the original **impairment calculations should be re-performed** using the actual cash flows.

(b)   Any **impairment** identified should be **recognised in the current period** unless the impairment has reversed.

2.11 Discount rate

The present value of the income-generating unit under review should be calculated by discounting the expected future cash flows of the unit.

(a)   The discount rate used should be an estimate of the rate that the market would expect on an equally risky investment.

(b)   It should exclude the effects of any risk for which the cash flows have been adjusted and should be calculated on a pre-tax basis.

2.12 Allocation of impairment loss

Allocation of any impairment loss calculated (ie where carrying amount exceeds value in use) should be allocated in stages

Step 1   To any **goodwill** in the unit

Step 2   To any **capitalised intangible asset**

Step 3   To the **tangible assets** (pro-rata or other method).

No asset with a readily ascertainable market value should be written down to below NRV.

2.13 Reversal of past impairments

Tangible fixed assets and investments are treated differently from goodwill and intangible assets.

2.13.1 Tangible fixed assets and investments

If, after an impairment loss has been recognised, the **recoverable amount** of a tangible fixed asset or investment (in subsidiaries, associates and joint ventures) **increases because of a change in economic conditions**, the resulting **reversal** of the impairment loss should be **recognised in the current period**. However, recognition is *only* **to the extent that it increases the carrying amount of the fixed asset up to the amount that it would have been had the original impairment not occurred**. The reversal of the impairment loss should be recognised in the **profit and loss account unless** it arises on a **previously revalued fixed asset** (see below).

Such events would be the reverse of those given above (Paragraph 2.8) to trigger an impairment review. Increases in value from the passage of time or through the passing of cash outflows do *not* give rise to the reversal of an impairment loss.

Important

> An increase in value above the original carrying value is a **revaluation**, and this is the case with goodwill and intangibles too.

2.13.2 Goodwill and intangible assets

The reversal of an impairment loss on intangible assets and goodwill should be **recognised in the current period if, and only if**:

(a)   an **external event** caused the recognition of the impairment loss in previous periods, and subsequent external events clearly and demonstrably reverse the effects of that event in a way that was not foreseen in the original impairment calculations; or

(b)   the impairment loss related to an intangible asset with a readily ascertainable market value and the **net realisable value based on that market value** has increased **to above the intangible asset's impaired carrying amount**.

The reversal of the impairment loss should be **recognised to the extent that it increases the carrying amount of the goodwill or intangible asset up to the amount that it would have been had the original impairment not occurred**. However, the reversal of an impairment loss recognised under (b) above should *not* be recognised **beyond the extent that it increases the carrying amount of the intangible asset to its net realisable value**.

Key term

> **Readily ascertainable market value**, in relation to an intangible asset, is the value that is established by reference to a market where:

(a)   The asset belongs to a homogeneous population of assets that are equivalent in all material respects

(b)   An active market, evidenced by frequent transactions, exists for that population of assets

(FRS 11)

Question

Reversal of impairment loss

An income-generating unit comprising a factory, plant and equipment etc and associated purchased goodwill becomes impaired because the product it makes is overtaken by a technologically more advanced model produced by a competitor. The recoverable amount of the income-generating unit falls to £60m, resulting in an impairment loss of £80m, allocated as follows.

	Carrying amounts before impairment £m	Carrying amounts after impairment £m
Goodwill	40	–
Patent (with no market value)	20	–
Tangible fixed assets	80	60
Total	140	60

After three years, the entity makes a technological breakthrough of its own, and the recoverable amount of the income-generating unit increases to £90m. The carrying amount of the tangible fixed assets had the impairment not occurred would have been £70m.

Required

Calculate the reversal of the impairment loss.

Answer

The reversal of the impairment loss is recognised to the extent that it increases the carrying amount of the tangible fixed assets to what it would have been had the impairment not taken place, ie a reversal of the impairment loss of £10m is recognised and the tangible fixed assets written back to £70m. Reversal of the impairment is not recognised in relation to the goodwill and patent because the effect of the external event that caused the original impairment has not reversed – the original product is still overtaken by a more advanced model.

The **reversal of past impairment losses** is **recognised** when the **recoverable amount** of a tangible fixed asset or investment in a subsidiary, an associate or a joint venture has **increased because of a change in economic conditions or in the expected use of the asset**. Increases in the recoverable amount of goodwill and intangible assets are recognised only when:

(a)   an external event caused the recognition of the impairment loss in previous periods; and

(b) subsequent external events clearly and demonstrably reverse the effects of that event in a way that was not foreseen in the original impairment calculations.

(a) **Impairment losses** are recognised in the **profit and loss account**, **unless** they arise on a **previously revalued fixed asset**.

(b) Impairment losses on **revalued fixed assets** are recognised in the **statement of total recognised gains and losses** until the carrying value of the asset falls **below depreciated historical** cost unless the impairment is clearly caused by a **consumption of economic benefits**, in which case the loss is recognised in the **profit and loss account**.

(c) Impairments **below depreciated historical** cost are recognised in the **profit and loss account**.

2.14 Presentation and disclosure

Impairment losses recognised in the profit and loss account should be included within **operating profit** under the **appropriate statutory heading**, and disclosed as an exceptional item if appropriate. Impairment losses recognised in the STRGL should be **disclosed separately** on the face of that statement.

In **the notes** to the financial statements in **accounting periods after the impairment**, the impairment loss should be treated as follows.

(a) For assets held on a **historical cost basis**, the impairment loss should be included **within cumulative depreciation**: the cost of the asset should not be reduced.

(b) For **revalued assets held at a market value** (eg existing use value or open market value), the impairment loss should be included **within the revalued carrying amount**.

(c) For **revalued assets held at depreciated replacement** cost, an impairment loss **charged to the profit and loss account** should be included **within cumulative depreciation**: the carrying amount of the asset should not be reduced; an **impairment loss charged to the STRGL** should be **deducted from the carrying amount** of the asset.

If the impairment loss is measured by reference to **value in use** of a fixed asset or income-generating unit, the **discount rate applied to the cash flows should be disclosed**. If a risk-free discount rate is used, some indication of the risk adjustments made to the cash flows should be given.

Where an impairment loss recognised in a previous period is **reversed** in the current period, the financial statements should **disclose the reason for the reversal**, including any changes in the assumptions upon which the calculation of recoverable amount is based.

Where an impairment loss would have been recognised in a previous period had the forecasts of future cash flows been more accurate but the impairment has reversed and the reversal of the loss is permitted to be recognised, the impairment now identified and its subsequent reversal should be disclosed.

Where, in the measurement of value in use, the period before a steady or declining long-term growth rate has been assumed extends to more than five years, the financial statements should **disclose the length of the longer period** and the circumstances justifying it.

Where, in the measurement of value in use, the long-term growth rate used has exceeded the long-term average growth rate for the country or countries in which the business operates, the financial statements should **disclose the growth rate assumed** and the circumstances justifying it.

2.15 Section summary

The main aspects of FRS 11 to remember are:

- **Indications** of impairment
- Identification of **income-generating** unit
- How an **impairment review** is carried out
- **Restoration of past losses** (tangibles vs intangibles)
- Impairment and restoration of **revalued fixed assets**

3 FRED 38 Impairment of assets

FAST FORWARD

FRED 38 implements IAS 36 *Impairment of assets*. The FRED would remove one of the requirements from FRS 11, namely that the accuracy of impairments needs to be checked by comparing actual cash flows against projected cash flows.

3.1 Background

As part of the first phase of the Business Combinations project (see Chapter 16), the IASB amended both IAS 38 *Intangible assets* and IAS 36 *Impairment of assets*. FREDs 37 and 38 propose the adoption of UK standards based on the current text of these standards. FRED 37 is covered in Section 5 of this chapter. FRED 38 will be discussed below in terms of the main changes to current UK practice.

3.2 Main changes

To justify the carrying of goodwill without systematic amortisation it is clear that a **robust test for impairment is required**. The impairment test must provide confidence in its ability to identify reductions in the carrying amount of acquired goodwill. There are two key differences between the impairment test set out in FRS 11 and that of IAS 36:

(a) The FRS 11 test attempts to **distinguish between acquired and internally generated goodwill** and to recognise only impairment of the acquired part. The proposed Standard **does not include** such a test;

(b) The FRS 11 impairment test includes a test to check the accuracy of impairment by **comparing actual cash flows against those projected; IAS 36 does not contain a similar test.**

4 SSAP 13 Accounting for research and development

FAST FORWARD

SSAP 13 on the other hand is a standard which is generally accepted and well understood. You should already be very familiar with its provisions, but make sure that you learn the disclosure requirements.

In many companies, especially those which produce food, or 'scientific' products such as medicines, or 'high-technology' products, the expenditure on research and development is considerable. When R & D is a large item of cost, its accounting treatment may have a significant influence on the profits of a business and its balance sheet valuation. SSAP 13 is relatively straightforward, and you have met it in your previous studies. A summary is given below, along with a revision question.

Knowledge brought forward from earlier studies

SSAP 13 Accounting research and development

Definitions

- **Pure/basic research** is experimental/theoretical work with no commercial end in view and no practical application.

- **Applied research** is original investigation directed towards a specific practical aim/objective.

- **Development** is the use of scientific/technical knowledge in order to produce new/substantially improved materials, devices, processes etc.

Accounting treatment

- **Pure and applied research** should be written off as incurred.

- **Development expenditure** should be written off in year of expenditure, *except* in certain circumstances when it *may* be deferred to future periods.

S	Separately defined project
E	Expenditure separately identifiable
C	Commercially viable
T	Technically feasible
O	Overall profit expected
R	Resources exist to complete the project

- Show **deferred development costs** as an intangible asset amortised from the beginning of commercial production, systematically by reference to sales, etc.

- Deferred costs should be **reviewed annually**; where the above criteria no longer apply, write off the cost immediately.

- Development expenditure previously written off can be **reinstated** if the uncertainties which led to it being written off no longer apply.

- **R & D fixed assets** should be capitalised and written off over their estimated economic lives.

- Deferral of costs should be **applied consistently** to all projects.

- SSAP 13 **does not apply to**:

  - Fixed assets used for R&D (except amortisation)
  - The cost of locating mineral deposits in extractive industries
  - Expenditure where there is a firm contract for reimbursement

Disclosure

- R&D activities should be disclosed in the **directors' report**.

- Private companies outside groups which include a plc are **exempt** from disclosing R & D expenditures (except amortisation) if they meet the criteria for a medium-sized company × 10.

- **Disclose**:

  - Movements on deferred development expenditure
  - R&D charged to the P&L a/c analysed between current year expenditure and amortisation
  - An accounting policy note

4.1 R & D in practice

In a recent survey of company accounts, it was found that 25% did not show the amount spent on R & D, even when it had been disclosed in the chairman's report that money had been spent during the period. This contradicts SSAP 13. It is obviously misleading for companies to state that they spend money on R & D unless the amount was **material**. If it was material the amount should be disclosed.

The importance of R & D disclosure was emphasised in another survey of what users really needed in financial statements. UK institutional investors said the top requirement was **future prospects and plans** (84%). R & D is seen to form a crucial quantitative element of prospects and plans. When specifically asked about R & D, 64% of UK investors said the data was very, or extremely, important to them. Unfortunately, the top companies analysed failed dismally to provide the information required. There is a wide variety of treatment and information given on R & D and improvements are required in the reporting of R & D.

The emergence of new and quickly growing **computer software companies** has brought SSAP 13, a previously uncontroversial standard, back into the spotlight. These companies have complained about the high level of write-offs of R & D costs, which has a significant impact on profits. Such costs have to be written off because they are often incurred on speculative software which is high risk and may never be produced commercially. It is unlikely, however, that the ASB will look at this topic in the near future.

| Question | R & D |

Forkbender Ltd develops and manufactures exotic cutlery and has the following projects in hand.

| | Project | | | | |
| | 1 | 2 | 3 | 4 | 5 |
	£'000	£'000	£'000	£'000	£'000
Deferred development expenditure b/f 1.1.X2	280	–	450	–	–
Development expenditure incurred during the year					
Salaries, wages and so on	35	29	–	60	20
Overhead costs	2	5	–	–	3
Materials and services	3	13	–	11	4
Patents and licences	1	2	–	–	–
Market research	–	10	–	2	–

Project 1 was originally expected to be highly profitable but this is now in doubt, since the scientist in charge of the project is now behind schedule, with the result that competitors are gaining ground.

Project 2: £370,000 development expenditure on this project has been written off in previous years. Directors now believe, on the best advice, that the project will in future earn revenue considerably in excess of all development costs and they therefore wish to reinstate the expenditure of previous years.

Project 3: commercial production started during the year. Sales were 20,000 units in 20X2 and future sales are expected to be: 20X3 30,000 units; 20X4 60,000 units; 20X5 40,000 units; 20X6 30,000 units. There are no sales expected after 20X6.

Project 4: these costs relate to a new project, which meets the criteria for deferral of expenditure and which is expected to last for three years.

Project 5 is another new project, involving the development of a 'loss leader', expected to raise the level of future sales.

The company's policy is to defer development costs, where permitted by SSAP 13. Expenditure carried forward is written off evenly over the expected sales life of projects, starting in the first year of sale.

Required

Show how the above projects should be treated in the accounting statements of Forkbender Ltd for the year ended 31 December 20X2 in accordance with best accounting practice. Justify your treatment of each project.

Answer

Project 1 expenditure, including that relating to previous years, should all be written off in 20X2, as there is now considerable doubt as to the profitability of the project.

Project 2 expenditure for 20X2 can be deferred and the expenditure relating to previous years can be reinstated.

Since commercial production has started under project 3 the expenditure previously deferred should now be amortised. This will be done over the estimated life of the product, as stated in the question.

Project 4 the development costs may be deferred.

Since project 5 is not expected to be profitable its development costs should not be deferred.

BALANCE SHEET AS AT 31 DECEMBER 20X2 (extract)

	£'000
FIXED ASSETS	
Intangible assets	
Development costs (Note 2)	850

NOTES TO THE ACCOUNTS

1   *Accounting policies*

     Research and development

     Research and development expenditure is written off as incurred, except that development expenditure incurred on an individual project is carried forward when its future recoverability can be foreseen with reasonable assurance. Any expenditure carried forward is amortised over the period of sales from the related project.

2   *Development costs*

	£'000	£'000
Balance brought forward 1 January 20X2		730
Development expenditure reinstated		370
Development expenditure incurred during 20X2	188	
Development expenditure amortised during 20X2	438	
		(250)
Balance carried forward 31 December 20X2		850

Note. SSAP 13 does not permit the inclusion of market research in deferred development expenditure. The costs might, however, be carried forward separately under the accruals principle.

Workings

	1	2	3	4	5	Total
	£'000	£'000	£'000	£'000	£'000	£'000
B/F	280	–	450	–	–	730
Expenditure previously written off, reinstated	–	370	–	–	–	370
Salaries etc.	35	29	–	60	20	144
Overheads	2	5	–	–	3	10
Materials etc.	3	13	–	11	4	31
Patents etc.	1	2	–	–	–	3
C/F	–	(419)	(360)	(71)	–	(850)
Written off	321	–	90	–	27	438

* *Note.* An alternative basis for amortisation would be:

$$\frac{20}{180} \times 450 = 50$$

The above basis is more prudent, however, in this case.

5 FRED 37 Intangible assets

FAST FORWARD

FRED 37 implements IAS 38 *Intangible assets*. It changes the definition of 'identifiable' and eliminates the choice of accounting treatment for development expenditure.

5.1 Background

As part of the first phase of the Business Combinations project (see Chapter 16), the IASB amended both IAS 38 *Intangible assets* and IAS 36 *Impairment of assets*. FREDs 37 and 38 proposed the adoption of UK standards based on the current text of these standards. FRED 38 is covered in Section 3 of this chapter. FRED 37 will be discussed below in terms of the main changes to current UK practice.

5.2 Definition of identifiable

The IASB reconsidered the definition of an intangible asset and affirmed the view that **identifiability** is the characteristic that conceptually **distinguishes other intangible assets from goodwill**.

IAS 38 does not define 'identifiable' but states an intangible asset meets the **identification criterion** when it:

(a) Is **separable,** ie is capable of being separated or divided from the entity and sold, transferred, licensed, rented or exchanged, either individually or together with a related contract asset or liability, or

(b) **Arises from contractual or other legal rights**, regardless of whether those rights are transferable or separable from the entity or from other rights and obligations.

This is in contrast to FRS 10 which defines identifiable assets as assets that are capable of being disposed of or discharged separately, without disposing of a business of the undertaking. FRED 37 therefore extends the definition of an intangible asset to include those that are not separable.

5.3 Useful economic life

The rebuttable presumption of a 20 year useful economic life is removed. There is no longer any requirement for an annual estimate of the recoverable amount of intangibles with a useful economic life of less than 20 years, unless there is an indication of impairment.

5.4 Development expenditure

SSAP 13 permits, but does not require, development costs to be capitalised. IAS 38 states that **internally generated intangible assets arising from development must be recognised if the criteria for recognition are met**. The criteria for the recognition of development expenditure as an asset are broadly comparable to SSAP 13 and limit recognition significantly.

Another change from SSAP 13 is the requirement in FRED 37 that an entity must **demonstrate how an intangible asset will generate probable future economic benefits** by using the principles set out FRED 38 *Impairment of assets.*

5.5 Website development costs

An Application Note to the draft FRS will replace UITF Abstract 29 on this topic. Website costs, **previously recognised as tangible assets**, that meet the requirements of the draft FRS will be **re-classified as intangible assets** and amortised over their remaining useful lives. Costs that meet the requirements for capitalisation of internally generated intangible assets must be capitalised in accordance with the proposed Application Note from the date the draft FRS becomes effective.

Chapter Roundup

- The treatment of **goodwill and intangibles** is a controversial and complex area. You must ensure that you can discuss the current thinking on the nature of fixed assets, intangible assets and goodwill and that you can discuss all the possible treatments of positive and negative goodwill in accounts and the arguments on brand accounting. You should be familiar with, and be able to explain, the ASB's requirements as set out in FRS 10 *Goodwill and intangible assets.*

- FRS 11 *Impairment of fixed assets and* goodwill was introduced to ensure that

    - Fixed assets and goodwill are recorded at no more than their **recoverable amount**
    - Any **impairment loss** is **correctly measured**
    - **Sufficient information** is disclosed

- **FRED 38** implements IAS 36 *Impairment of assets.* The FRED would remove one of the requirements from FRS 11, namely that the accuracy of impairment needs to be checked by comparing actual cash flows against projected cash flows.

- **SSAP 13** on the other hand is a standard which is generally accepted and well understood. You should already be very familiar with its provisions, but make sure that you learn the disclosure requirements.

- **FRED 37** implements IAS 38 *Intangible assets.* It changes the definition of 'identifiable' and eliminates the choice of accounting treatment for development expenditure.

Quick Quiz

1   What is the normal treatment prescribed by FRS 10 for positive purchased goodwill?

2   The useful economic life of goodwill or intangible assets is always 20 years or less. True or false?

3   Which of the following criteria need to be met in order that internally developed intangible assets can be capitalised per FRS 10 on the balance sheet? Circle any that apply.

    (a)   The asset is unique.
    (b)   The asset is a member of a group of homogeneous assets.
    (c)   There is an active market for that group of assets, evidenced by frequent transactions.

4   Per FRS 10, negative goodwill arising in the year on the acquisition of a subsidiary should be accounted for in the consolidated balance sheet in which of the following ways?

    A   Credited to the profit and loss reserve.

    B   Netted off against any positive goodwill arising on other acquisitions and the net balance shown on the face of the balance sheet as an intangible asset.

    C   Recognised on the face of the balance sheet as a negative intangible asset directly after any positive goodwill which has arisen on other acquisitions.

    D   Credited to a capital reserve.

5   What is the correct treatment for central assets under FRS 11?

6   A machine is presently recognised in the accounts at its historical cost NBV of £150,000. An impairment in value has been identified due to the machine becoming damaged in the year. Due to the damage the scrap value of the asset is now expected to be only £75,000 and £2,000 of selling expenses would need to be incurred. The alternative to selling the asset is to continue to use it in the business. The economic value is deemed to be £76,000 or £74,500 at present values.

    At what value should the asset be recognised in the balance sheet?

7   What is the accounting treatment of a laboratory purchased for R&D activity?

Answers to Quick Quiz

1   See KBF box.

2   False. This is a rebuttable presumption.

3   (b) and (c)

4   C

5   They should be apportioned across the income generating units on a systematic basis.

6

Recoverable amount is the higher of

Net realisable value   Value in use (using present values)

£73,000   £74,500
(£75,000 – £2,000)

ie value at £74,500

7   Per SSAP 13, capitalise the laboratory as a tangible fixed asset and depreciate over its useful life.

Now try the questions below from the Exam Question Bank

Number	Level	Marks	Time
Q4	Introductory	n/a	n/a
Q5	Introductory	n/a	n/a

Retirement benefits

Introduction

An increasing number of companies now provide a **pension** as part of their employees' remuneration package. In view of this trend, it was important to standardise best practice for the way in which pension costs are **recognised and disclosed** in the accounts of sponsoring companies, and the way in which pension schemes themselves draw up sets of accounts. SSAP 24 *Accounting for pension costs* was criticised for being too ambiguous, and FRS 17 *Retirement benefits* was published to address the criticisms.

Study guide

		Intellectual level
C6	**Employee benefits**	
(a)	Apply and discuss the accounting treatment of defined contribution and defined benefit plans	3
(b)	Account for gains and losses on settlements and curtailments	2
(c)	Account for the reporting of actuarial gains and losses	2
(d)	Determine going concern issues arising after the balance sheet date	3
F2	**Proposed changes to accounting standards**	
(a)	Identify the issues and deficiencies which have led to a proposed change to an accounting standard	2
(b)	Apply and discuss the implications of a proposed change to an accounting standard on the performance and balance sheet of an entity	2

Exam guide

This topic will be new to you at this level. It may be examined as part of a multi-standard scenario question, or perhaps you will be asked to outline the changes proposed in FRED 39.

1 Background

FAST FORWARD

Company pension schemes have become more and more important as supplements to or replacements for the state pension, as a means of support after retirement. With an increasingly large pensioned population, the importance of this topic can only increase.

Before we look at FRS 17, and to be absolutely clear as to how a pension scheme operates, let us examine a scheme in very simple terms.

Key term

Retirement benefits. All forms of consideration given by an employer in exchange for services rendered by employees that are payable after the completion of employment.

A **pension scheme** is an arrangement (other than accident insurance) to provide pension and/or other benefits for members on leaving service or retiring and, after a member's death, for his/her dependants.

(SSAP 24)

The basic roles of the participants are as follows.

(a)   The **trustees** administer the scheme and safeguard its assets.

(b)   The **company** pays over both its own contributions and, in practice, those of its employees (if they are required to contribute), deducted from their salaries.

(c)   The trustees invest the contributions with a **fund manager**, who in turn invests in the stock market or other assets for the scheme. The return is either reinvested or paid back to the scheme.

(d)   The scheme pays out **pensions to employees** who have reached retirement age and also pays **transfer values** to other funds when employees leave.

(e)   If allowed, the company contributions might be **refunded** to the company when the scheme is in surplus. Alternatively, the company's future contributions may be cut to use up a surplus.

(f)   The role of the **actuary** is very important. He or she is responsible for determining the future contributions required from the company, based on the value of the fund, expected rate of growth, profile of employees and so on.

Consider the diagram below.

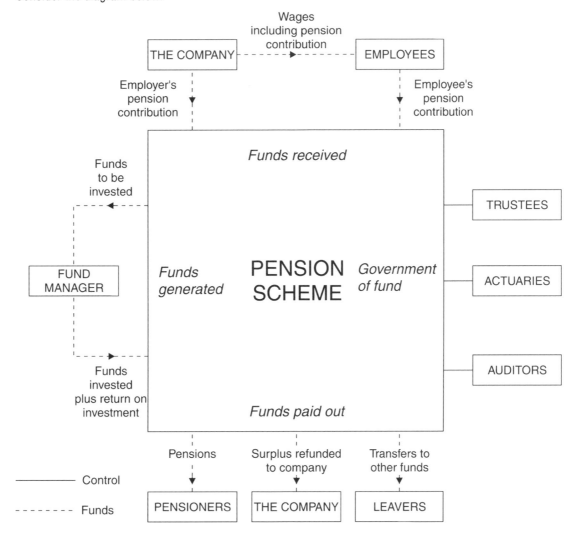

1.1 The conceptual nature of pension rights and costs

When a company employs a new worker and that worker is offered a chance to participate in the company's pension scheme, then the company is, in effect, saying that the contributions given by the employee and employer will secure an income in the future for the employee in the form of a **pension**.

The **cost of the pension** to the employer can be viewed in various ways. It could be described as a deferred salary to the employee. Alternatively, it is a deduction from the employee's true gross salary, used as a tax-efficient means of saving. The tax efficiency arises because the employer's contributions are not taxed on the employee, but they are a deduction from taxable profits for the employer. The income and capital gains made by the fund are tax free as well. It is only when the pension is received by the retired employee that the funds become taxable.

1.2 Accounting for pension costs

Accounting for pension costs is difficult. This is because of the **large amounts** involved, as well as the **long time scale**, **complicated estimates** and **uncertainty** surrounding the many assumptions which must be made. **Before SSAP 24**, the forerunner of FRS 17, the usual accounting practice was to charge the employer company's P&L account on the basis of the actual payments made to the pension fund. The company's reported profit was therefore subject to fluctuations as the contribution payments varied. Other disclosed information was sparse: little was said about commitments to pay pensions or any assets held in the pension funds to meet such obligations.

1.3 Types of scheme

There are two types of pension schemes.

1.3.1 Defined contribution schemes

Key term

> **Defined contribution scheme.** A pension or other retirement benefit scheme into which an employer pays regular contributions fixed as an amount or as a percentage of pay and will have no legal or constructive obligation to pay further contributions if the scheme does not have sufficient assets to pay all employee benefits relating to employee service in the current and prior periods.
>
> An individual member's benefits are determined by reference to contributions paid into the scheme in respect of that member, usually increased by an amount based on the investment return on those contributions.
>
> Defined contribution schemes may also provide death-in-service benefits. For the purposes of this definition, death-in-service benefits are not deemed to relate to employee service in the current and prior periods.

These schemes **do not present a problem** for the reporting company, as they should simply **charge the contributions** payable in respect of the accounting period **within operating profit**. If the amount actually paid is more or less than the amount payable, a prepayment or accrual will appear in the balance sheet in accordance with normal accounting practice.

The FRS 17 treatment of these schemes is identical to that required by SSAP 24.

1.3.2 Defined benefit schemes

Key term

> **Defined benefit scheme.** A pension or other retirement benefit scheme other than a defined contribution scheme.
>
> Usually, the scheme rules define the benefits independently of the contributions payable, and the benefits are not directly related to the investments of the scheme. The scheme may be funded or unfunded.

1.4 Problems

This type of scheme presents problems in respect of:

(a)   **Valuing** the scheme **assets**
(b)   **Estimating** the scheme **liabilities**
(c)   **Measuring** and recognising the **cost** to the employing company

The solutions to these problems in FRS 17 represent a substantial change from the previous treatment under SSAP 24.

1.5 UITF Abstract 13 *Accounting for ESOP Trusts*

Employee share ownership plans (ESOPs) are designed to facilitate employee shareholdings and are often used as vehicles for distributing shares to employees under remuneration schemes. In the light of FRS 5 *Reporting the substance of transactions* (see Chapter 11), questions arose regarding:

(a) The nature and extent of the sponsoring company's assets and liabilities
(b) The timing of expense recognition under such arrangements

In basic terms, the abstract requires that the assets and liabilities of the ESOP trust be brought **on to the balance sheet of the sponsoring company** where the company 'has *de facto* control of the shares held by the ESOP trust and bears their benefits or risks'.

The detailed structures of individual ESOPs are varied, as are the reasons for establishing them. However, the **main features** are normally as follows.

(a) The trust uses interest-free finance from the sponsoring company to purchase shares in that company which it 'warehouses' – holding them to sell or transfer to the employees of the company in future.

(b) The sponsoring company will guarantee any third party loans and pay interest, ie any shortfall in capital or revenue is made up by the company.

(c) Shares held by the ESOP trust are distributed to employees through an employee share scheme, by one of a variety of arrangements.

(d) Although the trustees of the ESOP trust must act in the interests of the beneficiaries, the schemes are generally designed to serve the interests of the sponsoring company. The sponsoring company therefore has *de facto* control.

The accounting requirements and disclosures required by the UITF consensus include the following.

(a) **Shares held by the ESOP trust** should be recognised as assets of the sponsoring company until the shares vest unconditionally in employees. The shares should be classified as 'own shares', either as fixed or current assets. They will generally be held for the continuing benefit of the sponsoring company's business and classified as **fixed assets.**

(b) Where the shares are classified as fixed assets, any **permanent diminution** in their value should be recognised immediately.

(c) Where the shares are **gifted conditionally** or are under option to employees at below the book value of the shares, 'the difference between book value and residual value should be charged as an operating cost over the period of service of the employees in respect of which the gifts or options are granted'.

(d) Any **borrowings** of the ESOP trust that are guaranteed (formally or informally) by the sponsoring company should be regarded as a liability of the company.

(e) **Dividend income** arising on the shares should be **excluded** in arriving at profit before tax and deducted from the aggregate of dividends paid and proposed. Until such time as the shares vest unconditionally in employees, the shares should also be excluded from earnings per share calculations as, under FRS 14 *Earnings per share*, they are treated as if they were cancelled.

Sufficient information should be **disclosed** as to enable readers of the sponsoring company's accounts to understand the significance of the ESOP trust in the context of the sponsoring company.

2 FRS 17 Retirement benefits

Criticisms of SSAP 24

(a)   There is too much scope for employers to adjust the pension cost in the short term.

(b)   There are too many different valuation methods.

(c)   The disclosure requirements do not necessarily lead to an adequate explanation of the pension costs and related balances.

(d)   It is inconsistent with international standards.

2.1 Objective of FRS 17

The objective of the FRS is to ensure that:

(a)   Financial statements reflect at fair value the assets and liabilities arising from an employer's retirement benefit obligations and any related funding

(b)   The operating costs of providing retirement benefits to employees are recognised in the accounting period(s) in which the benefits are earned by the employees, and the related finance costs and any other changes in value of the assets and liabilities are recognised in the accounting periods in which they arise

(c)   The financial statements contain adequate disclosure of the cost of providing retirement benefits and the related gains, losses, assets and liabilities

2.2 Scope

The FRS applies to **all financial statements that are intended to give a true and fair view** of a reporting employer's financial position and profit or loss (or income and expenditure) for a period.

The FRS covers **all retirement benefits** that an employer is committed to providing, whether the commitment is statutory, contractual or implicit in the employer's actions. It applies to retirement benefits arising overseas, as well as those arising in the UK and the Republic of Ireland. Retirement benefits include, for example, pensions and medical care during retirement.

The FRS covers **funded and unfunded retirement benefits**, including schemes that are operated on a pay-as-you-go basis, whereby benefits are paid by the employer in the period they fall due and no payments are made to fund benefits earned in the period.

The FRS requires a liability to be recognised as the benefits are earned, not when they are due to be paid. The fact that the employer is funded by central government (or any other body) is not a reason for the employer not to recognise its own liabilities arising under the FRS.

2.3 Multi-employer schemes

Multi-employer schemes are pension schemes are schemes which have been set up for a number of employers or for a whole industry. Such schemes **expose** participating employers to the actuarial **risks associated with other entities' employees**, both current and former.

Where more than one employer participates in a **defined contribution scheme**, the employer's cost is limited to the contributions payable, so **no special problems** arise.

Where more than one employer participates in a **defined benefit scheme**, the employer should **account for the scheme as a defined benefit** scheme except in limited circumstances.

(a) The employer's contributions are set in relation to the **current service period only**, and are therefore not affected by any surplus or deficit in the scheme relating to past service of its own employees or any other members of the scheme. In this case the employer should account for the contributions to the scheme as if it were a defined contribution scheme.

(b) The employer's contributions are affected by a surplus or deficit in the scheme but the employer is **unable to identify its share of the underlying assets and liabilities** in the scheme on a consistent and reasonable basis. If this is the case, the employer should account for the contributions to the scheme as if it were a defined contribution scheme but, in addition, disclose:

    (i) The fact that the scheme is a defined benefit scheme but that the employer is unable to identify its share of the underlying assets and liabilities

    (ii) Any available information about the existence of the surplus or deficit in the scheme and the implications of that surplus or deficit for the employer

Question
Group schemes

Many group schemes are run on a basis that does not enable individual companies within the group to identify their share of the underlying assets and liabilities.

How should the individual companies within the group account for such schemes?

Answer

In these circumstances, the individual companies (including the parent company) within the group will account for the scheme as a defined contribution scheme and will give the additional disclosures required above. From the point of view of the group entity, a group defined benefit scheme is not a multi-employer scheme and is treated as any other defined benefit scheme.

2.4 Defined contribution schemes

You met the definition of a defined contribution scheme earlier.

Key term

> **Defined contribution scheme.** A pension or other retirement benefit scheme into which an employer pays regular contributions fixed as an amount or as a percentage of pay and will have no legal or constructive obligation to pay further contributions if the scheme does not have sufficient assets to pay all employee benefits relating to employee service in the current and prior periods. *(FRS 17)*

The **cost of a defined contribution** scheme is **equal to the contributions payable** to the scheme for the accounting period. FRS 17 requires that the cost should be recognised **within operating profit** in the profit and loss account.

2.5 Defined benefit schemes

You also met the definition of a defined benefit scheme earlier.

Key term

> **Defined benefit scheme.** A pension or other retirement benefit scheme other than a defined contribution scheme *(FRS 17)*

2.6 Scheme assets

Scheme assets are measured at **market value** (previously actuarial value).

Assets in a defined benefit scheme should be measured at their **fair value at the balance sheet date.** FRS 17 defines fair value for each type of asset.

(a) For **quoted securities**, the **mid-market value** is taken as the fair value. For **unquoted securities**, an **estimate of fair value** is used. The fair value of unitised securities is taken to be the average of the bid and offer prices.

(b) **Property** should be valued at **open market value** or on another appropriate basis of valuation determined in accordance with the Appraisal and Valuation Manual published by the Royal Institution of Chartered Surveyors.

(c) **Insurance policies** that exactly match the amount and timing of some or all of the benefits payable under the scheme should be measured **at the same amount as the related obligations**. For **other insurance policies** there are a number of possible valuation methods. A method should be chosen which gives the **best approximation** to fair value given the circumstances of the scheme.

Scheme assets include current assets as well as investments. Any liabilities such as accrued expenses should be deducted. Notional funding of a pension scheme does not give rise to assets in a scheme for the purposes of the FRS.

2.7 Scheme liabilities

Scheme liabilities are discounted at a high-quality corporate bond rate.

Defined benefit scheme **liabilities** should be measured on an **actuarial basis using the projected unit method**. The scheme liabilities comprise:

(a) Any benefits promised under the formal terms of the scheme

(b) Any constructive obligations for further benefits where a public statement or past practice by the employer has created a valid expectation in the employees that such benefits will be granted

As there is no active market for defined benefit scheme liabilities, fair value must be estimated using actuarial techniques. FRS 17 has certain rules relating to the valuation.

(a) The benefits should be attributed to periods of service according to the scheme's benefit formula, except where the benefit formula attributes a disproportionate share of the total benefits to later years of service. In such cases, the benefit should be attributed on a straight-line basis over the period during which it is earned.

(b) The assumptions underlying the valuation should be mutually compatible and lead to the best estimate of the future cash flows that will arise under the scheme liabilities. The assumptions are ultimately the responsibility of the directors (or equivalent) but should be set upon advice given by an actuary. Any assumptions that are affected by economic conditions (financial assumptions) should reflect market expectations at the balance sheet date.

(c) The actuarial assumptions should reflect expected future events that will affect the cost of the benefits to which the employer is committed (either legally or through a constructive obligation) at the balance sheet date.

Question
Scheme liabilities

Which of the following expected future events will affect the cost of the benefits to which the employer is committed?

A   Expected cost of living increases provided for in the scheme rules
B   In the case of final salary schemes, any expected increase in salary
C   Expected future redundancies
D   Expected early retirement where the employee has that right under the scheme rules

Answer

A, B and D. Expected future redundancies are not reflected in the actuarial assumptions because the employer is not committed (either legally or constructively) to making such redundancies in advance. When the employer does become committed to making the redundancies, any impact on the defined benefit scheme is treated as a settlement and/or curtailment (see later).

2.8 Discounting

Defined benefit scheme **liabilities should be discounted** at a rate that reflects the time value of money and the characteristics of the liability. The rate should be assumed to be the **current rate of return on a high quality corporate bond** of equivalent currency and term to the scheme liabilities.

The discounting requirement is in line with other recent FRSs such as FRS 19, and reflects the fact that the scheme's liabilities are long-term and should take into account the time value of money.

2.9 Actuarial valuations

At intervals **not exceeding three years, full actuarial valuations** by a professionally qualified actuary should be obtained for a defined benefit scheme. The actuary should review the most recent actuarial valuation at the balance sheet date and update it to reflect current conditions.

The actuarial valuations required for the FRS may use different assumptions and measurement methods from those used for a scheme's funding valuation.

Full actuarial valuations under the FRS are not needed at every balance sheet date. Some aspects of the valuation will need to be updated at each balance sheet date, for example the fair value of the assets and financial assumptions such as the discount rate. Other assumptions, such as the expected leaving rate and mortality rate, may not need to be updated annually.

2.10 Recognition of defined benefit schemes in the balance sheet

2.10.1 Assets

The employer should **recognise an asset** to the extent that it is able to **recover** a surplus through **reduced contributions** in the future or through **refunds** from the scheme.

Key terms

A **surplus** in a defined benefit scheme is the excess of the value of the assets in the scheme over the present value of the scheme liabilities.

A **deficit** is the shortfall of the value of the assets below the present value of the scheme liabilities.

(FRS 17)

A surplus in the scheme gives rise to an asset of the employer to the extent that:

(a) The employer controls its use, ie has the ability to use the surplus to generate future economic benefits for itself, either in the form of a reduction in future contributions or a refund from the scheme, and

(b) That control is a result of past events (contributions paid by the employer and investment growth in excess of rights earned by the employees)

The amount of the asset that can be recovered is the present value of the liability expected to arise from future service by current and future scheme members less the present value of future employee contributions. The amount to be recovered from refunds should reflect only refunds that have been agreed by the pension scheme trustees at the balance sheet date.

2.10.2 Liability

Conversely, the employer has a **liability** if it has **a legal or constructive obligation to make good a deficit** in the defined benefit scheme. In general, the employer will either have a legal obligation under the terms of the scheme trust deed or will have by its past actions and statements created a constructive obligation as defined in FRS 12 *Provisions, contingent liabilities and contingent assets.*

2.11 Presentation in the balance sheet

The presentation is illustrated in the disclosure example at the end of this section. Note that **the defined benefit asset or liability is presented separately on the face of the balance sheet**, after accruals and deferred income, but before capital and reserves.

Unpaid contributions are presented as a creditor due within one year. Deferred tax relating to the asset or liability is not included with other deferred tax, but is offset against the defined benefit asset or liability.

2.12 Recognition of defined benefit schemes in the performance statements

The pension **cost** is the change in the defined benefit asset or liability, other than through contributions paid to the scheme. It is analysed into **periodic costs and non-periodic costs.**

Periodic costs	Non-periodic costs
Current service cost	Past service costs
Interest cost	Gains and losses on settlements or curtailments
Expected return on assets	
Actuarial gains and losses	

Look carefully at the following definitions. Read them through several times to make sure you understand them so the treatment will make sense.

Key terms

Current service cost. The increase in the present value of the scheme liabilities expected to arise from employee service in the current period.

Interest cost. The expected increase during the period in the present value of the scheme liabilities because the benefits are one period closer to settlement.

Expected return on assets. The average rate of return, including both income and changes in fair value but net of scheme expenses, expected over the remaining life of the related obligation on the actual assets held by the scheme.

Key terms

> **Actuarial gains and losses.** Changes in actuarial deficits or surpluses that arise because:
>
> (a) Events have not coincided with the actuarial assumptions made for the last valuation (experience gains and losses), or
>
> (b) The actuarial assumptions have changed
>
> **Past service costs.** The increase in the present value of the scheme liabilities related to employee service in prior periods arising in the current period as a result of the introduction of, or improvement to, retirement benefits.
>
> **Settlement.** An irrevocable action that relieves the employer (or the defined benefit scheme) of the primary responsibility for a pension obligation and eliminates significant risks relating to the obligation and the assets used to effect the settlement. Settlements include:
>
> (a) A lump-sum cash payment to scheme members in exchange for their rights to receive specified pension benefits
>
> (b) The purchase of an irrevocable annuity contract sufficient to cover vested benefits
>
> (c) The transfer of scheme assets and liabilities relating to a group of employees leaving the scheme
>
> **Curtailment.** An event that reduces the expected years of future service of present employees or reduces for a number of employees the accrual of defined benefits for some or all of their future service. Curtailments include:
>
> (a) Termination of employees' services earlier than expected, for example as a result of closing a factory or discontinuing a segment of a business
>
> (b) Termination of, or amendment to the terms of, a defined benefit scheme so that some or all future service by current employees will no longer qualify for benefits or will qualify only for reduced benefits
>
> *(FRS 17)*

Question
Past service cost

Can you think of an example of a past service cost?

Answer

Creation of a pension benefit for a spouse where benefit did not previously exist, or added on years of service on retirement.

2.12.1 Current service cost, interest cost and expected return on assets

These items should all be recognised in the profit and loss account.

(a) The **current service cost** should be based on the most recent actuarial valuation at the beginning of the period with the financial assumptions updated to reflect conditions at that date. **Include it within operating profit.** Any contributions from employees should be set off against it.

(b) The **interest cost** should be based on the discount rate and the present value of liabilities at the start of the period. It should also reflect changes in the scheme liabilities during the period. It should be shown **in the profit and loss account, adjacent to interest and netted off against the expected return on assets**.

(c)   The **expected return on assets** should be shown in the **profit and loss account, netted off against the interest cost.** It should be based on long-term expectations at the start of the period, for example, for quoted government or corporate bonds, the redemption yield × market value at the start of the period. It should reflect changes in assets through contributions paid in and benefits paid out of the scheme.

2.12.2 Actuarial gains and losses

> Actuarial gains and losses are **recognised immediately** in the STRGL, rather than spread forward in the P&L account.
>
> As a consequence, the **balance sheet reflects the surpius/deficit** in the scheme

Actuarial gains and losses arising from any new valuation and from updating the latest actuarial valuation to reflect conditions at the balance sheet date should be recognised in the **statement of total recognised gains and losses**. They should **never be re-cycled to the profit and loss account** in future periods.

2.12.3 Non-periodic costs

Past service costs should be **recognised in the profit and loss account on a straight-line basis over the period in which the increases in benefit vest.** If benefits vest immediately, recognise immediately.

Gains and losses on settlements and curtailments should be recognised **in the profit and loss account in operating profit** except where they attach to an exceptional item shown after operating profit. This would be the case with closure of business. This only refers to settlements and curtailments **not covered by actuarial assumptions.**

| Question | Events affecting pension plan |

Consider how the following events might affect a pension plan and how any gains or losses would be recognised. Fill in the table below.

Event	Effect and treatment
The law changes to recognise the rights of cohabitees to be treated as if they were a legally married couple.	
Unexpected falls in property values and global stock markets have adversely affected the value of the scheme assets.	
A company makes 40% of its workforce redundant.	

Answer

Event	Effect and treatment
The law changes to recognise the rights of cohabitees to be treated as if they were a legally married couple	This event has increased the pension liability, and to the extent that the additional benefits attach to past years' services, the past service cost should be recognised immediately.
Unexpected falls in property values and global stock markets have adversely affected the value of the scheme assets.	The difference between the estimated year-end value of the scheme net asset/liability based on expected return and the value from the year-end valuation will be recognised in the STRGL as an actuarial loss.
A company makes 40% of its workforce redundant.	This will reduce the scheme liabilities and a gain will result. This is a curtailment which would fall outside actuarial assumptions so it should be recognised in the profit and loss account. If the redundancies relate to the sale or termination of an operation or fundamental reorganisation or reconstruction, the gain would be included in the exceptional items. In other circumstances it should be included in operating expenses.

2.13 Disclosures

2.13.1 Defined benefit contribution schemes

(a)   The nature of the scheme (ie defined contribution)

(b)   The cost for the period

(c)   Any outstanding or prepaid contributions at the balance sheet date

2.13.2 Defined benefit schemes – a summary

(a)   The main assumptions underlying the scheme

(b)   An analysis of the assets in the scheme into broad classes and the expected rate of return on each class

(c)   An analysis of the amounts included:

    (i)   Within operating profit

    (ii)   Within other finance costs

    (iii)   Within the statement of total recognised gains and losses

(d)   A five-year history of:

    (i)   The difference between the expected and actual return on assets

    (ii)   Experience gains and losses arising on the scheme liabilities

    (iii)   The total actuarial gain or loss

(e)   An analysis of the movement in the surplus or deficit in the scheme over the period and a reconciliation of the surplus/deficit to the balance sheet asset/liability.

2.14 Step-by-step approach, example and summary

2.14.1 Step-by-step approach

Step 1   *Record opening asset and liability*

Step 2   *Interest cost*

DEBIT   Interest cost (x% × b/d obligation) (P&L)
CREDIT   PV defined benefit obligation (B/S working)

Step 3   *Expected return on plan assets*

DEBIT   Plan assets (B/S working)
CREDIT   Expected return (y% × b/d assets) (P&L)

Technically, the expected return is also time apportioned on contributions less benefits paid in the period.

Step 4   *Current service cost*

DEBIT   Current service cost (P&L)
CREDIT   PV defined benefit obligation (B/S working)

Step 5   *Contributions*

DEBIT   Plan assets (B/S)
CREDIT   Company cash

Step 6   *Benefits*

DEBIT   PV defined benefit obligation (B/S working)
CREDIT   Plan assets (B/S working)

Step 7   *Past service costs*

DEBIT   Past service cost (vested benefits) (P&L)
CREDIT   PV defined benefit obligation (B/S working)

Amortise unrecognised past service cost to the profit and loss account on a straight line basis over the average period until the benefits become vested (ie when the enhanced benefits are no longer conditional on future employment)

Step 8   *Calculate actuarial gains/losses using balance sheet workings*

Step 9   *Ensure disclosed in accordance with FRS 17 –* see the example below and the question immediately following.

The disclosure requirements in full are very extensive, and difficult to learn by heart. First look over this example, taken from the standard. Then try the questions which follow, to reinforce learning.

2.14.2 Example: FRS 17 disclosures

Below is an example, taken from the FRS, of the disclosures required.

Balance sheet presentation

	20X2 £m	20X1 £m
Net assets excluding pension asset	700	650
Pension asset	335	143
Net assets including pension asset	1,035	793

Reserves note

	20X2 £m	20X1 £m
Profit and loss reserve excluding pension asset	400	350
Pension reserve	335	143
Profit and loss reserve	735	493

Pension cost note

Composition of the scheme

The group operates a defined benefit scheme in the UK. A full actuarial valuation was carried out at 31 December 20X1 and updated to 31 December 20X2 by a qualified independent actuary. The major assumptions used by the actuary were:

	At 31.12.X2	At 31.12.X1	At 31.12.X0
Rate of increase in salaries	4.0%	5.5%	6.5%
Rate of increase in pensions in payment	2.0%	3.0%	3.5%
Discount rate	4.5%	7.0%	8.5%
Inflation assumption	2.5%	4.0%	5.0%

The assets in the scheme and the expected rate of return were:

	Long-term rate of return expected at 31/12/X2	Value at 31.12.X2 £m	Long-term rate of return expected at 31.12.X1	Value at 31.12.X1 £m	Long-term rate of return expected at 31.12.X0	Value at 31.12.X0 £m
Equities	7.3%	1,116	8.0%	721	9.3%	570
Bonds	5.5%	298	6.0%	192	8.0%	152
Property	6.0%	74	6.1%	49	7.9%	33
Total market value of assets		1,488		962		760
Present value of scheme liabilities		(1,009)		(758)		(608)
Surplus in the scheme		479		204		92
Related deferred tax liability		(144)		(61)		(28)
Net pension asset		335		143		64

Analysis of the amount charged to operating profit

	20X2 £m	20X1 £m
Service cost	34	25
Past service cost	12	–
Total operating charge	46	25

Analysis of amount credited to other finance income

	20X2 £m	20X1 £m
Expected return on pension scheme assets	73	68
Interest on pension liabilities	(53)	(57)
Net return	20	11

Analysis of amount recognised in statement of total recognised gains and losses (STRGL)

	20X2 £m	20X1 £m
Actual return less expected return on pension scheme assets	480	138
Experience gains and losses arising on the present value of the scheme liabilities	(58)	(6)
Changes in financial assumptions underlying the present value of the scheme liabilities	(146)	(41)
Actuarial gain/(loss) recognised in STRGL	276	91

Movement in surplus during the year

	20X2 £m	20X1 £m
Surplus in scheme at beginning of year	204	92
Movement in year:		
Current service cost	(34)	(25)
Contributions	25	35
Past service costs	(12)	
Other finance income	20	11
Actuarial gain/(loss)	276	91
Surplus in scheme at end of the year	479	204

The full actuarial valuation at 31 December 20X1 showed an increase in the surplus from £92 million to £204 million. Improvements in benefits costing £12 million were made in 20X1 and contributions reduced to £25 million (8 per cent of pensionable pay). It has been agreed with the trustees that contributions for the next three years will remain at that level.

History of experience gains and losses

	20X2	20X1	20X0	20W9	20W8
Difference between the expected and actual return on scheme assets:					
amount (£m)	480	138	(6)	94	(73)
Percentage of scheme assets	32%	14%	(1%)	16%	(26%)
Experience gains and losses on scheme liabilities:					
amount (£m)	(58)	(6)	34	25	(23)
Percentage of scheme liabilities	(4%)	(1%)	5%	2%	(2%)
Total amount recognised in statement of total recognised gains and losses:					
amount (£m)	276	91	1	66	(158)
Percentage of scheme liabilities	27%	12%	0%	5%	(14%)

Question

Davis Ltd has a defined benefit plan for its employees. The present value of the future benefit obligations and the fair value of the plan assets at 1 January 20X7 were both £1,000 million.

Further data concerning the years ended 31 December 20X7 and 20X8 are as follows:

	20X7 £m	20X8 £m	
Current service cost	130	140	
Benefit paid to former employees	150	180	
Contributions paid to plan	90	100	
Present value of benefit obligations at 31 December	1,100	1,380	As valued by professional actuaries
Fair value of plan assets at 31 December	1,190	1,372	
Gross yield on 'blue chip' Corporate bonds	10%	9%	
Expected return on plan assets	12%	10%	

In 20X8 the plan was amended to provide additional benefits from 1 January 20X8. The present value of the additional benefits was calculated by actuaries at £10 million with respect to current employees and £50 million for former employees.

Required

Calculate the amounts to be recognised in the profit and loss account, balance sheet and statement of total recognised gains and losses for 20X7 and 20X8 and prepare the 'movement in surplus' note.

Answer

PROFIT AND LOSS ACCOUNT (EXTRACT)

	20X7 £m	20X8 £m
Operating expenses		
Current service cost	130	140
Past service cost (W5)	–	60
Other finance charges (W4)	(20)	(20)

BALANCE SHEET (EXTRACT)

	20X7	20X8
Pension asset/(liability) (W1)	90	(8)
Pension reserve	90	(8)

STATEMENT OF TOTAL RECOGNISED GAINS AND LOSSES

	20X7	20X8
Actual return less expected return on pension scheme assets (W3)	130	143
Experience gains and losses arising on the scheme liabilities (W2)	(20)	(161)

MOVEMENT IN SURPLUS DURING THE YEAR

	20X7	20X8
Surplus in scheme at beginning of year		90
Movements in year		
Current cost	(130)	(140)
Contributions	90	100
Past service costs		(60)
Other finance income	20	20
Actuarial gain/loss	110	(18)
Surplus/deficit in scheme at end of year	90	(8)

Workings

1   *Balance sheet net asset/(liability)*

	£m
31.12.X7 (1,190 – 1,100)	90
31.12.X8 (1,372 – 1,380)	(8)

2   *Liability*

	£m
b/f 1.1.X7	1,000
Current service cost	130
Benefits paid	(150)
Interest (1,000 × 10%)	100
∴ experience loss on scheme liabilities	20
PV at 31.12.X7	1,100
Current service cost (X8)	140
Past service cost (W5)	60
Benefits paid	(180)
Interest (1,100 × 9%)	99
∴ experience loss on scheme liabilities	161
PV at 31.12.X8	1,380

3   *Fair value of assets*

	£m
b/f 1.1.X7	1,000
Benefits paid	(150)
Contributions paid	90
Expected return on assets (12% × 1,000)	120
∴ actual return less expected return	130
FV at 31.12.X7	1,190
Benefits paid	(180)
Contributions paid	100
Expected return on assets (10% × 1,190)	119
∴ Actual return less expected return	143
FV at 31.12.X8	1,372

4   *Other finance charges*

	20X7 £m	20X8 £m
Finance charges		
Interest (W2)	100	99
Expected return on assets (W3)	(120)	(119)
	(20) credit	(20) credit

5   *Past service cost 20X8*

	£m	
Re former employees	50	(recognised immediately)
Re current employees ($^{100}/_{10}$)	10	(recognised over period until benefits vest)
	60	

Question

The net pension liability of Sonya plc as at 1 January 20X3 comprised the following:

	£
Pension fund assets	10,000,000
Pension fund liabilities	(10,400,000)
	400,000

The following information relates to the year ended 31 December 20X3.

Current service cost	£800,000
Interest rate	5%
Expected return on assets	3%
Contributions paid	£1,020,000
Pensions paid	£560,000
Actual return on assets	£400,000
Actuarial valuation of liabilities at 31.12.X3	£11,000,000

Required

Show how the pension scheme assets, liabilities, gains and losses will be recognised in the financial statements for the year ended 31 December 20X3.

Answer

Balance sheet	£
Pension liability (W1)	(140,000)
Pension reserve	(140,000)
Profit and loss account	
Included in operating expenses	800,000
Other finance charges – 520,000 (journal (a)) – 300,000 (journal (c))	220,000
Statement of total recognised gains and losses	
Actual return less expected return on pension scheme (journal (f))	100,000
Experience gains and losses arising on the scheme liabilities (journal (g)	160,000

Working: Pension liability

	Journal	Asset £	Liability £
B/f		10,000,000	10,400,000
Current service cost	(a)		800,000
Interest	(b)		520,000
Expected return	(c)	300,000	
Contributions	(d)	1,020,000	
Pensions paid	(e)	(560,000)	(560,000)
		10,760,000	11,160,000
Actuarial gains	(f)/(g)	100,000	(160,000)
		10,860,000	11,000,000

Net deficit = £140,000

Journals			£	£
(a)	DEBIT	P&L account operating profits	800,000	
	CREDIT	Obligations		800,000
	Current service cost			
(b)	DEBIT	P&L account interest charge	520,000	
	CREDIT	Obligation		520,000
	Restatement of opening liability (10,400,000 × 5%)			
(c)	DEBIT	Pension fund assets	300,000	
	CREDIT	P&L account interest receivable		300,000
	Expected return (10,000,000 × 3%)			
(d)	DEBIT	Pension fund assets	1,020,000	
	CREDIT	Cash		1,020,000
	Contributions			
(e)	DEBIT	Obligations	560,000	
	CREDIT	Pension fund assets		560,000
	Pensions paid			
(f)	DEBIT	Pension fund assets	100,000	
	CREDIT	STRGL		100,000
	Re actual return (400,000 – 300,000)			
(g)	DEBIT	Pension fund obligations	160,000	
	CREDIT	STRGL		160,000
	Re actuarial gain obligations			

2.15 Benefits of FRS 17

(a) FRS 17 has brought the UK into line with **international practice** on measurement of pension scheme assets and liabilities. The only major difference is in the recognition of actuarial gains and losses. The FRS requires these to be recognised immediately they occur in the STRGL. IAS 19 requires actuarial gains and losses to be recognised in the profit and loss account to the extent that they exceed 10% of the greater of the gross assets or gross liabilities in the scheme. Recognition of actuarial gains and losses exceeding the 10% corridor may be spread forward over the expected average remaining working lives of the employees participating in the scheme.

(b) **Market values for assets are easier to understand** than actuarial values.

(c) The ASB believes that it has found a better way of **recognising the volatility** and risk inherent in a defined benefit pension scheme, **while protecting the P & L from massive swings** that could swamp the results of the employer's operations.

(d) By recognising the actuarial gains and losses immediately, a clear picture emerges in the accounts of the scheme's potential **impact on cash flows.**

(e) The **profit and loss account** and EPS are protected from market changes affecting the pension scheme. However, the ongoing operating and financing costs associated with providing a pension are recorded.

2.16 Potential problems with FRS 17

(a) **Market values** may **not** bear much relation to the **economic reality** of a pension scheme, since most scheme assets are held for the long term. A similar criticism could be made of the proposal to fair value financial instruments. Actuarial valuations take into account long term assumptions.

(b) The pension scheme **asset** (surplus) is treated as an **asset of the employer**, while the **legal position** is that it belongs to the **scheme members.**

(c) Market values cause **volatility**. Although the profit and loss account is protected from such fluctuations, the balance sheet may fluctuate.

(d) **The STRGL is often overlooked** by many users of accounts. The treatment could be viewed as a fudge, presenting the predictable in the profit and loss account and hiding the unpredictable.

(e) The standard is, arguably, even more **complex** than SSAP 24

2.17 UITF 35 Death-in-service and incapacity benefits

Abstract 35 was issued in May 2002. It clarifies the accounting required by FRS 17 *Retirement benefits* for the cost of death-in-service and incapacity benefits, where such benefits are provided through a defined benefit pension scheme.

The Abstract requires that, where the benefits are not wholly insured, the uninsured scheme liability and the cost for the accounting period should be measured, in line with other retirement benefits, using the projected unit method.

The effect is that the valuation of uninsured benefits reflects the current period's portion of the full benefits ultimately payable in respect of current members of the scheme; the cost of insured benefits is determined by the relevant insurance premiums.

Exam focus point

Keep an eye on the financial press to see how FRS 17 is working in practice.

3 FRED 39 Amendment

FAST FORWARD

FRED 39 contains proposals on termination benefits.

FRED 39 *Amendment to FRS 12 Provisions, contingent liabilities and contingent assets and Amendment to FRS 17 Retirement benefits* was issued in July 2005. It is part of a package of UK FREDs reflecting outputs from Phases I and II of the IASB project on business combinations. In this section we are concerned with the amendments to FRS 17, the amendments to FRS 12 being covered in Chapter 9. The amendments to FRS 17 are based on the IASB's Exposure Draft of proposed amendments to IAS 19 *Employee benefits*.

Key term

Termination benefits are defined as employee benefits provided in connection with the termination of an employee's employment. 'Involuntary' termination benefits arise from an entity's decision to terminate an employee's employment, whereas 'voluntary' termination benefits arise from an employee's decision to accept voluntary termination.

3.1 FRED 39 proposals

(a) Termination benefits are to be defined as employee benefits provided **in connection with the termination of an employee's employment**.

(b) Termination benefits may be **either 'involuntary'** (provided as a result of an entity's decision to terminate an employee's employment) **or 'voluntary'** (offered for a short period of time in exchange for an employee's decision to accept voluntary termination). (Note: most benefits offered to encourage employees to leave before retirement age benefits are normally covered under the existing rules of FRS 17.)

(c)   Benefits offered to encourage employees to leave service early are voluntary termination benefits **only if they are offered for a short period.**

(d)   **A liability and expense** for **voluntary** termination benefits should be **recognised** when the **employee accepts the entity's offer** to those termination benefits.

(e)   A liability and expense **for involuntary termination benefits**, except where provided in exchange for the employees' future services, should be **recognised when the entity has a plan of termination that it has communicated to the employees** and the plan meets the criteria specified in the Standard.

(f)   **Involuntary termination benefits** are provided in exchange for employees' future services if they:

   (i)   Are **incremental** to what the employees would otherwise be entitled to receive (ie benefits are not provided in accordance with the terms of an ongoing benefit plan)

   (ii)   Do not **vest** until the employment is **terminated**

   (iii) Are provided to employees who will be **retained beyond the minimum retention period**. The minimum retention period will normally be the period of notice an entity is required to provide employees in advance of terminating their employment

(g)   Where **involuntary** termination benefits are provided in exchange for employees' future service the termination benefits are **recognised as a liability and expense over the period of future service**.

(h)   Where termination benefits are provided as an **enhancement** of retirement benefits the liability and expense recognised initially includes **only the value of the additional benefits** that arise from the provision of the termination benefits.

Chapter Roundup

- **Company pension schemes** have become more and more important as supplements to or replacements for the state pension, as a means of support after retirement. With an increasingly large pensioned population, the importance of this topic can only increase. Retirement benefits are covered in FRS 17.

- **Scheme assets** are measured at **market value** (previously actuarial value).

- **Scheme liabilities** are discounted at a high-quality corporate bond rate.

- Actuarial gains and losses are **recognised immediately** in the STRGL, rather than spread forward in the P&L account.

- As a consequence, the **balance sheet reflects the surplus/deficit** in the scheme

- **FRED 39** contains proposals on termination benefits.

Quick Quiz

1 Assets of a pension scheme are valued at market value/actuarial value. (Delete as appropriate).

2 How is surplus defined?

3 Should the surplus be recognised as an asset?

4 Past service costs are not recognised because they are in the past.

True ☐

False ☐

5 How, under FRS 17, is the reserves note made up?

Answers to Quick Quiz

1 Market value

2 The excess of the value of the scheme assets over that of scheme liabilities.

3 Yes, to the extent that the employee is able to recover the surplus through reduced contributions or refunds from the scheme.

4 False. They relate to service in prior periods, but arise in current periods, for example as a result of improvements to benefits. They should be recognised in the P&L.

5

	£m
Profit and loss reserve excluding pension assets	X
Pension reserve	X
Profit and loss reserve	X

Now try the questions below from the Exam Question Bank

Number	Level	Marks	Time
Q6	Introductory	n/a	n/a

Taxation

Topic list	Syllabus reference
1 FRS 16 *Current tax*	C7
2 FRS 19 *Deferred tax*	C7

Introduction

FRS 16 *Current tax* is straightforward and should not cause too many problems. FRS 19 *Deferred tax* requires full provision for deferred tax.

Study guide

		Intellectual level
C7	**Income taxes**	
(a)	Apply and discuss the recognition and measurement of deferred tax liabilities and deferred tax assets	3
(b)	Determine the recognition of tax expenses or income and its inclusion in the financial statements	3

Exam guide

Be prepared for a whole question on deferred tax, as happened on the Pilot Paper, when you were asked to discuss the conceptual basis for its accounting treatment and to calculate the deferred tax provision after making adjustments.

1 FRS 16 Current tax

Key term

FRS 16 *Current tax* requires dividends, interest and other income or expenditure to be presented in the financial statements:

- Excluding the tax credit
- Including any withholding tax
- Including the effect of withholding tax suffered as part of the tax charge

Companies pay corporation tax at 30%, usually nine months after the year end. **FRS 16 Current tax** specifies how current tax should be reflected in the financial statements. This should be done in a **'consistent and transparent manner'**.

Specifically, the FRS deals with **tax credits** and **withholding tax**. Consider these definitions.

Key terms

Current tax. The amount of tax estimated to be payable or recoverable in respect of the taxable profit or loss for a period, along with adjustments to estimates in respect of previous periods.

Withholding tax. Tax on dividends or other income that is deducted by the payer of the income and paid to the tax authorities wholly on behalf of the recipient.

Tax credit. The tax credit given under UK tax legislation to the recipient of a dividend from a UK company. The credit is given to acknowledge that the income out of which the dividend has been paid has already been charged to tax, rather than because any withholding tax has been deducted at source. The tax credit may discharge or reduce the recipient's liability to tax on the dividend. Non-taxpayers may or may not be able to recover the tax credit.

You can see from these definitions that a tax credit is different from a withholding tax.

- A tax credit **gives credit for** tax paid by a company
- A **withholding tax withholds** the taxable part of the income

Accordingly, the tax credit and the withholding tax are treated differently in the financial statements.

1.1 Treatment in financial statements

Learn this treatment.

Outgoing dividends paid and proposed, interest or other amounts payable

- Include withholding tax
- Exclude tax credit

Incoming dividends, interest or other amounts payable

- Include withholding tax
- Exclude tax credit
- Include the effect of withholding tax suffered as part of the tax charge

1.2 Example: current tax

Taxus Ltd made a profit of £1,000,000. It received a dividend of £80,000 on which there was a tax credit of £20,000. From an overseas company it received a dividend of £3,000 on which 25% withholding tax had been deducted. The corporation tax charge was £300,000.

Required

Show how this information would be presented in the financial statements in accordance with FRS 16 *Current tax*.

Solution

	£
Operating profit	1,000,000
Income from fixed asset investments	
UK (note 1)	80,000
Foreign (note 2)	4,000
Profit before tax	1,084,000
Taxation (note 3)	301,000
Profit after tax	783,000

Notes

1　　Excludes tax credit.

2　　Includes withholding tax: £3,000 + £1,000 = £4,000. Read the question carefully – 25% had been deducted already.

3　　Add back withholding tax of £1,000.

1.3 Other requirements of FRS 16

Current tax should be recognised in the **profit and loss account**. But if it is attributable to a gain or loss that has been recognised in the statement of total recognised gains and losses, it should be recognised in that statement.

Current tax should be **measured** using tax rates and laws that have been enacted or **substantially enacted** by the balance sheet date.

Generally (apart from the treatment of withholding tax) income and expenses are **not adjusted** to reflect a **notional amount** of tax that would have been paid or received if the transaction had been taxable or allowable on a different basis. Income and expenses are included in pre-tax results on the basis of amounts **actually receivable or payable**.

1.4 Tax disclosure in the notes

This example, taken from the appendix to FRS 16, illustrates one method of showing by way of a note the tax items required to be disclosed under CA 2006 and the FRS.

	£'000	£'000
UK corporation tax		
Current tax on income for the period	X	
Adjustments in respect of prior periods	X	
	X	
Double taxation relief*	(X)	
		X
Foreign tax		
Current tax on income for the period	X	
Adjustments in respect of prior periods	X	
		X
Tax on profit on ordinary activities		X

*Don't worry about this – it's unlikely to come up in your exam.

1.5 SSAP *5 Accounting for value added tax*

SSAP 5 *Accounting for value added tax* is one of the most straightforward of all the SSAPs. A summary of the provisions is given here, but you should make sure you understand how VAT operates.

Knowledge brought forward from earlier studies

SSAP 5 Accounting for VAT

- **Turnover** shown in the P&L account should exclude VAT on taxable outputs. If gross turnover must be shown, then the VAT included in that figure must also be shown as a deduction in arriving at the turnover exclusive of VAT.

- **Irrecoverable VAT** allocated to fixed assets and other items separately disclosed should be included in their cost where material and practical.

- The **net amount due to or from Customs & Excise** should be included in the total for creditors or debtors, and need not be separately disclosed.

- **CA 2006** also requires disclosure of the cost of sales figure in the published accounts. This amount should exclude VAT on taxable inputs.

2 FRS 19 Deferred tax   Pilot paper

FAST FORWARD

FRS 19 requires **full provision,** although assets/liabilities may be discounted. In particular you should know about deferred tax and:

– Revalued assets
– Overseas earnings not yet remitted to the UK
– Discounting

You may already be aware from your studies of taxation that accounting profits and taxable profits are not the same. There are several reasons for this but they may conveniently be considered under two headings.

(a) **Permanent differences** arise because certain expenditure, such as entertainment of UK customers, is not allowed as a deduction for tax purposes although it is quite properly deducted in arriving at accounting profit. Similarly, certain income (such as UK dividend income) is not subject to corporation tax, although it forms part of accounting profit.

(b) **Timing differences** arise because certain items are included in the accounts of a period which is different from that in which they are dealt with for taxation purposes.

Deferred taxation is the tax attributable to timing differences.

Key term

> **Deferred tax.** Estimated future tax consequences of transactions and events recognised in the financial statements of the current and previous periods.

Deferred taxation is therefore a means of ironing out the tax inequalities arising from timing differences.

(a) In years when **corporation tax is saved** by timing differences such as accelerated capital allowances, a charge for deferred taxation is made in the P&L account and a provision set up in the balance sheet.

(b) In years when **timing differences reverse**, because the depreciation charge exceeds the capital allowances available, a deferred tax credit is made in the P&L account and the balance sheet provision is reduced.

Deferred tax is the subject of a new standard, FRS 19 *Deferred tax*. Before we look at the detailed requirements of FRS 19, we will explore some of the issues surrounding deferred tax.

You should be clear in your mind that the tax actually payable to the Inland Revenue is the **corporation tax liability**. The credit balance on the deferred taxation account represents an estimate of tax saved because of timing differences but expected ultimately to become payable when those differences reverse.

FRS 19 identifies the main categories in which timing differences can occur.

(a) **Accelerated capital allowances.** Tax deductions for the cost of a fixed asset are accelerated or decelerated, ie received before or after the cost of the fixed asset is recognised in the profit and loss account.

(b) **Pension liabilities** are accrued in the financial statements but are allowed for tax purposes only when paid or contributed at a later date.

(c) **Interest charges or development costs** are capitalised on the balance sheet but are treated as revenue expenditure and allowed as incurred for tax purposes.

(d) **Intragroup profits in stock**, unrealised at group level, are reversed on consolidation.

(e) **Revaluations.** An asset is revalued in the financial statements but the revaluation gain becomes taxable only if and when the asset is sold.

(f) **Unrelieved tax losses.** A tax loss is not relieved against past or present taxable profits but can be carried forward to reduce future taxable profits.

(g) **Unremitted earnings of subsidiaries.** The unremitted earnings of subsidiary and associated undertakings and joint ventures are recognised in the group results but will be subject to further taxation only if and when remitted to the parent undertaking.

Deferred taxation is therefore an accounting convention which is introduced in order to apply the accruals concept to income reporting where timing differences occur. However, **deferred tax assets** are not included in accounts as a rule, because it would not be prudent, given that the recovery of the tax is uncertain.

2.1 Basis of provision

A comprehensive tax allocation system is one in which deferred taxation is computed for every instance of timing differences: **full provision**. The opposite extreme would be the **nil provision** approach ('**flow through** method'), where only the tax payable in the period would be charged to that period.

Exam focus
point

In the Pilot paper, deferred tax was combined with financial instruments and retirement benefits.

It is important that you understand the issues properly so consider the example below.

2.2 Example: Full provision

Suppose that Girdo plc begins trading on 1 January 20X7. In its first year it makes profits of £5m, the depreciation charge is £1m and the capital allowances on those assets is £1.5m. The rate of corporation tax is 33%.

Solution

The tax liability is £1.485m again, but the debit in the P&L account is increased by the deferred tax liability of 33% × £0.5m = £165,000. The total charge to the P&L account is therefore £1,650,000 which is an effective tax rate of 33% on accounting profits (ie 33% × £5.0m). Again, no judgement is involved in using this method.

Question

Methods compared

Cuthbert Ltd buys a machine for £100,000 in 20X1. It is to be depreciated evenly over four years, has no scrap value, and will attract a 100% FYA. The company plans to buy a similar machine in 20X4 and its long term plans are for general expansion. Corporation tax is assumed to be 50% and pre-tax profit can be assumed to be £90,000 per annum before adjustments for tax in years 20X1-20X3. In 20X4 it will be £210,000. Calculate the figures for deferred tax for the years 20X1 to 20X4.

Answer

Full provision of deferred tax requires that at each year end the deferred tax account in the balance sheet contains full provision for tax on all timing differences to date, which are equal to the excess of FYAs claimed over depreciation charged. The deferred tax calculations are as follows.

	20X1	20X2	20X3	20X4
	£'000	£'000	£'000	£'000
WDV of machines (tax)				
NBV of machines (accounts)	75	50	25	75
Excess of NBV over WDV	75	50	25	75
(= accelerated capital allowances)				
Deferred tax provision				
(total) needed, at 50%	37.5	25	12.5	37.5
Deferred tax charge/(credit) for				
the year	37.5	(12.5)	(12.5)	25
(= movement required on provision)				
Tax payable (as above)	7.5	57.5	57.5	80
Deferred tax charge/(credit)	37.5	(12.5)	(12.5)	25
Tax charge in P & L a/c	45.0	45.0	45.0	105
Deferred tax provision in				
balance sheet	37.5	25.0	12.5	37.5

Note. The deferred tax figures could also be found as follows.

	FYA £'000	Depreciation £'000	Difference £'000	Deferred tax charge/(credit) (50% of difference) £'000
20X1	100	25	75	37.5
20X2	–	25	(25)	(12.5)
20X3	–	25	(25)	(12.5)
20X4	100	50	50	25

2.3 FRS 19 *Deferred tax*

In December 2000 the ASB published FRS 19. It requires entities to provide for tax timing differences on a **full, rather than partial provision basis.**

2.4 Objective

The objective of FRS 19 is to ensure that:

(a) Future tax consequences of past transactions and events are recognised as liabilities or assets in the financial statements

(b) The financial statements disclose any other special circumstances that may have an effect on future tax charges.

2.5 Scope

The FRS applies **to all financial statements that are intended to give a true and fair view** of a reporting entity's financial position and profit or loss (or income and expenditure) for a period.

The FRS applies to taxes calculated on the basis of taxable profits, including withholding taxes paid on behalf of the reporting entity.

2.6 Recognition of deferred tax assets and liabilities

Remember!

Deferred tax should be recognised in respect of all timing differences that have originated but not reversed by the balance sheet date.

Deferred tax should **not be recognised on permanent differences.**

Question

Timing differences

Can you remember some examples of timing differences?

Answer

- Accelerated capital allowances
- Pension liabilities accrued but taxed when paid
- Interest charges and development costs capitalised but allowed for tax purposes when incurred
- Unrealised intra-group stock profits reversed on consolidation
- Revaluation gains
- Tax losses
- Unremitted earnings of subsidiaries, associates and joint ventures recognised in group results.

Key term

> **Permanent differences.** Differences between an entity's taxable profits and its results as stated in the financial statements that arise because certain types of income and expenditure are non-taxable or disallowable, or because certain tax charges or allowances have no corresponding amount in the financial statements.

2.6.1 Allowances for fixed asset expenditure

Deferred tax **should be recognised** when the **allowances** for the cost of a fixed asset are **received before or after the cost of the fixed asset is recognised in the profit and loss account.** However, if and when **all conditions** for retaining the allowances have been met, the **deferred tax should be reversed.**

If an asset is not being depreciated (and has not otherwise been written down to a carrying value less than cost), the timing difference is the amount of capital allowances received.

Most capital allowances are received on a **conditional basis**, ie they are repayable (for example, via a balancing charge) if the assets to which they relate are sold for more than their tax written-down value. However, some, such as industrial buildings allowances, are repayable only if the assets to which they relate are sold within a specified period. Once that period has expired, all conditions for retaining the allowance have been met. At that point, deferred tax that has been recognised (ie on the excess of the allowance over any depreciation) is reversed.

Question
Industrial building allowance

An industrial building qualifies for an IBA when purchased in 20X1. The building is still held by the company in 20Z6. What happens to the deferred tax?

Answer

All the conditions for retaining tax allowances have been met. This means that the timing differences have become permanent and the deferred tax recognised should be reversed. Before the 25 year period has passed, deferred tax should be provided on the difference between the amount of the industrial building allowance and any depreciation charged on the asset.

2.6.2 Marked to market non-monetary assets

Deferred tax must be provided for when the timing difference arises on assets that are marked to market, with gains and losses recorded in the profit and loss account.

This reflects the view that, when gains and losses are recognised in the profit and loss account, it is because they are for the most part readily realisable. To give a true and fair view of the entity's performance, the additional tax that would be payable on realising the gains should also be recognised.

2.6.3 Revaluations

Deferred tax should not be recognised on timing differences arising when other non-monetary assets are **revalued**, unless, by the balance sheet date, the reporting entity has:

(a)   Entered into a **binding agreement to sell** the revalued assets
(b)   **Recognised the gains and losses** expected to arise on sale

Deferred tax **should not be recognised** on timing differences arising when non-monetary assets (other than marked to market assets) are revalued or sold if, on the basis of all available evidence, it is more likely than not that the taxable gain will be **rolled over**, being charged to tax only if and when the assets into which the gain has been rolled over are sold.

> Even if you have a binding agreement to sell and the gain/loss recognised is expected to arise on sale, those gains expected to be rolled over will not necessarily result in a future liability to tax and deferred tax should not be provided.

Gains subject to **holdover relief** do **not** receive the same exemption as those attributed to rollover relief.

The reason for this treatment is that, where rollover relief has been obtained, the entity retains the discretion to avoid paying tax on the chargeable gain. That tax will be paid only if and when the replacement assets are sold.

2.6.4 Unremitted earnings

Tax that could be payable (taking account of any double taxation relief) on any future remittance of the past earnings of a subsidiary, associate or joint venture **should be provided for only to the extent that**, at the balance sheet date:

(a) **Dividends** have been **accrued as receivable**

(b) **A binding agreement to distribute the past earnings in future** has been entered into by the subsidiary, associate or joint venture.

It is **considered unlikely** that there will be a binding agreement to distribute the past earnings of the subsidiary, associate or joint venture.

2.7 Deferred tax assets

Deferred tax assets should be recognised to the extent that they are considered **recoverable**, which will be the case if **it is more likely than not** that **suitable tax profits** will exist from which the reversal of the timing difference giving rise to the asset can be deducted.

The need for prudence would suggest that more evidence of the likelihood of future profits was needed for recognition of a deferred tax asset than for recognition of a deferred tax liability.

2.7.1 Suitable taxable profits

(a) The profits are generated by the same taxable entity and assessed by the same taxation authority.

(b) Set off is compliant with tax authority rules, for example carry back, carry forward relief.

(c) They arise from the future reversal of deferred tax liabilities recognised at the balance sheet date.

Account may be taken of tax planning opportunities, ie actions that the entity would take if necessary to create suitable taxable profits.

2.8 Recognition in the statements of performance

> Recognise deferred tax in the performance statement where related timing differences have been recognised.

Deferred tax should be **recognised in the profit and loss account** for the period, **except** to the extent that it is **attributable to a gain or loss** that is or has been **recognised** directly **in the statement of total recognised gains and losses.**

Where a gain or loss is or has been recognised directly in the statement of total recognised gains and losses, deferred tax attributable to that gain or loss should also be recognised directly in that statement.

2.9 Measurement – tax rates

Deferred tax should be measured at **the average tax rates expected to apply when timing differences reverse**, based on tax rates and laws **substantially enacted** by the balance sheet date.

Average tax rates only need to be calculated if different rates of tax are expected to apply to different levels of taxable income.

Tax rates are substantially enacted:

    (a)   Once a Bill has passed through the House of Commons but not the Lords

    (b)   When a resolution having statutory effect is passed under the Provisional Collection of Taxes Act 1968

2.10 Measurement – discounting

Reporting entities are **permitted but not required** to discount deferred tax assets and liabilities to reflect the time value of money.

The ASB believes that, just as other long-term liabilities such as provisions and debt are discounted, so too in principle should long-term deferred tax balances. The FRS therefore permits discounting and provides guidance on how it should be done. However, the ASB stopped short of making discounting mandatory, acknowledging that there is as yet **no internationally accepted methodology** for discounting deferred tax, and that for some entities **the costs might outweigh the benefits.** Entities are encouraged to select the more appropriate policy, taking account of factors such as materiality and the policies of other entities in their sector.

Question

Discounting

Can you think of a situation where it might be appropriate to discount deferred tax liabilities?

Answer

Where the reversal is fairly slow, for example with industrial buildings allowances.

Discounting should be **applied consistently** to all tax flows on timing differences where the effect is expected to be **material** and where the **tax flows have not already been discounted**. Certain timing differences such as those arising on provisions for pension costs or the lessor's investment in finance leases are measured by reference to cash flows that have already been discounted. The deferred tax provisions to which they give rise already incorporate discounting, so they are not eligible for further discounting.

No account should be taken of **future timing differences** including future tax losses.

The **scheduling of the reversals** should take account of the **remaining tax effect of transactions already reflected in the financial statements**, for example tax losses at the balance sheet date.

The **discount rate** should be the **post tax return** that could be obtained at the balance sheet date on **government bonds** with **similar maturity dates** and in **currencies similar to those of the deferred tax**

assets or liabilities. It may be possible to use average rates without introducing material errors. The examples below are taken from the FRS.

2.11 Example: Scheduling of reversal of accelerated capital allowances on a single asset

An entity purchases an asset for £100,000 at the start of 20X0. It is estimated that the asset will have a useful economic life of ten years and no residual value. Capital allowances can be claimed at a rate of 25 per cent of cost in each of the first four years.

At the end of 20X0, there is a timing difference of £15,000, which is the difference between the allowances of £25,000 received and the depreciation of £10,000. The timing difference is treated as reversing according to the following schedule (even if the entity expects to make losses at some point during the life of the asset):

Years from now:	1	2	3	4	5	6	7	8	9	Total
Depreciation (£'000)	10	10	10	10	10	10	10	10	10	90
Allowances (£'000)	25	25	25	–	–	–	–	–	–	75
(ACA)/ Reversal – leading to increase in PCTCT	(15)	(15)	(15)	10	10	10	10	10	10	15

	Published information			Post-tax return
Years to Maturity	**Coupon rate %**	**Bid Price**	**Bid Yield %**	**(bid yield less tax of 30%)**
1	6	99.37	6.67	4.7
3	7	102.82	6.01	4.2
5	6.5	104.27	5.55	3.9
9	7.2	114.16	5.29	3.7
30	6	114.00	5.09	3.6

Years from now	Timing difference (increase)/reversal £'000	Deferred tax (asset)/liabilit @ 30% £'000	Discount rate %	Deferred tax (asset)/liability Discounted £'000
1	(15)	(4.5)	4.7	(4.3)
2	(15)	(4.5)	4.4	(4.1)
3	(15)	(4.5)	4.2	(4)
4	10	3	4	2.6
5	10	3	3.9	2.5
6	10	3	3.8	2.4
7	10	3	3.8	2.3
8	10	3	3.2	2.2
9	10	3	3.2	2.2
Total	15	4.5		1.8

2.12 More complicated example: Discounting

This example is taken from an appendix to the FRS. It illustrates how deferred tax arising from accelerated capital allowances on a plant and machinery pool is discounted.

Assumptions

A company that operates solely in the UK depreciates its plant and machinery on a straight-line basis over 10 years. Residual value is estimated to be 1/11th of cost. The company receives capital allowances at a rate of 25 per cent per year on a reducing balance basis. It is taxed on its profits at 30 per cent.

The company has three groups of assets costing £1,100 each, purchased six years, three years and one year ago (in each case at the end of the financial year). The net book value of plant and machinery at the balance sheet date (year 0) is:

	£
Original cost	3,300
Cumulative depreciation	(1,000)
Net book value	2,300

The tax written-down values of the plant and machinery pool, and the consequential timing difference, at the balance sheet date are:

	£
Net book value	2,300
Tax written-down value	(1,114)
Timing difference at end of year 0	1,186

Scheduling the reversal of the deferred tax liability

The future reversals of the liability are scheduled in Table 1 below. The future depreciation of the existing pool of fixed assets (column b) is compared with the future writing-down allowances available on the pool (column c) to determine the years of reversal of the capital allowances (column d). When forecasting capital allowances for future periods, it is assumed that allowances will be claimed as early as possible and that the residual values of the assets will equal those forecast for depreciation purposes.

Table 1

Years from now	Depreciation	Capital allowances	Reversal of timing differences	Deferred tax liability (undiscounted)
	£	£	£	£
a	b	c	d = b − c	e = d × 30%
1	300	278	22	7
2	300	209	91	27
3	300	157	143	43
4	300	93	207	62
5	200	69	131	39
6	200	52	148	44
7	200	14	186	56
8	100	11	89	27
9	100	(17)	117	35
10	–	(52)	52	16
Total	2,000	814	1,186	356

Where do the capital allowances figures come from?

You will not need to calculate these figures in an exam, but it may help to know where they come from. Take the figure of £278 at the end of year 1.

At balance sheet date the three lots of assets will have had allowances for seven, four and two years respectively (as they were bought at the end of the financial years). So the tax written down values at the balance sheet dare are:

	£		£
Group 1	1,100	× 75%[7]	147
Group 2	1,100	× 75%[4]	348
Group 3	1,100	× 75%[2]	619
Total			1,114

The capital allowances arising in the next year are therefore (£1,114 × 25%) = £278.5

Discount rates

The prices of and yields on UK Treasury gilts are published in the *Financial Times*. An appropriate post-tax rate is obtained by deducting the rate of tax that the entity pays on investment income (30 per cent) from these returns.

Table 2

Years to Maturity	Published information			Post-tax return (bid yield less tax of 30%)
	Coupon rate %	Bid Price	Bid Yield %	
1	6	99.37	6.67	4.7
3	7	102.82	6.01	4.2
5	6.5	104.27	5.55	3.9
9	7.2	114.16	5.29	3.7
30	6	114.00	5.09	3.6

Appropriate rates of return for other maturity dates are estimated by interpolation. See column f of Table 3 below.

Discounting the liability

Table 3 below illustrates how the discounted liability of £290 is calculated. The guidance in the FRS notes that it may be possible to use simplifying assumptions without introducing material errors into the measurement of the discounted liability. In this example, all timing differences reversing in years 10 onwards are treated as reversing in year 10.

Table 3

Years from now	Deferred tax liability (undiscounted) £	Discount rate %		Deferred tax liability (discounted) £
a	e (from Table 1)	f (from Table 2)		$g = e/[(1 + f)^a]$
1	7	4.7		7
2	27	4.4	i	25
3	43	4.2		38
4	62	4.0	i	53
5	39	3.9		33
6	44	3.8	i	35
7	56	3.8	i	43
8	27	3.7	i	20
9	35	3.7		25
10+	16	3.7	i	11
Total	356			290

i = estimate based on interpolation of rates known for years 1, 3, 5, 9 and 30*

The discount reduces the deferred tax liability at year 0 by £66, ie from £ 356 to £290.

2.13 Presentation

In the **balance sheet** classify:

- Net deferred tax liabilities as 'provisions for liabilities and charges'
- Net deferred tax assets as debtors, as a separate subhead if material where taxes are levied by the same tax authority or in a group where tax losses of one entity can reduce the taxable profits of another.

Balances are to be **disclosed separately** on the face of the balance sheet **if** so **material** as to distort the financial statements.

In the **profit and loss account** classify as part of **tax on profit or loss on ordinary activities**.

2.14 Disclosures

FRS 19 has detailed disclosures relating to deferred tax, which are best learnt by studying the illustrative example below, taken from the Appendix.

Important!

> Note in particular that the FRS requires information to be disclosed about factors affecting current and future tax charges. A key element of this is a requirement to disclose a reconciliation of the current tax charge for the period to the charge that would arise if the profits reported in the financial statements were charged at a standard rate of tax.

2.15 Example: deferred tax

Red Ltd has three 100% owned subsidiaries, Yellow Ltd, Blue Ltd, and Green Inc.

(a) The following details relate to Yellow Ltd:

    (i) Red Ltd acquired its interest in Yellow Ltd on 1 January 20X3. The fair values of the assets were considered to be equal to their carrying values, with the exception of freehold property which was considered to be £1m in excess of its book value. This property is surplus to Yellow Ltd's requirements and the directors are looking for a buyer.

    (ii) Yellow Ltd has sold goods worth £6 million to Red since acquisition and made a profit of £2 million on the transaction. The stock of these goods recorded in Red's balance sheet at the year ended 30 September 20X3 was £3.6 million.

(b) Blue Ltd undertakes various projects from debt factoring to investing in property and commodities. The following details relate to Blue Ltd for the year ended 30 September 20X3:

    (i) Blue has a portfolio of readily marketable government securities which are held as current assets. These investments are stated at market value in the balance sheet with any gain or loss taken to the profit and loss account. These gains and losses are taxed when the investments are sold. Currently the accumulated unrealised gains are £8 million.

    (ii) Waddeson has calculated it requires a general provision of £2 million against its total loan portfolio. Tax relief is available when the specific loan is written off.

(c) Green Inc has unremitted earnings of $20 million which would give rise to additional tax payable of £1 million if remitted to the UK.

(d) Red Ltd has unrelieved trading losses as at 30 September 20X3 of £10 million. Assume a corporation tax rate of 30%.

Required

What are the deferred tax implications of the above information for the Red Ltd group of companies?

Solution

(a) (i) Fair value adjustments are treated in the same way as they would be if they were timing differences in the entity's own accounts. A revaluation would only create a deferred tax provision if there was a binding agreement to sell, which is not the case here.

      (ii) Provisions for unrealised profits are timing differences which create deferred tax assets and the deferred tax is provided at the supplying company's rate of tax. A deferred tax asset would arise of $(3.6 \times {}^2/_6)$ @ 30% = £360,000

(b) (i) The unrealised gains are timing differences which will reverse when the investments are sold therefore a deferred tax provision needs to be created of (£8m × 30%) = £2.4 million

      (ii) The general provision is a timing difference which will reverse when the currently unidentified loans go bad and the entity will then be entitled to tax relief. A deferred tax asset of (£2m at 30%) = £600,000 should be created.

(c) No provision is required for the additional tax payable of £1 million as there is no binding obligation to remit the earnings in the UK.

(d) Red Ltd's unrelieved trading losses can only be recognised as a deferred tax asset to the extent they are considered to be recoverable. In assessing the recoverability there needs to be evidence that there will be suitable taxable profits from which the losses can be deducted in the future. To the extent Nyman itself has a deferred tax provision for future taxable trading profits (eg ACAs) then an asset could be recognised.

2.16 International comparisons

The move to full provision accounting reflects an acceptance of the need to harmonise with international practice in the area of deferred tax. However, there are **differences** between the requirements of the FRS and those of the equivalent international standard IAS 12 *Income taxes*.

The **ASB does not agree** with the rationale underlying the **'temporary difference' approach** adopted in the IAS.

Key term

> **Temporary difference.** Any difference between the amount at which an asset or liability is recognised in financial statements and its tax base. The tax base is the amount that will be deductable or taxable in respect of the asset or liability in the future.

Temporary differences can include permanent as well as timing differences, and the ASB does not believe deferred tax should be provided on permanent differences.

In practical terms, the requirements of the FRS are similar to IAS 12's. Both standards require full provision on most timing differences, and both permit deferred tax assets to be recognised only if there is evidence that there will be taxable profits in the future against which the assets can be recovered.

2.17 Areas of difference

(a) The FRS does not require or permit deferred tax to be provided for when non-monetary assets are revalued.

(b) No deferred tax can be provided when a taxable gain is rolled over into replacement assets and will become taxable only if and when the assets are sold.

(c)   No deferred tax is provided when group accounts incorporate retained earnings of associates and joint ventures, which would become subject to further taxation on remittance to the parent company.

In each of the above cases there is no obligation to pay more tax until the entity commits itself to selling the assets or remitting the earnings.

2.18 Problems

The FRS makes a significant change. It will have the effect of **increasing the liabilities** reported by entities that at present have **large amounts of unprovided deferred tax** arising from capital allowances in excess of depreciation.

Criticisms that may be made of the FRS 19 approach include the following.

(a)   The provisions on **discounting** are somewhat **confusing**. The full reversal basis of discounting deferred tax liabilities may turn them into assets in the early years of an asset's life because capital allowances exceed depreciation before the timing differences reverse.

(b)   The standard is **complicated**, and there is **scope for manipulation and inconsistency**, since discounting is optional.

(c)   It is **open to question whether deferred tax is a liability** as defined in the *Statement of Principles*. It is not, strictly speaking, a present obligation arising as a result of a past event. However, it is being recognised as such under the FRS.

(d)   Arguably the flow-through or **nil provision method is closer to the ASB definition**, but this method, although much simpler, has been rejected to bring the standard closer to the IAS.

(e)   The standard may '**fall between two stools**', as it is different from IAS 12 and not really what the UK wants either.

2.19 Section summary

- Deferred tax is tax relating to timing differences.

- Full provision must be made for tax timing differences.

- Deferred tax must not be recognised on revaluation unless there is a commitment to sell, when a gain on sale is rolled over or on unremitted earnings of subsidiaries, associates or joint ventures.

- Discounting is allowed but not required.

Chapter Roundup

- **FRS 16 *Current tax*** requires dividends, interest and other income or expenditure to be presented in the financial statements:

  – Excluding the tax credit
  – Including any withholding tax
  – Including the effect of withholding tax suffered as part of the tax charge

- **FRS 19** requires **full provision,** although assets/liabilities may be discounted. In particular you should know about deferred tax and:

  – Revalued assets
  – Overseas earnings not yet remitted to the UK
  – Discounting

Quick Quiz

1 A company receives a dividend of £4,000 on which 20% withholding tax has been paid. At what amount should be dividend be shown in the financial statements?

2 What is the basis under which deferred tax must be computed?

3 Which method does FRS 19 require to be used?

4 Temporary differences are the same as timing differences

  True ☐

  False ☐

5 Under FRS 19 deferred tax assets and liabilities may/must be discounted. (Delete as applicable.)

Answers to Quick Quiz

1   £5,000

2   The full provision basis

3   Full provision

4   False. Temporary differences include permanent differences.

5   May

Now try the questions below from the Exam Question Bank

Number	Level	Marks	Time
Q7	Introductory	n/a	n/a

Financial instruments

Topic list	Syllabus reference
1 Financial instruments	C3
2 Presentation of financial instruments	C3
3 Recognition of financial instruments	C3
4 Measurement of financial instruments	C3
5 Hedging	C3
6 Disclosure of financial instruments	C3

Introduction

Financial instruments sounds like a daunting subject, and indeed this is a complex and controversial area. The numbers involved in financial instruments are often huge, but don't let this put you off. In this chapter we aim to simplify the topic as much as possible and to focus on the important issues.

The debate over **measurement and recognition** of financial instruments is very closely connected to the **off balance sheet finance debate** (see Chapter 11). Before the issue of FRS 25 and FRS 26 many financial instruments were not recognised or disclosed in financial statements at all.

The issues of disclosure and presentation are addressed in **FRS 25 and 29**. Recognition and measurement issues are dealt with in **FRS 26**. There has been plenty in the financial and accountancy press on this project – keep your eyes open for further press comment.

Study guide

		Intellectual level
C3	**Financial instruments**	
(a)	Apply and discuss the recognition and de-recognition of a financial asset or financial liability	2
(b)	Apply and discuss the classification of a financial asset or financial liability and their measurement	2
(c)	Apply and discuss the treatment of gains and losses arising on financial assets or financial liabilities	2
(d)	Apply and discuss the treatment of impairment of financial assets	2
(e)	Record the accounting for derivative financial instruments and simple embedded derivatives	2
(f)	Outline the principle of hedge accounting and account for fair value hedges and cash flow hedges, including hedge effectiveness	2

Exam guide

This is a highly controversial topic and therefore, likely to be examined, probably in Section B.

Exam focus point

> Although the very complexity of this topic makes it a highly likely subject for an exam question in Paper 2, there are limits as to how complicated and detailed a question the examiner can set with any realistic expectation of students being able to answer it. You should therefore concentrate on the essential points. Financial instruments have been tested within consolidation questions as well as single issue questions in Section B. Now it is more likely to be part of a mixed scenario.

1 Financial instruments

FAST FORWARD

> Financial instruments can be very complex, particularly **derivative instruments**, although **primary instruments** are more straightforward.

If you read the financial press you will probably be aware of **rapid international expansion** in the use of financial instruments. These vary from straightforward, traditional instruments, eg bonds, through to various forms of so-called 'derivative instruments'

We can perhaps summarise the reasons why a project on financial instruments was considered necessary as follows.

(a) The **significant growth of financial instruments** over recent years has outstripped the development of guidance for their accounting.

(b) The topic is of **international concern**, other national standard-setters are involved as well as the IASB.

(c) There have been recent **high-profile disasters** involving derivatives (eg Barings) which, while not caused by accounting failures, have raised questions about accounting and disclosure practices.

There are three standards on financial instruments, all issued as part of the ASB's convergence programme, and all of which implement IAS.

(a) FRS 25 *Financial instruments: presentation*, which deals with:

(i) The classification of financial instruments between liabilities and equity

(ii) Presentation of certain compound instruments

(b) FRS 29 *Financial instruments: disclosures,* which revised, simplified and incorporated disclosure requirements previously in FRS 25.

(c) FRS 26 *Financial Instruments: recognition and measurement*, which deals with:

(i) Recognition and derecognition

(ii) The measurement of financial instruments

(iii) Hedge accounting

Note: The recognition and derecognition rules were introduced in April 2006 by an amendment.

1.1 Definitions

The important definitions to learn are:

- **Financial asset**
- **Financial liability**
- **Equity instrument**

The most important definitions are common to all three standards.

Key terms

Financial instrument. Any contract that gives rise to both a financial asset of one entity and a financial liability or equity instrument of another entity.

Financial asset. Any asset that is:

(a) Cash

(b) An equity instrument of another entity

(c) A contractual right to receive cash or another financial asset from another entity; or to exchange financial instruments with another entity under conditions that are potentially favourable to the entity, or

(d) A contract that will or may be settled in the entity's own equity instruments and is:

(i) A non-derivative for which the entity is or may be obliged to receive a variable number of the entity's own equity instruments; or

(ii) A derivative that will or may be settled other than by the exchange of a fixed amount of cash or another financial asset for a fixed number of the entity's own equity instruments.

Financial liability. Any liability that is:

(a) A contractual obligation:

(i) To deliver cash or another financial asset to another entity, or

(ii) To exchange financial instruments with another entity under conditions that are potentially unfavourable; or

Key terms

(b)   a contract that will or may be settled in the entity's own equity instruments and is:

(i)   A non-derivative for which the entity is or may be obliged to deliver a variable number of the entity's own equity instruments; or

(ii)   A derivative that will or may be settled other than by the exchange of a fixed amount of cash or another financial asset for a fixed number of the entity's own equity instruments.

Equity instrument. Any contract that evidences a residual interest in the assets of an entity after deducting all of its liabilities.

Fair value is the amount for which an asset could be exchanged, or a liability settled, between knowledgeable, willing parties in an arm's length transaction

Derivative. A financial instrument or other contract with all three of the following characteristics:

(a)   Its value changes in response to the change in a specified interest rate, financial instrument price, commodity price, foreign exchange rate, index of prices or rates, credit rating or credit index, or other variable (sometimes called the 'underlying');

(b)   It requires no initial net investment or an initial net investment that is smaller than would be required for other types of contracts that would be expected to have a similar response to changes in market factors; and

(c)   It is settled at a future date.   *(FRS 25, FRS 26 and FRS 29)*

Exam focus point

These are very important – particularly the first three – so learn them.

1.1.1 More detail

We should clarify some points arising from these definitions. Firstly, one or two terms above should be themselves defined.

(a)   A '**contract**' need not be in writing, but it must comprise an agreement that has 'clear economic consequences' and which the parties to it cannot avoid, usually because the agreement is enforceable in law.

(b)   An '**entity**' here could be an individual, partnership, incorporated body or government agency.

The definitions of **financial assets and financial liabilities** may seem rather circular, referring as they do to the terms financial asset and financial instrument. The point is that there may be a chain of contractual rights and obligations, but it will lead ultimately to the receipt or payment of cash *or* the acquisition or issue of an equity instrument.

Examples of **financial assets** include:

(a)   Trade debtors
(b)   Options
(c)   Shares (when used as an investment)

Examples of **financial liabilities** include:

(a)   Trade creditors
(b)   Debenture loans payable
(c)   Redeemable preference (non-equity) shares
(d)   Forward contracts standing at a loss

As we have already noted, financial instruments include both of the following.

(a) **Primary instruments**: eg receivables, payables and equity securities

(b) **Derivative instruments**: eg financial options, futures and forwards, interest rate swaps and currency swaps, **whether recognised or unrecognised**

FRS 25 makes it clear that the following items are *not* financial instruments.

- **Physical assets**, eg stocks, property, plant and equipment, leased assets and intangible assets (patents, trademarks etc)

- **Prepaid expenses**, deferred revenue and most warranty obligations

- Liabilities or assets that are **not contractual** in nature

- Contractual rights/obligations that **do not involve transfer of a financial asset**, eg commodity futures contracts, operating leases

Question   Financial instruments

Can you give the reasons why the first two items listed above do not qualify as financial instruments?

Answer

Refer to the definitions of financial assets and liabilities given above.

(a) **Physical assets**: control of these creates an opportunity to generate an inflow of cash or other assets, but it does not give rise to a present right to receive cash or other financial assets.

(b) **Prepaid expenses, etc**: the future economic benefit is the receipt of goods/services rather than the right to receive cash or other financial assets.

(c) **Deferred revenue, warranty obligations**: the probable outflow of economic benefits is the delivery of goods/services rather than cash or another financial asset.

Contingent rights and obligations meet the definition of financial assets and financial liabilities respectively, even though many do not qualify for recognition in financial statements. This is because the contractual rights or obligations exist because of a past transaction or event (eg assumption of a guarantee).

1.2 Derivatives

A **derivative** is a financial instrument that **derives** its value from the price or rate of an underlying item. Common **examples** of derivatives include:

(a) **Forward contracts**: agreements to buy or sell an asset at a fixed price at a fixed future date

(b) **Futures contracts**: similar to forward contracts except that contracts are standardised and traded on an exchange

(c) **Options**: rights (but not obligations) for the option holder to exercise at a pre-determined price; the option writer loses out if the option is exercised

(d) **Swaps**: agreements to swap one set of cash flows for another (normally interest rate or currency swaps).

The nature of derivatives often gives rise to **particular problems**. The **value** of a derivative (and the amount at which it is eventually settled) depends on **movements** in an underlying item (such as an exchange rate). This means that settlement of a derivative can lead to a very different result from the one originally envisaged. A company which has derivatives is exposed to **uncertainty and risk** (potential for gain or loss) and this can have a very material effect on its financial performance, financial position and cash flows.

Yet because a derivative contract normally has **little or no initial cost**, under traditional accounting it **may not be recognised** in the financial statements at all. Alternatively it may be recognised at an amount which bears no relation to its current value. This is clearly **misleading** and leaves users of the financial statements unaware of the **level of risk** that the company faces. The IASs on which FRS 25 and 26 are based were developed in order to correct this situation.

1.3 Section summary

- Three accounting standards are relevant:
    - FRS 25 *Financial instruments: presentation*
    - FRS 26 *Financial instruments: measurement*
    - FRS 29 *Financial instruments: disclosures*

- The definitions of **financial asset, financial liability** and **equity instrument** are fundamental to FRS 25, FRS 26 and FRS 29.

- Financial instruments include:
    - **Primary** instruments
    - **Derivative** instruments

2 Presentation of financial instruments

The objective of FRS 25 is:

> 'to enhance financial statement users' understanding of the significance of on-balance-sheet and off-balance-sheet financial instruments to an entity's financial position, performance and cash flows.'

2.1 Scope

FRS 25 should be applied in the presentation and disclosure of **all types of financial instruments**, whether recognised or unrecognised.

Certain items are **excluded**.

- Interests in subsidiaries (FRS 2, FRS 5)

- Interests in associates (FRS 9)

- Interests in joint ventures (FRS 9)

- Pensions and other post-retirement benefits (FRS 17)

- Insurance contracts

- Contracts for contingent consideration in a business combination

- Contracts that require a payment based on climatic, geographic or other physical variables

- Financial instruments, contracts and obligations under share-based payment transactions (FRS 20)

2.2 Liabilities and equity

FAST FORWARD

Financial instruments must be classified as **liabilities** or **equity** according to their **substance**.

The main thrust of FRS 25 here is that financial instruments should be presented according to their **substance**, **not merely their legal form**. In particular, entities which issue financial instruments should classify them (or their component parts) as **either financial liabilities, or equity**.

The classification of a financial instrument as a liability or as equity depends on the following.

- The **substance of the contractual arrangement** on initial recognition
- The definitions of a financial liability and an equity instrument

FAST FORWARD

The critical feature of a financial liability is the **contractual obligation to deliver cash** or another financial instrument.

How should a **financial liability be distinguished from an equity instrument**? The critical feature of a **liability** is an **obligation** to transfer economic benefit. Therefore a financial instrument is a financial liability if there is a **contractual obligation** on the issuer either to deliver cash or another financial asset to the holder or to exchange another financial instrument with the holder under potentially unfavourable conditions to the issuer.

The financial liability exists **regardless of the way in which the contractual obligation will be settled**. The issuer's ability to satisfy an obligation may be restricted, eg by lack of access to foreign currency, but this is irrelevant as it does not remove the issuer's obligation or the holder's right under the instrument.

Where the above critical feature is *not* met, then the financial instrument is an **equity instrument**. FRS 25 explains that although the holder of an equity instrument may be entitled to a *pro rata* share of any distributions out of equity, the issuer does *not* have a contractual obligation to make such a distribution.

Although substance and legal form are often **consistent with each other**, this is not always the case. In particular, a financial instrument may have the legal form of equity, but in substance it is in fact a liability. Other instruments may combine features of both equity instruments and financial liabilities.

For example, many entities issue **preferred shares** which must be **redeemed** by the issuer for a fixed (or determinable) amount at a fixed (or determinable) future date. Alternatively, the holder may have the right to require the issuer to redeem the shares at or after a certain date for a fixed amount. In such cases, the issuer has an **obligation**. Therefore the instrument is a **financial liability** and should be classified as such.

The classification of the financial instrument is made when it is **first recognised** and this classification will continue until the financial instrument is removed from the entity's balance sheet.

2.3 Contingent settlement provisions

An entity may issue a financial instrument where the way in which it is settled depends on:

(a) The occurrence or non-occurrence of uncertain future events, or

(b) The outcome of uncertain circumstances,

that are beyond the control of both the holder and the issuer of the instrument. For example, an entity might have to deliver cash instead of issuing equity shares. In this situation it is not immediately clear whether the entity has an equity instrument or a financial liability.

Such financial instruments should be classified as **financial liabilities** unless the possibility of settlement is remote.

2.4 Settlement options

When a derivative financial instrument gives one party a **choice** over how it is settled (eg, the issuer can choose whether to settle in cash or by issuing shares) the instrument is a **financial asset** or a **financial liability** unless **all the alternative choices** would result in it being an equity instrument.

2.5 Compound financial instruments

> **Compound instruments** are split into **equity** and **liability** components and presented in the balance sheet accordingly.

Some financial instruments contain both a liability and an equity element. In such cases, FRS 25 requires the component parts of the instrument to be **classified separately**, according to the substance of the contractual arrangement and the definitions of a financial liability and an equity instrument.

One of the most common types of compound instrument is **convertible debt**. This creates a primary financial liability of the issuer and grants an option to the holder of the instrument to convert it into an equity instrument (usually ordinary shares) of the issuer. This is the economic equivalent of the issue of conventional debt plus a warrant to acquire shares in the future.

Although in theory there are several possible ways of calculating the split, FRS 25 requires the following method:

(a) Calculate the value for the liability component.

(b) Deduct this from the instrument as a whole to leave a residual value for the equity component.

The reasoning behind this approach is that an entity's equity is its residual interest in its assets amount after deducting all its liabilities.

The **sum of the carrying amounts** assigned to liability and equity will always be equal to the carrying amount that would be ascribed to the instrument **as a whole**.

2.6 Example: Valuation of compound instruments

Rathbone Co issues 2,000 convertible bonds at the start of 20X2. The bonds have a three year term, and are issued at par with a face value of £1,000 per bond, giving total proceeds of £2,000,000. Interest is payable annually in arrears at a nominal annual interest rate of 6%. Each bond is convertible at any time up to maturity into 250 common shares.

When the bonds are issued, the prevailing market interest rate for similar debt without conversion options is 9%. At the issue date, the market price of one common share is £3. The dividends expected over the three year term of the bonds amount to 14p per share at the end of each year. The risk-free annual interest rate for a three year term is 5%.

Required

What is the value of the equity component in the bond?

Solution

The liability component is valued first, and the difference between the proceeds of the bond issue and the fair value of the liability is assigned to the equity component. The present value of the liability component is calculated using a discount rate of 9%, the market interest rate for similar bonds having no conversion rights, as shown.

	£
Present value of the principal: £2,000,000 payable at the end of three years (£2m ×0.772)*	1,544,00
Present value of the interest: £120,000 payable annually in arrears for three years (£120,000 ×2.531)*	303,720
Total liability component	1,847,720
Equity component (balancing figure)	152,280
Proceeds of the bond issue	2,000,000

* These figures can be obtained from discount and annuity tables.

The split between the liability and equity components remains the same throughout the term of the instrument, even if there are changes in the **likelihood of the option being exercised.** This is because it is not always possible to predict how a holder will behave. The issuer continues to have an obligation to make future payments until conversion, maturity of the instrument or some other relevant transaction takes place.

2.7 Treasury shares

If an entity **reacquires its own equity instruments**, those instruments ('treasury shares') shall be **deducted from equity**. No gain or loss shall be recognised in profit or loss on the purchase, sale, issue or cancellation of an entity's own equity instruments. Consideration paid or received shall be recognised directly in equity.

2.8 Interest, dividends, losses and gains

As well as looking at balance sheet presentation, FRS 25 considers how financial instruments affect the profit and loss account (and movements in equity). The treatment varies according to whether interest, dividends, losses or gains relate to a financial liability or an equity instrument.

(a) Interest, dividends, losses and gains relating to a financial instrument (or component part) classified as a **financial liability** should be recognised as **income or expense** in profit or loss.

(b) Distributions to holders of a financial instrument classified as an **equity instrument** should be **debited directly to equity** by the issuer.

(c) **Transaction costs** of an equity transaction shall be accounted for as a **deduction from equity** (unless they are directly attributable to the acquisition of a business, in which case they are accounted for under FRS 2).

2.9 Offsetting a financial asset and a financial liability

A financial asset and financial liability should **only** be **offset**, with the net amount reported in the balance sheet, when an entity:

(a) has a **legally enforceable right of set off**, *and*

(b) intends to settle on a **net basis**, or to realise the asset and settle the liability simultaneously, ie at the same moment.

This will reflect the expected **future cash flows** of the entity in these specific circumstances. In all other cases, financial assets and financial liabilities are presented separately.

2.10 Current liabilities

A **long-term financial liability** due to be **settled within twelve months** of the balance sheet date should be classified as a **current liability**, even if an agreement to refinance, or to reschedule payments, on a long-term basis is completed after the balance sheet date and before the financial statements are authorised for issue.

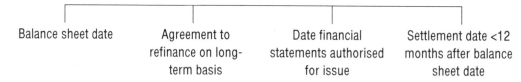

| Balance sheet date | Agreement to refinance on long-term basis | Date financial statements authorised for issue | Settlement date <12 months after balance sheet date |

A **long-term financial liability** that is payable on **demand** because the entity **breached** a **condition** of its loan agreement should be classified as **current** at the balance sheet date even if the **lender** has agreed **after the balance sheet date**, and **before** the financial statements are **authorised for issue**, **not** to **demand payment** as a consequence of the breach.

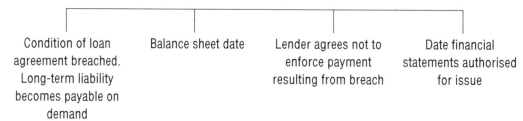

| Condition of loan agreement breached. Long-term liability becomes payable on demand | Balance sheet date | Lender agrees not to enforce payment resulting from breach | Date financial statements authorised for issue |

However, if the **lender** has **agreed** by the **balance sheet date** to provide a **period of grace** ending **at least twelve months after the balance sheet date** within which the entity can rectify the breach and during that time the lender cannot demand immediate repayment, the liability is classified as **non-current**.

2.11 Section summary

- Financial instruments must be classified as **liabilities** or **equity**

- The **substance** of the financial instrument is more important than its **legal form**

- The **critical feature of a financial liability** is the contractual obligation to deliver cash or another financial instrument

- **Compound instruments** are split into equity and liability parts and presented accordingly

- **Interest, dividends, losses and gains** are treated according to whether they relate to a financial asset or a financial liability

- Rules apply stating whether liabilities should be classified as **current or non current**

3 Recognition of financial instruments

FRS 26 *Financial instruments: recognition and measurement* establishes principles for recognising and measuring financial assets and financial liabilities.

3.1 Amendment

FAST FORWARD The Amendment to FRS 26 brings in the recognition and de-recognition rules of IAS 39.

In April 2006, the ASB issued *Amendment to FRS 26 (IAS 39) Financial instruments: measurement, recognition and derecognition*. This implements the recognition and derecognition rules in IAS 39. For items falling within the definition of financial instruments, recognition and derecognition are no longer governed by FRS 5.

In this section, FRS 26 will be known by its new name *Financial instruments: recognition and measurement*.

3.2 Initial recognition

Financial instruments should be recognised in the balance sheet when the entity becomes a party to the **contractual provisions of the instrument**.

Point to note

An important consequence of this is that all derivatives should be on the balance sheet.

Notice that this is **different** from the recognition criteria in the IASB *Framework,* the ASB *Statement of Principles* and in most other standards. Items are normally recognised when there is a probable inflow or outflow of resources and the item has a cost or value that can be measured reliably.

3.3 Example: initial recognition

An entity has entered into two separate contracts.

(a)   A firm commitment (an order) to buy a specific quantity of iron
(b)   A forward contract to buy a specific quantity of iron at a specified price on a specified date.

Contract (a) is a **normal trading contract**. The entity does not recognise a liability for the iron until the goods have actually been delivered. (Note that this contract is not a financial instrument because it involves a physical asset, rather than a financial asset.)

Contract (b) is a **financial instrument**. Under FRS 26 the entity recognises a financial liability (an obligation to deliver cash) on the **commitment date**, rather than waiting for the closing date on which the exchange takes place.

Note that planned future transactions, no matter how likely, are not assets and liabilities of an entity – the entity has not yet become a party to the contract.

3.4 Derecognition

Derecognition is the removal of a previously recognised financial instrument from an entity's balance sheet.

An entity should derecognise a **financial asset** when:

(a)   The **contractual rights** to the cash flows from the financial asset **expire**, or

(b)   The entity **transfers substantially all the risks and rewards of ownership** of the financial asset to another party.

Question   Risks and rewards

Can you think of an example of sales of financial assets in which:

(a)   An entity has transferred substantially all the risks and rewards of ownership?
(b)   An entity has retained substantially all the risks and rewards of ownership?

Answer

FRS 26 includes the following examples:

(a) (i)   An unconditional sale of a financial asset

(ii) A sale of a financial asset together with an option to repurchase the financial asset at its fair value at the time of repurchase

(b) (i)   A sale and repurchase transaction where the repurchase price is a fixed price or the sale price plus a lender's return

(ii) A sale of a financial asset together with a total return swap that transfers the market risk exposure back to the entity

Exam focus point

The principle here is that of **substance over form**.

An entity should derecognise a **financial liability** when it is **extinguished** – ie, when the obligation specified in the contract is discharged or cancelled or expires.

It is possible for only **part** of a financial asset or liability to be derecognised. This is allowed if the part comprises:

(a)   Only specifically identified cash flows; or

(b)   Only a fully proportionate (pro rata) share of the total cash flows.

For example, if an entity holds a bond it has the right to two separate sets of cash inflows: those relating to the principal and those relating to the interest. It could sell the right to receive the interest to another party while retaining the right to receive the principal.

On derecognition, the amount to be included in net profit or loss for the period is calculated as follows:

Formula to learn

	£	£
Carrying amount of asset/liability (or the portion of asset/liability) transferred		X
Less: Proceeds received/paid	X	
Any cumulative gain or loss reported in equity	X	
		(X)
Difference to net profit/loss		X

Where only part of a financial asset is derecognised, the carrying amount of the asset should be allocated between the part retained and the part transferred based on their relative fair values on the date of transfer. A gain or loss should be recognised based on the proceeds for the portion transferred.

3.5 Section summary

- **All financial assets** and **liabilities** should be **recognised on the balance sheet**, including derivatives.

- Financial assets should be derecognised when the **rights to the cash flows** from the asset **expire** or where **substantially all the risks and rewards of ownership are transferred** to another party.

- Financial liabilities should be derecognised when they are **extinguished**.

4 Measurement of financial instruments

FRS 26 *Financial instruments: recognition and measurement* was published in 2004, and amended in 2006 to include the IAS 39 rules on recognition and derecognition. It applies to listed entities or entities whose financial statements are prepared in accordance with the fair value accounting rules of CA 2006. Entities applying the FRSSE are exempt.

4.1 Initial measurement

Financial instruments are initially measured at the **fair value** of the consideration given or received (ie, **cost**) **plus** (in most cases) **transaction costs** that are **directly attributable** to the acquisition or issue of the financial instrument.

The **exception** to this rule is where a financial instrument is designated as **at fair value through profit or loss** (this term is explained below). In this case, **transaction costs** are **not** added to fair value at initial recognition.

The fair value of the consideration is normally the transaction price or market prices. If market prices are not reliable, the fair value may be **estimated** using a valuation technique (for example, by discounting cash flows).

4.2 Subsequent measurement

For the purposes of measuring a financial asset held subsequent to initial recognition, FRS 26 classifies financial assets into four categories defined here. Note particularly the **criteria** for a financial asset or liability at fair value through profit and loss.

Key terms

A financial asset or liability at **fair value through profit or loss meets** either of the following conditions:

(a)　It is classified as held for trading. A financial instrument is classified as held for trading if it is:

    (i)　Acquired or incurred principally for the purpose of selling or repurchasing it in the near term

    (ii)　Part of a portfolio of identified financial instruments that are managed together and for which there is evidence of a recent actual pattern of short-term profit-taking or

    (iii)　A derivative (unless it is a designated and effective hedging instrument)

(b)　Upon initial recognition it is designated by the entity as at fair value through profit or loss. An entity may only use this designation in severely restricted circumstances:

    (i)　It **eliminates** or significantly **reduces** a measurement or recognition **inconsistency** (mismatch) that would otherwise arise.

    (ii)　A **group** of financial assets/liabilities is **managed** and its performance is evaluated **on a fair value basis**.

Key terms

Held-to-maturity investments are non-derivative financial assets with fixed or determinable payments and fixed maturity that an entity has the positive intent and ability to hold to maturity other than:

(a)　Those that the entity upon initial recognition designates as at fair value through profit or loss
(b)　Those that the entity designates as available for sale and
(c)　Those that meet the definition of loans and receivables.

Loans and receivables are non-derivative financial assets with fixed determinable payments that are not quoted in an active market, other than:

(a)　Those that the entity intends to sell immediately or in the near term, which should be classified as held for trading and those that the entity upon initial recognition designates as at fair value through profit or loss

(b)　Those that the entity upon initial recognition designates as available-for-sale or

Key terms

> (c)   Those for which the holder may not recover substantially all of the initial investment, other than because of credit deterioration, which shall be classified as available for sale
>
> An interest acquired in a pool of assets that are not loans or receivables (for example, an interest in a mutual fund or a similar fund) is not a loan or a receivable.
>
> **Available-for-sale financial assets** are those financial assets that are not:
>
> (a)   Loans and receivables originated by the entity,
> (b)   Held-to-maturity investments, or
> (c)   Financial assets at fair value through profit or loss.   *(FRS 26)*

FAST FORWARD

> Subsequently they should be **re-measured to fair value** except for
>
> (a)   Loans and receivables not held for trading
> (b)   Other **held-to-maturity investments**
> (c)   **Financial assets** whose value **cannot be reliably measured**

After initial recognition, all financial assets should be **remeasured to fair value**, without any deduction for transaction costs that may be incurred on sale of other disposal, except for:

(a)   **Loans and receivables**

(b)   **Held to maturity investments**

(c)   Investments in **equity instruments** that do not have a quoted market price in an active market and whose **fair value cannot be reliably measured** and derivatives that are linked to and must be settled by delivery of such unquoted equity instruments

Loans and receivables and **held to maturity investments** should be measured at **amortised cost using the effective interest method**.

Key term

> Amortised cost of a financial asset or financial liability is the amount at which the financial asset or liability is measured at initial recognition minus principal repayments, plus or minus the cumulative amortisation of any difference between that initial amount and the maturity amount, and minus any write-down (directly or through the use of an allowance account) for impairment or uncollectability.
>
> The **effective interest method** is a method of calculating the amortised cost of a financial instrument and of allocating the interest income or interest expense over the relevant period.
>
> The **effective interest rate** is the rate that exactly discounts estimated future cash payments or receipts through the expected life of the financial instrument.   *(FRS 26)*

4.3 Example: Amortised cost

On 1 January 20X1 Abacus Co purchases a debt instrument for its fair value of £1,000. The debt instrument is due to mature on 31 December 20X5. The instrument has a principal amount of £1,250 and the instrument carries fixed interest at 4.72% that is paid annually. The effective interest rate is 10%.

How should Abacus Co account for the debt instrument over its five year term?

Solution

Abacus Co will receive interest of £59 (1,250 × 4.72%) each year and £1,250 when the instrument matures.

Abacus must allocate the discount of £250 and the interest receivable over the five year term at a constant rate on the carrying amount of the debt. To do this, it must apply the effective interest rate of 10%.

The following table shows the allocation over the years:

Year	Amortised cost at beginning of year	Profit and loss account: Interest income for year (@10%)	Interest received during year (cash inflow)	Amortised cost at end of year
	£	£	£	£
20X1	1,000	100	(59)	1,041
20X2	1,041	104	(59)	1,086
20X3	1,086	109	(59)	1,136
20X4	1,136	113	(59)	1,190
20X5	1,190	119	(1,250+59)	–

Each year the carrying amount of the financial asset is increased by the interest income for the year and reduced by the interest actually received during the year.

Investments whose **fair value cannot be reliably measured** should be measured at **cost**.

4.4 Classification

On initial recognition, certain financial instruments must be designated at fair value through profit and loss.

In contrast, it is quite difficult for an entity **not** to remeasure financial instruments to fair value.

Exam focus point

> Notice that derivatives **must** be remeasured to fair value. This is because it would be misleading to measure them at cost.

For a financial instrument to be held to maturity it must meet several extremely narrow criteria. The entity must have a **positive intent** and a **demonstrated ability** to hold the investment to maturity. These conditions are not met if:

(a) The entity intends to hold the financial asset for an undefined period

(b) The entity stands ready to sell the financial asset in response to changes in interest rates or risks, liquidity needs and similar factors (unless these situations could not possibly have been reasonably anticipated)

(c) The issuer has the right to settle the financial asset at an amount significantly below its amortised cost (because this right will almost certainly be exercised)

(d) It does not have the financial resources available to continue to finance the investment until maturity

(e) It is subject to an existing legal or other constraint that could frustrate its intention to hold the financial asset to maturity

In addition, an **equity** instrument is **unlikely** to meet the criteria for classification as held to maturity.

There is a **penalty** for selling or reclassifying a 'held-to-maturity' investment other than in certain very tightly defined circumstances. If this has occurred during the **current** financial year or during the **two preceding** financial years **no** financial asset can be classified as held-to-maturity.

If an entity can no longer hold an investment to maturity, it is no longer appropriate to use amortised cost and the asset must be re-measured to fair value. **All** remaining held-to-maturity investments must also be re-measured to fair value and classified as available-for-sale (see above).

4.5 Subsequent measurement of financial liabilities

After initial recognition, all financial liabilities should be measured at **amortised cost**, with the exception of financial liabilities at fair value through profit or loss (including most derivatives). These should be measured at **fair value**, but where the fair value **is not capable of reliable measurement**, they should be measured at **cost**.

Question

Deep discount bond

Galaxy Co issues a bond for £503,778 on 1 January 20X2. No interest is payable on the bond, but it will be redeemed on 31 December 20X4 for £600,000. The bond has **not** been designated as at fair value through profit or loss.

Required

Calculate the charge to the profit and loss account of Galaxy Co for the year ended 31 December 20X2 and the balance outstanding at 31 December 20X2.

Answer

The bond is a 'deep discount' bond and is a financial liability of Galaxy Co. It is measured at amortised cost. Although there is no interest as such, the difference between the initial cost of the bond and the price at which it will be redeemed is a finance cost. This must be allocated over the term of the bond at a constant rate on the carrying amount.

To calculate amortised cost we need to calculate the effective interest rate of the bond:

$\dfrac{600,000}{503,778}$ = 1.191 over three years.

To calculate **an annual rate**, we have to take the cube root, $(1.191)^{1/3}$, so the annual interest rate is 6%.

From tables, the interest rate is 6%.

The charge to the profit and loss account is £30,226 (503,778 × 6%)

The balance outstanding at 31 December 20X2 is £534,004 (503,778 + 30,226)

4.6 Gains and losses

Instruments at **fair value through profit or loss**: gains and losses are recognised **in profit or loss** (ie, in the profit and loss account).

Available for sale financial assets: gains and losses are recognised **in the statement of total recognised gains and losses.** When the asset is derecognised the cumulative gain or loss previously recognised in the STRGL should be recognised in profit and loss.

Financial instruments carried at **amortised cost**: gains and losses are recognised **in profit and loss** as a result of the amortisation process and when the asset is derecognised.

Financial assets and financial assets that are **hedged items**: special rules apply (discussed later in this chapter).

Question

Ellesmere Co entered into the following transactions during the year ended 31 December 20X3:

(1) Entered into a speculative interest rate option costing £10,000 on 1 January 20X3 to borrow £6,000,000 from AB Bank commencing 31 March 20X5 for 6 months at 4%. The value of the option at 31 December 20X3 was £15,250.

(2) Purchased 6% debentures in FG Co on 1 January 20X1 (their issue date) for £150,000 as an investment. Ellesmere Co intends to hold the debentures until their redemption at a premium in 5 year's time. The effective rate of interest of the bond is 8.0%.

(3) Purchased 50,000 shares in ST Co on 1 July 20X3 for £3.50 each as an investment. The share price on 31 December 20X3 was £3.75.

Required

Show the accounting treatment and relevant extracts from the financial statements for the year ended 31 December 20X3.

Answer

BALANCE SHEET EXTRACTS

	£
Financial assets:	
Interest rate option (W1)	15,250
4% debentures in MT Co (W2)	153,000
Shares in EG Co (W3)	187,500

PROFIT AND LOSS ACCOUNT EXTRACTS

	£
Finance income:	
Gain on interest rate option (W1)	5,250
Effective interest on 6% debentures (W2)	12,000

Workings

1   *Interest rate option*

This is a derivative and so it must be treated as at fair value through profit or loss.

Initial measurement (at cost):

DEBIT	Financial asset	£10,000	
CREDIT	Cash		£10,000

At 31.12.20X3 (re-measured to fair value)

DEBIT	Financial asset (£15,250 – £10,000)	£5,250	
CREDIT	Profit and loss account		£5,250

2   *Debentures*

On the basis of the information provided, this can be treated as a held-to-maturity investment.

Initial measurement (at cost):

DEBIT	Financial asset	£150,000	
CREDIT	Cash		£150,000

At 31.12.20X3 (amortised cost):

DEBIT	Financial asset (150,000 × 8%)	£12,000	
CREDIT	Finance income		£12,000
DEBIT	Cash (150,000 × 6%)	£9,000	
CREDIT	Financial asset		£9,000

Amortised cost at 31.12.20X3:

(150,000 + 12,000 – 9,000)	£153,000

3   *Shares*

These are treated as an available for sale financial asset (shares cannot normally be held to maturity and they are clearly not loans or receivables).

Initial measurement (at cost):

DEBIT	Financial asset (50,000 × £3.50)	£175,000	
CREDIT	Cash		£175,000

At 31.12.20X3 (re-measured to fair value)

DEBIT	Financial asset ((50,000 × £3.75) – £175,000))	£12,500	
CREDIT	Statement of total recognised gains and losses		£12,500

4.7 Impairment and uncollectability of financial assets

At each balance sheet date, an entity should assess whether there is any objective evidence that a financial asset or group of assets is impaired.

Question   Impairment

Give examples of indications that a financial asset or group of assets may be impaired.

Answer

FRS 26 lists the following:

(a)   Significant financial difficulty of the issuer

(b)   A breach of contract, such as a default in interest or principal payments

(c)   The lender granting a concession to the borrower that the lender would not otherwise consider, for reasons relating to the borrower's financial difficulty

(d)   It becomes probable that the borrower will enter bankruptcy

(e)   The disappearance of an active market for that financial asset because of financial difficulties

Where there is objective evidence of impairment, the entity should **determine the amount** of any impairment loss.

4.7.1 Financial assets carried at amortised cost

The impairment loss is the **difference** between the asset's **carrying amount** and its **recoverable amount**. The asset's recoverable amount is the present value of estimated future cash flows, discounted at the financial instrument's **original** effective interest rate.

The amount of the loss should be **recognised in profit or loss.**

If the impairment loss decreases at a later date (and the decrease relates to an event occurring **after** the impairment was recognised) the reversal is recognised in profit or loss. The carrying amount of the asset must not exceed the original amortised cost.

4.7.2 Financial assets carried at cost

Unquoted equity instruments are carried at cost if their fair value cannot be reliably measured. The impairment loss is the difference between the asset's **carrying amount** and the **present value of estimated future cash flows**, discounted at the current market rate of return for a similar financial instrument. Such impairment losses cannot be reversed.

4.7.3 Available for sale financial assets

Available for sale financial assets are carried at fair value and gains and losses are recognised in the statement of total recognised gains and losses. Any impairment loss on an available for sale financial asset should be **removed from statement of total recognised gains and losses** and **recognised in net profit or loss for the period** even though the financial asset has not been derecognised.

The impairment loss is the difference between its **acquisition cost** (net of any principal repayment and amortisation) and **current fair value** (for equity instruments) or recoverable amount (for debt instruments), less any impairment loss on that asset previously recognised in profit or loss.

Impairment losses relating to equity instruments cannot be reversed. Impairment losses relating to debt instruments may be reversed if, in a later period, the fair value of the instrument increases and the increase can be objectively related to an event occurring after the loss was recognised.

4.8 Example: Impairment

Broadfield Co purchased 5% debentures in X Co at 1 January 20X3 (their issue date) for £100,000. The term of the debentures was 5 years and the maturity value is £130,525. The effective rate of interest on the debentures is 10% and the company has classified them as a held-to-maturity financial asset.

At the end of 20X4 X Co went into liquidation. All interest had been paid until that date. On 31 December 20X4 the liquidator of X Co announced that no further interest would be paid and only 80% of the maturity value would be repaid, on the original repayment date.

The market interest rate on similar bonds is 8% on that date.

Required

(a)   What value should the debentures have been stated at just before the impairment became apparent?

(b)   At what value should the debentures be stated at 31 December 20X4, after the impairment?

(c)   How will the impairment be reported in the financial statements for the year ended 31 December 20X4?

Solution

(a) The debentures are classified as a held-to-maturity financial asset and so they would have been stated at amortised cost:

	£
Initial cost	100,000
Interest at 10%	10,000
Cash at 5%	(5,000)
At 31 December 20X3	105,000
Interest at 10%	10,500
Cash at 5%	(5,000)
At 31 December 20X4	110,500

(b) After the impairment, the debentures are stated at their recoverable amount (using the **original** effective interest rate of 10%, which, from tables, gives a discount factor of 0.751):

80% × £130,525 × 0.751 = £78,419

(c) The impairment of £32,081 (£110,500 – £78,419) should be recorded:

DEBIT Profit and loss account	£32,081	
CREDIT Financial asset		£32,081

Question

Finance cost 1

On 1 January 20X3 Deferred issued £600,000 loan notes. Issue costs were £200. The loan notes do not carry interest, but are redeemable at a premium of £152,389 on 31 December 20X4. The effective finance cost of the debentures is 12%.

What is the finance cost in respect of the loan notes for the year ended 31 December 20X4?

A £72,000
B £76,194
C £80,613
D £80,640

Answer

C The premium on redemption of the preferred shares represents a finance cost. The effective rate of interest must be applied so that the debt is measured at amortised cost (IAS 39).

At the time of issue, the loan notes are recognised at their net proceeds of £599,800 (600,000 – 200).

The finance cost for the year ended 31 December 20X4 is calculated as follows:

	B/f	Interest @ 12%	C/f
	£	£	£
20X3	599,800	71,976	671,776
20X4	671,776	80,613	752,389

Question

Finance cost 2

On 1 January 20X5, an entity issued a debt instrument with a coupon rate of 3.5% at a par value of £6,000,000. The directly attributable costs of issue were £120,000. The debt instrument is repayable on 31 December 2011 at a premium of £1,100,000.

What is the total amount of the finance cost associated with the debt instrument?

A   £1,470,000
B   £1,590,000
C   £2,570,000
D   £2,690,000

Answer

D

	£
Issue costs	120,000
Interest £6,000,000 × 3.5% × 7	1,470,000
Premium on redemption	1,100,000
Total finance cost	2,690,000

Question   Classification

During the financial year ended 28 February 20X5, MN issued the two financial instruments described below. For *each* of the instruments, identify whether it should be classified as debt or equity, **explaining in not more than 40 words each** the reason for your choice. In each case you should refer to the relevant International Accounting Standard or International Financial Reporting Standard.

(i)   Redeemable preferred shares with a coupon rate 8%. The shares are redeemable on 28 February 20X9 at premium of 10%

(ii)   A grant of share options to senior executives. The options may be exercised from 28 February 20X8.

Answer

(i)   **Debt.** The preference shares require regular distributions to the holders but more importantly have the debt characteristic of being redeemable. Therefore according to IAS 32 *Financial instruments: presentation* they must be classified as debt.

(ii)   **Equity.** According to IFRS 2 Share based payment the grant of share options must be recorded as equity in the balance sheet. It is an alternative method of payment to cash for the provision of the services of the directors.

Question   Hybrid financial instrument

On 1 January 20X1, EFG issued 10,000 5% convertible bonds at their par value of £50 each. The bonds will be redeemed on 1 January 20X6. Each bond is convertible at the option of the holder at any time during the five year period. Interest on the bond will be paid annually in arrears.

The prevailing market interest rate for similar debt without conversion options at the date of issue was 6%.

At what value should the equity element of the hybrid financial instrument be recognised in the financial statements of EFG at the date of issue?

Answer

Top tip The method to use here is to find the present value of the principal value of the bond, £500,000 (10,000 × £50) and the interest payments of £25,000 annually (5% × £500,000) at the market rate for non-convertible bonds of 6%, using the discount factor tables. The difference between this total and the principal amount of £500,000 is the equity element.

	£
Present value of principal £500,000 × 0.747	373,500
Present value of interest £25,000 × 4.212	105,300
Liability value	478,800
Principal amount	500,000
Equity element	21,200

4.9 Section summary

- On initial recognition, financial instruments are measured at **cost**.

- Subsequent measurement depends on how a financial asset is **classified**.

- Financial assets at **fair value through profit or loss** are measured at **fair value**; gains and losses are recognised in **profit or loss**.

- **Available for sale** assets are measured at **fair value**; gains and losses are taken to **the STRGL**.

- **Loans and receivables** and **held to maturity** investments are measured at **amortised cost**; gains and losses are recognised in **profit or loss**.

- Financial **liabilities** are normally measured at **amortised cost**, unless they have been classified as at fair value through profit and loss.

5 Hedging

FAST FORWARD

Hedging is allowed in certain strictly defined circumstances.

FRS 26 **requires hedge accounting** where there is a **designated hedging relationship** between a hedging instrument and a hedged item. It is **prohibited otherwise**.

Key terms

Hedging, for accounting purposes, means designating one or more hedging instruments so that their change in fair value is offset, in whole or in part, by the change in fair value or cash flows of a hedged item.

A **hedged item** is an asset, liability, firm commitment, or forecasted future transaction that:

(a)   exposes the entity to risk of changes in fair value or changes in future cash flows, and that
(b)   is designated as being hedged.

A **hedging instrument** is a designated derivative or (in limited circumstances) another financial asset or liability whose fair value or cash flows are expected to offset changes in the fair value or cash flows of a designated hedged item. (A non-derivative financial asset or liability may be designated as a hedging instrument for hedge accounting purposes only if it hedges the risk of changes in foreign currency exchange rates.)

Key term

Hedge effectiveness is the degree to which changes in the fair value or cash flows of the hedged item attributable to a hedged risk are offset by changes in the fair value or cash flows of the hedging instrument.

(*FRS 26*)

In simple terms, entities **hedge** to **reduce** their **exposure to risk** and uncertainty, such as changes in prices, interest rates or foreign exchange rates. Hedge accounting recognises hedging relationships by allowing (for example) losses on a hedged item to be offset against gains on a hedging instrument.

5.1 Example: Hedging

A company owns stocks of 20,000 gallons of oil which cost £400,000 on 1 December 20X3.

In order to hedge the fluctuation in the market value of the oil the company signs a futures contract to deliver 20,000 gallons of oil on 31 March 20X4 at the futures price of £22 per gallon.

The market price of oil on 31 December 20X3 is £23 per gallon and the futures price for delivery on 31 March 20X4 is £24 per gallon.

Required

Explain the impact of the transactions on the financial statements of the company:

(a)   Without hedge accounting
(b)   With hedge accounting

Solution

The futures contract was intended to protect the company from a fall in oil prices (which would have reduced the profit when the oil was eventually sold). However, oil prices have actually risen, so that the company has made a loss on the contract.

Without hedge accounting:

The futures contract is a derivative and therefore must be remeasured to fair value under FRS 26. The loss on the futures contract is recognised in the profit and loss account:

DEBIT	Profit and loss account (20,000 × 24 – 22)	£40,000	
CREDIT	Financial liability		£40,000

With hedge accounting:

The loss on the futures contract is recognised in the profit and loss account as before.

The stocks are revalued to fair value:

	£
Fair value at 31 December 20X4 (20,000 × 23)	460,000
Cost	(400,000)
Gain	60,000

The gain is also recognised in the profit and loss account:

DEBIT	Stock	£60,000	
CREDIT	Profit and loss account		£60,000

The net effect on the profit and loss account is a gain of £20,000 compared with a loss of £40,000 without hedge accounting.

The standard identifies three types of hedging relationship.

Key terms

> **Fair value hedge**: a hedge of the exposure to changes in the fair value of a recognised asset or liability, or an identified portion of such an asset or liability, that is attributable to a particular risk and could affect profit or loss.
>
> **Cash flow hedge**: a hedge of the exposure to variability in cash flows that
>
> (a)   is attributable to a particular risk associated with a recognised asset or liability (such as all or some future interest payments on variable rate debt) or a highly probable forecast transaction (such as an anticipated purchase or sale), and that
>
> (b)   could affect profit or loss.
>
> Hedge of a net investment in a foreign operation: IAS 21 defines a net investment in a foreign operation as the amount of the reporting entity's interest in the net assets of that operation.   (*FRS 26*)

The hedge in the example above is a **fair value hedge** (it hedges exposure to changes in the fair value of a recognised asset: the oil).

5.2 Conditions for hedge accounting

Before a hedging relationship qualifies for hedge accounting, **all** of the following **conditions** must be met.

(a)   The hedging relationship must be **designated at its inception as a hedge** based on the entity's risk management objective and strategy. There must be formal documentation (including identification of the hedged item, the hedging instrument, the nature of the risk that is to be hedged and how the entity will assess the hedging instrument's effectiveness in offsetting the exposure to changes in the hedged item's fair value or cash flows attributable to the hedged risk).

(b)   The hedge is expected to be **highly effective** in achieving offsetting changes in fair value or cash flows attributable to the hedged risk. (Note: the hedge need not necessarily be *fully* effective.)

(c)   For **cash flow hedges**, a **forecast transaction** that is the subject of the hedge must be **highly probable** and must present an exposure to variations in cash flows that could ultimately affect profit or loss.

(d)   The effectiveness of the hedge can be **measured reliably**.

(e)   The hedge is **assessed** on an ongoing basis (annually) and has been **effective during the reporting period**.

5.3 Accounting treatment

5.3.1 Fair value hedges

The **gain or loss** resulting from **re-measuring** the hedging instrument at fair value is **recognised in profit or loss**.

The gain or loss on the hedged item attributable to the hedged risk should **adjust the carrying amount** of the hedged item and be **recognised in profit or loss**.

5.3.2 Cash flow hedges

The portion of the gain or loss on the hedging instrument that is determined to be an **effective** hedge shall be **recognised through the statement of total recognised gains and losses**.

The **ineffective portion** of the gain or loss on the hedging instrument should be **recognised in profit or loss**.

When a hedging transaction results in the recognition of an asset or liability, changes in the value of the hedging instrument recognised in reserves either:

(a) Are adjusted against the carrying value of the asset or liability, or

(b) Affect the profit and loss account at the same time as the hedged item (for example, through depreciation or sale).

5.3.3 Example: Cash flow hedge

Bets Co signs a contract on 1 November 20X1 to purchase an asset on 1 November 20X2 for €60,000,000. Bets reports in US£ and hedges this transaction by entering into a forward contract to buy €60,000,000 on 1 November 20X2 at US£1: €1.5.

Spot and forward exchange rates at the following dates are:

	Spot	Forward (for delivery on 1.11.X2)
1.11.X1	US£1: €1.45	US£1: €1.5
31.12.X1	US£1: €1.20	US£1: €1.24
1.11.X2	US£1: €1.0	US£1: €1.0 (actual)

Required

Show the double entries relating to these transactions at 1 November 20X1, 31 December 20X1 and 1 November 20X2.

Solution

Entries at 1 November 20X1

The value of the forward contract at inception is zero so no entries recorded (other than any transaction costs), but risk disclosures will be made.

The contractual commitment to buy the asset would be disclosed if material (IAS 16).

Entries at 31 December 20X1

Gain on forward contract:

	£
Value of contract at 31.12.X1 (€60,000,000/1.24)	48,387,097
Value of contract at 1.11.X1 (€60,000,000/1.5)	40,000,000
Gain on contract	8,387,097

Compare to movement in value of asset (unrecognised):

Increase in £ cost of asset

| (€60,000,000/1.20 – €60,000,000/1.45) | £8,620,690 |

As this is higher, the hedge is deemed fully effective at this point:

DEBIT	Financial asset (Forward a/c)	£8,387,097	
CREDIT	Equity		£8,387,097

Entries at 1 November 20X2

Additional gain on forward contract

	£
Value of contract at 1.11.X2 (€60,000,000/1.0)	60,000,000
Value of contract at 31.12.X1 (€60,000,000/1.24)	48,387,097
Gain on contract	11,612,903

Compare to movement in value of asset (unrecognised):

Increase in £ cost of asset

(€60,000,000/1.0 – €60,000,000/1.2)   £10,000,000

Therefore, the hedge is not fully effective during this period, but is still highly effective (and hence hedge accounting can be used):

£10,000,000/ £11,612,903 = 86% which is within the 80% – 125% bandings.

DEBIT	Financial asset (Forward a/c)	£11,612,903	
CREDIT	Equity		£10,000,000
CREDIT	Profit and loss account		£1,612,903

Purchase of asset at market price

DEBIT	Asset (€60,000,000/1.0)	£60,000,000	
CREDIT	Cash		£60,000,000

Settlement of forward contract

DEBIT	Cash	£20,000,000	
CREDIT	Financial asset (Forward a/c)		£20,000,000

Realisation of gain on hedging instrument

The cumulative gain of £18,387,097 recognised in the statement of total recognised gains and losses.

- is transferred to the profit and loss account as the asset is used, ie over the asset's useful life; *or*

- adjusts the initial cost of the asset (reducing future depreciation).

5.3.4 Section summary

- **Hedge accounting** means designating one or more instruments so that their change in fair value is **offset** by the change in fair value or cash flows of another item.

- **Hedge accounting** is permitted in certain circumstances, provided the hedging relationship is **clearly defined**, **measurable** and actually **effective**.

- There are three types of hedge: **fair value** hedge; **cash flow** hedge; hedge of a **net investment in a foreign operation.**

- The accounting treatment of a hedge **depends on its type**.

6 Disclosure of financial instruments

Exam focus point

> Skim through for background only. Disclosures will not be tested in detail.

FAST FORWARD

> FRS 29 specifies the **disclosures** required for financial instruments. The standard requires qualitative and quantitative disclosures about exposure to risks arising from financial instruments and specifies minimum disclosures about credit risk, liquidity risk and market risk.

The IASB and ASB maintain that users of financial instruments need information about an entity's exposures to risks and how those risks are managed, as this information can **influence a user's assessment of the financial position and financial performance of an entity** or of the amount, timing and uncertainty of its **future cash flows.**

There have been new techniques and approaches to measuring risk management, which highlighted the need for guidance.

Accordingly, FRS 29 *Financial instruments: disclosures* was issued in December 2005. This embodies IFRS 7 of the same name, amended for UK entities.

6.1 General requirements

The extent of disclosure required depends on the extent of the entity's use of financial instruments and of its exposure to risk. It **adds to the requirements previously in FRS 25** by requiring:

- Enhanced balance sheet and income statement disclosures
- Disclosures about an allowance account when one is used to reduce the carrying amount of impaired financial instruments.

The standard requires **qualitative and quantitative disclosures about exposure to risks** arising from financial instruments, and specifies minimum disclosures about **credit risk**, **liquidity risk** and **market risk**.

6.2 Objective

The objective of the standard is to require entities to provide disclosures in their financial statements that enable users to evaluate:

(a) The significance of financial instruments for the entity's financial position and performance

(b) The nature and extent of risks arising from financial instruments to which the entity is exposed during the period and at the reporting date, and how the entity manages those risks.

The principles in FRS 29 complement the principles for recognising, measuring and presenting financial assets and financial liabilities in FRS 25 *Financial instruments: presentation* and FRS 26 *Financial instruments: recognition and measurement*.

6.3 Classes of financial instruments and levels of disclosure

The entity must group financial instruments into classes **appropriate to the nature of the information disclosed**. An entity must decide in the light of its circumstances how much detail it provides. Sufficient information must be provided to permit reconciliation to the line items presented in the balance sheet.

6.3.1 Balance sheet

The following must be disclosed.

(a) **Carrying amount** of financial assets and liabilities by FRS 26 category

(b) **Reason for any reclassification** between fair value and amortised cost (and vice versa)

(c) **Details** of the assets and exposure to risk where the entity has made a **transfer** such that part or all of the financial assets do not qualify for derecognition.

(d) The **carrying amount** of financial assets the entity has **pledged as collateral** for liabilities or contingent liabilities and the associated terms and conditions.

(e) When financial assets are impaired by credit losses and the entity records the impairment in a separate account (eg an **allowance account** used to record individual impairments or a similar account used to record a collective impairment of assets) rather than directly reducing the carrying amount of the asset, it must disclose a **reconciliation** of changes in that account during the period for each class of financial assets.

(f)   The **existence of multiple embedded derivatives**, where compound instruments contain these.

(g)   **Defaults and breaches**

6.3.2 Income statement and equity

The entity must disclose the following **items of income, expense, gains or losses**, either on the face of the financial statements or in the notes.

(a)   Net gains/losses by FRS 26 category (broken down as appropriate: eg interest, fair value changes, dividend income)

(b)   Interest income/expense

(c)   Impairments losses by class of financial asset

6.3.3 Other disclosures

Entities must disclose in the summary of **significant accounting policies** the measurement basis used in preparing the financial statements and the other accounting policies that are relevant to an understanding of the financial statements.

Disclosures must be made relating to **hedge accounting**, as follows:

(a)   **Description of hedge**

(b)   Description of financial instruments designated as **hedging instruments** and their fair value at the reporting date

(c)   The **nature of the risks** being hedged

(d)   For **cash flow hedges**, periods **when the cash flows will occur** and when will affect profit or loss

(e)   For **fair value hedges, gains or losses** on the **hedging instrument and the hedged item**.

(f)   The **ineffectiveness recognised in profit or loss** arising from cash flow hedges and net investments in foreign operations.

Disclosures must be made relating to **fair value**:

(a)   **By class** in a way that allows comparison to balance sheet value. (Financial assets and liabilities may only be offset to the extent that their carrying amounts are offset in the balance sheet.)

(b)   The **methods and assumptions** used, for example by reference to an active market, and any change in these assumptions. If the market for a financial instrument is not active, a valuation technique, as per FRS 26, must be used. There could be a difference between the fair value at initial recognition and the amount that would be determined using the valuation technique. The accounting policy for recognising that difference in profit or loss, the aggregate difference yet to be recognised in profit or loss at the beginning and end of the period and a reconciliation of the changes in the balance of this difference, should be disclosed, as in the following example.

6.3.4 Example: Fair value disclosures

Note: This is for illustrative purposes only – you will not need to prepare such a statement.

Background

On 1 January 20X1 an entity purchases for £15 million financial assets that are not traded in an active market. The entity has only one class of such financial assets.

The transaction price of £15 million is the fair value at initial recognition.

After initial recognition, the entity will apply a valuation technique to establish the financial assets fair value. This valuation technique includes variables other than data from observable markets.

At initial recognition, the same valuation technique would have resulted in an amount of £14 million, which differs from fair value by £1 million.

The entity has existing differences of £5 million at 1 January 20X1.

Application of requirements

The entity's 20X2 disclosure would include the following:

Accounting policies

The entity uses the following valuation technique to determine the fair value of financial instruments that are not traded in an active market: [description of technique, not included in this example]. Differences may arise between the fair value at initial recognition (which, in accordance with FRS 26, is generally the transaction price) and the amount determined at initial recognition using the valuation technique. Any such differences are [description of the entity's accounting policy].

In the notes to the financial statements

As discussed in note X, the entity uses [name of valuation technique]to measure the fair value of the following financial instruments that are not traded in an active market. However, in accordance with IAS 39, the fair value of an instrument at inception is generally the transaction price. If the transaction price differs from the amount determined at inception using the valuation technique, that difference is [description of the entity's accounting policy]. The differences yet to be recognised in profit or loss are as follows:

	31 Dec 20X2 £m	31 Dec 20X1 £m
Balance at beginning of year	5.3	5.0
New transactions		1.0
Amounts recognised in profit or loss during the year	(0.7)	(0.8)
Other increases		0.2
Other decreases	(0.1)	(0.1)
Balance at end of year	4.5	5.3

Disclosures of fair value are **not required** if carrying value is a reasonable approximation to fair value, or if fair value cannot be measured reliably.

6.4 Nature and extent of risks arising from financial instruments

In undertaking transactions in financial instruments, an entity may assume or transfer to another party one or more of **different types of financial risk** as defined below. The disclosures required by the standard show the extent to which an entity is exposed to these different types of risk, relating to both recognised and unrecognised financial instruments.

Credit risk	The risk that one party to a financial instrument will cause a financial loss for the other party by failing to discharge an obligation.
Currency risk	The risk that the fair value or future cash flows of a financial instrument will fluctuate because of changes in foreign exchange rates.
Interest rate risk	The risk that the fair value or future cash flows of a financial instrument will fluctuate because of changes in market interest rates.
Liquidity risk	The risk that an entity will encounter difficulty in meeting obligations associated with financial liabilities.
Loans payable	Loans payable are financial liabilities, other than short-term trade payables on normal credit terms.
Market risk	The risk that the fair value or future cash flows of a financial instrument will fluctuate because of changes in market prices. Market risk comprises three types of risk: **currency risk**, **interest rate risk** and **other price risk**.
Other price risk	The risk that the fair value or future cash flows of a financial instrument will fluctuate because of changes in market prices (other than those arising from **interest rate risk** or **currency risk**), whether those changes are caused by factors specific to the individual financial instrument or its issuer, or factors affecting all similar financial instruments traded in the market.
Past due	A financial asset is past due when a counterparty has failed to make a payment when contractually due.

6.4.1 Qualitative disclosures

For each type of risk arising from financial instruments, an entity must disclose:

(a)   The **exposures to risk** and how they arise

(b)   Its **objectives, policies and processes for managing the risk** and the methods used to measure the risk

(c)   Any **changes** in (a) or (b) from the previous period.

6.4.2 Quantitative disclosures

For each financial instrument risk, **summary quantitative data** about risk exposure must be disclosed. This should be based on the information provided internally to key management personnel. More information should be provided if this is unrepresentative.

Information about **credit risk** must be disclosed by class of financial instrument:

(a)   Maximum exposure at the balance sheet date

(b)   Any collateral pledged as security

(c)   Overdue debts

(d)   Impaired assets

(e)   Financial assets that are past due or impaired, giving an age analysis and a description of collateral held by the entity as security.

(f)   Collateral and other credit enhancements obtained, including the nature and carrying amount of the assets and policy for disposing of assets not readily convertible into cash.

For **liquidity risk** entities must disclose:

(a) A maturity analysis of financial liabilities

(b) A description of the way risk is managed.

Disclosures required in connection with **market risk** are:

(a) Sensitivity analysis, showing the effects on profit or loss of changes in each market risk

(b) If the sensitivity analysis reflects interdependencies between risk variables, such as interest rates and exchange rates the method, assumptions and limitations must be disclosed.

Chapter Roundup

- Financial instruments can be very complex, particularly **derivative instruments**, although **primary instruments** are more straightforward.

- The important definitions to learn are:

  - **Financial asset**
  - **Financial liability**
  - **Equity instrument**

- Financial instruments must be classified as **liabilities** or **equity** according to their **substance**.

- The critical feature of a financial liability is the **contractual obligation to deliver cash** or another financial instrument.

- **Compound instruments** are split into **equity** and **liability** components and presented in the balance sheet accordingly.

- **FRS 26** *Financial instruments: measurement* has been amended to include the recognition and derecognition rules of IAS 39.

- **Financial assets** should **initially** be measured at **cost = fair value**.

- Subsequently they should be **re-measured to fair value** except for

  (a) Loans and receivables not held for trading
  (b) Other **held-to-maturity investments**
  (c) **Financial assets** whose value **cannot be reliably measured**

- **Hedging** is allowed in certain strictly defined circumstances.

- **FRS 29** Specifies the **disclosures** required for financial instruments. The standard requires quantitative and qualitative disclosures about exposure to risks arising from financial instruments and specifies minimum disclosures about credit risk, liquidity risk and market risk.

Quick Quiz

1   Which three issues are dealt with by FRS 25?

2   Define the following.

   (a)   Financial asset
   (b)   Financial liability
   (c)   Equity instrument

3   What items are *not* financial instruments according to FRS 25?

4   What is the critical feature used to identify a financial liability?

5   How should compound instruments be classified?

6   Define interest rate risk and credit risk.

7   When should a financial asset be de-recognised?

8   How are financial instruments initially measured?

9   What is hedging?

10   Name the three types of hedging relationship identified by FRS 26.

Answers to quick quiz

1   Classification; presentation and offsetting. Disclosure is now dealt with by FRS 29.

2   See Key Terms, Section 1.1

3   Physical assets; prepaid expenses; non-contractual assets or liabilities; contractual rights not involving transfer of assets

4   The contractual obligation to deliver cash or another financial asset to the holder

5   By calculating the present value of the liability component and then deducting this from the instrument as a whole to leave a residual value for the equity component.

6   See Key Terms, Section 6.4

7   Financial assets should be derecognised when the rights to the cash flows from the asset expire or where substantially all the risks and rewards of ownership are transferred to another party.

8   At cost

9   See Key Terms, Section 5.1

10   Fair value hedge; cash flow hedge; hedge of a net investment in a foreign operation

Now try the questions below from the Exam Question Bank			
Number	**Level**	**Marks**	**Time**
Q8	Introductory	n/a	n/a
Q9	Introductory	n/a	n/a

Provisions, contingencies and events after the balance sheet date

Topic list	Syllabus reference
1 FRS 21 *Events after the balance sheet date*	C8
2 FRS 12 *Provisions, contingent liabilities and contingent assets*	C8
3 FRED 39 Amendment	C8, F2

Introduction

FRS 21 is a standard based on IAS 10 *Events after the balance sheet date*. Note the treatment of dividends. **Provisions** are an important area, covered by FRS 12 to which amendments are proposed.

Study guide

		Intellectual level
C8	**Provisions, contingencies, events after the balance sheet date**	
(a)	Apply and discuss the recognition, derecognition and measurement of provisions, contingent liabilities and contingent assets, including environmental provisions	3
(b)	Apply and discuss the accrual of restructuring provisions	3
(c)	Apply and discuss accounting for events after the balance sheet date	3
(d)	Determine going concern issues arising after the balance sheet date	3
F2	**Proposed changes to accounting standards**	
(a)	Identify the issues and deficiencies which have led to a proposed change to an accounting standard	2
(b)	Apply and discuss the implications of a proposed change to an accounting standard on the performance and balance sheet of an entity	2

Exam guide

These standards are likely to be tested as part of a scenario question. You may also be asked to advise the directors on the implications for the financial statements of the changes proposed in FRED 39.

1 FRS 21 Events after the balance sheet date

FAST FORWARD

> FRS 21 defines *events after the balance sheet date*.

The financial statements are significant indicators of a company's success or failure. It is important, therefore, that they include all the information necessary for an understanding of the company's position.

FRS 21 *Events after the balance sheet date* and FRS 12 *Provisions, contingent liabilities and contingent assets* both require the provision of additional information in order to facilitate such an understanding. FRS 21 deals with events *after* the balance sheet date which may affect the position at the balance sheet date. FRS 12 *Provisions, contingent liabilities and contingent assets* deals with matters which are **uncertain** at the balance sheet date.

The standard gives the following definition.

Key terms

Events after the balance sheet date are those events, both favourable and unfavourable, that occur between the balance sheet date and the date on which the financial statements are authorised for issue. Two types of events can be identified.

- Those that provide further evidence of conditions that existed at the balance sheet date (adjusting events after the balance sheet date)

- Those that are indicative of conditions that arose after the balance sheet date (non-adjusting events after the balance sheet date)
                                                                                                    (FRS 21)

1.1 Events after the balance sheet date

Between the balance sheet date and the date the financial statements are authorised (ie for issue outside the organisation), events may occur which show that assets and liabilities at the balance sheet date should be adjusted, or that disclosure of such events should be given.

1.2 Events requiring adjustment

The standard requires entities to **adjust** the amounts recognised in its financial statements to reflect adjusting events after the balance sheet date.

FAST FORWARD

> **Events** after the balance sheet date which provide **additional evidence** of conditions existing at the balance sheet date, will cause **adjustments** to be made to the assets and liabilities in the financial statements.

An **example** of additional evidence which becomes available after the balance sheet date is where a **customer goes bankrupt, thus confirming that the trade account receivable balance at the year end is uncollectable.**

FAST FORWARD

> Where events indicate that the **going concern concept** is no longer appropriate then the **accounts may have to be restated** on a break-up basis.

In relation to going concern, the standard states that, where operating results and the financial position have deteriorated after the balance sheet date, it may be necessary to reconsider whether the going concern assumption is appropriate in the preparation of the financial statements.

1.3 Examples of adjusting events

The following examples of adjusting events are given in FRS 21.

(a) The resolution after the balance sheet date of a court case giving rise to a liability

(b) Evidence of impairment of assets, such as news that a major customer is going into liquidation, or the sale of inventories (stocks) below cost

(c) Determination of the price of assets bought or sold before the balance sheet date

(d) Determination of employee bonuses or profit shares

(e) Discovery of fraud or errors showing that the financial statements were incorrect

1.4 Events not requiring adjustment

FAST FORWARD

> **Events** which **do not affect the situation at the balance sheet date** should **not be adjusted for**, but should be **disclosed** in the financial statements.

The standard then looks at events which do **not** require adjustment. Entities **must not adjust** the amounts recognised in their financial statements to reflect these non-adjusting events.

The **example** given by the standard of such an event is where the **value of an investment falls between the balance sheet date and the date the financial statements are authorised** for issue. The fall in value represents circumstances during the current period, not conditions existing at the previous balance sheet date, so it is not appropriate to adjust the value of the investment in the financial statements. Disclosure is an aid to users, however, indicating 'unusual changes' in the state of assets and liabilities after the balance sheet date.

The rule for **disclosure** of events occurring after the balance sheet date which relate to conditions that arose after that date, is that disclosure should be made if non-disclosure would hinder the user's ability to made **proper evaluations** and decision based on the financial statements. An example might be the acquisition of another business.

1.5 Examples of non-adjusting events

The following examples of non-adjusting events are given in FRS 21.

     (a)   Major business combination

     (b)   Announcement of a plan to discontinue an operation

     (c)   Major purchases and disposals of assets

     (d)   Destruction of a major production plant by a fire

     (e)   Announcement of or beginning of major restructuring

     (f)   Major share transactions

     (g)   Abnormally large changes in asset prices or foreign exchange rates

     (h)   Changes in tax rates having a significant effect on current and deferred tax assets and liabilities

     (i)   Entering into significant guarantees

     (j)   Commencing major litigation arising out of events after the balance sheet date

1.6 Dividends

Equity dividends proposed or declared after the balance sheet date should not be recognised as a liability at the balance sheet date. Such dividends are disclosed in the notes to the financial statements.

1.7 Disclosures

The following **disclosure requirements** are given **for events** which occur after the balance sheet date which do *not* require adjustment. If disclosure of events occurring after the balance sheet date is required, the following information should be provided.

     (a)   The nature of the event
     (b)   An estimate of the financial effect, or a statement that such an estimate cannot be made

Question   Adjustment

State whether the following events occurring after the balance sheet date require an adjustment to the assets and liabilities of the financial statements.

(a)   Purchase of an investment
(b)   A change in the rate of corporate tax, applicable to the previous year
(c)   An increase in pension benefits
(d)   Losses due to fire
(e)   A bad debt suddenly being paid
(f)   The receipt of proceeds of sales or other evidence concerning the net realisable value of inventory
(g)   A sudden decline in the value of property held as a long-term asset

Answer

(b), (e) and (f) are adjusting; the others are non-adjusting.

Question

Events

Fabricators Ltd, an engineering company, makes up its financial statements to 31 March in each year. The financial statements for the year ended 31 March 20X1 showed a turnover of £3m and trading profit of £400,000.

Before approval of the financial statements by the board of directors on 30 June 20X1 the following events took place.

(a)   The financial statements of Patchup Ltd for the year ended 28 February 20X1 were received which indicated a permanent decline in that company's financial position. Fabricators Ltd had bought shares in Patchup Ltd some years ago and this purchase was included in unquoted investments at its cost of £100,000. The financial statements received indicated that this investment was now worth only £50,000.

(b)   There was a fire at the company's warehouse on 30 April 20X1 when stock to the value of £500,000 was destroyed. It transpired that the stock in the warehouse was under-insured by some 50%.

(c)   It was announced on 1 June 20X1 that the company's design for tank cleaning equipment had been approved by the major oil companies and this could result in an increase in the annual turnover of some £1m with a relative effect on profits.

Answer

The treatment of the events arising in the case of Fabricators Ltd would be as follows.

(a)   The fall in value of the investment in Patchup Ltd has arisen over the previous year and that company's financial accounts for the year to 28 February 20X1 provide additional evidence of conditions that existed at the balance sheet date. The loss of £50,000 is material in terms of the trading profit figure and, as an adjusting event, should be reflected in the financial statements of Fabricators Ltd as an exceptional item in accordance with FRS 3.

(b)   The destruction of stock by fire on 30 April (one month after the balance sheet date) must be considered to be a non-adjusting event (ie this is 'a new condition which did not exist at the balance sheet date'). Since the loss is material, being £250,000, it should be disclosed by way of a note to the accounts. The note should describe the nature of the event and an estimate of its financial effect. Non-reporting of this event would prevent users of the financial statements from reaching a proper understanding of the financial position.

(c)   The approval on 1 June of the company's design for tank cleaning equipment creates a new condition which did not exist at the balance sheet date. This is, therefore, a non-adjusting event and if it is of such material significance that non-reporting would prevent a proper understanding of the financial position it should be disclosed by way of note. In this instance non-disclosure should not prevent a proper understanding of the financial position and disclosure by note may be unnecessary.

2 FRS 12 Provisions, contingent liabilities and contingent assets

Under FRS 12, a **provision** should be recognised

- When an entity has a **present obligation**, legal or constructive
- It is probable that a **transfer of economic benefits** will be required to settle it
- A **reliable estimate** can be made of its amount

As we have seen with regard to post balance sheet events, financial statements must include **all the information necessary for an understanding of the company's financial position**. Provisions, contingent liabilities and contingent assets are 'uncertainties' that must be accounted for consistently if are to achieve this understanding.

2.1 Objective

FRS 12 *Provisions, contingent liabilities and contingent assets* aims to ensure that appropriate **recognition criteria** and **measurement bases** are applied to provisions, contingent liabilities and contingent assets and that **sufficient information** is disclosed in the **notes** to the financial statements to enable users to understand their nature, timing and amount.

2.2 Provisions

You will be familiar with provisions for depreciation and doubtful debts from your earlier studies. The sorts of provisions addressed by FRS 12 are, however, rather different.

Before FRS 12, there was no accounting standard dealing with provisions. Companies wanting to show their results in the most favourable light used to make large **'one off' provisions** in years where a high level of underlying profits was generated. These provisions, often known as **'big bath'** provisions, were then available to shield expenditure in future years when perhaps the underlying profits were not as good.

In other words, **provisions were used for profit smoothing**. Profit smoothing is misleading.

Exam focus point

The key aim of FRS 12 is to ensure that provisions are made only where there are valid grounds for them.

FRS 12 views a provision as a **liability**.

Key terms

A **provision** is a **liability** of uncertain timing or amount.

A **liability** is an obligation of an entity to transfer economic benefits as a result of past transactions or events.   *(FRS 12)*

The FRS distinguishes provisions from other liabilities such as trade creditors and accruals. This is on the basis that for a provision there is **uncertainty** about the timing or amount of the future expenditure. Whilst uncertainty is clearly present in the case of certain accruals the uncertainty is generally much less than for provisions.

2.3 Recognition

FRS 12 states that a provision should be **recognised** as a liability in the financial statements when:

- An entity has a **present obligation** (legal or constructive) as a result of a past event
- It is probable that a **transfer of economic benefits** will be required to settle the obligation
- A **reliable estimate** can be made of the obligation

2.4 Meaning of obligation

It is fairly clear what a legal obligation is. However, you may not know what a **constructive obligation** is.

Key terms

FRS 12 defines a **constructive obligation** as

'An obligation that derives from an entity's actions where:

- by an established pattern of past practice, published policies or a sufficiently specific current statement the entity has indicated to other parties that it will accept certain responsibilities; and

- as a result, the entity has created a valid expectation on the part of those other parties that it will discharge those responsibilities.

Question

Recognising a provision

In which of the following circumstances might a provision be recognised?

(a)   On 13 December 20X9 the board of an entity decided to close down a division. The accounting date of the company is 31 December. Before 31 December 20X9 the decision was not communicated to any of those affected and no other steps were taken to implement the decision.

(b)   The board agreed a detailed closure plan on 20 December 20X9 and details were given to customers and employees.

(c)   A company is obliged to incur clean up costs for environmental damage (that has already been caused).

(d)   A company intends to carry out future expenditure to operate in a particular way in the future.

Answer

(a)   No provision would be recognised as the decision has not been communicated.

(b)   A provision would be made in the 20X9 financial statements.

(c)   A provision for such costs is appropriate.

(d)   No present obligation exists and under FRS 12 no provision would be appropriate. This is because the entity could avoid the future expenditure by its future actions, maybe by changing its method of operation.

2.4.1 Probable transfer of economic benefits

For the purpose of the FRS, a transfer of economic benefits is regarded as **'probable'** if the event is **more likely than not** to occur. This appears to indicate a probability of more than 50%. However, the standard makes it clear that where there is a number of similar obligations the probability should be based on considering the population as a whole, rather than one single item.

2.4.2 Example: transfer of economic benefits

If a company has entered into a warranty obligation then the probability of transfer of economic benefits may well be extremely small in respect of one specific item. However, when considering the population as a whole the probability of some transfer of economic benefits is quite likely to be much higher. If there is a **greater than 50% probability** of some transfer of economic benefits then a **provision** should be made for the **expected amount**.

2.4.3 Measurement of provisions

Important

> The amount recognised as a provision should be the best estimate of the expenditure required to settle the present obligation at the balance sheet date.

The estimates will be determined by the **judgement** of the entity's management supplemented by the experience of similar transactions.

Allowance is made for **uncertainty**. Where the provision being measured involves a large population of items, the obligation is estimated by weighting all possible outcomes by their discounted probabilities, ie **expected value**.

Question
Warranty

Parker plc sells goods with a warranty under which customers are covered for the cost of repairs of any manufacturing defect that becomes apparent within the first six months of purchase. The company's past experience and future expectations indicate the following pattern of likely repairs.

% of goods sold	Defects	Cost of repairs £m
75	None	–
20	Minor	1.0
5	Major	4.0

What is the expected cost of repairs?

Answer

The cost is found using 'expected values' (75% × £nil) + (20% × £1.0m) + (5% × £4.0m) = £400,000.

Where the effect of the **time value of money** is material, the amount of a provision should be the **present value** of the expenditure required to settle the obligation. An appropriate **discount** rate should be used.

The discount rate should be a **pre-tax rate** that reflects current market assessments of the time value of money. **The discount rate(s) should not reflect risks for which future cash flow estimates have been adjusted.**

The **unwinding of the discount** should be included as a financial item adjacent to interest but it should be **shown separately** from other interest either on the face of the profit and loss account or in a note.

2.4.4 Future events

Future events which are reasonably expected to occur (eg new legislation, changes in technology) may affect the amount required to settle the entity's obligation and should be taken into account.

2.4.5 Expected disposal of assets

Gains from the expected disposal of assets should not be taken into account in measuring a provision.

2.4.6 Reimbursements

Some or all of the expenditure needed to settle a provision may be expected to be recovered form a third party. If so, the **reimbursement should be recognised only when it is virtually certain that reimbursement will be received if the entity settles the obligation.**

- The reimbursement should be treated as a separate asset, and the amount recognised should not be greater than the provision itself.

- The provision and the amount recognised for reimbursement may be netted off in the profit and loss account.

2.4.7 Changes in provisions

Provisions should be renewed at each balance sheet date and adjusted to reflect the current best estimate. If it is no longer probable that a transfer of economic benefits will be required to settle the obligation, the provision should be reversed.

2.4.8 Use of provisions

A provision should be used only for expenditures for which the provision was originally recognised. Setting expenditures against a provision that was originally recognised for another purpose would conceal the impact of two different events.

2.4.9 Recognising an asset when recognising a provision

Normally the setting up of a provision should be charged immediately to the profit and loss account. But **if the incurring of the present obligation recognised as a provision gives access to future economic benefits an asset should be recognised.**

2.4.10 Example: Recognising an asset

An obligation for decommissioning costs is incurred by commissioning an oil rig. At the same time, the commissioning gives access to oil reserves over the years of the oil rig's operation. Therefore an asset representing future access to oil reserves is recognised at the same time as the provision for decommissioning costs.

2.4.11 Future operating losses

Provisions should not be recognised for future operating losses. They do not meet the definition of a liability and the general recognition criteria set out in the standard.

2.4.12 Onerous contracts

If an entity has a contract that is onerous, the present obligation under the contract **should be recognised and measured** as a provision. An example might be vacant leasehold property.

Key term

> An **onerous contract** is a contract entered into with another party under which the unavoidable costs of fulfilling the terms of the contract exceed any revenues expected to be received from the goods or services supplied or purchased directly or indirectly under the contract and where the entity would have to compensate the other party if it did not fulfil the terms of the contract.

2.4.13 Examples of possible provisions

It is easier to see what FRS 12 is driving at if you look at examples of those items which are possible provisions under this standard. Some of these we have already touched on.

(a) **Warranties**. These are argued to be genuine provisions as on past experience it is probable, ie more likely than not, that some claims will emerge. The provision must be estimated, however, on the basis of the class as a whole and not on individual claims. There is a clear legal obligation in this case.

229

(b)   **Major repairs**. In the past it has been quite popular for companies to provide for expenditure on a major overhaul to be accrued gradually over the intervening years between overhauls. Under FRS 12 this will no longer be possible as FRS 12 would argue that this is a mere intention to carry out repairs, not an obligation. The entity can always sell the asset in the meantime. The only solution is to treat major assets such as aircraft, ships, furnaces etc as a series of smaller assets where each part is depreciated over shorter lives. Thus any major overhaul may be argued to be replacement and therefore capital rather than revenue expenditure.

(c)   **Self insurance**. A number of companies have created a provision for self insurance based on the expected cost of making good fire damage etc instead of paying premiums to an insurance company. Under FRS 12 this provision would no longer be justifiable as the entity has no obligation until a fire or accident occurs. No obligation exists until that time.

(d)   **Environmental contamination**. If the company has an environment policy such that other parties would expect the company to clean up any contamination or if the company has broken current environmental legislation then a provision for environmental damage must be made.

(e)   **Decommissioning or abandonment costs**. When an oil company initially purchases an oilfield it is put under a legal obligation to decommission the site at the end of its life. Prior to FRS 12 most oil companies applied the SORP on *Accounting for abandonment costs* published by the Oil Industry Accounting Committee and they built up the provision gradually over the field so that no one year would be unduly burdened with the cost.

FRS 12, however, insists that a legal obligation exists on the initial expenditure on the field and therefore a liability exists immediately. This would appear to result in a large charge to profit and loss in the first year of operation of the field. However, the FRS takes the view that the cost of purchasing the field in the first place is not only the cost of the field itself but also the costs of putting it right again. Thus all the costs of abandonment may be capitalised.

(f)   **Restructuring**. This is considered in detail below.

2.4.14 Provisions for restructuring

One of the main purposes of FRS 12 was to target abuses of provisions for restructuring. Accordingly, FRS 12 lays down **strict criteria** to determine when such a provision can be made.

Key term

FRS 12 defines a **restructuring** as:

A programme that is planned and is controlled by management and materially changes either:

* The scope of a business undertaken by an entity, or
* The manner in which that business is conducted.

The FRS gives the following **examples** of events that may fall under the definition of restructuring.

* The **sale or termination** of a line of business

* The **closure of business locations** in a country or region or the **relocation** of business activities from one country region to another

* **Changes in management structure**, for example, the elimination of a layer of management

* **Fundamental reorganisations** that have a material effect on the **nature and focus** of the entity's operations

The question is whether or not an entity has an obligation – legal or constructive – at the balance sheet date.

- An entity must have a **detailed formal plan** for the restructuring.
- It must have **raised a valid expectation** in those affected that it will carry out the restructuring by starting to implement that plan or announcing its main features to those affected by it

Important

> **A mere management decision is not normally sufficient**. Management decisions may sometimes trigger off recognition, but only if earlier events such as negotiations with employee representatives and other interested parties have been concluded subject only to management approval.

Where the restructuring involves the **sale of an operation** then FRS 12 states that no obligation arises until the entity has entered into a **binding sale agreement**. This is because until this has occurred the entity will be able to change its mind and withdraw from the sale even if its intentions have been announced publicly.

2.4.15 Costs to be included within a restructuring provision

The FRS states that a restructuring provision should include only the **direct expenditures** arising from the restructuring, which are those that are both:

- **Necessarily entailed** by the restructuring; and
- Not associated with the **ongoing activities** of the entity.

The following costs should specifically **not** be included within a restructuring provision.

- **Retraining** or relocating continuing staff
- **Marketing**
- **Investment in new systems** and distribution networks

2.4.16 Disclosure

Disclosures for provisions fall into two parts.

- Disclosure of details of the **change in carrying value** of a provision from the beginning to the end of the year
- Disclosure of the **background** to the making of the provision and the uncertainties affecting its outcome

2.5 Contingent liabilities

Now you understand provisions it will be easier to understand contingent assets and liabilities.

Key term

> FRS 12 defines a **contingent liability** as:
>
> - A possible obligation that arises from past events and whose existence will be confirmed only by the occurrence or non-occurrence of one or more uncertain future events not wholly within the entity's control; or
> - A present obligation that arises from past events but is not recognised because:
>   - It is not probable that a transfer of economic benefits will be required to settle the obligation; or
>   - The amount of the obligation cannot be measured with sufficient reliability.

As a rule of thumb, probable means more than 50% likely. **If an obligation is probable, it is not a contingent liability** – instead, a **provision is needed**.

2.5.1 Treatment of contingent liabilities

An entity **should not recognise a contingent asset or liability**, but they **should be disclosed**.

Contingent liabilities **should not be recognised in financial statements** but they **should be disclosed**. The required disclosures are:

- A brief description of the nature of the contingent liability
- An estimate of its financial effect
- An indication of the uncertainties that exist
- The possibility of any reimbursement

2.6 Contingent assets

Key term

FRS 12 defines a **contingent asset** as:

A possible asset that arises from past events and whose existence will be confirmed by the occurrence of one or more uncertain future events not wholly within the entity's control.

A **contingent asset must not be recognised**. Only when the realisation of the related economic benefits is **virtually certain** should recognition take place. At that point, **the asset is no longer a contingent asset!**

2.6.1 Disclosure: contingent liabilities

A **brief description** must be provided of all material contingent liabilities unless they are likely to be remote. In addition, provide

- An estimate of their **financial effect**
- Details of **any uncertainties**

2.6.2 Disclosure: contingent assets

Contingent assets must only be disclosed in the notes if they are **probable**. In that case a brief description of the contingent asset should be provided along with an estimate of its likely financial effect.

2.6.3 'Let out'

FRS 12 permits reporting entities to avoid disclosure requirements relating to provisions, contingent liabilities and contingent assets if they would be expected to **seriously prejudice** the position of the entity in dispute with other parties. However, this should only be employed in **extremely rare** cases. Details of the general nature of the provision/contingencies must still be provided, together with an explanation of why it has not been disclosed.

You must practise the questions below to get the hang of FRS 12. But first, study the flow chart, taken from FRS 12, which is a good summary of its requirements.

Exam focus point

If you learn this flow chart you should be able to deal with most of the questions you are likely to meet in the exam.

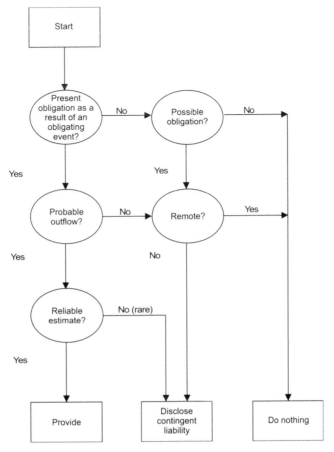

Question

Provide or not? (1)

During 20X0 Smack Ltd gives a guarantee of certain borrowings of Pony Ltd, whose financial condition at that time is sound. During 20X1, the financial condition of Pony Ltd deteriorates and at 30 June 20x1 Pony Ltd files for protection from its creditors.

What accounting treatment is required:

(a) At 31 December 20X0?
(b) At 31 December 20x1?

Answer

(a) At 31 December 20X0

There is a present obligation as a result of a past obligating event. The obligating event is the giving of the guarantee, which gives rise to a legal obligation. However, at 31 December 20X0 no transfer of economic benefits is probable in settlement of the obligation.

No provision is recognised. The guarantee is disclosed as a contingent liability unless the probability of any transfer is regarded as remote.

(b) At 31 December 20X1

As above, there is a present obligation as a result of a past obligating event, namely the giving of the guarantee.

At 31 December 20X1 it is probable that a transfer of economic events will be required to settle the obligation. A provision is therefore recognised for the best estimate of the obligation.

Question

Warren Ltd gives warranties at the time of sale to purchasers of its products. Under the terms of the warranty the manufacturer undertakes to make good, by repair or replacement, manufacturing defects that become apparent within a period of three years from the date of the sale. Should a provision be recognised?

Answer

Warren Ltd **cannot avoid** the cost of repairing or replacing all items of product that manifest manufacturing defects in respect of which warranties are given before the balance sheet date, and a provision for the cost of this should therefore be made.

Warren Ltd is obliged to repair or replace items that fail within the entire warranty period. Therefore, in respect of **this year's sales**, the obligation provided for at the balance sheet date should be the cost of making good items for which defects have been notified but not yet processed, **plus** an estimate of costs in respect of the other items sold for which there is sufficient evidence that manufacturing defects **will** manifest themselves during their remaining periods of warranty cover.

Question

After a wedding in 20X0 ten people died, possibly as a result of food poisoning from products sold by Callow Ltd. Legal proceedings are started seeking damages from Callow but it disputes liability. Up to the date of approval of the financial statements for the year to 31 December 20X0, Callow's lawyers advise that it is probable that it will not be found liable. However, when Callow prepares the financial statements for the year to 31 December 20X1 its lawyers advise that, owing to developments in the case, it is probable that it will be found liable.

What is the required accounting treatment:

(a)   At 31 December 20X0?

(b)   At 31 December 20X1?

Answer

(a)   *At 31 December 20X0*

On the basis of the evidence available when the financial statements were approved, there is no obligation as a result of past events. No provision is recognised. The matter is disclosed as a contingent liability unless the probability of any transfer is regarded as remote.

(b)   *At 31 December 20X1*

On the basis of the evidence available, there is a present obligation. A transfer of economic benefits in settlement is probable.

A provision is recognised for the best estimate of the amount needed to settle the present obligation.

2.7 Section summary

- The objective of FRS 12 is to ensure that **appropriate recognition criteria** and measurement bases are applied to **provisions and contingencies** and that **sufficient information** is disclosed.

- The FRS seeks to ensure that provisions are **only recognised** when a **measurable obligation** exists. It includes detailed rules that can be used to ascertain when an obligation exists and how to measure the obligation.

- The standard attempts to **eliminate** the **'profit smoothing'** which has gone on before it was issued.

3 FRED 39 Amendment

FAST FORWARD

FRED 29 proposes **amendments to FRS 12.**

- The standard would be re-named 'non-financial' liabilities and be extended to include all liabilities not covered by other standards.

- The terms contingent liability and contingent asset would be removed, and unconditional and conditional obligations introduced.

- Expected values would be used.

FRED 39 *Amendment to FRS 12 Provisions, contingent liabilities and contingent assets and Amendment to FRS 17 Retirement benefits* was issued in July 2005. It is part of a package of UK FREDs reflecting outputs from Phases I and II of the IASB project on business combinations. It is based on the IASB's proposals to amend IAS 37, which shares the same title and is nearly identical to FRS 12.

The most obvious change is that the term 'provision' is no longer used; instead it is proposed that the term 'non-financial liability' is used.

Key term

A **non-financial liability** is a liability other than a financial liability as defined in FRS 25 *Financial instruments: presentation.*

This section outlines the main changes from FRS 12.

3.1 Scope and terminology

FRS 12 defines a **provision** as a **liability of uncertain timing or amount.** FRED 39 does not use the term provision, but proposes the use of the term 'non-financial liability' as defined above. This includes items previously described as provisions, but also all other liabilities not covered by other accounting standards.

3.2 Contingent liabilities

3.2.1 FRS 12 treatment

FRS 12 defines a contingent liability **as a possible obligation or a present obligation that is not recognised.** A contingent liability that is a present obligation is not recognised either because it is not probable that an outflow of resources will be required to settle the obligation or because the amount of the obligation cannot be measured with sufficient reliability. The Standard does not permit contingent liabilities to be recognised but requires them to be disclosed, unless the possibility of any outflow of economic resources in settlement of the contingent liability is remote.

3.2.2 FRED 39 proposals

FRED 39 proposes changing the treatment as follows.

(a)   The term 'contingent liability' will be **omitted.**

(b)   The term 'contingency' will be used to refer to uncertainty about the **amount that will be required to settle a liability** rather than uncertainty about whether a liability exists.

(c)   The FRED specifies that a **liability** for which the settlement amount is contingent on one or more uncertain future events is **recognised independently of the probability** that the uncertain future event(s) will occur (or fail to occur).

The purpose of these amendments is twofold.

(a)   To clarify that **only present obligations** (rather than possible obligations) of an entity **give rise to liabilities** and that liabilities arise from **unconditional obligations**.

(b)   To require **uncertainty about future events** that affect the amount that will be required to settle a liability to be **reflected in the measurement of the liability**.

3.3 Contingent assets

3.3.1 FRS 12 treatment

FRS 12 defines a contingent asset as a **possible asset. It does not permit contingent assets to be recognised**, but requires them to be disclosed if an inflow of economic benefits is probable.

3.3.2 FRED 39 proposals

FRED 39 proposes changing the treatment as follows.

(a)   The **term 'contingent asset'** would be **eliminated**.

(b)   The term 'contingency' would be used to refer to **uncertainty about the amount** of the future economic benefits embodied in an asset, **rather than uncertainty** about **whether an asset exists**.

The purpose of this amendment is to clarify that only resources currently controlled by the entity as a result of a past transaction or event (rather than possible assets) give rise to assets, and that assets arise from unconditional rights.

3.4 Constructive obligations

3.4.1 FRS 12 treatment

FRS 12 defines a constructive obligation as an obligation that derives from an entity's actions when the entity has (a) indicated to other parties that it will accept particular responsibilities and (b) as a result has created a valid expectation on the part of those other parties that it will discharge those responsibilities.

3.4.2 FRED 39 proposals

(a)   The **definition** of a constructive obligation will be **amended** to clarify that the actions of an entity must result in **other parties having a valid expectation** that they can reasonably rely on the entity to discharge its responsibilities.

(b)   **Additional guidance** will be provided to help determine whether an entity has incurred a constructive obligation.

3.5 Probability recognition criterion

FRED 39 proposes **omitting the probability recognition** criterion (currently in FRS 12) from the Standard because, in all cases, an unconditional obligation satisfies the criterion. Therefore, **items that satisfy the definition of a liability are recognised unless they cannot be measured reliably.**

3.5.1 Rationale for proposed treatment

The Basis for Conclusions on the FRED emphasises that the probability recognition criterion is used in the IASB's *Framework* to determine whether it is probable that settlement of an item that has previously been determined to be a liability will require an outflow of economic benefits from the entity. In other words, the *Framework* requires an entity to determine **whether a liability exists** before considering whether that liability should be recognised. The Basis notes that in many cases, although there may be uncertainty about the amount and timing of the resources that will be required to settle a liability, there is **little or no uncertainty** that settlement will require *some* outflow of resources.

3.5.2 Example: product warranty

In the case of a product warranty, the question is not whether it is probable that the entity will be required to repair or replace the product. Rather, the question is whether the entity's *unconditional* obligation to provide warranty coverage for the duration of the warranty (ie to stand ready to honour warranty claims) will probably result in an outflow of economic benefits.

3.6 Measurement

The conditional obligation is measured as the **amount the entity would rationally pay to settle the obligation at the balance sheet date** or to transfer it to a third party. **Expected values** would be used, whether measuring a single obligation or a population of items.

3.7 Reimbursement

FRS 12 states that when expenditure required to settle a provision is expected to be reimbursed by another party, the reimbursement should be **recognised when it is virtually certain** that the reimbursement will be received. Consistently with the revised analysis of a contingent asset, FRED 39 proposes that **if an entity has an unconditional right to receive reimbursement, that right should be recognised as an asset if it can be measured reliably.**

3.8 Onerous contracts

FRED 39 provides additional recognition guidance relating to onerous contracts.

3.9 Restructuring provisions

3.9.1 FRS 12 treatment

FRS 12 states that an entity that (a) has a detailed formal plan for restructuring and (b) has raised a valid expectation in those affected that it will carry out the restructuring has a **constructive obligation**. Therefore, it **recognises a provision** for the direct expenditures arising from the restructuring.

3.9.2 FRED 39 proposals

FRED 39 proposes the following changes.

(a) The application guidance will be revised to specify that a non-financial liability for a cost associated with a restructuring is **recognised only when the definition of a liability has been satisfied for that cost**. Accordingly, a cost associated with a restructuring is recognised as a liability on the same basis as if that cost arose independently of a restructuring.

(b) **More specific guidance** will be given for costs associated with a restructuring.

3.10 Example of change from FRS 12

A entity is being sued for damages of £10 million. Legal proceedings have started, but the entity disputes liability. The entity estimates that it has a 20 per cent chance of losing the case. Under FRS 12, the entity would disclose a contingent liability in the notes to the accounts. Under the proposals in FRED 39, the entity has an unconditional obligation to stand ready to pay the damages if awarded. In this case, it would recognise a non-financial liability of £2 million.

Question   FRED 39

Shortly before 31 December 20X0, a patient dies in a hospital as a result of a mistake made during an operation. The hospital is aware that a mistake occurred. In these circumstances, the hospital's past experiences and lawyer's advice indicate that it is highly likely that the patient's relatives will start legal proceedings and, if the matter comes to court, that the hospital will be found guilty of negligence.

At the time that the financial statements are authorised for issue in early 20X1, the hospital has not received notice of legal proceedings against it.

Explain the accounting treatment required, in terms of recognition or otherwise and measurement.

Answer

There is a present obligation as a result of a past event, this being the operation in which negligence occurred. Accordingly, a non-financial liability is recognised.

Measurement of the liability reflects the likelihood that the hospital will be required to pay compensation because of the mistake, and the amount and timing of that compensation.

Chapter Roundup

- **FRS 21** defines *events after the balance sheet date.*

- **Events** after the balance sheet date which provide **additional evidence** of conditions existing at the balance sheet date, will cause **adjustments** to be made to the assets and liabilities in the financial statements.

- **Events** which **do not affect the situation at the balance sheet date** should **not be adjusted for**, but should be **disclosed** in the financial statements.

- Where events indicate that the **going concern concept** is no longer appropriate then the **accounts may have to be restated** on a break-up basis.

- Under FRS 12, a **provision** should be recognised
    - When an entity has a **present obligation**, legal or constructive
    - It is probable that a **transfer of economic benefits** will be required to settle it
    - A **reliable estimate** can be made of its amount

- An entity **should not recognise a contingent asset or liability**, but they **should be disclosed.**

- **FRED 29** proposes **amendments to FRS 12**.
    - The standard would be re-named 'non-financial' liabilities and be extended to include all liabilities not covered by other standards.
    - The terms contingent liability and contingent asset would be removed, and unconditional and conditional obligations introduced.
    - Expected values would be used.

Quick Quiz

1   Dividends declared after the balance sheet date are a liability under FRS 21.

    True   ☐

    False   ☐

2   FRS 12 requires that material contingent assets and liabilities, existing at the balance sheet date, should be treated as follows.

    A   Contingent assets and contingent liabilities must always be disclosed in the financial statements.

    B   Contingent assets must always be accrued and contingent liabilities must always be disclosed in the financial statements.

    C   Contingent liabilities must always be either accrued or disclosed and contingent assets must always be disclosed in the financial statements.

    D   Contingent liabilities must always be disclosed (unless remote) and contingent assets must sometimes be disclosed in the financial statements.

3   Castigliano plc has received a claim of £100,000 from one of its customers for defective yarn, which was sold in the year. The customer's claim is bona fide and Castigliano's solicitors have advised that it is probable that the claim will be successful.

Catigliano has insured itself against such a risk and the insurance company has agreed to reimburse Castigliano £80,000 of the cost. How should these transactions be represented in the balance sheet and profit and loss account?

4   How is the 'conditional obligation' measured under FRED 39?

Answers to Quick Quiz

1   False. Such dividends are disclosed in the notes.

2   D   Contingent liabilities must be disclosed.

Contingent assets are only disclosed if they are probable, but not virtually certain.

3   FRS 12 requires the reimbursement to be shown as a separate asset in the balance sheet. In the profit and loss account the expense relating to the provision may be presented net of the amount recognised for a reimbursement.

Therefore the most appropriate treatment would be

Balance sheet	P&L
Asset of £80,000	Net expense of
Provision	£20,000

4   At the amount the entity would rationally pay to settle the obligation at the balance sheet date or transfer it to a third party.

Now try the questions below from the Exam Question Bank

Number	Level	Marks	Time
Q10	Introductory	n/a	n/a

BPP)))
LEARNING MEDIA

Leases

10

Topic list	Syllabus reference
1 Forms of lease	C4
2 Lessee accounting	C4
3 Lessor accounting	C4
4 Criticism	C4

Introduction

Leasing transactions are extremely common in business and you will often come across them in both your business and personal capacity. You should be familiar with the more straightforward aspects of this topic from your earlier studies. Leasing is strongly associated with **off balance sheet finance** and SSAP 21 interacts with FRS 5 in **sale and leaseback transactions**.

Study guide

		Intellectual level
C4	**Leases**	
(a)	Apply and discuss the classification of leases and accounting by lessors and lessees	3
(b)	Apply and discuss the accounting for sale and leaseback transactions	3

Exam guide

As you can see from the Study Guide and Pilot paper, the emphasis is on sale and leaseback transactions or revenue recognition aspects rather than the mechanics of lease accounting.

1 Forms of lease

You should know the distinction between finance leases and operating leases from your earlier studies. Look back to your study material if anything in this summary is unfamiliar.

Knowledge brought forward from earlier studies

Finance lease

- Transfers substantially all the risks and rewards of ownership of an asset to the lessee

- Presumed if at the inception of a lease the PV of the minimum lease payments $\geq$ 90% of the FV of leased asset

- *PV*: calculate using the interest rate implicit in the lease

- The minimum lease payments are the minimum payments over the remaining part of the lease term (except charges for services and taxes to be paid by the lessor) *and*

    - (Lessee) any residual amounts guaranteed by him, *or*
    - (Lessor) any residual amounts guaranteed by the lessee or by an independent third party

- *Lease term*: the period for which the lessee has contracted to lease the asset (primary *and* secondary periods)

Operating lease

A lease other than a finance lease.

2 Lessee accounting

2.1 Finance leases

From the lessee's point of view there are two main **accounting problems**.

- Should the assets be **capitalised** as if it had been purchased?
- How should the **lease charge** allocated between different accounting periods?

2.1.1 SSAP 21 requirements

SSAP 21's requirements are not as tricky as they seem at first reading. You should understand the distinction between:

- **Finance leases**
- **Operating leases**

(a) A finance lease should be recorded in the balance sheet of a lessee as an asset and as an obligation to pay future rentals. At the inception of the lease the sum to be recorded both as an asset and as a liability should be the **present value of the minimum lease payments**, derived by discounting them at the interest rate implicit in the lease.

(b) In practice in the case of a finance lease the **fair value** of the asset will often be a sufficiently close approximation to the present value of the minimum lease payments and may in these circumstances be substituted for it.

(c) The combined benefit to a lessor of regional development and other **grants** together with **capital allowances**, which reduce tax liabilities, may enable the minimum lease payments under a finance lease to be reduced to a total which is less than the fair value of the asset. In these circumstances, the amount to be capitalised and depreciated should be restricted to the **minimum lease payments**. A negative finance charge should not be shown.

(d) **Rentals payable** should be apportioned between the **finance charge** and a **reduction of the outstanding obligation for future amounts payable**. The total finance charge under a finance lease should be allocated to accounting periods during the lease term so as to produce a **constant periodic rate of charge** on the remaining balance of the obligation for each accounting period, or a reasonable approximation thereto.

(e) An asset leased under a finance lease should be **depreciated** over the shorter of the lease term or its useful life. However, in the case of a hire purchase contract which has the characteristics of a finance lease, the asset should be depreciated over its useful life.

In interpreting the above these definitions from SSAP 21 should be borne in mind. We have seen that **the main argument in favour of capitalisation is substance over form**.

Finance leases are **capitalised** – an example of the application of substance over form.

Key terms

Fair value is the price at which an asset could be exchanged in an arm's length transaction less, where applicable, any grants receivable towards the purchase or use of the asset.

Finance charge is the amount borne by the lessee over the lease terms, representing the difference between the total of the minimum lease payments (including any residual amounts guaranteed by him) and the amount at which he records the leased asset at the inception of the lease.

The **interest rate implicit in a lease** is the discount rate which at the inception of the lease, when applied to the amounts which the lessor expects to receive and retain produces an amount (the present value) equal to the fair value of the leased asset. The amounts which the lessor expects to receive and retain comprise:

(a) The minimum lease payments to the lessor (as defined below); *plus*
(b) Any unguaranteed residual value; *less*
(c) Any part of (a) and (b) for which the lessor will be accountable to the lessee

If the interest rate implicit in the lease is not determinable, it should be estimated by reference to the rate which a lessee would be expected to pay on a similar lease.

2.1.2 Main arguments against capitalisation

FAST FORWARD

You must be able to discuss the **arguments for and against capitalisation** of finance leased assets.

(a)   **Legal position.** The benefit of a lease to a lessee is an intangible asset, not the ownership of the equipment. It may be misleading to users of accounts to capitalise the equipment when a lease is legally quite different from a loan used to purchase the equipment. Capitalising leases also raises the question of whether other executory contracts should be treated similarly, for example contracts of employment.

(b)   **Complexity**. Many small businesses will find that they do not have the expertise necessary for carrying out the calculations required for capitalisation.

(c)   **Subjectivity**. To some extent, capitalisation is a somewhat arbitrary process and this may lead to a lack of consistency between companies.

(d)   **Presentation**. The impact of leasing can be more usefully described in the notes to financial statements. These can be made readily comprehensible to users who may not understand the underlying calculations.

Important!

These are outweighed by the main argument in favour: **Substance over form**.

There are two main ways of **allocating the finance charge** between accounting periods:

- The actuarial method (before tax)
- The sum of the digits method.

Each of these is illustrated in an example later in this chapter. The actuarial method is to be preferred as it most exactly reflects the way in which the finance charges are incurred. The sum of the digits method produces a reasonable approximation to the actuarial method.

2.2 Operating leases

SSAP 21 requires that the rentals under operating leases should be written off as an expense on a straight line basis over the lease term even if the payments are not made on such a basis, unless another systematic and rational basis is justified by the circumstances.

2.3 Hire purchase contracts

Assets acquired under hire purchase agreements should be capitalised in the same way as those under finance leases if the HP contracts are of a financing nature. Otherwise (eg, if the option to purchase is not to be taken up) they should be accounted for on a basis similar to that used for operating leases.

2.4 Disclosure requirements: lessees

SSAP 21 requires lessees to disclose the following information.

(a)   The gross amounts of **assets held under finance leases*** together with the related accumulated depreciation, analysed by class of asset must be shown. This information may be consolidated with the corresponding information for owned assets, and not shown separately. In that case, the net amount of assets held under finance leases* included in the overall total should also be disclosed.

(b)   The amounts of **obligations related to finance leases*** (net of finance charges allocated to future periods) should be disclosed. These should be shown separately from other obligations and liabilities and should be analysed between amounts payable in the next year, amounts payable in the second to fifth years inclusive from the balance sheet date and the aggregate amounts payable thereafter.

(c) The **aggregate finance charges** allocated for the period in respect of finance leases must appear.

(d) Disclosure should be made of the amount of any **commitments** existing at the balance sheet date in respect of finance leases which have been entered into but whose inception occurs after the year end.

(e) The total of **operating lease rentals** charged as an expense in the profit and loss account should be disclosed, analysed between amounts payable in respect of hire of plant and machinery and in respect of other operating leases.

(f) In respect of **operating leases**, the lessee should disclose the payments which he is **committed** to make during the next year, analysed between those in which the commitment expires within that year, in the second to fifth years inclusive and over five years from the balance sheet date, showing separately the commitments in respect of leases of land and buildings and other operating leases.

* Including the equivalent information in respect of **hire purchase contracts**.

Exam focus point

Rather than learn this list by heart, take a look at a set of company accounts and see how those disclosures work in practice.

2.5 Apportionment of rental payments

When the lessee makes **a rental payment** it **will comprise two elements.**

(a) **An interest charge on the finance provided by the lessor**. This proportion of each payment is interest payable and interest receivable in the profit and loss accounts of the lessee and lessor respectively.

(b) **A repayment of part of the capital cost of the asset**. In the lessee's books this proportion of each rental payment must be debited to the lessor's account to reduce the outstanding liability. In the lessor's books, it must be credited to the lessee's account to reduce the amount owing (the debit of course is to cash).

The accounting problem is to decide what proportion of each instalment paid by the lessee **represents interest, and what proportion represents a repayment of the capital** advanced by the lessor. There are **three methods** you may encounter:

(a) The **level spread method**.
(b) The **actuarial method**.
(c) The **sum-of-the-digits method**.

Exam focus point

An examination question would always make it clear which method should be used. In theory, the aim is that the profit and loss account finance charge should produce a constant rate of return on outstanding leasing obligations.

The level spread method is based on the assumption that finance charges accrue evenly over the term of the lease agreement. For example, if an asset with a fair value of £3,000 is being 'acquired' on a finance lease for five payments of £700 each, the total interest is £(3,500 – 3,000) = £500. This is assumed to accrue evenly and therefore there is £100 interest comprised in each rental payment, the £600 balance of each instalment being the capital repayment.

The level spread method is quite **unscientific and takes no account of the commercial realities of the transaction.** You should use it in the examination only if you are specifically instructed to or if there is insufficient information to use another method.

The **actuarial method is the best and most scientific method**. It derives from the commonsense assumption that the **interest charged by a lessor company will equal the rate of return desired by the company, multiplied by the amount of capital it has invested.**

(a)   At the beginning of the lease the capital invested is equal to the fair value of the asset (less any initial deposit paid by the lessee).

(b)   This amount reduces as each instalment is paid. It follows that the interest accruing is greatest in the early part of the lease term, and gradually reduces as capital is repaid. In this section, we will look at a simple example of the actuarial method.

The sum-of-the-digits method approximates to the actuarial method, splitting the total interest (without reference to a rate of interest) in such a way that the greater proportion falls in the earlier years. The procedure is as follows.

(a)   **Assign a digit to each instalment.** The digit 1 should be assigned to the final instalment, 2 to the penultimate instalment and so on.

(b)   **Add the digits.** If there are twelve instalments, then the sum of the digits will be 78. For this reason, the sum of the digits method is sometimes called the *rule of 78.*

(c)   **Calculate the interest charge included in each instalment**. Do this by multiplying the total interest accruing over the lease term by the fraction:

$$\frac{\text{Digit applicable to the instalment}}{\text{Sum of the digits}}$$

2.6 Example: Apportionment methods

On 1 January 20X0 Bacchus Ltd, wine merchants, buys a small bottling and labelling machine from Silenus Limited on hire purchase terms. The cash price of the machine was £7,710 while the HP price was £10,000. The HP agreement required the immediate payment of a £2,000 deposit with the balance being settled in four equal annual instalments commencing on 31 December 20X0. The HP charge of £2,290 represents interest of 15% per annum, calculated on the remaining balance of the liability during each accounting period. Depreciation on the plant is to be provided for at the rate of 20% per annum on a straight line basis assuming a residual value of nil.

You are required to show the breakdown of each instalment between interest and capital, using in turn each of the apportionment methods described above.

Solution

In this example, enough detail is given to use any of the apportionment methods. In an examination question, you would normally be directed to use one method specifically.

(a)   *Level spread method*

The £2,290 interest charges are regarded as accruing evenly over the term of the HP agreement. Each instalment therefore contains £2,290/4 = £572.50 of interest. The break down is then as follows.

	1st instalment £	2nd instalment £	3rd instalment £	4th instalment £
Interest	572.50	572.50	572.50	572.50
Capital repayment (balance)	1,427.50	1,427.50	1,427.50	1,427.50
	2,000.00	2,000.00	2,000.00	2,000.00

(b)   *Sum-of-the-digits method*

Each instalment is allocated a digit as follows.

Instalment	Digit
1st (20X0)	4
2nd (20X1)	3
3rd (20X2)	2
4th (20X3)	1
	10

The £2,290 interest charges can then be apportioned.

		£
1st instalment	£2,290 × 4/10	916
2nd instalment	£2,290 × 3/10	687
3rd instalment	£2,290 × 2/10	458
4th instalment	£2,290 × 1/10	229
		2,290

The breakdown is then as follows.

	1st instalment £	2nd instalment £	3rd instalment £	4th instalment £
Interest	916	687	458	229
Capital repayment (balance)	1,084	1,313	1,542	1,771
	2,000	2,000	2,000	2,000

(c)   *Actuarial method*

Interest is calculated as 15% of the outstanding *capital* balance at the beginning of each year. The outstanding capital balance reduces each year by the capital element comprised in each instalment. The outstanding capital balance at 1 January 20X0 is £5,710 (£7,710 fair value less £2,000 deposit).

	Total £	Capital £	Interest £
Capital balance at 1 Jan 20X0		5,710	
1st instalment			
(interest = £5,710 × 15%)	2,000	1,144	856
Capital balance at 1 Jan 20X1		4,566	
2nd instalment			
(interest = £4,566 × 15%)	2,000	1,315	685
Capital balance at 1 Jan 20X2		3,251	
3rd instalment			
(interest = £3,251 × 15%)	2,000	1,512	488
Capital balance at 1 Jan 20X3		1,739	
4th instalment			
(interest = £1,739 × 15%)	2,000	1,739	261
	8,000		2,290
Capital balance at 1 Jan 20X4		–	

Question

On 31 December 20X3 Cradlebrake Ltd entered into a leasing arrangement with Heathcliffe Finance for a large packaging machine. The terms of the lease require quarterly payments in arrears for four years of £1,107.24. Cradlebrake depreciates all plant and machinery on a straight line basis. The engineering manager estimates that the packaging machine will last 4 years and will have no scrap value. The rate of interest implicit in the lease is 5% per quarter. The company intends to capitalise the machine and show as a liability the outstanding rentals (excluding interest).

You are required to calculate the relevant P&L account and balance sheet figures for incorporation in the annual accounts for the accounting periods ending 30 September 20X4, 20X5, 20X6, 20X7 and 20X8.

Answer

	Balance sheet		P&L account	
	Leased	Leasing	Depreciation	
	assets	creditor	charge	Interest
Year ending	£	£	£	£
30.9.X4	9,750	10,401	2,250	1,723
30.9.X5	6,750	7,870	3,000	1,898
30.9.X6	3,750	4,794	3,000	1,353
30.9.X7	750	1,055	3,000	690
30.9.X8	–	–	750	53

Working

Using the table towards the end of the Study Text, the present value of the payments under the lease is equal to £1,107.24 × 10.838 = £12,000 at the start of the lease.

Period	Liability at start of period	Finance charge	Rental payment	Liability at end of period
	£	£	£	£
1	12,000.00	600.00	(1,107.24)	11,492.76
2	11,492.76	574.64	(1,107.24)	10,960.16
3	10,960.16	548.01	(1,107.24)	10,400.93
4	10,400.93	520.05	(1,107.24)	9,813.74
5	9,813.74	490.69	(1,107.24)	9,197.19
6	9,197.19	459.86	(1,107.24)	8,549.81
7	8,549.81	427.49	(1,107.24)	7,870.06
8	7,870.06	393.50	(1,107.24)	7,156.32
9	7,156.32	357.82	(1,107.24)	6,406.90
10	6,406.90	320.34	(1,107.24)	5,620.00
11	5,620.00	281.00	(1,107.24)	4,793.76
12	4,793.76	239.69	(1,107.24)	3,926.21
13	3,926.21	196.31	(1,107.24)	3,015.28
14	3,015.28	150.76	(1,107.24)	2,058.80
15	2,058.80	102.94	(1,107.24)	1,054.50
16	1,054.50	52.74	(1,107.24)	Nil

The finance charges for each year can be found by adding together those for the appropriate quarters.

Where a large number of payments are involved, it is probably simpler to look at accounting periods rather than the periods within the lease. The liability at any point of the lease is equal to the present value of payments due thereafter. Thus the liability at 30.9.X4 when there are 13 instalments outstanding will be £1,107.24 × 9.394 (see cumulative discount table) = £10,401. The finance charge can then be found as follows.

	£
Rentals paid to 30.9.X4 (£1,107.24 × 3)	3,322
Capital repayment (reduction in liability)	
£12,000 – £10,401	1,599
Finance charge	1,723

The calculations for the remaining periods are shown below.

Year ending 30.9.X5
Liability at 30.9.X5 with 9 instalments to pay:
     £1,107.24 × 7.108 = £7,870; £10,401 – £7,870 = £2,531;
Interest = (4 × £1,107.24) – £2,531 = £1,898

Year ending 30.9.X6
Liability at 30.9.X6 with 5 instalments to pay:
     £1,107.24 × 4.329 = £4,794; £7,870 – £4,794 = £3,076
Interest = (4 × £1,107.24) – £3,076 = £1,353

Year ending 30.9.X7
Liability at 30.9.X7 with 1 instalment to pay:
     £1,107.24 × 0.952 = £1,055; £4,794 – £1,055 = £3,739
Interest = (4 × £1,107.24) – £3,739 = £690

Year ending 30.9.X8
Interest = £1,107.24 – £1,055 = £52

3 Lessor accounting

The following SSAP 21 definitions are relevant to lessor accounting.

Key terms

Initial direct costs are those costs incurred by the lessor that are directly associated with negotiating and consummating leasing transactions, such as commissions, legal fees, costs of credit investigations and costs of preparing and processing documents for new leases acquired.

Gross earnings comprise the lessor's gross finance income over the lease term, representing the difference between his gross investment in the lease and the cost of the leased asset less any grants receivable towards the purchase or use of the asset.

The **gross investment** in a lease at a point in time is the total of the minimum lease payments and any unguaranteed residual value accruing to the lessor.

The **net investment** in a lease at a point in time comprises:

(a)   The gross investment in a lease (as defined above)
(b)   Less gross earnings allocated to future periods.

The **net cash investment** in a lease at a point in time is the amount of funds invested in a lease by a lessor, and comprises the cost of the asset plus or minus the following related payments or receipts:

Key terms

(a)   Government/other grants receivable towards the purchase or use of the asset
(b)   Rentals received
(c)   Taxation payments and receipts, including the effect of capital allowances
(d)   Residual values, if any, at the end of the lease term
(e)   Interest payments (where applicable)
(f)   Interest received on cash surplus
(g)   Profit taken out of the lease

(SSAP 21)

3.1 Example: Gross investment

Willco Ltd has just purchased a lorry from Drogon Trucks Ltd for £50,000. The lorry has been leased to Newton Freight Ltd on a two year lease requiring annual payments in arrears of £13,500. Drogon Trucks have agreed to buy the truck back at open market value at the end of the lease. Newton Freight Ltd have guaranteed that the value of the lorry after two years will be not less than £30,000. A realistic estimate of its value at that time is £33,000, ie the unguaranteed residual value is £3,000.

What is the gross investment in the lease at the start of the lease?

Solution

At the start of the lease the 'minimum lease payments' will be the rentals due of £27,000 plus the guaranteed residual of £30,000 giving £57,000. The gross investment in the lease will be the minimum lease payments of £57,000 plus the unguaranteed residual of £3,000 (£33,000 – £30,000) giving £60,000.

It will be apparent from the definition of net investment above that when any residual amount receivable by the lessor is insignificant (as is usually the case in normal full payout leases) the net investment in the lease will be equal to the cost of the equipment less any grant receivable.

3.2 Standard accounting practice for lessors

The requirements of SSAP 21 for accounting by lessors are as follows.

(a)   The **amount due from the lessee** under a finance lease should be recorded in the balance sheet of a lessor as a *debtor* at the amount of the **net investment in the lease** after making provisions for items such as bad and doubtful rentals receivable.

(b)   The **total gross earnings** under a finance lease should normally be allocated to accounting periods to give a **constant rate of return** on the lessor's net cash investment in the lease in each period. In the case of a hire purchase contract which has characteristics similar to a finance lease, allocation of gross earnings so as to give a constant periodic rate of return on the finance company's net investment will in most cases be a suitable approximation to allocation based on the net cash investment.

In arriving at the constant periodic rate of return, a reasonable approximation may be made.

(c)   As an alternative to (b) above, an **allocation** may first be made out of gross earnings of an amount equal to the lessor's estimated cost of finance included in the net cash investment calculation, with the balance being recognised on a systematic basis.

(d)   **Tax free grants** which are available to the lessor against the purchase price of assets acquired for leasing should be spread over the period of the lease and dealt with by treating the grant as non-taxable income (see below).

(e)   An **asset** held for use in operating leases by a lessor should be recorded as a fixed asset and depreciated over its useful life.

(f) **Rental income from an operating lease**, excluding charges for services such as insurance and maintenance, should be recognised on **a straight-line basis** over the period of the lease, even if the payments are not made on such a basis, unless another systematic and rational basis is more representative of the time pattern in which the benefit from the leased asset is receivable.

(g) **Initial direct costs** incurred by a lessor in arranging a lease may be apportioned over the period of the lease on a systematic and rational basis.

3.3 Amendment to SSAP 21

You should understand the reasons why an **Amendment to SSAP 21** was required.

Until recently, SSAP 21 allowed an alternative treatment for the **tax free grants** mentioned in Paragraph 3.2(d) above. Such tax free grants were still spread over the period of the lease, but could be dealt with by grossing up the grant and including the grossed-up amount in arriving at profit before tax. Where this treatment was adopted, the lessor had to disclose the amount by which the profit before tax and the tax charge had been increased as a result of grossing up the grant.

3.4 Example: Net investment

Consider again the example first given in Paragraph 2.5, this time from the point of view of the lessor.

Solution

	Years ending 31 December				
	20X3	20X4	20X5	20X6	Total
	£	£	£	£	£
Rentals receivable	13,610	13,610	13,610	13,610	54,440
Capital repayment	13,610	10,225	11,248	12,377	47,460
Finance charge	–	3,385	2,362	1,233	6,980
Average sum outstanding during period		33,850	23,625	12,377	
Finance charge expressed as a % return on the average sum outstanding in the period		10%	10%	10%	

As suggested in the standard, this return is constant.

The lessor's balance sheet and notes will include the following amounts for each year.

	As at 31 December		
	20X3	20X4	20X5
	£	£	£
Debtors			
Net investment in finance lease	33,850	23,625	12,377
Of which the following is due in more than one year	23,625	12,377	–

Note that under the assumptions of this question the total net investments shown above are the same as the obligations shown in the lessee's balance sheet. This would not have been the case had the lessee based its disclosure on a present value found using its cost of borrowing rather than the implied rate in the lease.

The best methods of obtaining a **constant periodic rate of return** on the lessor's net *cash* investment are:

(a) The actuarial method *after* tax

(b) The investment period method (IPM)

The **main difference** between these two methods and the methods discussed above (actuarial method before tax and sum of the digits) is that the former methods take into account the impact of tax relief on the lessor's cash flow.

3.5 Disclosure requirements: lessors

The disclosure requirements of SSAP 21 are as follows.

(a)   The **net investment** in (i) finance leases and (ii) hire purchase contracts at each balance sheet date should be disclosed.

(b)   The **gross amounts of assets** held for use in operating leases*, and the related accumulated depreciation charges, should be disclosed.

(c)   Disclosure should be made of:

(i)   The **policy adopted** for accounting for operating leases* and finance leases* and, in detail, the policy for accounting for finance lease income*

(ii)   The **aggregate rentals receivable** in respect of an accounting period in relation to (i) finance leases* and (ii) operating leases*

(iii)   The **cost of assets acquired**, whether by purchase or finance leases*, for the purpose of letting under finance leases*

* Including the equivalent information in respect of **hire purchase contracts** which have characteristics similar to that type of lease.

3.6 Selling profit

A manufacturer or dealer lessor should not recognise a selling profit under an operating lease. The selling profit under a finance lease should be **restricted** to the excess of the fair value of the asset over the manufacturer's or dealer's cost less any grants receivable by the manufacturer or dealer towards the purchase, construction or use of the asset.

3.7 Sale and leaseback transactions

FAST FORWARD

You should be able to understand the treatment of **sale and leaseback** transactions.

These should be dealt with as follows.

(a)   **Accounting by the seller/lessee**

(i)   In a sale and leaseback transaction which results in a **finance lease**, any apparent profit or loss (that is, the difference between the sale price and the previous carrying value) should be deferred and amortised in the financial statements of the seller/lessee over the shorter of the lease term or the useful life of the asset.

(ii)   If the leaseback is an **operating lease**:

(1)   Recognise any profit or loss recognised immediately, provided it is clear that the transaction is established at a **fair value**

BPP
LEARNING MEDIA

(2) If the **sale price is below fair value**, any profit or loss should be recognised immediately except that if the apparent loss is compensated by future rentals at below market price it should to that extent be deferred and amortised over the remainder of the lease term (or, if shorter, the period during which the reduced rentals are chargeable)

(3) If the **sale price is above fair value**, the profit based on fair value may be recognised immediately. The balance of profit in excess of fair value should be deferred and amortised over the shorter of the remainder of the lease term and the period to the next rent review (if any). In some cases **where the sales price is significantly above fair value, the operating lease rentals are likely to have been adjusted for the excess price paid for the assets. According to FRS 5, the substance of the transaction is one of sale of an asset and a loan equalling the deferred income element**. The excess over fair value can be shown as a loan and part of the operating lease cost as a repayment of capital and interest on this amount.

(b) **Accounting by the buyer/lessor**

A buyer/lessor should account for a sale and leaseback in the same way as he accounts for other leases.

A leasing question may be connected to off balance sheet finance in general. In particular, you may be asked to discuss the links between SSAP 21 and FRS 5.

3.8 UITF 28 *Operating lease incentives*

Abstract 28 deals with the way in which both lessors and lessees should account for incentives given by the lessor to the lessee. The Abstract is based on a draft that was published for comment in October 2000, the proposals of which were supported by most of those who responded.

The Abstract reflects the UITF's view that the rental, net of any incentive, should be recognised as rental expense or income over the period of the lease or, as appropriate, the period to the next rent review.

The Abstract replaces Abstract 12 *Lessee accounting for reverse premiums and similar incentives*, which, as its title implies, deals only with accounting by the lessee. No major changes are made to the requirements of Abstract 12, the main purpose of the new Abstract being to extend the requirements to lessors, who are also covered by the equivalent international requirements.

4 Criticism

FAST FORWARD

You should be aware of the reasons why SSAP 21 has been **criticised**.

SSAP 21 has not been without its critics. Although it closed many loopholes in the treatment of leases, it is still open to abuse and manipulation. A great deal of this topic is tied up in the off balance sheet finance debate discussed in Chapter 9.

4.1 Unguaranteed residual value

Key term

Unguaranteed residual value is that portion of the residual value of the leased asset (estimated at the inception of the lease), the realisation of which by the lessor is not assured or is guaranteed solely by a party related to the lessor. *(SSAP 21)*

As we have already seen, to qualify as a finance lease the risks and rewards of ownership must be transferred to the lessee. One reward of ownership is any **residual value** in the asset at the end of the primary period. If the asset is returned to the lessor then it is he who receives this reward of ownership, not the lessee. This might prevent the lease from being a finance lease if this reward is significant (SSAP 21 allows insubstantial ownership risks and rewards not to pass).

SSAP 21 states that it should normally be presumed that a transfer of substantially all the risks and rewards of ownership occurs if, at the beginning of the lease, the present value of the minimum lease payments amounts to 90% or more of the fair value of the leased asset. This is an application of **discounting principles** to financial statements. The discounting equation is:

$$
\begin{array}{ccccc}
\text{Present value of} & & \text{Present value of} & & \\
\text{minimum lease} & + & \text{unguaranteed} & = & \text{Fair value of} \\
\text{payment} & & \text{residual amount} & & \text{leased asset} \\
& & \text{accruing to lessor} & &
\end{array}
$$

Note. Any **guaranteed residual amount** accruing to the lessor will be included in the minimum lease payments.

If there is an unguaranteed residual amount due to the lessor, it can be seen that its present value must be **less than 10% of the fair value** of the leased asset if the lease is to qualify as a finance lease, since only then will the present value of the minimum lease payments amount to 90% or more of that fair value under the 90% rule.

You should now be able to see the **scope for manipulation** involving lease classification.

(a) Whether or not a lease is classified as a finance lease can **hinge on the size of the unguaranteed residual amount** due to the lessor, and that figure will **only be an estimate**.

(b) A lessor might be persuaded to estimate a larger residual amount than he would otherwise have done and **cause the lease to fail the 90% test**, rather than lose the business.

(c) While the test is only intended to be presumptive and does not provide a precise mathematical definition of a finance lease, it would be a **brave auditor** who would contend that a lease which failed the test was still a finance lease.

4.2 Example: Unguaranteed residual value

A company enters into two leasing agreements.

	Lease A	Lease B
	£'000	£'000
Fair value of asset	210	120
Estimated residual value (due to lessor)	21	30
Minimum lease payments	238	108

How should each lease be classified?

Solution

You should note that it is unnecessary to perform any calculations for discounting in this example.

Lease A: it is obvious that the present value of the unguaranteed lease payments is less than £21,000, and therefore less than 10% of the fair value of the asset. This means that the present value of the minimum lease payments is over 90% of the fair value of the asset. Lease A is therefore a finance lease.

Lease B: the present value of the minimum lease payments is obviously less than £108,000 and therefore less than 90% of the fair value of the asset. Lease B is therefore an operating lease.

4.3 Implicit interest rate

It will often be the case that the lessee does not know the unguaranteed residual value placed on the asset by the lessor and he is therefore unaware of the interest rate implicit in the lease. In such a case, SSAP 21 allows the lessee to provide his **own estimate**, to calculate the implicit interest rate and perform the 90% test. It is obviously very easy to estimate a residual amount which fails the test. This situation would also lead to different results for the lessee and the lessor.

4.4 Omission of material assets and liabilities

The ASB and other standard setters regard existing leasing standards as deficient.

(a) They **omit material assets and liabilities** arising from operating lease contracts.

(b) The approach of SSAP 21 is **'all or nothing'**, while modern transactions are more complex than this.

(c) Classification of leases has important implications, eg for gearing, interest cover and return on capital employed. **Investment analysts** and credit rating agencies often **re-work** financial statements by calculating the assets and liabilities implicit in off balance sheet operating leases.

4.5 Discussion paper: Leases: implementation of a new approach

For some time, users have called for finance leases and operating leases to be treated consistently.

The ASB published a Discussion Paper *Leases: implementation of a new approach* in December 1999. The Discussion Paper presents a Position Paper that has been developed by the G4+1.

The paper recommends that **all leases should be reflected in financial statements in a consistent manner** and it explores the principles that should determine the extent of the assets and liabilities that lessees and lessors would recognise under leases.

At the beginning of a lease the lessee would **recognise an asset and a liability equivalent to the fair value of the rights and obligations that are conveyed by the lease** (usually the present value of the minimum payments required by the lease). Then the accounting for the lease asset and liability would **follow the normal requirements for accounting for fixed assets and debt**. The lessor would report financial assets (representing amounts receivable from the lessee) and residual interests as separate assets.

Leases that are now treated as operating leases and therefore off balance sheet would give rise to assets and liabilities. However, the difference may not be significant. **Where a lease is for a small part of an asset's useful economic life, only that part would be reflected in the lessee's balance sheet.**

The Discussion paper also examines the principles for accounting for more complex features of lease contracts. These include renewal options, contingent rentals, residual value guarantees and sale and leaseback transactions.

4.5.1 Sale and leaseback transactions

SSAP 21 requires a different treatment for sale and leaseback transactions depending on whether the leaseback is a finance or an operating lease. To recap:

- **Operating lease**: treat the transaction as a **sale**

- **Finance lease**: continue to recognise the **asset in the balance sheet**; recognise a **liability for the lease payment**

The Discussion Paper considers two possible approaches to accounting for sale and leaseback transactions.

(a)   **One transaction approach.** This views a sale and leaseback as **one transaction with a double purpose.**

    (i)   The raising of finance
    (ii)   The partial disposal of an interest in property

(b)   **Two transactions approach.** A sale and leaseback is viewed as **two separate transactions.**

    (i)   A sale of property
    (ii)   A subsequent lease of different property rights

The two transactions would be accounted for separately.

4.6 Example: Sale and leaseback transaction

Newlease Ltd sells a property for £240,000. The property has a carrying value of £200,000 and a fair value of £240,000.

Under the one transaction approach, the accounting entries are as follows.

DEBIT Cash	£240,000	
CREDIT Lease creditor		£240,000

The property remains in the balance sheet at its carrying value of £200,000. This is similar to the current treatment.

The two transactions approach splits the transaction into two components, as follows.

Sale

DEBIT Cash	£240,000	
CREDIT Asset		£200,000
CREDIT Profit on disposal		£40,000

Leaseback

DEBIT Asset	£240,000	
CREDIT Lease liability		£240,000

In effect, the asset has been revalued to its fair value of £240,000.

The Discussion Paper favours the **one transaction approach.** The main reason for this is that although there are technically two transactions, these are negotiated together.

A sale and leaseback is generally a **partial disposal**. At one extreme, the transaction may be a financing arrangement with only an immaterial part of the asset sold. At the other extreme, the transaction could be closer to a sale, with only an immaterial amount of finance raised. To deal with this situation, the Discussion Paper proposes the following accounting treatment.

Step 1   Recognise a liability for the lease payments.

Step 2   The excess of cash received over this liability is deemed to be consideration for the part of the asset that is sold.

Step 3   Apportion the carrying amount of the asset immediately before the transaction between the amount sold and the amount retained.

Step 4   The difference between the carrying amount apportioned as sold and the consideration calculated in Step 3 would be recognised as a gain or loss.

Step 5   The part of the asset that is retained, in other words the right to use the asset for the term of the lease would be carried as a proportion of the previous carrying amount, as calculated in Step 3.

4.7 Example: Sale and leaseback with 'partial disposal'

Goodlease Ltd has a building with a carrying value of £200,000 and a fair value of £240,000. It sells the property to Greatlease Ltd for £240,000 and leases it back. The liability for lease payments is £140,000.

As this is a partial disposal, we need to apportion the carrying amount of the asset between the part sold and the part retained. As the liability for lease payments is £140,000 and the total proceeds are £240,000, £100,000 of the proceeds can be deemed to have been received for selling part of the asset.

The accounting entries would be as follows.

DEBIT Cash	£240,000	
CREDIT Liability for lease payments		£140,000
CREDIT Asset (200 × 100/240)		£83,333
CREDIT Profit on disposal		£16,667

Note that the profit that would arise if the whole asset had been sold would be £240,000 − £200,000, ie £40,000. This needs to be apportioned to the part of the asset that has been sold, ie 100/240 × £40,000 = £16,667.

The carrying value of the building is now £200,000 − £83,333 = £116,667.

4.8 Not the last word

The Discussion Paper has met with some criticism. It has been argued (by KPMG's technical accounting director Kevin Singleton in *Accountancy,* March 2000) that FRS 5, with its emphasis on substance over form, can adequately deal with leases, and that ways will be found to bend the rules. The proposals would be particularly contentious for land and buildings, which are normally held on long leases. Lessees would have to recognise significant additional assets and liabilities in their balance sheets.

Exam focus point

The Pilot paper contained a question asking you to consider the effect of the treatment under the Discussion Paper.

Chapter Roundup

- SSAP 21's requirements are not as tricky as they seem at first reading. You should understand the distinction between:

    - **Finance leases**
    - **Operating leases**

- **Finance leases** are **capitalised** – an example of the application of substance over form.

- You should understand the reasons why an **Amendment to SSAP 21** was required.

- You should be able to understand the treatment of **sale and leaseback** transactions.

- You should be aware of the reasons why SSAP 21 has been **criticised**.

Quick Quiz

1   Distinguish between a finance lease and an operating lease.

2   List the arguments against lessees capitalising leased assets?

3   List the disclosure requirements for lessees.

4   Alpha plc enters into a lease with Omega Ltd of an aircraft which had a fair value of £240,000 at the inception of the lease. The terms of the lease require Alpha to pay 10 annual rentals of £36,000 in arrears.

Taking into account the residual value of the aircraft accruing to Omega Ltd at the end of 10 years, the interest rate implicit in the lease is approximately 10%.

The present value of the ten annual rentals of £36,000, discounted at the interest rate implicit in the lease, is £220,000.

Applying the provisions of SSAP 21 to this lease by how much will the assets of Alpha plc be increased?

5   SSAP 21 requires a lessee to capitalise a finance lease at the amount of the:

A   Arm's length price
B   Arm's length price less government grants
C   Minimum lease payments less residual value
D   Present value of the minimum lease payments

6   On 1 January 20X0 Melon plc entered into a finance lease in respect of a machine. The terms of the agreement were:

	£
Cash price	18,000
Deposit	(6,000)
	12,000
Interest (9% for two years)	2,160
Balance – payable in two annual instalments	
commencing 31 December 20X0	14,160

The rate of interest implicit in the contract is approximately 12%. Applying the provisions of SSAP 21, Accounting for leases and hire purchase contracts, what is the finance charge in the profit and loss account for the year ended 31 December 20X0?

7   What is the main change proposed by the ASB's Discussion Paper?

Answers to Quick Quiz

1   See paragraph 1

2   (a)   Legal position
     (b)   Complexity
     (c)   Subjectivity
     (d)   Presentation

3   See Paragraph 2.4.

4   £220,000. Per SSAP 21 the value should be the present value of the minimum base payments.

5   D

6   The rate of interest used should be the rate implicit in the lease. This rate takes account of the reducing balance on the amount outstanding.

     £12,000 × 12% = £1,440.

7   Leases that are now treated as operating leases and therefore off balance sheet would give rise to asset and liabilities.

Now try the questions below from the Exam Question Bank

Number	Level	Marks	Time
Q11	Introductory	n/a	n/a

Off balance sheet finance

Topic list	Syllabus reference
1 Off balance sheet finance explained	A2, B1
2 Substance over form	A2, B1
3 FRS 5 *Reporting the substance of transactions*	A2, B1
4 Common forms of off balance sheet finance	A2, B1
5 Revenue recognition	A2, B1

Introduction

This chapter deals with off balance sheet finance and substance over form. You need to know about these issues because they show how reports can be manipulated, an ethical issue. Also the fact that assets and liabilities may be presented – if those presenting them act unethically – according to their form rather than their substance, shows up the limitations of financial statements.

Study guide

		Intellectual level
A2	**Ethical requirements of reporting a true and fair view and the consequences of unethical behaviour**	
(a)	Appraise the potential ethical implications of professional and managerial decisions in the preparation of corporate reports	3
(b)	Assess the consequences of not upholding ethical principles in the preparation of corporate reports	3
B1	**The contribution and limitations of financial statements in meeting users' and capital markets' needs**	
(c)	Discuss the usefulness of corporate reports in making investment decisions	3

Exam guide

The issue of the substance of a transaction was examined in part of a Pilot Paper question dealing with ethics.

1 Off balance sheet finance explained

FAST FORWARD

> The subject of **off balance sheet finance** is a complex one which has plagued the accountancy profession. In practice, off balance sheet finance schemes are often very sophisticated and they are beyond the range of this syllabus. FRS 5 embodies the concept of **substance over form**.

Key term

> **Off balance sheet finance** is the funding or refinancing of a company's operations in such a way that, under legal requirements and existing accounting conventions, some or all of the finance may not be shown on its balance sheet.

Off balance sheet transactions may involve the **removal of assets** from the balance sheet, as well as liabilities, and they are likely to have a significant impact on the P&L account.

Why off balance sheet finance exists

(a) To **keep gearing low**, probably because of the views of some analysts and brokers.

(b) A company may need to keep its gearing down in order to **stay within the terms of loan covenants** imposed by lenders.

(c) A listed company with high borrowings is often expected (by analysts and others) to declare a **rights issue** in order to reduce gearing. This has an adverse effect on a company's share price and so off balance sheet financing is used to reduce gearing *and* the expectation of a rights issue.

(d) Analysts' short term views are a problem for companies **developing assets** which are not producing income during the development stage. Such companies will match the borrowings associated with such developing assets, along with the assets themselves, off balance sheet. They are brought back on balance sheet once income is being generated by the assets. This process keeps return on capital employed higher than it would have been during the development stage.

(e)   Groups of companies have **excluded subsidiaries** from consolidation in an off balance sheet transaction because they carry out completely different types of business and have different characteristics. The usual example is a leasing company (in say a retail group) which has a high level of gearing.

The overriding motivation is to **avoid misinterpretation**. The company does not trust the analysts or other users to understand the reasons for a transaction and so avoids any effect such transactions might have by taking them off balance sheet. Unfortunately, the position of the company is then **misstated** and the user of the accounts is misled.

Not all forms of 'off balance sheet finance' are undertaken for cosmetic or accounting reasons. Some transactions are carried out to **limit or isolate risk**, to reduce interest costs and so on. These transactions **are in the best interests of the company**, not merely a cosmetic repackaging of figures which would normally appear in the balance sheet. Also, not all off balance sheet financing schemes derive from an intention to mislead. There may be genuine reasons for exclusion.

1.1 The off balance sheet finance problem

The main argument used for disallowing off balance sheet finance is that the true **substance** of the transactions should be shown, not merely the **legal form**, particularly when it is exacerbated by poor disclosure.

2 Substance over form   **Pilot paper**

FAST FORWARD

> FRS 5 embodies the concept of **substance over form**.

Key term

> **Substance over form**: transactions and other events should be accounted for and presented in accordance with their substance and financial reality and not merely with their legal form.   *(IAS 1)*

The paragraphs below give examples of where the principle of substance over form is enforced, particularly in accounting standards.

2.1 SSAP 21 *Accounting for leases and hire purchase* contracts

There is an explicit requirement that if the lessor transfers substantially all the **risks and rewards of ownership** to the lessee, even though the legal title has not passed, the item being leased should be **shown as an asset** in the balance sheet of the lessee and the amount due to the lessor should be shown as a liability.

2.2 FRS 8 *Related party disclosures*

FRS 8 requires financial statements to disclose fully material transactions undertaken with a related party by the reporting entity, **regardless of any price charged**.

2.3 SSAP 9 *Stocks and long-term contracts*

In SSAP 9 there is a requirement to account for **attributable profits** on long-term contracts under the accruals convention. However, there may be a problem with realisation, since it is arguable whether we should account for profit which, although attributable to the work done, may not have yet been invoiced to the customer. It is argued that the convention of substance over form is applied to justify ignoring the strict legal position.

2.4 FRS 2 *Accounting for subsidiary undertakings*

This is perhaps the most important area of off balance sheet finance which has been prevented by the application of the **substance over form** concept. The use of quasi-subsidiaries was very common in the 1980s.

Key term

> A **quasi-subsidiary** of a reporting entity is a company, trust, partnership or other vehicle that, though not fulfilling the definition of a subsidiary, is directly or indirectly controlled by the reporting entity and gives rise to benefits for that entity that are in substance no different from those that would arise were the vehicle a subsidiary.
>
> *(FRS 5)*

The main off balance sheet transactions involving quasi-subsidiaries were:

(a)   **Sale of assets.** The sale of assets to a quasi-subsidiary was carried out to remove the associated borrowings from the balance sheet and so reduce gearing; or perhaps so that the company could credit a profit in such a transaction. The asset could then be rented back to the vendor company under an operating lease (no capitalisation required by the lessee).

(b)   **Purchase of companies or assets**. One reason for such a purchase through a quasi-subsidiary is if the acquired entity is expected to make losses in the near future. Post-acquisition losses can be avoided by postponing the date of acquisition to the date the holding company acquires the purchase from the quasi-subsidiary.

(c)   **Business activities conducted outside the group**. Such a subsidiary might have been excluded through a quasi-subsidiary or not consolidated under the 'dissimilar activities' requirement in FRS 2. Exclusion from consolidation might be undertaken because the activities are high risk and have high gearing.

CA 1989 introduced a new definition of a subsidiary based on **control** rather than just ownership rights and this definition (along with other related matters) was incorporated into FRS 2, thus substantially reducing the effectiveness of this method of off-balance sheet finance. FRS 5 defines control.

Key term

> **Control of another entity** is the ability to direct the financial and operating policies of that entity with a view to gaining economic benefit from its activities.
>
> *(FRS 5)*

2.5 FRS 9 Associates and joint ventures

FRS 9 was considered in Chapter 5. The aspect which is relevant to substance over form is the required treatment for **joint arrangements which are not** entities . The section of the standard dealing with such arrangements is headed 'a structure with the **form but not the substance of a joint venture'**. Such structures are **not** to be accounted for as joint ventures.

You may also hear the term **creative accounting** used in the context of reporting the substance of transactions. This can be defined simply as the manipulation of figures for a desired result. Remember, however, that it is very rare for a company, its directors or employees to manipulate results for the purpose of fraud. The major consideration is usually the effect the results will have on the company's share price. Some areas open to abuse (although some of these loopholes have been closed) are given below and you should by now understand how these can distort a company results.

(a)   Income recognition and cut-off
(b)   Use of merger accounting
(c)   Manipulation of reserves
(d)   Revaluations and depreciation
(e)   Window dressing
(f)   Changes in accounting policy

Question

Creative accounting

Creative accounting, off balance sheet finance and related matters (in particular how ratio analysis can be used to discover these practices) often come up in articles in, for example, the *Financial Times* and *The Economist*. Find a library, preferably a good technical library, which can provide you with copies of back issues of such newspapers or journals and look for articles on creative accounting. Alternatively look on the Web.

3 FRS 5 Reporting the substance of transactions

FAST FORWARD

Make sure that you have memorised the definitions for **assets and liabilities** and the criteria for their **recognition and derecognition** given in FRS 5.

3.1 FRS 5 *Reporting the substance of transactions*

FRS 5 *Reporting the substance of transactions* is a daunting document, running to well over 100 pages, although the standard section itself is relatively short. The overriding principle of FRS 5 is that transactions should be accounted for according to their **substance rather than their legal form**, as we discussed above.

As stated in Chapter 3 of the *Statement of Principles,* accounting for items according to substance and economic reality and not merely legal form is a key determinant of reliable information.

(a) For the majority of transactions there is **no difference** between the two and therefore no issue.

(b) For other transactions **substance and form diverge** and the choice of treatment can give different results due to non-recognition of an asset or liability even though benefits or obligations result.

FRS 5 makes clear that full disclosure is not enough: all transactions must be **accounted for** correctly, with full disclosure of related details as necessary to give the user of accounts a full understanding of the transactions.

3.2 Relationship to other standards

The interaction of FRS 5 **with other standards and statutory requirements** is also an important issue; whichever rules are the more specific should be applied. Leasing provides a good example. **Straightforward leases** which fall squarely within the terms of **SSAP 21** should continue to be accounted for without any need to refer to FRS 5. Where their terms are **more complex**, or the lease is only one element in a larger series of transactions, then **FRS 5** comes into play.

3.3 Basic principles

As stated above, FRS 5's fundamental principle is that the substance of an entity's transactions should be reflected in its accounts. The key considerations

- Whether a transaction has given rise to new assets and liabilities
- Whether it has changed any existing assets and liabilities.

The characteristics of transactions whose substance is not readily apparent are as follows.

(a)   The **legal title** to an item is separated from the ability to enjoy the principal benefits, and the exposure to the main risks associated with it.

(b)   The transaction is **linked to one or more others** so that the commercial effect of the transaction cannot be understood without reference to the complete series.

(c)   The transaction includes **one or more options**, under such terms that it makes it highly likely that the option(s) will be exercised.

Exam focus point

> The recognition and de-recognition principles of FRS 5 do not apply to financial assets and liabilities. These are now covered by the amended FRS 26 (see Chapter 8).

3.4 Definitions of assets and liabilities

Key terms

> **Assets** are rights or other access to future economic benefits controlled by an entity as a result of past transactions or events.
>
> **Liabilities** are an entity's obligations to transfer economic benefits as a result of past transactions or events.
>
> *(FRS 5)*

Identification of **who has the risks** relating to an asset will generally indicate **who has the benefits** and hence **who has the asset**. If an entity is, in certain circumstances unable to avoid an **outflow of benefits**, this will provide evidence that it has a liability.

Key terms

> **Control in the context of an asset** is the ability to obtain the future economic benefits relating to an asset and to restrict the access of others to those benefits.
>
> **Risk** is uncertainty as to the amount of benefits. The term includes both potential for gain and exposure to loss.
>
> *(FRS 5)*

3.5 Recognition

Key term

> **Recognition** is the process of incorporating an item into the primary financial statements with the appropriate headings. It involves depiction of the items in words and by a monetary amount and inclusion of that amount in the statement totals.
>
> *(FRS 5)*

The next key question is deciding **when** something which satisfies the definition of an asset or liability has to be recognised in the balance sheet.

Criterion 1   There is sufficient evidence of the existence of the item (including, where appropriate, evidence that a future inflow or outflow of benefit will occur)

Criterion 2   The item can be measured at a monetary amount with sufficient reliability.

3.6 Derecognition

This is the question of when to **remove from the balance sheet** the assets and liabilities which have previously been recognised. FRS 5 addresses this issue only in relation to assets, not liabilities, and its rules are designed to determine one of three outcomes.

- **Complete derecognition**
- **No derecognition**
- The in-between case, **partial derecognition**

The issue of derecognition is perhaps one of the most common aspects of off balance sheet transactions: **has an asset been sold or has it been used to secure borrowings**? The concept of partial derecognition attempts to deal with the in-between situation of where sufficient benefits and risks have been transferred to warrant at least some derecognition of an asset.

3.6.1 Complete derecognition

In the simplest case, where a transaction results in the transfer to another party of all the **significant benefits and risks** relating to an asset, the entire asset should cease to be recognised. In this context, the word 'significant' is explained further: it should not be judged in relation to all the conceivable benefits and risks that could exist, but only in relation to those that are **likely to occur in practice**.

3.6.2 No derecognition

At the other end of the spectrum, where a transaction results in **no significant change** to the benefits or to the risks relating to the asset in question, no sale can be recorded and the entire asset should continue to be recognised. Retaining **either** the benefits or the risks is sufficient to keep the asset on the balance sheet. This means that the elimination of risk by financing the asset on a **non-recourse basis** (ie finance secured only on the asset in question) will not remove it from the balance sheet; it would be necessary to dispose of the upside as well in order to justify recording a sale. A further possible treatment, the special case of a **'linked presentation'**, is discussed below.

The standard says that **any transaction** that is **in substance a financing** will **not qualify for derecognition**; the item will therefore stay on the balance sheet, and the finance will be introduced as a liability.

3.6.3 Partial derecognition

As can be seen, the above criteria are relatively restrictive. The standard therefore goes on to deal with circumstances where, although not all significant benefits and risks have been transferred, the transaction is more than a mere financing and has transferred enough of the benefits and risks to warrant at least some derecognition of the asset. It addresses three such cases.

(a) **Where an asset has been subdivided**

Where an identifiable part of an asset is separated and sold off, with the remainder being retained, the asset should be split and a partial sale recorded. Examples include the sale of a proportionate part of a loan receivable, where all future receipts are shared equally between the parties, or the stripping of interest payments from the principal of a loan instrument.

(b) **Where an item is sold for less than its full life**

The seller retains a residual value risk by offering to buy the asset back at a predetermined price at a later stage in the asset's life. Such an arrangement is sometimes offered in relation to commercial vehicles, aircraft, and so on. In such cases the original asset will have been replaced by a residual interest in the asset together with a liability for its obligation to pay the repurchase price.

(c) **Where an item is transferred for its full life but some risk or benefit is retained**

This may arise, for example, where a company gives a warranty or residual value guarantee in relation to the product being sold. This does not prevent the recording of the sale so long as the exposure under the warranty or guarantee can be assessed and provided for if necessary. Companies may also sometimes retain the possibility of an upward adjustment to the sale price of an asset based on its future performance, eg when a business is sold subject to an earn-out clause, but again this should not prevent the recognition of the sale.

In all of these cases of partial disposals, the amount of the initial profit or loss may be **uncertain**. The normal rules of prudence should be applied, but also that the uncertainty should be disclosed if it could have a material effect on the accounts.

3.7 Linked presentation

FAST FORWARD

You also need to understand the methods of presentation described in FRS 5, particularly *offset* and **linked presentation**.

A 'linked presentation' requires **non-recourse finance** to be shown on the face of the balance sheet as a deduction from the asset to which it relates (rather than in the liabilities section of the balance sheet), provided certain **stringent criteria** are met. This is really a question of how, rather than whether, to show the asset and liability in the balance sheet, so it is not the same as derecognition of these items, although there are some similarities in the result.

Linked presentation should be used when an asset is financed in such a way that:

(a)   the finance will be repaid only from **proceeds generated by the specific item** it finances and there is no possibility whatsoever of a claim on the entity being established other than against funds generated by that item; *and*

(b)   there is no provision whereby the entity may either **keep the item** on repayment of the finance or **reacquire** it at any time.

There are also several more specific conditions which elaborate on these principles.

An obvious example where linked presentation applies is when **debts are factored**. Debt factoring is discussed in more detail in the next section, but in simplified terms such a transaction would appear as follows.

	£'000
Current assets	
Debtors	500
Less non-returnable amounts received on sale of debtor	(425)
	75

In this case 85% of the debtor balances are received on a non-returnable basis.

Question

Linked presentation

The managing director of your company has read an article about FRS 5 relating to linked presentation. The company is seeking to structure a financing of its head office in such a way that the asset and the funding could be 'linked' on the balance sheet.

As the company's finance director, draft a reply to the managing director, stating whether this treatment is possible.

Answer

The 'linked presentation' is a layout that shows the amount of borrowing or proceeds raised that has been deducted from the original asset amount, on the assets side of the balance sheet. It was developed in response to the ASB's difficulties in settling an appropriate accounting treatment for securitisations, but the criteria for its use are expressed in general terms; it is not reserved solely for securitisations.

Nevertheless, the provisions of FRS 5 relating to linked presentation are drawn extremely strictly. And even though companies should in general interpret FRS 5 in terms of its spirit and reasoning, the ASB's intention in the case of linked presentation was to limit its application by requiring the criteria to be met 'to the letter' before a linked presentation could be adopted.

It is a question of fact whether the proposed financial transaction meets the criteria in FRS 5, although, apart from some securitisations and factoring arrangements, the transactions it does apply to are likely to be very rare. The main criteria are that the finance that is shown as linked should be non-recourse, ie secured only on the asset in question, and that the company must not keep the asset when the finance is paid off, or reacquire it at any time.

In this case, the transaction is unlikely to be effective, as presumably the company will want to continue to use its head office after the finance is repaid.

3.8 Offset

FRS 5 makes it clear that assets and liabilities which qualify for recognition should be accounted for individually, rather than netted off. Offset is allowed by the standard only where the debit and credit balances are **not really separate assets and liabilities**, eg where there are amounts due to and from the same third party and there is a legal right of set-off. The key consideration is whether the entity can **enforce** a right of set-off so that there is no possibility of having to pay the creditor balance without recovering the debtor amount.

The detailed criteria which permit offset and **all of which must apply** are set out in FRS.

(a)   The parties owe each other **determinable monetary amounts**, denominated either in the same currency or in different but freely convertible currencies.

(b)   The reporting entity has the ability to insist on a **net settlement**, which can be enforced in all situations of default by the other party.

(c)   The reporting entity's ability to insist on a net settlement is **assured beyond doubt**. This means that the debit balance must be receivable no later than the credit balance requires to be paid, otherwise the entity could be required to pay the other party and later find that it was unable to obtain payment itself. It also means that the ability to insist on a net settlement would survive the insolvency of the other party (which may require detailed examination in group situations).

3.9 Disclosure

FRS 5 has a general requirement to disclose transactions in sufficient detail to enable the reader to understand their **commercial effect**, whether or not they have given rise to the recognition of assets and liabilities. This means that where transactions or schemes give rise to assets and liabilities which are *not* recognised in the accounts, disclosure of their nature and effects still has to be considered in order to ensure that the accounts give a true and fair view.

A second general principle is that an explanation should be given where there are any assets or liabilities whose **nature is different** from that which the reader might expect of assets or liabilities appearing in the accounts under that description. There are specific disclosures in relation to the use of the linked presentation, the inclusion of quasi-subsidiaries in the accounts, and the various transactions dealt with in the application notes (see below).

Question

Explain the accounting treatment and disclosure requirements for off balance sheet finance.

Answer

In the past neither accounting standards nor company law provided fully effective means for outlawing all off balance sheet practices either by specifying an accounting treatment or by adequate disclosure. Some may consider that the requirement for accounts to provide a true and fair view implies that disclosure is required of the existence and financial effect of, say, a controlled non-subsidiary. On the other hand, it was common practice to rely on the letter of the law to avoid this.

The ASB strengthened the principle of 'substance over form' by introducing definitions of assets and liabilities that require recognition of most forms of off balance sheet financing. FRS 5 requires recognition of the true economic and commercial effects of such transactions regardless of the form that they take.

In addition, individual laws or standards outlaw specific practices. For example, the 1989 Companies Act, which implements the EC 7th Directive on consolidated accounts, amended the Companies Act 1985 so that it now applies tests regarding control over, rather than ownership of another company to determine whether or not it should be consolidated. This deals with the above situation, where control is exercised even in the absence of majority ownership. These changes were incorporated into FRS 2 by the ASB.

These moves indicate that there is decreasing sympathy in the accounting profession and in the business community for off balance sheet financing. Thus, we can expect the auditors to take a firmer line on this topic than in the past and the investment community and the financial press pay more attention to it.

Exam focus point

Examination questions are likely to ask for calculations, accounting treatment and disclosure for a variety of transactions, including sale and leaseback transactions and debt factoring agreements. Question practice in this area is very worthwhile.

3.10 Private finance initiative

In 1999 the ASB published an *Application Note to FRS 5 Reporting the substance of transactions*.

The accounting treatment of PFI has become the subject of much debate. To fulfil a PFI contract, a private sector 'operator' typically constructs a capital asset (eg a road, bridge, hospital, prison, computer system or school) and uses that asset to provide services to a public sector 'purchaser'. The key accounting question is:

- Whether the purchaser has an asset of the property used to provide the contracted services together with a corresponding liability to pay the operator for it; or, alternatively

- Whether the operator has an asset of the property used to provide the contracted services or a financial asset being a debt due from the purchaser.

FRS 5 has a two-stage test.

Stage 1 Exclude any separable elements of the contract that relate only to services (such as cleaning, laundry, catering etc), rather than to the capital asset. Any such **service** elements are not relevant to determining which party has the **asset** and should be ignored.

Stage 2 Assess what remains to see if the leasing standard (SSAP 21) or FRS 5 should be applied.

Accounting treatment for the recognition of assets and liabilities

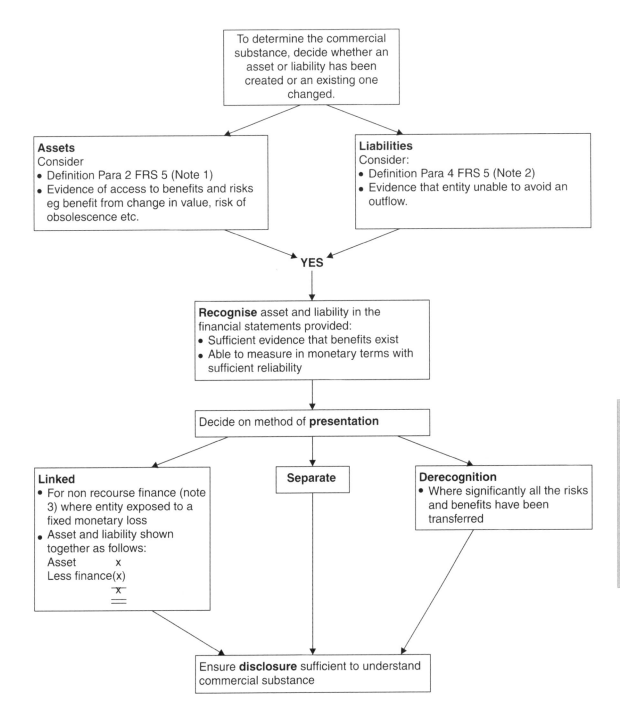

Notes

1   *Assets*: rights or other access to future economic benefits controlled by an entity as a result of past transactions or events.

2   *Liabilities*: an entity's obligations to transfer future economic benefits as a result of past transactions or events.

3   *Non-recourse finance*: there is no (or limited) recourse to the seller for losses.

3.11 Section summary

The diagram should help to explain a sensible approach to FRS 5 in examination questions. Important points to remember are:

- **Substance over form**
- Definitions of **assets** and **liabilities**
- Definition of **recognition**
- Different degrees of **derecognition**: complete, partial and none
- When **linked presentation** is used
- When **offset** is allowed

4 Common forms of off balance sheet finance

FAST FORWARD 〉〉

> The major types of off balance sheet finance are discussed in the **Application Notes** to FRS 5.

FRS 5 deals with certain specific aspects of off balance sheet finance in detailed **application notes**. These cover the following topics.

- Consignment stock
- Sale and repurchase agreements
- Factoring of debts
- Securitised assets
- Loan transfers

The application notes explain how to apply the standard to the particular transactions which they describe, and also contain specific disclosure requirements in relation to those transactions. The application notes are **not exhaustive** and they do not override the general principles of the standard itself, but they are regarded as authoritative insofar as they assist in interpreting it.

Note that in *all* cases **full disclosure** of the transaction should be given, whatever its accounting treatment. This will particularly hold where a **linked presentation** is used.

4.1 Consignment stock

Consignment stock is an arrangement where stock is held by one party (say a distributor) but is owned by another party (for example a manufacturer or a finance company). Consignment stock is common in the motor trade and is similar to goods sold on a 'sale or return' basis.

To identify the correct treatment, it is necessary to identify the point at which the distributor or dealer acquired the benefits of the asset (the stock) rather than the point at which legal title was acquired.

(a)   If the manufacturer has the right to require the return of the stock, and if that right is likely to be exercised, then the stock is *not* an asset of the dealer.

(b)   If the dealer is rarely required to return the stock, then this part of the transaction will have little commercial effect in practice and should be ignored for accounting purposes.

(c)   The potential liability would need to be disclosed in the accounts.

4.1.1 Summary of indications of asset status

The following analysis is given in FRS 5.

Indications that the stock is *not an asset* of the dealer at delivery	Indications that the stock *is an asset* of the dealer at delivery
Manufacturer can require dealer to **return stock** (or transfer stock to another dealer) without compensation; or	Manufacturer cannot require dealer to **return or transfer stock**; or
Penalty paid by the dealer to prevent returns/transfers of stock at the manufacturer's request.	**Financial incentives** given to persuade dealer to transfer stock at manufacturer's request.
Dealer has unfettered **right to return stock** to the manufacturer without penalty and actually exercises the right in practice.	Dealer has **no right to return stock** or is commercially compelled not to exercise its right of return.
Manufacturer bears **obsolescence risk**, eg: (a) obsolete stock is returned to the manufacturer without penalty; or (b) financial incentives given by manufacturer to prevent stock being returned to it (eg on a model change or if it becomes obsolete).	Dealer bears **obsolescence risk**, eg: (a) penalty charged if dealer returns stock to manufacturer; or (b) obsolete stock cannot be returned to the manufacturer and no compensation is paid by manufacturer for losses due to obsolescence.
Stock **transfer price** charged by manufacturer is based on manufacturer's list price at date of transfer of legal title.	Stock **transfer price** charged by manufacturer is based on manufacturer's list price at date of delivery.
Manufacturer bears **slow movement risk**, eg: transfer price set independently of time for which dealer holds stock, and there is no deposit.	Dealer bears **slow movement risk**, eg: (a) dealer is effectively charged interest as transfer price or other payments to manufacturer vary with time for which dealer holds stock; or (b) dealer makes a substantial interest-free deposit that varies with the levels of stock held.

4.1.2 Required accounting

Where it is concluded that the stock **is in substance an asset** of the dealer:

(a) Recognise the stock as such on the dealer's balance sheet, together with a corresponding liability to the manufacturer.

(b) Deduct any deposit from the liability and classify the excess as a trade creditor.

(c) Give full disclosure in the notes to the financial statements.

Where it is concluded that the stock is **not in substance an asset** of the dealer:

(a) Do not include the stock on the dealer's balance sheet until the transfer of title has crystallised.

(b) Include any deposit under 'other debtors'.

(c) Give full disclosure in the notes to the financial statements.

Question   Consignment stock

Daley Motors Ltd owns a number of car dealerships throughout Essex. The terms of the arrangement between the dealerships and the manufacturer are as follows.

(a)   Legal title passes when the cars are either used by Daley Ltd for demonstration purposes or sold to a third party.

(b)   The dealer has the right to return vehicles to the manufacturer without penalty. (Daley Ltd has rarely exercised this right in the past.)

(c)   The transfer price is based on the manufacturer's list price at the date of delivery.

(d)   Daley Ltd makes a substantial interest-free deposit based on the number of cars held.

Should the asset and liability be recognised at the date of delivery?

Answer

(a)   Legal form is irrelevant.
(b)   Yes: only because rarely exercised (otherwise 'no').
(c)   Yes: per FRS 5.
(d)   Yes: the dealership is effectively forgoing the interest which could be earned on the cash sum.

4.2 Sale and repurchase agreements

These are arrangements under which the company sells an asset to another person on terms that allow the company to **repurchase the asset** in certain circumstances. A common example is the sale and repurchase of maturing whisky stocks. The key question is whether the transaction is a **straightforward sale**, or whether it is, in effect, a **secured loan**. It is necessary to look at the arrangement to determine who has the rights to the economic benefits that the asset generates, and the terms on which the asset is to be repurchased.

If the seller has the right to the benefits of the **use of the asset**, and the repurchase terms are such that the **repurchase is likely** to take place, the transaction should be accounted for as a **loan**.

4.2.1 Summary of indications of the sale of the asset

FRS 5 gives the following summary.

Indications of *sale* of original asset to buyer (nevertheless, the seller may retain a different asset)	Indications of *no sale* of original asset to buyer (secured loan)
	Sale price does not equal market value at date of sale.
No commitment for seller to repurchase asset, eg call option where there is a real possibility the option will fail to be exercised.	Commitment for seller to repurchase asset, eg: • put and call option with the same exercise price; • either a put or a call option with no genuine commercial possibility that the option will fail to be exercised; or • seller requires asset back to use in its business, or asset is in effect the only source of seller's future sales.

Indications of *sale* of original asset to buyer (nevertheless, the seller may retain a different asset)	Indications of *no sale* of original asset to buyer (secured loan)
Risk of **changes in asset value** borne by buyer such that buyer does not receive solely a lender's return, eg both sale and repurchase price equal market value at date of sale/repurchase	Risk of **changes in asset value** borne by seller such that buyer receives solely a lender's return, eg: • Repurchase price equals sale price plus costs plus interest • Original purchase price adjusted retrospectively to pass variations in the value of the asset to the seller • Seller provides residual value guarantee to buyer or subordinated debt to protect buyer from falls in the value of the asset.
Nature of the asset is such that it will be used over the life of the agreement, and seller has no rights to **determine its use**. Seller has no rights to determine asset's development or future sale.	Seller retains right to **determine asset's use**, development or sale, or rights to profits therefrom.

4.2.2 Required accounting

Where the substance of the transaction is that of a **secured loan**:

(a) The seller should continue to recognise the original asset and record the proceeds received from the buyer as a liability

(b) Interest, however designated, should be accrued

(c) The carrying amount of the asset should be reviewed and provided against if necessary

(d) Full disclosure should be made in the notes to the financial statements

Where the transaction is a **sale and leaseback**, no profit should be recognised on entering in to the arrangement and no adjustment made to the carrying value of the asset. As stated in the guidance notes to SSAP 21, this represents the substance of the transactions, 'namely the raising of finance secured on an asset that continues to be held and that is not disposed of'.

Where the **seller has a new asset or liability** (eg merely a call option to repurchase the original asset), it should recognise or disclose that new asset or liability on a prudent basis in accordance with the provisions of FRS 12. In particular, the seller should recognise (and not merely disclose) a liability for any kind of unconditional obligation it has entered into.

Question	Sale and repurchase

A construction company, Mecanto plc, agrees to sell to Hamlows Bank some of the land within its landbank. The terms of the sale are as follows.

(a) The sales price is to be at open market value.

(b) Mecanto plc has the right to develop the land on the basis that it will pay all the outgoings on the land plus an annual fee of 5% of the purchase price.

(c) Mecanto has the option to buy back the land at any time within the next five years. The repurchase price is based on:

(i) Original purchase price
(ii) Expenses relating to the purchase

(iii)   An interest charge of base rate + 2%

(iv)   Fewer amounts received from Mecanto by Hamlows.

(d)   At the end of five years Hamlows Bank may offer the land for sale generally. Any shortfall on the proceeds relative to the agreed purchase price agreed with Mecanto has to be settled by Mecanto in cash.

Should the asset continue to be recognised and the sales proceeds treated as a loan?

Answer

(a)   No: the sales price is as for an arms' length transaction.

(b)   Yes: Mecanto has control over the asset.
Yes: Mecanto has to pay a fee based on cash received.

(c)   Yes: interest is charged on the proceeds paid to Mecanto.
Yes: the repurchase price is based on the lender's return

(d)   Yes: options ensure that Mecanto bears all the risk (both favourable and unfavourable) of changes in the market value of the land.

4.3 Factoring of debts

Where debts are factored, the original creditor **sells the debts to the factor**. The sales price may be fixed at the outset or may be adjusted later. It is also common for the factor to offer a credit facility that allows the seller to draw upon a proportion of the amounts owed.

In order to determine the correct accounting treatment it is necessary to consider whether the benefit of the debts has been passed on to the factor, or whether the factor is, in effect, providing a loan on the security of the debtors. If the seller has to **pay interest** on the difference between the amounts advanced to him and the amounts that the factor has received, and if the seller bears the **risks of non-payment** by the debtor, then the indications would be that the transaction is, in effect, a loan. Depending on the circumstances, either a linked presentation or separate presentation may be appropriate.

4.3.1 Summary of indications of appropriate treatment

FRS 5 gives the following summary of indicators of the appropriate treatment.

Indications that derecognition is appropriate (debts are *not* an *asset* of the seller)	Indications that a *linked presentation* is appropriate	Indications that a separate presentation is appropriate (debts are an *asset* of the seller)
Transfer is for a single non-returnable fixed sum.	Some non-returnable proceeds received, but seller has rights to further sums from the factor (or vice versa) whose amount depends on whether or when debtors pay.	Finance cost varies with speed of collection of debts, eg: • by adjustment to consideration for original transfer or • subsequent transfers priced to recover costs of earlier transfers.
There is **no recourse** to the seller for losses.	There is either **no recourse** for losses, or such recourse has a fixed monetary ceiling.	There is **full recourse** to the seller for losses.

Indications that derecognition is appropriate (debts are *not an asset* of the seller)	Indications that a *linked presentation* is appropriate	Indications that a separate presentation is appropriate (debts are an *asset* of the seller)
Factor is paid **all amounts** received from the factored debts (and no more). Seller has no rights to further sums from the factor.	Factor is paid only out of **amounts collected** from the factored debts, and seller has no right or obligation to repurchase debts.	Seller is required to **repay** amounts received from the factor on or before a set date, regardless of timing or amounts of collections from debtors.

4.3.2 Required accounting

Derecognition. Where the seller has retained no significant benefits and risks relating to the debts and has no obligation to repay amounts received from the factors, the debtors should be removed from its balance sheet and no liability shown in respect of the proceeds received from the factor. A profit or loss should be recognised, calculated as the difference between the carrying amount of the debts and the proceeds received.

Linked presentation. Where the conditions for a linked presentation are met, the proceeds received, to the extent they are non-returnable, should be shown deducted from the gross amount of the factored debts (after providing for bad debts, credit-protection charges and any accrued interest) in the face of the balance sheet. The interest element of the factor's charges should be recognised as it accrues and included in the P&L account with other interest charges.

Separate presentation. Where neither derecognition nor a linked presentation is appropriate, a separate presentation should be adopted: a gross asset (equivalent in amount to the gross amount of the debts) should be shown on the balance sheet of the seller within assets, and a corresponding liability in respect of the proceeds received from the factor should be shown within liabilities. The interest element of the factor's charges should be recognised as it accrues and included in the P&L account with other interest charges. Other factoring costs should be similarly accrued and included in the P&L account within the appropriate caption.

4.4 Securitised assets

Securitisation is very common in the financial services industry, and the assets that are most commonly securitised are mortgages and credit card accounts, although hire purchase loans, trade debts and even property and stocks are sometimes securitised. **Blocks of assets** are thus financed, rather than the company's general business.

The normal procedure is for the assets to be transferred by the person who held them (the originator) to a special purpose company (the issuer) in exchange for cash. The issuer will use the proceeds of an issue of debentures or loan notes to pay for the assets. The shares in the issuer are usually held by a third party so that it does not need to be consolidated. The issuer will usually have a very small share capital, and so most of the risk will be borne by the people who lent it the money through the debentures to pay for the assets. For this reason there is usually some form of insurance taken out on the assets to give some security for the lenders.

4.4.1 Summary of indications as to accounting treatment

FRS 5 gives the following summary of indications of the appropriate treatment.

Indications that derecognition is appropriate (securitised assets are *not an asset* of the seller)	Indications that a *linked presentation* is appropriate	Indications that a separate presentation is appropriate (securitised assets are *assets* of the originator)
Originator's individual financial statements		
Transaction price is **arm's length price** for an outright sale.	Transaction price **is not arm's length price** for an outright sale.	Transaction price is **not arm's length price** for an outright sale.
Transfer is for a **single, non-returnable fixed sum**.	Some **non-returnable proceeds** received, but originator has rights to further sums from the issuer, the amount of which depends on the performance of the securitised assets.	Proceeds received are **returnable**, or there is a provision whereby the originator may keep the securitised assets on repayment of the loan notes or re-acquire them.
There is **no recourse** to the originator for losses.	There is either **no recourse** for losses, or such recourse has a fixed monetary ceiling.	There is or may be **full recourse** to the originator for losses, eg: • Originator's directors are unable or unwilling to state that it is not obliged to fund any losses • Noteholders have not agreed in writing that they will seek repayment only from funds generated by the securitised assets
Originator's consolidated financial statements		
Issuer is owned by an **independent third party** that made a substantial capital investment, has control of the issuer, and has the benefits and risks of its net assets.	Issuer is a **quasi-subsidiary** of the originator, but the conditions for a linked presentation are met from the point of view of the group.	Issuer is a **subsidiary** of the originator.

4.4.2 Required accounting: originator's financial statements

Derecognition. Where the originator has retained no significant benefits and risks relating to the securitised assets and has no obligation to repay the proceeds of the note issue, the asset should be removed from its balance sheet, and no liability shown in respect of the proceeds of the note issue. A profit or loss should be recognised, calculated as the difference between the carrying amount of the assets and the proceeds received.

Linked presentation. Where the conditions for a linked presentation are met, the proceeds of the note issue (to the extent they are non-returnable) should be shown deducted from the securitised assets on the face of the balance sheet within a single asset caption. Profit should be recognised and presented in the manner set out in FRS 5. The disclosure requirements are extensive, including a description of the securitised assets and all relevant terms, income and expenses, claims on proceeds, etc.

Separate presentation. Where neither derecognition nor a linked presentation is appropriate, a separate presentation should be adopted, ie a gross asset (equal in amount to the gross amount of the securitised assets) should be shown on the balance sheet of the originator within assets, and a corresponding liability in respect of the proceeds of the note issue shown within liabilities. No gain or loss should be recognised at the time the securitisation is entered into (unless adjustment to the carrying value of the asset independent of the securitisation is required).

4.4.3 Required accounting: issuer's financial statements

The requirements set out in the paragraphs above for the originator's individual financial statements also apply to the issuer's financial statements. In most cases the issuer will be required to adopt a **separate presentation**, in which case the provisions of the previous paragraph will apply.

4.5 Loan transfers

These are arrangements where a loan is transferred to a transferee from an original lender. This will usually be done by the **assignment of rights and obligations** by the lender, or the **creation of a new agreement** between the borrower and the transferee. The same principles apply to loan transfers as to debt factoring and securitised assets.

4.5.1 Summary of indications of appropriate treatment

FRS 5 gives the following summary.

Indications that *derecognition* is appropriate (off lender's balance sheet)	Indications that a *linked presentation* is appropriate	Indications that a *separate presentation* is appropriate (on lender's balance sheet
Transfer is for a single, non-returnable fixed sum.	Some non-returnable proceeds received, but lender has rights to further sums whose amount depends on whether or when the borrowers pay.	The proceeds received are returnable in the event of losses occurring on the loans.
There is no recourse to the lender for losses from any cause.	There is either no recourse for losses, or such recourse has a fixed monetary ceiling.	There is full recourse to the lender for losses.
Transferee is paid all amounts received from the loans (and no more), as and when received. Lender has no rights to further sums from the loans or the transferee.	Transferee is paid only out of amounts received from the loans, and lender has no right or obligation to repurchase them.	Lender is required to repay amounts received from the transferee on or before a set date, regardless of the timing or amount of payments by the borrowers.

4.5.2 Required accounting

Derecognition. Where the lender has retained no significant benefits and risks relating to the loans and has no obligation to repay the transferee, the loans should be removed from its balance sheet and no liability shown in respect of the amounts received from the transferee. A profit or loss may arise for the lender. Where the profit or loss is realised in cash it should be recognised, calculated as the difference between the carrying amount of the loans and the cash proceeds received. Where, however, the lender's profit or loss is not realised in cash and there are doubts as to its amount, full provision should be made for any expected loss but recognition of any gain, to the extent it is in doubt, should be deferred until cash has been received.

Linked presentation. Where the conditions for a linked presentation are met, the proceeds received, to the extent they are non-returnable, should be shown deducted from the gross amount of the loans on the face of the balance sheet. Profit should be recognised and presented as set out in FRS 5.

Separate presentation. Where neither derecognition not a linked presentation is appropriate, a separate presentation should be adopted, ie a gross asset (equivalent in amount to the gross amount of the loans) should be shown on the balance sheet of the lender within assets, and a corresponding liability in respect of the amounts received from the transferee should be shown within creditors. No gain or loss should be recognised at the time of the transfer (unless adjustment to the carrying value of the loan independent of the transfer is required).

<table>
<tr><td>Exam focus
point</td><td>In spite of FRS 5 and its application notes, there are still opportunities to manipulate results.</td></tr>
</table>

4.6 UITF Abstract 32 *Employee benefit trusts and other intermediate payment arrangements*

This Abstract was published in 2001. It applies where an entity sets up and provides funds to an employee benefit trust (or other intermediary) and the trust's accumulated assets are used to remunerate the entity's employees (or other service providers).

Abstract 32 clarifies how the principles of FRS 5 *Reporting the substance of transactions* should be applied to determine:

(a)   Whether a payment to the intermediary should be charged as an expense when the payment is made

(b)   If the payment is not an expense, what assets and liabilities the sponsoring entity should recognise after the payment

The Abstract requires that when an entity transfers funds to an employee benefit trust or other intermediary there should be a rebuttable presumption that the entity has exchanged one asset (usually cash) for another (such as restricted cash) and that the payment itself does not represent an immediate expense. The expense is incurred when a liability for the employee costs arises. This means that in most circumstances sponsoring entities should recognise the assets (and any liabilities) of employee benefit trusts as their own until, for example, the assets vest unconditionally in identified beneficiaries.

4.7 UITF Abstract 36 *Contracts for sale of capacity*

In some industries, entities enter into contracts that convey the right to use some or all of the capacity of a physical assets. For example, in the telecommunications and electricity industries, entities may buy and sell capacity on each others' network. Some contracts give the right to use identifiable physical assets, whilst others convey the right to use a specified amount of capacity.

This type of transaction gives rise to three questions.

(a)   Should the seller **report the transaction as a sale** of an asset or should the seller **continue to recognise existing assets** in their entirety?

(b)   Should gains and losses arising be **presented as operating revenues/costs**, or should they be presented as gains /losses on disposal of fixed assets?

(c)   How should transactions involving **exchanges** of network capacity be accounted for?

UITF Abstract 36, which was issued in 2003, addresses these issues. In general terms, the principles of FRS 5 are applied.

4.7.1 Reporting the transaction as a sale

A seller of a right to use capacity should **not** report the transaction as the **sale of an asset** or component of a larger asset unless all of the following **conditions** can be satisfied.

(a) The purchaser's right of use is **exclusive and irrevocable**.

(b) The asset component is **specific and separable**. (The buyer's exclusivity is guaranteed and the seller has no right to substitute other assets.)

(c) The term of the contract is for a **major part of the asset's useful economic life**.

(d) The attributable cost or carrying value can be **measured reliably**.

(e) **No significant risks are retained** by the seller.

4.7.2 Turnover or disposal of fixed asset

If a transaction is reported as the sale of an asset, the proceeds will generally be reported as a **fixed asset disposal**. Only if the assets were designated as held for resale may the proceeds be reported as turnover.

4.7.3 Exchanges of network capacity

An entity may sell capacity on a network in exchange for receiving capacity on another entity's network in cases where the two capacities are of similar value. These types of transactions are often referred to as **reciprocal transactions**. They fall into two categories.

(a) Contracts to provide capacity in exchange for receiving capacity (no cash involved)

(b) Transactions entered into wholly or in part for a cash consideration

The UITF states that turnover or gains in respect of reciprocal transactions should be **recognised only** if the assets or services provided or received have a **readily ascertainable market value**.

No accounting recognition should be given to transactions that are **artificial or lacking in substance**.

FRS 5 is counted as one of the ASB's successes. However, it is not without its critics. It is very long, dense and in places difficult to understand. Moreover, the linked presentation requirement is controversial, and some commentators think it is wrong.

5 Revenue recognition

Revenue recognition is an important problem, so the ASB has issued a Discussion Paper about it.

5.1 The problem

The recognition and measurement of revenue are of fundamental importance to proper financial reporting. Furthermore, revenue recognition has been in the news recently. There has been much discussion about the range of different accounting policies adopted by software companies, with pressure from analysts and shareholders to achieve greater consistency of reporting in that sector. The Auditing Practices Board issued a Consultation Paper at the end of June focusing on 'aggressive earnings management', with revenue recognition being one of the concerns at the heart of that debate.

The basic problem is that, with the increasing complexity of business activities, **traditional drivers of revenue**—such as 'earning', realisation, accruals/matching and prudence—are becoming harder to apply.

Faced with difficult questions over revenue recognition, different companies are finding different answers, and **practices** are developing that are in some respects **inconsistent** from one industry to another and within a single industry. The ASB believes that this inconsistency is not merely a practical issue: it also reflects different views of what revenue should represent, and of how financial statements should portray a business's operating activities.

Nor is this a problem confined to the UK and the Republic of Ireland. Although revenue accounting standards elsewhere are based on underlying concepts, those concepts are not always explored in sufficient depth to ensure their consistent application. For example, in the USA accounting for revenue is driven by underlying concepts of revenue being both **earned** and **realised**, but considerable judgement can be required in interpreting and applying these concepts.

5.2 ASB Discussion Paper

In 2001, the ASB published a Discussion Paper *Revenue recognition*. The Paper does not discuss revenue recognition issues arising in specific industries, such as the software industry. Rather, it **focuses on the underlying proble**m, which is that, with the increasing complexity of business activities, traditional drivers of revenue are becoming harder to apply.

The ASB aims to develop a single accounting standard that sets out general principles for revenue recognition, but in sufficient depth to avoid some of the inconsistencies that exist at present. It hopes to **establish a framework** that can be used consistently to address revenue issues arising in different contexts. It's main content is summarised below.

5.2.1 Chapter 1: What should revenue represent?

This chapter asks what 'revenue' – which may be referred to by various names, including sales, fees, interest, dividends and royalties – should represent in financial statements. It proposes the following definitions.

Key term

> In the context of a business operating cycle, **revenue** is the class of gains, before deduction of associated costs, arising as a result of **benefit being transferred to a customer** in an **exchange transaction** (ie under a contract).

An **operating cycle** is a sequence of business activities, carried out with a view to profit, which involves the **transfer of benefit to customers in exchange for consideration** (ie payment).

5.2.2 Chapter 2: Revenue and contractual performance

Chapter 2 develops this definition of revenue, by exploring how benefit is transferred to customers in exchange transactions. It concludes that benefit is transferred when the seller honours the promises it has made under the contract – in other words, 'performs' its contractual obligations. In that light, the chapter builds on the definition of revenue from Chapter 1.

In the context of a business operating cycle, revenue arises as a result of benefit being transferred to a customer through the **seller's performance under a contract**.

5.2.3 Chapter 3: Accounting for incomplete contractual performance

Chapter 3 extends this discussion of performance to contracts where the seller's contractual performance is incomplete. It concludes that **full performance is only sometimes necessary for revenue to arise**, and suggests the following general principle for determining the extent to which revenue should be recognised on the basis of partial performance.

Where contractual performance **is incomplete**, revenue should be recognised **to the extent that the seller has performed** and that performance has resulted **in benefit accruing to the customer**.

The Chapter then considers, at a very high level, various techniques by which this general principle might be applied in practice. It acknowledges, however, that dealing with **incomplete performance is likely to be the biggest single difficulty arising in practice,** and that the application of the above proposal to specific industries will be an important part of the next stage of this project.

5.2.4 Chapter 4: Rights of return and post performance options

Chapter 4 considers how the approach developed above is affected by customer rights of return, which in effect give a customer the ability to unwind a contract after performance by the supplier has occurred. The chapter proposes the following two possible approaches to accounting for rights of return and asks for views on which is more appropriate.

(a) **Expected sale approach.** Where goods are transferred along with a right of return, revenue should be recognised on the transfer of benefit, with an appropriate adjustment to reflect the risk of returns.

(b) **Accounting policy approach.** Where goods are transferred along with a right of return, an entity should select and consistently apply whichever of the following accounting policies is **most appropriate** to its circumstances.

(i) *Either* revenue should be recognised on the transfer of benefit, with an appropriate adjustment to reflect the risk of returns

(ii) *Or* revenue should be recognised on the expiry of the right to return

The most appropriate accounting policy should be judged by reference to the objectives and constraints set out in FRS 18 *Accounting policies,* giving due weight to the objective of comparability between entities operating within the same industry.

5.2.5 Chapter 5: Measuring consideration

Chapter 5 discusses measurement principles as opposed to recognition principles. It makes the following proposal for measurement of revenue.

Revenue should be **measured as the change in fair value** arising from the **seller's performance** of:

(a) **Assets** representing rights or other access to consideration, and
(b) **Liabilities** in respect of consideration received in advance of performance

Because revenue is restricted to gains that arise from the seller's performance, measurement of revenue is not distorted by the timing of payment from a customer. **Changes** to the value of consideration **that do not arise from performance**, for example, the **time value of money** where a customer pays a long time in advance, **do not form part of the measurement of revenue.**

Chapter 5 also considers barter transactions and asks if these should give rise to revenue. What is important is the role that the transaction has in the entity's operating cycle.

A transaction is with a customer – and hence gives rise to revenue – if, on its completion, the entity has been rewarded for **eliminating the risks previously outstanding in the relevant operating cycle.**

5.2.6 Chapter 6: Other issues relating to contracts and performance

This chapter considers

- Pre-performance options
- Which activities constitute performance
- 'Two-way' trading arrangements

It asks how customer payments for options should be dealt with and puts forward the following proposals.

When a customer pays for an **option** to require future performance from a seller, that payment gives rise to a liability which should be **released as revenue only when the future performance to which it relates occurs.**

Because the number of options that will lapse unexercised cannot be known with certainty, the relationship between proceeds and **performance should be estimated at the outset and estimates should be revised over the period of performance**.

The chapter goes on to consider which activities of a seller should be taken into account when assessing the extent to which performance has occurred. It concludes that in order to be considered as part of the performance of the contract, it must be a **necessary part of the contract.** It must be specific to the customer and it must be an activity that would not have taken place had the contract not existed.

Two contracts should be accounted for separately if they are genuinely independent of one another. However, they should be treated as one larger contract if one is conditional or dependent on the other, either legally or economically.

This kind of economic dependence may arise if, for example, contract prices are set so far from fair value that there is no realistic prospect that the second contract will not follow from the first.

5.2.7 Chapter 7: Agency

This chapter considers certain aspects of agency agreements. Its main proposals are as follows.

(a) When a **principal transacts with a customer through a disclosed agent**, the principal's revenue should reflect the **full consideration payable by the customer** in the transaction. The principal should treat any **commission** or other amounts payable to the agent **separately as an expense and not as a reduction of revenue.**

(b) When an **entity acts as a disclosed agent**, its revenue should reflect the amount of **commission or other income receivable** from its principal.

(c) When an entity acts as an **undisclosed agent**, it should **account for revenue in the same way as a principal.**

5.3 FRED 28 *Inventories; Construction and service contracts*

As part of the ASB's programme of convergence between FRS and IFRS (see Chapter 23), in May 2002 it issued FRED 28 *Inventories; Construction and service contracts.*

5.3.1 Main points

This FRED covers material from three IAS: IAS 2 *Inventories,* IAS 11 *Construction contracts* and a small amount of material from IAS 18 *Revenue.*

There are no major differences between the accounting required by the proposals in FRED 28 and the existing requirements of SSAP 9.

The topic of revenue recognition is being considered by the ASB and other standard setters, and is currently the subject of a Discussion Paper (see paragraphs 5.1-5.21). For this reason, the ASB does not currently propose that the UK should adopt the full text of IAS 18.

The main difference between SSAP 9 and FRED 28 is in the **terminology**, most obviously in the title. International accounting standards talk about 'inventory' rather than 'stocks' and 'construction and service contracts' rather than 'long-term contracts'. **Stocks and long-term contracts are not examinable at. Paper P2**, so we focus below on the material from IAS 18 on revenue recognition, which will be new to you.

5.3.2 Main changes proposed to existing UK requirements

There are **no major differences** between the accounting required in FRED 28 and the existing requirements of SSAP 9. However, SSAP 9 requires 'prudently calculated attributable profit' to be recognised in the profit and loss account when the outcome of a contract can be assessed with 'reasonable certainty'. Appendix I to the standard, contains similar references to prudence and reasonable certainty. FRED 28 requires the recognition of contract revenue and contract costs when the outcome of a contract can be **estimated reliably**. In emphasising reliability rather than prudence, the approach of the draft standard is more in keeping with the ASB's *Statement of Principles* and FRS 18 *Accounting policies*.

FRED 28 requires that **amounts received from the customer before the related work is performed** are recognised as a **separate liability** ('advances'). However, there are **no requirements relating to the further analysis** of the remaining balance sheet amount. (Paragraph 42 requires it to be presented as a single asset or liability, the 'gross amount due to/from customers for contract work'.) SSAP 9 requires the separate disclosure of 'amounts recoverable on contracts' (a debtor), 'payments on account' (a creditor), 'long-term contract balances' (stock) and foreseeable losses (a provision or creditor).

FRED 28 allows the requirements of the standard to be applied to the **separately identifiable components of a single contract or to a group of contracts together**, if that would reflect the substance of a contract or a group of contracts. SSAP 9 itself does not include an equivalent requirement.

The appendix to SSAP 9 indicates that, in some businesses, it will be most appropriate to treat parts of a long-term contract separately, but does not mention the combination of more than one contract. A similar treatment to that of the draft standard should be achieved by applying SSAP 9 in the context of FRS 5 *Reporting the substance of transactions*.

The remainder of this section deals with the material on contracts for services from IAS 18.

5.3.3 Rendering of services

The rendering of services typically involves the performance by the entity of a contractually agreed task over an agreed period of time. The services may be rendered within a single period or over more than one period.

Some contracts for the rendering of services are directly related to construction contracts, for example those for the services of project managers and architects. These are dealt with in accordance with the requirements for construction contracts.

When the outcome of a transaction involving the rendering of services can be estimated reliably, the associated revenue should be recognised by reference to the **stage of completion of the transaction** at the balance sheet date. The outcome of a transaction can be estimated reliably when *all* these conditions are satisfied.

  (a) The amount of revenue can be **measured reliably**

  (b) It is probable that the **economic benefits** associated with the transaction will flow to the entity

  (c) The **stage of completion** of the transaction at the balance sheet date can be measured reliably

  (d) The **costs incurred** for the transaction and the costs to complete the transaction can be measured reliably

The parties to the transaction will normally have to agree the following before an entity can make reliable estimates.

  (a) Each party's **enforceable rights** regarding the service to be provided and received by the parties

(b)   The **consideration** to be exchanged

(c)   The **manner and terms of settlement**

There are various methods of determining the stage of completion of a transaction, but for practical purposes, when services are performed by an indeterminate number of acts over a period of time, revenue should be recognised on a **straight line basis** over the period, unless there is evidence for the use of a more appropriate method. If one act is of more significance than the others, then the significant act should be carried out *before* revenue is recognised.

In uncertain situations, when the outcome of the transaction involving the rendering of services cannot be estimated reliably, the standard recommends a **no loss/no gain approach**. Revenue is recognised only to the extent of the expenses recognised that are recoverable.

This is particularly likely during the **early stages of a transaction**, but it is still probable that the entity will recover the costs incurred. So the revenue recognised in such a period will be equal to the expenses incurred, with no profit.

Obviously, if the costs are not likely to be reimbursed, then they must be recognised as an expense immediately. **When the uncertainties cease to exist**, revenue should be recognised as above.

Exam focus point	See also the treatment of service contracts in UITF 40, below. This has just been issued and is very topical.

5.4 Amendment to FRS 5: Revenue recognition

FAST FORWARD

> The ASB has also issued an **Application Note on revenue recognition** in the form of an **Amendment to FRS 5**. This gives both general principles and specialist guidance.

There is no specific UK standard which deals exclusively with revenue recognition, although it has featured in a number of standards including SSAP 9, the former SSAP 2, FRS 18 and UITF Abstract 26.

The IASB has a standard on Revenue (IAS 18), and is currently working on a project that will lead to a revision of both IAS 18 and the *Framework*. The intention is to publish an Exposure Draft in 2004. IASB is currently exploring an approach to revenue recognition which focuses on changes in assets and liabilities.

The ASB issued a Discussion Paper in July 2001, which is covered above. However, the ASB has no plans to produce an Exposure Draft or FRS on the subject because of its policy of only issuing full standards on topics of major concern that have been developed jointly with the IASB.

Nevertheless, the ASB has noted that **questions continue to arise** in relation to transactions affecting revenue recognition, and has therefore issued guidance on a number of aspects of the topic. This guidance takes the form of an **Application Note to FRS 5** *Reporting the substance of transactions*, which was published in November 2003.

The Application Note sets out a number of **basic principles**, which may be summarised as follows.

5.4.1 Exchange transaction

A seller enters into exchange transactions with its customers under **contractual arrangements** (formal or informal) under which it obtains the **right to be paid**.

Turnover is the revenue resulting from exchange transactions under which the seller transfers to customers the **goods or services that it is in business to provide.**

Payments derived from **other exchange transactions** (eg fixed asset sales) **do not normally give rise to turnover** as they do not fall within the class of transactions above (ie 'goods or services that it is in business to provide').

5.4.2 Reporting of revenue

At the point of performance of its contractual obligations, an entity will recognise either:

(a)   An **increase in assets**, or

(b)   A **decrease in liabilities** (eg where an entity previously received payment in advance of performance and is now released from the liability)

The asset increase or liability decrease is simultaneously reported as **revenue**.

5.4.3 Payment in advance of performance

When a seller receives payment from a customer in advance of performance, it recognises a **liability:**

(a)   This liability equals the consideration received and represents the seller's contractual obligation to provide goods or services to that value.

(b)   When performance takes place, the gross amount of the reduction in liability is simultaneously reported as revenue.

5.4.4 Measurement of revenue

Revenue (represented by the seller's new asset or by derecognition of a liability) should be measured at the **fair value of the consideration receivable.**

Fair value (FV) is defined as the amount at which goods or services could be exchanged in an arm's length transaction between informed and willing parties, other than in a forced or liquidation sale.

The FV of the consideration receivable will normally be the amount specified in the contractual arrangement as adjusted for:

- Discounts
- The time value of money and risk (where material)

The statement also gives **detailed guidance** on the following five areas.

(a)   Long-term contractual performance

(b)   Separation and linking of contractual arrangements

(c)   Bill and hold arrangements

(d)   Sales with rights of return

(e)   Presentation of turnover as a principal or agent.

These are the main areas which have been subject to **differing interpretation** in practice. The intention is to ensure that entities report turnover in accordance with the **substance of their contractual arrangements** with customers, and **at the point at which their performance entitles them to recognise** either an **increase in assets** or a **decrease in liabilities**.

5.4.5 Long-term contractual performance

A contractual arrangement may require a seller to design, manufacture or construct a single substantial asset or provide a service for a customer which is significant to the business and which straddles the seller's year-end.

The Application note proposes the following approach to such transactions.

(a)   Assess how changes in a seller's assets or liabilities, and related turnover, that arise from its performance under an incomplete long-term contract, should be recorded in the seller's financial statements.

287

(b)   Amounts recognised should represent the **stage of completion of contractual obligations, derived from an assessment of the fair value of goods or services provided** to the reporting date as **proportion of the total fair value of the contract**. This is preferred to considering expenditure to date as a proportion of total expenditure.

(c)   Fair values should represent those applicable on **inception of contract** (except where contractual terms specify that changes in prices will be passed on to the customer).

(d)   **Payments in instalments** may be (but will not necessarily be) **indicative** of extent to which seller has performed its contractual obligations.

(e)   Where payment is received in **arrears**, seller should take the following into account when valuing changes in assets or liabilities and related turnover:

   (i)   Risk

   (ii)   Time value of money

(f)   Where contractual arrangements give the customer the **right to cancel** at an interim stage of contract completion, the seller should have regard to the effect of **additional risk** arising.

5.4.6 Separation and linking of contractual arrangements

A single contractual arrangement may require a seller to provide a number of different goods or services (or 'components') to its customers. Three possibilities arise.

(a)   The components are unrelated and capable of being sold separately.

(b)   Two or more components are so closely related that their individual sale is not commercially feasible from viewpoint of either party.

(c)   A number of goods or services are provided in which the amount payable is set below the price at which the items would be sold individually.

The approach to be followed in the case of such arrangement is to **determine whether 'unbundling' or 'bundling' is appropriate.**

(a)   **Unbundling.** This arises when the seller, as a result of performance, decides to recognise a change in its assets or liabilities, and turnover, in respect of its right to be paid for each component on an individual basis.

(b)   **Bundling.** This is where a seller combines two or more components and recognises turnover on that basis.

In each case the commercial substance of the transaction needs to be considered.

Question	'Bundling' and 'unbundling'

State whether 'bundling' or 'unbundling' is appropriate in each of the following situations.

(a)   Fiona buys an 'off the shelf' software package from Seager Software Ltd. Seager Software offers separately a support service that provides helpline assistance and advice about the package's operation.

(b)   Total Software Solutions plc enters into a contractual arrangement for the supply of bespoke software, together with its maintenance and the customer's right to future upgrades for a period of three years.

Answer

(a)   An analysis of the arrangement shows that Fiona has no commercial obligation or requirement to purchase the support service; it is not needed in order that the software package operates satisfactorily. Seager Software Ltd's performance is made up from two components and it should recognise turnover separately for each.

(b)   An analysis of the arrangement shows that the maintenance and upgrades are required in order to ensure that the software continues to operate satisfactorily throughout the three year period and that these services are offered only by the supplier of the software, Total Software Solutions plc. The commercial substance of the arrangement is therefore that the customer is paying for a three year service agreement. The seller should treat all three components as linked, and recognise turnover on a long-term contractual basis.

5.4.7 Bill and hold arrangements

A seller may enter into a contractual arrangement with a customer for the supply of goods where there is **transfer of title but physical delivery is delayed to a later date.** These are commonly known as 'bill and hold' arrangements. It is necessary to determine whether, at any point, the seller has the right to recognise changes in its assets or liabilities, and turnover, in relation to the bill and hold arrangement.

In order to recognise these changes, the seller needs to have performed its contractual obligations by **transferring to the customer the principal benefits and risks of the goods**.

Benefits include:

(a)   The right to obtain the goods as and when required

(b)   The sole right to the goods for their sale to a third party, and the future cash flows from such a sale

(c)   Insulation from changes in prices charged by the seller (for example, arising from revisions to the seller's standard price list)

Risks include:

(a)   Slow movement (resulting in increased holding costs) and obsolescence

(b)   Being compelled to take delivery of goods that have become obsolescent or not readily saleable

For changes in assets/liabilities and turnover to be recognised, the contractual arrangements between seller and customer should include *all* of the following characteristics.

(a)   The bill and hold terms should **fulfil the commercial objectives of the customer**.

(b)   Subject to any normal rights of return, the **seller should have the right to be paid regardless of whether the goods are shipped**, at the customer's request, to its delivery address.

(c)   The **seller should not have retained any performance obligations** other than the safekeeping of the goods, and their shipment when the customer requests this.

(d)   The **goods should be identified separately from the seller's other stock** and should not be capable of being used to fill other orders that are received between the date of the bill and hold sale and shipment of the goods to the customer.

(e)   The goods should be **complete and ready for delivery**.

5.4.8 Sales with right of return

The terms of contractual arrangements may allow customers to return goods that they have purchased and either obtain a refund or be released from the obligation to pay. Rights of return may be included explicitly or implicitly within contractual arrangements, or arise through statutory requirements.

Including rights of return in a contractual arrangement **may affect either the quantification of the seller's right to be paid** (compared with a transaction which does not have these rights), **or the point at which the seller should recognise that right**. In some cases, 'right of return' could oblige the seller to defer recognition of the sales transaction so long as the seller retains substantially all of the risks associated with the related goods.

The seller's recognition of its right to be paid and contractual obligation to transfer economic benefits to its customer in respect of rights of return are linked transactions. In consequence, **changes in the seller's assets or liabilities should reflect the loss expected to arise from the rights of return. Turnover should exclude the sales value of estimated returns.**

The seller will generally be able reliably to estimate the sales value of returns, having regard to risk, which may be less than its maximum potential obligation. This may be derived from historic experience of comparable sales.

In extreme cases **where no reliable estimate can be made, substantially all of the risks of the related goods remain with the seller and turnover should not be recognised**. Any payments received should be included within creditors as **payments in advance**.

5.4.9 Presentation of turnover as principle or agent

A seller may act on its own account (as 'principal') when contracting with customers for the supply of goods or services. Alternatively a seller may act as an intermediary ('agent'), earning a fee or commission in return for arranging the provision of goods or services on behalf of a principal.

It is necessary to determine whether a seller should be regarded as acting as principal or agent in relation to an exchange transaction with a customer. **For a seller to account for exchange transactions as a principal, the seller should normally have exposure to all significant benefits and risks** associated with at least one of the following.

(a)   **Selling price**. The seller must be able to establish the selling price, directly or indirectly (for example through provision of additional goods or services).

(b)   **Stock**. The seller must be exposed to risks of damage, slow movement and obsolescence and changes in suppliers' prices.

Other indications that the **seller acts as principal** include:

(a)   Performance of part of the services, or modification to the goods supplied
(b)   Assumption of credit risk
(c)   Discretion in supplier selection
(d)   No disclosure of agency relationship

Other indications that the **seller acts as agent** include the following.

(a)   Once the customer's order has been confirmed with a third party, the seller has no further involvement in performance of ultimate supplier's contractual obligations.

(b)   The amount the seller earns is predetermined (a fixed fee or percentage of amount billed to customer).

(c)   The seller bears no stock or credit risk.

(d)   The seller has disclosed the fact that it is acting as agent.

Question

Consider whether the seller is acting as principal or agent in the following situations.

(a)   Buildit Ltd acts as a building contractor for the construction of a new office block. An analysis of the arrangement shows that the terms of the Buildit's contract with its customer include a negotiated selling price, credit risk for amounts due from the customer, primary responsibility for the construction and quality of the new building and discretion as to whether it carries out the work itself or employs subcontractors.

(b)   Kwikbreak.com acts as an online retailer from a website, where it advertises discounted holidays. An analysis of the arrangement shows that it acts as an intermediary between its customers and the ultimate sellers of the holidays and that it does not set the selling price. Its contractual terms of business include an exclusion of any liability to its customers once they have been put in touch with the ultimate sellers. Kwikbreak.com is paid a fee for each customer that purchases a holiday from an ultimate seller and has no involvement in the transaction after it has put the customer in touch with the ultimate seller.

Answer

(a)   Buildit Ltd is acting as principal and should account for the gross amount of turnover, regardless of whether it carries out the work itself or employs subcontractors to carry out part or all of the construction activities.

(b)   Kwikbreak.com is acting as agent and its turnover should include only the fees it receives from the ultimate seller.

5.5 UITF Abstract 40 *Revenue recognition and service contracts*

5.5.1 Background and main issue

Since Application Note G was issued some questions have been raised about accounting for revenue from service contracts. The main situation about which issues have been raised is long-term contracts, ie when revenue may (under SSAP 9) be recognised as contract activity progresses or on contract completion. **Service contracts do not fall within the SSAP 9 definition**. To deal with this problem, UITF 40 *Revenue recognition and service contracts* was issued in March 2005, effective for accounting periods ending on or after 22 June 2005.

5.5.2 Consensus

Application Note G requires a seller to recognise revenue to the extent that the seller obtains a right to consideration in exchange for its performance – this may be when some, but not all, of its contractual obligations have been fulfilled. If the seller has performed some, but not all, of its contractual obligations, it is required to recognise revenue to the extent that it has obtained the right to consideration through its performance. The UITF concluded that **the principles of revenue recognition in Application Note G are the same for long-term and other contracts for services**. The overriding consideration is whether the seller has performed, or partially performed, its contractual obligations.

5.5.3 Additional guidance

Abstract 40 provides additional guidance on the considerations that should inform the choice of appropriate accounting polices. These should have regard to the substance of contracts. A principal conclusion is that **where the substance of a contract is that the seller's contractual obligations are**

performed gradually over time, revenue should be recognised as contract activity progresses to reflect the seller's partial performance of its contractual obligations. In these circumstances it is inappropriate to defer recognition of revenue until contract completion. The amount of revenue should reflect the accrual of the right to consideration as contract activity progresses, taking account of both the value of the work performed and any uncertainties as to the amount that the customer will accept and pay. When, on the other hand, the right to consideration is contingent on a specified future event or outcome outside the seller's control, revenue is not recognised until that event occurs.

5.5.4 International comparison

The accounting required by Abstract 40 is similar to IAS 18 *Revenue* in relation to the rendering of services.

Chapter Roundup

- The subject of **off balance sheet finance** is a complex one which has plagued the accountancy profession. In practice, off balance sheet finance schemes are often very sophisticated and they are beyond the range of this syllabus. FRS 5 embodies the concept of **substance over form**.

- **FRS 5** embodies the concept of **substance over form**.

- Make sure that you have memorised the definitions for **assets and liabilities** and the criteria for their **recognition and derecognition** given in FRS 5.

- You also need to understand the methods of presentation described in FRS 5, particularly *offset* and **linked presentation**.

- The major types of off balance sheet finance are discussed in the **Application Notes** to FRS 5.

- **Revenue recognition** is an important problem, so the ASB has issued a Discussion Paper about it.

- The ASB has also issued an **Application Note on revenue recognition** in the form of an **Amendment to FRS 5**. This gives both general principles and specialist guidance.

Quick Quiz

1   Off balance sheet transactions are always fraudulent.

    True ☐

    False ☐

2   Give three examples of ways in which the principle of substance over form is enforced.

3   When should an asset be recognised on the balance sheet?

4   Assets must be recognised or not appear at all.

    True ☐

    False ☐

5   What is 'linked presentation'?

6   FRS 5 allows offset of assets and liabilities only in very limited cases.

Fill in the blanks.

(a)   The parties owe each other ……………………………………………….. amounts.

(b)   The reporting entity has the ability to insist on a ……………………………………

(c)   The above is ……………………………………………………………………………..

7   Factotem Ltd brings in a debt factor. The terms of the agreement are that the factor pays Factotem 90% of the value of the outstanding debtors. Interest is charged on this amount. The factor then collects the debts and reduces this amount accordingly. Factotem is responsible for any uncollected debts. What is the substance of the transaction?

8   The ASB's Discussion Paper on revenue recognition deals with specific industries.

    True ☐

    False ☐

9   Why would a sale of fixed assets not give rise to revenue?

Answers to Quick Quiz

1   False. There may be genuine reasons for excluding items from the balance sheet.

2   (a)   Leasing
     (b)   Quasi subsidiaries
     (c)   Joint arrangement which are not entities.

3   See Paragraph 3.5.

4   False. FRS 5 allows the in-between case of partial derecognition.

5   This requires non-recourse finance to be shown on the face of the balance sheet as a deduction from the asset to which it relates, rather than in the liabilities section.

6   (a)   Determinable monetary amounts
     (b)   Net settlement
     (c)   Assured beyond doubt

7   The form is likely to be that Factotem has sold its debtors to the factor. The substance is that Factotem is still responsible for bad debts and the factor has provided a commercial loan with the debtors as security.

8   False. It is a discussion of the underlying principles.

9   Under the ASB's recent Application Note to FRS 5, such a transaction would not give rise to revenue because it does not fall within the category of goods or services that the entity is in business to provide.

Now try the questions below from the Exam Question Bank

Number	Level	Marks	Time
Q12	Introductory	n/a	n/a

Part C
Reporting financial performance

Performance measures

Topic list	Syllabus reference
1 Performance measurement	B1
2 Financial performance measures	B1
3 Non-financial performance measures	B1
4 Benefits and problems of performance measures	B1
5 Accounting theory and practice	B3

Introduction

This chapter looks at a number of aspects of performance reporting standards.
Alternative performance measures are considered, including non-financial
measures. Finally the potential weakness of the reported profit figure is
considered. You should consider matters covered here in conjunction with
those covered in Chapter 11 on the substance of transactions, where some
weaknesses in conventional financial reporting are also shown up.

Study guide

		Intellectual level
B1	**The contribution and limitations of financial statements in meeting user's and capital markets' needs**	
(a)	Evaluate the consistency and clarity of corporate reports	3
(b)	Assess the insight into financial and operational risks provided by corporate reports	3
(c)	Discuss the usefulness of corporate reports in making investment decisions	3
B3	**Critical evaluation of principles and practices**	
(b)	Identify the relationship between accounting theory and practice	3
(c)	Critically evaluate accounting principles and practices used in corporate reporting	3

Exam guide

Weaknesses in current financial reporting may come up as part of a discussion on the impact of change. Perhaps alternative types of reporting will be presented, and you will need to point out strengths and weaknesses.

1 Performance measurement

FAST FORWARD

Key areas for performance measurement are **profitability, activity** and **productivity**. Profitability is often a key objective but other **'success factors'** are also critical. **Benchmarking** is increasingly common.

Performance measurement aims to establish **how well** something or somebody is doing in relation to the **planned activity** and **desired results**. The 'thing' may be a machine, a factory, a subsidiary company or an organisation as a whole. The 'body' may be an individual employee, a manager, or a group of people.

A typical business requires performance measurement in the following areas.

(a)   In relation to **external parties** (customers, market, suppliers, competitors)
(b)   **Across the organisation** as a whole (divisional performance measurement)
(c)   **Within** each of the main sub-divisions of the business
(d)   At the level of **individual activities**

Measurement can be in terms of **profitability, activity** and **productivity**.

Point of reference	Comment
Profitability	Profit has two components: cost and income. All parts of an organisation and all activities within it incur costs, and so their success needs to be judged in relation to cost. Only some parts of an organisation receive income, and their success should be judged in terms of both cost and income.

Point of reference	Comment
Activity	All parts of an organisation are also engaged in activities (activities cause costs). Activity measures could include the following. • Number of orders received from customers, a measure of the effectiveness of marketing • Number of deliveries made, a measure of the effectiveness of distribution • Number of production runs achieved by a particular factory Each of these items could be measured in terms of physical numbers, monetary value, or time spent.
Productivity	This is the quantity of the product or service produced in relation to the resources put in, for example so many units produced per hour, or per employee, or per tonne of material. It defines how *efficiently* resources are being used.

Question

Performance measurement

An invoicing assistant works in a department with three colleagues. She is paid £8,000 per annum. The department typically handles 10,000 invoices per week. One morning she spends half an hour on the phone to her grandfather, who lives in Australia, at the company's expense. The cost of the call proves to be £32.

Required

From this scenario identify as many different performance measures as possible, explaining what each is intended to measure. Make any further assumptions you wish.

Answer

Invoices per employee per week: 2,500 (activity)
Staff cost per invoice: £0.06 (cost/profitability)
Invoices per hour: 2,500/(7 × 5) = 71.4 (productivity)
Cost of idle time: £32 + £2.14 = £34.14 (cost/profitability)

You may have thought of other measures and probably have slight rounding differences.

1.1 Profit and other objectives

A traditional view has been that a desire to achieve greater profitability often entails a **sacrifice** in some other aspect of performance. One obvious example is quality: if cheaper materials are used to make a product or less highly trained workers deliver a service, money will be saved (increasing profits), but quality will fall.

In other cases there may not be a clear link between an objective and the profitability objective. A company may aim to improve **working conditions** for its staff, and measure its success in terms of the cost of improved facilities, falls in staff turnover, or absenteeism and so on. Some of the successes are directly contrary to profitability, while others can only with difficulty be linked to extra productivity.

A third example is where a company aims to fulfil its **social and moral responsibilities**, for example by incurring costs to make a manufacturing process more environmentally friendly.

1.2 Control and performance measurement

Performance measurement is a vital part of **control**: it is the part of the control process where **feedback** is compared with the plan, and it is also a means of **feedforward control** in the sense that it sets targets to be aimed at in the future.

> An exam question might refer to the need to exercise control over the process of performance measurement and ask how measurement itself acted as a control mechanism.

1.3 Measuring productivity

Earlier we identified **productivity** as a key area for measurement of a business, so let us see how that might be 'controlled', in other words how we can make sure that the 'right' productivity gets measured.

Key term

> **Productivity** expresses a relationship between outputs from a system and the inputs which go into their creation, as output ÷ input.

The lower the input and the higher the output, the higher will be the resulting productivity. However it needs to be understood by those measuring and those being measured that **high productivity is not a virtue** in itself. It might be possible to produce a larger number of items by spreading the inputs available more thinly, but **if the final output does not then serve its intended purpose** high productivity is worthless.

Inputs should be measured accurately and fairly.

(a)   In some cases it is very **easy** to measure inputs: the material inputs for a mass-produced product can be **weighed** or **counted** and a standard established. The more finished items that can be got out of standard inputs the more productive the process is.

(b)   Sometimes it can be more **difficult**, however, perhaps because **people** do not keep accurate records of the time they put into a task (or falsify records), or because satisfactory outputs depend upon **quality** of input rather than quantity.

(c)   Arguably, a fair measure should be **neutral**, that is, not manipulated by the measurer to encourage certain behaviour. An example might be the exclusion from time measurements of an arbitrary allowance for time that management considers to be 'wasted' chatting to colleagues.

Outputs must also be measured fairly and accurately.

(a)   In a manufacturing context outputs are likely to consist of finished products, but a fair measurement should also take account of goods subsequently **returned** for repair or replacement.

(b)   In a service context (for example, the delivery of products or after-sales care), outputs can be difficult to define: *how* **satisfied** is a satisfied customer, for example?

The measure needs to exhibit all the qualities of **good information**. For example it needs to be understood by those using it to make decisions, it needs to be available to them on time so that they can act if necessary, it should not cost more to obtain and calculate the measurement than the benefit derived from it, and so on.

The measurement should be **interpreted in context**. Low productivity in a particular month may be an isolated occurrence or part of a worsening trend. High productivity in one part of the factory may be overburdening workers in the next part of the process, causing them to cut corners and produce less satisfactory finished output.

As a **means of control**, productivity measures can be used in the following ways.

(a) They can be linked to, and so help to achieve, the organisation's overall **strategy** and **objectives**. (A certain level of productivity may, in fact, be an objective itself.)

(b) Once established they can be used to **predict** future performance.

(c) They can indicate when and **where action is needed** to correct a process that is out of control.

(d) They can be used as a **motivation** device if appropriate incentives are offered for achieving productivity targets (or disincentives for failing to achieve them).

1.4 Critical success factors

The use of critical success factors (CSFs) can help to determine the information requirements of senior management.

Key term

> **Critical success factors** are the few key areas of the job where things must go right for the organisation to flourish. They are all critical to the furtherance of the organisation's aims and the organisation cannot afford to fall behind in any of these areas.

There are usually **fewer than ten** of these factors that any one executive should monitor. They are very **time dependent**, so they should be **re-examined** as often as necessary to keep abreast of the current business climate.

Critical success factors are derived from the concerns of senior management and cover such areas as industry trends, market positioning and the wider business environment. Here are four sources of CSFs.

(a) The **industry** that the business is in

(b) The **company** itself and its situation within the industry

(c) The **environment**, for example consumer trends and the economy

(d) **Temporal organisational factors** (areas of corporate activity which are currently **unacceptable** and represent a cause of concern, such as high stock levels)

 Case Study

A famous study of GEC examined a management reporting system that produced reports on the following factors.

(a) Profitability
(b) Market share
(c) Productivity
(d) Product leadership

(e) Personnel development
(f) Employee attitudes
(g) Public responsibility
(h) Balance between short-range and long-range goals

One approach to asking users to define the factors which are critical to success in performing their functions or making decisions is as follows.

Step 1 List the organisation's corporate objectives and goals.

Step 2 Determine which factors are critical for accomplishing the objectives.

Step 3 Determine a small number of prime measures for each factor.

Two separate types of critical success factor can be identified. A **monitoring** CSF is used to keep abreast of existing activities and operations. A **building** CSF helps to measure the progress of new initiatives and is more likely to be relevant at senior executive level.

1.5 Behavioural implications of performance measurement

If people **know** that their performance is being measured then this will affect the standard of their performance, particularly if they know that they will be **rewarded** for achieving a certain level of performance.

Ideally, performance measures will be devised that reward behaviour that maximises the **corporate good**. In practice, however, it is not quite so simple.

(a)   There is a danger that managers and staff will concentrate **only** upon what they know is being measured. This is not a problem if every important issue has a measure attached to it, but such a system is difficult to devise and implement.

(b)   Individuals have their own **personal goals**, but performance that satisfies their own sense of what is important will not necessarily work towards the corporate good.

Point (b) is the problem of **goal congruence**.

1.6 Attitudes

There are a number of factors which may affect the **attitude** of staff to their work.

(a)   The feeling of **belonging** to a group with similar aims can be a great motivating force.

(b)   The feeling of having **fulfilled one's personal potential** by introducing a new method or receiving praise from a customer can motivate staff.

(c)   The amount of **resources** available will affect how staff work. If resources provided are inadequate they will feel as if their task is almost impossible.

(d)   **Pay**, **promotion** prospects and bonuses will also be influencing factors.

Staff attitude can be measured in a number of ways.

(a)   By the level of **quality** of their work and their **productivity** relative to other staff.
(b)   By responses to **customer questionnaires** about the attitude of staff.
(c)   By reviews written by **colleagues** and **bosses**.

2 Financial performance measures

Financial measures (or *monetary* measures) are very familiar to you. Here are some examples, accompanied by comments from a single page of the *Financial Times*.

Measure	Example
Profit	Profit is the commonest measure of all. Profit maximisation is usually cited as the main objective of most business organisations: 'ICI increased pre-tax profits to £233m'; 'General Motors... yesterday reported better-than-expected first-quarter net income of $513 (£333m).
Revenue	'the US businesses contributed £113.9m of total group turnover of £409m'.
Costs	'Sterling's fall benefited pre-tax profits by about £50m while savings from the cost-cutting programme instituted in 1991 were running at around £100m a quarter'; 'The group interest charge rose from £48m to £61m'.

Measure	Example
Share price	'The group's shares rose 31p to 1,278p despite the market's fall'.
Cash flow	'Cash flow was also continuing to improve, with cash and marketable securities totalling $8.4bn on March 31, up from $8bn at December 31'.

Note here that monetary amounts stated are only given meaning in **relation to something else**. Here is a list of yard-sticks against which financial results are usually placed so as to become measures, perhaps in the form of **variances.**

- Budgeted **sales**, **costs** and **profits**
- **Standards** in a standard costing system
- The **trend** over time (last year/this year, say)
- The results of **other parts** of the business
- The results of **other businesses**
- The **economy** in general
- **Future potential**

2.1 Modern trends: customer profitability analysis

In certain circumstances a useful approach to performance evaluation may be the analysis of **profitability by customer** or customer group. Profitability can vary widely between different customers because various overhead costs are, to some extent, variable and **'customer-driven'**. These overheads include things like discounts and distribution costs.

Customer profitability analysis relates these variabilities in cost to individual customers or customer groups. Managers can use this information to check whether or not individual customers are actually profitable to sell to, and to assess whether profitability can be improved for any customer by switching effort from one type of overhead activity to another, or by reducing spending on some overhead activities.

2.2 Modern trends: activity based costing

The implications of ABC for performance measurement are highly significant. For example if a large part of production overheads used to be known as 'warehousing', but are now recognised as 'materials handling costs' that are incurred in relation to the number of production runs, then a materials handling rate per production run can be established. Many such insights will become possible using ABC and they are useful not only for costing products, but also as a **measurement** that will help in the **management** of costs.

2.3 Modern trends: benchmarking

Benchmarking has been described as 'the formalisation of the basic notion of comparing practices. It is a **systematic analysis of one's own performance against that of another organisation** … the overall objective of benchmarking is to improve performance by learning from the experience of others' (Smith). Benchmarking, which is becoming increasingly popular, therefore aims to **achieve competitive advantage** by **learning from others' experiences and mistakes**, finding **best practice** and translating this best practice into **use in the organisation**.

2.4 Types of benchmarking

External benchmarking involves comparing the performance of an organisation with that of a **direct competitor** – ideally one that is acknowledged to be the 'best in class' (**competitive benchmarking**) or comparing the performance of an internal function with those of the best **external practitioners of those functions**, regardless of the industry within which they operate (**functional benchmarking**). Given that the benchmark is the 'best' in a particular field, it provides a meaningful target towards which the organisation should aim.

Internal benchmarking, on the other hand, involves comparing the performance of **one part of a business with that of a different part of the same business** with the aim of establishing best practice throughout an organisation. Some external benchmarking is still required, however, in order to establish best practice.

2.5 Why benchmark?

'Perhaps performance measures, when done correctly, help everyone in the company focus on the right things in the right place at the right time. However ... there are many stories of dysfunctional behaviour – the telephone company which pledged to have at least 90% of payphones working, then achieving this figure by simply removing all public payphones from those areas most often vandalised. Or the bus operator which, plagued by delays, decided to pay bonuses to drivers who arrived at the terminus on time. As a result, most buses arrived at the terminus on time – however, drivers no longer tended to stop for passengers along the way!

Measuring performance by itself has no meaning. Meaning can only be achieved through comparison, either against poor performance, which usually provides no true indication of future or competitive position, or through benchmarking.'   (*Management Accounting*)

2.6 Limitations

Both approaches to benchmarking suffer from a number of **limitations**.

(a)   **Limitations of external benchmarking**

- Deciding which activities to benchmark
- Identifying which organisation is the 'best in class' at an activity
- **Persuading that organisation to share information**
- Successful practices in one organisation may not transfer successfully to another

(b)   The principal limitation of **internal benchmarking** centres on the **relevance of the other part of the business**.

- The amount of resources devoted to the units may differ.
- There may be local differences (use of different computer hardware).
- Inputs and outputs may be difficult to define.

Benchmarking **works**, it is claimed, **for the following reasons**.

(a)   The comparisons are carried out by the **managers who have to live with any changes implemented** as a result of the exercise.

(b)   Benchmarking focuses on improvement in key areas and sets **targets** which are **challenging but 'achievable'**. What is *really* achievable can be discovered by examining what others have achieved: managers are thus able to accept that they are not being asked to perform miracles.

Benchmarking can also provide **early warning of competitive disadvantage** and should lead to a greater incidence of **teamworking** and **cross-functional learning**.

3 Non-financial performance measures

FAST FORWARD

An imaginative approach to performance measurement is becoming a necessity in the modern business environment, and many businesses now recognise the need to supplement traditional financial measures with other, **non-financial indicators**.

3.1 Quantitative and qualitative performance measures

Both quantitative and qualitative performance measures are equally valuable.

As you know it is possible to distinguish between **quantitative** information, which is capable of being expressed in numbers, and **qualitative** information, which can only be expressed in numerical terms with difficulty.

An example of a **quantitative** performance measure is 'You have been late for work *twice* this week and it's only Tuesday!'. An example of a **qualitative** performance measure is 'My bed is *very* comfortable'.

The first measure is likely to find its way into a staff appraisal report. The second would feature in a bed manufacturer's customer satisfaction survey. Both are indicators of whether their subjects are doing as good a job as they are required to do.

Qualitative measures are by nature **subjective** and **judgmental** but this does not mean that they are not valuable. They are especially valuable when they are derived from several different sources because then they can be expressed in a mixture of quantitative and qualitative terms which is more meaningful overall.

Consider the following statement.

'Seven out of ten customers think our beds are very comfortable.'

This is a **quantitative** measure of customer satisfaction as well as a **qualitative** measure of the perceived performance of the beds. (But it does not mean that only 70% of the total beds produced are comfortable, nor that each bed is 70% comfortable and 30% uncomfortable: 'very' is the measure of comfort.)

3.2 Non-financial indicators (NFIs)

Financial measures do not convey the full picture of a company's performance, especially in a **modern business environment**.

'In today's worldwide competitive environment companies are competing in terms of product quality, delivery, reliability, after-sales service and customer satisfaction. None of these variables is directly measured by the traditional responsibility accounting system, despite the fact that they represent the major goals of world-class manufacturing companies.'

Many companies are discovering the usefulness of quantitative and qualitative **non-financial indicators (NFIs)** such as the following.

- Quality
- Lead times
- Rework
- Number of customer complaints and warranty claims
- Delivery to time
- Non-productive hours
- System (machine) down time, and so on

Unlike traditional variance reports, measures such as these can be provided quickly for managers, per shift, **daily** or even **hourly** as required. They are likely to be easy to calculate, and easier for non-financial managers to understand and therefore to use effectively.

The beauty of non-financial indicators is that **anything can be compared** if it is **meaningful** to do so. The measures should be **tailored** to the circumstances so that, for example, number of coffee breaks per 20 pages of Study Text might indicate to you how hard you are studying!

Many suitable measures combine elements from the chart shown below. The chart is not intended to be prescriptive or exhaustive.

Errors/failure	Time	Quantity	People
Defects	Second	Range of products	Employees
Equipment failures	Minute	Parts/components	Employee skills
Warranty claims	Hour	Units produced	Customers
Complaints	Shift	Units sold	Competitors
Returns	Cycle	Services performed	Suppliers
Stockouts	Day	kg/litres/metres	
Lateness/waiting	Month	m²/m³	
Misinformation	Year	Documents	
Miscalculation		Deliveries	
Absenteeism		Enquiries	

Traditional measures derived from these lists like 'kg (of material) per unit produced' or 'units produced per hour' are fairly obvious, but what may at first seem a fairly **unlikely combination** may also be very revealing. 'Absenteeism per customer', for example, may be of no significance at all or it may reveal that a particularly difficult customer is being avoided, and hence that some action is needed.

There is clearly a need for the information provider to work more closely with the managers who will be using the information to make sure that their needs are properly understood. The measures used are likely to be **developed and refined over time**. It may be that some will serve the purpose of drawing attention to areas in need of improvement but will be of no further relevance once remedial action has been taken. A flexible, responsive approach is essential.

Question

Non-financial indicators

Using the above chart make up five non-financial indicators and explain how each might be useful.

Answer

Here are five indicators, showing you how to use the chart, but there are many other possibilities.

(a) Services performed late v total services performed
(b) Total units sold v total units sold by competitors (indicating market share)
(c) Warranty claims per month
(d) Documents processed per employee
(e) Equipment failures per 1,000 units produced

Don't forget to explain how the ones that you chose might be useful.

3.3 NFIs and financial measures

FAST FORWARD

Financial measures generally derive from the accounting system (or other businesses' accounting systems).

Non-monetary measures also include **ratios**, **percentages** and **indices**.

Arguably, NFIs are less likely to be **manipulated** than traditional profit-related measures and they should, therefore, offer a means of counteracting short-termism, since short-term profit at any (non-monetary) expense is rarely an advisable goal. The ultimate goal of commercial organisations in the long run is likely to remain the maximisation of **profit**, however, and so the financial aspect cannot be ignored.

There is a danger that too many such measures could be reported, leading to **information overload** for managers, providing information that is not truly useful, or that sends conflicting signals. A further danger of NFIs is that they might lead managers to pursue detailed **operational goals** and become blind to the **overall strategy** in which those goals are set.

A **combination** of financial and non-financial indicators is therefore likely to be most successful.

Question   Operational performance

What do the following indicate about an organisation's operational performance?

(a)   Actual late deliveries as a percentage of total orders are greater than the budgeted figure.
(b)   Actual process losses as a percentage of input are greater than the budgeted figure.
(c)   Actual sales volumes are lower than budgeted sales volumes.

Answer

(a)   This could indicate problems with either production planning or distribution.

(b)   This could indicate faulty material, poor quality work or machine faults.

(c)   This could indicate a fall in demand or too great a proportion of replacements or too many losses in process so that production cannot meet demand.

3.4 Ratios

Ratios (covered in Chapter 13) are a useful way of measuring performance for a number of reasons.

(a)   It is easier to look at **changes over time** by comparing ratios in one time period with the corresponding ratios for periods in the past.

(b)   Ratios are often **easier to understand than absolute measures** of physical quantities or money values. For example, it is easier to understand that 'productivity in March was 94%' than 'there was an adverse labour efficiency variance in March of £3,600'.

(c)   Ratios **relate one item to another**, and so help to put performance into context. For example the profit/sales ratio sets profit in the context of how much has been earned per £1 of sales, and so shows how wide or narrow profit margins are.

(d)   Ratios can be used as **targets**. In particular, targets can be set for ROI, profit/sales, asset turnover, capacity fill and productivity. Managers will then take decisions which will enable them to achieve their targets.

(e)   Ratios provide a way of **summarising** an organisation's results, and **comparing** them with similar organisations. For example, the results of one investment centre/profit centre/company can be compared directly with the results of another.

3.5 Percentages

A **percentage** expresses one number as a proportion of another and gives meaning to absolute numbers. Examples are as follows.

(a)   **Market share**. A company may aim to achieve a 25% share of the total market for its product, and measure both its marketing department and the quality of the product against this.

(b)   **Capacity levels** are usually measured in this way. 'Factory A is working at 20% below full capacity' is an example which indicates relative inefficiency.

(c)   **Wastage** is sometimes expressed in percentage terms. 'Normal loss' may be 10%, a measure of *in*efficiency.

(d)   **Staff turnover** is often measured in this way. In the catering industry for example, staff turnover is typically greater than 100%, and so a hotel with a lower percentage could take this as an indicator both of the experience of its staff and of how well it is treating them.

3.6 Indices

FAST FORWARD

Indices can be used in a variety of ways in performance measurement, for example in **forecasting** and for **inter-company comparisons**.

Indices show how a particular variable has changed **relative to a base value**. The base value is usually the level of the variable at an earlier date. The 'variable' may be just one particular item, such as material X, or several items, such as 'raw materials' generally.

In its simplest form an index is calculated as (current value/base value) × 100. Thus if materials cost £15 per kg in 20X0 and now (20X3) cost £27 per kg, the 20X0 value would be expressed in index form as 100 (15/15 × 100) and the 20X3 value as 180 (27/15 × 100). If you find it easier to think of this as a percentage, then do so.

4 Benefits and problems of performance measures

FAST FORWARD

A recent article by the examiner considers the **benefits and problems of performance measures**.

George Brown's article on performance measurement ('Accountability and performance measurement' *ACCA Students' Newsletter,* August 1998) includes Berry, Broadbent and Otley's list of **benefits of performance measures**.

1   'Clarifying the objectives of the organisation
2   Developing agreed measures of activity
3   Greater understanding of the processes
4   Facilitating comparison of performance in different organisations
5   Facilitating the setting of targets for the organisation and its managers
6   Promoting accountability of the organisation to its stakeholders'

Their list of **problems of performance measures** is also included in the article.

Problem	Comment
Tunnel vision	Undue focus on performance measures to the detriment of other areas
Sub-optimisation	Focus on some objectives so that others are not achieved
Myopia	Short-sightedness leading to the neglect of longer-term objectives
Measure fixation	Measures and behaviour in order to achieve specific performance indicators which may not be effective
Misrepresentation	'Creative' reporting to suggest that a result is acceptable
Misinterpretation	Failure to recognise the complexity of the environment in which the organisation operates

Problem	Comment
Gaming	Deliberate distortion of a measure to secure some strategic advantage
Ossification	An unwillingness to change the performance measure scheme once it has been set up

The article suggests ways in which the **problems may be reduced**, and they are summarised here.

    (a)   **Involvement of staff** at all levels in the development and implementation of the scheme should help to reduce gaming and tunnel vision.

    (b)   A **flexible use** of performance measures should help to reduce measure fixation and misrepresentation.

    (c)   Keeping the performance measurement system under **constant review** should help to overcome the problems of ossification and gaming.

    (d)   Give careful consideration to the **dimensions of performance**. Quantifying all objectives should help to overcome sub-optimisation, while a focus on measuring customer satisfaction should reduce tunnel vision and sub-optimisation.

    (e)   Consideration should be given to the **audit of the system**. Expert interpretation of the performance measurement scheme should help to provide an idea of the incidence of the problems, while a careful audit of the data used should help to reduce the incidence and impact of measure fixation, misinterpretation and gaming.

    (f)   **Recognition of the key feature** necessary in any scheme (a long-term view/perspective amongst staff, a sensible number of measures, benchmarks which are independent of past activity) should help to overcome the range of problems listed above.

5 Accounting theory and practice

FAST FORWARD

Accounting is not an exact science. **Results may be manipulated**.

5.1 The nature of profit

You will know from your earlier studies that accounting 'profit' is an arbitrary figure, subject to the whims and biases of accountants and the variety of treatments in accounting standards. Go back to the contents page and pick out all the topics which demonstrate or indicate how company results are manipulated. Isn't it nearly all of them? Let us briefly mention some of them again.

5.1.1 SSAP 4 Accounting for government grants

SSAP 4 allows capital grants to be credited to revenue over the expected life of the asset in two ways.

    (a)   By reducing the acquisition cost of the fixed asset by the amount of the grant and providing depreciation on the reduced amount

    (b)   By treating the amount of the grant as a deferred credit and transferring a portion of it to revenue annually

The final profit figure is the same under both methods but the depreciation charge disclosed will be different, as will the carrying value of the asset.

5.1.2 SSAP 9 Stocks and long-term contracts

Companies are allowed to use different methods of valuing stock under SSAP 9, which means that the final stock figure in the balance sheet will be different under each method. Profit will be affected by the closing stock valuation, particularly where the level of stock fluctuates to a great extent.

5.1.3 FRS 15 Tangible fixed assets

As with SSAP 9, FRS 15 allows different accounting bases for depreciation. Choosing to use the reducing balance method rather than the straight line method can front-load the depreciation charge for assets. It is also the case that the subjectivity surrounding the estimated economic lives of assets can lead to manipulation of profits. (Note. Remember that some companies refuse to depreciate some assets at all – mainly freehold property.)

5.1.4 SSAP 13 Accounting for research and development

Development costs can be capitalised under SSAP 13, whereas all research costs should be written off. Although the criteria for capitalisation are quite strict, there is room for manipulation.

You should note that the ASB is trying to stop abuses such as those described here by forcing companies to follow general tenets (FRS 5, *Statement of Principles*) and also by restricting abusive practice, eg merger accounting and FRS 6.

5.2 Other problems with financial analysis

Two frequent problems affecting financial analysis are discussed here.

- Seasonal fluctuations
- Window dressing

5.2.1 Seasonal fluctuations

Many companies are located in industries where trade is seasonal. For example:

- Firework manufacturers
- Swimwear manufacturers
- Ice cream makers
- Umbrella manufacturers
- Gas companies
- Travel agents
- Flower suppliers and deliverers
- Football clubs

Year on year the seasonal fluctuations affecting such companies does not matter; a year end has to be chosen and as long as the fluctuations are at roughly the same time every year, then there should be no problem. Occasionally a perverse sense of humour will cause a company to choose an accounting period ending in the middle of the busy season: this may affect the cut off because the busy season might be slightly early or late.

A major difficulty can arise if companies affected by seasonal fluctuations change their accounting date. A shorter period (normally) may encompass part, all or none of the busy season. Whatever happens, the figures will be distorted and the comparatives will be meaningless. Analysts would not know how to extrapolate the figures from the shorter period to produce a comparison for the previous year. Weightings could be used, but these are likely to be inaccurate.

 Case Study

An example of the problems this can cause occurred when. British Gas plc changed its accounting period to 31 December from 31 March. The company published two reports and accounts.

- For the year to 31 March 1991
- For the year to 31 December 1991

thus including the first three months of the calendar year in both reports. As a note to the later accounts, the company produced a profit and loss account for the last nine months of the calendar year.

Although the British Gas auditors did not qualify the audit report, the Review Panel was not very happy about this double counting of results. The nine month profit and loss account did not meet the provisions of CA 1985 'either as to its location or its contents, nor did it contain the relevant earnings per share figure'. British Gas had to promise that, in their 1992 results, the 1991 comparative would be for the nine months period only.

The effect here is obvious. The first three months of the calendar year are when British Gas earns a high proportion of its profits (winter!). If the 1991 results had covered the period from 1 April only, then the profits would have been reduced by more than an average loss of three months' profit. By using a 12 month period, British Gas avoided the risk of the period's results looking too bad.

5.2.2 Window dressing

Window dressing transactions were made largely redundant by SSAP 17, the predecessor of FRS 21 *Events after the balance sheet date* for post balance sheet events. SSAP 17 stated that non-adjusting events requiring disclosure include the reversal or maturity after the balance sheet date of transactions, the substance of which was primarily to alter the appearance of the balance sheet. This gives a good description of window dressing transactions. Note that window dressing transactions were not outlawed, but full disclosure would render such transactions useless.

One example of window dressing is a situation where a large cheque is written against one group company's positive bank balance in favour of another group company with a large overdraft. The cheque is put through at the year end and then cancelled at the beginning of the next year, thus concealing the overdraft in the consolidated balance sheet (where positive and negative bank balances cannot be netted off).

CA 2006 requires coterminous accounting periods for all group companies. This is to avoid window dressing, for example where a subsidiary with a period end three months later than that of the group makes a profit in one part of its year and a loss in the other. By choosing whatever method will produce the best results, the company could book a result which will be wholly or partly reversed in the next period.

You may be able to think of other examples of window dressing and you should look for any potential examples which come up in examination questions.

Summary of limitations of financial analysis

(a)   Information problems

　　(i)   The base information is often out of date, so timeliness of information leads to problems of interpretation.

　　(ii)   Historic cost information may not be the most appropriate information for the decision for which the analysis is being undertaken.

　　(iii)   Information in published accounts is generally summarised information and detailed information may be needed.

　　(iv)   Analysis of accounting information only identifies symptoms not causes and thus is of limited use.

(b)   Comparison problems: inter-temporal

    (i)   Effects of price changes make comparisons difficult unless adjustments are made.

    (ii)   Impacts of changes in technology on the price of assets, the likely return and the future markets.

    (iii)   Impacts of a changing environment on the results reflected in the accounting information.

    (iv)   Potential effects of changes in accounting policies on the reported results.

    (v)   Problems associated with establishing a normal base year to compare other years with.

(c)   Comparison problems: inter-firm

    (i)   Selection of industry norms and the usefulness of norms based on averages.

    (ii)   Different firms having different financial and business risk profiles and the impact on analysis.

    (iii)   Different firms using different accounting policies.

    (iv)   Impacts of the size of the business and its comparators on risk, structure and returns.

    (v)   Impacts of different environments on results, for example different countries or home-based versus multinational firms.

You should use this summary as a type of checklist.

Chapter Roundup

- Key areas for performance measurement are **profitability, activity** and **productivity**. Profitability is often a key objective but other **'success factors'** are also critical. **Benchmarking** is increasingly common.

- Both quantitative and qualitative performance measures are equally valuable.

- Financial measures generally derive from the accounting system (or other businesses' accounting systems).

- An imaginative approach to performance measurement is becoming a necessity in the modern business environment, and many businesses now recognise the need to supplement traditional financial measures with other, **non-financial indicators.**

- Non-monetary measures also include **ratios**, **percentages** and **indices**.

- **Indices** can be used in a variety of ways in performance measurement, for example in **forecasting** and for **inter-company comparisons**.

- A recent article by the examiner considers the **benefits and problems of performance measures**.

- Accounting is not an exact science. **Results may be manipulated**.

Quick Quiz

1   What is the aim of performance management?

2   What is a critical success factor?

3   Which of the following are examples of non-financial indicators? Circle all that apply.

- Number of customer complaints
- Lead times
- Cash flow
- Delivery to time
- Revenue

4   Financial indicators are superior to non-financial indicators.

True ☐

False ☐

Answers to Quick Quiz

1   To establish how well something or somebody is doing in relation to the planned activity and desired results.

2   An area of the job where things must go right for the organisation to flourish.

3   Number of customer complaints
    Lead times
    Delivery to time

4   False. A combination of financial and non-financial indicators is desirable.

Number	Level	Marks	Time
Q13	Introductory	n/a	n/a

Now try the questions below from the Exam Question Bank

Ratio and trend analysis

13

Topic list	Syllabus reference
1 Sources of information and the role of regulation	G2
2 The broad categories of ratios	G2
3 Profitability and return on capital	G2
4 Liquidity and working capital	G2
5 Long-term solvency: debt and gearing	G2
6 Shareholders' investment ratios	G2

Introduction

You should be very familiar with many of the **ratios** discussed in this chapter from your earlier studies. They are covered in full again here, because it is very unusual for a P2 exam not to have some financial analysis in it somewhere. Such questions will often draw in more complex matters, which we will look at in the next few chapters.

You must be able to **explain the results** of your analysis in the P2 exam: numbers alone are never enough.

Study guide

		Intellectual level
G2	**Analysis and interpretation of financial information and measurement of performance**	
(a)	Select and calculate relevant indicators of financial and non-financial performance	3
(b)	Identify and evaluate significant features and issues in financial statements	3
(c)	Highlight inconsistencies in financial information through analysis and application of knowledge	3
(d)	Make inferences from the analysis of the information, taking into account the limitation of the information, the analytical methods used and the business environment in which the entity operates	3

Exam guide

An analytical approach will be required. At this level, you are assumed to know how to calculate ratios, so there won't be much number-crunching on this type of question.

1 Sources of information and the role of regulation

FAST FORWARD

Keep the various **sources of financial information** in mind and the effects of insider dealing, the efficient market hypothesis and Stock Exchange regulations.

The accounts of a business are designed to provide users with information about its performance and financial position. The bare figures, however, are not particularly useful and it is only through **comparisons** (usually of ratios) that their significance can be established. Comparisons may be made with previous financial periods, with other similar businesses or with averages for the particular industry. The choice will depend on the purpose for which the comparison is being made and the information that is available.

Various groups are interested in the performance and financial position of a company.

(a) **Management** will use comparisons to ensure that the business is performing efficiently and according to plan

(b) **Employees**, trade unions and so on

(c) **Government**

(d) Present and potential **investors** assess the company to judge if it is a good investment

(e) **Lenders** and **suppliers** will want to judge its creditworthiness

This text is concerned with financial rather than management accounting and the ratios discussed here are therefore likely to be calculated by external users. The main sources of information available to external users are:

(a) Published accounts and interim statements
(b) Documents filed at Companies House
(c) Statistics published by the government
(d) Other published sources eg *Investors Chronicle*, *The Economist*, Extel

1.1 Financial analysis

The **lack of detailed information** available to the outsider is a considerable disadvantage in undertaking ratio analysis. The first difficulty is that there may simply be insufficient data to calculate all of the required ratios. A second concerns the availability of a suitable 'yardstick' with which the calculated ratios may be compared.

1.2 Inter-temporal analysis

Looking first at inter-temporal or trend analysis (comparisons for the same business over time), some of the **problems** include:

(a) Changes in the nature of the business
(b) Unrealistic depreciation rates under historical cost accounting
(c) The changing value of the pound
(d) Changes in accounting policies

Other factors will include changes in government incentive packages, changes from purchasing equipment to leasing and so on.

1.3 Cross-sectional analysis

When undertaking 'cross-sectional' analysis (making comparisons with other companies) the position is even more difficult because of the problem of identifying companies that are comparable. **Comparability** between companies may be impaired because of:

(a) Different degrees of diversification

(b) Different production and purchasing policies (if an investor was analysing the smaller car manufacturers, he would find that some of them buy in engines from one of the 'majors' whilst others develop and manufacture their own)

(c) Different financing policies (eg leasing as opposed to buying)

(d) Different accounting policies (one of the most serious problems particularly in relation to fixed assets and stock valuation)

(e) Different effects of government incentives

The major **inter-company comparison organisations** (whose results are intended for the use of participating companies and are not generally available) go to considerable length to adjust accounts to comparable bases. The external user will rarely be in a position to make such adjustments. Although the position is now improved by increases in disclosure requirements (especially the more detailed P&L accounts required by CA 2006 and FRS 3), direct comparisons between companies will inevitably, on occasion, continue to give rise to misleading results.

1.4 Social and political considerations

Social considerations tend to be **shortlived** or 'fashionable' and therefore each set of statements can be affected by a different movement or fad. In recent years, the social aspect much in evidence has been that of environmental issues. Companies have gone for a 'green' image, although this has been more in evidence in glossy pictures than in the accounts themselves.

Political considerations have been more far reaching. The new regulatory regime was set up by statute (CA 1989), which was a direct result of UK membership of the EU, and politicians have kept the pressure up after disasters like Polly Peck and BCCI. In general, however, self-regulation is encouraged in the UK through bodies such as the Competition Commission, Stock Exchange and Takeover Panel.

1.5 Multinational companies

Multinational companies have great difficulties sometimes because of the need to comply with **legislation** in a large number of countries. As well as different reporting requirements, different rules of incorporation exist, as well as different directors' rules, tax legislation and so on. Sometimes the local rules can be so harsh that companies will avoid them altogether. In California, for example, multinational companies with operations there are taxed on their *world wide* profits, not just their US profits. Local tax regimes may also require information about the group as a whole because of the impact of internal transfer pricing on tax.

Different local reporting requirements will also make **consolidation** more difficult. The results of subsidiaries must be translated, not only to the company's base currency, but also using the accounting rules used by head office. This is a requirement in the UK in company law as 'uniform accounting policies' are called for.

1.6 The efficient market hypothesis and the Stock Exchange

It has been argued that the UK and US stock markets are **efficient capital markets**, that is, markets in which:

(a)   The prices of securities bought and sold reflect all the relevant information which is available to the buyers and sellers. In other words, share prices change quickly to reflect all new information about future prospects

(b)   No individual dominates the market

(c)   Transaction costs of buying and selling are not so high as to discourage trading significantly

If the stock market is efficient, share prices should vary in a **rational way**, ie reflecting the known profits or losses of a company and the state of return required based on interest states.

Research in both Britain and the USA has suggested that market prices anticipate mergers several months before they are formally announced, and the conclusion drawn is that the stock market in these countries *do* exhibit **semi-strong efficiency**. It has also been argued that the market displays sufficient efficiency for investors to see through 'window dressing' of accounts by companies which use accounting conventions to overstate profits (ie creative accounting).

Evidence suggests that stock markets show efficiency that is **at least weak form**, but tending more towards a semi-strong form. In other words, current share prices reflect all or most publicly available information about companies and their securities. However, it is very difficult to assess the market's efficiency in relation to shares which are not usually actively traded.

Fundamental analysis and **technical analysis** carried out by analysts and investment managers play an important role in creating an efficient stock market. This is because an efficient market depends on the widespread availability of cheap information about companies, their shares and market conditions, and this is what the firms of market makers and other financial institutions *do* provide for their clients and for the general investing public. In a market which demonstrates strong-form efficiency, such analysis would not identify profitable opportunities, ie where shares are undervalued, because such information would already be known and reflected in the share price.

On the other hand, the crash of October 1987, in which share prices fell suddenly by 20% to 40% on the world's stock markets, raised serious questions about the validity of the **fundamental theory of share values** and the efficient market hypothesis. If these theories are correct, how can shares that were valued at one level on one day suddenly be worth 40% less the next day, without any change in expectations of corporate profits and dividends? On the other hand, a widely feared crash late in 1989 failed to happen, suggesting that stock markets may not be altogether out of touch with the underlying values of companies.

2 The broad categories of ratios

FAST FORWARD

Much of the material here on **basic ratios** should have been revision for you. The next few chapters will cover much more complicated aspects of financial analysis.

Ratio analysis involves comparing **one figure against another** to produce a ratio, and assessing whether the ratio indicates a weakness or strength in the company's affairs.

Exam focus point

You are unlikely to be asked to calculate many ratios in the Paper 2 exam, or directly at any rate. If, say, you were asked to comment on a company's past or potential future performance, you would be expected to select your own ratios in order to do so. The skill here is picking the key ratios in the context of the question and not calculating a lot of useless ratios.

2.1 The broad categories of ratios

FAST FORWARD

Make sure that you can **define** all the ratios. Look out for variations in definitions of ratios which might appear in questions.

Broadly speaking, basic ratios can be grouped into five categories.

- Profitability and return
- Short-term solvency and liquidity
- Long-term solvency and stability
- Efficiency (turnover ratios)
- Shareholders' investment ratios

Ratio analysis on its own is **not sufficient** for interpreting company accounts, and that there are other items of information which should be looked at, for example:

(a) **Comments** in the chairman's report, the directors' report and the operating and financial review (see Chapter 1)

(b) The age and nature of the **company's assets**

(c) Current and future **developments** in the company's markets, at home and overseas, recent acquisitions or disposals of a subsidiary by the company

(d) Any other **noticeable features** of the report and accounts, such as post balance sheet events, contingent liabilities, a qualified auditors' report, the company's taxation position, and so on

The following sections summarise what you already know about ratio analysis from your earlier studies. You should then perform the comprehensive questions given in this chapter. The following three chapters look at more complex areas of analysis and interpretation, which build on the knowledge in this chapter.

Exam focus point

It cannot be emphasised enough that a deeper level of analysis is required for Paper P2. You **must** answer the question from the viewpoint of the person needing the ratios – banker, prospective investor/predator.

3 Profitability and return on capital

One profit figure that should be calculated and compared over time is **PBIT, profit before interest and tax**, the amount of profit which the company earned before having to pay interest to the providers of loan capital. By providers of loan capital, we usually mean longer-term loan capital, such as debentures and medium-term bank loans, which will be shown in the balance sheet as 'creditors: amounts falling due after more than one year'. Also, tax is affected by unusual variations which have a distorting effect.

3.1 Profit before interest and tax

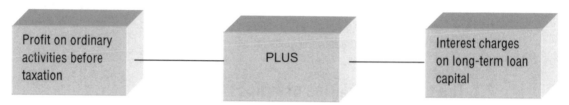

Published accounts do not always give sufficient detail on interest payable to determine how much is interest on long-term finance.

Knowledge brought forward from earlier studies

Profitability

Return on capital employed

$$ROCE = \frac{PBIT}{Capital\,employed} = \frac{PBIT}{Total\,assets\,less\,current\,liabilities}$$

When **interpreting** ROCE look for the following.

- How risky is the business?
- How capital intensive is it?
- What ROCE do similar businesses have?

Knowledge brought forward from earlier studies (cont'd)

Problems: which items to consider to achieve comparability:

- Revaluation reserves
- Policies, eg goodwill, R & D
- Bank overdraft: short/long-term liability
- Investments and related income: exclude

The following **considerations** are important.

- Change year to year
- Comparison to similar companies
- Comparison with current market borrowing rates

Return on equity

$$ROE = \frac{Profit\,after\,tax\,and\,pref\,div}{Ordinary\,share\,capital + reserves}\%$$

This gives a more **restricted view** of capital than ROCE, but the same principles apply.

Secondary ratios

Profit margin × Asset turnover = ROCE

Profit margin

$$\text{Profit margin} = \frac{\text{PBIT}}{\text{Turnover}}\% \qquad \text{Gross profit margin} = \frac{\text{Gross profit}}{\text{Turnover}}\%$$

It is useful to compare profit margin to gross profit % to investigate movements which do not match. Take into account:

- **Gross profit margin**

    - Sales prices, sales volume and sales mix

    - Purchase prices and related costs (discount, carriage etc)

    - Production costs, both direct (materials, labour) and indirect (overheads both fixed and variable)

    - Stock levels and stock valuation, including errors, cut-off and stock-out costs

- **Net profit margin**

    - Sales expenses in relation to sales levels
    - Administrative expenses, including salary levels
    - Distribution expenses in relation to sales levels

    Depreciation should be considered as a separate item for each expense category.

Asset turnover

$$\text{Asset turnover} = \frac{\text{Turnover}}{\text{Total assets less current liabilities}}$$

This measures the **efficiency** of the use of assets. Amend to just fixed assets for capital intensive businesses.

3.2 A warning about comments on profit margin and asset turnover

It might be tempting to think that a high profit margin is good, and a low asset turnover means sluggish trading. In broad terms, this is so. But there is **a trade-off** between profit margin and asset turnover, and you cannot look at one without allowing for the other.

(a)   A high profit margin means a high profit per £1 of sales, but if this also means that sales prices are high, there is a strong possibility that sales turnover will be depressed, and so asset turnover lower.

(b)   A high asset turnover means that the company is generating a lot of sales, but to do this it might have to keep its prices down and so accept a low profit margin per £1 of sales.

4 Liquidity and working capital

Profitability is of course an important aspect of a company's performance and debt or gearing is another. Neither, however, addresses directly the key issue of liquidity in the **short term**.

Liquidity is the amount of cash a company can put its hands on quickly to settle its debts (and possibly to meet other unforeseen demands for cash payments too). Liquid funds consist of:

(a) Cash

(b) Short-term investments for which there is a ready market (short-term investments are distinct from investments in shares in subsidiaries or associated companies)

(c) Fixed-term deposits with a bank or building society, for example, a six month high-interest deposit with a bank

(d) Trade debtors (because they will pay what they owe within a reasonably short period of time)

(e) Bills of exchange receivable (because like ordinary trade debtors, these represent amounts of cash due to be received within a relatively short period of time)

A company can obtain liquid assets from sources other than sales, such as the issue of shares for cash, a new loan or the sale of fixed assets. But a company cannot rely on these at all times, and in general obtaining liquid funds depends on making sales and profits. Even so, **profits do not always lead to increases in liquidity**. This is mainly because funds generated from trading may be immediately invested in fixed assets or paid out as dividends.

Efficiency ratios indicate how well a business is controlling aspects of its working capital.

> ### Knowledge brought forward from earlier studies

> *Liquidity and working capital*
>
> This was very topical in the late 1980s as interest rates were high, and there was a recession Can a company meet its short-term debts.
>
> *Current ratio*
>
> $$\text{Current ratio} = \frac{\text{Current assets}}{\text{Current liabilities}}$$
>
> Assume assets realised at book level $\therefore$ theoretical. 2:1 acceptable? 1.5:1? It depends on the industry.
>
> *Quick ratio*
>
> $$\text{Quick ratio (acid test)} = \frac{\text{Current assets - Stock}}{\text{Current liabilities}}$$
>
> Eliminates illiquid and subjectively valued stock. Care is needed: it could be high if **overtrading** with debtors, but no cash. Is 1:1 OK? Many supermarkets operate on 0.3.
>
> *Collection period*
>
> $$\text{Average collection period} = \frac{\text{Trade debtors}}{\text{Credit turnover}} \times 365$$
>
> Is it **consistent** with quick/current ratio? If not, investigate.
>
> *Stock turnover*
>
> $$\text{Stock turnover} = \frac{\text{Cost of sales}}{\text{Stock}} \qquad \text{Stock days} = \frac{\text{Stock}}{\text{Cost of sales}} \times 365$$

Higher the better? But remember:

- Lead times
- Seasonal fluctuations in orders
- Alternative uses of warehouse space
- Bulk buying discounts
- Likelihood of stock perishing or becoming obsolete

Creditors' payment period

$$\text{Creditors' payment period} = \frac{\text{Trade creditors}}{\text{Purchases}} \times 365$$

Use **cost of sales** if purchases are not disclosed.

Cash cycle

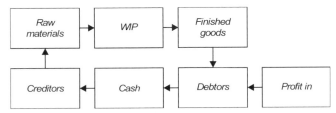

- Cash flow timing does not match sales/cost of sales timing as credit is taken
- Holding stock delays the time between payments for goods and sales receipts

Reasons for changes in liquidity

- **Credit control** efficiency altered
- Altering **payment period** of creditors as a source of funding
- Reduce **stock holdings** to maintain liquidity

5 Long-term solvency: debt and gearing

Debt and gearing ratios are concerned with a company's **long-term stability**: how much the company owes in relation to its size, whether it is getting into heavier debt or improving its situation, and whether its debt burden seems heavy or light.

(a) When a company is heavily in debt, banks and other potential lenders may be unwilling to advance further funds.

(b) When a company is earning only a modest profit before interest and tax, and has a heavy debt burden, there will be very little profit left (if any) over for shareholders after the interest charges have been paid. And so if interest rates were to go up (on bank overdrafts and so on) or the company were to borrow even more, it might soon be incurring interest charges in excess of PBIT. This might eventually lead to the liquidation of the company.

Debt and gearing

Debt/equity

$$\text{Debt/equity ratio} = \frac{\text{Interest bearing net debts}}{\text{Shareholders' funds}}\%\,(>100\%=\text{high})$$

There is **no definitive answer**; elements included are subjective. The following could have an impact.

- Convertible loan stock
- Preference shares
- Deferred tax
- Goodwill and development expenditure capitalisation
- Revaluation reserve

Gearing ratio

$$\text{Gearing ratio} = \frac{\text{Prior charge capital}}{\text{Total capital}}$$

Interest cover

$$\text{Interest cover} = \frac{\text{PBIT(incl int receivable)}}{\text{Interest payable}}$$

Is this a better way to **measure gearing**? Company must generate enough profit to cover interest. Is a figure of 3+ safe?

5.1 The implications of high or low gearing

Gearing is, amongst other things, an attempt to quantify the **degree of risk** involved in holding equity shares in a company, both in terms of the company's ability to remain in business and in terms of expected ordinary dividends from the company. The problem with a highly geared company is that, by definition, there is a lot of debt. Debt generally carries a fixed rate of interest (or fixed rate of dividend if in the form of preference shares), hence there is a given (and large) amount to be paid out from profits to holders of debt before arriving at a residue available for distribution to the holders of equity.

The more highly geared the company, the greater the risk that little (if anything) will be available to distribute by way of dividend to the ordinary shareholders. The more highly geared the company, the greater the percentage change in profit available for ordinary shareholders for any given percentage change in profit before interest and tax. The relationship similarly holds when profits increase. This means that there will be greater **volatility** of amounts available for ordinary shareholders, and presumably therefore greater volatility in dividends paid to those shareholders, where a company is highly geared. That is the risk. You may do extremely well or extremely badly without a particularly large movement in the PBIT of the company.

The risk of a company's ability to remain in business was referred to earlier. Gearing is relevant to this. A highly geared company has a large amount of interest to pay annually. If those borrowings are 'secured' in any way (and debentures in particular are secured), then the holders of the debt are perfectly entitled to force the company to realise assets to pay their interest if funds are not available from other sources. Clearly, the more highly geared a company, the more likely this is to occur when and if profits fall. Note that problems related to **off balance sheet finance** hiding the level of gearing have gradually become rarer, due to standards such as FRS 2 and SSAP 21.

Companies will only be able to increase their gearing if they have **suitable assets** to offer for security. Companies with assets which are depreciated rapidly or which are at high risk of obsolescence will be unable to offer sufficient security, eg computer software companies. On the other hand, a property company will have plenty of assets to offer as security whose value is fairly stable (but note the effect of a property slump as in the late 1980s).

Ideally, the following **gearing profiles** would apply, so that only certain types of company could have higher gearing.

Type of company	Assets	Profits
Highly geared companies	Holding value, long-term	Stable, steady trends
Low geared companies	Rapid depreciation/change	Erratic, volatile

5.2 The effect of GAAP on gearing

FAST FORWARD

Always remember that 'profit' and 'net assets' are fairly **arbitrary figures**, affected by different accounting policies and manipulation.

Variations in accounting policy can have a significant impact on gearing and it will be necessary to consider the individual policies of companies. The main areas which are likely to require consideration area as follows.

(a)   FRS 25 *Financial instruments: disclosure and presentation* has halted the practice of classifying an instrument as equity when the true nature is that of debt and also of accounting for debt at an amount lower than its repayable amount (see Chapter 18).

(b)   Revaluation of fixed assets will have an impact on equity and it will be necessary to consider the frequency of such revaluations (see Chapter 4).

(c)   Assets held under leases may be excluded from a company's balance sheet if the leases are classified as operating leases (see Chapter 10).

(d)   The treatment of deferred development expenditure will have an impact on gearing, ie capitalise or write off (see Chapter 5 on SSAP 13).

(e)   The structure of group accounts and methods of consolidation will also have a substantial impact on gearing.

6 Shareholders' investment ratios

These are the ratios which help equity shareholders and other investors to assess the value and quality of an investment in the **ordinary shares** of a company.

The value of an investment in ordinary shares in a **listed company** is its market value, and so investment ratios must have regard not only to information in the company's published accounts, but also to the current price.

Earnings per share is a valuable indicator of an ordinary share's performance and you should refer to Chapter 14 to study its calculation.

Knowledge brought forward from earlier studies

Investors' ratios

Dividend yield

$$\text{Dividend yield} = \frac{\text{Div per share}}{\text{Mid-market price}}\%$$

- **Low yield**: the company retains a large proportion of profits to reinvest
- **High yield**: this is a risky company or slow-growing

Knowledge brought forward from earlier studies (cont'd)

Dividend cover

$$\text{Dividend cover} = \frac{\text{EPS}}{\text{Net div per share}}$$

Or $$\frac{\text{Profit after tax and pref div}}{\text{Div on ordinary shares}}$$

This shows **how safe the dividend is**, or the extent of profit retention. Variations are due to maintaining dividend when profits are declining.

P/E ratio

$$\text{P/E ratio} = \frac{\text{Mid - market price}}{\text{EPS}}$$

The **higher the better** here: it reflects the confidence of the market. A rise in EPS will cause an increase in P/E ratio, but maybe not to same extent: Look at the context of the market and industry norms.

Earnings yield

$$\text{Earnings yield} = \frac{\text{EPS}}{\text{Mid - market price}}$$

This shows the dividend yield if there is no retention of profit. It allows you to compare companies with **different dividend policies**, showing growth rather than earnings.

Net assets per share

$$\text{Net assets per share} = \frac{\text{Net assets}}{\text{No of shares}}$$

This is a **crude measure** of value of a company, liable to distortion.

See also **EPS** and **dividend per share**

Exam focus point

It cannot be overemphasised that question practice is *vital* in this area. By answering as many questions as possible you will become more and more adept at spotting the major issues in these types of question – which means you will gain most of the marks!

Question

RST plc is considering purchasing an interest in its competitor XYZ Ltd. The managing director of RST plc has obtained the three most recent P&L accounts and balance sheets of XYZ Ltd as shown below.

XYZ LIMITED
PROFIT AND LOSS ACCOUNTS FOR YEARS ENDED 31 DECEMBER

	20X0	20X1	20X2
	£'000	£'000	£'000
Turnover	18,000	18,900	19,845
Cost of sales	10,440	10,340	11,890
Gross profit	7,560	8,560	7,955
Distribution costs	1,565	1,670	1,405
Administrative expenses	1,409	1,503	1,591
Operating profit	4,586	5,387	4,959
Interest payable on bank overdraft	104	215	450
Interest payable on 12% debentures	600	600	600
Profit on ordinary activities before taxation	3,882	4,572	3,909
Taxation on ordinary activities	1,380	2,000	1,838
Profit on ordinary activities after taxation	2,502	2,572	2,071
Proposed dividend	1,600	1,693	1,800
Retained profit	902	879	271

XYZ LIMITED
BALANCE SHEETS AS AT 31 DECEMBER

	20X0		20X1		20X2	
	£'000	£'000	£'000	£'000	£'000	£'000
Fixed assets						
Land and buildings	11,460		12,121		11,081	
Plant and machinery	8,896		9,020		9,130	
		20,356		21,141		20,211
Current assets						
Stock	1,775		2,663		3,995	
Trade debtors	1,440		2,260		3,164	
Cash	50		53		55	
	3,265		4,976		7,214	
Current liabilities						
Trade creditors	390		388		446	
Bank	1,300		2,300		3,400	
Taxation	897		1,420		1,195	
Proposed dividend	1,600		1,696		1,800	
	4,187		5,804		6,841	
Net current assets/(liabilities)		(922)		(828)		373
12% debentures 20X5 – 20X8		(5,000)		(5,000)		(5,000)
		14,434		15,313		15,584
Share capital		8,000		8,000		8,000
Profit and loss account		6,434		7,313		7,584
		14,434		15,313		15,584

Required

Prepare a report for the managing director of RST plc commenting on the financial position of XYZ Ltd and highlighting any areas that require further investigation.

(Marks will be awarded for ratios and other financial statistics where appropriate.)

Answer

To: MD of RST plc
From: An Accountant
Date: XX.XX.XX
Subject: *The financial position of XYZ Ltd*

Introduction

This report has been prepared on the basis of the three most recent P&L accounts and balance sheets of XYZ Ltd covering the years 20X0 to 20X2 inclusive. Ratio analysis used in this report is based on the calculations shown in the appendix attached.

Performance

Sales have increased at a steady 5% per annum over the three year period.

In contrast, the gross profit percentage has increased from 42% in 20X0 to 45% in 20X1 before dropping back to 40% in 20X2. Similarly, operating profit as a percentage of sales was 26% in 20X0, 28.5% in 20X1 and 25% in 20X2. This may indicate some misallocation of costs between 20X1 and 20X2 and should be investigated or it may be indicative of a longer downward trend in profitability.

Return on capital employed, as one would expect, has shown a similar pattern with an increase in 20X1 with a subsequent fall in 20X2 to a level below that of 20X0.

Debt and liquidity

The debt ratio measures the ratio of a company's total debt to its total assets. Although we have no information as to the norm for the industry as a whole, the debt ratios appear reasonable. However, it should be noted that it has risen steadily over the three year period.

When reviewing XYZ Ltd's liquidity the situation has improved over the period. The current ratio measures a company's ability to meet its current liabilities out of current assets. A ratio of at least 1 should therefore be expected. XYZ Ltd did not meet this expectation in 20X0 and 20X1.

This ratio can be misleading as stock is included in current assets. Because stock can take some time to convert into liquid assets a second ratio, the quick ratio, is calculated which excludes stock. As can be seen, the quick ratio, although improving, is low and this shows that current liabilities cannot be met from current assets if stock is excluded. As a major part of current liabilities is the bank overdraft, the company is obviously relying on the bank's continuing support with short-term funding. It would be useful to find out the terms of the bank funding and the projected cash flow requirements for future funding.

Efficiency ratios

The efficiency ratios, debtors ratio and stock turnover, give a useful indication of how the company is managing its current assets.

As can be seen from the appendix the debtors collection period has increased over the three years from 29 days to 58 days. This may indicate that the company is failing to follow up its debts efficiently or that it has given increased credit terms to some or all of its customers.

Looking at stock turnover, this has also risen from 62 days to 122 days. This may be an indication of over-stocking, stocking up on the expectation of a substantial sales increase or the holding of obsolete or slow-moving stock items which should be written down. More investigation needs to be done on both debtors and stock.

The financing of additional debtors and stock has been achieved in the main through the bank overdraft as the trade creditors figure has not increased significantly.

Conclusion

The review of the three year financial statements for XYZ Ltd has given rise to a number of queries which need to be resolved before a useful conclusion can be reached on the financial position of XYZ Ltd. It may also be useful to compare XYZ Ltd's ratios to those of other companies in the same industry in order to obtain some idea of the industry norms.

APPENDIX TO MEMORANDUM

	20X0	*20X1*	*20X2*
% sales increase		5%	5%
Gross profit %	42%	45%	40%
Operating profit %	25.5%	28.5%	25%

Return on capital employed

$$= \frac{\text{Profit before interest and tax}}{\text{Capital employed}} \times 100\%$$

	20X0	*20X1*	*20X2*
	$\frac{4,586-104}{14,434+5,000}$	$\frac{5,387-215}{15,313+5,000}$	$\frac{4,959-450}{15,584+5,000}$
	= 23%	= 25.5%	= 21.9%

Debt ratio

$$= \frac{\text{Total debt}}{\text{Total assets}} \times 100\%$$

	$\frac{4,187+5,000}{20,356+3,265}$	$\frac{5,804+5,000}{21,114+4,976}$	$\frac{6,841+5,000}{20,211+7,214}$
	= 38.9%	= 41.4%	= 43.2%

Current ratio

$$= \frac{\text{Current assets}}{\text{Current liabilities}}$$

	$\frac{3,265}{4,187}$	$\frac{4,976}{5,804}$	$\frac{7,214}{6,814}$
	= 0.78	= 0.86	= 1.06

Quick ratio

$$= \frac{\text{Current assets} - \text{stock}}{\text{Current liabilities}}$$

	$\frac{3,265-1,775}{4,187}$	$\frac{4,976-2,663}{5,804}$	$\frac{7,214-3,995}{6,814}$
	= 0.36	= 0.40	= 0.47

Debtors ratio

$$= \frac{\text{Trade debtors}}{\text{Sales}} \times 365 \text{ days}$$

	$\frac{1,440}{18,000}$	$\frac{2,260}{18,900}$	$\frac{3,164}{19,845}$
	= 29.2 days	= 43.6 days	= 58.2 days

Stock turnover

$$= \frac{\text{Stock}}{\text{Cost of sales}} \times 365 \text{ days}$$

	$\frac{1,775}{10,440}$	$\frac{2,663}{10,340}$	$\frac{3,995}{11,890}$
	= 62 days	= 94 days	= 122.6 days

Question   Ratio analysis (2)

You are the management accountant of Fry plc. Laurie plc is a competitor in the same industry and it has been operating for 20 years. Summaries of Laurie plc's P&L accounts and balance sheets for the previous three years are given below.

SUMMARISED PROFIT AND LOSS ACCOUNTS
FOR THE YEAR ENDED 31 DECEMBER

	20X0	20X1	20X2
	£m	£m	£m
Turnover	840	981	913
Cost of sales	554	645	590
Gross profit	286	336	323
Selling, distribution and administration expenses	186	214	219
Profit before interest	100	122	104
Interest	6	15	19
Profit on ordinary activities before taxation	94	107	85
Taxation	45	52	45
Profit on ordinary activities after taxation	49	55	40
Dividends	24	24	24
Retained profit for year	25	31	16

SUMMARISED BALANCE SHEETS AS AT 31 DECEMBER

	20X0	20X1	20X2
	£m	£m	£m
Fixed assets			
Intangible assets	36	40	48
Tangible assets at net book value	176	206	216
	212	246	264
Current assets			
Stocks	237	303	294
Debtors	105	141	160
Bank	52	58	52
	606	748	770
Creditors: amounts falling due within one year			
Trade creditors	53	75	75
Other creditors	80	105	111
	133	180	186
Creditors: amounts falling due after more than one year			
Long-term loans	74	138	138
	207	318	324
Shareholders' interest			
Ordinary share capital	100	100	100
Retained profits	299	330	346
	606	748	770

You may assume that the index of retail prices has remained constant between 20X0 and 20X2.

Required

Write a report to the finance director of Fry plc:

(a)   Analysing the performance of Laurie plc and showing any calculations in an appendix to this report

(b)   Summarising five areas which require further investigation, including reference to other pieces of information which would complement your analysis of the performance of Laurie plc

Answer

(a) To: Finance Director
     From: Management accountant
     Subject: *Performance of Laurie plc 20X0 to 20X2*

An appendix is attached to this report which shows the ratios calculated as part of the performance review.

Profitability

The gross profit margin has remained relatively static over the three year period, although it has risen by approximately 1% in 20X2. ROCE, while improving very slightly in 20X1 to 21.5% has dropped dramatically in 20X2 to 17.8%. The net profit margin has also fallen in 20X2, in spite of the improvement in the gross profit margin. This marks a rise in expenses which suggests that they are not being well controlled. The utilisation of assets compared to the turnover generated has also declined reflecting the drop in trading activity between 20X1 and 20X2.

Trading levels

It is apparent that there was a dramatic increase in trading activity between 20X0 and 20X1, but then a significant fall in 20X2. Turnover rose by 17% in 20X1 but fell by 7% in 20X2. The reasons for this fluctuation are unclear. It may be the effect of some kind of one-off event, or it may be the effect of a change in product mix. Whatever the reason, it appears that improved credit terms granted to customers (debtors payment period up from 46 to 64 days) has not stopped the drop in sales.

Working capital

Both the current ratio and quick ratio demonstrate an adequate working capital situation, although the quick ratio has shown a slight decline. There has been an increased investment over the period in stocks and debtors which has been only partly financed by longer payment periods to trade creditors and a rise in other creditors (mainly between 20X0 and 20X1).

Capital structure

The level of gearing of the company increased when a further £64m was raised in long term loans in 20X1 to add to the £74m already in the balance sheet. Although this does not seem to be a particularly high level of gearing, the debt/equity ratio did rise from 18.5% to 32.0% in 20X1. The interest charge has risen to £19m from £6m in 20X0. The 20X1 charge was £15m, suggesting that either the interest rate on the loan is flexible, or that the full interest charge was not incurred in 20X1. The new long-term loan appears to have funded the expansion in both fixed and current assets in 20X1.

APPENDIX

Ratio	Working	20X0	20X1	20X2
Gross profit margin	(1)	34.0%	34.3%	35.4%
ROCE	(2)	21.1%	21.5%	17.8%
Profit margin	(3)	11.9%	12.4%	11.4%
Assets turnover	(4)	1.78	1.73	1.56
Gearing ratio	(5)	15.6%	24.3%	23.6%
Debt/equity ratio	(6)	18.5%	32.0%	30.9%
Interest cover	(7)	16.7	8.1	5.5
Current ratio	(8)	3.0	2.8	2.7
Quick ratio	(9)	1.2	1.1	1.1
Debtor's payment period (days)	(10)	46	52	64
Stock turnover period (days)	(11)	156	171	182
Creditor's turnover period	(12)	35	42	46

Workings (all in £m)

		20X0	20X1	20X2
1	Gross profit margin	$\dfrac{286}{840}$	$\dfrac{336}{981}$	$\dfrac{323}{913}$
2	ROCE *	$\dfrac{100}{473}$	$\dfrac{122}{568}$	$\dfrac{104}{584}$
3	Profit margin	$\dfrac{100}{840}$	$\dfrac{122}{981}$	$\dfrac{104}{913}$
4	Assets turnover	$\dfrac{840}{473}$	$\dfrac{981}{568}$	$\dfrac{913}{584}$
5	Gearing ratio	$\dfrac{74}{74 + 399}$	$\dfrac{138}{138 + 430}$	$\dfrac{138}{138 + 446}$
6	Debt/equity ratio	$\dfrac{74}{399}$	$\dfrac{138}{430}$	$\dfrac{138}{446}$
7	Interest cover	$\dfrac{100}{6}$	$\dfrac{122}{15}$	$\dfrac{104}{19}$
8	Current ratio	$\dfrac{394}{133}$	$\dfrac{502}{180}$	$\dfrac{506}{186}$
9	Quick ratio	$\dfrac{157}{133}$	$\dfrac{199}{180}$	$\dfrac{212}{186}$
10	Debtors' payment period	$\dfrac{105}{840} \times 365$	$\dfrac{141}{981} \times 365$	$\dfrac{160}{913} \times 365$
11	Stock turnover period	$\dfrac{237}{554} \times 365$	$\dfrac{303}{645} \times 365$	$\dfrac{294}{590} \times 365$
12	Creditors' payment period	$\dfrac{53}{554} \times 365$	$\dfrac{75}{645} \times 365$	$\dfrac{75}{590} \times 365$

* ROCE has been calculated here as:

$$\frac{\text{Profit on ordinary activities before interest and taxation (PBIT)}}{\text{Capital employed}}$$

where capital employed = shareholders' funds plus creditors falling due after one year and any long-term provision for liabilities and charges. It is possible to calculate ROCE using net profit after taxation and interest, but this admits variations and distortions into the ratio which are not affected by *trading* activity.

(b)   Areas for further investigation include the following.

   (i)   *Long-term loan*

   There is no indication as to why this loan was raised and how it was used to finance the business. Further details are needed of interest rate(s), security given and repayment dates.

   (ii)   *Trading activity*

   The level of sales has fluctuated in quite a strange way and this requires further investigation and explanation. Factors to consider would include pricing policies, product mix, market share and any unique occurrence which would affect sales.

   (iii)   *Further breakdown*

   It would be useful to break down some of the information in the financial statements, perhaps into a management accounting format. Examples would be:

   (1)   Sales by segment, market or geographical area
   (2)   Cost of sales split, into raw materials, labour and overheads
   (3)   Stocks broken down into raw materials, work in progress and finished goods
   (4)   Expenses analysed between administrative expenses, sales and distribution costs

(iv) *Accounting policies*

Accounting policies may have a significant effect on certain items. In particular, it would be useful to know what the accounting policies are in relation to intangible assets (and what these assets consist of), and whether there has been any change in accounting policies.

(v) *Dividend policy*

The company has maintained the level of dividend paid to shareholders (although it has not been raised during the three year period). Presumably the company would have been able to reduce the amount of long-term debt taken on if it had retained part or all of the dividend during this period. It would be interesting to examine the share price movement during the period and calculate the dividend cover.

Tutorial note. Other matters raised could have included:

(1) working capital problems, particularly stock turnover and control over debtors; and

(2) EPS (which cannot be calculated here as the number of shares is not given) and other related investor statistics, such as the P/E ratio.

Chapter Roundup

- Keep the various **sources of financial information** in mind and the effects of insider dealing, the efficient market hypothesis and Stock Exchange regulations.

- Much of the material here on **basic ratios** should have been revision for you. The next few chapters will cover much more complicated aspects of financial analysis.

- Make sure that you can **define** all the ratios. Look out for variations in definitions of ratios which might appear in questions.

- Always remember that 'profit' and 'net assets' are fairly **arbitrary figures**, affected by different accounting policies and manipulation.

Quick Quiz

1   Apart from ratio analysis, what other information might be helpful in interpreting a company's accounts?

2   In a period when profits are fluctuating, what effect does a company's level of gearing have on the profits available for ordinary shareholders?

3   Name three areas where variations in accounting policy can have a significant impact on gearing.

4   The acid test or quick ratio should include:

   A   Stocks of finished goods
   B   Raw materials and consumables
   C   Long-tem loans
   D   Trade debtors

5   The asset turnover of Taplow Ltd is 110% that of Stoke Ltd.

   The return on capital of Taplow Ltd is 80% of that of Stoke Ltd.

   Calculate Taplow Ltd's profit margin expressed as a percentage of Stoke Ltd's.

6   Deal Ltd has the following capital structure:

	£'000
£1 ordinary shares	55,000
6% £1 Preference shares	15,000
Reserves	12,000
	82,000
8% debentures	30,000
	112,000

   What is the most appropriate measure of the debt/equity ratio for a potential equity investor?

7   Below is an extract of the profit and loss account of Public plc.

	£	£
Operating profit		1,260,000
Interest payable on loan stock		60,000
Profit before tax		1,200,000
Taxation at 30%		360,000
Profit after taxation		840,000
Dividends: preference	65,000	
ordinary	100,000	
		(165,000)
		675,000

   Treating the preference shares as part of the borrowing of the company, what is the interest cover?

Answers to Quick Quiz

1   See Para 1.2.

2   There is more risk that there will be little to distribute by way of a dividend as the percentage change in profit available for shareholders fluctuates more.

3   (a)   Classification of debt and equity instruments
    (b)   Revaluation of fixed assets
    (c)   Classification of leases
    (d)   Treatment of deferred development expenditure
    (e)   Structure of group accounts

4   D   Acid test ratio = $\dfrac{CA - \text{stock}}{CL}$

5   $\dfrac{80}{110} = 73\%$

6   Debt   =   30 + 15 = 45
    Equity =   55 + 12 = 67
    ∴ 45/67 × 100 = 67.2%

7   Interest cover = $\dfrac{PBIT}{\text{Interest} + \text{Pref dividends} \times 100/70}$

    $= \dfrac{1,200 + 60}{60 + (65 \times 100 / 70)}$

    The preference dividend is paid from post tax profits and therefore needs grossing up by the tax rate.

Now try the questions below from the Exam Question Bank

Number	Level	Marks	Time
Q14	Examination	25	45 mins

Reporting financial performance 1

14

Topic list	Syllabus reference
1 FRS 3 *Reporting financial performance*	C1
2 FRS 22 *Earnings per share*	C1
3 FRS 28 *Corresponding amounts*	C1

Introduction

We have already discussed the problems perceived by companies when they report their results, and how they feel 'obliged' to **manipulate** those results to avoid adverse reaction in the market. **FRS 3** represents the ASB's attempt to prevent some of the worst abuses.

Earnings per share is covered briefly here – the detail is not important as it has been covered at an earlier level.

Study guide

		Intellectual level
C1	**Performance reporting**	
(a)	Prepare reports relating to corporate performance for external stakeholders	3

Exam guide

Proposed changes to FRS 3 are covered in a later chapter.

1 FRS 3 Reporting financial performance

FAST FORWARD

It is important that you appreciate how great an impact **FRS 3** has on reporting financial performance. You may be called on to discuss the changes and comment on them.

Try to remember the **important terms**.

- Reserve accounting
- All inclusive concept
- Exceptional items
- Prior year adjustments
- Discontinued operations
- Total recognised gains and losses

The P&L account is arguably the most significant single indicator of a company's success or failure. It is very important to ensure that it is not presented in such a way as to be misleading. This could happen either through an inadvertent lack of consistency within a company or between different companies; or it could arise as a result of deliberate manipulation of accounting figures by unscrupulous directors.

One particular area where this might happen is the practice known as **reserve accounting**. This involves deducting items of expenditure not from the profits for the current year, but from the balance of accumulated profits brought forward. By eliminating such items from the **current** year's P&L account a more favourable presentation of the year's results may be achieved; only a close inspection of the previous year's balance sheet will disclose that the figure for reserves brought forward has been manipulated.

Possible **justifications** for excluding items in this way from the current year's P&L account include the following.

(a) The item might have **arisen in a previous year** without becoming apparent until the current year. It is really a charge against previous year's profits and would have appeared in an earlier year's P&L account if the directors had been aware of it.

(b) The item is **unique in nature** and unlikely to recur. It would be a misleading distortion of the trend of reported profits if such an item were charged against the current year's profits.

Each of these arguments may be valid in certain circumstances, but it is clear that scope is available for unscrupulous manipulation of the P&L account unless those circumstances are very clearly defined. The old SSAP 6 attempted to standardise the treatment of **prior year adjustments** and **extraordinary items**, which are respectively the two categories of items referred to above.

You have covered FRS 3 in your earlier studies, but here is a reminder of its main reading.

1.1 Exceptional and extraordinary items

FRS 3 practically outlawed extraordinary items.

Exceptional and extraordinary items

Exceptional items

Exceptional items are **material items** which derive from events or transactions that fall **within the ordinary activities** of the reporting entity and which need to be disclosed by virtue of their **size or incidence** if the financial statements are to give a true and fair view. Show on the face of the P&L a./c:

- Profit *and* loss (no offset) on the sale/termination of an operation

- Costs of a fundamental reorganisation or restructuring that has a material effect on the nature and focus of the reporting entity's operations

- Profit *and* loss (no offset) on disposal of fixed assets (difference between sale proceeds and the carrying value of the investment)

Other exceptional items should be allocated to the appropriate **statutory format heading** and attributed to continuing or discontinued operations as appropriate. If sufficiently material disclose on the face of the P&L a/c.

Extraordinary items

Extraordinary items are material items possessing a **high degree of abnormality** which arise from events or transactions that fall **outside the ordinary activities** of the reporting entity and which are not expected to recur. Note that **ordinary activities** include infrequent and unusual events.

- Largely **redundant** as the ASB has stated that such items are not expected to appear in P&L accounts in future.

- Should be shown on the **face of the P&L account** before dividends and other minority interests; tax and MI in the extraordinary item shown separately; a description should be given in the notes.

1.2 The profit and loss account

The face of the P&L account was altered by FRS 3 to give further information.

The P & L account

Structure

- All statutory headings from turnover to operating profit are subdivided: **continuing vs discontinued operations.**

- Turnover and operating profit are fully analysed: **existing vs newly acquired operations.**

- Only figures for turnover and operating profit need to be shown on the **face of the P&L account**; others are by note.

Discontinued operations

A discontinued operation needs *all* these conditions

Knowledge brought forward from earlier studies (continued)

- Sale/termination must be **completed** before the earlier of 3 months after the y/e or the date the FS approved (terminations not completed by this date: disclose by note)

- Former activity must have **ceased permanently**

- Sales/termination has a **material effect** on the **nature and focus** of the entity's operations and represents a **material reduction** in its operating facilities resulting from either a:
    - Withdrawal from a market (business/geographical), or
    - Material reduction in turnover in its continuing markets

- Assets, liabilities, results of operations and activities are **clearly distinguishable**, physically, operationally and for financial reporting purposes

Accounting for the discontinuation involves the following.

- The **results** of the discontinued operation up to the date of sale/termination or the balance sheet date should be shown under each of the relevant P&L account headings.

- **Profit/loss on (or costs of) discontinuation**: disclose as exceptional item after operating profit, before interest

- Figures for the **previous year** must be adjusted for any activities which are now discontinued in the current year

- Once a business is committed to dispose of an operation (eg by signing a sale agreement) it should **provide for direct costs of sale or termination**; and any **operating losses** up to the date of sale/termination.
    - If the operation continues during the whole of the accounting period then the provision should be included under the continuing column
    - If the operation is discontinued in the next accounting period, the provision will be utilised and disclosed

Acquisitions

- Business combinations that are accounted for as **mergers** and/or as **acquisitions.**
- Associates that **become subsidiaries**, on further acquisition of shares.
- **Start-ups** and **acquisitions of associates** are *not* acquisitions.

1.3 Statement and notes

A new statement and various notes were introduced by FRS 3.

Knowledge brought forward from earlier studies

Statement and notes

Statement of total recognised gains and losses

Presented with the same prominence as the P&L account, balance sheet and cash flow statement, as a **primary statement**.

- **Contents**

Profit for the year (per P&L a/c)	X
Items taken directly to reserves (not goodwill written off to reserves)	X
Unrealised surplus on revaluation of fixed assets	X
Surplus/deficit on revaluation of investment properties	X
Currency translation differences on foreign currency net investments	X
Total recognised gains and losses for the year	X
Prior period adjustments (see later)	(X)
Total gains and losses recognised since last annual report	X

- Once an unrealised gain or loss is recognised in the statement, transfer for inclusion in the P&L when it **becomes realised** at a later date is *not* allowed.

- **Transactions with shareholders** are excluded (dividends paid and proposed, share issues, redemptions): these transactions do not represent gains/losses.

- Where the profit/loss for the year is the **only recognised gain/loss**, state this below the P&L account.

- In the consolidated statement of total recognised gains and losses, include the investor's share of the total recognised gains and losses of its associates, shown separately under each heading if the amounts are material, either in the statement or a note.

Reconciliation of movements in shareholders' funds

- In the notes to the accounts *or* a primary statement

- Pulls together **financial performance** as shown in the:

  - P&L account
  - Other movements in shareholders' funds as in STRGL
  - All other changes in shareholders' funds

- **Example**

Profit for the financial year	X
* Dividends	(X)
	X
Other recognised gains and losses (per STRGL)	X
* New share capital	X
Net addition to shareholders' funds	X
Opening shareholders' funds	X
Closing shareholders' funds	X
* Items not appearing in the primary statements	

Note of historical cost profits and losses

Reported profit is not the same as HC profit where **alternative accounting rules** are used. If the difference is material, then include a **reconciliation** statement after the STRGL or the P&L account. Reconcile profit before tax; however, the retained profit for the year must also be restated.

1.4 Prior period adjustments

FRS 3 defines prior period adjustments and states when they should be used.

Knowledge brought forward from earlier studies

Prior period adjustments

- **Definition**: material adjustments applicable to prior periods arising from changes in accounting policies or from the correction of fundamental errors; it does *not* include normal recurring adjustments or corrections of account estimates made in prior periods.

- **Accounting treatment**

    ○   Restate prior year P&L account and balance sheet
    ○   Restate opening reserves balance
    ○   Include in the reconciliation of movements in shareholders' funds
    ○   Note at the foot of the STRGL of the current period

- **Fundamental error**: an error which is so significant that the truth and fairness of the financial statements is not achieved.

- **Change in accounting policy**: based on the fundamental accounting concept of **consistency**; reasons for a change in policy:

    −   Gives fairer presentation of financial position/result
    −   Introduction of, or change to a standard/legislation

The following exercises will be useful revision.

 Question   Discontinued operation

B&C plc's P&L account for the year ended 31 December 20X2, with comparatives, is as follows.

	20X2	20X1
	£'000	£'000
Turnover	200,000	180,000
Cost of sales	(60,000)	(80,000)
Gross profit	140,000	100,000
Distribution costs	(25,000)	(20,000)
Administration expenses	(50,000)	(45,000)
Operating profit	65,000	35,000

During the year the company sold a material business operation with all activities ceasing on 14 February 20X3. The loss on the sale of the operation amounted to £2.2m. The results of the operation for 20X1 and 20X2 were as follows.

	20X2	20X1
	£'000	£'000
Turnover	22,000	26,000
Operating loss	(7,000)	(6,000)

In addition, the company acquired a business which contributed £7m to turnover and an operating profit of £1.5m.

Required

Prepare the profit and loss account and related notes for the year ended 31 December 20X2 complying with the requirements of FRS 3 as far as possible.

Answer

B&C PROFIT AND LOSS ACCOUNT FOR THE YEAR ENDED 31 DECEMBER

	20X2		20X1	
	£'000	£'000	£'000	£'000
Turnover				
Continuing operations				
(200 – 22 – 7)/(180 – 26)		171.0		154
Acquisitions		7.0		–
		178.0		154
Discontinued		22.0		26
		200.0		180
Cost of sales		(60.0)		(80)
Gross profit		140.0		100
Distribution costs		(25.0)		(20)
Administration expenses (50 – 2.2)		(47.8)		(45)
Operating profit				
Continuing operations	72.7		41	
Acquisitions	1.5		–	
	74.2		41	
Discontinued	(7.0)		(6)	
		67.2		35
Loss on sale of operation		(2.2)		–
		65.0		35

Note to the P&L account

	20X2			20X1 (as restated)		
	Continuing	Discontinued	Total	Continuing	Discontinued	Total
	£'000	£'000	£'000	£'000	£'000	£'000
Cost of sales	X	X	60.0	X	X	80
Net operating expenses						
Distribution costs	X	X	25.0	X	X	20
Admin expenses	X	X	47.8	X	X	45
	X	X	72.8	X	X	65

Question   STRGL and reconciliation

Extracts from Z Ltd's P&L account for the year ended 31 December 20X1 were as follows.

	£'000
Profit after tax	512
Dividend	(120)
Retained profit	392

During the year the following important events took place.

(a)   Assets were revalued upward by £120,000.

(b)   £300,000 share capital was issued during the year.

(c)   Certain stock items were written down by £45,000.

(d)   The company's investment properties previously revalued by £81,000 were written down by £110,000. This deficit is expected to be temporary.

(e)   Opening shareholders' funds = £4m

Show how the events for the year would be shown in the statement of total recognised gains and losses and the reconciliation of movements in shareholders' funds.

Answer

	£'000
Profit after tax	512
Asset	120
Devaluation of investments properties *	(110)
	522

* An amendment to SSAP 19 allows a temporary debit balance on the investment revaluation reserve (IRR).

RECONCILIATION OF MOVEMENTS IN SHAREHOLDERS' FUNDS

	£'000
Profit after tax	512
Dividend	(120)
	392
Other recognised gains and losses (522 − 512)	10
New share capital	300
Net addition to shareholders' funds	702
Opening shareholders' funds	4,000
Closing shareholders' funds	4,702

Question

Historical cost profit reconciliations

A Ltd reported a profit before tax of £162,000 for the year ended 31 December 20X1. During the year the following transactions in fixed assets took place.

(a)   An asset with a book value of £40,000 was revalued to £75,000. The remaining useful life is estimated to be five years.

(b)   An asset (with a five year useful life at the date of revaluation) had been revalued upwards by £20,000 (book value £30,000). It was sold during the current year (one year after revaluation) for £48,000.

Show the reconciliation of profit to historical cost profit for the year ended 31 Dec 20X1.

Answer

RECONCILIATION OF PROFIT TO HISTORICAL COST PROFIT
FOR THE YEAR ENDED 31 DECEMBER 20X1

	£'000
Reported profit on ordinary activities before taxation	162
Realisation of property revaluation gains	20
Difference between historical cost depreciation charge and the actual depreciation charge of the year calculated on the revalued amount (75,000 − 40,000)/5	7
	189

Question   Change of accounting policy

Wick Ltd was established on 1 January 20X0. In the first three years' accounts deferred development expenditure was carried forward as an asset in the balance sheet. During 20X3 the directors decided that for the current and future years, all development expenditure should be written off as it is incurred. This decision has not resulted from any change in the expected outcome of development projects on hand, but rather from a desire to favour the prudence concept. The following information is available.

(a) Movements on the deferred development account:

Year	Deferred development expenditure incurred during year £'000	Transfer from deferred development expenditure account to P & L account £'000
20X0	525	–
20X1	780	215
20X2	995	360

(b) The 20X2 accounts showed the following.

	£'000
Retained reserves b/f	2,955
Retained profit for the year	1,825
Retained profits carried forward	4,780

(c) The retained profit for 20X3 after charging the actual development expenditure for the year was £2,030,000.

Required

Show how the change in accounting policy should be reflected in the statement of reserves in the company's 20X3 accounts. Ignore taxation.

Answer

If the new accounting policy had been adopted since the company was incorporated, the additional profit and loss account charges for development expenditure would have been as follows.

	£'000
20X0	525
20X1 (780 – 215)	565
	1,090
20X2 (995 – 360)	635
	1,725

This means that the reserves brought forward at 1 January 20X3 would have been £1,725,000 less than the reported figure of £4,780,000; while the reserves brought forward at 1 January 20X2 would have been £1,090,000 less than the reported figure of £2,955,000. The statement of reserves in Wick Ltd's 20X3 accounts should, therefore, appear as follows.

STATEMENT OF RESERVES (EXTRACT)

	20X3 £'000	20X2 £'000	
Retained profits at the beginning of year			
Previously reported	4,780	2,955	
Prior year adjustment (note 1)	1,725	1,090	
Restated	3,055	1,865	
Retained profits for the year	2,030	1,190	(note 2)
Retained profits at the end of the year	5,085	3,055	

Notes

1   The accounts should include a note explaining the reasons for and consequences of the changes in accounting policy. (See above workings for 20X3 and 20X2.)

2   The retained profit shown for 20X2 is after charging the additional development expenditure of £635,000.

1.5 Effect of FRS 3

First of all, FRS 3 makes **extraordinary items virtually non-existent**. All exceptional items, apart from a few important exceptions, will be included under the relevant P&L heading. Those exceptional items requiring disclosure on the face of the P&L account are indicators of important events during the accounting period and they would usually have been shown under extraordinary items under the old SSAP 6. FRS 3 introduced **new definitions** for most of the important terms.

The effect on **prior year adjustments** is negligible. The effect on **EPS** will be studied in Section 2.

A **new format** for the P&L account was introduced, splitting continuing and discontinued operations. The definitions of these terms will again prevent manipulation. **Disclosure** is much fuller than under SSAP 6, where only a one line extraordinary item was given.

A **statement of total recognised gains and losses** (STRGL) must be provided. The ASB's aim here has been to turn attention away from particular numbers or indicators and to encourage users to make their own judgements about a company's performance based on the set of information given. This statement cannot be lost in the notes as the reserve movement note was under SSAP 6, because it must be given equal prominence with the other primary statements. (Note that one of the main reasons why this statement came into existence was the collapse of Polly Peck. The size of the exchange movements going through reserves was considerable and, although they had been disclosed, they had not been highlighted.) The really important figure here is that of **total gains and losses** for the year. This will probably be of great importance to all users in the future, as much as the profit for the year.

Consideration was given to extending the statement of recognised gains and losses to provide a **reconciliation of movements in shareholders' funds** for the period. Instead, a separate reconciliation was suggested, which could be shown as either a note or a primary statement. This statement includes dividends and goodwill written off. Note that dividends are shown as a deduction from profit for the financial year rather than from total recognised gains and losses, because dividends cannot be paid out of unrealised profits.

FRS 3 has been **criticised** and the following points show the major criticisms.

(a)   Restricting extraordinary items and calculating EPS after extraordinary items will make earnings and EPS too **volatile** to obtain meaningful results over time. Analysts will probably exclude items they consider extraordinary for their purposes, thus undermining the impact of FRS 3.

(b)   The old and new primary statements and the new notes are not necessarily easy to relate to each other. The formats could have been adjusted to allow the **relationships to be clearer**.

(c)   FRS 3, by introducing new statements and notes, has made financial statements even **more confusing** for the lay user, particularly since the non-columnar layout is allowed.

(d)   Allowing companies to prepare **alternative EPS figures** will lead to confusion as different methods will be used in each case. Analysts also believe that the market, by its very nature, will aim for one 'across the board' earnings figure (see Section 4).

You may be able to think of other problems associated with FRS 3 but remember that it has many advantages, not the least of which is the fact that it discloses *more* information. You will be able to see this if you obtain some recent sets of company accounts. It also reflects the ASB's aim to avoid the use of just one earnings measure, such as EPS.

Exam focus point

Although you may be faced with a question based specifically on FRS 3, you may also find that questions requiring a consolidated P&L account will involve FRS 3 disclosures.

2 FRS 22 Earnings per share

FAST FORWARD

Earnings per share is a measure of the amount of profits earned by a company for each ordinary share. Earnings are profits after tax and preferred dividends.

Exam focus point

You studied earnings per share for earlier papers. The examiner has stated that it is not going to form the basis of a full question. However, you may have to talk about the potential for manipulation.

FRS 22 *Earnings per share* was published in December 2004 as part of the ASB's convergence programme. It implements IAS 33 of the same name. The objective of FRS 22 is to improve the **comparison** of the performance of different entities in the same period and of the same entity in different accounting periods.

2.1 Definitions

The following definitions are given in FRS 22.

Key terms

Ordinary share: an equity instrument that is subordinate to all other classes of equity instruments.

Potential ordinary share: a financial instrument or other contract that may entitle its holder to ordinary shares.

Options, warrants and their equivalents: financial instruments that give the holder the right to purchase ordinary shares.

Contingently issuable ordinary shares are ordinary shares issuable for little or no cash or other consideration upon the satisfaction of certain conditions in a contingent share agreement.

Contingent share agreement: an agreement to issue shares that is dependent on the satisfaction of specified conditions.

Dilution is a reduction in earnings per share or an increase in loss per share resulting from the assumption that convertible instruments are converted, that options or warrants are exercised, or that ordinary shares are issued upon the satisfaction of certain conditions.

Antidilution is an increase in earnings per share or a reduction in loss per share resulting from the assumption that convertible instruments are converted, that options or warrants are exercised, or that ordinary shares are issued upon the satisfaction of certain conditions.

(FRS 22)

2.1.1 Ordinary shares

There may be more than one class of ordinary shares, but ordinary shares of the same class will have the same rights to receive dividends. Ordinary shares participate in the net profit for the period **only after other types of shares**, eg preference shares.

2.1.2 Potential ordinary shares

FRS 22 identifies the following examples of financial instrument and other contracts generating potential ordinary shares.

(a) **Debts** (financial liabilities) **or equity instruments**, including preference shares, that are convertible into ordinary shares

(b) **Share warrants and options**

(c) Shares that would be issued upon the satisfaction of **certain conditions** resulting from contractual arrangements, such as the purchase of a business or other assets

2.2 Scope

FRS 22 has the following **scope restrictions**.

(a) Only companies with (potential) ordinary shares which are **publicly traded** need to present EPS (including companies in the process of being listed).

(b) EPS need only be presented on the basis of **consolidated results** where the parent's results are shown as well.

(b) Where companies **choose** to present EPS, even when they have no (potential) ordinary shares which are traded, they must do so according to FRS 22.

(c) Entities applying the Financial Reporting Standard for Smaller Entities (FRSSE) are exempt, as are entities applying FRS 6 *Acquisitions and mergers*

2.3 Basic EPS

FAST FORWARD

> **Basic EPS** is calculated by dividing the net profit or loss for the period attributable to ordinary shareholders by the weighted average number of ordinary shares outstanding during the period.
>
> You should know how to calculate **basic EPS** and how to deal with related complications (issue of shares for cash, bonus issue, share splits/reverse share splits, rights issues).

Basic EPS should be calculated for **profit or loss attributable to ordinary equity holders** of the parent entity and **profit or loss from continuing operations** attributable to those equity holders (if this is presented).

Basic EPS should be calculated by dividing the **net profit** or loss for the period attributable to ordinary equity holders by the **weighted average number of ordinary shares** outstanding during the period.

$$\frac{\text{Net profit/(loss) attribtable to ordinary shareholders}}{\text{Weighted average number of ordinary shares outstanding during the period}}$$

2.3.1 Earnings

Earnings includes **all items of income and expense** (including tax and minority interests) *less* net profit attributable to **preference shareholders**, including preference dividends.

Preference dividends deducted from net profit consist of the following:

(a) Preference dividends on non-cumulative preference shares declared in respect of the period.

(b) Preference dividends for cumulative preference shares required for the period, *whether or not* they have been declared (*excluding* those paid/declared during the period in respect of previous periods).

If an entity purchases its own preference shares for more than their carrying amount the excess should be treated as a return to the preference shareholders and deducted from profit or loss attributable to ordinary equity holders.

2.3.2 Per share

The number of ordinary shares used should be the weighted average number of ordinary shares during the period. This figure (for all periods presented) should be **adjusted for events**, other than the conversion of potential ordinary shares, that have changed the number of shares outstanding without a corresponding change in resources.

The **time-weighting factor** is the number of days the shares were outstanding compared with the total number of days in the period. A reasonable approximation is usually adequate.

Shares are usually included in the weighted average number of shares from the **date consideration is receivable** which is usually the date of issue. In other cases consider the specific terms attached to their issue (consider the substance of any contract). The treatment for the issue of ordinary shares in different circumstances is as follows.

Consideration	Start date for inclusion
In exchange for cash	When cash is receivable
On the voluntary reinvestment of dividends on ordinary or preferred shares	The dividend payment date
As a result of the conversion of a debt instrument to ordinary shares	Date interest ceases accruing
In place of interest or principal on other financial instruments	Date interest ceases accruing
In exchange for the settlement of a liability of the entity	The settlement date
As consideration for the acquisition of an asset other than cash	The date on which the acquisition is recognised
For the rendering of services to the entity	As services are rendered

Ordinary shares issued as **purchase consideration** in an acquisition should be included as of the date of acquisition because the acquired entity's results will also be included from that date.

Where a **merger** takes place the number of ordinary shares used for the calculation is the aggregate of the weighted average number of shares of the combined entities, adjusted to equivalent shares of the entity whose shares are outstanding after the combination.

Ordinary shares that will be issued on the **conversion** of a mandatorily convertible instrument are included in the calculation from the **date the contract is entered into**.

If ordinary shares are **partly paid**, they are treated as a fraction of an ordinary share to the extent they are entitled to dividends relative to fully paid ordinary shares.

Contingently issuable shares (including those subject to recall) are included in the computation when all necessary conditions for issue have been satisfied.

2.4 Effect on basic EPS of changes in capital structure

2.4.1 New issues/buy backs

When there has been an issue of new shares or a buy-back of shares, the corresponding figures for EPS for the previous year will be comparable with the current year because, as the weighted average of shares has risen or fallen, there has been a **corresponding increase or decrease in resources**. Money has been received when shares were issued, and money has been paid out to repurchase shares. It is assumed that the sale or purchase has been made at full market price.

There are other events, however, which change the number of shares outstanding, **without a corresponding change in resources**. In these circumstances (four of which are considered by FRS 22) it is necessary to make adjustments so that the current and prior period EPS figures are comparable.

2.4.2 Capitalisation/bonus issue and share split/reverse share split

These two types of event can be considered together as they have a similar effect. In both cases, ordinary shares are issued to existing shareholders for **no additional consideration**. The number of ordinary shares has increased without an increase in resources.

This problem is solved by **adjusting the number of ordinary shares outstanding before the event** for the proportionate change in the number of shares outstanding as if the event had occurred at the beginning of the earliest period reported.

2.4.3 Rights issue

A rights issue of shares is an issue of new shares to existing shareholders **at a price below the current market value**. The offer of new shares is made on the basis of x new shares for every y shares currently held, eg a 1 for 3 rights issue is an offer of 1 new share at the offer price for every 3 shares currently held. This means that there is a bonus element included.

To arrive at figures for EPS when a rights issue is made, we first calculate the **theoretical ex-rights price**. This is a weighted average value per share.

The procedures for calculating the EPS for the current year and a corresponding figure for the previous year are as follows.

(a)   The **EPS for the corresponding previous period** should be multiplied by the following fraction. (*Note*. The market price on the last day of quotation is taken as the fair value immediately prior to exercise of the rights, as required by the standard.)

$$\frac{\text{Theoretical ex-rights price}}{\text{Market price on last day of quotation (with rights)}}$$

(b)   To obtain the **EPS for the current year** you should:

(i)   multiply the number of shares before the rights issue by the fraction of the year before the date of issue and by the following fraction.

$$\frac{\text{Market price on last day of quotation with rights}}{\text{Theoretical ex-rights price}}$$

(ii)   multiply the number of shares after the rights issue by the fraction of the year after the date of issue and add to the figure arrived at in (i).

The total earnings should then be divided by the total number of shares so calculated.

 Question   Were you awake?

Give the formula for the 'bonus element' of a rights issue.

Answer

$$\frac{\text{Actual cum-rights price}}{\text{Theoretical ex-rights price}}$$

Question	Basic EPS

Macarone Co has produced the following net profit figures.

	£m
20X6	1.1
20X7	1.5
20X8	1.8

On 1 January 20X7 the number of shares outstanding was 500,000. During 20X7 the company announced a rights issue with the following details.

Rights:	1 new share for each 5 outstanding (100,000 new shares in total)
Exercise price:	£5.00
Last date to exercise rights:	1 March 20X7

The market (fair) value of one share in Marcoli immediately prior to exercise on 1 March 20X7 = £11.00.

Required

Calculate the EPS for 20X6, 20X7 and 20X8.

Answer

Computation of theoretical ex-rights price

This computation uses the total fair value and number of shares.

$$\frac{\text{Fair value of all outstanding shares + total received from exercise of rights}}{\text{No shares outstanding prior to exercise + no shares issued in exercise}}$$

$$= \frac{(£11.00 \times 500,000) + (\$5.00 \times 100,000)}{500,000 + 100,000} = £10.00$$

Computation of EPS

		20X6 £	20X7 £	20X8 £
20X6	EPS as originally reported $\dfrac{£1,100,000}{500,000}$	2.20		
20X6	EPS restated for rights issue = $\dfrac{£1,100,000}{500,000} \times \dfrac{10}{11}$	2.00		
20X7	EPS including effects of rights issue $\dfrac{£1,500,000}{(500,000 \times 2/12 \times 11/10) + (600,000 \times 10/12)}$		2.54	
20X8	$EPS = \dfrac{£1,800,000}{600,000}$			3.00

2.5 Diluted EPS

FAST FORWARD

Diluted EPS is calculated by adjusting the net profit attributable to ordinary shareholders and the weighted average number of shares outstanding for the effects of all dilutive potential ordinary shares.

You must be able to deal with **options** and all other **dilutive potential ordinary shares**.

At the end of an accounting period, a company may have in issue some **securities** which do not (at present) have any 'claim' to a share of equity earnings, but **may give rise to such a claim in the future**.

(a) A **separate class of equity shares** which at present is not entitled to any dividend, but will be entitled after some future date.

(b) **Convertible loan stock** or **convertible preferred shares** which give their holders the right at some future date to exchange their securities for ordinary shares of the company, at a pre-determined conversion rate.

(c) **Options** or **warrants**.

In such circumstances, the future number of shares ranking for dividend might increase, which in turn results in a fall in the EPS. In other words, a **future increase** in the **number of equity shares will cause a dilution or 'watering down' of equity**, and it is possible to calculate a **diluted earnings per share** (ie the EPS that would have been obtained during the financial period if the dilution had already taken place). This will indicate to investors the possible effects of a future dilution.

2.5.1 Earnings

The earnings calculated for basic EPS should be adjusted by the **post-tax** (including deferred tax) effect of the following.

(a) Any **dividends** on dilutive potential ordinary shares that were deducted to arrive at earnings for basic EPS.

(b) **Interest recognised** in the period for the dilutive potential ordinary shares.

(c) Any **other changes in income or expenses** (fees and discount, premium accounted for as yield adjustments) that would result from the conversion of the dilutive potential ordinary shares.

The conversion of some potential ordinary shares may lead to changes in **other income or expenses**. For example, the reduction of interest expense related to potential ordinary shares and the resulting increase in net profit for the period may lead to an increase in the expense relating to a non-discretionary employee profit-sharing plan. When calculating diluted EPS, the net profit or loss for the period is adjusted for any such consequential changes in income or expense.

2.5.2 Per share

The number of ordinary shares is the weighted average number of ordinary shares calculated for basic EPS plus the weighted average number of ordinary shares that would be issued on the conversion of all the **dilutive potential ordinary shares** into ordinary shares.

It should be assumed that dilutive ordinary shares were converted into ordinary shares at the **beginning of the period** or, if later, at the actual date of issue. There are two other points.

(a) The computation assumes the most **advantageous conversion rate** or exercise rate from the standpoint of the holder of the potential ordinary shares.

(b) A **subsidiary, joint venture or associate** may issue potential ordinary shares that are convertible into either ordinary shares of the subsidiary, joint venture or associate, or ordinary shares of the reporting entity. If these potential ordinary shares have a dilutive effect on the consolidated basic EPS of the reporting entity, they are included in the calculation of diluted EPS.

2.5.3 Example: diluted EPS

In 20X7 Farrah plc had a basic EPS of 105p based on earnings of £105,000 and 100,000 ordinary £1 shares. It also had in issue £40,000 15% Convertible Loan Stock which is convertible in two years' time at the rate of 4 ordinary shares for every £5 of stock. The rate of tax is 30%. In 20X7 gross profit of £150,000 was recorded.

Required

Calculate the diluted EPS.

Solution

Diluted EPS is calculated as follows.

Step 1 **Number of shares**: the additional equity on conversion of the loan stock will be 40,000 × 4/5 = 32,000 shares

Step 2 **Earnings**: Farrah plc will save interest payments of £6,000 but this increase in profits will be taxed. Hence the earnings figure may be recalculated:

	£
Gross profit £(150,000 + 6,000)	156,000
Taxation (30%)	46,800
Profit after tax	109,200

Step 3 **Calculation**: Diluted EPS = $\dfrac{£109,200}{132,000}$ = 82.7p

Step 4 **Dilution**: the dilution in earnings would be 105p − 82.7p = 22.3p per share.

Question   EPS 1

Ardent Co has 5,000,000 ordinary shares of 25 pence each in issue, and also had in issue in 20X4:

(a)   £1,000,000 of 14% convertible loan stock, convertible in three years' time at the rate of 2 shares per £10 of stock.

(b)   £2,000,000 of 10% convertible loan stock, convertible in one year's time at the rate of 3 shares per £5 of stock.

The total earnings in 20X4 were £1,750,000.

The rate of income tax is 35%.

Required

Calculate the EPS and diluted EPS.

Answer

(a)   EPS = $\dfrac{£1,750,000}{5\,\text{million}}$ = 35 pence

(b)   On dilution, the (maximum) number of shares in issue would be:

	Shares
Current	5,000,000
On conversion of 14% stock	200,000
On conversion of 10% stock	1,200,000
	6,400,000

	£	£
Current earnings		1,750,000
Add interest saved (140,000 + 200,000)	340,000	
Less tax thereon at 35%	119,000	
		221,000
Revised earnings		1,971,000

Fully diluted EPS $= \dfrac{£1,971,000}{6.4 \text{ million}} = 30.8$ pence

2.6 Presentation

A entity should present on the **face of the income statement** basic and diluted EPS for:

(a)   profit or loss from continuing operations; and

(b)   profit or loss for the period

for each class of ordinary share that has a different right to share in the net profit for the period.

The basic and diluted EPS should be presented with **equal prominence** for all periods presented.

Basic and diluted EPS for any **discontinued operations** must also be presented.

Disclosure must still be made where the EPS figures (basic and/or diluted) are **negative** (ie a loss per share).

2.7 Alternative EPS figures

An entity may present **alternative EPS figures if it wishes**. However, FRS 22 lays out certain rules where this takes place.

(a)   The weighted average number of shares as calculated under FRS 22 **must** be used.

(b)   A **reconciliation** must be given between the component of profit used in the alternative EPS (if it is not a line item in the income statement) and the line item for profit reported in the income statement.

(c)   The entity must indicate the basis on which the **numerator** is determined.

(d)   Basic and diluted EPS must be shown with **equal prominence**.

2.8 Significance of earnings per share

Earnings per share (EPS) is one of the most frequently quoted statistics in financial analysis. Because of the widespread use of the price earnings **(P/E) ratio** as a yardstick for investment decisions, it became increasingly important.

It seems that reported and forecast EPS can, through the P/E ratio, have a **significant effect on a company's share price**. Thus, a share price might fall if it looks as if EPS is going to be low. This is not very rational, as EPS can depend on many, often subjective, assumptions used in preparing a historical statement, namely the income statement. It does not necessarily bear any relation to the value of a company, and of its shares. Nevertheless, the market is sensitive to EPS.

EPS has also served as a means of assessing the **stewardship and management** role performed by company directors and managers. Remuneration packages might be linked to EPS growth, thereby increasing the pressure on management to improve EPS. The danger of this, however, is that management effort may go into distorting results to produce a favourable EPS.

2.9 The P2 exam

Because EPS was covered at an earlier level, it is assumed knowledge. You are unlikely to have to deal with the complications except as they relate to manipulation by the directors, particularly of the earnings figure. Have a go at the case study question Wingit at the end of the text.

2.10 Section summary

EPS is an important measure for investors.

- **Basic EPS** is straightforward, although it may require adjustments for **changes in capital structure**

- **Diluted EPS** is more complex.

- In an exam you may have to deal with ways in which EPS can be manipulated.

3 FRS 28 Corresponding amounts

FRS 28 requires **corresponding amounts** to be shown for items in the primary financial statements and notes to the financial statements. Where corresponding amounts are not directly comparable with the amount shown for the current year, they must be **adjusted**, with the basis of the adjustment disclosed in a note.

FRS 28 *Corresponding amounts* was issued in October 2005, in response to draft proposals from the DTI.

3.1 Background

In March 2005 the Department of Trade and Industry (DTI) issued a Consultation Document *Company Reporting: Extending use of Summary Financial Statements and Other Minor Changes.*

The draft Regulations propose to remove from the law the requirements to restate corresponding amounts where they are not comparable – although it will remain a legal requirement to provide corresponding amounts, and the law will permit restatement where they are not comparable.

The ASB intends entities using IFRS-based UK accounting standards to be able to take advantage of the same exemptions as entities adopting IFRS. In certain circumstances entities adopting IFRS are exempted from restating corresponding amounts when applying standards. As a consequence of the amendments proposed in the draft Regulations it will fall to accounting standards to prescribe whether corresponding amounts should be restated. This will enable the ASB, where appropriate, to permit the same exemptions as permitted under IFRS.

3.2 FRS 28 requirements

FRS 28, which builds on the DTI's proposals, replicates most of the current legal requirements on corresponding amounts.

The requirements are as follows.

- (a) Corresponding amounts should be shown for **items in the primary financial statements and the notes** to the financial statements.

- (b) Where corresponding amounts are **not directly comparable** with the amount to be shown in respect of the current financial year, they should be **adjusted**.

- (c) Most of the **exemptions** from showing corresponding amounts given in the Companies Act 2006 should be **maintained**.

(d)   The requirements of the proposed FRS apply unless an accounting standards or UITF Abstract permits or requires an alternative treatment.

3.3 Exemptions

The Companies Act 2006 currently provides a number of specific exemptions from providing corresponding amounts to items in the notes to the financial statements The exemptions are mainly replicated in the FRS.

3.3.1 No exemptions for directors' transactions

The exemption provided in the Companies Act 2006 not to present corresponding amounts for loans and other dealings in favour of directors and others is excluded in the FRS. The corresponding amounts for these items can often be easily provided and would enhance the usefulness of the financial statements. It is difficult to justify these specific exemptions as there is no general exemption for related party transactions.

3.4 Effect

FRS 28 will make no change to the presentation of corresponding amounts, rather it brings the rules, previously only set out in the Companies Act, within the scope of accounting standards.

Chapter Roundup

- It is important that you appreciate how great an impact **FRS 3** has on reporting financial performance. You may be called on to discuss the changes and comment on them.

- Try to remember the **important terms**.
    - Reserve accounting
    - All inclusive concept
    - Exceptional items
    - Prior year adjustments
    - Discontinued operations
    - Total recognised gains and losses

- **Earnings per share** is a measure of the amount of profits earned by a company for each ordinary share. Earnings are profits after tax and preferred dividends.

- **Basic EPS** is calculated by dividing the net profit or loss for the period attributable to ordinary shareholders by the weighted average number of ordinary shares outstanding during the period.

- You should know how to calculate **basic EPS** and how to deal with related complications (issue of shares for cash, bonus issue, share splits/reverse share splits, rights issues).

- **Diluted EPS** is calculated by adjusting the net profit attributable to ordinary shareholders and the weighted average number of shares outstanding for the effects of all dilutive potential ordinary shares.

- **FRS 28** requires **corresponding amounts** to be shown for items in the primary financial statements and notes to the financial statements. Where corresponding amounts are not directly comparable with the amount shown for the current year, they must be **adjusted**, with the basis of the adjustment disclosed in a note.

Quick Quiz

1   Reserve Ltd profit and loss account for the year ended 31 December 20X9 was as follows.

	£'000
Turnover	420
Costs and expenses	(180)
Operating profit	240
Interest	(20)
Profit before tax	220
Taxation	(70)
Profit after tax	150
Dividends	(60)
Retained profit	90

What amount would be included in the statement of total recognised gains and losses for the year ended 31 December 20X9?

2   Which of the following items has no impact on the STRGL?

A   Rights issue of ordinary shares
B   Impairment in the value of a tangible fixed asset previously revalued
C   Prior year adjustment
D   Upward revaluation of a fixed asset investment

3   How is basic EPS calculated?

4   Give the formula for the 'bonus element' of a rights issue.

5   Define 'dilutive potential ordinary share'.

Answers to Quick Quiz

1   £150,000. Ignore all transactions with shareholders, ie dividends.

2   A   Statement of total recognised gains and losses (STRGL) does not include transactions with shareholders.

Part of the impairment in the value of a tangible fixed asset previously revalued will reduce the total recognised gains and losses. The amount of the impairment taken to the STRGL is the difference between the carrying value of the asset and the depreciated historic cost.

The other items will be stated as such on the STRGL.

3   See KBF box.

4   Actual cum-rights price

Theoretical ex-rights price

5   See Paragraph 3.8.

| Now try the questions below from the Exam Question Bank |

Number	Level	Marks	Time
Q15	Introductory	n/a	n/a

PART C REPORTING FINANCIAL PERFORMANCE

Reporting financial performance 2

Topic list	Syllabus reference
1 Segmental reporting	C1
2 Related party disclosures	C1
3 Share-based payment	C10
4 FRS 18 Accounting policies	G1

Introduction

Section 1 covers segmental reporting, which you have looked at in your earlier studies. The ASB has issued a **discussion paper on segmental reporting** in response to an IASB proposal. Section 2 deals with related party disclosures, and Section 3 deals with FRS 20, a recent standard on share based payment.

Study guide

		Intellectual level
C1	**Performance reporting**	
(a)	Prepare reports relating to corporate performance for external stakeholders	3
G1	**The creation of suitable accounting policies**	
(a)	Develop accounting policies for an entity which meets the entity's reporting requirements	3
(b)	Identify accounting treatments adopted in financial statements and assess their suitability and acceptability	3

Exam guide

This examiner is fond of testing share-based payment as part of a scenario question.

1 Segmental reporting

FAST FORWARD

SSAP 25 *Segmental Reporting* requires listed companies to provide a breakdown of their operations in different geographical and business areas.

CA 2006 and the Stock Exchange both require the disclosure of segmental information. The **purpose** of SSAP 25 *Segmental reporting* is twofold.

(a) It provides guidance to all companies on how best to comply with **Companies Act requirements** on segmental information.

(b) It requires plcs and large private companies to disclose **more segmental information** than CA 2006 requires.

A summary is given below as you have studied SSAP 25 for Paper F7.

1.1 Reasons for segmental information

Segmental information is considered **useful** for the following reasons.

(a) Segmental information can **explain factors** which have contributed to company results.
(b) Users can compare the results of **different products** from year to year.
(c) Users can compare performance with companies **within the same market**.
(d) Users can assess the **future risks and rewards** associated with the business.

1.2 Arguments against reporting by segment

Those who argue against this form of disclosure generally emphasise the practical problems, which include:

(a) **identifying segments** for reporting purposes;
(b) **allocating common income and costs** among the different segments;
(c) reporting **inter-segment transactions**;
(d) providing information in such a way as to **eliminate misunderstanding** by investors;
(e) avoiding any **potential damage** that may be done to the reporting entity by disclosing information about individual segments.

Knowledge brought forward from earlier studies

SSAP 25 and CA 2006 on segmental reporting

Reportable segment: definition

- **SSAP 25**

    - A **class of business** is a distinguishable component of an enterprise that provides a separate product or a separate group of related products or services.

    - A **geographical segment** is an area comprising an individual country or group of countries in which a company operates or to which it supplies products or services.

- **CA 2006 (directors' opinion)**

    - A **class of business** is a component of an enterprise that differs substantially from other elements of the business.

    - A **geographical segment** is a market supplied by a business which differs substantially from other geographical markets supplied.

- $\geq$ 10% of third party turnover/net assets/profit should be used to **identify a segment**.

Scope

- SSAP 25 **applies only** to plcs, banks/insurance companies, and companies exceeding medium-sized company criteria $\times$ 10.

- Companies can dispense with the disclosure of segmental information if, in the opinion of the directors, it would be **seriously prejudicial** to the interests of the company: a statement to that effect is required.

Disclosure

An example of disclosure is shown on the next two pages. Note the individual disclosures for the following.

- **Turnover**

    - Geographical
    - Class of business

- **Results for the year** (SSAP 25 only)

    - PBIT

    - Interest is stated separately

    - Common costs relate to more than one segment and should be apportioned or deducted from the total

- **Capital employed**

    - Treat interest-bearing assets/liabilities as interest was treated
    - Common assets/liabilities should be treated as common costs were treated

- **Associated companies** are shown separately with extra disclosure for associates' results where they are $\geq$ 20% of the entity's net assets/results.

- The **average number of employees** by category of employee should be disclosed (CA 2006).

CLASSES OF BUSINESS

	Industry A 20X2 £'000	Industry A 20X1 £'000	Industry B 20X2 £'000	Industry B 20X1 £'000	Other Industries 20X2 £'000	Other Industries 20X1 £'000	Group 20X2 £'000	Group 20X1 £'000
Turnover								
Total sales	33,000	30,000	42,000	38,000	26,000	23,000	101,000	91,000
Inter-segment sales	(4,000)	-	-	-	(12,000)	(14,000)	(16,000)	(14,000)
Sales to third parties	29,000	30,000	42,000	38,000	14,000	9,000	85,000	77,000
Profit before taxation								
Segment profit	3,000	2,500	4,500	4,000	1,800	1,500	9,300	8,000
Common costs							(300)	(300)
Operating profit							9,000	7,700
Net interest							(400)	(500)
							8,600	7,200
Group share of the profit before taxation of associated undertakings	1,000	1,000	1,400	1,200	-	-	2,400	2,200
Group profit before taxation							11,000	9,400
Net assets								
Segment net assets	17,600	15,000	24,000	25,000	19,400	19,000	61,000	59,000
Unallocated assets*							3,000	3,000
							64,000	62,000
Group share of the net assets of associated undertakings	10,200	8,000	8,800	9,000	-	-	19,000	17,000
Total net assets							83,000	79,000

* Unallocated assets consist of assets at the group's head office in London amounting to £2.4 million (19X1: £2.5 million) and at the group's regional office in Hong Kong amounting to £0.6 million (19X1: £0.5 million).

GEOGRAPHICAL SEGMENTS

	United Kingdom		North America		Far East		Other		Group	
	20X2 £'000	20X1 £'000	20X2 £'000	20X1 £'000	20X2 £'000	20X1 £'000	20X2 £'000	20X1 £'000	20X2 £'000	20X1 £'000
Turnover										
Turnover by destination										
Sales to third parties	34,000	31,000	16,000	14,500	25,000	23,000	10,000	8,500	85,000	77,000
Turnover by origin										
Total sales	38,000	34,000	29,000	27,500	23,000	23,000	12,000	10,500	102,000	95,000
Inter-segment sales	–	–	(8,000)	(9,000)	(9,000)	(9,000)	–	–	(17,000)	(18,000)
Sales to third parties	38,000	34,000	21,000	18,500	14,000	14,000	12,000	10,500	85,000	77,000
Profit before taxation										
Segment profit	4,000	2,900	2,500	2,300	1,800	1,900	1,000	900	9,300	8,000
Common costs									(300)	(300)
Operating profit									9,000	7,700
Net interest									(400)	(500)
									8,600	7,200
Group share of the profit before taxation of associated undertakings	950	1,000	1,450	1,200	–	–	–	–	2,400	2,200
Group profit before taxation									11,000	9,400
Net assets										
Segment net assets	16,000	15,000	25,000	26,000	16,000	15,000	4,000	3,000	61,000	59,000
Unallocated assets★									3,000	3,000
									64,000	62,000
Group share of the net assets of associated undertakings	8,500	7,000	10,500	10,000	–	–	–	–	19,000	17,000
Total net assets									83,000	79,000

★ Unallocated assets consist of assets at the group's head office in London amounting to £2.4 million (19X1: £2.5 million) and at the group's regional office in Hong Kong amounting to £0.6 million (19X1: £0.5 million).

2 Related party disclosures

The basics of this should be familiar to you from your earlier studies.

FAST FORWARD

FRS 8 is primarily a disclosure standard. It is concerned to improve the quality of information provided by published accounts and also to strengthen their stewardship roles.

Knowledge brought forward from earlier studies

FRS 8

FRS 8 covers related party disclosures.

Definition: related parties

Two or more parties are related parties when at any time during the financial period:

- One party has direct or indirect control of the other party, *or*

- The parties are subject to common control from the same source, *or*

- One party has influence over the financial and operating policies of the other party to an extent that the other party might be inhibited from pursuing at all times its own separate interests, *or*

- The parties, in entering a transaction, are subject to influence from the same source to such an extent that one of the parties to the transaction has subordinated its own separate interests

The FRS states that the most important factor in deciding whether two parties are related is the *substance* of their relationship.

'Deemed' and 'presumed' related parties

Examples of related parties are divided into two categories (lists not exhaustive).

- Those where the nature of the relationship is *deemed* to result in the parties being related

    - Ultimate/intermediate parent(s), (fellow) subsidiaries
    - Associates, JVs of itself or any of above
    - Investor/venturer to entity's associate/JV
    - Directors of entity/parent(s), plus immediate family
    - Pension fund of entity or its related parties

- Those where the nature of the relationship is *presumed* to result in the parties being related unless there is evidence to the contrary

    - Key management of entity/parent plus their direct families

    - Owns/controls > 20% voting rights in entity (nominees, direct family, holdings etc)

    - Concert parties exercising control/influence

    - Entity managed by the reporting entity under a management contract

    - Partnerships, companies, trusts, other entities of which directors/people listed above have a controlling interest

Further definitions

- *Control*: the ability to direct the financial and operating policies of an entity with a view to gaining economic benefits from its activities

Knowledge brought forward from earlier studies (continued)

- *Related party transactions*: the transfer of assets or liabilities or the performance of services by, to or for a related party irrespective of whether a price is charged

Disclosure of transactions and balances

Financial statements should disclose material transactions undertaken with a related party by the entity, irrespective of whether a price is charged, as follows.

- Names of the related parties
- Description of the relationship between the parties
- Description of the transactions
- Amounts involved
- Any other explanations required
- Amounts due to/from related parties at the B/S date
- Amounts w/off related party debts

Disclosure can be on aggregate basis for similar transactions.

Disclosure of control

When the reporting entity is controlled by another party, there should be disclosure of the name of that party and, if different, that of the ultimate controlling party (if not known, that fact should be disclosed). Disclose irrespective of whether any transactions have taken place between the controlling parties and the reporting entity.

Exemptions from disclosure

FRS 8 does *not* require disclosure of the following.

- In consolidated financial statements, of any transactions or balances between group entities that have been eliminated on consolidation

- In a parent's own financial statements when those statements are presented together with its consolidated financial statements

- In the financial statements of > 90% voting subsidiary undertakings, of transactions with entities that are part of the group or investees of the group qualifying as related parties, *if* consolidated a/cs are available (state exemption taken)

- Of pension contributions paid to a pension fund

- Of emoluments in respect of services as an employee of the reporting entity

CA 2006 and the SE require disclosures covering transactions with directors, substantial shareholders and associates.

Exam focus point

The Pilot Paper contained a question on related parties, which was fairly straightforward.

Question

FRS 8

Fancy Feet Ltd is a UK company which supplies handmade leather shoes to a chain of high street shoe shops. The company is also the sole importer of some famous high quality Greek stoneware which is supplied to an upmarket shop in London's West End.

Fancy Feet Ltd was set up 30 years ago by Georgios Kostades who left Greece when he fell out with the military government. The company is owned and run by Mr Kostades and his three children.

The shoes are purchased from a French company, the shares of which are owned by the Kostades Family Trust (Monaco).

Required

Identify the financial accounting issues arising out of the above scenario.

Answer

(a)   The basis on which Fancy Feet trades with the Greek supplier and the French company owned by the Kostades family trust.

(b)   Whether the overseas companies trade on commercial terms with the UK company or do the foreign entities control the UK company.

(c)   Who owns the Greek company: is this a related party under the provisions of FRS 8?

(d)   Should the nature of trade suggest a related party controls Fancy Feet Ltd? Detailed disclosures will be required in the accounts.

2.1 FRED 25 Related party disclosures

FAST FORWARD

> **FRED 25** proposes limited changes to FRS 8.

As part of the ASB's programme of convergence between FRS and IFRS (see Chapter 23), in May 2002, it published FRED 25 *Related party disclosures*.

IAS 24 *Related party disclosures* covers similar ground to FRS 8. This standard has now been revised, and FRED 25 essentially adopts the revised IAS. The main difference between FRED 25 and IAS 24 is that **FRED 25** retains the requirement that an **entity's controlling party should be named**, while IAS 24 does not.

2.1.1 Summary of changes from current UK requirements

Implementation of FRED 25 would mean:

(a)   Changes in the **definitions** of related parties

(b)   Changes in the **detail of the disclosure requirements**. For example, the FRED does not propose that the names of the transacting related parties should be disclosed

(c)   Changes in the **exemptions from disclosure**. For example, the proposed exemption for subsidiaries' disclosure extends only to wholly-owned subsidiaries, while FRS 8 exempts 90% subsidiaries. However, the proposed exemption will cover all related party transactions and balances

3 Share-based payment

FAST FORWARD

Share-based payment transactions should be recognised in the financial statements. You need to understand and be able to advise on:

- Recognition
- Measurement
- Disclosure

of both equity settled and cash settled transactions.

3.1 Background

Transactions whereby entities purchase goods or services from other parties, such as suppliers and employees, by **issuing shares or share options** to those other parties are **increasingly common.** Share schemes are a common feature of director and executive remuneration and in some countries the authorities may offer tax incentives to encourage more companies to offer shares to employees. Companies whose shares or share options are regarded as a valuable 'currency' commonly use share-based payment to obtain employee and professional services.

The increasing use of share-based payment has raised questions about the accounting treatment of such transactions in company financial statements.

Share options are often granted to employees at an exercise price that is equal to or higher than the market price of the shares at the date the option is granted. Consequently the options have no intrinsic value and so **no transaction is recorded in the financial statements**.

This leads to an **anomaly:** if a company pays its employees in cash, an expense is recognised in the income statement, but if the payment is in share options, no expense is recognised.

Arguments against recognition of share-based payment in the financial statements

There are a number of arguments against recognition. The ASB and the IASB has considered and rejected the arguments below.

(a) **No cost therefore no charge**

There is no cost to the entity because the granting of shares or options does not require the entity to sacrifice cash or other assets. Therefore a charge should not be recognised.

This argument is unsound because it ignores the fact that a transaction has occurred. The employees have provided valuable services to the entity in return for valuable shares or options.

(b) **Earnings per share is hit twice**

It is argued that the charge to the income statement for the employee services consumed reduces the entity's earnings, while at the same time there is an increase in the number of shares issued.

However, the dual impact on earnings per share simply reflects the two economic events that have occurred.

(i) The entity has issued shares or options, thus increasing the denominator of the earnings per share calculation.

(ii) It has also consumed the resources it received for those shares or options, thus reducing the numerator.

(c) **Adverse economic consequences**

It could be argued that entities might be discouraged from introducing or continuing employee share plans if they were required to recognise them on the financial statements. However, if this happened, it might be because the requirement for entities to account properly for employee share plans had revealed the economic consequences of such plans.

A situation where entities are able to obtain and consume resources by issuing valuable shares or options without having to account for such transactions could be perceived as a **distortion**.

3.2 FRS 20 *Share-based payment*

In April 2004, the ASB, issued FRS 20 *Share based payment*. This implements IFRS 2 of the same name.

3.3 Objective and scope

FRS 20 requires an entity to **reflect the effects of share-based payment transactions** in its profit or loss and financial position.

FRS 20 applies to all share-based payment transactions. There are three types.

(a) **Equity-settled share-based payment transactions**, in which the entity receives goods or services in exchange for equity instruments of the entity (including shares or share options)

(b) **Cash-settled share-based payment transactions**, in which the entity receives goods or services in exchange for amounts of cash that are based on the price (or value) of the entity's shares or other equity instruments of the entity

(c) Transactions in which the entity receives or acquires goods or services and either the entity or the supplier has a **choice** as to whether the entity settles the transaction in cash (or other assets) or by issuing equity instruments

Certain transactions are **outside the scope** of the FRS:

(a) Transactions with employees and others in their capacity as a holder of equity instruments of the entity (for example, where an employee receives additional shares in a rights issue to all shareholders)

(b) The issue of equity instruments in exchange for control of another entity in a business combination

Key terms

> **Share-based payment transaction** A transaction in which the entity receives goods or services as consideration for equity instruments of the entity (including shares or share options), or acquires goods or services by incurring liabilities to the supplier of those goods or services for amounts that are based on the price of the entity's shares or other equity instruments of the entity.
>
> **Share-based payment arrangement** An agreement between the entity and another party (including an employee) to enter into a share-based payment transaction, which thereby entitles the other party to receive cash or other assets of the entity for amounts that are based on the price of the entity's shares or other equity instruments of the entity, or to receive equity instruments of the entity, provided the specified vesting conditions, if any, are met.
>
> **Equity instrument** A contract that evidences a residual interest in the assets of an entity after deducting all of its liabilities.
>
> **Equity instrument granted** The right (conditional or unconditional) to an equity instrument of the entity conferred by the entity on another party, under a share-based payment arrangement.

Key terms

Share option A contract that gives the holder the right, but not the obligation, to subscribe to the entity's shares at a fixed or determinable price for a specified period of time.

Fair value The amount for which an asset could be exchanged, a liability settled, or an equity instrument granted could be exchanged, between knowledgeable, willing parties in an arm's length transaction.

Grant date The date at which the entity and another party (including an employee) agree to a share-based payment arrangement, being when the entity and the other party have a shared understanding of the terms and conditions of the arrangement. At grant date the entity confers on the other party (the counterparty) the right to cash, other assets, or equity instruments of the entity, provided the specified vesting conditions, if any, are met. If that agreement is subject to an approval process (for example, by shareholders), grant date is the date when that approval is obtained.

Intrinsic value The difference between the fair value of the shares to which the counterparty has the (conditional or unconditional) right to subscribe or which it has the right to receive, and the price (if any) the other party is (or will be) required to pay for those shares. For example, a share option with an exercise price of £15 on a share with a fair value of £20, has an intrinsic value of £5.

Measurement date The date at which the fair value of the equity instruments granted is measured. For transactions with employees and others providing similar services, the measurement date is grant date. For transactions with parties other than employees (and those providing similar services), the measurement date is the date the entity obtains the goods or the counterparty renders service.

Vest To become an entitlement. Under a share-based payment arrangement, a counterparty's right to receive cash, other assets, or equity instruments of the entity vests upon satisfaction of any specified vesting conditions.

Vesting conditions The conditions that must be satisfied for the counterparty to become entitled to receive cash, other assets or equity instruments of the entity, under a share-based payment arrangement. Vesting conditions include service conditions, which require the other party to complete a specified period of service, and performance conditions, which require specified performance targets to be met (such as a specified increase in the entity's profit over a specified period of time).

Vesting period The period during which all the specified vesting conditions of a share-based payment arrangement are to be satisfied.

(FRS 20)

3.4 Recognition: the basic principle

An entity should **recognise goods or services received or acquired in a share-based payment transaction when it obtains the goods or as the services are received.** Goods or services received or acquired in a share-based payment transaction **should be recognised as expenses unless they qualify for recognition as assets**. For example, services are normally recognised as expenses (because they are normally rendered immediately), while goods are recognised as assets.

If the goods or services were received or acquired in an **equity-settled** share-based payment transaction the entity should recognise **a corresponding increase in equity** (reserves). If the goods or services were received or acquired in a **cash-settled** share-based payment transaction the entity should recognise a **liability.**

3.5 Equity-settled share-based payment transactions

3.5.1 Measurement

The issue here is how to measure the 'cost' of the goods and services received and the equity instruments (eg, the share options) granted in return.

The general principle in FRS 20 is that when an entity recognises the goods or services received and the corresponding increase in equity, it should measure these at the **fair value of the goods or services received**. Where the transaction is with **parties other than employees**, there is a rebuttable presumption that the fair value of the goods or services received can be estimated reliably.

If the fair value of the goods or services received cannot be measured reliably, the entity should measure their value by reference to the **fair value of the equity instruments granted.**

Where the transaction is with a party other than an employee fair value should be measured at the date the entity obtains the goods or the counterparty renders service.

Where shares, share options or other equity instruments are granted to **employees** as part of their remuneration package, it is not normally possible to measure directly the services received. For this reason, the entity should measure the fair value of the employee services received by reference to the **fair value of the equity instruments granted**. The fair value of those equity instruments should be measured at **grant date**.

3.5.2 Determining the fair value of equity instruments granted

Where a transaction is measured by reference to the fair value of the equity instruments granted, fair value is based on **market prices** if available, taking into account the terms and conditions upon which those equity instruments were granted.

If market prices are not available, the entity should estimate the fair value of the equity instruments granted using a **valuation technique**. (These are beyond the scope of this exam.)

3.5.3 Transactions in which services are received

The issue here is **when** to recognise the transaction. When equity instruments are granted they may vest immediately, but often the counterparty has to meet specified conditions first. For example, an employee may have to complete a specified period of service. This means that the effect of the transaction normally has to be allocated over more than one accounting period.

If the equity instruments granted **vest immediately**, (ie, the counterparty is not required to complete a specified period of service before becoming unconditionally entitled to the equity instruments) it is presumed that the services have already been received (in the absence of evidence to the contrary). The entity should **recognise the services received in full**, with a corresponding increase in equity, **on the grant date**.

If the equity instruments granted do not vest until the counterparty completes a specified period of service, the entity should account for those services **as they are rendered** by the counterparty during the vesting period. For example if an employee is granted share options on condition that he or she completes three years' service, then the services to be rendered by the employee as consideration for the share options will be received in the future, over that three-year vesting period.

The entity should recognise an amount for the goods or services received during the vesting period based on the **best available estimate** of the **number of equity instruments expected to vest**. It should **revise** that estimate if subsequent information indicates that the number of equity instruments expected to vest differs from previous estimates. On **vesting date**, the entity should revise the estimate to **equal the number of equity instruments that actually vest**.

Once the goods and services received and the corresponding increase in equity have been recognised, the entity should make no subsequent adjustment to total equity after vesting date.

3.6 Example: Equity-settled share-based payment transaction

On 1 January 20X1 an entity grants 100 share options to each of its 400 employees. Each grant is conditional upon the employee working for the entity until 31 December 20X3. The fair value of each share option is £20.

During 20X1 20 employees leave and the entity estimates that 20% of the employees will leave during the three year period.

During 20X2 a further 25 employees leave and the entity now estimates that 25% of its employees will leave during the three year period.

During 20X3 a further 10 employees leave.

Required

Calculate the remuneration expense that will be recognised in respect of the share-based payment transaction for each of the three years ended 31 December 20X3.

Solution

FRS 20 requires the entity to recognise the remuneration expense, based on the fair value of the share options granted, as the services are received during the three year vesting period.

In 20X1 and 20X2 the entity estimates the number of options expected to vest (by estimating the number of employees likely to leave) and bases the amount that it recognises for the year on this estimate.

In 20X3 it recognises an amount based on the number of options that actually vest. A total of 55 employees left during the three year period and therefore 34,500 options (400 – 55 × 100) vested.

The amount recognised as an expense for each of the three years is calculated as follows:

		Cumulative expense at year-end £	Expense for year £
20X1	40,000 × 80% × 20 × 1/3	213,333	213,333
20X2	40,000 × 75% × 20 × 2/3	400,000	186,667
20X3	34,500 × 20	690,000	290,000

Question   Share options

During its financial year ended 31 January 20X6, TSQ issued share options to several of its senior employees. The options vest immediately upon issue.

Which *one* of the following describes the accounting entry that is required to recognise the options?

A	DEBIT the statement of changes in equity	CREDIT liabilities
B	DEBIT the statement of changes in equity	CREDIT equity
C	DEBIT the income statement	CREDIT liabilities
D	DEBIT the income statement	CREDIT equity

Answer

D   Under FRS 20, a charge must be made to the income statement

Question

On 1 January 20X3 an entity grants 250 share options to each of its 200 employees. The only condition attached to the grant is that the employees should continue to work for the entity until 31 December 20X6. Five employees leave during the year.

The market price of each option was £12 at 1 January 20X3 and £15 at 31 December 20X3.

Required

Show how this transaction will be reflected in the financial statements for the year ended 31 December 20X3.

Answer

The remuneration expense for the year is based on the fair value of the options granted at the grant date (1 January 20X3). As five of the 200 employees left during the year it is reasonable to assume that 20 employees will leave during the four year vesting period and that therefore 45,000 options (250 × 180) will actually vest.

Therefore the entity recognises a remuneration expense of £135,000 (45,000 × 12 × ¼) in the income statement and a corresponding increase in equity of the same amount.

3.7 Cash-settled share-based payment transactions

Examples of this type of transaction include:

(a) **Share appreciation rights** granted to employees: the employees become entitled to a future cash payment (rather than an equity instrument), based on the increase in the entity's share price from a specified level over a specified period of time or

(b) An entity might grant to its employees a right to receive a future cash payment by granting to them a **right to shares that are redeemable**

The basic principle is that the entity measures the goods or services acquired and the liability incurred at the **fair value of the liability**.

The entity should **remeasure** the fair value of the liability **at each reporting date** until the liability is settled **and at the date of settlement**. Any **changes** in fair value are recognised in **profit or loss** for the period.

The entity should recognise the services received, and a liability to pay for those services, **as the employees render service.** For example, if share appreciation rights do not vest until the employees have completed a specified period of service, the entity should recognise the services received and the related liability, over that period.

3.8 Example: Cash-settled share-based payment transaction

On 1 January 20X1 an entity grants 100 cash share appreciation rights (SARS) to each of its 500 employees, on condition that the employees continue to work for the entity until 31 December 20X3.

During 20X1 35 employees leave. The entity estimates that a further 60 will leave during 20X2 and 20X3.

During 20X2 40 employees leave and the entity estimates that a further 25 will leave during 20X3.

During 20X3 22 employees leave.

At 31 December 20X3 150 employees exercise their SARs. Another 140 employees exercise their SARs at 31 December 20X4 and the remaining 113 employees exercise their SARs at the end of 20X5.

The fair values of the SARs for each year in which a liability exists are shown below, together with the intrinsic values at the dates of exercise.

	Fair value £	Intrinsic value £
20X1	14.40	
20X2	15.50	
20X3	18.20	15.00
20X4	21.40	20.00
20X5		25.00

Required

Calculate the amount to be recognised in the income statement for each of the five years ended 31 December 20X5 and the liability to be recognised in the balance sheet at 31 December for each of the five years.

Solution

For the three years to the vesting date of 31 December 20X3 the expense is based on the entity's estimate of the number of SARSs that will actually vest (as for an equity-settled transaction). However, the fair value of the liability is **re-measured** at each year-end.

The intrinsic value of the SARs at the date of exercise is the amount of cash actually paid.

	Liability at year-end £	£	Expense for year £
20X1 Expected to vest (500 – 95):			
405 × 100 × 14.40 × 1/3	194,400		194,400
20X2 Expected to vest (500 – 100):			
400 × 100 × 15.50 × 2/3	413,333		218,933
20X3 Exercised:			
150 ×100 × 15.00		225,000	
Not yet exercised (500 – 97 – 150):			
253 × 100 × 18.20	460,460	47,127	
			272,127
20X4 Exercised:			
140 × 100 × 20.00		280,000	
Not yet exercised (253 – 140):			
113 × 100 × 21.40	241,820	(218,640)	
			61,360
20X5 Exercised:			
113 × 100 × 25.00		282,500	
	Nil	(241,820)	
			40,680
			787,500

Transactions which either the entity or the other party has a choice of settling in cash or by issuing equity instruments

If the entity has incurred a liability to settle in cash or other assets it should account for the transaction as a cash-settled share-based payment transaction

If no such liability has been incurred the entity should account for the transaction as an equity-settled share-based payment transaction.

3.9 Deferred tax implications

3.9.1 Issue

An entity may receive a tax deduction that differs from related cumulative remuneration expense, and may arise in a later accounting period.

For example, an entity recognises an expense for share options granted under FRS 20, but does not receive a tax deduction until the options are exercised and receives the tax deduction at the share price on the exercise date.

3.9.2 Measurement

The deferred tax asset timing difference is measured as:

Tax-deductible element of share-based payment expenses to date	X
Less: tax deduction to date	(0)
Timing difference	X
Deferred tax asset at X%	X

In line with FRS 19 all of the deferred tax is charged to the profit and loss account.

3.9.3 Example: Deferred tax implications of share-based payment

On 1 January 20X2, Beaton plc granted 5,000 share options to an employee vesting two years later on 31 December 20X3. The fair value of each option measured at the grant date was £3.

Tax law in the jurisdiction in which the entity operates allows a tax deduction of the intrinsic value of the options on exercise. The intrinsic value of the share options was £1.20 at 31 December 20X2 and £3.40 at 31 December 20X3 on which date the options were exercised.

Assume a tax rate of 30%.

Required

Show the deferred tax accounting treatment of the above transaction at 31 December 20X2, 31 December 20X3 (before exercise), and on exercise.

Solution

	31/12/20X1	*31/12/20X2 before exercise*
	£	£
Tax deductible element of share based payment expense to date		
(5,000 × £1.20 ÷ 2)(5,000 × £3.40)	3,000	17,000
Less: tax deduction to date	–	–
Timing difference	3,000	17,000
Deferred tax asset @ 30%	900	5,100

On exercise, the deferred tax asset is replaced by a current tax one. The double entry is:

DEBIT	Deferred tax (P/L)	5,100	
CREDIT	Deferred tax asset		5,100

} reversal

DEBIT	Current tax asset	5,100	
CREDIT	Current tax (P/L)		5,100

3.10 Section summary

FRS 20 requires entities to **recognise** the goods or services received as a result of **share based payment transactions.**

- **Equity settled transactions**: DEBIT Asset/Expense, CREDIT **Equity**
- **Cash settled transactions**: DEBIT Asset/Expense, CREDIT **Liability**
- Transactions are **recognised when goods/services are obtained/received** (usually over the performance period)
- Transactions are **measured at fair value**

3.11 UITF 37 Purchases and sales of own shares

The *Statement of Principles* addresses the treatment of increases or decreases in an entity's ownership interest that result from transactions with owners in their capacity as owners. Such transactions are referred to as 'contributions from owners'' and 'distributions to owners'; these elements of financial statements do not give rise to gains or losses. Distributions to owners include the payment of dividends and the return of capital. The Statement gives the purchase by a company of its own shares as an example of a return of capital, which is reflected in financial statements by reducing the amount of ownership interest. Ownership interest is defined as a residual interest, ie the amount that results from deducting all of an entity's liabilities from all of its assets.

An entity's purchase of its own shares gives rise to a **reduction in the entity's ownership interest, not an asset**. Transactions in own shares do not give rise to gains or losses in the issuing entity's profit and loss account or statement of total recognised gains and losses.

This is reflected in FRS 4. Whether a transaction in own shares relates to equity or non-equity shares, there is no effect on reported profit as it is a transaction affecting only shareholders' interests. Any difference between the carrying amount of shareholders' funds attributable to non-equity shares and the consideration paid for their purchase is reported as an appropriation of profits in the same manner as FRS 4 requires for finance costs in respect of non-equity shares.

UITF 37 states that:

(a) **Consideration paid for an entity's own shares** should be **deducted** in arriving at **shareholders' funds**.

(b) **No gain or loss** should be recognised in the **profit and loss account** or statement of total recognised gains and losses on the purchase, sale or cancellation of an entity's own shares.

(c) **Consideration** paid or received for the purchase or sale of an entity's own shares should be shown as **separate amounts** in the reconciliation of movements in shareholders' funds.

(d) The **amounts of reductions to shareholders' funds** for an entity's own shares held, and the number of own shares held, should be **disclosed separately**.

Where shares in a holding company are purchased, held or sold by a subsidiary, the requirements apply in the holding company's consolidated financial statements.

3.12 UITF Abstract 38 *Accounting for ESOP trusts*

This Abstract supersedes UITF Abstract 13 of the same name. Abstract 13 dealt with two issues.

(a) The **nature and extent** of the sponsoring company's assets and liabilities that should be recognised under employee share ownership plans (ESOPs

(b) The **timing** of expense recognition under such arrangements

Abstract 38 addresses (a) above. The principal change from Abstract 13 concerns the treatment of an interest in an entity's own shares arising through an ESOP trust. Abstract 13 required that such shares should be recognised as assets of the sponsoring entity. This Abstract reflects the principle in UITF Abstract 37 *Purchases and sales of own shares*, which is consistent with International Financial Reporting Standards (IFRSs), that an **entity that reacquires its own equity instruments should present them as a deduction in arriving at shareholders' funds rather than as assets**. The sponsoring company of an ESOP trust should recognise the assets and liabilities of the trust in its own accounts whenever it has de facto control of those assets and liabilities:

(a)   Until such time as the company's own shares held by the ESOP trust vest unconditionally in employees, the consideration paid for the shares should be deducted in arriving at shareholders' funds.

(b)   Other assets and liabilities (including borrowings) of the ESOP trust should be recognised as assets and liabilities of the sponsoring company.

(c)   Consideration paid or received for the purchase or sale of the company's own shares in an ESOP trust should be shown as separate amounts in the reconciliation of movements in shareholders' funds.

(d)   No gain or loss should be recognised in the profit and loss account or statement of total recognised gains and losses on the purchase, sale, issue or cancellation of the company's own shares.

(e)   Finance costs and any administration expenses should be charged as they accrue and not as funding payments are made to the ESOP trust.

(f)   Any dividend income arising on own shares should be excluded in arriving at profit before tax and deducted from the aggregate of dividends paid and proposed. The deduction should be disclosed if material. Under FRS 14 *Earnings per share*, the shares are treated as if they were cancelled when calculating earnings per share.

3.13 ED Amendment to FRS 20

The ED *Amendment to FRS 20 Share-based payment: Vesting conditions and cancellations* was issued in March 2006. It sets out equivalent proposed amendments to those proposed by the IASB (issued in February 2006)

3.13.1 Proposals

FRS 20 would be amended to define vesting conditions and clarify the accounting treatment of cancellations by parties other than the entity. **These proposals are being made because of uncertainties as to how the standard applies to employee share purchase plans.**

The proposed amendment would require cancellations by the employee to be treated in the same way as cancellations by the employer, resulting in an **accelerated charge to profit and loss account of the unamortised balance of the options granted.**

The ASB is concerned that this is a little harsh, if not penal for Save As You Earn Schemes.

4 FRS 18 Accounting policies

FAST FORWARD ❯❯ FRS 18 *Accounting policies* replaced SSAP 2.

Exam focus point

> You may be required to discuss the differences between SSAP 2 and FRS 18 in the exam. The examiner could ask you to highlight and discuss the improvements that FRS 18 has made on the old SSAP, or relate FRS 18 to the accounting framework provided by the *Statement of Principles*.

FRS 18 *Accounting policies* replaced SSAP 2 *Disclosure of accounting policies*.

4.1 Bedrocks of accounting

FAST FORWARD ❯❯ Prudence and consistency are now less important.

The most obvious change is the relegation of two fundamental accounting concepts.

- Prudence
- Consistency

These concepts are now **desirable features** of financial statements.

FAST FORWARD ❯❯ **Going concern and accruals** are the **bedrocks** of accounting.

The bedrocks of accounting are:

- **Accruals** (matching)
- **Going concern**

FRS 18 places great **importance** upon these concepts. There is no tangible increase in emphasis on accruals (except that it is a great deal more important than prudence and consistency). Going concern is a different matter.

Entities are required to **consider going concern** and disclose the following

(a) **Material uncertainties.** Conditions or events which present **significant doubts** about the entity's ability to continue as a going concern.

(b) **Foreseeable future.** Where the future has been restricted to **less than one year** from the approval of the financial statements.

(c) **Going concern.** Where the financial statements are **not prepared on a going concern basis**, the reason for this and the method under which they have been prepared.

4.2 Statement of Principles

FRS 18 is designed to sit alongside the *Statement of Principles* framework. This helps explain the downplaying of the previously important prudence and consistency concepts.

The preparers of financial statements must now consider

- Relevance
- Reliability
- Comparability
- Understandability

There is an assumption that, in considering these objectives, the concepts of **prudence and consistency will be followed** in the majority of cases anyway. The objectives will need to be weighed against each other and a course of action taken which **best fits all four.**

All four objectives overlap and none of them should be compromised by the accounting policies adopted by the entity. By fulfilling the reliability and comparability objectives an accounting policy is likely to fulfil the consistency concept. If a policy provides information which is relevant and reliable then it is likely that amounts are not overstated and so the prudence concept is indirectly adhered to.

4.3 Accounting policies

FRS 18 prescribes the **regular consideration of the entity's accounting policies**. The **best** accounting policy should be adopted at all times. This is the major reason for downplaying consistency (and to a lesser extent prudence). An entity **cannot retain** an accounting policy merely because it was used last year or because it gives a prudent view.

However, the entity should consider how a **change** in accounting policy may affect **comparability**. Essentially a **balance** must be struck between selecting the **most appropriate policies** and presenting **coherent and useful** financial statements. The overriding guidance is that the financial statements should give a **true and fair view** of the entity's business. Chopping and changing accounting policies year on year is likely to jeopardise the true and fair view but so too is retaining accounting policies which do not present the most useful information to the users of the accounts.

4.3.1 Disclosure

FRS 18 requires the disclosure of:

- A **description of each accounting policy** which is material to the entity's financial statements
- A description of any significant estimation technique
- **Changes** to accounting policies
- The effects of any material change to an estimation technique

4.3.2 Estimation techniques

FAST FORWARD

An important distinction is made between **accounting policies and estimation techniques**.

An estimation technique is material **only where a large range** of monetary values may be arrived at. The entity should vary the assumptions it uses, to assess how sensitive monetary values are under that technique. In most cases the range of values will be relatively narrow. Consider the useful life of motor vehicles, for example.

4.3.3 Changes to accounting policies

The disclosure of new accounting policies also requires:

- An explanation of the **reason for change**
- The **effects of a prior period adjustment** on the previous years results (in accordance with FRS 3)
- The **effects of the change in policy** on the previous year's results

If it is **not possible** to disclose the last two points then the **reason** for this should be disclosed instead.

Exam focus point

You need to be confident about the application of FRS 18. Make sure that you can **identify** a change in accounting policy and the **reason** that it is a change in accounting policy as opposed to a change in estimation technique. You will have to **discuss** the decision you have reached **and justify** your conclusions.

The most complex aspect to FRS 18 is the **application of the terms and definitions** within the standard. SSAP 2 defined accounting policies and accounting bases. There was some confusion as to what an accounting base was. FRS 18 has dispensed with the term accounting base. However, the term which seems to replace it, **estimation technique**, may prove difficult to apply in practice.

It is essential that you **learn the following definitions**. However, once you have read them you should **apply them** to the questions later in this section to make sure that you understand them.

Key term

Accounting policies. The principles, conventions, rules and practices applied by an entity that prescribe how transactions and other events are to be reflected in its financial statements.

Accounting policies are **not** estimation techniques.

An accounting policy includes the

- Recognition
- Presentation
- And measurement basis

Of assets, liabilities, gains, losses and changes to shareholders' funds.

Key term

Estimation technique. The methods used by an entity to establish the estimated monetary amounts associated with the measurement bases selected for assets, liabilities, gains, losses and changes to shareholders' funds.

Estimation techniques are used to **implement the measurement basis** of an accounting policy. The accounting policy specifies the measurement basis and the estimation technique is used when there is an uncertainty over this amount.

The method of **depreciation is an estimation technique**. The accounting policy is to spread the cost of the asset over its useful economic life. Depreciation is the measurement basis. The estimation technique would be, say, straight line depreciation as opposed to reducing balance.

A change of estimation technique should **not** be accounted for as a prior period adjustment unless the following apply.

- It is the correction of a fundamental error
- The Companies Act, an accounting standard or a UITF Abstract **requires the change to be accounted** for as a prior period adjustment.

4.4 Application of FRS 18

FAST FORWARD

FRS 18 was written in the light of the *Statement of Principles.*

FRS 18 gives a number of examples of its application in an appendix to the standard. When a change is required to an accounting policy then **three criteria** must be **considered** to ensure that the change is affecting the accounting policy and not an estimation technique.

Criterion 1   Recognition

Criterion 2   Presentation

Criterion 3   Measurement basis

If **any one of the criteria apply** then a change has been made to the accounting policy. If they do **not** apply then a change to an estimation technique has taken place.

You should note that where an **accounting standard gives a choice** of treatments (ie SSAP 9 states that stock can be recognised on a FIFO or weighted average cost basis) then adopting the alternative treatment is a **change of accounting policy.** Also note that FRS 15 states that a **change in depreciation method is not** a change in accounting policy.

Example	Recognition	Change to Presentation	Change to Measurement basis?	Change of Accounting Policy
1 Changing from capitalisation of finance costs associated with the construction of fixed assets to charging them through the profit and loss	Yes	Yes	No	Yes
2 A reassessment of an entity's cost centres means that all three will have production overheads allocated to them instead of just two	No	No	No	No
3 Overheads are reclassified from distribution to cost of sales	No	Yes	No	Yes
4 Change from straight-line depreciation to machine hours	No	No	No	No
5 Reallocate depreciation from administration to cost of sales	No	Yes	No	Yes
6 A provision is revised upwards and the estimates of future cash flows are now discounted in accordance with FRS 12. They were not discounted previously as the amounts involved were not material	No	No	No	No
7 Deferred tax is now reported on a discounted basis. It was previously undiscounted	No	No	Yes	Yes
8 A foreign subsidiary's profit and loss account is now to be translated at the closing rate. It was previously translated at the average rate	No	No	Yes	Yes
9 Fungible stocks are to be measured on the weighted average cost basis instead of the previously used FIFO basis	No	No	Yes	Yes

4.5 Fungible assets

Key term

> **Fungible assets** are similar assets which are grouped together as there is no reason to view them separately in economic terms. Shares and items of stock are examples of fungible assets.

The last example (Example 9) is based on a **change to fungible assets**. The standard states that when fungible assets are considered in **aggregate** a change from weighted average cost to FIFO (or vice versa),

BPP
LEARNING MEDIA

is a change to the **measurement base**. The standard also recommends that fungible assets should **always be considered in aggregate** in order to enhance **comparability** of financial statements.

Question — Change of accounting policy (1)

Question: change of accounting policy (1)

The board of Beezlebub plc decide to change the depreciation method they use on their plant and machinery from 30% reducing balance to 20% straight line to better reflect the way the assets are used within the business. Is this a change of accounting policy ?

Answer

No. This is a change to the **estimation technique**. The same measurement basis is used. The historic cost is allocated over the asset's estimated useful life.

Question — Change of accounting policy (2)

The board of Beezlebub plc also decide to change their stock valuation. They replace their FIFO valuation method for an AVCO method to better reflect the way that stock is used within the business. Is this a change in accounting policy?

Answer

Yes. This is a change to the **measurement basis**. The paragraphs on fungible assets discuss this further.

Question — Change of accounting policy (3)

The board of Beezlebub plc decide in the following year that the development costs the business incurs should not be capitalised and presented on the balance sheet. Instead they agree that all development expenditure should be expended in the profit and loss account. Is this an accounting policy change?

Answer

Yes. The choice to capitalise or not is given in SSAP 13. The criteria affected by this decision are **recognition and presentation.**

Question — Change of accounting policy (4)

Beezlebub plc's board are also considering reallocating the depreciation charges made on its large fleet of company cars to administration expenses, they were previously shown in cost of sales. Is this an accounting policy change?

Answer

Yes. Beezlebub would be changing the way they **presented** the depreciation figure.

4.6 SORPs

If an entity's financial statements **fall within the scope of a SORP** the entity should **identify** the SORP and state **whether** it has been **complied with**. Any departure from the SORP must be **disclosed together with the reason for the departure**. The effect of the departure does not need to be quantified unless quantification would provide a **true and fair view.**

An entity can **choose** to comply with a SORP even if its financial statements do not fall within its scope. Entities **should disclose this fact** in their financial statements.

4.7 Section summary

- FRS 18 requires an entity to conduct a review on an annual basis in order to ensure that it is using the most appropriate accounting policies. The three criteria:

    - Recognition
    - Presentation
    - Measurement basis

- Are considered in order to establish whether there has been a change of accounting policy or merely a change of estimation technique. The objectives of:

    - Reliability
    - Relevance
    - Comparability
    - Understandability

- Must be fulfilled by the accounting policies adopted. This requirement helps prevent entities from changing accounting policies too often.

- Prudence and consistency have a lesser role in the accounting policy framework but despite this, FRS 18 is not a major departure from the old SSAP 2.

Chapter Roundup

- **SSAP 25** *Segmental Reporting* requires listed companies to provide a breakdown of their operations in different geographical and business areas.

- **FRS 8** is primarily a disclosure standard. It is concerned to improve the quality of information provided by published accounts and also to strengthen their stewardship roles.

- **FRED 25** proposes limited changes to FRS 8.

- **Share-based payment** transactions should be recognised in the financial statements. You need to understand and be able to advise on:

  - Recognition
  - Measurement
  - Disclosure

  of both equity settled and cash settled transactions.

- **FRS 18** *Accounting policies* replaced SSAP 2.

- Prudence and consistency are now less important.

- **Going concern and accruals** are the **bedrocks** of accounting.

- An important distinction is made between **accounting policies and estimation techniques**.

- **FRS 18** was written in the light of the *Statement of Principles.*

Quick Quiz

1   Why is segmental reporting considered useful?

2   What are the arguments against segmental reporting?

3   What are the key issues in segmental reporting identified by the ASB's discussion draft?

4   A managing director of a company is deemed a related party.

   True   ☐

   False   ☐

5   Under FRED 25, names of the transacting parties in a related party transaction need to be disclosed.

   True   ☐

   False   ☐

6   What is grant date?

7   If an entity has entered into an equity-settled share based payment transaction, what should it recognise in its financial statements?

8   Where an entity has granted share options to its employees in return for services, how is the transaction measured?

9   An employee is granted share options on condition that he completes five years' service. When should the transaction be recognised?

10   FRS 18 abolished the concept of prudence.

   True   ☐

   False   ☐

Answers to Quick Quiz

Answers to quick quiz

1   See Paragraph 1.1.

2   See Paragraph 1.2.

3   (a)   Division of operations into segments

     (b)   The information to be given for each segment

     (c)   Whether the information is verifiable and easy to understand

4   False. He is presumed to be a related party unless there is evidence to the contrary.

5   False. They do not need to be disclosed under the FRED, although they do under FRS 8.

6   The date on which the entity and another party (including an employee) agree to a share-based payment agreement, being when the entity and the other party have a shared understanding of the terms and conditions of the agreement.

7   The goods or services received and a corresponding increase in equity.

8   By reference to the fair value of the equity instruments granted, measured at grant date.

9   The entity should account for the employee's services as they are rendered, over the five year vesting period.

10   False. Prudence has been relegated to the status of a desirable feature.

Now try the questions below from the Exam Question Bank

Number	Level	Marks	Time
Q16	Examination	25	45 mins

Part D
Group financial statements

Simple groups and fair value

Topic list	Syllabus reference
1 Revision: definition of a subsidiary	D1
2 Revision: exclusion/exemption	D1
3 Revision: other provisions of FRS 2	D1
4 Revision: summary of techniques	D1
5 FRED 36 Business combinations	D1
6 FRS 7 Fair values in acquisition accounting	D1

Introduction

You will have covered basic groups in your earlier studies, including the important **legislation**, **definitions** and **standards**. This is the first of six chapters on consolidation.

At this level, the emphasis is on the more **complex aspects** of consolidation compared to the simple consolidation in your earlier studies. In this chapter, you can revise briefly the main provisions of FRS 2 *Accounting for subsidiary undertakings* and the CA 2006 provisions relating to group accounts. You can also revise some of the basic principles of consolidation by carrying out an exercise. If you have problems with this exercise, then you should go back and **revise** from your earlier study material.

Note. In all the chapters on consolidation, all undertakings are **incorporated** (ie limited companies) unless stated otherwise.

Study guide

		Intellectual level
D1	**Group accounting including cash flow statements**	
(a)	Apply the method of accounting for business combinations including complex group structures	3
(b)	Apply the principles relating to the cost of a business combination	3
(c)	Apply the recognition and measurement criteria for identifiable acquired assets and liabilities and goodwill, including piecemeal acquisitions	3
F2	**Proposed changes to accounting standards**	
(a)	Identify the issues and deficiencies which have led to a proposed change to an accounting standard	2
(b)	Apply and discuss the implications of a proposed change to an accounting standard on the performance and balance sheet of an entity	2

Exam guide

The Pilot Paper asked you to comment on the proposed changes to accounting for business combinations.

1 Revision: definition of a subsidiary

FAST FORWARD

You should go back to your earlier study material (if necessary) and make sure you know:

- the CA 2006 and FRS 2 **definitions** of parent and subsidiary undertakings;

- CA 2006 requirements for **exemption** from consolidation and **exclusion** of subsidiaries;

- the accounting requirements for **non-consolidated** subsidiaries;

- FRS 2's regulations for **acquisition accounting**;

- the treatment of **intra-group profits** and the situations where it arises; and

- how to prepare **simple consolidated accounts**, including the basic treatment of goodwill and minority interests.

From your earlier studies, as well as being able to prepare a simple group balance sheet and P&L account, you should also know:

(a) The requirements of the CA 2006 and FRS 2 *Accounting for subsidiary undertakings* regarding groups of companies

(b) The different methods which could be used to prepare group accounts

(c) The basic meaning and function of acquisition, equity and merger accounting

(d) The methods of dealing with intra-group profits

If a company has a subsidiary at its year end, it must prepare group accounts which must be in the form of **consolidated accounts**.

Definition of a subsidiary

The Companies Act 2006 defines a subsidiary undertaking as one in which the parent:

- Has a majority of the **voting rights**

- Is a **member** and can appoint/remove a **majority of the board of directors** (entitled to the majority of voting rights)

- Is a member and controls alone a majority of the voting rights **by agreement** with other members

- Has the right to exercise a **dominant influence** through the Memorandum and Articles or a control contract

- It has the **power to exercise or actually exercises dominant influence**, as defined below

Further definition was required to stop the increasing practice of the use of the non-consolidated (quasi) subsidiary. The following extra definitions were added by FRS 2.

- **Control**: the ability of an undertaking to direct the financial and operating policies of another undertaking with a view to gaining economic benefits from its activities.

- **Dominant influence**: the ability to direct the financial and operating policies of another undertaking with a view to gaining benefits from its activities.

- **On a unified basis**: two or more undertakings are managed on a unified basis if the whole of the operations of the undertakings are integrated and managed as a single unit.

- **Held on a long-term basis**: any interest held other than exclusively with a view to subsequent resale.

2 Revision: exclusion/exemption

FRS 2 and CA 2006 have **different rules** on the exclusion of subsidiaries from consolidated accounts. The rules on exemptions are much more uncontroversial and straightforward.

Exclusion/exemption

Exclusion of a subsidiary

There may be situations where consolidation would not give a true and fair view of the group's affairs: this would be exceptional.

Knowledge brought forward from earlier studies (cont'd)

- FRS 2 **requires** exclusion from consolidation under the following circumstances.

Reason	Accounting treatment
Severe long-term restrictions	Balance sheet: equity method up to date of severe restrictions subject to any write-down for impairment P&L a/c: dividends received only

| Held exclusively for subsequent resale; never been consolidated | Current asset at the lower of cost and net realisable value |
| Dissimilar activities | Equity method (see Chapter 17) |

- CA 2006 **permits** exclusion from consolidation in all of the circumstances cited above. CA 2006 permits exclusion for additional reasons, dismissed as invalid by the ASB.
  - The subsidiary's inclusion is not material.
  - Information cannot be obtained without disproportionate expense or undue delay.

Exemptions

- Where a company has a subsidiary but is itself at least **50% owned** by another company established in an **EU member** state, it is exempt from preparing group accounts if the intermediate holding company:
  - Does not have shares or debentures listed on a recognised SE in a member state, or
  - Is included in the audited consolidated financial statements of an EU parent

- **Minority shareholders** can request consolidation if they hold over 50% of the remaining shares in the company or 5% of the total shares.

- **Small and medium-sized groups** are not required to produce group accounts (unless they are plcs, banks etc) and cannot be required to do so by the minority shareholders.

- There is an **exemption for intermediate parent undertakings** whose immediate parents are **not governed by the law of a European Economic Area (EEA) state**.

3 Revision: other provisions of FRS 2

The following revises some of the other important points in FRS 2 which you ought to remember.

Other provisions of FRS 2

- **Uniform accounting policies** should be used throughout the group.
  - Subsidiaries should be adjusted on consolidation
  - If this is not possible, make full disclosure of the different policies and their effects

- **Accounting period and dates**: the financial statements of all group companies should be prepared to the same accounting date and for the same accounting period; subsidiaries can prepare three months before if necessary and with appropriate adjustments and disclosure.

- **Material purchase of a subsidiary**: disclose sufficient information about the results of the subsidiary acquired to enable shareholders to appreciate its effect.

- **Effective date for acquisitions and disposals** of a subsidiary should be the date on which control passes.

- **Intra group transactions**

  - Profits/losses on any intra group transactions should be eliminated in full

  - Elimination of the profit/loss should be set against the interests held by the group and MI in respective proportion to their holdings in the relevant undertaking

4 Revision: summary of techniques

Consider the nature of the **current definitions and accounting requirements**. You should be able to discuss why they are so complex and detailed.

The summary given below is very brief but it encompasses all the major, but basic, rules of consolidation for, firstly, the consolidated balance sheet.

Knowledge brought forward from earlier studies

Summary of technique: consolidated balance sheet

- **Net assets**: 100% P plus 100% S.

- **Share capital**: P only.

- **Reserves**: 100% P plus group share of post-acquisition retained reserves of S less consolidation adjustments.

- **Minority interest**: MI share of S's consolidated assets.

The method of consolidation is as follows.

- Determine the **group structure**.

- Consider **adjustments** for:

    - Dividends
    - Provisions for unrealised profits
    - Revaluation to fair value
    - Inter-company stock and cash in transit

- Combine **net assets**, cancelling any **intra-group balances**.

    - Current accounts
    - Proposed dividends of subsidiary
    - Debentures

- **Share capital** of P only

- Calculate the **minority interest** in net assets

MI % of share capital	X
MI % of reserves	X
MI % of revaluations to fair value	X
MI % of unrealised profit	(X)
	X

- Calculate the **goodwill**

Cost of investment		X
Pre-acquisition dividend		(X)
Assets acquired		
Share capital	X	
Pre-acquisition reserves	X	
Revaluation to fair value	X	
Group share	X%	(X)
Goodwill		X

Knowledge brought forward from earlier studies (continued)

If cost is **greater than** the share of net assets acquired then the difference is **positive** goodwill, which should be:

- Capitalised and amortised over its estimated useful life through the P&L account or

- Capitalised and retained in the balance sheet without amortising in those rare cases where its useful economic life is deemed indefinite (subject to annual impairment review).

If cost is **less than** the share of net assets acquired then the difference is **negative** goodwill.

- This should be

    - Disclosed in the intangible fixed assets category directly under positive goodwill

    - Recognised in the P&L account in the periods where **non-monetary assets** are depreciated or sold

- **Calculate reserves**

P per question		X
Post-acquisition dividends not yet accounted for		X
Proposed dividends not yet accounted for		(X)
PUP for sales made by P		(X)
		X
S per question	X	
Dividends to be proposed	(X)	
PUP for sales made by S	(X)	
Additional depreciation: transfer of fixed assets	(X)	
Less reserves at acquisition	(X)	
Group share	X%	X
Goodwill amortisation		(X)
		X

The technique for the preparation of a **consolidated P&L account** is given below, with two additional (and very important) points.

Knowledge brought forward from earlier studies

Summary of technique: consolidated P&L account

Adjustments required for consolidation of a subsidiary are as follows.

- Eliminate **intra-group sales and purchases**.

- Eliminate any **unrealised profits** on intra-group purchases still in stock at the year end.

- Eliminate any **intra-group dividends** received and paid, ie show only H's dividends.

- Show the **MI** as a separate line after profit after tax.

- Include the group share of any **extraordinary items** (very rare) in the subsidiary's accounts where material in a group context.

For the inclusion of a subsidiary carry out the following.

- **Combine all P and S results** from turnover to profit after tax (where the acquisition is mid-year, use a time apportioned basis).

- Exclude any **investment income** that is intra-group.

- **Calculate MI**:

    - Where there are no preference shares: MI = % × profit after tax
    - Where there are preference shares an additional working is required

Pre-acquisition dividends

There are two ways to calculate the pre-acquisition element of a dividend.

- To the extent that post-acquisition profits are **insufficient** to cover the dividend, the distribution must be out of pre-acquisition profits; this method is more commonly used in practice.

- **Apportion** the dividend on a time basis between the pre– and post-acquisition periods, so that only post-acquisition dividends are taken to H's reserves; this method is recommended in ACCA exams.

    - For **pre-acquisition dividends**: *Debit* Dividend receivable/cash, *Credit* Cost of investment.
    - For **post-acquisition dividends**: *Debit* Dividend receivable/cash, *Credit* P&L a/c.

Unrealised profits/losses

Only where **S sells to P**, allocate the unrealised profit between MI and P: *Debit* Group reserves, *Debit* Minority interest, *Credit* Stock.

After you have tried the following question and refreshed your memory on the topics listed above, we will move on to consider the usefulness and adequacy of current definitions, international definitions and the audit implications of consolidation and group accounts.

Question   Simple groups

Boo Ltd has owned 80% of Goose Ltd's equity since its incorporation. On 31 December 20X8 it despatched goods which cost £80,000 to Goose, at an invoiced cost of £100,000. Goose received the goods on 2 January 20X9 and recorded the transaction then. The two companies' draft accounts as at 31 December 20X8 are shown below.

PROFIT AND LOSS ACCOUNTS

	Boo	Goose
	£'000	£'000
Sales	5,000	1,000
Cost of sales	2,900	600
Gross profit	2,100	400
Other expenses	1,700	320
Net profit	400	80
Tax	130	25
Profit after tax	270	55
Dividends proposed	130	40
Retained profit for the year	140	15
Retained profit brought forward	260	185
Retained profit carried forward	400	200

BALANCE SHEETS

	Boo £'000	Goose £'000
Fixed assets		
Tangible assets	1,920	200
Investment in Goose	80	–
	2,000	200
Current assets		
Stock	500	120
Trade debtors	650	40
Bank and cash	390	35
	1,540	195
Current liabilities		
Trade creditors	910	30
Dividend payable	100	40
Tax	130	25
	1,140	95
Net current assets	400	100
	2,400	300
Capital and reserves		
Share capital	2,000	100
P&L account	400	200
	2,400	300

Required

Prepare draft consolidated financial statements.

(Assume all dividends were proposed before the year end.)

Answer

BOO GROUP
CONSOLIDATED PROFIT AND LOSS ACCOUNT
FOR THE YEAR ENDED 31 DECEMBER 20X8

	£'000
Sales (5,000 + 1,000 – 100)	5,900
Cost of sales (2,900 + 600 – 80)	3,420
Gross profit	2,480
Other expenses (1,700 + 320)	2,020
Net profit	460
Tax (130 + 25)	155
Profit after tax	305
Minority interest (20% × £55,000)	11
Group profit for the year	294
Dividend proposed (Boo only)	130
Retained profit for the year	164
Retained profit brought forward	408
Retained profit carried forward	572

CONSOLIDATED BALANCE SHEET AS AT 31 DECEMBER 20X8

	£'000	£'000
Fixed assets (1,920 + 200)		2,120
Current assets		
Stock (500 + 120 + 80)	700	
Trade debtors (650 – 100 + 40)	590	
Bank and cash (390 + 35)	425	
	1,715	
Current liabilities		
Trade creditors (910 + 30)	940	
Dividend payable: Boo Ltd	100	
to minority in Goose Ltd	8	
Tax (130 + 25)	155	
	1,203	
Net current assets		512
		2,632
Capital and reserves		
Share capital (Boo only)		2,000
P&L account (W)		572
Shareholders' funds		2,572
Minority interest (20% × 300)		60
		2,632
Working: group reserves		
Per question	400	200
Closing stock in transit (at cost)	80	
Inter company sale	(100)	
Dividend receivable: 80% × 40	32	
Share of Goose: 80% × 200	160	
	572	

This working is, of course, only necessary when you are not required to prepare the consolidated P & L account. Here, it serves as a proof of the consolidated P & L account as well as of the reserves figure in the balance sheet.

Exam focus point

The consolidation questions in the Paper P2 exam are likely to be much more difficult than those in Paper F7. The examiner will not bother to test basic consolidation techniques directly, although they may come up in a question: rather he will ask about one of the more complex areas which we will look at in the next few chapters.

5 FRED 36 Business combinations

FAST FORWARD

FRED 36 proposes major changes in accounting for business combinations.
- Merger accounting will no longer be permitted.
- Goodwill is no longer to be amortised but is subject to annual impairment tests.
- Goodwill is to be shown gross of non-controlling ('minority') interests.
- Negative goodwill is to be recognised as a gain in profit and loss accounts.

5.1 Background

The IASB is carrying out a major review of the treatment of business combinations, and its requirements regarding the first phase of this review were issued as IFRS 3 in March 2004. The second phase has now been issued as an Exposure Draft by the IASB, and the ASB has issued four FREDs reflecting both the first and second phases:

FRED 36 *Business combinations* (discussed below)
FRED 37 *Intangible assets* (discussed in Chapter 5)
FRED 38 *Impairment of assets* (discussed in Chapter 4)
FRED 39 *Amendments to FRS 12 and FRS 17* (discussed in Chapters 9 and 6 respectively)

5.2 Main changes to UK accounting practices

FRED 36 *Business combinations* was issued in July 2005. It is based on the Exposure Draft of Proposed Amendments to IFRS 3 issued by the IASB in June 2005 and the Exposure Draft of Proposed Amendments to IAS 27.

5.2.1 Merger accounting

Merger accounting will no longer be permitted. Under FRED 36, all business combinations are to be treated as acquisitions.

5.2.2 Objective of acquisition accounting

Exam focus
point

Under the proposals, **minority interests** will be known as **non-controlling interests.**

In the UK, to date, accounting has been based on the 'parent entity concept'. Under the **parent entity concept** the extent of **non-controlling interests** and transactions with non-controlling interests are **separately identified** in the primary financial statements.

FRED 36 treats the group as a **single economic entity** ('entity concept') and any outside equity interest in a subsidiary is treated as part of the overall ownership interest in the group. As a consequence of this **changes in a parent's ownership interest, that do not result in a change of control, are to be recognised as changes in equity. No gain or loss will be recognised in the profit and loss account.** (Changes in ownership interest, or group composition are covered in Chapter 19.)

5.2.3 Goodwill: recognition

Under current UK accounting practice the objective of acquisition accounting is to reflect the **cost of the acquisition.** To the extent to which it is not represented by identifiable assets and liabilities (measured at their fair value), goodwill arises and is reported in the financial statements. **FRED 36** sets out a conceptually different version of acquisition accounting and requires the financial statements to reflect the **fair value of the acquired business.**

FRS 2 requires that goodwill arising on acquisition should only be recognised with respect to the part of the subsidiary undertaking that is attributable to the interest held by the parent entity. Under **FRED 36, goodwill is to be recognised in full**; that is 100% of goodwill is recognised even if less than 100% is acquired. In other words, goodwill is to be shown **gross of non-controlling (minority) interest.**

The **ASB** has expressed **reservations** about this. Recognition of goodwill attributable only to the parent's interest is consistent with the view that non-controlling interests, who do not hold shares in the parent entity, have no direct interests in the parent or group, but only in the subsidiary. As such, they have no interest in the consolidated financial statements of the parent entity, and therefore need not recognise a hypothetical amount of goodwill allocated for their interest in the group.

5.2.4 Goodwill: subsequent measurement

Under FRS 10 *Goodwill and intangible assets* goodwill is charged to the profit and loss account only to the extent that the carrying value of goodwill is not supported by the current value of goodwill within the acquired business. Systematic amortisation is a practical means of recognising the reduction in value of goodwill that has a limited useful economic life.

Under FRED 36 goodwill, after initial recognition, is to be **measured at cost less impairment losses, and amortisation is not to be permitted.** The IASB concluded that more useful information would be provided if goodwill was not amortised but subjected to a rigorous and operational impairment test.

Again, the ASB has **reservations** about this. Neither annual impairment nor amortisation is likely to result in a conclusive value for the carrying amount of goodwill. The ASB is seeking views on whether the UK IFRS-based standard should be amended and an **option** introduced **allowing amortisation** of goodwill.

5.2.5 Negative goodwill

FRS 10 requires negative goodwill to be recognised in the profit and loss account in the periods in which the non-monetary assets acquired are depreciated or sold, with any excess being written back in the profit and loss account over the period expected to benefit from that negative goodwill.

Under FRED 36, negative goodwill is no longer called negative goodwill. It is recognised immediately as a gain in the income statement.

The ASB is concerned whether this is appropriate, other than in cases where there has been a bargain purchase.

5.2.6 Costs incurred in connection with an acquisition

These are not to be accounted for as part of the cost of the investment.

5.2.7 Group reconstructions

The draft IFRS whose requirements are given in FRED 36 does not apply to entities under common control, including group reconstructions. By contrast, FRS 6 allowed merger accounting to be applied to group reconstructions. (Group reconstructions are covered in Chapter 19.)

The ASB is considering whether it should **retain some of the provisions of FRS 6** and prescribe how UK group reconstructions should be accounted for.

5.2.8 Fair value hierarchy

The **fair value hierarchy** groups into three broad categories (levels) the inputs that should be used to estimate fair value. The hierarchy gives the highest priority to inputs that reflect quoted prices in active markets and lowest priority to an entity's own internal estimates and assumptions.

This may lead to some assets being given different values to those under FRS 7. For example, FRS 7 requires stocks and work-in-progress to be valued at the lower of replacement cost and net realisable value, whereas applying the hierarchy might lead to a valuation reflecting selling price less cost to complete and selling expenses.

6 FRS 7 *Fair values in acquisition accounting*

FAST FORWARD

The accounting requirements and disclosures of the fair value exercise are covered by **FRS 7,** which outlaws the use of provisions for future losses and for reorganisation costs on acquisition of a subsidiary.

FRS 10 *Goodwill and intangible assets* defines **goodwill** as the difference between the purchase consideration paid by the acquiring company and the aggregate of the 'fair values' of the identifiable assets and liabilities acquired. The balance sheet of a subsidiary company at the date it is acquired may not be a guide to the fair value of its net assets. For example, the market value of a freehold building may have risen greatly since it was acquired, but it may appear in the balance sheet at historical cost less accumulated depreciation.

6.1 Fair value calculations

Until now we have calculated goodwill as the difference between the cost of the investment and the **book value** of net assets acquired by the group. If this calculation is to comply with the definition in FRS 10 we must ensure that the book value of the subsidiary's net assets is the same as their **fair value**.

There are two possible ways of achieving this.

(a)   The subsidiary company might **incorporate any necessary revaluations** in its own books of account. In this case, we can proceed directly to the consolidation, taking asset values and reserves figures straight from the subsidiary company's balance sheet.

(b)   The revaluations may be made as a **consolidation adjustment** without being incorporated in the subsidiary company's books. In this case, we must make the necessary adjustments to the subsidiary's balance sheet as a working. Only then can we proceed to the consolidation.

Note. Remember that when depreciating assets are revalued there may be a corresponding alteration in the amount of depreciation charged and accumulated.

6.2 Example: Fair value adjustments

H Ltd acquired 75% of the ordinary shares of S Ltd on 1 September 20X5. At that date the fair value of S Ltd's fixed assets was £23,000 greater than their net book value, and the balance of retained profits was £21,000. The balance sheets of both companies at 31 August 20X6 are given below. S Ltd has not incorporated any revaluation in its books of account.

H LIMITED
BALANCE SHEET AS AT 31 AUGUST 20X6

	£
Fixed assets	
Tangible assets	63,000
Investment in S Ltd at cost	51,000
	114,000
Net current assets	62,000
	176,000
Capital and reserves	
Ordinary shares of £1 each	80,000
Retained profits	96,000
	176,000

S LIMITED
BALANCE SHEET AS AT 31 AUGUST 20X6

	£
Tangible fixed assets	28,000
Net current assets	33,000
	61,000
Capital and reserves	
Ordinary shares of £1 each	20,000
Retained profits	41,000
	61,000

If S Ltd had revalued its fixed assets at 1 September 20X5, an addition of £3,000 would have been made to the depreciation charged in the P&L account for 20X5/X6.

Required

Prepare H Ltd's consolidated balance sheet as at 31 August 20X6.

Note. Goodwill is deemed to have an indefinite useful life and is therefore to remain in the balance sheet.

Solution

S Ltd has not incorporated the revaluation in its draft balance sheet. Before beginning the consolidation workings we must therefore adjust the company's balance of profits at the date of acquisition and at the balance sheet date.

S Ltd adjusted balance of retained profits

	£	£
Balance per accounts at 1 September 20X5		21,000
Consolidation adjustment: revaluation surplus		23,000
∴ Pre-acquisition profits for consolidation purposes		44,000
Profit for year ended 31 August 20X6		
Per draft accounts £(41,000 − 21,000)	20,000	
Consolidation adjustment: increase in depreciation charge	(3,000)	
		17,000
Adjusted balance of retained profits at 31 August 20X6		61,000

In the consolidated balance sheet, S Ltd's fixed assets will appear at their revalued amount: £(28,000 + 23,000 − 3,000) = £48,000. The consolidation workings can now be drawn up.

1   *Minority interest*

	£
Share capital (25% × £20,000)	5,000
Revenue reserves (25% × £61,000)	15,250
	20,250

2   *Goodwill*

	£	£
Cost of investment		51,000
Share of net assets acquired as represented by		
Ordinary share capital	20,000	
Revenue reserves		
£(21,000 + 23,000)	44,000	
	64,000	
Group share (75%)		48,000
Goodwill		3,000

3   *Revenue reserves*

	H Ltd	S Ltd
	£	£
Per question	96,000	41,000
Depreciation increase		(3,000)
Pre-acquisition		(21,000)
		17,000
Share of S Ltd 75% × 17,000	12,750	
	108,750	

H LIMITED CONSOLIDATED BALANCE SHEET AS AT 31 AUGUST 20X6

	£
Intangible fixed asset: goodwill	3,000
Tangible fixed assets £(63,000 + 48,000)	111,000
Net current assets	95,000
	209,000
Capital and reserves	
Ordinary shares of £1 each	80,000
Retained profits	108,750
Shareholders' funds	188,750
Minority interest	20,250
	209,000

6.3 FRS 7 *Fair values in acquisition accounting*

FRS 7 was published in September 1994. The main problem is the practice of attributing the **lowest values possible** to the net assets acquired so that the goodwill figure is correspondingly increased. Goodwill is generally deducted direct from reserves, the P&L account is by-passed, and profits are enhanced when the low asset values are subsequently charged against them in depreciation.

The commonest method of reducing the net assets acquired has been by establishing **provisions for reorganisation and restructuring costs**, reflecting the changes the acquirer intends to make to the business it has acquired. Since such provisions allow the subsequent expenditure to by-pass the P&L account, the costs disappear into a 'black hole' as far as reported profits are concerned; and the profits of the acquirer benefit from the increased earnings resulting from the reorganisation, without bearing the costs involved.

In attributing fair values to assets and liabilities acquired, FRS 7 states that the basic principle is that fair values should reflect the **circumstances at the time of the acquisition**, and should not reflect either the acquirer's intentions or events subsequent to the acquisition. Thus, the assets and liabilities recognised are restricted to those of the acquired entity that existed at the date of acquisition, and **exclude** both provisions for reorganisation costs to be carried out by the acquirer and provisions for future losses. Such items are to be treated as part of the post-acquisition results of the enlarged group.

FRS 7 also sets out specific rules on how fair values should be determined for the main categories of asset and liability. The underlying principle remains that fair values should reflect the price at which an asset or liability could be **exchanged in an arm's length transaction**. For long-term monetary assets and liabilities, fair values may be derived by **discounting**.

The standard also describes how the value attributed to the **consideration** given for the acquisition should be determined, and the acquisition expenses that may be included as part of the cost.

6.4 Objective

The objective of FRS 7 is to ensure that when a business entity is acquired by another, all the assets and liabilities that existed in the acquired entity at the date of acquisition are recorded at fair values reflecting their **condition at that date**. Any changes to the acquired assets and liabilities, and the resulting gains and losses, that arise after control of the acquired entity has passed to the acquirer should be reported as part of the post-acquisition profits of the group.

6.5 Definitions

The following definitions are given by FRS 7; particularly note the definition of fair value.

Key terms

> **Acquisition:** a business combination that is accounted for by using the acquisition method of accounting.
>
> **Business combination**: the bringing together of separate entities into one economic entity as a result of one entity uniting with, or obtaining control over the net assets and operations of, another.
>
> **Date of acquisition**: the date on which control of the acquired entity passes to the acquirer. This is the date from which the acquired entity is accounted for by the acquirer as a subsidiary undertaking under FRS 2.
>
> **Fair value**: the amount at which an asset or liability could be exchanged in an arm's length transaction between informed and willing parties, other than in a forced or liquidation sale.
>
> **Identifiable assets and liabilities**: the assets and liabilities of the acquired entity that are capable of being disposed of or settled separately, without disposing of a business of the entity.
>
> **Recoverable amount**: the greater of the net realisable value of an asset and, where appropriate, the value in use.
>
> **Value in use**: the present value of the future cash flows obtainable as a result of an asset's continued use, including those resulting from the ultimate disposal of the asset. *(FRS 7)*

6.6 Scope

FRS 7 applies to all financial statements that are intended to give a true and fair view. Although the FRS is framed in terms of the acquisition of a subsidiary undertaking by a parent company that prepares consolidated financial statements, it also applies where an **individual company** entity acquires a business other than a subsidiary undertaking. This last point means that companies cannot avoid the provisions of FRS 7 when taking over an unincorporated entity or joint venture vehicle.

6.7 Determining the fair values of identifiable assets and liabilities acquired

The basic principles stated by FRS 7 are that:

(a) All identifiable assets and liabilities should be **recognised** which are in existence at the date of acquisition

(b) Such recognised assets and liabilities should be **measured at fair values** which reflect the conditions existing at the date of acquisition

Most importantly, the FRS lists those items which do *not* affect fair values at the date of acquisition, and which are therefore to be treated as **post-acquisition items.**

(a) Changes resulting from the acquirer's **intentions or future actions**

(b) Impairments or other changes, resulting from **events subsequent to the acquisition**

(c) Provisions or accruals for **future operating losses** or for **reorganisation and integration costs** expected to be incurred as a result of the acquisition, whether they relate to the acquired entity or to the acquirer

In general terms, fair values should be determined in accordance with the acquirer's **accounting policies** for similar assets and liabilities. The standard does, however, go on to describe how the major categories of assets and liabilities should be assessed for fair values.

    (a)   **Tangible assets**: fair value based on:

        (i)   Market value, if similar assets are sold on the open market, or

        (ii)   Depreciated replacement cost, reflecting normal business practice.

However, fair value ≤ replacement cost.

    (b)   **Intangible assets**, where recognised: fair value should be based on replacement costs, which will normally be estimated market value.

    (c)   **Stocks and work in progress**

        (i)   For stocks which are replaced by purchasing in a ready market (commodities, dealing stock etc), the fair value is market value.

        (ii)   For other stocks, with no ready market (most manufacturing stocks), fair value is represented by the current cost to the acquired company of reproducing the stocks.

    (d)   **Quoted investments**: value at market price, adjusted where necessary for unusual price fluctuations or the size of the holding.

    (e)   **Monetary assets and liabilities**: fair values should take into account the amounts expected to be received or paid and their timing. Reference should be made to market prices (where available) or to the current price if acquiring similar assets or entering into similar obligations, or to the discounted present value.

    (f)   **Contingencies**: reasonable estimates of the expected outcome may be used.

    (g)   **Pensions and other post-retirement benefits**: the fair value of a deficiency, a surplus (to the extent it is expected to be realised) or accrued obligation should be recognised as an asset/liability of the acquiring group. Any changes on acquisition should be treated as post-acquisition items.

    (h)   **Deferred tax** recognised in a fair value exercise should be measured in accordance with the requirements of FRS 19. Thus deferred tax would not be recognised on an adjustment to recognise a non-monetary asset acquired with the business at its fair value on acquisition.

6.8 Business sold or held with a view to subsequent resale

The fair value exercise for such an entity, 'sold as a single unit, within approximately one year of acquisition', should be carried out on the basis of a **single asset investment**.

'Its fair value should be based on the net proceeds of the sale, adjusted for the fair value of any assets or liabilities transferred into or out of the business, unless such adjusted net proceeds are demonstrably different from the fair value at the date of acquisition as a result of a post-acquisition event.'

Any relevant part of the business can be treated in this way if it is separately identifiable, ie it does not have to be a separate subsidiary undertaking.

Where the **first financial statements** after the date of acquisition come for approval, but the business has not been sold, the above treatment can still be applied if:

    (a)   A purchaser has been identified or is being sought

    (b)   The disposal is expected to occur within one year of the date of acquisition

The interest (or its assets) should be shown in current assets. On determination of the sales price, the original estimate of fair value should be **adjusted** to reflect the actual sales proceeds.

6.9 Investigation period and goodwill adjustments

FRS 7 states that:

> 'The recognition and measurement of assets and liabilities acquired should be completed, if possible, by the date on which the first post-acquisition financial statements of the acquirer are approved by the directors.'

Where this has not been possible, **provisional valuations** should be made, amended if necessary in the next financial statements with a corresponding adjustment to goodwill. Such adjustments should be incorporated into the financial statements in the **full year following acquisition**. After that, any adjustments (except for the correction of fundamental errors by prior year adjustment) should be recognised as profits or losses as they are identified.

6.10 Determining the fair value of purchase consideration

The cost of acquisition is the amount of **cash paid and the fair value of other purchase consideration** given by the acquirer, together with the expenses of the acquisition. Where a subsidiary undertaking is acquired in stages, the cost of acquisition is the total of the costs of the interests acquired, determined as at the date of each transaction.

The main likely components of purchase consideration are as follows.

    (a)   **Ordinary shares**

        (i)   Quoted shares should be valued at market price on the date of acquisition.

        (ii)   Where there is no suitable market, estimate the value using:

            •   the value of similar quoted securities; *or*
            •   the present value of the future cash flows of the instrument used; *or*
            •   any cash alternative which was offered.

    (b)   **Other securities**: the value should be based on similar principles to those given in (a).

    (c)   **Cash or monetary amounts**: value at the amount paid or payable.

    (d)   **Non-monetary assets**: value at market price, estimated realisable value, independent valuation or based on other available evidence.

    (e)   **Deferred consideration**: discount the amounts calculated on the above principles (in (a) to (d)). An appropriate discount rate is that which the acquirer could obtain for a similar borrowing.

    (f)   **Contingent consideration**: use the probable amount. When the actual amount is known, it should be recorded in the financial statements and goodwill adjusted accordingly.

Acquisition costs (the fees and expenses mentioned above) should be included in the cost of the investment. Internal costs and the costs of issuing capital instruments should *not* be capitalised, according to the provisions of FRS 26, ie they must be written off to the P&L account.

6.11 Summary and assessment

The most important effect of FRS 7 is the ban it imposes on making provisions for **future trading losses** of acquired companies and the costs of any related **rationalisation or reorganisation**, unless outgoing management had already incurred those liabilities. This is a controversial area, demonstrated by the dissenting view of one member of the ASB. However, this approach has been followed in FRS 12 *Provisions, contingent liabilities and contingent assets*.

Some argue that the ASB's approach **ignores the commercial reality** of the transaction by treating as an expense the costs of reorganisation that the acquirer regards as part of the capital cost of the acquisition; and that within defined limits a provision for planned post-acquisition expenditure should be permitted to be included in the net assets acquired.

The Hundred Group of finance directors gave an example. If you buy a house for, say £100,000 that you know needs £50,000 spent on it to bring it into good condition and make it equivalent to a property that sells for £150,000, then you would treat the £50,000 renovation expense as part of the cost of the house and not as part of ordinary outgoings. The group states that FRS 7 goes beyond standards set in other countries, including the US. It also recommends that abuses in this area should be dealt with by tightening existing accounting standards and through 'proper policing' by external auditors (the standard is seen to undermine the professional judgement of the auditor) and 'not by distorting accounting concepts'.

The ASB rejected this view, saying that an intention to incur revenue expenditure subsequent to the acquisition could not properly be regarded as a liability of the acquired business at the date of acquisition.

> 'Acquisition accounting should reflect the business that is acquired as it stands at the date of acquisition and ought not to take account of the changes that an acquirer might intend to make subsequently. Nor could the ASB accept the proposition that some of the inadequacies of the present system could be met by better disclosure. In the ASB's view deficient accounting cannot be put right by disclosure alone.'

Exam focus point

Questions on FRS 7 will probably involve fair values of deferred and contingent consideration and discussions on the use of provisions. You are likely to be asked about the more contentious items in P2.

6.12 Section summary

Factors to consider when arriving at a fair value are as follows.

- **Deferred consideration**: time value of money
- **Contingent consideration**: expected amount payable/receivable
- Use of **hindsight**
- **Pension surpluses/deficiencies** unrecorded by subsidiary
- Net assets acquired should be identified and recognised using the **acquirer's accounting policies**
- No adjustments should be made for the **acquirer's future intentions**
- **Deferred tax implications** should be considered

Question   FRS 7 (1)

H Ltd acquired 100% of S Ltd for £1,000,000. At the date of acquisition S Ltd had net assets of £500,000. However, H Ltd would need to spend £200,000 on reorganising S Ltd to successfully incorporate the company into the group. The group's policy is to amortise goodwill over 5 years with a full year's amortisation in the year of acquisition.

The P&L account of H Ltd in the first year following the acquisition are as follows.

	H Ltd £'000	S Ltd £'000
Operating profit	700	400
Reorganisation costs	–	200
Profit before tax	700	200
Tax	200	70
Profit after tax	500	130

Requirement

Calculate the goodwill and prepare the consolidated P&L account in accordance with FRS 7

Answer

Goodwill

	£'000
Cost of investment	1,000
Net assets acquired	500
Provision for reorganisation	–
Goodwill	500

Profit and loss account

	£'000
Operating profit	1,100
Goodwill amortisation (700/5/500/5)	(100)
Reorganisation	200
Release provision	
Profit before tax	800
Tax	270
Profit after tax	530
Profit b/fwd	–
Retained profit reserves c/f	530

Question

FRS 7 (2)

Tyzo plc prepares accounts to 31 December. On 1 September 20X7 Tyzo plc acquired 6 million £1 shares in Kono plc at £2.00 per share. The purchase was financed by an additional issue of loan stock at an interest rate of 10%. At that date Kono plc produced the following interim financial statements.

	£m		£m
Tangible fixed assets (note 1)	16.0	Trade creditors	3.2
Stocks (note 2)	4.0	Taxation	0.6
Debtors	2.9	Bank overdraft	3.9
Cash in hand	1.2	Long-term loans (note 3)	4.0
		Share capital (£1 shares)	8.0
		Profit and loss account	4.4
	24.1		24.1

Notes

1   The following information relates to the tangible fixed assets of Kono plc at 1 September 20X7.

	£m
Gross replacement cost	28.4
Net replacement cost	16.6
Economic value	18.0
Net realisable value	8.0

The fixed assets of Kono plc at 1 September 20X7 had a total purchase cost to Kono plc of £27.0 million. They were all being depreciated at 25% per annum pro rata on that cost. This policy is also appropriate for the consolidated financial statements of Tyzo plc. No fixed assets of Kono plc which were included in the interim financial statements drawn up as at 1 September 20X7 were disposed of by Kono plc prior to 31 December 20X7. No fixed asset was fully depreciated by 31 December 20X7.

2   The stocks of Kono plc which were shown in the interim financial statements at cost to Kono plc of £4 million would have cost £4.2 million to replace at 1 September 20X7 and had an estimated net realisable value at that date of £4.8 million. Of the stock of Kono plc in hand at 1 September 20X7, goods costing Kono plc £3.0 million were sold for £3.6 million between 1 September 20X7 and 31 December 20X7.

3   The long-term loan of Kono plc carries a rate of interest of 10% per annum, payable on 31 August annually in arrears. The loan is redeemable at par on 31 August 20Y1. The interest cost is representative of current market rates. The accrued interest payable by Kono plc at 31 December 20X7 is included in the trade creditors of Kono plc at that date.

4   On 1 September 20X7 Tyzo plc took a decision to rationalise the group so as to integrate Kono plc. The costs of the rationalisation (which were to be borne by Tyzo plc) were estimated to total £3.0 million and the process was due to start on 1 March 20X8. No provision for these costs has been made in any of the financial statements given above.

Required

Compute the goodwill on consolidation of Kono plc that will be included in the consolidated financial statements of the Tyzo plc group for the year ended 31 December 20X7, explaining your treatment of the items mentioned above. You should refer to the provisions of relevant accounting standards.

Answer

Goodwill on consolidation of Kono Ltd

	£m	£m
Consideration (£2.00 × 6m)		12.0
Group share of fair value of net assets acquired		
Share capital	8.0	
Pre-acquisition reserves	4.4	
Fair value adjustments		
Tangible fixed assets (16.6 – 16.0)	0.6	
Stocks (4.2 – 4.0)	0.2	
	13.2	
Group share	75%	9.9
Goodwill		2.1

Notes on treatment

(a)   It is assumed that the market value (ie fair value) of the loan stock issued to fund the purchase of the shares in Kono plc is equal to the price of £12.0m. FRS 2 requires goodwill to be calculated by comparing the fair value of the consideration given with the fair value of the separable net assets of the acquired business or company.

(b) Share capital and pre-acquisition profits represent the book value of the net assets of Kono plc at the date of acquisition. Adjustments are then required to this book value in order to give the fair value of the net assets at the date of acquisition. For short-term monetary items, fair value is their carrying value on acquisition.

(c) FRS 7 states that the fair value of tangible fixed assets should be determined by market value or, if information on a market price is not available (as is the case here), then by reference to depreciated replacement cost, reflecting normal business practice. The net replacement cost (ie £16.6m) represents the gross replacement cost less depreciation based on that amount, and so further adjustment for extra depreciation is unnecessary.

(d) FRS 7 also states that stocks which cannot be replaced by purchasing in a ready market (eg commodities) should be valued at current cost to the acquired company of reproducing the stocks. In this case that amount is £4.2m.

(e) The fair value of the loan is the present value of the total amount payable, ie on maturity and in interest. If the quoted interest rate was used as a discount factor, this would give the current par value.

(f) The rationalisation costs must be reported in post-acquisition results under FRS 7, so no adjustment is required in the goodwill calculation.

Chapter Roundup

- You should go back to your earlier study material (if necessary) and make sure you know:
  - The CA 2006 and FRS 2 **definitions** of parent and subsidiary undertakings;
  - CA 2006 requirements for **exemption** from consolidation and **exclusion** of subsidiaries;
  - The accounting requirements for **non-consolidated** subsidiaries;
  - FRS 2's regulations for **acquisition accounting**;
  - The treatment of **intra-group profits** and the situations where it arises; and
  - How to prepare **simple consolidated accounts**, including the basic treatment of goodwill and minority interests.

- Consider the nature of the **current definitions and accounting requirements**. You should be able to discuss why they are so complex and detailed.

- FRED 36 proposes major changes in accounting for business combinations.
  - Merger accounting will no longer be permitted.
  - Goodwill is no longer amortised but is subject to annual impairment tests.
  - Goodwill is to be shown gross of non-controlling ('minority') interests.
  - Negative goodwill is to be recognised as a gain in the profit and loss account.

- The accounting requirements and disclosures of the fair value exercise are covered by **FRS 7**, which outlaws the use of provisions for future losses and for reorganisation costs on acquisition of a subsidiary.

Quick Quiz

1   **Fill in the blanks** in the statements below, using the words in the box.

Per FRS 2, A is a parent of B if:

(a)   A holds (1) .... in B
(b)   A can appoint or remove (2) ....
(c)   A has the right to exercise (3) .... over B
(d)   B is a (4) .... of A

• Sub-subsidiary	• Dominant influence
• Directors holding a majority of the voting rights	• A majority of the voting rights

2   If a company holds 20% or more of the shares of another company, it has a participating interest. True or false?

3   What is dominant influence?

4   Sometimes an undertaking **may** be excluded from consolidation. Sometimes it **must** be excluded. Write 'may' or 'must' against the appropriation circumstance.

(a)   Inclusion is not material.

(b)   The subsidiary is held exclusively for resale and has not been consolidated previously.

(c)   The subsidiary's activities are so different from those of other undertakings to be consolidated that its inclusion would be incompatible with the requirement to give a true and fair view.

5   How should a subsidiary excluded on the grounds of temporary control be accounted for in the consolidated balance sheet?

6   What are the components making up the figure of minority interest in a consolidated balance sheet?

7   Fill in the blanks to show the adjustment required before consolidation in cases where a holding company has not accounted for dividends receivable from a subsidiary.

DEBIT
CREDIT
With

8   The following diagram shows the structure of the Alpha group.

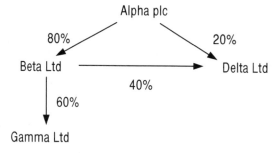

Which are the subsidiaries of Alpha plc?

A   Beta Ltd
B   Beta Ltd and Gamma Ltd
C   Beta Ltd and Delta Ltd
D   Beta Ltd, Gamma Ltd and Delta Ltd

9   Goodwill is always positive. True or false?

10 The following figures relate to Sanderstead plc and its subsidiary Croydon Ltd for the year ended 31 December 20X9.

	Sanderstead plc £	Croydon Ltd £
Turnover	600,000	300,000
Cost of sales	(400,000)	(200,000)
Gross profit	200,000	100,000

During the year, Sanderstead plc sold goods to Croydon Ltd for £20,000 making a profit of £5,000. These goods were all sold by Croydon Ltd before the year end.

What are the amounts for turnover and gross profit in the consolidated profit and loss accounts of Sanderstead plc for the year ended 31 December 20X9?

11 Under FRED 36 amortisation of goodwill will be permitted as an option.

True or false?

12 How is 'fair value' defined by FRS 7?

13 Which items does FRS 7 state must be treated as post-acquisition?

14 How is the cost of an acquisition made up?

15 On 31 March, Vellow Ltd purchased 1,800,000 of the 2,000,000 ordinary shares of £1 each in Yapton Ltd paying £1.20 per share.

At that date the values of the separable net assets of Yapton Ltd were:

Aggregate book value	£1,800,000
Aggregate fair value	£1,700,000

What is the values of the goodwill on consolidation as at 31 March?

16 On 31 March, Vellow Ltd purchased 1,800,000 of the 2,000,000 ordinary shares of £1 each in Yapton Ltd paying £1.20 per share.

At that date the value of the separable net assets of Yapton Ltd were:

Aggregate book value	£1,800,000
Aggregate fair value	£1,700,000

What is the value of the minority interest as at 31 March?

Answers to Quick Quiz

1   (a)   A majority of the voting rights
           (b)   Directors holding a majority of the voting rights
           (c)   Dominant influence
           (d)   Sub-subsidiary

2   False. Significant influence is presumed but the presumption may be rebutted.

3   Influence that can be exercised to achieve the operating and financial policies desired by the holder of the influence, notwithstanding the rights or influence of any other party.

4   (a)   May
           (b)   Must
           (c)   Must

5   It should be included under current assets at the lower of cost and NRV.

6   The minority's share of ordinary shares, preference shares and reserves.

7   DEBIT   Debtors (dividend receivable)
           CREDIT   Revenue reserves

        With the parent company's share of the dividend receivable in the parent's books.

8   D   Alpha has control over Beta's 40% holding in Delta and has a 20% direct holding. Thus Delta is a subsidiary.

9   False. Goodwill can be negative if the purchaser has 'got a bargain'.

10

	£
Turnover (1,600 + 300 – 20)	880
Cost of sales (400 +200 – 20)	580
Gross profit	300

11   False. Goodwill will not be amortised, but will be subject to annual impairment reviews.

12   The amount at which an asset or liability could be exchanged in an arm's length transaction between informed and willing parties other than in forced liquidation sale.

13   See Paragraph 1.7.

14   The amount of cash paid
        The fair value of other purchase consideration given by the acquirer
        The expenses of the acquisition

15

	£'000
Cost	2,160
Fair value of separable net assets acquired	
90% × 1,700,000	1,530
	630

16   10% × £1,700,000 = £170,000.

Now try the questions below from the Exam Question Bank

Number	Level	Marks	Time
Q17	Introductory	n/a	n/a
Q18	Introductory	n/a	n/a

Associates
and joint ventures

17

Topic list	Syllabus reference
1 FRS 9 *Associates and joint ventures:* summary	D1
2 Examples	D1
3 Questions	D1

Introduction

Some investments are not subsidiaries but they may be much more than trade investments. The most important of these are associates and joint ventures, which are the subject of this chapter and of one of the ASB's recent standards FRS 9 *Associates and joint ventures.*

Study guide

		Intellectual level
D1	**Group accounting including cash flow statements**	
(f)	Account for and apply the equity method of accounting for associates	3
(g)	Outline and apply the key definitions and accounting methods which relate to interests in joint ventures	3

Exam guide

Associates and joint ventures are likely to be tested as part of the compulsory group accounts in Section A. Typically you may be asked to account for a change in status from associate to subsidiary in a piecemeal acquisition, or subsidiary to associate in a disposal.

FAST FORWARD

Associates and **joint ventures** are entities in which an investor holds a **substantial but not controlling interest**.

1 FRS 9 Associates and joint ventures: summary

FAST FORWARD

They are the subject of an accounting standard: **FRS 9** *Associates and joint ventures.*

You have covered FRS 9 in your earlier studies. Here we remind you of its requirements and give you some questions to practise. You must look back to your earlier studies if you are unsure.

Knowledge brought forward from earlier studies

Definition of associate

- **Associates.** FRS 9: an associate exists where:

    - Investor holds a participating interest
    - Investor exercises significant influence

    Participating interest. An interest held in the shares of another entity on a long-term basis for the purpose of securing a contribution to the investor's activities by the exercise of control or influence arising from or related to that interest.

    Significant influence. This essentially involves participation in the financial and operating policy decisions (including dividend policy). Representation on the board is indicative but not conclusive.

- **Presumptions**

    - If ≥ 20% of equity voting rights, presumption of significant influence unless clearly demonstrated otherwise

    - If < 20% of equity voting rights, presumption of no significant influence unless clearly demonstrated otherwise

    In applying the above test, holdings of the parent company and subsidiaries should be aggregated but holdings via another associated company should be excluded.

Accounting treatment

- **Consolidated balance sheet.** Associated undertakings should be accounted for under the equity method of accounting

  Interest in associated

Investing group's share of net assets other than goodwill of the associate (after attributing FVs to net assets at time of acquisition)	X
Investing group's share of any goodwill in the associate financial statements	X
Premium paid (or discount) on the acquisition insofar as it has not already been written off or amortised	X/(X)
Investment in associate	X

- **Additional disclosures** are required where the investor's share exceeds 15% of the gross assets, liabilities or operating result of the investing group

–	Turnover	–	Current assets
–	Fixed assets	–	Current liabilities (< 1 year and > 1 year)

  If the investor's share exceeds 25% of gross assets etc, the investor's share of the following must be shown

–	Turnover	–	Fixed assets
–	Profit before tax	–	Current assets
–	Tax	–	Liabilities < 1 year
–	Profit after tax	–	Liabilities > 1 year

- **Consolidated P&L**

  - Group share of associate's operating results immediately after group operating profit
  - Amortisation of goodwill (if any)
  - Group share of associate's profit before tax included within the amounts for the group
  - Group share of tax charge of associate disclosed separately within the group tax charge

Joint ventures

- A joint venture is an entity in which the reporting entity holds an **interest on a long-term basis** and is **jointly controlled** by the **reporting entity and one or more** other venturers under a contractual arrangement.

- **Joint control**. A reporting entity jointly controls a venture with one or more other entities if none of the entities alone can control that entity but all together can do so and decisions on financial and operating policy essential to the activities, economic performance and financial position of that venture require each venturer's consent.

Knowledge brought forward from earlier studies (continued)

- Joint ventures are included in consolidated financial statements using the **gross equity method**, ie like associates but:

    - In consolidated P&L joint venture's turnover should not be shown as part of the group turnover

    - In consolidated B/S group share of gross assets and liabilities underlying the net equity amount should be shown as amplification of the net amount

    - Except for profit before tax in the P&L, any supplementary information given for joint ventures, either in the P&L or B/S must be shown clearly separate from accounts for the group and must not be included in group total

- **Joint arrangements**. Participants in a joint arrangement that is not an entity (ie not a subsidiary, joint venture or associate) should account for their own assets, liabilities and cash flows measured according to the terms of the agreement governing the arrangement.

1.1 Summary

The table below, taken from the FRS, describes the **different sorts of interest that a reporting entity may have in other entities or arrangements**. The sections marked with an asterisk (*) are covered by the FRS. The defining relationships described in the table form the basis for the definitions used in the FRS.

Entity/ arrangement	Nature of relationship	Description of the defining relationship – the full definitions are given in the FRS
Subsidiary	Investor controls its investee	Control is the ability of an entity to direct the operating and financial policies of another entity with a view to gaining economic benefits from its activities. To have control an entity must have both: (a) the ability to deploy the economic resources of the investee or to direct it; and (b) the ability to ensure that any resulting benefits accrue to itself (with corresponding exposure to losses) and to restrict the access of others to those benefits.
* Joint arrangement that is not an entity	Entities participate in an arrangement to carry on part of their own trades or businesses	A joint arrangement, whether or not subject to joint control, does not constitute an entity unless it carries on a trade or business of its own.
* Joint venture	Investor holds a long-term interest and shares control under a contractual arrangement	The joint venture agreement can override the rights normally conferred by ownership interests with the effect that: • acting together, the venturers can control the venture and there are procedures for such joint action • each venturer has (implicitly or explicitly) a veto over strategic policy decisions. There is usually a procedure for settling disputes between venturers and, possibly, for terminating the joint venture.

Entity/ arrangement	Nature of relationship	Description of the defining relationship – the full definitions are given in the FRS
* Associate	Investor holds a participating interest and exercises significant influence	The investor has a long-term interest and is actively involved, and influential, in the direction of its investee through its participation in policy decisions covering the aspects of policy relevant to the investor, including decisions on strategic issues such as: (i) the expansion or contraction of the business, participation in other entities or changes in products, markets and activities of its investee; and (ii) determining the balance between dividend and reinvestment.
Simple investment		The investor's interest does not quality the investee as an associate, a joint venture or a subsidiary because the investor has limited influence or its interest is not long-term.

The table below, also taken from the FRS, sets out the **treatments in consolidated financial statements** for the different interests that a reporting entity may have in other entities and for joint arrangements that are not entities – the sections marked with an asterisk (*) are covered by the FRS.

FAST FORWARD

Associates are to be included in the investor's consolidated financial statements using the **equity method**.

- The investor's share of its associates' results should be included immediately after group operating profit.

- The investor's share of its associates' turnover may be shown as a memorandum item.

Joint ventures are to be included in the venturer's consolidated financial statements by the **gross equity method**.

This requires, in addition to the amounts included under the equity method, disclosure of the venturer's share of its joint ventures' turnover, gross assets and gross liabilities.

Other **joint arrangements**, such as cost-sharing arrangements and one-off construction projects, are to be included in their participants' individual and consolidated financial statements by **each participant including directly** its share of the assets, liabilities and cash flows arising from the arrangements.

Type of investment	Treatment in consolidated financial statements
Subsidiaries	The investor should consolidate the assets, liabilities, results and cash flows of its subsidiaries.
* Joint arrangements that are not entities	Each party should account for its own share of the assets, liabilities and cash flows in the joint arrangement, measured according to the terms of that arrangement, for example pro rata to their respective interests.
Joint ventures	The venturer should use the gross equity method showing in addition to the amounts included under the equity method, on the face on the balance sheet, the venturer's share of the gross assets and liabilities of its joint ventures, and, in the profit and loss account, the venturer's share of their turnover distinguished from that of the group. Where the venturer conducts a major part of its business through joint ventures, it may show fuller information provided all amounts are distinguished from those of the group.

Type of investment	Treatment in consolidated financial statements
Associates	The investor should include its associates in its consolidated financial statements using the equity method. In the investor's consolidated profit and loss account the investor's share of its associates' operating results should be included immediately after group operating results. From the level of profit before tax, the investor's share of the relevant amounts for associates should be included within the amounts for the group. In the consolidated statement of total recognised gains and losses the investor's share of the total recognised gains and losses of its associates should be included, shown separately under each heading, if material. In the balance sheet the investor's share of the net assets of its associates should be included and separately disclosed. The cash flow statement should include the cash flows between the investor and its associates. Goodwill arising on the investor's acquisition of its associates, less any amortisation or write-down, should be included in the carrying amount for the associates but should be disclosed separately. In the profit and loss account the amortisation or write-down of such goodwill should be separately disclosed as part of the investor's share of its associates' results.
Simple investments	The investor includes its interests as investments at either cost or valuation.

2 Examples

The following example of consolidated financial statements is taken from Appendix IV of FRS 9.

The format is illustrative only. The amounts shown for 'Associates' and 'joint ventures' are subdivisions of the item for which the statutory prescribed heading is 'Income from interests in associated undertakings'. The subdivisions may be shown in a note rather than on the face of the profit and loss account.

CONSOLIDATED PROFIT AND LOSS ACCOUNT

	£m	£m
Turnover: group and share of joint ventures	320	
Less: share of joint ventures' turnover	(120)	
Group turnover		200
Cost of sales		(120)
Gross profit		80
Administrative expenses		(40)
Group operating profit		40
Share of operating profit in		
Joint ventures	30	
Associates	24	
		54
		94
Interest receivable (group)		6
Interest payable		
Group	(26)	
Joint ventures	(10)	
Associates	(12)	
		(48)
Profit on ordinary activities before tax		52
*Tax on profit on ordinary activities**		(12)
Profit on ordinary activities after tax		40
Minority interests		(6)
Profit on ordinary activities after taxation and minority interest		34
Equity dividends		(10)
Retained profit for group and its share of associates and joint ventures		24

*Tax relates to the following:	Parent and subsidiaries	(5)
	Joint ventures	(5)
	Associates	(2)

CONSOLIDATED BALANCE SHEET

	£m	£m	£m
Fixed assets			
Tangible assets		480	
Investments			
Investments in joint ventures:			
Share of gross assets	130		
Share of gross liabilities	(80)		
		50	
Investments in associates		20	
			550
Current assets			
Stock		15	
Debtors		75	
Cash at bank and in hand		10	
		100	
Creditors (due within one year)		(50)	
Net current assets			50
Total assets less current liabilities			600
Creditors (due after more than one year)			(250)
Provisions for liabilities and charges			(10)
Equity minority interest			(40)
			300

	£m	£m	£m
Capital and reserves			
Called up share capital			50
Share premium account			150
Profit and loss account			100
Shareholders' funds (all equity)			300

Notes

In the example, there is no individual associate or joint venture that accounts for more than 25 per cent of any of the following for the investor group (excluding any amount for associates and joint ventures).

- Gross assets
- Gross liabilities
- Turnover
- Operating results (on a three-year average)

Additional disclosures for joint ventures (which in aggregate exceed the 15 per cent threshold)

	£m	£m
Share of assets		
Share of fixed assets	100	
Share of current assets	30	
		130
Share of liabilities		
Liabilities due within one year or less	(10)	
Liabilities due after more than one year	(70)	
		(80)
Share of net assets		50

Additional disclosures for associates (which in aggregate exceed the 15 per cent threshold)

	£m	£m
Share of turnover of associates		90
Share of assets		
Share of fixed assets	4	
Share of current assets	28	
		32
Share of liabilities		
Liabilities due within one year or less	(3)	
Liabilities due after more than one year	(9)	
		(12)
Share of net assets		20

2.1 Further aspects of FRS 9 applying to both joint ventures and associates

2.1.1 Principles of consolidation

As has been mentioned, when calculating the amounts to be included in the investor's consolidated financial statements, whether using the equity method for associates or the gross equity method for joint ventures, the **same principles should be applied as are applied in the consolidation of subsidiaries**. This has the following implications.

(a)   **Fair values** are to be attributed to assets and liabilities on acquisition. Goodwill should be treated as per FRS 10.

(b)   In arriving at the amounts to be included by the equity method, the same **accounting policies** as those of the investor should be applied.

(c)   The financial statements of the investor and the associate or joint venture should be prepared to the **same accounting date** and for the **same accounting period**; associates/joint ventures can prepare three months before if necessary with appropriate adjustments and disclosure.

(d)   Profits or losses resulting from **transactions between the investor and its associate/joint venture** may be included in the carrying amount of assets in either party. Where this is the case, the part relating to the **investor's share should be eliminated**. Any impairment of those or similar assets must be taken into account if evidence of it is given by the transactions in question.

2.1.2 Investor is a group

Where the investor is a group, it share of its associate or joint venture is the aggregate of the holdings of the parent and its subsidiaries in that entity. The holdings of any of the group's other associates or joint ventures should be ignored for this purpose. Where an associate or joint venture itself has subsidiaries, associates or joint ventures, the results and net assets to be taken into account by the equity method are those reported in that investee's consolidated financial statements (including the investee's share of the results and net assets of its associates and joint ventures), after any adjustment necessary to give effect to the investor's accounting policies.

2.1.3 Options, convertibles and non-equity shares

The investor may hold options, convertibles or non-equity shares in its associate or joint venture. In certain circumstances, the conditions attaching to such holdings are such that the investor should take them into account in reflecting its interest in its investee under the equity or gross equity method. In such cases, the costs of exercising the options or converting the convertibles, or future payments in relation to the non-equity shares, should also be taken into account.

2.1.4 Impairment

In cases where there is impairment in any goodwill attributable to an associate or joint venture the **goodwill should be written down** and the amount written off in the accounting period separately disclosed.

2.1.5 Commencement and cessation of relationship

The following points apply with regard to commencement or cessation of an associate or joint venture relationship.

(a)   An investment **becomes an associate** on the date on which the investor begins:

    (i)   To hold a **participating interest**

    (ii)   To exercise **significant influence**

(b)   An investment **ceases to be an associate** on the date when it **ceases to fulfil** either of the above.

(c)   An investment **becomes a joint venture** on the date on which the investor begins to **control it jointly** with other investors, provided it has a long-term interest.

(d)   On the date when an investor **ceases to have joint control**, the investment **ceases to be a joint venture.**

(e)   The **carrying amount** (percentage of investment retained) should be reviewed and, if necessary, written down to the **recoverable amount**.

2.2 Joint arrangements that are not entities

A reporting entity may operate through a structure that has the appearance of a joint venture but not the reality. It may thus be a separate entity in which the participants hold a long-term interest and exercise joint management, but there may be no common interest because each venturer operates independently of the other venturers within that structure. The framework entity acts merely as an agent for the ventures with each venturer able to identify and control its share of the assets, liabilities and cash flows arising within the entity. **Such arrangements have the form but not the substance of a joint venture**.

The accounting treatment for such joint arrangements required by FRS 9 is that **each venturer should account directly for its share of the assets, liabilities and cash flows held within that structure**. This treatment reflects the substance rather than the form of the arrangement.

2.3 Investors that do not prepare consolidated accounts

A reporting entity may have an associate or joint venture, but no subsidiaries. It will thus not prepare group accounts. In such cases it should present the relevant amounts for associates and joint ventures, as appropriate, by preparing a **separate set of financial statements** or by showing the relevant amounts, together with the effects of including them, as additional information to its own financial statements. Investing entities that are exempt from preparing consolidated financial statements, or would be exempt if they had subsidiaries, are exempt from this requirement.

3 Questions

You should be familiar enough with FRS 9 to get the following questions right. If not, look back to your earlier study material.

| Question | Treatment of items |

How should a holding company treat the following items in the financial statements for an associated company, when preparing group accounts?

(a)   Turnover
(b)   Inter-company profits
(c)   Goodwill

Answer

(a)   The holding company should not aggregate the turnover of an associated company with its own turnover.

(b)   Wherever the effect is material, adjustments similar to those adopted for the purpose of presenting consolidated financial statements should be made to exclude from the investing group's consolidated financial statements such items as unrealised profits on stocks transferred to or from associated companies.

(c)   The investing group's balance sheet should disclose 'interest in associated companies'. The amount disclosed under this heading should include both the investing group's share of any goodwill in the associated companies' own financial statements and any premium paid on acquisition of the interests in the associated companies in so far as it has not already been written off or amortised.

Question

Ross plc is a long established business in office supplies. The nature of its business has expanded and diversified to take account of technological changes which have taken place in recent years. Now in addition to stationery and office furniture, it also supplies photocopiers, fax machines and more recently new computer based technologies. The expansion has occurred organically but also through acquisition of existing companies and joint ventures. Ross plc's investments are as follows.

(a) *Joey Ltd*. Ross has a 40% interest in the issued share capital of Joey Ltd and representation on the board. Joey Ltd manufactures office furniture and a large proportion of what it produces is sold to Ross. Ross is therefore actively involved in decisions regarding product ranges, designs and pricing to ensure they get the products they want.

(b) *Rachel NRG*. Rachel NRG is a joint venture company which commenced operations on 1 June 20X7. The joint venturers in Rachel are Ross plc and Monica Inc, a company also in office automation, specialising in computer products. The purpose of the joint venture was to distribute their products to Asia Pacific where the demand for office automation is growing rapidly. Ross and Monica have an equal interest in Rachel.

(c) *Phoebe Ltd*. Phoebe Ltd's principal activities is the supply and fitting of bathroom suites. Its managing director is Mrs Janice Chandler, wife of Mr Paul Chandler, a director of Ross plc. Ross plc has a 25% interest in the share capital of Phoebe and the remaining shares are held by various members of the Chandler family. Mr Chandler is on the board of Phoebe as a non-executive director and this was approved at the last AGM by all the voting members of the Chandler family. The activities of Phoebe and Ross are in totally different markets, the share interest is there for historic reasons and Ross has not exercised its voting rights for several years. During the year Ross plc sold one of the company's executive cars to Phoebe Ltd for an agreed open market value of £30,000.

The following are extracts from the financial statements of Joey, Rachel and Phoebe for the year ended 31 March 20X8.

	Joey	Rachel	Phoebe
	£'000	£'000	£'000
Turnover	4,068	17,720	7,640
Operating costs	3,872	16,834	6,980
Operating profit	196	886	660
Interest payable	–	280	30
Profit before tax	196	606	630
Tax	40	152	200
Profit after tax	156	454	430
Fixed assets	360	1,720	260
Current assets	2,940	2,130	834
Creditors falling due within one year	(2,214)	(710)	(252)
Creditors falling due after one year	(26)	(1,810)	(400)
	1,060	1,330	442
Cost of investment	600	500	400

Sales of office furniture from Joey to Ross amounted to £160,000 during the year. 10% of the goods remain in the closing stock of Ross. These goods had been sold at a mark up of 25% on cost.

Required

Produce extracts from the consolidated profit and loss account and balance sheet of Ross for the year ended 31 March 20X8 indicating clearly the treatments for Joey, Rachel and Phoebe and where each item would appear.

Answer

EXTRACTS FROM THE CONSOLIDATED PROFIT AND LOSS ACCOUNT
FOR THE YEAR ENDED 31 MARCH 20X8

	£'000	£'000
Turnover	X	
Less share of joint ventures' turnover	(8,860)	
Group turnover		X
Group operating profit		X
Share of operating profit in		
Joint ventures	443	
Associates (W1)	77.2	
Interest payable		
Group	X	
Joint ventures	(140)	
Profit before tax		X
Tax (see below)		X
Profit after tax		X
Tax relates to		
Parent and subsidiary		X
Joint ventures		76
Associates		16

EXTRACTS FROM THE CONSOLIDATED BALANCE SHEET AS AT 31 MARCH 20X8

	£'000	£'000
Fixed assets		
Investments		
Investments in joint ventures		
Share of gross assets	1,925	
Share of gross liabilities	1,260	
		665.0
Investments in associates (W2)		422.8
Other investments		400.0

Workings

1   *Share of associate company profit*

	£'000
Profit of Joey per question	196.0
Less PUP (160,000 × 10% × 25/125)	3.2
	192.8
Group share (40%) (rounded)	77.2

2   *Investment in associates*

	£'000
Net assets per question	1,060.0
Less PUP (W1)	(3.2)
	1,056.8
Group share (40%) (rounded)	422.8

Question

Comic plc, the holding company of the Comic Group, acquired 25% of the ordinary shares of Strip plc on 1 September 20X0 for £54 million. Strip plc carried on business as a property investment company. The draft accounts as at 31 August 20X1 are as follows.

PROFIT AND LOSS ACCOUNTS FOR THE YEAR ENDED 31 AUGUST 20X1

	Comic Group £m	Strip plc £m
Sales	175.0	200
Profit before interest and tax	90.0	80
Exceptional profit on sale of property	20.0	
Interest	(2.0)	(20)
	108.0	60
Taxation	(23.2)	(20)
	84.8	40
Proposed dividends	(61.0)	–
	23.8	40

BALANCE SHEETS AS AT 31 AUGUST 20X1

	Comic Group £m	Strip plc £m
Fixed assets		
Tangible fixed assets	135	200
Investment in Strip plc	54	–
Current assets		
Stock	72	210
Debtors	105	50
Current liabilities		
Creditors	(95)	(20)
Overdraft	(14)	(100)
Net current assets	68	140
	257	340
Capital and reserves		
Ordinary shares of £1 each	135	50
Reserves	122	90
10% loan	–	200
	257	340

On 1 September 20X0 Comic plc sold a property with a book value of £40 million to Strip plc at its market value of £60 million. The tax suffered on this gain was £7 million. Strip plc obtained the funds to pay the £60 million by raising a loan which is included in the 10% loan that appears in its balance sheet at 31 August 20X1.

Premiums on acquisition are amortised over 5 years. The dividends were proposed before the year end.

Required

Prepare:

(a) The consolidated profit and loss account of the Comic Group for the year ended 31 August 20X1 and a consolidated balance sheet as at that date

(b) Relevant notes to comply with the requirements of FRS 9 *Associates and joint ventures*

Answer

(a) COMIC GROUP
CONSOLIDATED PROFIT AND LOSS ACCOUNT
FOR THE YEAR ENDED 31 AUGUST 20X1

	£m	£m
Group turnover		175.00
Group operating profit		90.00
Share of operating profit in associate 20 – 5.8		14.20
		104.20
Profit on sales of property		15.00
Interest payable		
Group	2	
Associate	5	
		(7.00)
		112.20
Taxation		
Group	21.45	
Associate	5.00	
		(26.45)
		85.75
Dividends		(61.00)
Retained profit for the year		24.75

COMIC GROUP
CONSOLIDATED BALANCE SHEET
AS AT 31 AUGUST 20X1

	Notes	£m	£m
Fixed assets			
Tangible assets			135.00
Interest in associated company	2, 5		54.95
			189.95
Current assets			
Stock		72	
Debtors		105	
		177	
Current liabilities			
Creditors		95	
Bank overdraft		14	
		109	
Net current assets			68.00
			257.95
Capital and reserves			
Ordinary shares £1 each			135.00
Reserves	4		122.95
			257.95

(b) NOTES TO THE ACCOUNTS

1 *Retained profit*

	£m
Retained by Comic and its subsidiaries	14.75
Retained by Strip plc	10.00
	24.75

2   *Interest in associate*

	£m
Group's share of net assets (25% × (340 − 200))	35.00
Less unrealised profit (25% × 13)	(3.25)
Unamortised goodwill (29 − 5.8)	23.20
	54.95

Additional disclosures for associates

The group has one associate, Strip plc, in which the group's share exceeds 25 per cent with respect to the group.

	£m	£m
Share of turnover of associate		50
Share of assets		
Share of fixed assets (W5)		45
Share of current assets		65
		110
Share of liabilities		
Liabilities due within one year or less (W6)	(28.25)	
Liabilities due after more than one year	(50.00)	
		(78.25)
		31.75

Workings

1   *Premium on acquisition*

	£m
Share capital	50
Reserves at date of acquisition (90 − 40)	50
	100
Group share (25%)	25
Cost	54
Premium on acquisition	29
Amortisation (29,000 ÷ 5)	5.8

2   *Reserves*

	Comic £m	Strip £m
Per question	122.00	
Post acquisition (per P&L)		40
Unrealised profit	(3.25)	
Share of Strip: 40 × 25%	10.00	
Less amortisation of goodwill	(5.80)	
	122.95	

3   *Working: exceptional profit*

	£m
Profit per Comic's profit and loss account	20
Less unrealised profit	
(25% × 20)	(5)
	15

4   *Group tax charge*

	£m
Comic per question	23.20
Less tax on unrealised element of exceptional profit	
(7 × 25%)	(1.75)
	21.45

5 *Share of Strip's fixed assets*

	£m
Strip fixed assets per question	200
Unrealised profit	(20)
	180
× 25%	45

6 *Share of Strip's liabilities within one year*

	£m
Strip liabilities per question	120
Tax element of unrealised profit	(7)
	113
× 25%	28.25

3.1 UITF Abstract 31 Exchanges of businesses or other non-monetary assets for an interest in a subsidiary, joint venture or associate

This UITF abstract was published in 2001. It deals with increasingly common transactions where an entity exchanges a business (or other non-monetary assets) for equity in a subsidiary, joint venture or associate. An example is where an entity forms a joint venture combining one of its businesses with that of another entity. An important issue is whether such transactions should be reported at **fair values or book values**; this affects the amounts of profits or losses and goodwill that are recognised in relation to the exchange.

The Abstract requires such transactions to be analysed in terms of **net changes in ownership interests**. The part of the business exchanged that **the entity still owns** indirectly through its new shareholding should remain at **book value**. In contrast, the entity's share of **net assets** acquired through its **new shareholding** should be accounted for at **fair value**. Goodwill is recognised in respect of the entity's newly acquired interest; a gain or loss is recognised in respect of the part of the business exchanged that the entity no longer directly or indirectly owns.

Chapter Roundup

- **Associates** and **joint ventures** are entities in which an investor holds a **substantial but not controlling interest**.

- They are the subject of an accounting standard: **FRS 9 *Associates and joint ventures.***

- **Associates** are to be included in the investor's consolidated financial statements using the **equity method**.

    - The investor's share of its associates' results should be included immediately after group operating profit.

    - The investor's share of its associates' turnover may be shown as a memorandum item.

- **Joint ventures** are to be included in the venturer's consolidated financial statements by the **gross equity method**.

- This requires, in addition to the amounts included under the equity method, disclosure of the venturer's share of its joint ventures' turnover, gross assets and gross liabilities.

- Other **joint arrangements**, such as cost-sharing arrangements and one-off construction projects, are to be included in their participants' individual and consolidated financial statements by **each participant including directly** its share of the assets, liabilities and cash flows arising from the arrangements.

Quick Quiz

1   What types of interest does FRS 9 identify?

2   A group of companies has the following shareholdings.

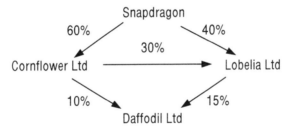

For consolidation purposes what, prima facie, is the relationship of Lobelia Ltd and Daffodil Ltd to Snapdragon plc?

3   What additional disclosures are required by FRS 9 when the '25% threshold' is reached (ie not also required when the '15% threshold' is reached). Circle any that apply.

    (a)   Fixed assets
    (b)   Liabilities due within one year
    (c)   Profit before tax
    (d)   Turnover
    (e)   Profit after tax

4   Constable plc owns 40% of Turner plc which it treats as an associated company in accordance with FRS 9. Constable plc also owns 60% of Whistler Ltd. Constable has held both of these shareholdings for more than one year. Turnover of each company for the year ended 30 June 20X0 was as follows.

	£m
Constable	400
Turner	200
Whistler	100

What figure should be shown as turnover in the consolidated profit and loss account of Constable plc?

5   Under the equity method of accounting, the balance sheet of an investing group will disclose, in respect of its associate:

A   Dividends receivable but not share of net assets of the associate

B   Share of net assets of the associate but not dividends receivable

C   Share of net assets of the associate and dividends receivable

D   Cost of investment plus goodwill on acquisition less amounts written off but not dividends receivable

Answers to Quick Quiz

1   Associates

Joint ventures

Joint arrangements that are not entities

2   Lobelia Ltd subsidiary; Daffodil Ltd associate

Shares held by subsidiary companies count in full. Snapdragon has control of Cornflower's 30% holding in Lobelia. It owns 40% itself, 40 + 30 gives control. Snapdragon therefore controls Lobelia's 15% in Daffodil and Cornflower's 10% in Daffodil (10 + 15 = 25 = associate).

3   (c) and (e)

4   Turnover will be 100% H + 100% S only. Associates are introduced in to the consolidated profit and loss account as a share of their operating profits in the first instance.

	£m
Constable	400
Whistler (subsidiary)	100
	500

5   C   Dividends receivable from associates will be included within 'amounts owed by associated companies' and not necessarily disclosed separately. In simple terms, dividends from associates do not 'cancel out' like those from subsidiaries.

Now try the questions below from the Exam Question Bank

Number	Level	Marks	Time
Q19	Introductory	n/a	n/a

Complex groups

Topic list	Syllabus reference
1 Multi-company structures	D1
2 Consolidating sub-subsidiaries	D1
3 Direct holdings in sub-subsidiaries	D1

Introduction

This chapter introduces the first of several more complicated consolidation topics. The best way to tackle these questions is to be logical and to carry out the consolidation on a **step by step** basis.

In questions of this nature, it is very helpful to sketch a **diagram of the group structure**, as we have done. This clarifies the situation and it should point you in the right direction: always sketch the group structure as your first working and double check it against the information in the question.

Study guide

		Intellectual level
D1	**Group accounting including cash flow statements**	
(a)	Apply the method of accounting for business combinations including complex group structures	3

Exam guide

If the groups questions does not involve an acquisition or disposal or a cash flow statement, then it is likely to involve a complex group.

1 Multi-company structures

In this section we shall consider how the principles of balance sheet consolidation may be applied to more complex structures of companies within a group.

    (a)   **Several subsidiary companies**

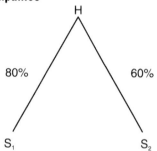

        You have already seen this type of structure in your previous studies.

    (b)   **Sub-subsidiaries**

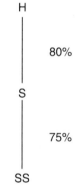

        H holds a controlling interest in S which in turn holds a controlling interest in SS. SS is therefore a subsidiary of a subsidiary of H; in other words, a *sub-subsidiary* of H.

(c)   **Direct holdings in sub-subsidiaries: 'D' shaped groups**

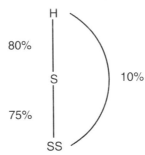

In this example, SS is a sub-subsidiary of H with additional shares held directly by H.

In practice, groups are usually larger, and therefore more complex, but the procedures for consolidation of large groups will not differ from those we shall now describe for smaller ones.

1.1 A holding company which has several subsidiaries

FAST FORWARD

When a holding company has **several subsidiaries**, the consolidated balance sheet shows a single figure for minority interests and for goodwill arising on consolidation.

Where a company H has several subsidiaries S_1, S_2, S_3 and so on, the technique for consolidation is exactly as described already. **Cancellation** is from the holding company, which has assets of investments in subsidiaries S_1, S_2, S_3, to each of the several subsidiaries.

The consolidated balance sheet will show:

(a)   A single figure for **minority interest**
(b)   Separate totals for **goodwill** arising

A single working should be used for each of the constituents of the consolidated balance sheet: one working for goodwill, one for minority interest, one for revenue reserves, and so on, but on the consolidated balance sheet itself the separate portions of goodwill arising must each be accounted for in compliance with FRS 10.

1.2 Sub-subsidiaries

FAST FORWARD

There may also be a figure for 'capital reserve arising on consolidation'. In cases where there are several subsidiary companies the technique is to open up a **single minority interest working and a single goodwill working.**

When dealing with **sub-subsidiaries**, you are often required to calculate effective interest.

A slightly different problem arises when there are sub-subsidiaries in the group, which is how should we **identify the minority interest** in the reserves of the group? Suppose H owns 80% of the equity of S, and that S in turn owns 60% of the equity of SS.

It would appear that in this situation:

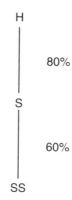

H
|
80%
|
S
|
60%
|
SS

(a) H owns 80% of 60% = 48% of SS.
(b) The minority interest in S owns 20% of 60% = 12% of SS.
(c) The minority interest in SS itself owns the remaining 40% of the SS equity.

SS is nevertheless a **sub-subsidiary** of H, because it is a subsidiary of S which in turn is a subsidiary of H. The chain of control thus makes SS a sub-subsidiary of H which owns only 48% of its equity.

The total minority in SS may be checked by considering a **dividend** of £100 paid by SS where S then distributes its share of this dividend in full to its own shareholders.

		£
S will receive	£60	
H will receive	80% × £60 =	48
Leaving for the total minority in SS		52
		100

1.3 Date of effective control

The **date of acquisition** is important when dealing with sub-subsidiaries. Remember that it is the post-acquisition reserves from a **group perspective** which are important.

The date the sub-subsidiary comes under the **control of the holding company** is one of the following.

(a) The date H acquired S if S already holds shares in SS
(b) If S acquires shares in SS later, then that later date

2 Consolidating sub-subsidiaries

The basic consolidation method is as follows.

(a) **Net assets**: show what the group controls.

(b) **Capital and reserves**: show who owns the net assets included in the top half of the balance sheet. Reserves, therefore, are based on **effective holdings**.

As indicated earlier, the major problem on consolidation is to identify the minority interest share of the reserves of S and (especially) SS.

2.1 Example: Consolidating sub-subsidiaries

The draft balance sheets of H Ltd, S Ltd and SS Ltd on 30 June 20X7 were as follows.

	H Ltd £	H Ltd £	S Ltd £	S Ltd £	SS Ltd £	SS Ltd £
Fixed assets						
Tangible assets		105,000		125,000		180,000
Investments, at cost						
80,000 shares in S Ltd		120,000		–		–
60,000 shares in SS Ltd		–		110,000		–
Current assets	80,000		70,000		60,000	
Creditors	30,000		35,000		25,000	
		50,000		35,000		35,000
		275,000		270,000		215,000
Capital and reserves						
Ordinary shares of £1 each		80,000		100,000		100,000
Reserves		195,000		170,000		115,000
		275,000		270,000		215,000

H Ltd acquired its shares in S Ltd when the reserves of S Ltd stood at £40,000; and

S Ltd acquired its shares in SS Ltd when the reserves of SS Ltd stood at £50,000.

For the moment, we will assume that both acquisitions occurred on the same date.

Required

Prepare the draft consolidated balance sheet of H Group.

Note. Goodwill should be capitalised, but amortisation can be ignored.

Solution

Having calculated the minority interest and the H group interest (see 1.2 above), the workings can be constructed. You should, however, note the following.

(a) **Minority interest working**: bring in the total minority interests in S Ltd's share capital and reserves (20%), and the total minority interests in SS Ltd's share capital and reserves (52%). Bring in the goodwill arising on S Ltd's acquisition of SS Ltd.

(b) **Goodwill working**: compare the costs of investments with the effective group interests acquired (80% of S Ltd and 60% of SS Ltd).

(c) **Reserves working**: bring in the share of S Ltd's and SS Ltd's post-acquisition reserves in the normal way.

1 *Minority interests*

	£	£
S Ltd		
Share capital (20% × £100,000)		20,000
Reserves (20% × £170,000)		34,000
Goodwill on acquisition of SS Ltd (20% × 20,000)		4,000
Investment in SS Ltd (20% × £110,000)		(22,000)
		36,000
SS Ltd		
Share capital (52% × £100,000)	52,000	
Reserves (52% × £115,000)	59,800	
		111,800
		147,800

Note. The rationale behind the treatment of goodwill is that on consolidation all assets are consolidated gross and minority interests shown separately. Goodwill is just another asset and should be treated in the same way.

2   *Goodwill*

	£	£	£
S Ltd			
Cost of investment			120,000
Share of net assets acquired as represented by			
Ordinary share capital		100,000	
Reserves		40,000	
		140,000	
Group share (80%)			112,000
Goodwill			8,000
SS Ltd			
Cost of investment		110,000	
Share of net assets acquired			
Ordinary share capital	100,000		
Reserves	50,000		
	150,000		
SS share (60%)		90,000	
Goodwill			20,000
Net goodwill			28,000

3   *Reserves*

	£
H Ltd	195,000
Share of S Ltd's post acquisition retained reserves	
£(170,000 − 40,000) × 80%	104,000
Share of SS Ltd's post acquisition retained reserves	
£(115,000 − 50,000) × 48%	31,200
	330,200

Note. This working could be presented as in earlier chapters.

H LIMITED
CONSOLIDATED BALANCE SHEET AT 30 JUNE 20X7

	£	£
Fixed assets		
Goodwill		28,000
Tangible assets		410,000
Current assets	210,000	
Creditors	90,000	
		120,000
		558,000
Capital and reserves		
Ordinary shares of £1 each fully paid		80,000
Reserves		330,200
		410,200
Minority interest		147,800
		558,000

2.2 Date of acquisition

Care must be taken when consolidating sub-subsidiaries, because (usually) either:

(a)   The holding company acquired the subsidiary **before** the subsidiary bought the sub-
      subsidiary

(b)   The holding company acquired the subsidiary **after** the subsidiary bought the sub-
      subsidiary

The rule to remember here, when considering pre– and post-acquisition profits, is that we are only interested in the consolidated results of the **holding company**. We will use the example above (using the single-stage method of consolidation) to demonstrate the required approach.

2.3 Example: Subsidiary acquired first

Using the figures in Paragraph 2.1, assume that:

(a)   H Ltd purchased its holding in S Ltd on 1 July 20X4
(b)   S Ltd purchased its holding in SS Ltd on 1 July 20X5

The same reserve figures applied on the date of acquisition.

Solution

The solution would be the same as that given above. Contrast this with the situation in the next example.

2.4 Example: Sub-subsidiary acquired first

Again using the figures in Paragraph 2.4, assume that:

(a)   S Ltd purchased its holding in SS Ltd on 1 July 20X4
(b)   H Ltd purchased its holding in S Ltd on 1 July 20X5

The reserve figures on the respective dates of acquisition are the same, but on the date H Ltd purchased its holding in S Ltd, the reserves of *SS Ltd* were £60,000.

Solution

The point here is that SS Ltd only became part of the H group on 1 July 20X5, *not* on 1 July 20X4. This means that only the reserves of SS Ltd arising *after* 1 July 20X5 can be included in the post-acquisition reserves of H Ltd group. Goodwill arising on the acquisition will be calculated by comparing the cost of the investment to the consolidated separable net assets of S (as represented by share capital and consolidated reserves, net of all goodwill).

H LIMITED
CONSOLIDATED BALANCE SHEET AS AT 30 JUNE 20X7

	£	£
Fixed assets		
Goodwill (W1)		19,200
Tangible		410,000
Current assets	210,000	
Creditors	90,000	
		120,000
		549,200

	£	£
Capital and reserves		
Ordinary shares £1 each		80,000
Reserves (W3)		325,400
Shareholders' funds		405,400
Minority interest (W2)		143,800
		549,200

Workings

		£	£
1	*Goodwill*		
	S Ltd		
	Cost of investment		120,000
	Share of net assets acquired		
	Ordinary share capital	100,000	
	Consolidated reserves:		
	S	40,000	
	SS (60 – 50) × 60%	6,000	
	Goodwill (see para 2.6)	(20,000)	
		126,000	
	80%		(100,800)
	Goodwill		19,200

Alternative working:

	£	£	£
S Ltd (as in Paragraph 2.5)			8,000
SS Ltd			
Cost of investment (80% × 110)		88,000	
Share of net assets acquired			
Ordinary share capital	100,000		
Reserves	60,000		
	160,000		
Group share (48%)		76,800	
			11,200
Goodwill			19,200

		£
2	*Minority interests*	
	As para 2.5	147,800
	Deduct 20% of goodwill on acquisition of SS	4,000
		143,800

		£
3	*Reserves*	
	H Ltd (as above)	195,000
	S Ltd (as above)	104,000
	SS Ltd (115 – 60) × 48%	26,400
		325,400

Question

The balance sheets of Antelope Ltd, Yak Ltd and Zebra Ltd at 31 March 20X4 are summarised as follows.

	Antelope Ltd £	Antelope Ltd £	Yak Ltd £	Yak Ltd £	Zebra Ltd £	Zebra Ltd £
Fixed assets						
Freehold property		100,000		100,000		
Plant and machinery		210,000		80,000		3,000
		310,000		180,000		3,000
Investments in subsidiaries						
Shares, at cost	80,000		2,200			–
Loan account	–		3,800			–
Current accounts	10,000		12,200			–
		90,000		18,200		3,000
Current assets						
Stocks	200,000		24,500		15,000	
Debtors	140,000		50,000		1,000	
Cash at bank	60,000		16,500		4,000	
	400,000		91,000		20,000	
Creditors						
Trade creditors	130,000		40,200		800	
Due to Antelope Ltd	–		12,800		600	
Due to Yak Ltd	–		–		12,600	
Taxation	40,000		7,000		–	
Unclaimed dividends	400		–		–	
Proposed dividends	50,000		–		–	
	220,400		60,000		14,000	
Net current assets		179,600		31,000		6,000
		579,600		229,200		9,000
Capital and reserves						
Ordinary share capital		200,000		100,000		10,000
Reserves		379,600		129,200		(1,000)
		579,600		229,200		9,000

Antelope Ltd acquired 75% of the shares of Yak Ltd in 20X1 when the credit balance on the reserves of that company was £40,000. No dividends have been paid since that date. Yak Ltd acquired 80% of the shares in Zebra Ltd in 20X3 when there was a debit balance on the reserves of that company of £3,000. Subsequently £500 was received by Zebra Ltd and credited to its reserves, representing the recovery of a bad debt written off before the acquisition of Zebra's shares by Yak Ltd. During the year to 31 March 20X4 Yak Ltd purchased stock from Antelope Ltd for £20,000 which included a profit mark-up of £4,000 for Antelope Ltd. At 31 March 20X4 one half of this amount was still held in the stocks of Yak Ltd. Group accounting policies are to make a full provision for unrealised inter-company profits, and to treat goodwill in accordance with FRS 10. Any dividends were proposed before the year end.

Prepare the draft consolidated balance sheet of Antelope Ltd at 31 March 20X4.

Answer

The loan account and current accounts of the three companies are self-cancelling assets and liabilities. The minority interests are as follows.

Direct minority interest in Yak Ltd		25%
Direct minority interest in Zebra Ltd	20%	
Indirect minority interest in Zebra Ltd (25% of 80%)	20%	
Total minority interest in Zebra Ltd		40%

Antelope Ltd

75%

Yak Ltd ——— Minority Interest (direct) 25%

80%

Zebra Ltd ——— Minority Interest (direct) 20%

The group therefore owns a 75% interest in Yak Ltd and a 60% interest in Zebra Ltd.

1 *Minority interests*

	£	£
Yak Ltd		
Share capital (25% × £100,000)		25,000
Reserves (25% × £129,200)		32,300
Negative goodwill on acquisition of Zebra (3,800 × 25%)		(950)
Investment in Zebra Ltd (25% × £2,200)		(550)
		55,800
Zebra Ltd		
Share capital (40% × £10,000)	4,000	
Reserves (40% × £(1,000))	(400)	
		3,600
		59,400

2 *Goodwill*

	£	£	£
Yak Ltd			
Cost of investment			80,000
Share of net assets acquired as represented by			
Share capital		100,000	
Reserves		40,000	
		140,000	
Group share (75%)			105,000
Negative goodwill c/f			(25,000)
Zebra Ltd			
Cost of investment		2,200	
Share of net assets acquired as represented by			
Share capital	10,000		
Reserves (£3,000) + £500	(2,500)		
	7,500		
Yak's share (80%)		6,000	
Negative goodwill			(3,800)
Total negative goodwill			(28,800)

3   *Reserves*

	Antelope	Yak	Zebra
	£	£	£
Per question	379,600	129,200	(1,000)
Unrealised profit on stock: 4,000 × 1/2	(2,000)		
Pre-acquisition		(40,000)	(−2,500)
		89,200	1,500
Share of Yak £89,200 × 75%	66,900		
Share of Zebra £1,500 × 60%	900		
	445,400		

ANTELOPE LIMITED
CONSOLIDATED BALANCE SHEET AS AT 31 MARCH 20X4

	£	£
Fixed assets		
Negative goodwill		(28,800)
Freehold property		200,000
Plant and machinery		293,000
		464,200
Current assets		
Stocks £(239,500 – 2,000)	237,500	
Debtors	191,000	
Cash and bank	80,500	
	509,000	
Creditors: amounts falling due within one year		
Trade creditors	171,000	
Taxation	47,000	
Unclaimed dividends	400	
Proposed dividends	50,000	
	268,400	
Net current assets		240,600
		704,800

ANTELOPE LIMITED
CONSOLIDATED BALANCE SHEET AS AT 31 MARCH 20X4

	£
Capital and reserves	
Ordinary share capital	200,000
Reserves	445,400
Shareholders' funds	645,400
Minority interests	59,400
	704,800

Attention!

For further practice on dealing with goodwill in subsidiaries, try Question 21, Armoury, in the Exam Question Bank.

2.5 Section summary

You should follow this **step-by-step approach** in all questions using the single-stage method. This applies to Section 3 below as well.

Step 1   Sketch the **group structure** and check it to the question

Step 2   **Add details** to the sketch of dates of acquisition, holdings acquired (percentage and nominal values) and cost

Step 3   **Minority interest working**: total MI in subsidiary plus total MI in sub-subsidiary

Step 4   **Goodwill working**: compare costs of investment with the **effective** group interests acquired. Check the question: how is goodwill to be treated? If the sub-subsidiary has already been acquired by the subsidiary, goodwill should be calculated by comparing the cost of the investments to the consolidated separable net assets of the subsidiary (net of all goodwill). If the sub-subsidiary is acquired post acquisition, include goodwill arising in the consolidated balance sheet.

Step 5   **Reserves working**: group share of subsidiary and sub-subsidiary post-acquisition reserves (effective holdings again)

Step 6   Prepare the **consolidated balance sheet** (and P&L account if required).

3 Direct holdings in sub-subsidiaries

Consider the following structure, sometimes called a **'D-shaped' group**.

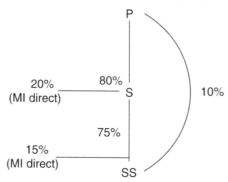

In practice several consolidations might be carried out, using procedures which are the same as in the **'two-stage' method** of consolidation for sub-subsidiaries:

(a)   S with SS
(b)   H with the S group
(c)   H with SS (for the direct holding of 10%)

In an examination however, the **single-stage method** is recommended as it will save you valuable time. In the structure above, there is:

(a)	A **direct** minority in S of		20%
(b)	A **direct** minority in SS of	15%	
(c)	An **indirect** minority in SS of 20% × 75% =	15%	
			30%

Once again, you could check a **dividend distribution** of £100 from SS.

	£
S will receive £75	
H will receive 80% of £75 =	60
H will receive 10% of £100 =	10
	70
Leaving for the total minority in SS	30

Having ascertained the structure and minority interests, proceed as for a typical sub-subsidiary situation by the single-stage method.

Question

'D'-shaped group

The draft balance sheets of Hulk Ltd, Molehill Ltd and Pimple Ltd as at 31 May 20X5 are as follows.

	Hulk Ltd £	Hulk Ltd £	Molehill Ltd £	Molehill Ltd £	Pimple Ltd £	Pimple Ltd £
Fixed assets						
Tangible assets		90,000		60,000		60,000
Investments in subsidiaries at cost						
Shares in Molehill Ltd	90,000		–		–	
Shares in Pimple Ltd	25,000		42,000		–	
		115,000		42,000		–
		205,000		102,000		60,000
Current assets	40,000		50,000		40,000	
Creditors due within one year						
Proposed dividends	30,000		20,000		10,000	
Other creditors	20,000		20,000		15,000	
	50,000		40,000		25,000	
Net current assets (liabilities)		(10,000)		10,000		15,000
		195,000		112,000		75,000
Creditors (falling due after one year)						
12% loan stock		–		10,000		–
		195,000		102,000		75,000
Capital and reserves						
Ordinary shares of £1, allotted and fully paid		100,000		50,000		50,000
Share premium account		50,000		20,000		–
Profit and loss reserves		45,000		32,000		25,000
		195,000		102,000		75,000

(a) Hulk Ltd acquired 60% of the shares in Molehill on 1 January 20X3 when the balance on that company's profit and loss reserves was £8,000 (credit) and there was no share premium account.

(b) Hulk acquired 20% of the shares of Pimple Ltd and Molehill acquired 60% of the shares of Pimple Ltd on 1 January 20X4 when that company's profit and loss reserves stood at £15,000.

(c) There has been no payment of dividends by either Molehill or Pimple since they became subsidiaries.

(d) The proposed dividends have not yet been recorded in the books of the shareholding companies as dividends receivable.

(e) Goodwill arising on consolidation is assumed to have an indefinite life and is therefore capitalised in the balance sheet.

Required

Prepare the consolidated balance sheet of Hulk Ltd as at 31 May 20X5 using the single-stage method.

Answer

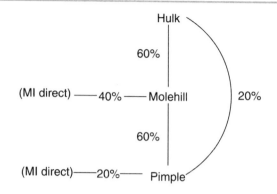

The direct minority interest in Molehill Ltd is		40%
The direct minority interest in Pimple Ltd is	20%	
The indirect minority interest in Pimple Ltd is (40% of 60%)	24%	
The total minority interest in Pimple Ltd is		44%

The group share of Molehill Ltd is 60% and of Pimple Ltd is (100 – 44)% = 56%

Dividends receivable

In Molehill Ltd's books:

DEBIT	Dividends receivable	£6,000	
CREDIT	Profit and loss reserves		£6,000

Being 60% of Pimple Ltd's proposed dividend

In Hulk Ltd's books:

DEBIT	Dividends receivable	£14,000	
CREDIT	Profit and loss reserves		£14,000

Being 20% of Pimple Ltd's proposed dividend plus 60% of Molehill Ltd's proposed dividend

1   *Minority interests*

	£	£
Molehill Ltd		
Share capital (40% × £50,000)		20,000
Share premium (40% × £20,000)		8,000
Reserves (40% × £(32,000 + 6,000))		15,200
Goodwill on acquisition of Pimple (40% × 3,000)		1,200
Investment in Pimple (40% × £42,000)		(16,800)
		27,600
Pimple Ltd		
Share capital (44% × £50,000)	22,000	
Reserves (44% × £25,000)	11,000	
		33,000
		60,600

2   *Goodwill*

	£	£	£
Molehill Ltd			
Cost of investment			90,000
Share of net assets acquired represented by			
Share capital		50,000	
Reserves		8,000	
		58,000	
Group share (60%)			34,800
Goodwill			55,200
Pimple Ltd			
Cost of direct holding		25,000	
Share of net assets acquired represented by			
Share capital	50,000		
Reserves	15,000		
	65,000		
Group share (direct interest – 20%)		13,000	
Goodwill			12,000
Cost of indirect holding		42,000	
Share of net assets acquired (60% × 65,000)		39,000	
			3,000
Total goodwill			70,200

3   *Reserves*

	Hulk	Molehill	Pimple
	£	£	£
Per question	45,000	32,000	25,000
Dividends receivable	14,000	6,000	–
Pre-acquisition		(8,000)	(15,000)
		30,000	10,000
Share of Molehill: £30,000 × 60%	18,000		
Share of Pimple: £10,000 × 56%	5,600		
	82,600		

4   *Share premium account*

	£
Hulk Ltd	50,000
Molehill Ltd: all post-acquisition (£20,000 × 60%)	12,000
	62,000

HULK LIMITED
CONSOLIDATED BALANCE SHEET AT 31 MAY 20X5

	£	£
Fixed assets		
Intangible asset: goodwill		70,200
Tangible assets		210,000
Current assets	130,000	
Creditors: amounts falling due within one year		
Minority proposed dividend	10,000	
Proposed dividend	30,000	
Other creditors	55,000	
	95,000	
Net current assets		35,000
Creditors: amounts falling due after more than one year		
12% loan stock		10,000
		305,200
Capital and reserves		
Ordinary shares of £1 allotted and fully paid		100,000
Share premium		62,000
Profit and loss reserves		82,600
Shareholders' funds		244,600
Minority interests		60,600
		305,200

Chapter Roundup

- When a holding company has **several subsidiaries**, the consolidated balance sheet shows a single figure for minority interests and for goodwill arising on consolidation.

- There may also be a figure for 'capital reserve arising on consolidation'. In cases where there are several subsidiary companies the technique is to open up a **single minority interest working and a single goodwill working.**

- When dealing with **sub-subsidiaries**, you are often required to calculate effective interest.

- The **date of acquisition** is important when dealing with sub-subsidiaries. Remember that it is the post-acquisition reserves from a **group perspective** which are important.

Quick Quiz

1   Anna plc owns 80% of Bella Ltd and 15% of Emma Ltd. Bella Ltd owns 80 % of Camilla Ltd and 40% of Emma Ltd. Camilla Ltd owns 60% of Dora Ltd. Which are the subsidiaries of Anna plc? Circle any that apply.

   A   Bella Ltd
   B   Camilla Ltd
   C   Dora Ltd
   D   Emma Ltd

2   The following diagram shows the structure of the Quince Group.

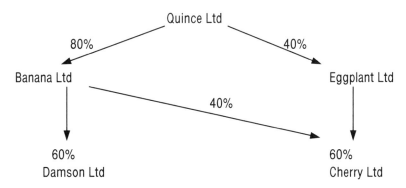

3   Which of these are the subsidiaries of Quince Ltd? Circle any that apply.

   A   Banana Ltd
   B   Cherry Ltd
   C   Damson Ltd
   D   Eggplant Ltd

   What is the basic consolidation method for sub-subsidiaries?

Answers to Quick Quiz

1   All of them. Simply consider which company controls another.

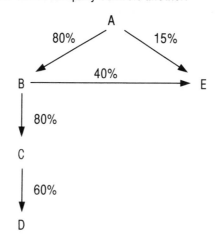

Anna controls Bella, it controls its 40% shareholdings in Emma, and 40 + 15% give control.

2   A and C. For the purposes of determining subsidiary status, shareholdings held by subsidiaries count in full, but shares held by associates do not count at all. Simply consider which company controls another. As Banana controls Damson, and as Quince controls Banana, it must control Damson. Quince does not control Eggplant.

3   (a)   Net assets: show what the group controls.

     (b)   Capital and reserves: show who owns the net assets included in the top half of the balance sheet. Reserves, therefore, are based on effective holdings.

Now try the questions below from the Exam Question Bank

Number	Level	Marks	Time
Q20	Introductory	–	–

Changes in group structures

Topic list	Syllabus reference
1 Piecemeal acquisitions	D3
2 Disposals	D3
3 Discontinued operations	C2, D2

Introduction

Complex consolidation issues are very likely to come up in this, the final stage of your studies on financial accounting. Your approach should be the same as for more simple consolidation questions: **methodical and logical**. If you understand the basic principles of consolidation, you should be able to tackle these complicated questions.

Study guide

		Intellectual level
C2	**Non-current assets**	
(b)	Apply and discuss the treatment of non-current assets held for sale	3
D2	**Continuing and discontinued interests**	
(a)	Prepare group financial statements where activities have been classified as discontinued or have been acquired or disposed in the period	3
(b)	Apply and discuss the treatment of a subsidiary which has been acquired exclusively with a view to subsequent disposal	3
D3	**Changes in group structure**	
(a)	Discuss the reasons behind a group reorganisation	3
(b)	Evaluate and assess the principal terms of a proposed group reorganisation	3

Exam guide

Although FRED 32 is only an exposure draft in the UK, you should know it in detail. The international equivalent, IFRS 5, is a full standard, and the two are generally tested at the same level.

> **FAST FORWARD**
>
> Transactions of the type described in this chapter can be very complicated and certainly look rather daunting. Remember and apply the **basic techniques** and you should find such questions easier than you expected.

1 Piecemeal acquisitions

> **FAST FORWARD**
>
> **Piecemeal acquisitions** can lead to a company becoming a fixed asset investment, an associate and then a subsidiary over time. Make sure you can deal with each of these situations.
>
> In piecemeal acquisitions, use the **rule-of-thumb** in Paragraph 1.2 below to decide whether the step-by-step method or the one-computation-at-the-date-of-control method is more appropriate.

A holding company may acquire a controlling interest in the shares of a subsidiary as a result of **several successive share purchases**, rather than by purchasing the shares all on the same day. For the purpose of consolidation, it is necessary to decide which reserves of the subsidiary are pre-acquisition profits; but since the acquisition has occurred in several stages, it is not immediately clear how to decide what they are.

If a controlling interest is achieved by means of a build-up of share acquisitions over a period of time, the present reserves may include elements which are **pre-acquisition** as regards some blocks of shares held, but **post-acquisition** as regards other blocks of shares.

There are two possible ways of dealing with the subsidiary in the accounts.

(a) Only take account of the subsidiary when **control** is achieved, in accordance with FRS 2.

(b) If the company has **already been equity accounted** for when it was an associate, then account for the **additional interest separately**.

Remember, whether the company is accounted for as an associate (equity accounted) does not depend just on the percentage of shares acquired but on whether the investor **actually exercises significant influence.** The significance of the approach taken lies in the different procedures adopted for consolidation when the partly-bought company eventually **becomes a subsidiary.** The exercise involves looking back at previous share purchases to decide on how to consolidate now that a subsidiary status (controlling interest) has been achieved.

1.1 Example: Piecemeal acquisition

Suppose that X Ltd bought 20,000 ordinary £1 shares in Y Ltd in 20X1 when the reserves of Y Ltd stood at £27,000 and a further 20,000 shares in 20X2 when the reserves of Y Ltd were £42,000. Finally, a purchase of 30,000 shares in 20X3 when the reserves of Y Ltd were £60,000 gave X Ltd a controlling interest over the 100,000 shares of Y Ltd. The cost of the shares purchased was £30,000 in 20X1, £34,000 in 20X2 and £56,000 for the final 30,000 shares in 20X3.

What are the pre-acquisition and post-acquisition profits of the group in Y Ltd, and what is the goodwill arising on consolidation at the date of the final acquisition in 20X3? Assume that no dividends were paid in these three years.

Solution: Y Ltd accounted for as an associate

Purchase	% of shares in Y Ltd bought	% of shares in Y Ltd now held
20X1	20%	20%
20X2	20%	40%
20X3	30%	70% (controlling interest)

X Ltd exercises significant influence over the financial and operating policies of Y Ltd.

If X Ltd accounted for Y Ltd as an associate, we would use the **step-by-step method.** This method calculates pre-acquisition profits by computing the proportion of reserves attaching to the shares at the time of **each individual purchase.**

		£
20X1	Pre-acquisition profits of 20,000 shares (20% of £27,000)	5,400
20X2	Pre-acquisition profits of next 20,000 shares (20% of £42,000)	8,400
20X3	Pre-acquisition profits of final 30,000 shares (30% of £60,000)	18,000
	Total pre-acquisition profits	31,800

Note that post-acquisition profits would be:

		£
(a)	on shares bought in 20X1:	
	20% of profits since 20X1 = 20% of £(60,000 – 27,000) =	6,600
(b)	on shares bought in 20X2:	
	20% of profits since 20X2 = 20% of £(60,000 – 42,000) =	3,600
	(since no dividends were paid out on profits in this time)	10,200

Reserve working: share of Y Ltd's post acquisition retained reserves = (£60,000 × 70%) – £31,800 = £10,200.

This step-by-step calculation is only required when the company (Y Ltd) becomes a subsidiary in 20X3 and subsequent years.

Goodwill arising on consolidation would be the excess of the cost of the shares bought over their called-up value, less pre-acquisition profits: £(120,000 – 70,000 – 31,800) = £18,200.

Solution: Y Ltd not accounted for as an associate

If X Ltd did not exercise a significant influence when it bought the shares of Y Ltd in 20X1 and 20X2, but only gained control when it made its final purchase in 20X3, the pre-acquisition profits would be calculated on the basis of reserves at the date of acquisition of control, ie in our example on the basis of reserves of £60,000 at the date of acquisition in 20X3.

Reserve working: share of Y Ltd's pre-acquisition retained reserves = £60,000 × 70% = £42,000.

Goodwill on consolidation would be the excess of the cost of shares over their called-up value, less pre-acquisition profits = £(120,000 – 70,000 – 42,000) = £8,000.

1.2 Suggested method

The decisive factor is whether or not the company has been equity accounted for when it was an associate. A rule-of-thumb approach to piecemeal acquisitions might be suggested as follows.

(a) Ignore share purchases which keep the buying company's share of equity **below 20%**: make no step-by-step method calculations before the bought company becomes an associated company. This is an rough and ready assumption that significant influence is not exercised on holdings of less than 20%.

(b) When the purchase of shares first takes a company's **holding above 20% (and up to 50%)**, treat all the shares purchased up to this date as a single block of purchases for the purpose of calculating pre-acquisition profits.

(c) For **future (significant) purchases** up to the time when control is eventually acquired, the step-by-step method should be applied.

Exam focus point

> This question may not arise: control may be achieved after the first purchase, with a further purchase afterwards.

Question   Piecemeal acquisition

A Ltd acquired shares in Z Ltd, which has issued and fully paid share capital of 100,000 £1 ordinary shares, on three separate dates.

Date	Number of shares bought in the purchase	Cost £	Reserves of Z Ltd at date of purchase £
1 February 20X0	10,000	16,000	40,000
1 November 20X0	25,000	42,000	60,000
1 April 20X1	20,000	40,000	80,000

Required

Calculate the pre-acquisition profits of the A group in Z Ltd when Z Ltd eventually became a subsidiary on 1 April 20X1.

Answer

Step	Date	% of shares bought	% of total holding	
1	1 February 20X0	10%	10%	Ignore
2	1 November 20X0	25%	35%	Z Ltd achieves associated company status
3	1 April 20X1	20%	55%	Z Ltd becomes a subsidiary

A step-by-step calculation of pre-acquisition profits, assuming significant influence is exercised, would regard the first step as the purchase of shares which made Z Ltd an associated company: step 2.

	£
Pre-acquisition profits	
35% of reserves at 1 November 20X0 (35% of £60,000)	21,000
Plus 20% of reserves at 1 April 20X1 (20% of £80,000)	16,000
Total pre-acquisition profits	37,000
The minority interest at 1 April 20X1 is 45% of £80,000 =	£36,000
Post-acquisition profits are therefore £(80,000 – 37,000 – 36,000) =	£7,000

1.3 Piecemeal acquisition of a sub-subsidiary

Care may be needed in deciding the group's share of **pre-acquisition profits** when shares in a sub-subsidiary are acquired on several dates.

1.4 Example 1: Piecemeal acquisition of a sub-subsidiary

Suppose H Ltd buys 60% of the shares of S Ltd on 1 April 20X3 and 20% of the shares of SS Ltd on 1 October 20X3. S Ltd bought 70% of the shares of SS Ltd on 1 January 20X3.

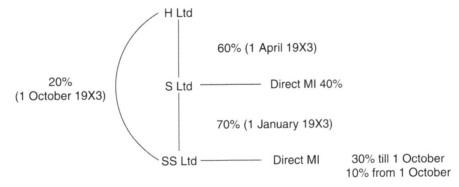

Solution

Pre-acquisition profits of H Ltd in SS Ltd would be calculated as follows, by the single-stage method of consolidation:

(a)   60% × 70% = 42% of the reserves of SS Ltd at 1 April 20X3 (when the indirect minority is 40% × 70% = 28% and the total minority interest is 58%); *plus*

(b)   20% of the reserves of SS Ltd at 1 October 20X3 when the additional shares are bought.

1.5 Example 2: Piecemeal acquisition of a sub-subsidiary

Suppose instead that H Ltd buys 80% of the shares of S Ltd on 1 April 20X4 and 30% of the shares of SS Ltd on 1 November 20X4. S Ltd bought 40% of the shares of SS Ltd on 1 January 20X4.

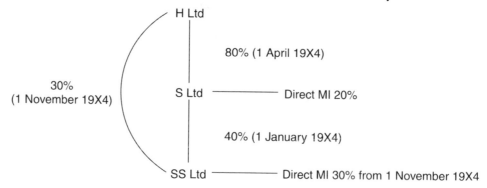

Solution

In this example, SS Ltd does not come under the control of the group until 1 November 20X4 and SS Ltd is unlikely to have been equity accounted (since the original shares were bought by S Ltd before it became a subsidiary of H Ltd). The most appropriate assumption would be to calculate the pre-acquisition reserves in SS Ltd on the basis of reserves at the date of acquiring control, 1 November 20X4, so that the pre-acquisition profits in SS Ltd would be 62% of the reserves at that date.

(The indirect minority interest in SS Ltd is 20% of 40% = 8%. Therefore, the total minority interest is 38% and the group interest is 62%.)

Question	Piecemeal acquisition of a sub-subsidiary

Juniper plc made the following share purchases in gaining control of Berry plc.

Date	Voting rights and shares acquired
1.4.X2	20%
1.4.X3	25%
1.4.X4	10%

The reserves of Berry plc were as follows.

Date	Reserves plc £'000
31.3.X2	300
31.3.X3	1,200
31.3.X4	1,500
31.3.X5	1,800

Berry plc has paid no dividends since 20X2.

Required

(a)   Calculate the post-acquisition reserves for the consolidated accounts as at 31 March 20X5.
(b)   Calculate the pre-acquisition reserves.
(c)   Calculate the minority interest.

Answer

Year ended	% of shares held	Year-end reserves £'000	Post-acquisition £'000	
31.3.X2	–	300	–	
31.3.X3	20%	1,200	180	(20% × 900)
31.3.X3	45%	1,500	135	(45% × 300)
31.3.X5	55%	1,800	165	(55% × 300)
			480	

	£'000
Minority interest 45% × 1,800	810
Post-acquisition reserves, as above	480
Remainder, being pre-acquisition reserves	510
	1,800

Check

Year ended	Year-end reserves £'000	Increase in reserves £'000	Pre-acquisition	Pre-acquisition reserves £'000
31.3.X2	300		55%	165
31.3.X3	1,200	900	35% (55% – 20%)	315
31.3.X4	1,500	300	10% (55% – 45%)	30
Pre-acquisition reserves, as above				510

Note. This 'piecemeal acquisition' method is suitable only where the subsidiary has previously been equity accounted for as an associate.

1.6 Section summary

Where there is a build up of share acquisitions over time:

- What are the **pre-acquisition** profits?
- If the company has been equity accounted for when it was an associate use the **step-by-step method**.
- If it is not, use reserves at the **date control is achieved.**
- Use the same principles for piecemeal acquisitions of **sub-subsidiaries**.

2 Disposals

FAST FORWARD

Disposals can drop a subsidiary holding to associate status, fixed asset investment status and to zero, or a the parent might still retain a subsidiary undertaking with a reduced holding. Once again, you should be able to deal with all these situations. Remember particularly how to deal with **goodwill**.

A holding company may dispose of a subsidiary in total, or reduce the holding to the level of an associate or an investment.

2.1 Effective date of disposal

FRS 2 defines the effective date of disposal in terms of **when control passes**: 'the date for accounting for an undertaking ceasing to be a subsidiary undertaking is the date on which its former parent undertaking relinquishes its control over that undertaking'. **FRS 3** requires that the results of discontinued operations should be shown separately in the P&L account in the year of disposal (see Chapter 14). **FRS 2** states that the consolidated P&L account should include the results of a subsidiary undertaking up to the date of its disposal. We are not concerned with FRS 3 disclosure in this section, only the FRS 2 calculations.

2.2 Goodwill

When a subsidiary is disposed of, the group needs to deal with any goodwill (positive or negative) which arose when the subsidiary was purchased. If the goodwill was **written off to reserves**, it could by-pass the P&L account, thus causing a misstatement of the profit or loss on disposal.

2.3 Disposals and partial disposals

When only part of an investment is sold, but an **associate or subsidiary status** is retained, then it is necessary to decide how to account for the disposal.

2.4 Disposal: subsidiary, status retained

If the holding is still a subsidiary then it must still be **consolidated line by line**. The consolidated accounts are only adjusted in reserves and in the minority interest. A comparison of the sale proceeds and the consolidated net asset value attributable to the shares sold at the date of disposal will give the profit or loss on disposal.

2.5 Example: Partial disposals

Chalk plc bought 100% of the voting share capital of Cheese plc on 1 January 20X2 for £160,000. Cheese plc earned and retained £240,000 from that date until 31 December 20X7. At that date the balance sheets of the company and the group were as follows.

	Chalk plc £'000	Cheese plc £'000	Consolidated £'000
Investment in Cheese	160	–	–
Other net assets	800	400	1,200
	960	400	1,200
Share capital	400	160	400
Reserves	560	240	800
	960	400	1,200

On 1 January 20X8 Chalk plc sold 40% of its shareholding in Cheese plc for £280,000. The profit on disposal (ignoring tax) is calculated as follows.

	Holding company £'000	Group £'000
Sale proceeds	280	280
40% of investment/net assets	64	160
Gain on sale	216	120

Solution: subsidiary status

The balance sheets immediately after the sale will appear as follows.

	Chalk plc £'000	Cheese plc £'000	Consolidated £'000
Investment in Cheese	96	–	–
Other net assets	1,080	400	1,480
	1,176	400	1,480
Minority interest			(160)
			1,320

	Chalk plc £'000	Cheese plc £'000	Consolidated £'000
Share capital	400	160	400
Reserves	776	240	920
	1,176	400	1,320

2.6 Disposal: subsidiary to associate status

The only difference when a subsidiary becomes an associate is that the balance sheet only carries the underlying asset on **one line**. Otherwise, the same principles apply.

Solution: associate status

Using the above example, assume that Chalk plc sold 60% of its holding in Cheese plc for £440,000. The gain or loss on disposal would be calculated as follows.

	Holding company £'000	Group £'000
Sale proceeds	440	440
60% of investment/net assets	96	240
Profit on sale	344	200

The balance sheets would now appear as follows.

	Chalk plc £'000	Cheese plc £'000	Consolidated £'000
Investment in Cheese	64	–	160
Other net assets	1,240	400	1,240
	1,304	400	1,400
Share capital	400	160	400
Reserves	904	240	1,000
	1,304	400	1,400

2.7 Disposal: subsidiary to investment status

In these circumstances dividend income only is shown in the P&L account after the date of disposal. The investment should be left in the balance sheet at the **equity valuation at the date of disposal**. Consider whether any write down is required.

2.8 Summary of accounting treatment

Calculate the gain or loss on disposal.

(a) **In holding company**

	£
Sale proceeds	X
Less cost of investment	X
Profit/(loss): (taxable)	X/(X)

(b) **In group accounts**

	£	£
Sale proceeds		X
Less: net assets now disposed of	X	
goodwill not yet w/off through P & L a/c	X	
		X
Profit/(loss)		X/(X)
Add goodwill previously written off through P & L a/c		X
		X

For a **full disposal**, apply the following treatment.

(a)   **P&L account**

(i)   Consolidate results to the date of disposal.

(ii)   Show the group gain or loss as an exceptional item after operating profit and before interest.

(b)   **Balance sheet**

There will be no minority interest and no consolidation as there is no subsidiary at the date the balance sheet is being prepared.

For **partial disposals**, use the following treatments.

(a)   **Subsidiary to subsidiary**

(i)   The **minority interest in the P&L account** will be based on percentage before and after disposal, ie time apportion.

(ii)   The **minority interest in the balance sheet** is based on the year end percentage.

(b)   **Subsidiary to associate**

(i)   **P&L account**

(1)   Treat the undertaking as a subsidiary up to the date of disposal, ie consolidate for the correct number of months and show the minority interest in that amount.

(2)   Treat as an associate thereafter.

(ii)   **Balance sheet**: use an equity valuation based on the year end holding.

(c)   **Subsidiary to trade investment**

(i)   P&L account

(1)   Treat the undertaking as a subsidiary up to the date of disposal.
(2)   Show dividend income only thereafter.

(ii)   **Balance sheet**: leave the investment valued at its equity valuation at the date of disposal but consider whether any write-down is required.

The following comprehensive exercise should help you get to grips with disposal problems. Try to complete the whole exercise without looking at the solution, and then check your answer very carefully. Give yourself at least an hour.

Exam focus point

Questions are likely to involve part-disposals leaving investments with both subsidiary and associate status.

 Question

Disposal

Smith Ltd bought 80% of the share capital of Jones Ltd for £324,000 a number of years ago. At that date Jones Ltd's P&L account balance stood at £180,000. The balance sheets at 30 September 20X8 and the summarised P&L accounts to that date are given below.

	Smith Ltd £'000	Jones Ltd £'000
Fixed assets	360	270
Investment in Jones Ltd	324	–
Net current assets	270	270
	954	540

	Smith Ltd £'000	Jones Ltd £'000
Share capital and reserves		
£1 ordinary shares	540	180
Profit and loss account	414	360
	954	540
Profit before tax	153	126
Tax	45	36
Retained profit	108	90
Retained profit b/f	306	270
Retained profit c/f	414	360

No entries have been made in the accounts for any of the following transactions.

Assume that profits accrue evenly throughout the year and that any goodwill has been amortised through the profit and loss account.

Ignore taxation.

Required

Prepare the consolidated balance sheet and P&L account at 30 September 20X8 in each of the following circumstances.

(a) Smith Ltd sells its entire holding in Jones Ltd for £650,000 on 30 September 20X8.

(b) Smith Ltd sells its entire holding in Jones Ltd for £650,000 on 30 June 20X8.

(c) Smith Ltd sells one quarter of its holding in Jones Ltd for £160,000 on 30 June 20X8.

(d) Smith Ltd sells one half of its holding in Jones Ltd for £340,000 on 30 June 20X8, and the remaining holding is to be dealt with:

    (i) As an associate
    (ii) As a trade investment

Answer

(a) *Complete disposal at year end*

CONSOLIDATED BALANCE SHEET
AS AT 30 SEPTEMBER 20X8

	£'000
Fixed assets	360
Net current assets (270 + 650)	920
	1,280
Share capital and reserves	
£1 ordinary shares	540
Profit and loss account (W3)	740
	1,280

CONSOLIDATED PROFIT AND LOSS ACCOUNT
FOR THE YEAR ENDED 30 SEPTEMBER 20X8

	£'000
Profit before tax (153 + 126)	279
Exceptional item (W1)	218
Tax (45 + 36)	81
	416
Minority interest (20% × 90)	18
Profit attributable to members of Smith Ltd	398
Retained profit brought forward	342
Retained profit carried forward (W3)	740

Workings

1   *Group profit on disposal*

	£'000
Sales proceeds	650
Less net assets of Jones now sold (540 × 80%)	432
	218

	£'000
Note: goodwill	
Cost	324
Acquired 80% × (180 + 180)	288
	36

2   *Retained profit brought forward*

	£'000
Smith	306
Jones: 80% × (270 − 180)	72
Goodwill fully amortised (W1)	(36)
	342

3   *Retained profit carried forward*

	£'000
Smith	414
Profit on disposal (W1)	326
	740

(b)   *Complete disposal mid-year*

CONSOLIDATED BALANCE SHEET
AS AT 30 SEPTEMBER 20X8

	£'000
Fixed assets	360
Net current assets (270 + 650)	920
	1,280
Share capital and reserves	
£1 ordinary shares	540
Profit and loss account (W3)	740
	1,280

CONSOLIDATED PROFIT AND LOSS ACCOUNT
FOR THE YEAR ENDED 31 SEPTEMBER 20X8

	£'000
Profit before tax (153 + (9/12 × 126))	247.5
Exceptional item (W1)	236.0
Tax (45 + (36 × 9/12))	72.0
Profit after tax	411.5
Minority interest	
(20% × 90 × 9/12)	13.5
Profit attributable to members of Smith Ltd	398.0
Retained profit brought forward (W2)	342.0
Retained profit carried forward (W3)	740.0

Workings

1   *Group profit on disposal*

	£'000
Sale proceeds	650
Less net assets of Jones now sold	
$((540 - 90) + (9/12 \times 90)) \times 80\%$	414
	236

2   *Retained profit brought forward*

	£'000
Smith	306
Jones: $80\% \times (270 - 180)$	72
Goodwill fully amortised	(36)
	342

3   *Retained profit carried forward*

	£'000
Smith	414
Profit on disposal (W1)	326
	740

(c)   *Partial disposal: subsidiary to subsidiary*

CONSOLIDATED BALANCE SHEET AS AT 30 SEPTEMBER 20X8

	£'000
Fixed assets (360 + 270)	630
Net current assets (270 + 160 + 270)	700
	1,330
Share capital and reserves	
£1 ordinary shares	540
Profit and loss account (W3)	574
	1,114
Minority interest (40% × 540)	216
	1,330

CONSOLIDATED PROFIT AND LOSS ACCOUNT
FOR THE YEAR ENDED 30 SEPTEMBER 20X8

	£'000	£'000
Profit before tax (153 +126)		279.0
Exceptional item (W1)		56.5
Tax (45 + 36)		81.0
Profit after tax		254.5
Minority interest		
20% × 90 × 9/12	13.5	
40% × 90 × 3/12	9.0	
		22.5
Profit attributable to members of Smith Ltd		232.0
Retained profit brought forward (W2)		342.0
Retained profit carried forward (W3)		574.0

Workings

1   *Group profit on disposal*

	£'000
Sale proceeds	160.0
Less net assets of Jones now sold	
20% × ((540 − 90) + (9/12 × 90))	103.5
	56.5

2   *Retained profit brought forward*

	£'000
Smith	306
Jones: 80% × (270 − 180)	72
Goodwill fully amortised	(36)
	342

3   *Retained profit carried forward*

	£'000
Smith	414
Profit on disposal (W1)	79
Jones 60% × (360 − 180)	108
Goodwill fully amortised	(27)
	574

(d)   (i)   *Partial disposal: subsidiary to associate*

CONSOLIDATED BALANCE SHEET AS AT 30 SEPTEMBER 20X8

	£'000
Fixed assets	360
Investment in associated undertaking (40% × 540)	216
Net current assets (270 + 340)	610
	1,186
Share capital and reserves	
£1 ordinary shares	540
Profit and loss account (W3)	646
	1,186

CONSOLIDATED PROFIT AND LOSS ACCOUNT
FOR THE YEAR ENDED 30 SEPTEMBER 20X8

	£'000
Profit before tax*	
(153 + (9/12 × 126)) + (3/12 × 126 × 40%)	260.1
Exceptional item (W1)	133.0
Tax (45+ (9/12 × 36)) + (3/12 × 36 × 40%)	75.6
Profit after tax	317.5
Minority interest (20% × 90 × 9/12)	13.5
Profit attributable to members of Smith Ltd	304.0
Retained profit brought forward (W2)	342.0
Retained profit carried forward (W3)	646.0

*Note. Per FRS 9 *Associates and joint ventures* disclosure should be made of group's share of associate's operating profit. However, PBT is used here for the sake of simplicity.

Workings

1   *Group profit on disposal*

		£'000
Sale proceeds		340
Less: net assets of Jones now sold		
40% × ((540 − 90) + ((9/12 × 90))		207
		133

2   *Retained profit brought forward*

	£'000
Smith	306
Jones 80% × (270 − 180)	72
Goodwill fully amortised	(36)
	342

3   *Retained profit carried forward*

	£'000
Smith	414
Profit on disposal (W1)	178
Jones 40% × (360 − 180)	72
Goodwill fully amortised	(18)
	646

(ii)   Partial disposal: subsidiary to trade investment

CONSOLIDATED BALANCE SHEET
AS AT 30 SEPTEMBER 20X8

	£'000
Fixed assets	360
Investment (40% × (180 + 270 + ((9/12 × 90)))	207
Net current assets	610
	1,177
Share capital and reserves	
£1 ordinary shares	540
Profit and loss account	637
	1,177

CONSOLIDATED PROFIT AND LOSS ACCOUNT
FOR THE YEAR ENDED 30 SEPTEMBER 20X8

	£'000
Profit before tax (153 + (9/12 × 126))	247.5
Exceptional item (See (d)(i) above)	133.0
Tax (45 + (9/12 × 36))	72.0
Profit after tax	308.5
Minority interest	13.5
Profit attributable to members of Smith Ltd	295.0
Retained profit brought forward	342.0
Retained profit carried forward (W)	637.0

Working

Retained profit carried forward

	£'000
Smith	414
Profit on disposal	178
Jones 40% × (270 + (9/12 × 90) − 180)	63
Goodwill fully amortised	(18)
	637

2.9 Dividends

The retained reserves/net assets at the date of disposal of the subsidiary should be calculated deducting only those dividends to which the **holding company is entitled**, in other words dividends paid up to the date of disposal and dividends proposed if the shares are sold *ex-dividend*.

At the date of disposal this would be as follows.

	£
Retained profits brought forward	X
Profits after tax and extraordinary items to date of disposal	X
Dividends paid/proposed at date of disposal	(X)
	X

2.10 Section summary

Disposals are likely to occur frequently in Paper P2 consolidation questions.

- The effective date of disposal is when **control passes**.

- Treatment of **goodwill** is according to FRS 2.

- Disposals may be **full** or **partial**, to subsidiary, associate or investment status.

- **Gain or loss** on disposal is calculated for the holding company and the group.

- **FRS 3** disclosure requirements are important.

3 Discontinued operations

3.1 Background

FRED 32 *Disposal of non-current assets* and *presentation of discontinued* operations was published in July 2003. It was the result of a short-term convergence project with the US Financial Accounting Standards Board (FASB). In due course as part of its programme to converge UK standards with IFRSs, the ASB proposes to issue a UK standard based on this exposure draft, which would replace FRS 3 and introduce new requirements for non-current assets held for disposal.

FRED 32 requires assets and groups of assets that are 'held for sale' to be **presented separately** on the face of the balance sheet and the results of discontinued operations to be presented separately in the income statement. This is required so that users of financial statements will be better able to make **projections** about the financial position, profits and cash flows of the entity.

Key term

> **Disposal group**: a group of assets to be disposed of, by sale or otherwise, together as a group in a single transaction, and liabilities directly associated with those assets that will be transferred in the transaction. (In practice a disposal group could be a subsidiary, a cash-generating unit or a single operation within an entity.)   (*FRED 32*)

FRED 32 does not apply to certain assets covered by other accounting standards:

(a)   Goodwill
(b)   Deferred tax assets
(c)   Financial assets
(d)   Assets arising from employee benefits
(e)   Financial assets arising under leases

3.2 Classification of assets held for sale

FAST FORWARD

> **FRED 32** requires assets **'held for sale'** to be **presented separately** on the face of the balance sheet.

A non-current asset (or disposal group) should be classified as **held for sale** if its carrying amount will be recovered **principally through a sale transaction** rather than **through continuing use**. A number of detailed criteria must be met:

(a)   The asset must be **available for immediate sale** in its present condition.

(b)   Its sale must be **highly probable** (ie significantly more likely than not).

For the sale to be highly probable, the following must apply.

(a)   Management must be **committed** to a plan to sell the asset.

(b)   The asset should be available for immediate sale in its present condition.

(c)   There must be an active programme to **locate a buyer.**

(d)   The asset must be marketed for sale at a **price that is reasonable** in relation to its current fair value.

(e)   The sale should be highly probable and should be expected to take place **within one year** from the date of classification.

(f)   It is unlikely that significant changes to the plan will be made or that the plan will be withdrawn.

An asset (or disposal group) can still be classified as held for sale, even if the sale has not actually taken place within one year. However, the delay must have been **caused by events or circumstances beyond the entity's control** and there must be sufficient evidence that the entity is still committed to sell the asset or disposal group. Otherwise the entity must cease to classify the asset as held for sale.

If an entity acquires a disposal group (eg a subsidiary) exclusively with a view to its subsequent disposal it can classify the asset as held for sale only if the sale is expected to take place within one year and it is highly probable that all the other criteria will be met within a short time (normally three months).

An asset that is to be **abandoned** should not be classified as held for sale. This is because its carrying amount will be recovered principally through continuing use. However, a disposal group to be abandoned may meet the definition of a discontinued operation and therefore separate disclosure may be required (see below).

Question

Held for sale?

On 1 December 20X3, a company became committed to a plan to sell a manufacturing facility and has already found a potential buyer. The company does not intend to discontinue the operations currently carried out in the facility. At 31 December 20X3 there is a backlog of uncompleted customer orders. The subsidiary will not be able to transfer the facility to the buyer until after it ceases to operate the facility and has eliminated the backlog of uncompleted customer orders. This is not expected to occur until spring 20X4.

Required

Can the manufacturing facility be classified as 'held for sale' at 31 December 20X3?

Answer

The facility will not be transferred until the backlog of orders is completed; this demonstrates that the facility is not available for immediate sale in its present condition. The facility cannot be classified as 'held for sale' at 31 December 20X3. It must be treated in the same way as other items of property, plant and equipment: it should continue to be depreciated and should not be separately disclosed.

3.3 Measurement of assets held for sale

Key terms

> **Fair value:** the amount for which an asset could be exchanged, or a liability settled, between knowledgeable, willing parties in an arm's length transaction.
>
> **Costs to sell:** the incremental costs directly attributable to the disposal of an asset (or disposal group), excluding finance costs and income tax expense.
>
> **Recoverable amount:** the higher of an asset's fair value less costs to sell and its value in use.
>
> **Value in use:** the present value of estimated future cash flows expected to arise from the continuing use of an asset and from its disposal at the end of its useful life.

A non-current asset (or disposal group) that is held for sale should be measured at the **lower of** its **carrying amount** and **fair value less costs to sell**. Fair value less costs to sell is equivalent to net realisable value.

An impairment loss should be recognised where fair value less costs to sell is lower than carrying amount. Note that this is an exception to the normal rule. FRS 11 *Impairment of fixed assets and goodwill* requires an entity to recognise an impairment loss only where an asset's recoverable amount is lower than its carrying value. Recoverable amount is defined as the higher of net realisable value and value in use. FRS 11 does not apply to assets held for sale.

A gain must be recognised for any subsequent increase in fair value less costs to sell, but not in excess of the cumulative impairment loss that has been recognised under this FRS or FRS 11.

Non-current assets held for sale **should not be depreciated**, even if they are still being used by the entity.

A non-current asset (or disposal group) that is **no longer classified as held for sale** (for example, because the sale has not taken place within one year) is measured at the **lower of**:

(a)   Its **carrying amount** before it was classified as held for sale, adjusted for any depreciation that would have been charged had the asset not been held for sale

(b)   Its **recoverable amount** at the date of the decision not to sell

3.4 Presenting discontinued operations

FAST FORWARD

> The results of **discontinued operations** should be **presented separately** in the income statement.

Key terms

> **Discontinued operation:** a component of an entity that has either been disposed of, or is classified as held for sale, and:
>
> (a)   The operations and cash flows of that component have been (or will be) eliminated from the ongoing operations of the entity as a result of its disposal
>
> (b)   The entity will have no significant continuing involvement in that component after its disposal
>
> **Component of an entity:** operations and cash flows that can be clearly distinguished, operationally and for financial reporting purposes, from the rest of the entity.   *(FRED 32)*

An entity should **present and disclose information** that enables users of the financial statements to evaluate the financial effects of **discontinued operations** and disposals of non-current assets or disposal groups.

An entity should also disclose for all periods presented:

(a)   The revenue, expenses and pre-tax profit or loss of discontinued operations

(b)   The related income tax expense

(c)   The gain or loss recognised on the measurement to fair value less costs to sell or on the disposal of the assets or the discontinued operation

(d)   The related income tax expense

This may be presented either on the face of the income statement or in the notes. If it is presented on the face of the income statement it should be presented in a section identified as relating to discontinued operations, ie separately from continuing operations. This analysis is not required where the discontinued operation is a newly acquired subsidiary that has been classified as held for sale.

An entity should disclose the **net cash flows** attributable to the operating, investing and financing activities of discontinued operations. These disclosures may be presented either on the face of the cash flow statement or in the notes.

Gains and losses on the remeasurement of a non-current asset or disposal group that is not a component of an entity should be included in profit or loss from continuing operations.

Illustration

The following illustration is taken from the implementation guidance to IFRS 5, the International Standard based on an equivalent exposure draft. Profit for the period from discontinued operations would be analysed in the notes.

XYZ GROUP
INCOME STATEMENT
FOR THE YEAR ENDED 31 DECEMBER 20X2

	20X2 $'000	20X1 $'000
Continuing operations		
Revenue	X	X
Cost of sales	(X)	(X)
Gross profit	X	X
Other income	X	X
Distribution costs	(X)	(X)
Administrative expenses	(X)	(X)
Other expenses	(X)	(X)
Finance costs	(X)	(X)

	20X2	20X1
	$'000	$'000
Share of profit of associates	X	X
Profit before tax	X	X
Income tax expense	(X)	(X)
Profit for the period from continuing operations	X	X
Discontinued operations		
Profit for the period from discontinued operations	X	X
Profit for the period	X	X
Attributable to:		
Equity holders of the parent	X	X
Minority interest	X	X
	X	X

An alternative to this presentation would be to analyse the profit from discontinued operations in a separate column on the face of the income statement.

Question

On 20 October 20X3 the directors of a parent company made a public announcement of plans to close a steel works. The closure means that the group will no longer carry out this type of operation, which until recently has represented about 10% of its total turnover. The works will be gradually shut down over a period of several months, with complete closure expected in July 20X4. At 31 December output had been significantly reduced and some redundancies had already taken place. The cash flows, revenues and expenses relating to the steel works can be clearly distinguished from those of the subsidiary's other operations.

Required

How should the closure be treated in the financial statements for the year ended 31 December 20X3?

Answer

Because the steel works is being closed, rather than sold, it cannot be classified as 'held for sale'. In addition, the steel works is not a discontinued operation. Although at 31 December 20X3 the group was firmly committed to the closure, this has not yet taken place and therefore the steel works must be included in continuing operations. Information about the planned closure could be disclosed in the notes to the financial statements.

3.5 Presentation of a non-current asset or disposal group classified as held for sale

Non-current assets and disposal groups classified as held for sale should be **presented separately** from other assets in the balance sheet. The liabilities of a disposal group should be presented separately from other liabilities in the balance sheet.

(a)   Assets and liabilities held for sale **should not be offset**.

(b)   The **major classes** of assets and liabilities held for sale should be **separately disclosed** either on the face of the balance sheet or in the notes.

3.6 Additional disclosures

In the period in which a non-current asset (or disposal group) has been either classified as held for sale or sold the following should be disclosed.

(a) A description of the **facts and circumstances** of the disposal and the expected manner and timing of the disposal

(b) Any **gain or loss** recognised when the item was classified as held for sale

(c) If applicable, the **segment** in which the non-current asset (or disposal group) is presented in accordance with SSAP 25 *Segment reporting.*

Where an asset previously classified as held for sale is **no longer held for sale**, the entity should disclose a description of the facts and circumstances leading to the decision and its effect on results.

Chapter Roundup

- Transactions of the type described in this chapter can be very complicated and certainly look rather daunting. Remember and apply the **basic techniques** and you should find such questions easier than you expected.

- **Piecemeal acquisitions** can lead to a company becoming a fixed asset investment, an associate and then a subsidiary over time. Make sure you can deal with each of these situations.

- In piecemeal acquisitions, use the **rule-of-thumb** in Paragraph 1.8 to decide whether the step-by-step method or the one-computation-at-the-date-of-control method is more appropriate.

- **Disposals** can drop a subsidiary holding to associate status, fixed asset investment status and to zero, or a the parent might still retain a subsidiary undertaking with a reduced holding. Once again, you should be able to deal with all these situations. Remember particularly how to deal with **goodwill**.

- **FRED 32** requires assets **'held for sale'** to be **presented separately** on the face of the balance sheet.

- The results of **discontinued operations** should be **presented separately** in the income statement.

Quick Quiz

1   What is the general rule in determining pre– and post-acquisition reserves in a piecemeal acquisition?

2   When a subsidiary is disposed of, what is the required treatment of any goodwill which arose when the subsidiary was purchased?

3   Corrie Ltd acquired 70% of the 100,000 £1 ordinary shares of Brookie Ltd on 1 January 20X7 for £115,000. It sold its entire holding on 30 June 20X9 for £150,000. At acquisition Brookie Ltd had reserves of £44,000. By 1 January 20X9 the reserves had mounted to £72,000. Profit for the year ended 31 December 20X9 was £20,000, after paying a final dividend in November 20X9 of £5,000.

     What is the reported exceptional item in the individual company profit and loss account?

4   Muggins Ltd had a 40% stake in Gumm Ltd which it has acquired 2 years ago for £108,000. Goodwill on acquisition was to be capitalised and amortised over five years.

     The whole shareholding was sold on 31 December 20X9 for £150,000. Balance sheets were as follows

	31.12.20X7	31.12.20X9
	£'000	£'000
£1 ordinary shares	100	100
Share premium account	10	10
Revaluation reserve	60	90
Profit and loss account	50	120
	220	320

     What is the reported consolidated profit on disposal?

5   Complete the 'after' diagrams in the following cases

     New top holding company

     Subsidiary moved up

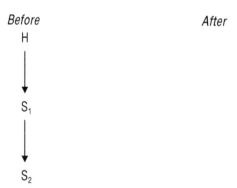

6   Why would a subsidiary be moved up?

7   Why would a subsidiary be moved down?

8   When can a non-current asset be classified as held for sale?

9   How should an asset held for sale be measured?

10   How does FRED 32 define a discontinued operation?

Answers to Quick Quiz

1 See Paragraph 1.2.

2 Any goodwill not yet written off to the profit and loss account must be deducted from the gain on disposal in the group accounts.

3 The individual company gain is simply the proceeds less the cost.

This gain will be subject to tax at the prevailing CT rate, but the tax charge is added to 'Taxation' in the profit and loss account and does not affect the reported exceptional item.

No details of goodwill policy are given. If you assume goodwill is capitalised and not amortised, the group gain would be £6,650.

		£
ie	Proceeds	150,000
	Less NA disposed 70% [100 + 72 + ½ × (25)]	(129,150)
	Less goodwill [115 – 70% (100 + 44)]	(14,200)
		6,650

4

	£'000
Proceeds	150
Less NA sold 40% (320)	(128)
Less unamortised goodwill 3/5 (108 – 40% (220)]	(12)
	10

Alternative calculation:

	£'000
Proceeds	150
Less cost	(108)
	42
Less increase in net assets 40% (320 – 220)	(40)
Plus amortised goodwill 2/5 [108 – 40% (220)]	8
	10

5 New top holding company

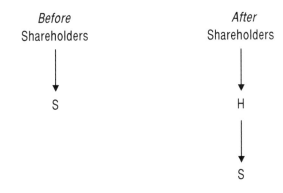

Before
Shareholders

↓

S

After
Shareholders

↓

H

↓

S

Subsidiary moved up:

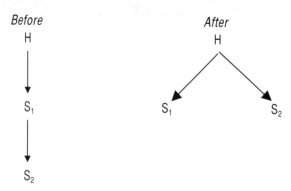

6   To allow S1 to be sold while S2 is retained, or to split diverse business.

7   To form a top group where the holding company is foreign and the subsidiaries are UK companies.

8   See Paragraph 3.2.

9   At the lower of its carrying amount and fair value less costs to sell

10   See Paragraph 3.4, key terms

Now try the questions below from the Exam Question Bank

Number	Level	Marks	Time
Q21	Examination	25	45 mins
Q22	Examination	25	45 mins
Q23	Introductory	n/a	n/a

Foreign currency translation

20

Introduction

Many of the largest companies in the UK, while based there, have subsidiaries and other interests all over the world: they are truly **global companies** and so foreign currency consolidations take place frequently in practice.

FRS 23 governs foreign currency translation and FRS 24 governs hyperinflation.

Study guide

		Intellectual level
D4	**Foreign transactions and entities**	
(a)	Outline and apply the translation of foreign currency amounts and transactions into the functional currency and the presentation currency	3
(b)	Account for the consolidation of foreign operations and their disposal	3
(c)	Describe the principal objectives of establishing a standard for enterprises reporting in the currency of a hyperinflationary economy	1

Exam guide

Foreign currency consolidation questions are likely to appear frequently in Paper P2. Students have always found such questions difficult but, as with most financial accounting topics, you only need to adopt a **logical approach** and to **practice plenty of questions**.

1 Foreign currency translation

> **FAST FORWARD**
>
> Questions on foreign currency translation have always been popular with examiners. In general you are required to prepare **consolidated accounts** for a group which includes a foreign subsidiary.

If a company trades overseas, it will buy or sell assets in **foreign currencies**. For example, an Indian company might buy materials from Canada, and pay for them in pounds sterling, and then sell its finished goods in Germany, receiving payment in Euros, or perhaps in some other currency. If the company owes money in a foreign currency at the end of the accounting year, or holds assets which were bought in a foreign currency, those liabilities or assets must be translated into the local currency (in this text £), in order to be shown in the books of account.

A company might have a subsidiary abroad (ie a foreign entity that it owns), and the subsidiary will trade in its own local currency. The subsidiary will keep books of account and prepare its annual accounts in its own currency. However, at the year end, the holding company must 'consolidate' the results of the overseas subsidiary into its group accounts, so that somehow, the assets and liabilities and the **annual profits of the subsidiary must be translated from the foreign currency into £.**

If foreign currency exchange rates remained constant, there would be no accounting problem. As you will be aware, however, foreign exchange rates are continually changing, and it is not inconceivable for example, that the rate of exchange between the Polish zlotych and sterling might be Z6.2 to £1 at the start of the accounting year, and Z5.6 to £1 at the end of the year (in this example, a 10% increase in the relative strength of the zlotych).

There are two distinct types of foreign currency transaction, **conversion and translation**.

1.1 Conversion gains and losses

Conversion is the process of exchanging amounts of one foreign currency for another. For example, suppose a local company buys a large consignment of goods from a supplier in Germany. The order is placed on 1 May and the agreed price is €124,250. At the time of delivery the rate of foreign exchange was €3.50 to £1. The local company would record the amount owed in its books as follows.

DEBIT   Inventory (stock) account (124,250 ÷ 3.5)   £35,500

CREDIT   Payables (creditors) account   £35,500

When the local company comes to pay the supplier, it needs to obtain some foreign currency. By this time, however, if the rate of exchange has altered to €3.55 to £1, the cost of raising €124,250 would be (÷ 3.55) £35,000. The company would need to spend only £35,000 to settle a debt for inventories 'costing' £35,500. Since it would be administratively difficult to alter the value of the inventories in the company's books of account, it is more appropriate to record a profit on conversion of £500.

DEBIT	Payables account	£35,500	
CREDIT	Cash		£35,000
CREDIT	Profit on conversion		£500

Profits (or losses) on conversion would be included in the income statement for the year in which conversion (whether payment or receipt) takes place.

Suppose that another home company sells goods to a Chinese company, and it is agreed that payment should be made in Chinese Yuan at a price of Y116,000. We will further assume that the exchange rate at the time of sale is Y10.75 to £1, but when the debt is eventually paid, the rate has altered to Y10.8 to £1. The company would record the sale as follows.

DEBIT	Receivables (debtors) account (116,000 ÷ 10.75)	£10,800	
CREDIT	Sales account		£10,800

When the Y116,000 are paid, the local company will convert them into £, to obtain (÷ 10.8) £10,750. In this example, there has been a loss on conversion of £50 which will be written off to the income statement:

DEBIT	Cash	£10,750	
DEBIT	Loss on conversion	£50	
CREDIT	Payables account		£10,800

There are **no accounting difficulties** concerned with foreign currency conversion gains or losses, and the procedures described above are uncontroversial.

1.2 Translation

Foreign currency translation, as distinct from conversion, does not involve the act of exchanging one currency for another. **Translation is required at the end of an accounting period when a company still holds assets or liabilities in its balance sheet which were obtained or incurred in a foreign currency.**

These assets or liabilities might consist of any of the following.

(a) An individual home company holding individual **assets** or **liabilities** originating in a foreign currency 'deal'.

(b) An individual home company with a separate **branch** of the business operating abroad which keeps its own books of account in the local currency.

(c) A home company which wishes to consolidate the **results of a foreign subsidiary**.

There has been great **uncertainty** about the method which should be used to translate the following.

- Value of assets and liabilities from a foreign currency into £ for the year end balance sheet

- Profits of an independent foreign branch or subsidiary into £ for the annual income statement

Suppose, for example, that a Belgian subsidiary purchases a piece of property for €2,100,000 on 31 December 20X7. The rate of exchange at this time was €70 to £1. During 20X8, the subsidiary charged depreciation on the building of €16,800, so that at 31 December 20X8, the subsidiary recorded the asset as follows.

475

	€
Property at cost	2,100,000
Less accumulated depreciation	16,800
Net book value	2,083,200

At this date, the rate of exchange has changed to €60 to £1.

The local holding company must translate the asset's value into £, but there is a **choice of exchange rates**.

(a)   Should the rate of exchange for translation be the rate which existed at the date of purchase, which would give a net book value of 2,083,200 ÷ 70 = £29,760?

(b)   Should the rate of exchange for translation be the rate existing at the end of 20X8 (the closing rate of €60 to £1)? This would give a net book value of £34,720.

Similarly, should depreciation be charged in the group income statement at the rate of €70 to £1 (the historical rate), €60 to £1 (the closing rate), or at an average rate for the year (say, €64 to £1)?

1.3 Consolidated accounts

If a parent has a subsidiary whose accounts are presented in a foreign currency, those accounts must be translated into the local currency before they can be included in the consolidated financial statements.

- Should the subsidiary's accounts be translated as if the subsidiary is an extension of the parent?

- Or should they be translated as if the subsidiary is a separate business?

Where the affairs of a foreign operation are very closely interlinked with those of the investing company, it should be included in the consolidated financial statements as if the transactions had been entered into by the investing company in its own currency. Non-monetary assets and depreciation are translated at **historical rate** and sales, purchase and expenses at **average rate**. **Exchange differences** arising on retranslation are reported as part of **profit or loss** on ordinary activities.

Where a foreign operation is effectively a separate business, the **closing rate** is used for most items in the financial statements. **Exchange differences** are taken **directly** to **equity**.

We will look at the consolidation of foreign subsidiaries in much more detail in Section 3 of this chapter.

2 FRS 23: Individual company stage

The questions discussed above are addressed by FRS 23 *The effects of changes in foreign exchange rates.* FRS 23 was published in 2004, as part of the ASB's convergence project.

We will examine those matters which affect single company accounts here.

2.1 Definitions

These are some of the definitions given by FRS 23.

Key terms

> **Foreign currency.** A currency other than the functional currency of the entity.
>
> **Functional currency.** The currency of the primary economic environment in which the entity operates.
>
> **Presentation currency.** The currency in which the financial statements are presented.
>
> **Exchange rate.** The ratio of exchange for two currencies.

Key term

> **Exchange difference**. The difference resulting from translating a given number of units of one currency into another currency at different exchange rates.
>
> **Closing rate**. The spot exchange rate at the balance sheet date.
>
> **Spot exchange rate**. The exchange rate for immediate delivery.
>
> **Monetary items**. Units of currency held and assets and liabilities to be received or paid in a fixed or determinable number of units of currency. *(FRS 23)*

Each entity – whether an individual company, a parent of a group, or an operation within a group (such as a subsidiary, associate or branch) – should determine its **functional currency** and **measure its results and financial position in that currency**.

FAST FORWARD

You may have to make the decision yourself as to whether the subsidiary has the same functional currency as the parent or a different functional currency from the parent. This determines whether the subsidiary is treated as an **extension of the parent** or as a **net investment**.

For most individual companies the functional currency will be the currency of the country in which they are located and in which they carry out most of their transactions. Determining the functional currency is much more likely to be an issue where an entity operates as part of a group. FRS 23 contains detailed guidance on how to determine an entity's functional currency and we will look at this in more detail in Section 3.

An entity can present its financial statements in any currency (or currencies) it chooses. FRS 23 deals with the situation in which financial statements are presented in a currency other than the functional currency.

Again, this is unlikely to be an issue for most individual companies. Their presentation currency will normally be the same as their functional currency (the currency of the country in which they operate). A company's presentation currency may be different from its functional currency if it operates within a group and we will look at this in Section 3.

2.2 Foreign currency transactions: initial recognition

FRS 23 states that a foreign currency transaction should be recorded, on initial recognition in the functional currency, by applying the exchange rate between the reporting currency and the foreign currency **at the date of the transaction** to the foreign currency amount.

An **average rate** for a period may be used if exchange rates do not fluctuate significantly.

2.3 Reporting at subsequent balance sheet dates

The following rules apply at each subsequent balance sheet date.

(a) Report foreign currency **monetary items** using the **closing rate**

(b) Report **non-monetary items** (eg non-current (fixed) assets, inventories) which are carried at **historical cost** in a foreign currency using the **exchange rate at the date of the transaction** (historical rate)

(c) Report **non-monetary items** which are carried at **fair value** in a foreign currency using the exchange rates that existed **when the values were determined.**

2.4 Recognition of exchange differences

You must be able to calculate **exchange differences** and also to explain the differences between the methods. You should be able to discuss the treatment of **foreign currency borrowings** to finance overseas investment.

Exchange differences occur when there is a **change in the exchange rate** between the transaction date and the date of settlement of monetary items arising from a foreign currency transaction.

Exchange differences arising on the settlement of monetary items (receivables, payables, loans, cash in a foreign currency) or on translating an entity's monetary items at rates different from those at which they were translated initially, or reported in previous financial statements, should be **recognised in profit or loss** in the period in which they arise.

There are two situations to consider.

(a)   The transaction is **settled in the same period** as that in which it occurred: all the exchange difference is recognised in that period.

(b)   The transaction is **settled in a subsequent accounting period**: the exchange difference recognised in each intervening period up to the period of settlement is determined by the change in exchange rates during that period.

In other words, where a monetary item has not been settled at the end of a period, it should be **restated using the closing exchange rate** and any gain or loss taken to the income statement (=profit and loss account).

Question

Single company

White Cliffs plc, whose year end is 31 December, buys some goods from Rinka SA of France on 30 September. The invoice value is €40,000 and is due for settlement in equal instalments on 30 November and 31 January. The exchange rate moved as follows.

	€ = £1
30 September	1.60
30 November	1.80
31 December	1.90
31 January	1.85

Required

State the accounting entries in the books of White Cliffs plc.

Answer

The purchase will be recorded in the books of White Cliffs plc using the rate of exchange ruling on 30 September.

DEBIT	Purchases	£25,000	
CREDIT	Trade payables		£25,000

Being the £ cost of goods purchased for €40,000 (€40,000 ÷ €1.60/£1)

On 30 November, White Cliffs must pay €20,000. This will cost €20,000 ÷ €1.80/£1 = £11,111 and the company has therefore made an exchange gain of £12,500 – £11,111 = £1,389.

DEBIT	Trade payables (creditors)	£12,500	
CREDIT	Exchange gains: P & L account		£1,389
CREDIT	Cash		£11,111

On 31 December, the balance sheet date, the outstanding liability will be recalculated using the rate applicable to that date: €20,000 ÷ €1.90/£1 = £10,526. A further exchange gain of £1,974 has been made and will be recorded as follows.

DEBIT	Trade payables	£1,974	
CREDIT	Exchange gains: P & L account		£1,974

The total exchange gain of £3,363 will be included in the operating profit for the year ending 31 December.

On 31 January, White Cliffs must pay the second instalment of €20,000. This will cost them £10,811 (€20,000 ÷ €1.85/£1).

DEBIT	Trade payables	£10,526	
	Exchange losses: P & L account	£285	
CREDIT	Cash		£10,811

When a gain or loss on a non-monetary item is recognised **in the statement of total recognised gains and losses** (for example, where property is revalued), any **related exchange differences** should also be **recognised in the statement of total recognised gains and losses.**

3 FRS 23: Consolidated financial statements stage

The following definitions are relevant here.

Key terms

> **Foreign operation.** A subsidiary, associate, joint venture or branch of a reporting entity, the activities of which are based or conducted in a country or currency other than those of the reporting entity.
>
> **Net investment in a foreign operation.** The amount of the reporting entity's interest in the net assets of that operation.
> *(FRS 23)*

3.1 Determining functional currency

A holding or parent company with foreign operations must **translate the financial statements** of those operations into its own reporting currency before they can be consolidated into the group accounts. There are two methods: **the method used depends** upon **whether** the foreign operation has the **same functional currency as the parent**.

FRS 23 states that an entity should consider the following factors in determining its functional currency:

(a) The currency that mainly **influences sales prices** for goods and services (often the currency in which prices are denominated and settled)

(b) The currency of the **country whose competitive forces and regulations** mainly determine the sales prices of its goods and services

(c) The currency that mainly **influences labour, material and other costs** of providing goods or services (often the currency in which prices are denominated and settled)

Sometimes the functional currency of an entity is not immediately obvious. Management must then exercise judgement and may also need to consider:

(a)   The currency in which **funds from financing activities** (raising loans and issuing equity) are generated

(b)   The currency in which **receipts from operating activities** are usually retained

Where a parent has a foreign operation a number of factors are considered:

(a)   Whether the activities of the foreign operation are carried out as an **extension of the parent**, rather than being carried out with a **significant degree of autonomy**.

(b)   Whether **transactions with the parent** are a high or a low proportion of the foreign operation's activities.

(c)   Whether **cash flows** from the activities of the foreign operation **directly affect the cash flows of the parent** and are readily available for remittance to it.

(d)   Whether the activities of the foreign operation are **financed from its own cash flows** or by **borrowing from the parent**.

To sum up: in order to determine the functional currency of a foreign operation it is necessary to consider the **relationship** between the foreign operation and its parent:

- If the foreign operation carries out its business as though it were an **extension of the parent's operations**, it almost certainly has the **same functional currency** as the parent.

- If the foreign operation is **semi-autonomous** it almost certainly has **a different functional currency** from the parent.

The translation method used has to reflect the economic reality of the relationship between the reporting entity (the parent) and the foreign operation.

3.1.1 Same functional currency as the reporting entity

In this situation, the foreign operation normally carries on its business as though it were an **extension of the reporting entity's operations.** For example, it may only sell goods imported from, and remit the proceeds directly to, the reporting entity.

Any **movement in the exchange rate** between the reporting currency and the foreign operation's currency will have an **immediate impact** on the reporting entity's cash flows from the foreign operations. In other words, changes in the exchange rate affect the **individual monetary items** held by the foreign operation, *not* the reporting entity's net investment in that operation.

3.1.2 Different functional currency from the reporting entity

In this situation, although the reporting entity may be able to exercise control, the foreign operation normally operates in a **semi-autonomous** way. It accumulates cash and other monetary items, generates income and incurs expenses, and may also arrange borrowings, all **in its own local currency**.

A change in the exchange rate will produce **little or no direct effect on the present and future cash flows** from operations of either the foreign operation or the reporting entity. Rather, the change in exchange rate affects the reporting entity's **net investment** in the foreign operation, not the individual monetary and non-monetary items held by the foreign operation.

3.2 Accounting treatment: same functional currency as the reporting entity

The same standards and procedures identified in Section 2 above for individual company accounts should be applied to the financial statements of a foreign operation, **as if the transactions of the foreign operation had been those of the parent**.

We can summarise the treatment here.

(a) **Income statement (profit and loss account)**: translate using actual rates. An average for a period may be used, but not where there is significant fluctuation and the average is therefore unreliable.

(b) **Non-monetary items**: translate using an historical rate at the date of purchase (or revaluation to fair value, or reduction to realisable/recoverable amount). This includes inventories and long-term assets (and their depreciation).

(c) **Monetary items**: translate at the closing rate.

(d) **Exchange differences**: report as part of profit for the year.

3.3 Accounting treatment: different functional currency from the reporting entity

The financial statements of the foreign operation must be translated to the functional currency of the parent. Different procedures must be followed here, because the functional currency of the parent is the **presentation currency** of the foreign operation.

(a) The **assets and liabilities** shown in the foreign operation's balance sheet are translated at the **closing rate** at the balance sheet date, regardless of the date on which those items originated. The balancing figure on the translated balance sheet represents the reporting entity's net investment in the foreign operation.

(b) Amounts in the **income statement** should be translated at the rate ruling at the date of the transaction (an **average rate** will usually be used for practical purposes).

(c) **Exchange differences** arising from the re-translation at the end of each year of the parent's net investment should be **taken to the statement of total recognised gains and losses**, not through the income statement (P & L) for the year, until the disposal of the net investment.

FAST FORWARD

Practising examination questions is the best way of learning this topic.

3.4 Example: Different functional currency from the reporting entity

A company, Stone plc, set up a foreign subsidiary on 30 June 20X7. Stone subscribed €24,000 for share capital when the exchange rate was €2 = £1. The subsidiary, Brick Inc, borrowed €72,000 and bought a non-monetary asset for €96,000. Stone plc prepared its accounts on 31 December 20X7 and by that time the exchange rate had moved to €3 = £1. As a result of highly unusual circumstances, Brick Inc sold its asset early in 20X8 for €96,000. It repaid its loan and was liquidated. Stone's capital of €24,000 was repaid in February 20X8 when the exchange rate was €3 = £1.

Required

Account for the above transactions

(a) As if the entity has the same functional currency as the parent (the functional currency method)

(b)   As if the entity has a different functional currency from the parent (the presentation currency method)

Solution

From the above it can be seen that Stone plc will record its initial investment at £12,000 which is the starting cost of its shares. The balance sheet of Brick Inc at 31 December 20X7 is summarised below.

	€'000
Non-monetary asset	96
Share capital	24
Loan	72
	96

This may be translated as follows.

	£'000
Non-monetary asset	
(€2 = £1)	
(€3 = £1)	32
Equity (balancing figure)	8
Loan (€3 = £1)	24
	32

Exchange gain/(loss) for 20X7	(4)

The exchange gain and loss are the differences between the value of the original investment (£12,000) and the total of equity (share capital and retained earnings) as disclosed by the above balance sheets.

On liquidation, Stone plc will receive £8,000 (€24,000 converted at €3 = £1).

3.5 Some practical points

The following points apply.

(a)   For consolidation purposes calculations are simpler if a subsidiary's share capital is translated at the **historical rate** (the rate when the investing company acquired its interest) and Retained earnings are found as a balancing figure.

(b)   **Dividends declared** by a subsidiary should always be translated at the **closing rate** in the income statement and at the actual rate on the date of payment. This is because the investing company will record the items at these rates in its own books.

3.6 Summary

A summary of the translation method is given below, which shows the main steps to follow in the consolidation process.

Exam focus point	You should learn this summary.

	Translation
Step 1 Translate the closing balance sheet (net assets/shareholders' funds) and use this for preparing the consolidated balance sheet in the normal way.	Under **closing rate** at the year end for all items (see note).
Step 2 Translate the income statement (profit and loss account). (In all cases, dividends should be translated at the rate ruling when the dividend was paid or, in the case of declared dividends proposed, the closing rate at the year end.)	Use the **average rate** for the year for all items (but see comment on dividends). The figures obtained can then be used in preparing the consolidated income statement (P & L).
Step 3 Translate the shareholders' funds (net assets) at the beginning of the year.	Use the **closing rate** at the beginning of the year (the opening rate for the current year).

Step 4
 	
Calculate the total exchange difference for the year as follows.
 	
         £
 	
Closing net assets
at closing rate (Step 1)   X
Less opening net
Assets at opening rate
(Step 3) $\underline{X}$
         X
 	
Less retained profit
per translated income
statement (Step 2) $\underline{X}$
Exchange differences $\underline{\underline{X}}$
Group share (%)   X
 	
It may be necessary to adjust for any profits or losses taken direct to retained earnings (reserves) during the year.
	This stage will be **unnecessary** unless you are asked to state the total exchange differences or are asked to prepare a statement of the movement on retained earnings (reserves), where the ex-change difference will be shown.
	
	For **exam purposes** you can translate the closing shareholders' funds as follows.
	
	(a) Share capital + pre-acquisition retained earnings (reserves) at historical rate.
	
	(b) Post-acquisition retained earnings (reserves) as a balancing figure.

As mentioned above, the share capital may be translated at the historical rate. The retained earnings (reserves) will then be the balancing figure. The advantage of this method is that it simplifies the 'cancellation' of the share capital on consolidation.

Exam focus point

Because FRS 23 implements an international accounting standard (IAS 21) it uses international terminology, and it is likely that international layouts will be required for the financial statements. The main points to note are:

- Balance sheet has all the assets in the top half and equity and liabilities in the bottom half. Follow the format given in the question.

- The terminology is different: debtors = receivables; stocks = inventories; creditors = payables; profit and loss account = income statement.

Question

Consolidated financial statements

The abridged balance sheets and income statements of Darius plc and its foreign subsidiary, Xerxes Inc, appear below.

DRAFT BALANCE SHEET AS AT 31 DECEMBER 20X9

	Darius Co		Xerxes Inc	
	£	£	€	€
Assets				
Non-current (fixed) assets				
Plant at cost	600		500	
Less depreciation	(250)		(200)	
		350		300
Investment in Xerxes				
100 € shares		25		–
		375		300
Current assets				
Inventories (stocks)	225		200	
Receivables (debtors)	150		100	
		375		300
		750		600
Equity and liabilities				
Equity				
Ordinary £1/1€ shares	300		100	
Retained earnings	300		280	
		600		380
Long-term loans		50		110
Current liabilities		100		110
		750		600

INCOME STATEMENTS (P & L ACCOUNTS)
FOR THE YEAR ENDED 31 DECEMBER 20X9

	Darius Co	Xerxes Inc
	£	€
Profit before tax	200	160
Tax	100	80
Profit after tax, retained	100	80

The following further information is given.

(a) Darius plc has had its interest in Xerxes Inc since the incorporation of the company.

(b) Depreciation is 8% per annum on cost.

(c) There have been no loan repayments or movements in non-current assets during the year. The opening inventory of Xerxes Inc was €120. Assume that inventory turnover times are very short.

(d) Exchange rates: €4 to £1 when Xerxes Inc was incorporated
€2.5 to £1 when Xerxes Inc acquired its long-term assets
€2 to £1 on 31 December 20X8
€1.6 to £1 average rate of exchange year ending 31 December 20X9
€1 to £1 on 31 December 20X9.

Required

Prepare the summarised consolidated financial statements of Darius plc.

Answer

Step 1   The balance sheet of Xerxes Inc at 31 December 20X9, other than equity (share capital and retained earnings), should be translated at €1 = £1.

SUMMARISED BALANCE SHEET AT 31 DECEMBER 20X9

	£	£
Non-current assets (NBV)		300
Current assets		
Inventories	200	
Receivables	100	
		300
		600
Non-current liabilities		110
Current liabilities		110

∴ Shareholders' funds = 600 − 110 − 110 = 380

Since Darius plc acquired the whole of the issued share capital on incorporation, the post-acquisition retained earnings (reserves) including exchange differences will be the value of shareholders' funds arrived at above, less the original cost to Darius plc of £25. Post-acquisition retained earnings = £380 − £25 = £355.

SUMMARISED CONSOLIDATED BALANCE SHEET AS AT 31 DECEMBER 20X9

		£	£
Assets			
Non-current assets (NBV)	£(350 + 300)		650
Current assets			
Inventories	£(225 + 200)	425	
Receivables	£(150 + 100)	250	
			675
			1,325
Equity and liabilities			
Equity			
Ordinary £1 shares (Darius only)			300
Retained earnings	£(300 + 355)		655
			955
Non-current liabilities: loans	£(50 + 110)		160
Current liabilities	£(100 + 110)		210
			1,325

Note. It is quite unnecessary to know the amount of the exchange differences when preparing the consolidated balance sheet.

Step 2   The income statement should be translated at average rate (€1.6 = £1).

SUMMARISED INCOME STATEMENT
FOR THE YEAR ENDED 31 DECEMBER 20X9

	£
Profit before tax	100
Tax	50
Profit after tax, retained	50

SUMMARISED CONSOLIDATED INCOME STATEMENT
FOR THE YEAR ENDED 31 DECEMBER 20X9

		£
Profit before tax	£(200 + 100)	300
Tax	£(100 + 50)	150
Profit after tax, retained	£(100 + 50)	150

Step 3 The equity interest at the beginning of the year can be found as follows.

	€
Equity value at 31 December 20X9	380
Retained profit for year	80
Equity value at 31 December 20X8	300
Translated at €2 = £1, this gives	£150

Step 4 The exchange difference can now be calculated.

	£
Equity interest at 31 December 20X9 (stage 1)	380
Equity interest at 1 January 20X9 (stage 3)	150
	230
Less retained profit (stage 2)	50
Exchange gain	180

CONSOLIDATED STATEMENT OF MOVEMENTS ON RETAINED EARNINGS (RESERVES)
FOR THE YEAR ENDED 31 DECEMBER 20X9

	£
Consolidated retained earnings at 31 December 20X8	325
Exchange gains arising on consolidation	180
Retained profit for the year	150
Consolidated retained earnings at 31 December 20X9	655

(*Note*. The post-acquisition retained earnings of Xerxes Inc at the beginning of the year must have been £150 − £25 = £125 and the retained earnings of Darius plc must have been £300 − £100 = £200. The consolidated retained earnings must therefore have been £325.)

3.7 Analysis of exchange differences

The exchange differences in the above exercise could be reconciled by splitting them into their component parts.

Exam focus point

> Such a split is not required by FRS 23, nor is it required in your exam, but it may help your understanding of the subject.

- **Presentation currency method**: the exchange difference consists of those exchange gains/losses arising from:

  - Translating **income/expense items** at the exchange rates at the date of transactions, whereas **assets/liabilities** are translated at the closing rate

  - Translating the **opening net investment** (opening net assets) in the foreign entity at a closing rate different from the closing date at which it was previously reported.

- **Functional currency method**: exchange differences will arise because income/expenses are translated at the actual (or average rate) but monetary assets/liabilities at a closing rate

This can be demonstrated using the above question.

Using the opening balance sheet and translating at €2 = £1 and €1 = £1 gives the following.

	€2 = £1 £	€ = £1 £	Difference £
Non-current assets at NBV	170	340	170
Inventories	60	120	60
Net current monetary liabilities	(25)	(50)	(25)
	205	410	205
Shareholders' funds	150	300	150
Loans	55	110	55
	205	410	205

Translating the income statement using €1.60 = £1 and €1 = £1 gives the following results.

	€1.60 = £1 £	€1 = £1 £	Difference £
Profit before tax, depreciation and increase in inventory values	75	120	45
Increase in inventory values	50	80	30
	125	200	75
Depreciation	(25)	(40)	(15)
	100	160	60
Tax	(50)	(80)	(30)
Profit after tax, retained	50	80	30

The overall position is then:

	£	£
Gain on non-current assets (£170 – £15)		155
Loss on loan		(55)
Gain on inventories (£60 + £30)	90	
Loss on net monetary current assets/ Liabilities (all other differences) (£45 – £30 – £25)	(10)	
		80
Net exchange gain: as above		180

3.8 Minority interests

In problems involving minority interests the following points should be noted.

(a)   The figure for **minority interests in the balance sheet** will be the appropriate proportion of the translated equity (share capital and retained earnings) of the subsidiary. In addition, it may be necessary to show the proposed dividend payable to the minorities as a liability. The proposed dividend should be translated at the closing rate for this purpose.

(b)   The **minority interest in the income statement** will be the appropriate proportion of dollar profits available for distribution. If the functional currency of the subsidiary is the same as that of the parent, this profit will be arrived at *after* charging or crediting the exchange differences.

3.9 Example: Minority interests

The summarised accounts of Camrumite Inc are shown below.

BALANCE SHEET AS AT 31 DECEMBER 20X3

	€
Non-current assets	10,000
Net monetary assets	5,000
	15,000
Equity	15,000

INCOME STATEMENT FOR THE YEAR ENDED 31 DECEMBER 20X3

	€
Profit after tax	3,080
Proposed final dividend	1,680
Retained profit	1,400

60% of the issued capital of Camrumite Inc is owned by Bates Co, a company based in another country.

There have been no movements in long-term assets during the year. The depreciation charge for the year was €560.

The exchange rate has moved as follows.

Date on which non-current assets were acquired	€8 = £1
1 January 20X3	€5 = £1
Average for the year ended 31.12.X3	€7 = £1
31 December 20X3	€8 = £1

You are required to calculate the figures for minority interests to be included in the consolidated accounts of Bates Co using:

(a)   The functional currency method.
(b)   The presentation currency method.

Show the movements on the minority interest accounts during the year.

Solution

Translating the shareholders' funds using the closing rate as at 31 December 20X3 gives €15,000 ÷ 8 = £1,875. The minority interest in the balance sheet will be 40% × £1,875 = £750.

The proposed dividend translated at the closing rate is €1,680 ÷ 8 = £210. The amount payable to the minority shareholders is 40% × £210 = £84.

The profit after tax translated at the average rate is €3,080 ÷ 7 = £440. The minority interest in the income statement is therefore 40% × £440 = £176.

At the beginning of the year the share capital and Retained earnings must have been €15,000 − €1,400 = €13,600. Translating this at the rate ruling on 1 January 20X3 gives €13,600 ÷ 5 = £2,720. The minority interest at 1 January 20X3 was 40% × £2,720 = £1,088.

	£	£
Shareholders' funds as at 1 January 20X3		2,720
Add: profit for year	440	
less dividends	210	
		230
		2,950
Less shareholders' funds at 31 December 20X3		1,875
Exchange loss		1,075
Minority interest therein £1,075 × 40%		430

The minority interest can be summarised as follows.

	£
Balance at 1 January 20X3	1,088
Minority interest in profit for the year	176
Minority interest in exchange losses	(430)
	834
Balance at 31 December 20X3	750
Dividend payable to minority	84
	834

3.10 Further matters relating to foreign operations

3.10.1 Goodwill and fair value adjustments

Goodwill and fair value adjustments arising on the acquisition of a foreign operation should be treated as assets and liabilities of the acquired entity. This means that they should be expressed in the functional currency of the foreign operation and translated at the **closing rate**.

Below is a suggested layout for workings for goodwill and retained reserves (earnings) with some numbers inserted for illustrative purposes:

Retained reserves

	£'000
Pink	35,000
Blue post acquisition (3,800 × 90%)	3,420
Less provision for unrealised profit (90% × 250)	(225)
Foreign exchange gain on goodwill (see below)	420
	38,615

Goodwill

	F000	F000	Rate	£'000
Cost of combination (12,000 × 6)		72,000		
Less				
Share capital	40,000			
Pre acquisition ret'd earnings	26,000			
	66,000 × 90%	(59,400)		
At 1.4.20X1		12,600	6	2,100
Foreign exchange gain		–	Bal	420
At 31.3.20X7		12,600	5	2,520

3.10.2 Consolidation procedures

Follow normal consolidation procedures, except that where an exchange difference arises on **long– or short-term intra-group monetary items**, these cannot be offset against other intra-group balances. This is because these are commitments to convert one currency into another, thus exposing the reporting entity to a gain or loss through currency fluctuations.

If the foreign operation's **balance sheet date** is different from that of the parent, it is acceptable to use the accounts made up to that date for consolidation, as long as adjustments are made for any significant changes in rates in the interim.

3.10.3 Hyperinflationary economies

We will look at FRS 24 *Financial reporting in hyperinflationary economies* in Section 5. The financial statements of a foreign operation operating in a hyperinflationary economy must be adjusted under FRS 24 before they are translated into the parents' reporting currency and then consolidated. When the economy **ceases to be hyperinflationary**, and the foreign operation ceases to apply FRS 24, the amounts restated to the price level at the date the entity ceased to restate its financial statements should be used as the historical costs for translation purposes.

3.10.4 Disposal of foreign entity

When a parent disposes of a foreign entity, the cumulative amount of deemed exchange differences relating to that foreign entity should be **recognised as an income or expense** in the same period in which the gain or loss on disposal is recognised. Effectively, this means that these exchange differences are recognised once by taking them to Retained earnings and then are recognised for a second time ('recycled') by transferring them to the income statement on disposal of the foreign operation.

3.10.5 In the parent's accounts

In the parent company's own accounts, exchange differences arising on a **monetary item** that is effectively part of the parent's net investment in the foreign entity should be recognised **in profit or loss** in the separate financial statements of the reporting entity or the individual financial statements of the foreign operation, as appropriate.

3.11 Change in functional currency

The functional currency of an entity can be changed only if there is a change to the underlying transactions, events and conditions that are relevant to the entity. For example, an entity's functional currency may change if there is a change in the currency that mainly influences the sales price of goods and services.

Where there is a change in an entity's functional currency, the entity translate all items into the new functional currency **prospectively** (ie, from the date of the change) using the exchange rate at the date of the change.

3.12 Tax effects of exchange differences

FRS 16 *Current tax* and FRS 19 *Deferred tax* should be applied when there are tax effects arising from gain or losses on foreign currency transactions and exchange differences arising on the translation of the financial statements of foreign operations.

3.13 Foreign associated undertakings

Foreign associates will be companies with substantial autonomy from the group and so their **functional currency will be different** from that of the parent.

3.14 Section summary

- Where the functional currency of a foreign operation is the **same** as that of the parent/reporting entity

    - Operation is normally a direct extension of the investing company

    - Translate assets and liabilities at **closing rate (monetary items)** and **historical rate (non-monetary)**

    - Translate income statement at actual **(average) rate** and **historical rate (non-monetary items)**

    - Exchange differences are **part of profit**

- Where the functional currency of a foreign operation is **different** from that of the parent/reporting entity

    - Operation is semi-autonomous
    - Translate assets and liabilities at **closing rate**
    - Translate income statement at **average rate**
    - Exchange differences through **Retained earnings/equity**

4 A criticism of FRS 23

> **FRS 23** is criticised for a variety of reasons.

Although FRS 23 is an improvement over the previous situation, it is still criticised.

The average rate can be used to translate the income statement where it approximates to actual rates. Any other rate meeting this requirement can be used, including (presumably) the closing rate. This is a weakness of FRS 23 and the problem of a **lack of comparability** between companies is exacerbated.

Arguments for the use of the **closing rate** include the following.

(a) The use of the closing rate is simpler as it avoids the need to find an average rate weighted by the volume of transactions.

(b) The use of the closing rate will preserve the relationships in the foreign currency financial statements between income statement items and balance sheet items. (This is stated as one of the reasons for choosing the closing rate method at all.)

On the other hand, the **average rate** method has the following advantages.

(a) Profits accrue over a whole period, so the average rate will reflect the true events.
(b) There is no need to restate interim results.
(c) It is less volatile than the closing rate method.
(d) It gives greater comparability between companies with overlapping accounting periods.

5 Hyperinflation

> FRS 24 requires financial statements of entities operating within a **hyperinflationary economy** to be **restated** in terms of measuring units **current at the balance sheet date**.

In a hyperinflationary economy, **money loses its purchasing power very quickly**. Comparisons of transactions at different points in time, even within the same accounting period, are misleading. It is therefore considered inappropriate for entities to prepare financial statements without making adjustments for the **fall in the purchasing power of money over time**.

FRS 24 *Financial reporting in hyperinflationary economies* was published in December 2004 as part of the ASB's convergence project. It applies to the **primary financial statements** of entities (including consolidated accounts and cash flow statements) whose functional currency is the currency of a hyperinflationary economy. In this section, we will identify the hyperinflationary currency as £H.

The standard does not define a **hyperinflationary economy** in exact terms, although it indicates the characteristics of such an economy, for example, where the cumulative inflation rate over three years approaches or exceeds 100%.

Question

What other factors might indicate a hyperinflationary economy?

Answer

These are examples, but the list is not exhaustive.

(a)   The population prefers to retain its wealth in non-monetary assets or in a relatively stable foreign currency. Amounts of local currency held are immediately invested to maintain purchasing power.

(b)   The population regards monetary amounts not in terms of the local currency but in terms of a relatively stable foreign currency. Prices may be quoted in that currency.

(c)   Sales/purchases on credit take place at prices that compensate for the expected loss of purchasing power during the credit period, if that period is short.

(d)   Interest rates, wages and prices are linked to a price index.

The reported value of **non-monetary assets**, in terms of current measuring units, increases over time. For example, if a fixed asset is purchased for £H1,000 when the price index is 100, and the price index subsequently rises to 200, the value of the asset in terms of current measuring units (ignoring accumulated depreciation) will rise to £H2,000.

In contrast, the value of **monetary assets and liabilities**, such as a debt for 300 units, is unaffected by changes in the prices index, because it is an actual money amount payable or receivable. If a debtor owes £H300 when the price index is 100, and the debt is still unpaid when the price index has risen to 150, the debtor still owes just £H300. The purchasing power of monetary assets, however, will decline over time as the general level of prices goes up.

5.1 Requirement to restate financial statements in terms of measuring units current at the balance sheet date

In most countries, financial statements are produced on the basis of either:

(a)   **Historical cost**, except to the extent that some assets (eg property and investments) may be revalued, or

(b)   **Current cost**, which reflects the changes in the values of specific assets held by the entity.

In a hyperinflationary economy, neither of these methods of financial reporting are meaningful unless adjustments are made for the fall in the purchasing power of money. FRS 24 therefore requires that the **primary financial statements** of entities in a hyperinflationary economy should be produced by restating the figures prepared on either a historical cost basis or a current cost basis in terms of **measuring units current at the balance sheet date**.

Key term

> **Measuring unit current at the balance sheet date**. This is a unit of local currency with a purchasing power as at the date of the balance sheet, in terms of a general prices index.

Financial statements that are not restated (ie that are prepared on a historical cost basis or current cost basis without adjustments) may be presented as **additional statements** by the entity, but this is discouraged. The primary financial statements are those that have been restated.

After the assets, liabilities, equity and income statement of the entity have been restated, there will be a **net gain or loss on monetary assets and liabilities (the 'net monetary position')** and this should be recognised separately in the income statement for the period.

5.2 Making the adjustments

FRS 24 recognises that the resulting financial statements, after restating all items in terms of measuring units current at the balance sheet date, will **lack precise accuracy**. However, it is more important that certain procedures and judgements should be applied consistently from year to year. The implementation guidelines to the Standard suggest what these procedures should be.

5.3 Balance sheet: historical cost

Where the entity produces its accounts on a historical cost basis, the following procedures should be applied.

(a) Items that are not already expressed in terms of measuring units current at the balance sheet date should be restated, using a **general prices index**, so that they are valued in measuring units current at the balance sheet date.

(b) **Monetary assets and liabilities** are not restated, because they are already expressed in terms of measuring units current at the balance sheet date.

(c) Assets that are **already stated at market value or net realisable value** need not be restated, because they too are already valued in measuring units current at the balance sheet date.

(d) Any assets or liabilities **linked by agreement to changes in the general level of prices**, such as indexed-linked loans or bonds, should be adjusted in accordance with the terms of the agreement to establish the amount outstanding as at the balance sheet date.

(e) All **other non-monetary assets**, ie tangible fixed assets, intangible fixed assets (including accumulated depreciation/amortisation) investments and stocks, should be restated in terms of measuring units as at the balance sheet date, by applying a general prices index.

The **method of restating** these assets should normally be to multiply the original cost of the assets by a factor: [prices index at balance sheet date/prices index at date of acquisition of the asset]. For example, if an item of machinery was purchased for £H2,000 units when the prices index was 400 and the prices index at the balance sheet date is 1,000, the restated value of the long-term asset (before accumulated depreciation) would be:

£H2,000 × [1,000/400] = £H5,000

If, in the above example, the non current asset has been held for half its useful life and has no residual value, the **accumulated depreciation** would be restated as £H2,500. (The depreciation charge for the year should be the amount of depreciation based on historical cost, multiplied by the same factor as above: 1,000/400.)

If an asset has been **revalued** since it was originally purchased (eg a property), it should be restated in measuring units at the balance sheet date by applying a factor: (prices index at balance sheet date/prices index at revaluation date) to the revalued amount of the asset.

If the restated amount of a non-monetary asset **exceeds its recoverable value** (ie its net realisable value or market value), its value should be reduced accordingly.

The **owners' equity** (all components) as at the start of the accounting period should be restated using a general prices index from the beginning of the period.

5.4 Income statement: historical cost

In the income statement, all amounts of income and expense should be **restated in terms of measuring units current at the balance sheet date**. All amounts therefore need to be restated by a factor that allows for the change in the prices index since the item of income or expense was first recorded.

5.5 Gain or loss on net monetary position

In a period of inflation, an entity that holds monetary assets (cash, debtors) will suffer a fall in the purchasing power of these assets. By the same token, in a period of inflation, the value of monetary liabilities, such as a bank overdraft or bank loan, declines in terms of current purchasing power.

(a)   If an entity has an **excess of monetary assets over monetary liabilities**, it will suffer a loss over time on its net monetary position, in a period of inflation, in terms of measuring units as at 'today's date'.

(b)   If an entity has an **excess of monetary liabilities over monetary assets**, it will make a gain on its net monetary position, in a period of inflation.

5.6 Example: Hyperinflationary accounts

An entity maintains an unchanged balance sheet position over time. At 1 January, when the general prices index was 100, its balance sheet was as follows.

	£H
Assets	
Non-monetary assets	2,000
Monetary assets	2,000
	4,000
Liabilities and equity	
Monetary liabilities	1,000
Equity	3,000
	4,000

Suppose that the general prices index rises to 150 at 31 December.

Required

Show the adjustments required in the balance sheet.

Solution

Restating this balance sheet in terms of measuring units when the prices index is 50% higher gives the following.

	£H
Assets	
Non-monetary assets ($\times$ 150/100)	3,000
Monetary assets	2,000
	5,000
Liabilities and equity	
Monetary liabilities	1,000
Equity ($\times$ 150/100)	4,500
	5,500

The entity has suffered a loss on its net monetary position of £H500, in terms of measuring units at the current date £H(5,500 – 5,000). This is because it has held net monetary assets of £H1,000 during the period.

In the financial statements of an entity reporting in the currency of a hyperinflationary economy, the gain or loss on the net monetary position:

(a) may be derived as the **difference between total assets and total equity and liabilities**, after restating the non-monetary assets, owners' equity, income statement items and index-linked items, *or*

(b) may be estimated by **applying the change in the general prices index** for the period to the weighted average of the net monetary position of the entity in the period.

The gain or loss on the net monetary position should be **included in net income** and disclosed separately. (Any adjustment that was made to index-linked items can be set off against this net monetary gain or loss.)

5.7 Economies ceasing to be hyperinflation economies

When an economy ceases to be a hyperinflation economy, entities reporting in the currency of the economy are no longer required to produce financial statements in compliance with FRS 24.

Suppose for example that in 20X4 an entity reports in compliance with FRS 24, but in 20X5 it reverts to historical cost accounting because the economy is no longer a hyperinflation economy. As a starting point for reverting to historical cost accounts reporting, the entity should use the amounts expressed in terms of measuring units as at the end of 20X4 as the basis for its carrying amounts in 20X5 and subsequent years.

5.8 Disclosures

FRS 24 calls for the following disclosures.

- The fact that the **financial statements have been restated** for the changes in general purchasing power.

- Whether the financial statements as shown are based on **historical cost or current cost**.

- The **identity of the prices index** used to make the restatements, its level at the balance sheet date and the movement in the index during the current and the previous reporting periods.

In financial statements prepared under FRS 24, corresponding figures for the previous year should be **restated using the general prices index**.

5.9 Hyper-inflation and changes in foreign exchange rates

FRS 23 *The effects of changes in foreign exchange rates* was covered in an earlier chapter. A parent may have a foreign operation whose functional currency is the currency of a hyperinflationary economy. When the parent prepares consolidated financial statements it should:

(a) **Restate the financial statements** of the foreign operation in accordance with FRS 24, **before**

(b) **Translating all amounts** from the foreign operation's functional currency to the presentation currency **at the closing rate**.

The following example is a simple illustration of the problems that can arise where a foreign subsidiary operates in a hyper-inflationary economy.

5.10 Example: 'Disappearing assets'

A company has a subsidiary in a country which suffers from hyper-inflation. On 31 December 20X2 the subsidiary acquired freehold land for £H1,000,000. At that date the exchange rate was £H4 = £1 and the relevant price index was 100.

At 31 December 20X3 the exchange rate was £H10 = £1 and the price index was 300.

Required

Show the value at which the freehold land is included in the consolidated financial statements of the parent at 31 December 20X3 if the subsidiary's financial statements:

(a)   Are not restated to reflect current price levels
(b)   Are restated to reflect current price levels

Solution

(a)   **Without restatement**

Assuming that the subsidiary has a different functional currency (£H) from that of its parent (£) the balance sheet is translated at the closing rate.

At 31 December 20X3 the land is included at £100,000 (£H1,000,000 @ 10).

At 31 December 20X2 (the date of purchase) its was stated at £250,000 (£H1,000,000 @ 4). Therefore there has been an exchange loss of £150,000 (which may significantly reduce equity) and the land appears to have fallen to only 40% of its original value.

(b)   **With restatement**

At 31 December 20X3 the land is included at £300,000 (£H1,000,000 × 300/100 @ 10).

The value of the land is now adjusted so that it reflects the effect of inflation over the year and the 'disappearing assets' problem is overcome.

Where the financial statements of an entity whose functional currency is that of a hyperinflationary economy are translated into a different presentation currency, **comparative amounts** should be those that were presented as current year amounts in the relevant prior year financial statements (ie, **not adjusted** for subsequent changes in the price level or subsequent changes in exchange rates).

5.11 Section summary

- FRS 24 does not define **hyperinflationary economies**, but they have various characteristics

- Financial statements should be **restated based on a measuring unit current** at the balance sheet date

   - **Monetary assets/liabilities** do not need to be restated
   - **Non-monetary assets/liabilities** must be restated by applying a general prices index
   - **Items of income/expense** must be restated
   - **Gain/loss on net monetary items** must be reported in the income statement

Chapter Roundup

- Questions on foreign currency translation have always been popular with examiners. In general you are required to prepare **consolidated accounts** for a group which includes a foreign subsidiary.

- You may have to make the decision yourself as to whether the subsidiary has the same functional currency as the parent or a different functional currency from the parent. This determines whether the subsidiary is treated as an **extension of the parent** or as a **net investment.**

- You must be able to calculate **exchange differences** and also to explain the differences between the methods. You should be able to discuss the treatment of **foreign currency borrowings** to finance overseas investment.

- **Practising** examination questions is the best way of learning this topic.

- **FRS 23** is criticised for a variety of reasons.

- **FRS 24** requires financial statements of entities operating within a **hyperinflationary economy** to be **restated** in terms of measuring units **current at the balance sheet date**.

Quick Quiz

1   What is the difference between conversion and translation?

2   Define 'monetary' items according to FRS 23.

3   How should foreign currency transactions be recognised initially in an individual enterprise's accounts?

4   What factors must management take into account when determining the functional currency of a foreign operation?

5   How should goodwill and fair value adjustments be treated on consolidation of a foreign operation?

6   When can an entity's functional currency be changed?

Answers to Quick Quiz

1   (a)   Conversion is the process of exchanging one currency for another.
    (b)   Translation is the restatement of the value of one currency in another currency.

2   Money held and assets and liabilities to be received or paid in fixed or determinable amounts of money.

3   Use the exchange rate at the date of the transaction. An average rate for a period can be used if the exchange rates did not fluctuate significantly.

4   See Section 3.2

5   Treat as assets/liabilities of the foreign operation and translate at the closing rate.

6   Only if there is a change to the underlying transactions relevant to the entity.

Now try the questions below from the Exam Question Bank

Number	Level	Marks	Time
Q24	Examination	36	65 mins

Group cash flow statements

Topic list	Syllabus reference
1 FRS 1 *Cash flow statements: single company*	D1
2 Consolidated cash flow statements	D1

Introduction

A cash flow statement is an additional primary statement of **great value** to users of financial statements for the extra information it provides.

You should be familiar with the basic principles, techniques and definitions relating to cash flow statements from your earlier studies. This chapter develops the principles and preparation techniques to include **consolidated statements** and **foreign currency problems**.

Study guide

		Intellectual level
D1	**Group accounting including cash flow statements**	
(h)	Prepare and discuss group cash flow statements	3

Exam guide

A group cash flow statement is likely to appear as the first half of a compulsory 50 mark question.

1 FRS 1 Cash flow statements: single company

FAST FORWARD

> You must be able to produce a single company cash flow statement. You should also know the scope, formats and definitions given in FRS 1 (revised).

We have covered this in your earlier studies, so only a summary is given here. However, if you have any problems with the question at the end of this section, look back to your earlier study material.

Knowledge brought forward from earlier studies

FRS 1 (Revised) Cash flow statements

- Information on cash flows assists the user in assessing company's viability.

    - Shows enterprise's cash generation ability
    - Shows enterprise's cash utilisation needs

- *Format of statement*

    Inflows and outflows of cash of an enterprise are classified between the major economic activities.

    - Operating activities
    - Dividends from associates and joint ventures
    - Returns on investments and servicing of finance
    - Taxation
    - Capital expenditure and financial investment
    - Acquisitions and disposals
    - Equity dividends paid
    - Management of liquid resources
    - Financing

    The last two headings can be shown in a single section provided a subtotal is given for each heading.

- *Notes*

    FRS 1 requires two reconciliations.

    - Operating profit to net cash flow from operating activities
    - Movement in cash in the period to movement in net debt

    Give either adjoining the statement or in a separate note.

- *Definitions*
    - Cash: cash in hand and deposits repayable on demand … less overdrafts … repayable on demand. Deposits are repayable on demand if they can be withdrawn at any time without notice and without penalty or if a maturity/period of notice of ≤ 24 hours or one working day has been agreed. Includes cash in hand and deposits in foreign currencies.
    - Liquid resources: current asset investments held as readily disposable stores of value. A readily disposable investment is one that:
        - Is disposable by the reporting entity without curtailing or disrupting its business, and is either:
        - Readily convertible into known amounts of cash at or close to its carrying amount,
        or
        - Traded in an active market
    - Net debt: the borrowings of the reporting entity less cash and liquid resources; may be 'net funds' rather than 'net debt'.
- *Direct and indirect methods*

    The cash flow statement may be presented using either the direct or indirect method.
    - Direct method: the components of operating cash flows (cash from customers, payments to suppliers, other cash payments) are reported under this method; encouraged because of the value of the extra information given but not required because of the recognised extra costs involved in extracting the operating cash flows
    - Indirect method: the net cash flow from operating activities is arrived at by starting with the operating profit and adjusting it for non-cash charges and credits

1.1 Summary of techniques

Remember the steps involved in preparation of a cash flow statement.

Step 1   Set out the proforma leaving plenty of space.

Step 2   Complete the reconciliation of operating profit to net cash inflow, as far as possible.

Step 3   Calculate the following where appropriate.

- Tax paid
- Dividends paid
- Purchase and sale of fixed assets
- Issues of shares
- Repayment of loans

Step 4   Work out the profit if not already given using: opening and closing balances, tax charge and dividends.

Step 5   Complete the note of gross cash flows. Alternatively the information may go straight into the statement.

Step 6   Slot the figures into the statement.

Step 7   Complete the note of the analysis of changes in net debt.

Step 8   Complete the reconciliation of net cash flow to movement in net debt.

Question

The summarised accounts of Ashley plc for the year ended 31 December 20X8 are as follows.

ASHLEY PLC
BALANCE SHEET AS AT 31 DECEMBER 20X8

	20X8		20X7	
	£'000	£'000	£'000	£'000
Fixed assets				
Tangible assets		628		514
Current assets				
Stocks	214		210	
Debtors	168		147	
Cash	7		–	
	389		357	
Creditors: amounts falling due within one year				
Trade creditors	136		121	
Tax payable	39		28	
Dividends payable	18		16	
Overdraft	–		14	
	193		179	
Net current assets		196		178
Total assets less current liabilities		824		692
Creditors: amounts falling due after more than one year				
10% debentures		(80)		(50)
		744		642
Capital and reserves				
Share capital (£1 ords)		250		200
Share premium account		70		60
Revaluation reserve		110		100
Profit and loss account		314		282
		744		642

ASHLEY PLC
PROFIT AND LOSS ACCOUNT
FOR THE YEAR ENDED 31 DECEMBER 20X8

	£'000
Sales	600
Cost of sales	(319)
Gross profit	281
Other expenses (including depreciation of £42,000)	(194)
Profit before tax	87
Tax	(31)
Profit after tax	56
Dividends	(24)
Retained profit for the year	32

You are additionally informed that there have been no disposals of fixed assets during the year. New debentures were issued on 1 January 20X8. Wages for the year amounted to £86,000.

Required

Produce a cash flow statement using the direct method suitable for inclusion in the financial statements, as per FRS 1 (revised 1996).

Answer

ASHLEY PLC
CASH FLOW STATEMENT FOR THE YEAR ENDED 31 DECEMBER 20X8

	£'000	£'000
Operating activities		
Cash received from customers (147 + 600 – 168)	579	
Cash payments to suppliers (121 + 381 (W1) – 136)	(366)	
Cash payments to and on behalf of employees	(86)	
		127
Returns on investments and servicing of finance		
Interest paid		(8)
Taxation		
UK corporation tax paid (W2)		(20)
Capital expenditure		
Purchase of tangible fixed assets (W3)		(146)
		(47)
Equity dividends paid (16 + 24 – 18)		(22)
Financing		
Issue of share capital	60	
Issue of debentures	30	
Net cash inflow from financing		90
Increase in cash		21

NOTES TO THE CASH FLOW STATEMENT

1   Reconciliation of operating profit to net cash inflow from operating activities

	£'000
Operating profit (87 + 8)	95
Depreciation	42
Increase in stock	(4)
Increase in debtors	(21)
Increase in creditors	15
	127

2   Reconciliation of net cash flow to movement in net debt

	£'000
Net cash inflow for the period	21
Cash received from debenture issue	(30)
Change in net debt	(9)
Net debt at 1 January 20X8	(64)
Net debt at 31 December 20X8	(73)

3   Analysis of changes in net debt

	At 1 January 2 0X8 £'000	Cash lows £'000	At 31 December 20X8 £'000
Cash at bank	–	7	7
Overdrafts	(14)	14	–
		21	
Debt due after 1 year	(50)	(30)	(80)
Total	(64)	(9)	(73)

Workings

1   *Purchases*

	£'000
Cost of sales	319
Opening stock	(210)
Closing stock	214
Expenses (194 – 42 – 86 – 8 debenture interest)	58
	381

2   *Taxation*

TAXATION

	£'000		£'000
∴ Tax paid	20	Balance b/f	28
Balance c/f	39	Charge for year	31
	59		59

3   *Purchase of fixed assets*

	£'000
Opening fixed assets	514
Less depreciation	(42)
Add revaluation (110 – 100)	10
	482
Closing fixed assets	628
Difference = additions	146

2 Consolidated cash flow statements   Pilot paper

FAST FORWARD

Consolidated cash flows should not present a great problem if you understand how to deal with acquisitions and disposals of subsidiaries, minority interests and dividends.

The following format is given in the standard for a group cash flow statement.

XYZ GROUP PLC
CASH FLOW STATEMENT FOR THE YEAR ENDED 31 DECEMBER 20X6

	£'000	£'000
Cash flow from operating activities (note 1)		15,672
Dividends received from associates		350
Returns on investments and servicing of finance* (note 2)		(2,239)
Taxation		(2,887)
Capital expenditure and financial investment (note 2)		(865)
Acquisitions and disposals (note 2)		(17,824)
Equity dividends paid		(2,606)
Cash outflow before use of liquid resources and financing		(10,399)
Management of liquid resources (note 2)		700
Financing (note 2) Issue of shares	600	
Increase in debt	2,347	
		2,947
Decrease in cash in the period		(6,752)

Reconciliation of net cash flow to movement in net debt (note 3)

	£'000	£'000
Decrease in cash in the period	(6,752)	
Cash inflow from increase in debt and lease financing	(2,347)	
Cash inflow from decrease in liquid resources	(700)	
Change in net debt resulting from cash flows		(9,799)
Loans and finance leases acquired with subsidiary		(3,817)
New finance leases		(2,845)
Translation difference		643
Movement in net debt in the period		(15,818)
Net debt at 1.1.X6		(15,215)
Net debt at 31.12.X6		(31,033)

* This heading would include any dividends received *other than* those from equity accounted entities included in operating activities.

NOTES TO THE CASH FLOW STATEMENT

Exam focus point

All notes are included for completeness, but in the exam you will only need Note 1, which should be shown as a working.

1   *Reconciliation of operating profit to operating cash flows*

	Continuing		Dis-continued	Total
	£'000	£'000	£'000	£'000
Operating profit		18,829	(1,616)	17,213
Depreciation charges		3,108	380	3,488
Cash flow relating to previous year restructuring provision (note 4)			(560)	(560)
Increase in stocks		(11,193)	(87)	(11,280)
Increase in debtors		(3,754)	(20)	(3,774)
Increase in creditors		9,672	913	10,585
Net cash inflow from continuing operating activities		16,662		
Net cash outflow in respect of discontinued activities			(990)	
Net cash inflow from operating activities				15,672

2   *Analysis of cash flows for headings netted in the cash flow statement*

	£'000	£'000
Returns on investments and servicing of finance		
Interest received	508	
Interest paid	(1,939)	
Preference dividend paid	(450)	
Interest element of finance lease rental payments	(358)	
Net cash outflow for returns on investments and servicing of finance		(2,239)
Capital expenditure and financial investment		
Purchase of tangible fixed assets	(3,512)	
Sale of trade investment	1,595	
Sale of plant and machinery	1,052	
Net cash outflow for capital expenditure and financial investment		(865)
Acquisitions and disposals		
Purchase of subsidiary undertaking	(12,705)	
Net overdrafts acquired with subsidiary	(5,516)	
Sale of business	4,208	
Purchase of interest in a joint venture	(3,811)	

	£'000	£'000
Net cash outflow for acquisitions and disposals		(17,824)
Management of liquid resources *		
Cash withdrawn from 7 day deposit	200	
Purchase of government securities	(5,000)	
Sale of government securities	4,300	
Sale of corporate bonds	1,200	
Net cash inflow from management of liquid resources		700
Financing		
Issue of ordinary share capital		600
Debt due within a year		
Increase in short-term borrowings	2,006	
Repayment of secured loan	(850)	
Debt due beyond a year		
New secured loan repayable in 20Y0	1,091	
New unsecured loan repayable in 20X8	1,442	
Capital element of finance lease rental payments	(1,342)	
		2,347
Net cash inflow from financing		2,947

* XYZ Group plc includes as liquid resources term deposits of less than a year, government securities and AA rated corporate bonds.

3   Analysis of net debt

	At 1 Jan 20X6 £'000	Cash flow £'000	Acquisition* (excl. cash and overdrafts) £'000	Other non-cash changes £'000	Exchange movement £'000	At 31 Dec 20X6 £'000
Cash in hand, at bank	235	(1,250)			1,392	377
Overdrafts	(2,528)	(5,502)			(1,422)	(9,452)
		(6,752)				
Debt due after 1 year	(9,640)	(2,533)	(1,749)	2,560	(792)	(12,154)
Debt due within 1 year	(352)	(1,156)	(837)	(2,560)	1,465	(3,440)
Finance leases	(4,170)	1,342	(1,231)	(2,845)		(6,904)
		(2,347)				
Current asset investments	1,240	(700)				540
Total	(15,215)	(9,799)	(3,817)	(2,845)	643	(31,033)

4   Cash flows relating to exceptional items

The operating cash outflows include under discontinued activities an outflow of £560,000, which relates to the £1,600,000 exceptional provision for a fundamental restructuring made in the 20X5 accounts.

5   Major non-cash transactions

(a)   During the year the group entered into finance lease arrangements in respect of assets with a total capital value at the inception of the leases of £2,845,000.

(b)   Part of the consideration for the purchases of subsidiary undertakings and the sale of a business that occurred during the year comprised shares and loan notes respectively. Further details of the acquisitions and the disposal are set out below.

6   *Purchase of subsidiary undertakings*

	£'000
Net assets acquired	
Tangible fixed assets	12,194
Investments	1
Stocks	9,384
Debtors	13,856
Taxation recoverable	1,309
Cash at bank and in hand	1,439
Creditors	(21,715)
Bank overdrafts	(6,955)
Loans and finance leases	(3,817)
Deferred taxation	(165)
Minority shareholders' interests	(9)
	5,522
Goodwill	16,702
	22,224
Satisfied by	
Shares allotted	9,519
Cash	12,705
	22,224

The subsidiary undertakings acquired during the year contributed £1,502,000 to the group's net operating cash flows, paid £1,308,000 in respect of net returns on investments and servicing of finance, paid £522,000 in respect of taxation and utilised £2,208,000 for capital expenditure.

7   *Sale of business*

	£'000
Net assets disposed of	
Fixed assets	775
Stocks	5,386
Debtors	474
	6,635
Loss on disposal	(1,227)
	5,408
Satisfied by	
Loan notes	1,200
Cash	4,208
	5,408

The business sold during the year contributed £200,000 to the group's net operating cash flows, paid £252,000 in respect of net returns on investments and servicing of finance, paid £145,000 in respect of taxation and utilised £209,000 for capital expenditure.

Cash flows that are **internal to the group** should be eliminated in the preparation of a consolidated cash flow statement. Where a subsidiary undertaking **joins or leaves** a group during a financial year the cash flows of the group should include the cash flows of the subsidiary undertaking concerned for the same period as that for which the group's P&L account includes the results of the subsidiary undertaking.

2.1 Acquisitions and disposals of subsidiary undertakings

A note to the cash flow statement should show a summary of the effects of acquisitions and disposals of subsidiary undertakings indicating how much of the **consideration comprised cash**. Material effects on amounts reported under each of the standard headings reflecting the cash flows of a subsidiary undertaking acquired or disposed of in the period should be disclosed, as far as practicable. This information could be given by dividing cash flows between continuing and discontinued operations and acquisitions.

2.2 Consolidation adjustments and minority interests

The group cash flow statement should only deal with flows of cash and cash equivalents external to the group, so all intra-group cash flows should be eliminated. **Dividends paid to minority interests** should be included under the heading 'returns on investments and servicing of finance' and disclosed separately.

2.3 Example: Minority interests

The following are extracts of the consolidated results for Jarvis plc for the year ended 31 December 20X2.

CONSOLIDATED PROFIT AND LOSS ACCOUNT (EXTRACT)

	£'000
Group profit before tax	90
Taxation	(30)
Profit after tax	60
Minority interest	(15)
Retained profit	45

CONSOLIDATED BALANCE SHEET (EXTRACT)

	20X1	20X2
	£'000	£'000
Minority interest	300	306

Calculate the dividends paid to the minority interest during the year.

Solution

The minority interest share of profit after tax represents retained profit plus dividends paid.

MINORITY INTERESTS

	£'000		£'000
Dividend paid	9	Balance b/fwd	300
Balance c/fwd	306	Profit and loss account	15
	315		315

2.4 Associated undertakings

Only the actual cash flows from sales or purchases between the group and the associate, and investments in and dividends from the entity should be included. Dividends should be included as a separate item between operating activities and **returns on investments and servicing of finance**. Any other cash flows between the investment its associates should be included under the appropriate cash flow heading for the activity giving rise to the cash flow. (Note that this is the treatment prescribed by FRS 9 *Associates and joint ventures*, covered in Chapter 17.)

2.5 Example: Associated company

The following are extracts of the consolidated results of Pripon plc for the year ended 31 December 20X2.

CONSOLIDATED PROFIT AND LOSS ACCOUNT (EXTRACT)

	£'000	£'000
Operating profit of group		150
Share of associated undertaking profit		60
		210
Tax: group	75	
share of associate	30	
		105
Profit after tax		105

CONSOLIDATED BALANCE SHEET (EXTRACTS)

	20X1	20X2
	£'000	£'000
Investment in associated undertaking	264	276

Calculate the dividend received from the associated company.

Solution

The associated undertaking profit before tax represents retained profit plus dividend plus tax.

ASSOCIATE

	£'000		£'000
Balance b/fwd	264	Dividend from associate	18
Profit before tax	60	Tax	30
		Balance c/fwd	276
	324		324

2.6 Finance lease transactions

When rentals under a finance lease are paid the **capital and interest elements are split out** and included under the 'financing' and 'servicing of finance' headings respectively.

2.7 Section summary

The preparation of consolidated cash flow statements will, in many respects, be the same as those for single companies, with the following **additional complications.**

- Acquisitions and disposals of subsidiary undertaking
- Cancellation of intra-group transactions
- Minority interests
- Associated undertakings
- Finance leases

509

Question

Consolidated cash flow statement

Topiary plc is a 40 year old company producing garden statues carved from marble. In 20V9 it acquired a 100% interest in a marble importing company, Hardstuff Ltd; in 20W9 it acquired a 40% interest in a competitor, Landscapes Ltd; and on 1 January 20X7 it acquired a 75% interest in Garden Furniture Designs. The draft consolidated accounts for the Topiary Group are as follows.

DRAFT CONSOLIDATED PROFIT AND LOSS ACCOUNT
FOR THE YEAR ENDED 31 DECEMBER 20X7

	£'000	£'000
Group operating profit		4,455
Share of operating profit in associates		1,485
Income from fixed asset investment		465
Interest payable (group)		(450)
Profit on ordinary activities before taxation		5,955
Tax on profit on ordinary activities		
Corporation tax	1,308	
Deferred taxation	312	
Tax attributable to income of associated undertakings	435	
		(2,055)
Profit on ordinary activities after taxation		3,900
Minority interests		(300)
Profit for the financial year		3,600
Dividends paid and proposed		(1,200)
Retained profit for the year		2,400

DRAFT CONSOLIDATED BALANCE SHEET
AS AT 31 DECEMBER

	20X6		20X7	
	£'000	£'000	£'000	£'000
Fixed assets				
Tangible assets				
Buildings at net book value		6,600		6,225
Machinery: cost	4,200		9,000	
aggregate depreciation	(3,300)		(3,600)	
net book value		900		5,400
		7,500		11,625
Investments in associated undertaking		3,000		3,300
Fixed asset investments		1,230		1,230
		11,730		16,155
Current assets				
Stocks		3,000		5,925
Trade debtors		3,825		5,550
Cash		5,460		13,410
		12,285		24,885
Creditors: amounts falling due within one year				
Trade creditors		840		1,500
Obligations under finance leases		600		720
Corporation tax		651		1,386
Dividends		600		900
Accrued interest and finance charges		90		120
		2,781		4,626
Net current assets				
Total assets less current liabilities		9,504		20,259
Creditors: amounts falling due after more		21,234		36,414
than one year				
Obligations under finance leases		510		2,130
Loans		1,500		4,380
Provisions for liabilities				
Deferred taxation		39		90
Net assets		19,185		29,814
Capital and reserves				
Called up share capital in 25p shares		6,000		11,820
Share premium account		6,285		8,649
Profit and loss account		6,900		9,000
Total shareholders' equity		19,185		29,469
Minority interest		–		345
		19,185		29,814

Notes

1 There had been no acquisitions or disposals of buildings during the year.

Machinery costing £1.5m was sold for £1.5m resulting in a profit of £300,000. New machinery was acquired in 20X7 including additions of £2.55m acquired under finance leases.

2   *Information relating to the acquisition of Garden Furniture Designs*

	£'000
Machinery	495
Stocks	96
Trade debtors	84
Cash	336
Trade creditors	(204)
Corporation tax	(51)
	756
Minority interest	(189)
	567
Goodwill	300
	867
2,640,000 shares issued as part consideration	825
Balance of consideration paid in cash	42
	867

It is group policy to write off goodwill to reserves.

3   Loans were issued at a discount in 20X7 and the carrying amount of the loans at 31 December 20X7 included £120,000 representing the finance cost attributable to the discount and allocated in respect of the current reporting period.

Required

Prepare a consolidated cash flow statement for the Topiary Group for the year ended 31 December 20X7 as required by FRS 1 (revised) with supporting notes for the following.

(a)   Reconciliation of operating profit to net cash flow from operating activities
(b)   Analysis of cash flows netted in the cash flow statement
(c)   Analysis of changes in net debt

Answer

(a)   TOPIARY PLC
       CONSOLIDATED CASH FLOW STATEMENT
       FOR THE YEAR ENDED 31 DECEMBER 20X7

	Note	£'000	£'000
Cash flows from operating activities	1		1,116
Dividend received from associate (W2)	1		750
Returns on investments and servicing of finance	2		21
Taxation (W9)			(885)
Capital expenditure and financial investment	2		(1,755)
Acquisitions and disposals	2		294
Equity dividends paid (600 + 1,200 – 900)			(900)
Cash outflow before financing			(1,359)
Financing	2		
Issue of shares		7,359	
Increase in debt		1,950	
			9,309
Increase in cash in the period			7,950

	Note	£'000	£'000
Reconciliation of net cash flow to movement in net funds	3		
Increase in cash in the period			7,950
Cash inflow from loan issue			(2,760)
Capital element of finance lease instalments			810
Movement resulting from cash flows			6,000
Non-cash movements			
Accretion of finance costs			(120)
Additions to fixed assets under finance leases			(2,550)
Movement in net funds in period			3,330
Net funds at 1.1.X7			2,850
Net funds at 31.12.X7			6,180

NOTES TO THE CASH FLOW STATEMENT

1   Reconciliation of operating profit to operating cash flows

	£'000	£'000
Operating profit		4,455
Depreciation charges (W1)		975
Profit on sale of machinery		(300)
Increase in stocks (5,925 – 3,000 – 96)		(2,829)
Increase in debtors (5,500 – 3,825 – 84)		(1,641)
Increase in creditors (1,500 – 840 – 204)		456
Net cash inflow from operating activities		1,116

2   Analysis of cash flows for headings netted in the cash flow statement

	£'000	£'000
Returns on investments and servicing of finance		
Interest paid (W3)*	(300)	
Dividends from fixed asset investment	465	
Dividends paid to minority interest (W4)	(144)	
		21
Capital expenditure and financial investment		
Purchase of tangible fixed assets (W5)	(3,255)	
Sale of tangible fixed assets	1,500	
		(1,755)
Acquisitions and disposals		
Purchase of subsidiary undertaking		
Cash received on acquisition		336
Less cash consideration		(42)
Cash inflow		(294)
Financing		
Issue of ordinary share capital (W6)		7,359
Debt due beyond a year (W7)	2,760	
Capital element of finance lease rental payments (W8)	(810)	
		1,950
		9,309

* There is not sufficient information in the question to identify separately interest on finance leases.

3   *Analysis of changes in net funds*

	At 1 Jan 20X7 £'000	Cash flow £'000	Other changes £'000	At 31 Dec 20X7 £'000
Cash at bank	5,460	7,950	–	13,410
Debt due > 1yr	(1,500)	(2,760)	(120)	(4,380)
Finance leases	(1,110)	810	(2,550)	(2,850)
	–	(1,950)		–
	2,850	6,000	(2,670)	6,810

Workings

1   *Depreciation charges*

	£'000	£'000
Freehold buildings (6,600 – 6,225)		375
Plant		
Closing balance	3,600	
Opening balance	3,300	
	300	
Depreciation on disposal	300	
		600
		975

2   *Dividends from associates*

	£'000	£'000
Opening balance		3,000
Share of profit	1,485	
Taxation	(435)	
		1,050
		4,050
Closing balance		3,300
		750

3   *Interest*

	£'000
Accrued interest b/f	90
P & L account	450
Discount	(120)
Less accrued interest c/f	(120)
	300

4   *Minority interests*

	£'000
Opening balance	–
Profit for year	300
On acquisition	189
	489
Closing balance	(345)
Cash outflow	144

5   *Purchase of tangible fixed assets: machinery*

	£'000	£'000
Cost at 31 December 20X7		9,000
Cost at 1 January 20X7		4,200
		4,800
Disposal		1,500
		6,300
On acquisition	495	
Leased	2,550	
		(3,045)
Cash outflow		3,255

6   *Issue of ordinary share capital*

	£'000	£'000
Closing balance		
Shares	11,820	
Premium	8,649	
		20,469
Non-cash consideration		
Shares	660	
Premium	165	
		(825)
Opening balance		
Shares	6,000	
Premium	6,285	
		(12,285)
Cash inflow		7,359

7   *Issue of loan stock*

	£'000
Closing balance	4,380
Opening balance	1,500
	2,880
Finance cost	120
Cash inflow	2,760

8   *Capital payments under leases*

	£'000	£'000
Opening balances		
Current		600
Long-term		510
		1,110
New lease commitment		2,550
Closing balances		
Current	720	
Long-term	2,130	
		(2,850)
Cash outflow		810

9   *Taxation*

	£'000	£'000
Opening balance		
Corporation tax	651	
Deferred tax	39	
		690
Profit and loss account transfer (1,308 + 312)		1,620
Closing balances		
Corporation tax	1,386	
Deferred tax	90	
		(1,476)
		834
On acquisition		51
Cash outflow		885

Chapter Roundup

- You must be able to produce a single company cash flow statement. You should also know the scope, formats and definitions given in FRS 1 (revised).

- Consolidated cash flows should not present a great problem if you understand how to deal with acquisitions and disposals of subsidiaries, minority interests and dividends.

Quick Quiz

1   List the standard headings of a cash flow statement under the revised FRS 1.

2   How should an acquisition or disposal of a subsidiary be shown in the cash flow statement?

3   How should an associate be reported in the cash flow statement?

4   What is the net cash inflow from financing giving the following?

Receipts	£	Payments	£
Share issue	5,000	Loan repayments	2,200
Loan	9,000	Expense of share issue	500

Included in loan repayments are £300 interest.

5   Extracts from Net Ltd accounts are given below.

	20X9	20X8
	£'000	£'000
Current assets		
Treasury bills	140	120
Cash	40	30
Creditors after one year:		
Debenture loans	200	500
Ordinary share capital	200	100
Share premium account	120	20

What amount will be shown as the change in net debt for the year from 20X8 to 20X9?

Answers to Quick Quiz

1   See Knowledge Brought Forward box.

2   A note to the cash flow statement should show a summary of the effects of acquisitions and disposals of subsidiary undertakings indicating how much of the consideration comprised cash.

3   Only the actual cash flows from sales or purchases between the group and the associate, and investment in and dividends from the entity should be included.

4

			£'000
Inflows:	Issue		5,000
	Loan		9,000
			14,000
Outflows:	Shares expenses		(500)
	Loan repayments		
	(net of interest)		(1,900)
			11,600

5

	£'000
Cash inflow	10
Cash used to acquire liquid resources	20
Cash used to repurchase debentures	300
	330

Now try the questions below from the Exam Question Bank

Number	Level	Marks	Time
Q25	Examination	25	45 mins
Q30	Examination	50	90 mins

Part E
Specialised entities

Reporting for specialised entities

Topic list	Syllabus reference
1 Not-for-profit sector: primary aims	E1
2 Not-for-profit sector: regulatory framework	E1
3 Not-for-profit sector: performance measurement	E2
4 Smaller entities	E2
5 Life assurance	E2

Introduction

You should be aware that not-for-profit entities and smaller entities may have different accounting needs from the larger profit-making entities that you are used to. This chapter gives you the background you need to set you thinking about whether a one-size-fits-all set of standards is adequate.

Study guide

		Intellectual level
E1	**Financial reporting in specialised, not-for-profit and public sector entities**	
(b)	Apply knowledge from the syllabus to straightforward transactions and events arising in specialised, not-for-profit and public sector entities	3
E2	**Reporting requirements of small and medium entities (SMEs)**	
(a)	Outline the principal considerations in developing a set of accounting standards for SMEs	3
(b)	Discuss solutions to the problem of differential financial reporting	3

Exam guide

This could be tested in essay form, or you could be given a scenario of a not-for-profit entity and have to apply your knowledge from the rest of the syllabus to it. The examiner has said that he will give you the information you need for a question on specialised entities.

1 Not-for-profit sector: primary aims

FAST FORWARD

> The not-for-profit sector can include **public sector entities** and **private** not-for-profit entities such as **charities**.
>
> Not-for-profit entities **have different** goals from profit-making entities, but they still need to be **properly managed** and their accounts need to give a true and fair view.

What organisations do we have in mind when we refer to **Not-for-profit and public sector entities**? These are the most obvious examples:

(a) Central government departments and agencies

(b) Local or federal government departments

(c) Publicly-funded bodies providing healthcare (in the UK this would be the NHS) and social housing

(d) Further and higher education institutions

(e) Charitable bodies

The first four are **public sector entities**. Charities are **private** not-for-profit entities.

Not-for-profit entities have different goals and purposes to profit-making entities and are responsible to different stakeholders. However, they are dealing in very large sums of money and it is important that they are properly managed and that their accounts present fairly the results of their operations.

Until recently, **public sector** accounts were prepared on a **cash basis**. A transition is still in progress which will get them operating on an **accruals basis**, in line with normal practice in the private sector.

1.1 Conceptual framework for not-for profit entities

The IASB and the FASB are currently in a project to produce a new, improved conceptual framework for financial reporting, entitled: *The Objective of Financial Reporting and Qualitative Characteristics of Decision-Useful Financial Reporting Information*. This project is being undertaken in phases. Phase G is entitled *Application to not-for-profit entities in the private and public sector*. A monitoring group, including ASB members, set up to advise on this has made the following points:

(a) Not-for profit entities have different objectives, different operating environments and other different characteristics to private sector businesses.

(b)   The following issues exist regarding application of the proposals to not-for-profit entities:
- Insufficient emphasis on accountability/stewardship
- A need to broaden the definition of users and user groups
- The emphasis on future cash flows is inappropriate to not-for-profit entities
- Insufficient emphasis on budgeting

1.2 Accountability/stewardship

Not-for-profit entities are not reporting to shareholders, but it is very important that they can account for funds received and show how they have been spent. In some cases, resources may be contributed for specific purposes and management is required to show that they have been utilised for that purpose. Perhaps most importantly, taxpayers are entitled to see how the government is spending their money.

1.3 Users and user groups

The primary user group for not-for-profit entities is providers of funds. In the case of public bodies, such as government departments, this primary group will consist of taxpayers. In the case of private bodies such as charities it will be financial supporters, and also potential future financial supporters. There is also a case for saying that a second primary user group should be recognised, being the recipients of the goods and services provided by the not-for-profit entity.

1.4 Cash flow focus

The new framework, like the existing framework, emphasises the need to provide information which will enable users to assess an entity's ability to generate net cash inflows. Not-for-profit entities also need to generate cash flows, but other aspects are generally more significant – for instance, the resources the entity has available to deliver future goods and services, the cost and effectiveness of those it has delivered in the past and the degree to which it is meeting its objectives.

1.5 Budgeting

The IASB has decided to leave consideration of whether financial reporting should include forecast information until later in the project. However, for not-for-profit entities, budgets and variance analyses are more important. In some cases, funding is supplied on the basis of a formal, published budget.

2 Not-for-profit sector: regulatory framework

FAST FORWARD

The IASB and the FASB are working on a **Framework** for reporting which is to include not-for-profit entities.

The ASB gives approval to bodies which develop SORPs.

Regulation of not-for-profit entities, principally local and national governments and governmental agencies, is by the **ASB** assisted by two specialist advisory committees – the Financial Sector and Other Special Industries Committee (FSOSIC) and the Committee on Accounting for Public Benefit Entities (CAPE). These bodies advise the ASB on proposals for Statements of Recommended Practice (SORPs) put forward by specialist bodies developing accounting practice for their sectors.

The ASB gives approval to bodies which wish to develop SORPs. They are developed in accordance with ASB guidelines and the ASB will then give a statement granting approval to the SORP.

These are some SORPs prepared by independent bodies to which the ASB has given its statement:

Authorised Unit Trust Schemes and Authorised Open-Ended Investment Companies

The Investment Management Association

Derivatives
British Bankers Association

Accounting and Reporting by Charities
Charity Commission for England and Wales

Accounting for Further and Higher Education
Universities UK

Accounting for Insurance Business
Association of British Insurers

Limited Liability Partnerships
The Consultative Committee of Accountancy Bodies

Accounting by Registered Social Landlords
National Housing Federation

Code of Practice on Local Authority Accounting in the UK
Chartered Institute of Public Finance and Accountancy

You do not need to remember any of these, but this gives you some idea of the bodies which prepare SORPs. The ASB approval signifies that the SORP complies with current UK accounting standards, the ASB's Statement of Principles and GAAP, apart from any departures arising from the Government's requirements.

2.1 Characteristics of Not-for-profit Entities

As part of its preliminary report on the new Framework, the IASB, advised by the ASB, sets out some of the characteristics of not-for-profit entities as follows:

2.2 Private Sector

Not-for-profit entities in the private sector have the following characteristics:

- Their objective is to provide goods and services to various recipients and not to make a profit
- They are generally characterised by the absence of defined ownership interests (shares) that can be sold, transferred or redeemed
- They may have a wide group of stakeholders to consider (including the public at large in some cases)
- Their revenues generally arise from contributions (donations or membership dues) rather than sales
- Their capital assets are typically acquired and held to deliver services without the intention of earning a return on them

2.3 Public sector

Nor-for-profit entities in the public sector have similar key characteristics to those in the private sector. They are typically established by legislation and:

- Their objective is to provide goods and services to various recipients or to develop or implement policy on behalf of governments and not to make a profit
- They are characterised by the absence of defined ownership interests that can be sold, transferred or redeemed
- They typically have a wide group of stakeholders to consider (including the public at large)

- Their revenues are generally derived from taxes or other similar contributions obtained through the exercise of coercive powers

- Their capital assets are typically acquired and held to deliver services without the intention of earning a return on them

2.4 Not-for-profit entities – specific issues

Public sector bodies are **moving from cash to accruals based** accounting.

While the general trend is to get not-for-profit entities producing accounts which are based as far as possible on the provisions of FRSs and which are generally comparable to those produced for profit-making entities, there are two issues which have yet to be resolved.

2.4.1 Cost of transition

While there has been a general assumption that for public sector entities the move to the accruals basis will result in more relevant and better quality financial reporting, no actual cost-benefit analysis has been undertaken on this.

One of the arguments in favour of the adoption of the accruals basis is that it will be possible to compare the cost of providing a service against the same cost in the private sector. It will then be possible to see how goods and services can be most cheaply sourced.

However, it is questionable whether governments get a good deal anyway when they involve themselves with the private sector and the move to accruals accounting has not gained universal acceptance. The governments of Germany, Italy and Holland have so far made no plans for the transition and the governments of China, Japan, Malaysia and Singapore have decided against it. The main issue is the huge cost involved in terms of the number of qualified accountants required. For developing countries this cost is considered to be prohibitive.

2.4.2 Definition of a liability

The *Framework* defines a liability as 'a present obligation of the entity arising from past events, the settlement of which is expected to result in an outflow from the entity of resources embodying economic benefits'. A liability is recognised when the amount of the outflow can be reliably measured.

Public benefit entities are subject to a commitment to provide public benefits, but there is an issue to be resolved over whether this commitment meets the definition of a liability. In this situation there has been no 'exchange'. The entity has not received any goods or services for which it is required to make 'settlement'. A distinction can be drawn between 'general commitments to provide public benefits' and 'specific commitments to provide public benefits'. The specific commitment can be regarded as a 'present obligation', but it can be argued that the obligation only arises when the entity formally undertakes to provide something such as a non-performance-related grant. (If the grant were performance-related, the entity would be able to withdraw from the agreement if the performance targets were not reached.)

There is also the issue of 'reliable measurement'. Governments in particular often find themselves funding projects which go a long way over budget, suggesting that reliable measurement was not obtained at the outset.

This issue is still being debated by the CAPE. It is of major importance in the financial reporting of the social policies of governments.

2.5 Charities

Financial reporting by UK charities is regulated by a Statement of Recommended Practice (SORP), which was last revised in 2005, generally referred to as SORP 2005. This SORP is the work of the Charity Commission, and they review it each year, taking into account changes in the financial environment.

SORP 2005 is a summary of how accounting standards, charity law and company law impact on charity financial reporting. UK charities are not currently allowed to adopt IFRS. They are required to report under UK standards. The Charities SORP will continue to be reviewed to take into account changes in UK standards, including those arising from the convergence process with IFRS. The SORP deals with accruals-based accounts, although smaller charities with a gross income of below £100,000 per annum are still allowed to prepare cash-based receipts and payments accounts.

In addition to a balance sheet, charities also produce a Statement of Financial Activities (SOFA), an Annual Report to the Charity Commission and sometimes an income and expenditure account. The Statement of Financial Activities is the primary statement showing the results of the charity's activities for the period.

The SoFA shows **Incoming resources**, **Resources expended**, and the resultant **Net movement in funds**. Under incoming resources, income from all sources of funds are listed. These can include:

- Subscription or membership fees
- Public donations
- Donations from patrons
- Government grants
- Income from sale of goods
- Investment income
- Publication sales
- Royalties

The resources expended will show the amount spent directly in furtherance of the Charity's objects. It will also show items which form part of any income statement, such as salaries, depreciation, travelling and entertaining, audit and other professional fees. These items can be very substantial.

Charities, especially the larger charities, now operate very much in the way that profit-making entities do. They run high-profile campaigns which cost money and they employ professional people who have to be paid. At the same time, their stakeholders will want to see that most of their donation is not going on running the business, rather than achieving the aims for which funds were donated.

One of the problems charities experience is that, even although the accruals basis is being applied, they will still have income and expenditure recognised in different periods, due to the difficulty of correlating them. The extreme example is a campaign to persuade people to leave money to the charity in their will. The costs will have to be recognised, but there is no way to predict when the income will arise.

3 Not-for-profit sector: performance measurement

Not-for-profit and public sector entities produce financial statements in the same way as profit-making entities do but, while they are expected to remain solvent, their performance cannot be measured simply by the bottom line.

A public sector entity is not expected to show a profit or to underspend its budget. In practice, government and local government departments know that if they underspend the budget, next year's allocation will be correspondingly reduced. This leads to a rash of digging up the roads and other expenditure just before the end of the financial year as councils strive to spend any remaining funds.

Private and public sector entities are judged principally on the basis of what they have achieved, not how much or how little they have spent in achieving it. So how is performance measured?

3.1 Public sector entities

These will have performance measures laid down by government. The emphasis is on economy, efficiency and effectiveness. Departments and local councils have to show how they have spent public money and what level of service they have achieved. Performance measurement will be based on Key Performance Indicators (KPIs). Examples of these for a local council could be:

- Number of homeless people rehoused
- % of rubbish collections made on time
- Number of children in care adopted

Public sector entities use the services of outside contractors for a variety of functions. They then have to be able to show that they have obtained the best possible value for what they have spent on outside services. This principle is usually referred to as Value For Money (VFM). In the UK, local authorities are required to report under a system known as Best Value. They have to show that they applied 'fair competition' in awarding contracts.

Best Value is based on the principle of the 'four Cs':

1   Challenging why, how and by whom a service is provided
2   Comparing performance against other local authorities
3   Consulting service users, the local community etc
4   Using fair Competition to secure efficient and effective services

3.2 Charities

While charities must demonstrate that they have made proper use of whatever funds they have received, their stakeholders will be more interested in what they have achieved in terms of their stated mission. People who donate money to a relief fund for earthquake victims will want to know what help has been given to survivors, before enquiring how well the organisation has managed its funds. Although it must be said that any mismanagement of funds by a charity is taken very seriously by the donating public.

Some charities produce 'impact reports' which highlight what the charity set out to achieve, what it has achieved and what it has yet to do. Stakeholders should know what the organisation is aiming to achieve and how it is succeeding. Each charity will have its own performance indicators which enable it to measure this.

3.3 Activity

Choose a charity with which you are familiar and produce a possible set of performance indicators for it.

4 Smaller Entities

FAST FORWARD

The *FRS for Smaller Entities* aims to close the big GAAP/little GAAP debate by giving small entities basic accounting and disclosure rules to follow.

4.1 Big GAAP/little GAAP

This is a current debate in the financial accounting world. Most UK companies are **small companies**, generally owned and managed by one person or a family. The owners have invested their own money in the business and there are no outside shareholders to protect. Large companies, by contrast, particularly plcs, may have shareholders who have invested their money, possibly through a pension fund, with no knowledge whatever of the company. These shareholders need protection and the regulations for such companies need to be more stringent.

It could therefore be argued that company accounts should be of **two types**: 'simple' ones for small companies with fewer regulations and disclosure requirements and 'complicated' ones for larger companies with extensive and detailed requirements. This is the 'big GAAP/little GAAP' divide.

4.2 FRS for Smaller Entities

In 1997 the ASB published the *Financial Reporting Standard for Smaller Entities*. This has been revised several times to take account of new FRSs. The latest revision was January 2005. It brings together in one brief document all the **accounting guidance** which UK small businesses will require to draw up their financial statements.

The FRSSE is applicable to all companies that satisfy the definition of a small company in companies legislation and is available to other entities that would meet that definition if they were companies. A company that chooses to comply with the FRSSE is exempt from all other accounting standards and UITF Abstracts.

The FRSSE contains in a simplified form the requirements from existing accounting standards that are relevant to the majority of smaller entities. The latest version (see Paragraph 4.3) also incorporates the requirements of applicable **company law**.

In order to keep the FRSSE as user-friendly as possible some of the requirements in accounting standards relating to more complex transactions have not been included in the FRSSE, as they do not affect most smaller entities. Where guidance is needed on a matter not contained in the FRSSE, regard should be paid to existing practice as set out in the relevant accounting standards.

4.2.1 Measurement

The measurement bases in the FRSSE are the same as, or a simplification of, those in existing accounting standards. For example, under the FRSSE a lessee that is a small company could account for the finance charges on a finance lease on a straight-line basis over the life of the lease, rather than, as in SSAP 21, using a constant periodic rate of return.

4.2.2 Disclosure requirements

One of the many ways in which the FRSSE should reduce the burden for preparers of smaller entities' financial statements is likely to be its *reduced* disclosure requirements. For example, the FRSSE does not require an analysis of turnover and profits into continuing operations, acquisitions and discontinued operations, nor a reconciliation of movements in shareholders' funds.

4.2.3 Related parties

The disclosure requirements for related party transactions in the FRSSE represent a useful dispensation for smaller entities compared with those in FRS 8 *Related party disclosures*. Under FRS 8, related party transactions that are material to the related party, where that related party is an individual, are required to be disclosed in the accounts of the reporting entity even if the transaction is not material to the entity. This is not so for smaller entities adopting the FRSSE, as they need disclose only those related party transactions that are material in relation to the reporting entity.

4.2.4 Cash flow statement

Since small entities are already exempt from the requirements of FRS 1 *Cash flow statements* the FRSSE does not include a requirement for a cash flow statement. The ASB nevertheless believes that a cash flow statement is an important aid to the understanding of an entity's financial position and performance and the FRSSE therefore includes a 'voluntary disclosures' section, recommending that smaller entities present a simplified cash flow statement using the indirect method (ie starting with operating profit and reconciling it to the total cash generated (or utilised) in the period).

4.2.5 Small groups

Small groups are not required by law to prepare consolidated accounts, and therefore in practice not many do so, at least on a statutory basis. The Working Party and the Board, however, agreed with respondents that it would be unfair to those small groups that voluntarily prepare group accounts, if they were not able to take advantage of the provisions in the FRSSE. To import all the necessary requirements from accounting standards and UITF Abstracts into the FRSSE to deal with consolidated accounts would have added substantially to its length and complexity, even though it would have been of interest to only a small percentage of entities. Accordingly, the Working Party and the Board preferred to extend the FRSSE in certain areas and then require small groups adopting the FRSSE to follow those accounting standards and UITF Abstracts that deal with consolidated financial statements. This approach was supported by the majority of respondents to the Exposure Draft commenting on the matter.

4.2.6 Criticisms of the FRSSE

Criticisms of the FRSSE have been as follows.

(a)   The FRSSE is unlikely to make it **easier or cheaper** to prepare financial statements.

(b)   The case in favour of relaxing **measurement** GAAP for smaller companies has not yet been made convincingly. If it is ultimately decided that the only exemptions are to be from disclosure, rather than from measurement, this could be achieved more easily by simply stating in the individual FRSs and SSAPs what disclosure requirements apply to all companies and what applies only to large ones.

(c)   There is concern that the FRSSE could allow smaller companies to use **different accounting measurements**, eg the straight line method rather than the current actuarial method for finance charges.

(d)   It is questionable whether accounts prepared under the FRSSE would give a **true and fair view** under company law. The true and fair view requirement applies to all companies, whatever their size.

(e)   The present document is not a **'stand-alone' document**. Users would still need to refer to 'mainstream' standards if they are to prepare financial statements which show a true and fair view.

However, some commentators back the concept of a financial reporting standard for smaller entities; they feel that the FRSSE provides a satisfactory and workable solution to the problems of smaller entities caused by the **increasing complexity** of accounting standards.

4.3 January 2005 'one stop shop' FRSSE

The ASB published in April 2005 an updated Financial Reporting Standard for Smaller Entities (FRSSE) which is effective for accounting periods beginning on or after 1 January 2005. The standard was developed from the 'one stop shop' proposals set out in the March 2004 Discussion Paper and the recent Exposure Draft.

4.3.1 Company law incorporated

For the convenience of small companies using the FRSSE, this version **reflects the accounting requirements of applicable company law**. These are clearly distinguished from the requirements of accounting standards by the use of small capitals throughout the text.

Recent amendments to the Companies Act introduced a requirement, in reporting transactions, to have regard to their substance in accordance with generally accepted accounting principles or practice. One effect of this is that some preference shares will be shown as liabilities. The FRSSE has been amended to reflect this change.

4.3.2 Updated for new accounting standards

The FRSSE has also been updated to reflect where appropriate the accounting standards and UITF Abstracts issued, or amended, between the last update and October 2004:

(a) The basic principles of **FRS 5 Application Note G** *Revenue recognition* are incorporated into a new section. Guidance on bill and hold arrangements, sales with rights of return and presentation of turnover as principal or as agent is included in an appendix.

(b) The section on post balance sheet events has been updated to reflect the language used in **FRS 21** *Events after the balance sheet date*.

(c) The change to the effective date of the **transitional arrangements** for accounting for defined benefit **pension schemes** is incorporated.

(d) The treatment of costs incurred in bidding for and securing contracts to supply goods or services set out in **UITF Abstract 34** *Pre-contract costs* has been incorporated.

Respondents to the Exposure Draft suggested that the FRSSE should reflect the recently issued **UITF Abstract 40** *Revenue recognition and service contracts*. This specific proposal will be subject to consultation in a future update. In the meantime, to assist entities using the FRSSE, the requirements of the Abstract are reflected as guidance in an appendix.

The FRSSE continues to be available for smaller entities to **prepare consolidated accounts**. The relevant legal requirements for small companies on the **form and content of group accounts** are summarised together with references to the relevant accounting standards.

4.3.3 Further changes

In April 2006, the ASB issued an exposure draft of further amendments to the FRSSE.

Since the FRSSE was last updated, eight new FRSs have been issued. There have also been two amendments to FRSs and two new UITF Abstracts. In considering whether these changes in financial reporting are appropriate for smaller entities, the Board has been advised by its specialist Committee on Accounting for Smaller Entities (CASE).

The Exposure Draft also considers FRS 20 (on share-based payment), which was not addressed in the last amendment to the FRSSE, and recent changes in company law financial reporting requirements. In particular, the Board is seeking views on its proposal to apply in full the requirements of FRS 20.

The Exposure Draft is expected to lead to the fifth periodic revision to the FRSSE.

4.4 Small company limits

The thresholds for small companies, ie those eligible to use the FRSSE increased in 2004 to:

(a) Turnover not more than £5.6m

(b) Balance sheet total not more than £2.8m

(c) Number of employees unchanged from the limit of 50

4.5 International developments: IASB Exposure Draft

4.5.1 The ED

In February 2007, the IASB published an **exposure draft** of a proposed *IFRS for small and medium-sized entities*. In April 2007 this was published in the UK as a Consultation Paper. This invites comments on eleven questions:

(a) The proposed *IFRS for SMEs* is intended to be a **stand-alone document**. Is additional information needed to make it more self-contained?

(b) Are there other recognition or measurement simplifications that the Board should consider?

(c) Are there recognition and measurement simplifications that the Board should re-consider?

(d) Should *all* **accounting policy options** in full IFRS be available to SMEs?

(e) Should SMEs be allowed to **choose** either the **expense model** or the **capitalisation model** for borrowing costs, and why?

(f) Should any **additional topics** be omitted from the IFRS for SMEs and replaced by a cross reference?

(g) The proposed *IFRS for SMEs* is intended as a stand-alone document, but it contains cross **references** to full IFRS in specific circumstances. Is this appropriate?

(h) Are there specific areas for which SMEs are likely to need **additional guidance**?

(i) Should there be **disclosure requirements** in addition to those specified in the draft implementation guidance *Illustrative Financial Statements and Disclosure Checklist?*

(j) Is the **transition guidance** adequate?

(k) The IASB expects to amend the *IFRS for SMEs* **every other year**. Is this adequate?

4.5.2 Pluses and minuses of the ED

Pluses

(a) It is virtually a '**one stop shop**'.
(b) It is **structured according to topics**, which should make it practical to use.
(c) It is written in an **accessible style**.
(d) There is **considerable reduction in disclosure requirements**.
(e) Guidance **not relevant** to SMEs is **excluded**.

Minuses

(a) It **does not focus on the smallest companies**.
(b) The scope extends to 'non-publicly accountable' entities. Potentially, the **scope is too wide**.
(c) The standard will be **onerous** for small companies.
(d) **Further simplifications could be made**. These might include:

(i) Amortisation for goodwill and intangibles
(ii) No requirement to value intangibles separately from goodwill on a business combination.
(iii) No recognition of deferred tax.
(iv) No measurement rules for equity-settled share-based payment.
(v) No requirement for consolidated accounts (as for EU SMEs currently)
(vi) All leases accounted for as operating leases with enhanced disclosures
(vii) Fair value measurement when readily determinable without undue cost or effort.

4.5.3 The ASB's view

The ASB made the following statement on its website:

> 'The ASB is of the opinion that there are three main implications that need to be considered by constituents. Firstly, constituents need to consider what other role the IFRS for SMEs may play within the ASB's convergence project ie is it suitable for a mid-tier of companies above the current range for the FRSSE but below those currently required to apply full IFRS? Secondly, is the IFRS for SMEs an appropriate replacement for the FRSSE? Finally, if the IFRS for SMEs is to be considered a suitable basis for middle tier companies, or as a replacement for the FRSSE, what changes will need to be made to it? The ASB is inviting constituents' views on these implications, which also includes a question on the relative costs and benefits of the ASB adopting the proposed IFRS for SMEs.

> The ASB's previous tentative decision on UK convergence was to support a two-tier approach, with the lower level potentially (and ideally) being based on the outcome of the IASB's IFRS for SMEs project. Consequently, the ASB has decided to defer any final decisions on convergence until feedback from the above ITC has been analysed and discussed by the ASB; at which time a judgement can be made as to whether or not it is suitable for the needs of the UK and Republic of Ireland.'

5 FRS 27: Life assurance

5.1 Issue

FRS 27 *Life assurance* was issued in December 2004. The standard was issued in response to a request from the UK Government for the ASB to look into accounting for with-profits business by life assurers. It builds on the new regulatory capital regime introduced by the Financial Services Authority (FSA).

FAST FORWARD

> **FRS 27** aims is to provide a better understanding of both the liabilities and capital management of life assurers.

5.2 Measurement

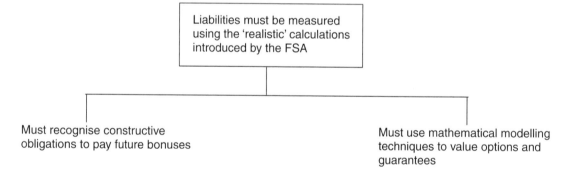

Liabilities must be measured using the 'realistic' calculations introduced by the FSA

Must recognise constructive obligations to pay future bonuses

Must use mathematical modelling techniques to value options and guarantees

5.3 New disclosure requirements

Capital statement	– Analysing shareholders' funds and other components of regulatory capital across the entity
Narrative explanation	– Regulatory requirements – Capital held to meet requirements – Extent to which capital in one part of the entity's insurance business is available to meet risks and requirements in other parts
Further disclosure	– Sensitivity of capital and liabilities to changes in market conditions – Assumptions made, including those relating to future management actions

5.4 Implementation

The ASB has a signed voluntary agreement with major life assurers and banks that they will adopt FRS 27 within an IFRS framework.

5.5 International

There is no direct equivalent to FRS 27. The IASB are working on insurance accounting and issued IFRS 4 on insurance contracts to establish some basic principles. The ASB will contribute to the IASB's continuing work in this area.

Chapter Roundup

- The not-for-profit sector can include **public sector entities** and **private** not-for-profit entities such as **charities**.

- Not-for-profit entities **have different** goals from profit-making entities, but they still need to be **properly managed** and their accounts need to give a true and fair view.

- The IASB and the FASB are working on a **Framework** for reporting which is to include not-for-profit entities.

- The ASB gives approval to bodies which develop SORPs.

- Public sector bodies are **moving from cash to accruals based** accounting.

- The **FRSSE** is a standard for smaller entities

- The *FRS for Smaller Entities* aims to close the big GAAP/little GAAP debate by giving small entities basic accounting and disclosure rules to follow.

- **FRS 27** aims to provide a better understanding of both the liabilities and the capital management of life assurers

Quick Quiz

1   Charities are public sector entities. True or false?

2   Why do not-for-profit entities need to keep accounts if they are not reporting to shareholders?

3   What are the two issues which need to be resolved before not-for-profit entities can move to FRS?

4   What is the purpose of the FRSSE?

Answers to Quick Quiz

1   False. Charities are private not-for-profit entities.

2   They often deal in large sums of money. Managers and taxpayers need to know it is being properly spent.

3   (a)   The transition from cash to accruals-based accounting.
     (b)   The definition of a liability.

4   It brings together in one document all the accounting guidance which UK small businesses will require to draw up their financial statements.

Now try the questions below from the Exam Question Bank

Number	Level	Marks	Time
Q26	Introductory	n/a	n/a

Part F
Evaluating current developments

23

International issues

Topic list	Syllabus reference
1 International harmonisation	H2
2 Convergence	H2
3 Accounting overseas	H3
4 Financial reporting in the USA	H3
5 UK GAAP vs IAS vs US GAAP	H3
6 IASB work plan	H3

Introduction

As business expands on an **international scale** so financial reporting must be viewed as it operates on an international rather than a national level. In studying the impact of the international environment we will look at the influences on accounting in a number of countries. These influences vary from country to country and include legal, political, socio-cultural and economic conditions prevailing at any time.

Study guide

		Intellectual level
H2	**Convergence between national and international reporting standards**	
(a)	Evaluate the implications, nationally and globally, of convergence with International Financial Reporting Standards	3
(b)	Discuss the implementation issues arising from convergence process	3
H3	**Comparison of national reporting requirements**	
(a)	Identify the reasons for major differences in accounting practices, including culture	2
(b)	Discuss the influence of national regulators on international financial reporting	2

Exam guide

In view of the developments in convergence, this is a 'hot topic', and, as such, ripe for examination. This topic comprised the bulk of a question on the Pilot Paper.

1 International harmonisation

> **FAST FORWARD**
>
> **Harmonisation** in accounting is likely to come from international accounting standards. There are enormous difficulties to overcome, both technical and political and progress, but progress is being made.

Before we look at any other countries in particular, we must consider what barriers there are to international harmonisation and why harmonisation is considered so desirable, before looking at comparative accounting systems.

1.1 Barriers to harmonisation

> **FAST FORWARD**
>
> You should be able to discuss the **barriers to harmonisation** and the advantages of and **progress towards harmonisation**.

There are undoubtedly many barriers to international harmonisation: if there were not then greater progress would probably have been made by now. The main problems are as follows.

(a) **Different purposes of financial reporting**. In some countries the purpose is solely for tax assessment, while in others it is for investor decision-making.

(b) **Different legal systems**. These prevent the development of certain accounting practices and restrict the options available.

(c) **Different user groups**. Countries have different ideas about who the relevant user groups are and their respective importance. In the USA investor and creditor groups are given prominence, while in Europe employees enjoy a higher profile.

(d) **Needs of developing countries**. Developing countries are obviously behind in the standard setting process and they need to develop the basic standards and principles already in place in most developed countries.

(e) **Nationalism** is demonstrated in an unwillingness to accept another country's standard.

(f) **Cultural differences** result in objectives for accounting systems differing from country to country.

(g) **Unique circumstances**. Some countries may be experiencing unusual circumstances which affect all aspects of everyday life and impinge on the ability of companies to produce proper reports, for example hyperinflation, civil war, currency restriction and so on.

(h) **The lack of strong accountancy bodies**. Many countries do not have strong independent accountancy or business bodies which would press for better standards and greater harmonisation.

These are difficult problems to overcome, and yet attempts are being made continually to do so. We must therefore consider what the perceived advantages of harmonisation are, which justify so much effort.

1.2 Advantages of global harmonisation

The advantages of harmonisation will be based on the benefits to users and preparers of accounts, as follows.

(a) **Investors**, both individual and corporate, would like to be able to compare the financial results of different companies internationally as well as nationally in making investment decisions. Differences in accounting practice and reporting can prove to be a barrier to such cross-border analysis. There is a growing amount of investment across borders and there are few financial analysts able to follow shares in international markets. For example, it is not easy for an analyst familiar with UK accounting principles to analyse the financial statements of a Dutch or German company. Harmonisation would therefore be of benefit to such analysts.

(b) **Multinational companies** would benefit from harmonisation for many reasons including the following.

   (i) Better access would be gained to foreign investor funds.

   (ii) Management control would be improved, because harmonisation would aid internal communication of financial information.

   (iii) Appraisal of foreign enterprises for take-overs and mergers would be more straightforward.

   (iv) It would be easier to comply with the reporting requirements of overseas stock exchanges.

   (v) Consolidation of foreign subsidiaries and associated companies would be easier.

   (vi) A reduction in audit costs might be achieved.

   (vii) Transfer of accounting staff across national borders would be easier.

(c) **Governments of developing countries** would save time and money if they could adopt international standards and, if these were used internally, governments of developing countries could attempt to control the activities of foreign multinational companies in their own country. These companies could not 'hide' behind foreign accounting practices which are difficult to understand.

(d) **Tax authorities**. It will be easier to calculate the tax liability of investors, including multinationals who receive income from overseas sources.

(e) **Regional economic groups** usually promote trade within a specific geographical region. This would be aided by common accounting practices within the region.

(f) **Large international accounting firms** would benefit as accounting and auditing would be much easier if similar accounting practices existed throughout the world.

1.3 Progress with harmonisation to date

The barriers to harmonisation may be daunting but some progress has been made. There are various bodies which are working on different aspects of harmonisation and these are discussed below. The most important of these bodies, in the light of recent developments, is the IASB.

1.4 International Accounting Standards Board (IASB)

The function and role of the IASB was covered in your earlier studies. In particular, the effect of the IASB's *Framework for the Preparation and Presentation of Financial Statements* on the UK standard setting regime has been profound.

The IASB is tackling the issue of harmonisation through a review of its International Accounting Standards (IASs). This review was embodied in a Statement of Intent *Comparability of Financial Statements*, published in mid-1990. This statement laid out proposed revisions of certain IASs and the programme of amendment should be completed soon.

The IASB has been around for over 30 years. The current list of IFRS and IAS is as follows.

International Accounting Standards	
IAS 1 (revised)	Presentation of financial statements
IAS 2 (revised)	Inventories
IAS 7	Cash flow statements
IAS 8 (revised)	Accounting policies, changes in accounting estimates and errors
IAS 10 (revised)	Events after the balance sheet date
IAS 11	Construction contracts
IAS 12 (revised)	Income taxes
IAS 14 (revised)	Segment reporting
IAS 16 (revised)	Property, plant and equipment
IAS 17 (revised)	Leases
IAS 18	Revenue
IAS 19 (revised)	Employee benefits
IAS 20	Accounting for government grants and disclosure of government assistance
IAS 21	The effects of changes in foreign exchange rates
IAS 23	Borrowing costs
IAS 24 (revised)	Related party disclosures
IAS 26	Accounting and reporting by retirement benefit plans
IAS 27 (revised)	Consolidated and separate financial statements
IAS 28	Investments in associates
IAS 29	Financial reporting in hyperinflationary economies
IAS 30	Disclosure in the financial statements of banks and similar financial institutions
IAS 31	Interests in joint ventures
IAS 32	Financial instruments: presentation
IAS 33	Earnings per share
IAS 34	Interim financial reporting
IAS 36 (revised)	Impairment of assets
IAS 37	Provisions, contingent liabilities and contingent assets
IAS 38 (revised)	Intangible assets

International Accounting Standards	
IAS 39	Financial instruments: recognition and measurement
IAS 40	Investment property
IAS 41	Agriculture
IFRS 1	First-time application of International Financial Reporting Standards
IFRS 2	Share based payment
IFRS 3	Business combinations
IFRS 4	Insurance contracts
IFRS 5	Non-current assets held for sale and discontinued operations
IFRS 6	Exploration for and evaluation of mineral resources
IFRS 7	Financial instruments: disclosures
IFRS 8	Operating segments

1.5 IASB and current developments

America and Japan have been two of the developed countries which have been most reluctant to accept accounts prepared under IASs, but recent developments suggest that such financial statements may soon be acceptable on these important stock exchanges. The Japanese situation was discussed above.

In **America**, the Securities and Exchange Commission (SEC) agreed in 1993 to allow foreign issuers (of shares, etc) to follow IASB treatments on business combinations, goodwill and subsidiaries in hyper-inflationary economies, and to file cash flow statements under IAS 7. The SEC also allowed foreign issuers to use proportional consolidations (favoured by the IASB) to report interests in joint ventures. The overall effect is that, where IASB treatments differ from US GAAP, these treatments will now be acceptable. The SEC is now supporting the IASB because it wants to attract foreign listings.

This SEC decision was supported by the findings of a report by Professor Trevor Harris of the University of Columbia on the reporting practices of several large multi-national companies. His report concludes that on both measurement issues and disclosure, the revised IASs had reduced differences between IASs and US GAAP where differences still existed. IAS treatments or disclosures were often as good as or even better than US GAAP. In addition, in early 1996, the FASB and IASB approved similar draft codes on the disclosure of EPS.

This **close conformity between IASs and US GAAP** could, however, **cause problems for the IASB**. Some countries will see these moves as an attempt to force an international version of US GAAP on the rest of the world. It is not only developing countries which have reservations; the IOSCO review of IASs highlighted a number of European and Japanese issues which are outstanding. The IASC agreement with IOSCO has added substance to the perception that the IASC attaches more importance to American issues than to those of Europe or Japan.

The IASB therefore runs a fine balancing act between various strong interests. It must maintain support from all areas in order to ensure that pronouncements are accepted worldwide and this is a difficult political talk. The main methods of achieving this will be by:

(a) Ensuring the quality of the IASB's technical work

(b) Involving national standard-setting bodies (and multi-national companies) in the IASB's work

This will also help to ensure that IASs are 'marketed' as the best approach based on accepted principles, rather than 'lowest-common denominator' standards.

1.6 ASB and international standards

The ASB considers the development of international standards of **fundamental importance**. In addition, the ASB meets on a formal, and regular basis with standard-setters around the world.

FRS 20 *Share based payment* is almost identical to IFRS 2 of the same name.

1.7 The EC regulation

FAST FORWARD

From 2005 consolidated accounts of all listed companies **have been obliged to comply with IAS.**

As we have already seen, the EC regulations form one part of a broader programme for the harmonisation of company law in member states. The commission is uniquely the only organisation to produce **international** standards of accounting practice which are legally enforceable, in the form of directives which must be included in the national legislation of member states. The directives have been criticised as they might become constraints on the application of world-wide standards and bring accounting standardisation and harmonisation into the political arena.

FAST FORWARD

This led to the publication of the **Convergence Handbook.**

Since 2005 consolidated accounts of listed companies have been required to comply with international accounting standards. The implications of this proposal are far reaching. A detailed comparison of international and national accounting standards has been carried out, called *The Convergence Handbook.* In conjunction with other developments, this has led to the development of a Strategy for Convergence (see Section 2).

Many commentators believe that, in the light of the above, it is only a matter of time before national standard setting bodies like the ASB are, in effect, replaced by the IASB and national standards fall into disuse. However, national standards were designed for the national environment, which includes small companies (see Chapter 1). Moreover, the IASB will need input and expertise from valued national standard setters like the ASB.

1.8 The situation today and in the future

Many organisations committed to global harmonisation have done a great deal of work towards this goal. It is the case at present, however, that fundamental disagreements exist between countries and organisations about the way forward. One of the major gulfs is between the reporting requirements in developed countries and those in non-developed countries. It will be some time before these difficulties can be overcome. The IASB is likely to be the lead body in attempting to do so, as discussed above.

2 Convergence   Pilot paper

As explained in Section 1, The **Convergence Handbook** is a detailed comparison between International Accounting Standards (IASs) and UK financial reporting requirements. Implementation of the Handbook's recommendations will require changes to UK accounting standards or IASs— and in many cases to both.

The ASB asked for the research to be carried out in the light of the **European Commission's** regulation that, in order to improve the harmonisation of accounting within the single market, consolidated accounts of listed companies should be required to **comply with IASs by 2005.**

The ASB's intention in asking for a comparison to be made was to reveal in detail the differences between the two sets of accounting requirements. This will enable the financial and business community in the UK and in the Republic of Ireland to examine the differences and inform the ASB whether they would wish the domestic requirements to be altered to conform with IASs. Alternatively, where the UK requirements are thought to be of a higher quality, the ASB can seek to persuade IASB to change IASs.

2.1 Recommendations for convergence

It is outside the scope of your syllabus to go into all the differences between UK GAAP and IAS. However, an outline of the Handbook's recommendations is given here.

The authors believe that there is now a **strong case for greater convergence** of UK GAAP and IAS and that any changes should happen quickly.

Complete convergence could be achieved by the ASB replacing all current accounting standards with FRSs that are identical to IAS. However, the authors do not support this approach, as some IAS are simply inferior to FRSs.

Alternatively, complete convergence could be achieved by the IASB replacing all current IAS with UK standards. Even if this approach were acceptable internationally (unlikely), the authors believe that some IAS are superior or more up to date than FRSs and are not constrained by company law. The authors believe that **convergence should be achieved by changes to both UK standards and IAS.**

The Handbook's recommended approach is twofold.

Stage 1   The **ASB** should undertake a **convergence project** to deal with **revisions to UK GAAP** and seek any necessary changes in company law.

Stage 2   The **IASB** should undertake a further **improvements project** to deal with the **revisions to IAS**.

2.2 Recent developments: FREDs, FRSs, IAS and Discussion Paper

FAST FORWARD

The **convergence project** is well underway with a number of FREDs based on IAS, new standards and revisions to IAS.

The ASB's **Discussion Paper on Convergence** sets out the strategy. The aim is to minimise the burden of change. The strategy is twofold.

- New standards effective in 2005/06 to enhance UK financial reporting
- 'Step changes', replacing UK standards as and when IASB projects are completed

Rather than 'sit tight' using its own Standards until 2005, the ASB has been **revising** a number of **UK Standards** to bring them into line with the (revised and improved) IAS. To this end, in May 2002 it has published for comment nine Financial Reporting Exposure Drafts. It also published three Consultation Papers, two of which describe certain changes proposed by the IASB to its standards and one of which gives guidance on first-time application. This is a record in terms of the amount of material issued in such a short time. The documents are as follows.

FRED 23   *Financial instruments: hedge accounting* *

FRED 24   *The effects of changes in foreign exchange rates; Financial reporting in hyperinflationary economies* *

FRED 25   *Related party disclosures*

FRED 26   *Earnings per share* *

FRED 27   *Events after the balance sheet date* *

FRED 28   *Inventories*

FRED 29   *Property, plant and equipment; Borrowing costs*

FRED 30   *Financial instruments: Disclosure and Presentation; recognition and measurement* *

FRED 31   *Share-based payment* *

Consultation Paper *IASB proposals to amend certain International Accounting Standards* *

Consultation Paper *IASB proposals for first-time application of International Financial Reporting Standards* *

Consultation Paper *IASB proposals on business combinations, impairment and intangible assets* *

2.3 Moving on

The items marked with an asterisk (*) have been developed further, since they were first issued.

(a)   FRED 24 has now become FRS 23 *The effects of changes in foreign exchange rates* and FRS 24 *Financial reporting in hyperinflationary economies*

(b)   FRED 26 *Earnings per share* is now FRS 22 of the same name.

(c)   FRED 30 has now become FRS 25 *Financial instruments: presentation IFRS 7 Financial Instruments: disclosure* and FRS 26 *Financial instruments: recognition and measurement*, FRS 26.

(d)   FRED 27 *Events after the balance sheet date* has now become a full standard (FRS 21), covered in Chapter 9.

(e)   FRED 31 *Share based payment* has now become a full standard (FRS 20) (identical to IFRS 2, covered in Chapter 15).

(f)   The Consultation Paper on first-time application of IFRS is now IFRS 1 *First time adoption of International Financial Reporting Standards* and is covered in Chapter 14.

(g)   The changes proposed in the other consultation papers have been effected by revising IAS 1, 2, 8, 10, 16, 17, 24, 27, 28, 33, 36, 38 and 40 and issuing IFRS 3 *Business combinations*.

Exam focus point

You will need to know these in terms of the main changes from UK practice.

2.4 Discussion Paper: UK accounting standards: a strategy for convergence with IFRS

In March 2004, the ASB issued a Discussion Paper *UK accounting standards: a strategy for convergence with IFRS*. The EU Regulation requiring the accounts of UK listed companies to comply with international standards has **significant consequences for the ASB** and for the future of **UK accounting standards**.

The objective of the Discussion Paper is to set out the ASB's views on the possible development of UK accounting standards and to consult on its plans.

The approach taken by the ASB reflects two fundamental propositions.

(a)   There can be no **case for the use in the UK of two sets of wholly different accounting standards in the medium term**.

(b)   should **not** seek to issue **new standards** that are **more demanding or restrictive than** International Financial Reporting Standards ('**IFRS**')

The intention of the ASB is to bring UK accounting standards into line with IFRS as quickly as possible, whilst:

(a)   **Avoiding the burden of excessive changes** in any one year

(b)   Minimising the cases in which an entity using UK standards may be required to make **successive changes of accounting policy** in respect of the same matter

2.5 Phased approach

Accordingly, the ASB has proposed a **phased approach** to the convergence.

Phase 1   New standards effective in 2005 and 2006 that will **enhance** existing UK financial reporting requirements and keep them in step with changes in the law.

Phase 2   A series of 'step changes', replacing one or more existing UK accounting standards with standards **based on IFRS as prospective IASB projects are completed**.

In order to avoid two changes of accounting policy on the same issue within a short period, the Paper discusses a number of ongoing IASB projects for which the ASB recommends retaining the equivalent UK standards at present.

2.6 Phase 1: standards for 2005 to 2006

The new standards effective in 2005 and 2006 will address the following areas.

(a)   **Share options.** FRS 20 *Share based payment* (see Chapter 15) is based on IFRS 2 of the same name.

(b)   **Financial instruments.** Standards will be issued based on IAS 32 and much of IAS 39 from 2005. This is covered in FRS 26, second supplement (see Chapter 8).

(c)   **Retirement benefits.** FRS 17 (see Chapter 6) will replace SSAP 24 in 2005 so that, consistent with IASB proposals for IAS 19 *Employee benefits*, actuarial gains and losses are fully recognised in the period in which they arise.

(d)   **Events after the balance sheet date** (post balance sheet events). FRS 21 *Events after the balance sheet date* (see Chapter 9) was issued in May 2004. The standard replaces SSAP 17 from 2005 and brings UK GAAP into line with the revised IAS 10.

(e)   **Earnings per share.** A UK standard (applicable to listed companies only) based on IAS 33 ie FRS 22.

(f)   **Related party disclosures.** A standard based on IAS 24 will replace FRS 8 from 2006. This will follow FRED 25 (see Chapter 15).

(g)   **Subsidiary undertakings.** An exposure draft was published in May 2004 proposing a minor amendment arising from the Government's expected change to the legal definition of a subsidiary undertaking (see Chapter 16).

(h)   **Agriculture and leases.** After considering responses to the discussion paper, the ASB may issue exposure drafts for a UK standard based on IAS 41 *Agriculture* and revised disclosures in respect of operating lease commitments based on those in IAS 17 *Leases*.

2.7 Phase 2: Standards to be retained

Phase 2 involves replacing one or more existing UK standards with standards based on IFRS as IASB projects are completed. The Discussion Paper mentions a number of ongoing IASB projects for which the ASB recommends retaining the equivalent UK standards at present.

(a)   **FRS 5.** This plays a critical role in the context of UK financial reporting and should be retained until it becomes clear that its most important requirements, including those on revenue recognition, have adequate counterparts under IFRS.

(b)   **SSAP 9 and FRS 5 Application Note G (Revenue recognition).** The ASB favours retaining these until the IASB's project on revenue recognition results in a standard. Then UK standards based on IAS 2 and IAS 11 would be introduced, as well as the new standard on revenue recognition.

(c)   **Financial instruments.** The ASB does not intend to implement the sections of IAS 39 relating to recognition and derecognition at this time; it believes that the requirements of FRS 5, which cover a wider scope than the derecognition of financial assets dealt with in IAS 39, should be retained for the present. Further delays relate to fair value and hedging.

2.8 Phase 2: 'Step changes' awaiting completion of IASB projects

In most of these cases, an IASB project would affect several UK standards. Implementing the changes would therefore entail replacing several UK standards at the same time with new standards based on IFRS. Thus UK standards would converge with IFRS in a series of significant, but discrete, steps rather than a number of piecemeal changes being introduced over a number of years.

(a)   **Reporting comprehensive income.** FRS 3 was introduced to combat the focus on one measure of performance, such as EPS by requiring a STRGL as well as a profit and loss account. It also prohibits 'recycling' gains and losses, that is transferring them to the profit and loss account in a subsequent period, for example, when the gain or loss is 'realised'. UK standards are in contrast to US standards, which sometimes require it and IFRS, which sometimes allow it, eg IAS 39 and IAS 21. This issue remains unresolved. The ASB does not therefore propose IFRS based standards to replace FRS 1 *Cash flow statements*, FRS 3 *Reporting financial performance* or SSAP 25 *Segmental reporting*. It would also be necessary to retain FRS 18 *Accounting policies*, as the corresponding requirements in IFRS are contained in IAS 1 *Presentation of financial statements* and IAS 8 *Accounting policies, changes in accounting estimates and errors* which may also be revised as a result of the project on comprehensive income.

(b)   **Disposal of non-current assets and presentation of discontinued operations.** IFRS 5 on this topic has been published. However, as it is part of reporting comprehensive income and would also require changes to FRS 15, the ASB is awaiting the outcome of this project and revisions to IAS 16 *Property, plant and equipment*.

(c)   **Fixed assets and investment properties.** There is an international project on measurement. Until completion of this, FRS 15 and SSAP 19 are to be retained.

(d)   **Business combinations, impairment and intangibles.** The first phase of the IASB project is reflected in IFRS 3 *Business combinations*. The IASB is continuing its work on accounting for business combinations and further international exposure drafts will be published. Introduction of standards based on IFRS resulting from the completed IASB project would be likely to involve replacing SSAP 13, FRS 6, FRS 7, FRS 10 and FRS 11. The ASB will await the completion of the IASB business combinations project before introducing UK standards based on IFRS.

(e)   **Provisions, contingent liabilities and contingent assets.** The IASB is considering modifying IAS 37, so the ASB will await the revised IAS before revising FRS 12.

(f)   **Government grants.** IAS 20 on government grants is to be withdrawn, therefore it will not be brought into the UK in its present form.

(g)   **Consolidation, associates and joint ventures.** This is the subject of an IASB project, therefore FRS 2 and FRS 9 will be retained for now.

(h)   **Taxation and leasing.** Replacement of or changes to FRS 16 and 19 are awaiting the completion of IASB and FASB considerations.

(i) **Insurance.** IFRS 4 on insurance has recently been published, but may be subject to further changes, and therefore its requirements will not at this stage be introduced into the UK.

(j) **Small companies.** As mentioned in Chapter 1, the IASB's consideration of smaller companies is at an early stage (discussion paper), so the FRSSE will be retained for now.

2.9 Role of the ASB

The ASB plans to continue to devote significant resources to **working with, and influencing the work of**, the IASB, the International Financial Reporting Interpretations Committee ('IFRIC') and other international bodies, including the European Financial Reporting Advisory Group ('EFRAG'). The ASB will continue to maintain its dialogue with constituents in the UK and Republic of Ireland and encourage them to make their views known directly to such bodies.

The ASB also intends to:

(a) Address issues that arise in the context of UK standards either through UK accounting standards or through its Urgent Issues Task Force

(b) Maintain the FRSSE

(c) Oversee the development of Statements of Recommended Practice ('SORPs') where these give appropriate sectoral guidance.

Exam focus point

> This information is up to date as of June 2007. It is vital that you read *Student Accountant* to keep up to date with developments in this area. It will also help you in practice to know what's coming next, in this rapidly changing financial reporting environment.

The role of the ASB is discussed in an exposure draft of a policy statement (see Chapter 24).

3 Accounting overseas

FAST FORWARD

> We have concentrated on certain countries in our **comparison** between UK and overseas accounts, but you should be able to highlight the differences to UK accounting if you are presented with a set of accounts from any other country.

3.1 Europe

You would expect that countries which are members of the EU, and which are therefore bound by European Commission directives (particularly the 4th and 7th), would have very similar reporting and accounting requirements. This is not necessarily the case, however, and many influences have shaped financial reporting practices, even events as far back as the Second World War. In an effort to understand what differences exist between European countries, we will examine four areas and their impact on financial reporting:

- The legal system
- The taxation system
- The forms of organisations
- The accounting profession

We have limited the scope of our comparison to France and Germany, which will give you a good idea of the differences which can exist across Europe.

Exam focus point

> The discussion that follows on the differences in these four areas is useful background reading, so that you can understand why international differences exist. Try to get an overview.

3.2 Legal system

European countries have historically had either a **common law system**, such as in the UK, or a **Roman codified system**, such as in France and Germany. These different systems have had a direct effect on the development of the variety of accounting practices found in Europe.

In **France** the Roman codified system is made up of commercial codes and related decrees and amendments. The significant influence of legislation on French financial accounting reflects the national planning policy of the government, which requires a high level of standardised accounting practice and reporting. This process is aided by the use of a national plan. The plan has been adopted by almost all enterprises in the country, and provides:

(a) A national uniform chart of accounts
(b) Definitions and explanations of terminology
(c) Details of bookkeeping entries
(d) Principles of accounting measurement (valuation)
(e) Standard forms of financial statements
(f) Details of permitted cost accounting methods

The main principles of the French plan reflect **conservatism** and adherence to legal form rather than economic substance. This is similar to the situation in Germany, whose system influenced the French during the 1930s and 1940s.

In **Germany** the provision of detailed accounting requirements by law has a long history, during which period these **legal regulations** have remained dominant in the field of prescribing basic accounting practices. The majority of the current legislation is laid down in the Commercial Code (first established in 1897), the Corporation Act 1965 and tax laws. The Commercial Code regulates the maintenance of accounting records in accordance with 'principles of proper bookkeeping' and the preparation of periodic financial statements. The Corporation Act 1965 regulates the accounting standards and practices that should be adopted in preparing financial statements.

A feature of German financial accounting which is important is the legal and revenue reserves that are required, plus the **'secret reserves'**, which exist because revaluation of appreciating assets is not allowed and depreciation in line with the tax rules is often in excess of that which is required to measure the periodic cost of depreciating assets. Such reserves have no exact UK equivalent.

3.3 Taxation system

In some European countries the tax system, in line with the legal system, has a **considerable effect** on financial accounting practices while in others, including the UK, it has only a minor indirect influence.

The **French** tax system is an imputation system and has a very strong influence on French accounting practices including the values incorporated in financial statements. **Accounting profit measurement rules are the same as those for tax profit measurement**, mainly because for an item to be allowed as a tax deduction it must be included in the financial accounts. Depreciation rules, for example, are based on tax rules and assets are only revalued in line with tax regulations. Voluntary revaluations are permitted but are unlikely to occur as income tax is payable on the unrealised profit on revaluation. A French company's tax return will therefore look like a detailed copy of the financial statements.

In **Germany** the tax system is an integral part of the legal system. For example, there is a fundamental legal principle that values of profit/assets and liabilities in financial accounts may be no higher or lower, respectively, than their counterparts allowed for tax purposes. The financial accounts should agree with the tax requirements, and so changes in accounting practice are often made in the name of changes in the accounting requirements of the tax system.

The **emphasis on compliance** with the tax rules and regulations limits the usefulness of German financial statements for decision making by readers. The reported profit and the valuations contained in the statements will reflect the most favourable tax position. This may not reflect the economic profitability and position of the company, making them too conservative for readers to (say) estimate the future net cash flows due to the company. This is obviously not the objective of German financial reporting.

3.4 Forms of organisation

The types of organisation and their ownership will also have varying effects on a nation's accounting practices. In some countries ownership is mainly in the **hands of a family** and finance is provided by the banks. Both these parties have access to internal financial information concerning the business and therefore there is little demand for the development of forms of external financial reporting.

In other countries the ownership of the business organisation is in the hands of **external widely dispersed shareholders** (as in the UK and US). Such providers of finance will probably not have direct access to internal financial information and will therefore demand some form of external reporting to provide them with the information they require to make investment decisions. The existence and importance of shareholders will determine the influence of the national stock exchange.

A wide spectrum of organisations exist in **France** including:

- Partnerships (Société en nom Collectif)
- Companies (Société Anonyme (SA) and Société à Responsibilité Limitée (SARL))
- Family holdings

The accounts produced by all these organisations are governed by the National Plan; the stock exchange (Bourse) has not had a particularly strong influence over financial reporting practices.

There are various forms of organisations in **Germany** and the distinction is important because financial reporting and disclosure requirements are dependent on the organisational form of business. Public companies consist of the following.

(a) 'Aktiengesellschaft' (AG). This is similar to a large UK public company, although the shares are usually 'bearer'. These companies have a supervisory body; 50% is appointed by shareholders and 50% by employees. This board appoints a management board and approves the annual accounts.

(b) 'Kommanditgesellschaft auf Aktien' (KGaA). This is a form of limited partnership and company combined. One shareholder is liable to the creditors in full, while the others enjoy limited liability. It is not a particularly popular form of company.

Another form of company is a 'Gesellschaft mit beschränkter Haftung' (GmbH). It is not quoted on the stock exchange and is subject to different legal reporting requirements. It is similar to, but not the same as, a UK private company. There are numerous organisations operating as partnerships or sole traders. Banks and other lenders are an important source of finance in Germany, and therefore the **German stock exchange**, while being an efficient medium for raising new finance, **does not appear to have a great influence** on financial reporting.

3.5 Accounting profession

The accounting profession in a country has **varying levels of influence** on national accounting practices. However, care must be taken in interpreting the influence of the accounting profession because in some countries an 'accountant' may not be considered to be part of the 'profession'.

In **France**, the accounting profession is split into two distinct organisations:

- **Accountants** (Ordre des Experts Comptables et des Comptables Agrées)
- **Auditors** (Compaigne Nationale des Commissaires aux Agrées)

Most members of the auditors' organisation are also members of the more important accountants' organisation. Examinations, work experience and articles are similar to those of the UK accountancy bodies, but there are only an estimated 11,000 qualified accountants in France. The profession's main influence is through the issue of non-mandatory opinions and recommendations of accounting principles relevant to the implementation of the National Plan.

The main professional body in **Germany** is the Institute of Certified Public Accountants (Institut der Wirtschafsprüfer). Members of this institute carry out all the statutory audits, and are required to have very high educational and experience qualifications. The Institute issues a form of auditing standard but this is tied very closely to legislation. As well as auditing, members are mainly involved in tax and business management, with no obvious significant role in establishing financial accounting principles and practices. There is no independent accounting standard-setting body.

3.6 Former communist and developing countries

The sophisticated regulatory frameworks discussed above, along with those in the UK and the USA, contrast sharply with the situation in former communist and developing countries. The problems in these countries are covered briefly here.

In socialist countries the economic system has usually been **resource constrained** and enterprise management operating within such an environment required quantity data on resource availability and resource utilisation. The accounting function was **passive**. Price signals were not influential and enterprises did not need to be 'profitable'. There was not the same call for accounting development and innovation that exists where accounting is **active** (as in capitalist countries).

For the country trying to recover from events such as revolution or war, such a system is appropriate but after the short-term resource problems have been solved the economy needs to develop along the lines of the demand constrained economy. Many socialist and former socialist countries are currently attempting to move to such a system which includes enterprise independence and market conditions of supply and demand. Accounting will therefore (hopefully) develop in these socialist countries into a more active information source.

Developing countries are often defined as such by using *per capita* **gross national product**, relating development to economic growth and social improvements. The general characteristics of such countries include unbalanced distribution of wealth, few exports (agricultural/mineral), basic but developing domestic industries, long-term balance of payments deficits, authoritarian political systems and inadequate education.

Both developing and former socialist countries have the same problems in relation to financial accounting and many will be overcome in the same way. In general, most of these countries are **adopting financial reporting systems** from developed countries and adjusting them to suit the individual needs of the country concerned. This is a long and slow process as such sophisticated reporting systems are rarely suitable and require a great deal of modification. The local workers do not have the requisite skills, which have to be imported from abroad. More sophisticated financial reporting may be required by multinational companies who have subsidiaries or investments in such countries.

3.7 Other countries

Of the other **main developed countries**, such as Canada, Australia and New Zealand, some have developed framework projects like the IASB and some have detailed standards, often with the force of law.

The country which has had most impact on world financial reporting, however, is the USA (as we shall see in the next section).

US GAAP accounts

In recent years, only two German companies, Daimler Benz and Veba, have filed accounts prepared under US GAAP, although other German companies are likely to follow suit. Why should German companies take the trouble to produce such accounts, and what do you think was the impact on reported results?

Answer

The reasons given by Veba for producing US GAAP accounts were based on the fact that, although Veba still earns 70% of its revenues within Germany, only about 44% of its equity is held in Germany, with 15% held in the US. The company saw the need to become 'more international' and US GAAP accounts would increase transparency and shareholder value. An article in the *Financial Times* on 28 March 1996 stated the following.

> 'Converting accounts to US accounting standards has been problematic for German companies, many of whom prefer the inscrutability of the German accounting system. It enables them to build up reserves which might otherwise be paid out to shareholders.
>
> Mr Kurt Lauk, Veba's finance director, said he had conducted 'difficult' negotiations with the Securities and Exchange Commission, the agency supervising the New York Stock Exchange, for two years before all differences were resolved.
>
> Mr Lauk said Veba had chosen GAAP over the rival IAS accounting standard, widely used by large European companies, because the latter did not permit a listing in New York.'

The likely effect and reported results can be difficult to judge. One might expect that German accounting rules, generally perceived as more conservative than UK/US GAAP, would produce lower profits and shareholder funds. This was the case recently when BMW reported its results, including Rover, a British subsidiary.

> 'BMW, the German carmaker, yesterday reported that Rover, its UK subsidiary, lost DM355m (£157m) last year, in spite of having earlier reported a 9 per cent rise in profits before interest and tax to £91m for the same period.
>
> The discrepancy came from the 'stricter valuation criteria' applied by BMW compared with its UK subsidiary, according to the German company.'   (*Financial Times*, 3 April 1996)

This is not always the case, however, as was demonstrated when Daimler Benz first produced US GAAP accounts. Analysts were shocked when a substantial loss was reported under US GAAP rather than the modest profit under German rules. (DM 949m loss vs DM 168m profit, 1991 half year results). This was partly because the company was caught during a slump, but it demonstrates how dramatic the differences can be under the different accounting regimes.

4 Financial reporting in the USA

Standard setting in the USA is characterised by a **plethora of highly detailed legislative rules**. These have largely obscured the concept of 'fair presentation', despite the development of a conceptual framework as discussed below. The Financial Accounting Standards Board (FASB) has produced well over 100 Statements of Financial Accounting Standards (SFASs).

4.1 A conceptual framework in the USA

The FASB has been developing a conceptual framework since 1973. According to the FASB, the conceptual framework was expected:

(a) To **guide the body** responsible for establishing standards

(b) To provide a **frame of reference** for resolving accounting questions in the absence of a specific promulgated standard

(c) To determine **bounds for judgement** in preparing financial statements

(d) To increase financial statement **users' understanding** of and confidence in financial statements

(e) To enhance **comparability**

4.2 Comparison with UK/IASB view

The ASB has acknowledged that, in drafting the *Statement of Principles,* it drew heavily on the **work done in previous projects** in other countries, mainly the FASB concept statements *and* the IASB *Framework.* This is particularly true of the early chapters, and indeed Chapter 1 opens with the statement that 'the objective of financial statements is to provide information ... that is useful to a wide range of users in making economic decisions', almost a repetition of the FASB wording. The ASB has, however, extended this function to include showing the results of the stewardship of management.

The IASB's *Framework* was **based very closely** on the FASB's concept statements, and it is perceived as an attempt by the IASC to justify the *status quo*; the IASB tried to make the proposed framework consistent with current external financial reporting practice. The ASB stated that it would use the IASB *Framework* as much as possible in its own work on the conceptual framework. It remains to be seen whether the flaws in both the FASB's concept statements and the IASB's *Framework* will be tackled adequately by the ASB.

5 UK GAAP vs IAS vs US GAAP

Your syllabus requires you to identify **major differences** between UK GAAP, IASs and US GAAP. An **overview** is given in the table below.

Exam focus point

> A **detailed knowledge of IAS and US GAAP is not necessary.** Such questions tend to be both interesting and relatively straightforward, requiring only a general overview of IAS and US GAAP.

Subject	UK GAAP	US GAAP	IAS
Goodwill	FRS 10 requires goodwill to be amortised over its expected life. In some cases the life may be indefinite, in which case there is no amortisation. There is a rebuttable presumption that the life of goodwill will be no more than 20 years. If more than 20 years perform annual impairment reviews.	Goodwill must be capitalised and is then carried in the balance sheet, subject to annual impairment reviews.	IFRS 3 requires goodwill to be calculated and then carried in the balance sheet, subject to annual impairment reviews.

Subject	UK GAAP	US GAAP	IAS
Merger accounting **Uniting of interests 'merger accounting'**	Merger accounting must be used if the criteria in FRS 6 are met.	All business combinations must be accounted for as acquisitions; 'pooling of interests' cannot be used.	IFRS 3 prohibits uniting of interest accounting; all combinations must be treated as acquisitions
Research and development	SSAP 13 permits but does not require capitalisation. No time period is specified.	Development expenditure must be written off to the income statement under all circumstances.	Development costs recognised as an asset should be amortised normally over a maximum of 5 years.
Capitalisation of borrowing costs	FRS 15 permits capitalisation of borrowing costs but does not require it. The policy as regards capitalisation must be consistent.	Under US GAAP, interest must be capitalised in certain circumstances.	IAS 23 states that such costs should be recognised as an expense, but allows capitalisation as an alternative.
Stock (inventory) valuation	The LIFO method is not permitted under UK GAAP, so the stock must be valued using a method such as FIFO (first in first out)	In the USA stock may be valued using the LIFO (last in first out) method. Under this method, assuming prices are rising, closing stock has a lower value than using FIFO	IAS 2 no longer permits LIFO as an allowed alternative; FIFO or AVCO must be used.

6 IASB Work plan

Below is the latest (March 2007) version of the IASB Work plan. Not all the topics are covered in this text.

IASB Work Plan - projected timetable as at 31 March 2007

The timetable shows the current best estimate of document publication dates. The effective date of amendments and new standards is usually 6-18 months after publication date. However, except for the items listed in the section 'Amendments to standards', the effective date of IFRSs resulting from the current work plan will be no earlier than financial periods beginning 1 January 2009. In appropriate circumstances, early adoption of new standards will be allowed.

		MoU milestone by 2008	2007 Q2	2007 Q3	2007 Q4	2008 H1	2008 H2	Timing yet to be determined
ACTIVE AGENDA								
Projects in Memorandum of Understanding (MoU) with the FASB [1]								
Short-term convergence projects								
Government grants [2]	(IASB)	*Determine whether major differences should be eliminated and substantially complete work*						Pending work on Liabilities
Joint ventures	(IASB)		ED			IFRS		
Impairment	(Joint)							Staff work in progress
Income tax	(Joint)				ED		IFRS	
Investment properties	(FASB)							
Research and development	(FASB)							
Subsequent events	(FASB)							
Other convergence projects								
Business combinations		*Converged standards*		IFRS				
Consolidations		*Work towards converged standards*		DP			ED	IFRS
Fair value measurement guidance		*Converged guidance*		RT			ED	IFRS
Financial statement presentation [3] Phase A			IFRS					
Phase B		*One or more due process documents*			DP		ED	IFRS
Revenue recognition		*One or more due process documents*			DP			ED, IFRS
Post-retirement benefits (including pensions)		*One or more due process documents*			DP			ED, IFRS
Leases		*Agenda decision*				DP		

	2007			2008	2008	Timing yet to be determined
	Q2	Q3	Q4	H1	H2	
Conceptual Framework						
Phase A: Objectives and qualitative characteristics		ED				
Phase B: Elements and recognition				DP		
Phase C: Measurement						DP
Phase D: Reporting entity	DP					
Phase E: Presentation and disclosure						DP
Phase F: Purpose and status						DP
Phase G: Application to not-for-profit entities						DP
Phase H: Remaining issues [4]						TBD
Other projects						
Small and medium-sized entities				IFRS		
Insurance contracts	DP				ED	IFRS
Liabilities [5]					IFRS	
Emission trading schemes [2]						
Amendments to standards						
Financial instruments: puttable instruments (IAS 32)		IFRS				
Earnings per share: treasury stock method (IAS 33)		ED			IFRS	
First-time adoption: cost of investment in subsidiary (IFRS 1)			IFRS			
Share-based payment: vesting conditions and cancellations (IFRS 2)	IFRS					
Related party disclosures (IAS 24)				IFRS		

RESEARCH AGENDA

projects yet to be added to the ACTIVE AGENDA but included in the MoU with the FASB (except as shown)

	MoU milestone by 2008	Q2	Q3	Q4	H1	H2	Timing yet to be determined
Derecognition	*Consider staff research*			RR			
Financial instruments (replacement of existing standards)	*One or more due process documents*			DP			
Intangible assets	*Consider research and make agenda decision*			AD			
Liabilities and equity [6]	*One or more due process documents*		DP				
Management commentary	*Not in MoU*						TBD
Extractive activities	*Not in MoU*				DP		

Abbreviations used in the IASB Work Plan:

DP	Discussion Paper	TBD	The type of initial document (DP or ED) is yet to be determined
ED	Exposure Draft		
RT	Round-table discussion	RR	Research report
IFRS	International Financial Reporting Standard	AD	Agenda decision

Notes:

1   The Memorandum of Understanding (MoU) sets out the milestones that the FASB and the IASB have agreed to achieve in order to demonstrate standard-setting convergence, which is one part of the process towards removal of the requirement imposed on foreign registrants with the SEC to reconcile their financial statements to US GAAP.

2   Work on government grants and emission rights has been deferred pending the conclusion of work on other relevant projects.

3   The Financial Statement Presentation project was formerly known as the Performance Reporting project.

4   The IASB and the FASB will publish individual chapters as they complete each phase. Each board will evaluate the practical implications of doing so in the context of its own GAAP hierarchy.

5   The Liabilities project is the amendments to IAS 37. It was formerly known as the Non-financial Liabilities project.

6   Project is being conducted as a 'modified joint' project, ie the IASB expects to make a formal agenda decision and begin work when the FASB has completed work on an initial discussion document.

555

Chapter Roundup

- **Harmonisation** in accounting is likely to come from international accounting standards, but not in the near future. There are enormous difficulties to overcome, both technical and political.

- You should be able to discuss the **barriers to harmonisation** and the advantages of and **progress towards harmonisation**.

- **From 2005** consolidated accounts of all listed companies **have been obliged to comply with IAS.**

- This led to the publication of the **Convergence Handbook.**

- The **convergence project** is well underway with a number of FREDs based on IAS, new standards and revisions to IAS.

- The ASB's **Discussion Paper on Convergence** sets out the strategy. The aim is to minimise the burden of change. The strategy is twofold.

    – New standards effective in 2005/06 to enhance UK financial reporting
    – 'Step changes', replacing UK standards as and when IASB projects are completed

- We have concentrated on certain countries in our **comparison** between UK and overseas accounts, but you should be able to highlight the differences to UK accounting if you are presented with a set of accounts from any other country.

Quick Quiz

1   Which preparers and users of accounts can be expected to benefit from global harmonisation of accounting?

2   How many IASs are in existence at the moment? How many IFRSs?

3   Fill in the blanks: IFRS ...... is almost identical to FRS ......

4   Why was The Convergence Handbook published?

5   German financial statements may be less useful than UK ones for decision-making purposes. Why?

6   Goodwill has been identified as an area where UK GAAP differs from US GAAP. In what way?

7   US GAAP permits but does not require capitalisation of development expenditure. True or false?

8   Fill in the blanks.

    The LIFO method of stock valuation is not permitted under ....

    LIFO is permitted under ....

9   What other areas of difference are there between UK GAAP, US GAAP and IAS?

10   Why were so many new FREDs published in recent years?

11   International rules on discontinued operations will be introduced in the UK in 2005.

    True ☐
    False ☐

Answers to Quick Quiz

1   Investors, multinational companies, governments of developing countries, the authorities (overseas income), regional economic groups, large international accounting firms.

2   41 IASs, 7 IFRSs

3   IFRS 2 is almost identical to FRS 20.

4   To determine, in the light of the EC harmonisation proposal, whether domestic requirements should change to fit in with IAS or vice versa.

5   Because of the emphasis on compliance with tax rules.

6   UK GAAP allows the possibility of an indefinite useful life, while US GAAP does not.

7   False. Under US GAAP, development expenditure must be written off to the profit and loss account under all circumstances.

8   Not permitted under UK GAAP and now under IAS. Permitted under US GAAP and IASs.

9   Merger accounting, capitalisation of borrowing of costs, research and development.

10   To bring UK Standards into line with IAS in good time for the changeover to IAS in 2005.

11   False. An IAS-based standard awaits the outcome of the project on reporting comprehensive income.

Now try the questions below from the Exam Question Bank

Number	Level	Marks	Time
Q27	Examination	25	45 mins

24

Current developments

Topic list	Syllabus reference
1 Managing the change to IFRS	F1
2 Current issues in corporate reporting	F2, G4
3 Impact of changes in accounting policies and standards	G1, G4

Introduction

This chapter deals with a number of current issues and developments.
Section 2 highlights the latest developments in FRSs, FREDs and Discussion
Papers. These are dealt with within the relevant chapters of this text.

Study guide

		Intellectual level
F1	**The effect of changes in accounting standards on accounting systems**	
(a)	Apply and discuss the accounting implications of the first time adoption of a body of new accounting standards	3
(b)	Outline the issues in implementing a change to new accounting standards, including organisational, behavioural and procedural changes within the entity	3
F2	**Proposed changes to accounting standards**	
(a)	Identify the issues and deficiencies which have led to a proposed change to an accounting standard	2
(b)	Apply and discuss the implications of a proposed change to an accounting standard on the performance and balance sheet of an entity	2
H4	**Current reporting issues**	
(a)	Discuss current issues in corporate reporting	3

Exam guide

Current issues may come up in the context of a question requiring advice. For example, in the scenario question involving groups, perhaps you might have to explain the difference that the proposed changes will make.

Current issues are summarised here, but discussed in detail in the context of the topic to which they relate.

1 Managing the change to IFRS

FAST FORWARD
> The change to IFRS will need to be carefully managed

1.1 Managing the change to IFRS

The implementation of the change to IFRS is likely to entail careful management in most companies. Here are some of the **change management considerations** that should be addressed.

(a) **Accurate assessment of the task involved**. Underestimation or wishful thinking may hamper the effectiveness of the conversion and may ultimately prove inefficient.

(b) **Proper planning**. This should take place at the overall project level, but a **detailed** task **analysis** could be drawn up to **control work performed**.

(c) **Human resource management**. The project must be properly structured and staffed.

(d) **Training**. Where there are **skills gaps**, remedial training should be provided.

(e) **Monitoring and accountability**. A relaxed 'it will be alright on the night' attitude could spell danger. Implementation **progress** should be **monitored** and **regular meetings** set up so that participants can **personally account for what they are doing** as well as **flag up any problems** as early as possible. **Project drift should be avoided**.

(f) **Achieving milestones**. Successful completion of key steps and tasks should be appropriately acknowledged, ie what managers call 'celebrating success', so as to **sustain motivation and performance**.

(g) **Physical resourcing.** The need for IT **equipment** and **office space** should be properly assessed.

(h) **Process review**. Care should be taken not to perceive the change as a one-off quick fix. Any charge in **future systems** and processes should be assessed and properly implemented.

(i) **Follow-up procedures**. As with general good management practice, the **follow up procedures** should be planned in to **make sure that the changes stick** and that any further changes are identified and addressed.

2 Current issues in corporate reporting

You should know which are the **current issues** and concentrate your studying on these.

The examiner for P2 is very keen indeed on current issues and has said that there will be even more emphasis than previously on these issues.

The P2 examiner has given the following guidance on current issues:

'The IASB's work programme will be the basis for many of the current issue discursive questions asked in the paper. However the work programme will not be the exclusive source of questions.'

The Pilot Paper had part of a question on the business combination proposals.

2.1 Hot topics

The IASB workplan, as at March 2007 is reproduced in the previous chapter. Below are the examinable current issues, with an indication of where to find them. Most are dealt with in the chapters on the individual topic.

Hot topic	Where to find it
IASB Discussion Paper on fair value measurement	See below
IASB Discussion Paper on Conceptual Framework (Joint IASB FASB project)	Chapter 1
Consultation Paper on IASB's Exposure Draft on SMEs	Chapter 22
Proposed changes to accounting for business combinations (FRED 36)	Chapter 16
Proposed changes to FRS 12 and FRS 17 (FRED 39)	Chapter 9 and 6
Proposed standard on intangible assets (FRED 37)	Chapter 4
Proposed standard on impairment (FRED 38)	Chapter 5

2.2 Older FREDs

The examiner has stated that he will not examine older FREDs in detail, if at all. Only brief details are therefore given on the following older FREDs, the exception being FRED 32 because discontinued operations is a full syllabus topic. There has been no progress on developing new standards from them, since the IASB's priorities have changed to working more closely with FASB.

FRED	Main change	Brief details in...
25	Related parties – changes to definitions, disclosures and exemptions.	Chapter 15
28	Inventories- implements IAS 2	Chapter 11
29	Brings in IAS 16 *Property, plant and equipment* and IAS 23 *Borrowing costs*. Value to the business model replaced with fair value model.	Chapter 4

2.3 Exposure Draft: Accounting standard-setting in a changing environment: the role of the Accounting Standards Board

The **ASB** has issued an ED examining its own **role**.

In March 2005, the ASB published an Exposure Draft of its Policy Statement *Accounting Standard-setting in a Changing Environment: The Role of the Accounting Standards Board*. The Exposure Draft sets out the ASB's views on its future role.

2005 has ushered in significant changes in the standard setting environment. The draft Policy Statement argues that **the most significant future role of the ASB will be in contributing to the development, with the International Accounting Standards Board (IASB) and others, of a set of high quality global accounting standards**. The ASB has the capacity as an established national standard-setter to be a valuable source of accounting thought and insight for the IASB and an influential voice in debates on new accounting standards.

2.3.1 Fundamental aim and activities

The ASB believes that its fundamental aim remains appropriate:

> 'To contribute to the establishment and improvement of standards of financial accounting and reporting for the benefit of users, preparers and auditors of financial information.'

Supporting this aim the ASB has identified the following as its major activities.

(a)   Contributing to the **development and implementation** of International Financial Reporting Standards (**IFRS**)

(b)   **Influencing European Union policy** on accounting standards, including the endorsement of IFRS

(c)   **Achieving convergence** of UK accounting standards with IFRS

(d)   **Improving other aspects** of UK accounting standards

(e)   **Improving communication** between companies and investors, including developing and implementing standards for the OFR

2.3.2 Communication and influence

The draft policy statement stresses the importance of **effective communication, including communication with IASB, other national standard-setters, EFRAG and constituents**.

In relation to influencing the IASB the ED suggests the ASB has a role as the natural focus for a debate on accounting issues in the UK. **A two way dialogue** with UK constituents will allow the ASB to formulate its own views on IASB proposals, but also reflect on the views and concerns of UK constituents. The ASB can then provide its comments to the IASB in a constructive manner that also demonstrates an understanding of IASB thinking, as a result of its continual contact with IASB at various levels.

The ASB also provides a **focus for a UK voice in Europe**. For example the ASB is actively involved in EFRAG's research-type projects and will work with other European standard-setters to share views and support the development of these projects.

2.3.3 Convergence

The ASB aims to work towards the convergence of UK accounting standards and IFRS, with a current aim of **bringing UK standards fully into line within a period of three to four years**. This process has already started and the ASB's Technical Plan (also published in March) sets out in detail the publications expected for the remainder of 2005 and the strategy the ASB plans to adopt in relation to the introduction of other UK IFRS-based accounting standards. However, the ASB will not commit itself, as a matter of policy, to converging with all IFRS, although any exceptions are expected to be extremely rare.

In setting UK IFRS-based accounting standards the ASB **may vary the requirements from those in the equivalent IFRS, where it is justifiable to do so**. This will generally involve making a standard more appropriate for the entities that have to apply it, or giving a later implementation date. However, this will not result in multiple sets of accounting standards for different classes of entities: the standards will all be based on the same core set of principles: only in relatively minor respects (such as disclosure) will the requirements differ.

2.3.4 Future of SORPs

The ASB has also set out its thoughts on the future of its SORP regime, how the process of dealing with urgent issues might change and the development of reporting standards for other area of corporate reporting complementary to financial reporting.

2.4 Fair Value Measurements: IASB Discussion Paper

In November 2006, the IASB published a Discussion Paper, *Fair value measurements.* The Discussion Paper arose as a result of the Memorandum of Understanding between the IASB and FASB (February 2006) reaffirming their commitment to the convergence of IFRSs and US GAAP.

2.4.1 Objective

The objective of the project is to codify, clarify and simplify existing guidance that is dispersed widely in IFRSs. The intention is not therefore to expand the use of fair value in financial reporting.
The Discussion Paper focuses on the recent US Statement of Financial Accounting Standards No. 157 *Fair Value Measurements* (SFAS 157) as a starting point, on which work was well advanced before the Memorandum of Understanding was published.

2.4.2 Definitions

SFAS 157 defines fair value as 'the price that would be received to sell an asset or paid to transfer a liability in an orderly transaction between market participants at the measurement date.'
The IFRS definition is generally 'the amount for which an asset could be exchanged, or a liability settled, between knowledgeable, willing parties in an arm's length transaction'.

2.4.3 Differences between definitions

There are three key differences between the SFAS 157 and IFRS definitions:

(a)   The SFAS definition is explicitly an exit (selling) price, whereas the IFRS definition is neither explicitly an exit price nor an entry (buying) price.

(b)   The SFAS definition refers explicitly to market participants, whereas the IFRS definition refers to knowledgeable, willing parties in an arm's length transaction.

(c)   For liabilities, the SFAS definition rests on the notion that the liability is transferred (the liability to the counterparty continues; it is not settled with the counterparty). The IFRS definition refers to the amount at which a liability could be settled between knowledgeable, willing parties in an arm's length transaction.

2.4.4 Valuation techniques

SFAS 157 establishes a three-level hierarchy for the inputs that valuation techniques use to measure fair value:

Level 1   Quoted prices (unadjusted) in active markets for identical assets or liabilities that the reporting entity has the ability to access at the measurement date

Level 2   Inputs other than quoted prices included within Level 1 that are observable for the asset or liability, either directly or indirectly, eg quoted prices for similar assets in active markets or for identical or similar assets in non active markets or use of quoted interest rates for valuation purposes

Level 3   Unobservable inputs for the asset or liability, ie using the entity's own assumptions about market exit value.

The Discussion Paper analyses each of these principles in detail and provides a copy of the SFAS in order to seek a public opinion on this as a starting point for an IFRS ED to be published in early 2008.

2.4.5 Is the project necessary?

The IASB is already considering the matter of the measurement basis for assets and liabilities in financial reporting as part of its conceptual framework project. It could therefore be argued that it is not necessary to have a separate project on fair value. The conceptual framework might be the more appropriate forum for discussing **when** fair value should be used **as well as how to define and measure it.**

However, it has been argued that a concise definition and clear measurement framework is needed because there is so much inconsistency in this area, and this may form the basis for discussions in the conceptual framework project.

Exam focus point

Keep your eye out for articles on these topics in *Student Accountant*, a good indication that the topic will be examined.

3 Impact of changes in accounting policies and standards

FAST FORWARD

Accounting policies may be adopted for the purpose of **manipulation.**

Changes in accounting standards can have a significant impact on the financial statements.

We discussed the disclosure of accounting policies in your earlier studies. The choice of accounting policy and the effect of its implementation are almost as important as its disclosure in that the results of a company can be altered significantly by the choice of accounting policy.

3.1 The effect of choice of accounting policies

Where accounting standards allow alternative treatment of items in the accounts, then the accounting policy note should declare which policy has been chosen. It should then be applied consistently.

Consider, though, the **radically different effects produced by the different treatment of some items**. An example is the treatment of development expenditure under SSAP 13. Although the criteria for capitalising development expenditure are very strict, the choice of whether to capitalise and amortise or write off such costs can have a significant impact on profit. Consider the size of the R & D expenditure of the large drugs companies and you can see how important such an accounting policy could be.

You should be able to think of other examples of how the choice of accounting policy can affect the financial statements.

3.2 Changes in accounting policy

The effect of a change of accounting policy is treated as a prior year adjustment according to FRS 3 *Reporting financial performance*. This just means that the comparative figures are adjusted for the change in accounting policy for comparative purposes and an adjustment is put through reserves.

FRS 3 states that, as consistency is a fundamental accounting concept, any change in policy may:

> 'only be made if it can be justified on the grounds that the new policy is preferable to the one it replaces because it will give a fairer presentation of the result and of the financial position of a reporting entity.'

The problem with this situation is that the directors may be able to **manipulate the results** through change(s) of accounting policies. This would be done to avoid the effect of an old accounting policy or gain the effect of a new one. It is likely to be done in a sensitive period, perhaps when the company's profits are low or the company is about to announce a rights issue. The management would have to convince the auditors that the new policy was much better, but it is not difficult to produce reasons in such cases.

The effect of such a change is **very short-term**. Most analysts and sophisticated users will discount its effect immediately, except to the extent that it will affect any dividend (because of the effect on distributable profits). It may help to avoid breaches of banking covenants because of the effect on certain ratios.

Obviously, the accounting policy for any item in the accounts could only be changed once in quite a long period of time. No auditors would allow another change, even back to the old policy, unless there was a wholly exceptional reason.

The managers of a company can choose accounting policies **initially** to suit the company or the type of results they want to get. Any changes in accounting policy must be justified, but some managers might try to change accounting policies just to manipulate the results.

As the UK moves to IFRS, and as **choices of accounting treatment are eliminated** in IFRS, accounting policy changes may become less significant.

3.3 Changes in accounting standards

FAST FORWARD

You will probably be asked to **advise the directors** on the implication of a change in accounting standards, or on the effect of using the correct accounting treatment.

The effect of a change of accounting standard can be far reaching. For example when, in the interests of convergence with IFRS, FRS 17 *Retirement benefits* was introduced, the figures became much more volatile than previously. If FRED 36 *Business combinations* becomes a full standard, goodwill arising on consolidation will no longer be amortised, but will be reviewed annually for impairment. Impairment tests are more subjective than amortisation, although both methods have their drawbacks.

3.4 The impact of change and the P2 examination

Judging from the Pilot Paper and from the approach taken by the P2 examiner in the past, this topic is likely to be examined regularly. Usually you will be in the position of advising the directors. The directors may have adopted an accounting treatment that is incorrect. You will need to advise them of the correct accounting treatment and show, usually with supporting calculations, the effect on the financial statements of adopting the correct treatment.

Ethics are an important aspect of the ACCA's qualification. If the directors, in adopting certain accounting treatments, are acting unethically, you may need to discuss this. This happened in Question 1 of the Pilot paper.

Alternatively the treatment may not be wrong, but a matter of accounting policy which the directors wish to change. As before, you will be asked to explain, with supporting calculations, the effect of the change.

You are very likely to be asked to explain the significance of a proposed change in accounting standards. For example, the Pilot Paper required you to discuss the effect of the changes proposed in FRED 36.

3.5 Practise case study questions

The impact of change in standards, policies or treatment is unlikely to comprise a whole question. It is more likely to come up as part of a longer question. For example, it may come up as part of the compulsory 50 mark case study question, the first part of which will always be on groups. You should therefore practise this type of question. Have a go at Question 1 of the Pilot Paper at the end of this Study Text, and the questions Planet and Wingit in the Exam Question Bank. Further questions of this type can be found in BPP Learning Media's Practice & Revision Kit for this Paper.

Chapter Roundup

- The **change to IFRS** will need to be **carefully managed**.
    - You should know which are the **current issues** and concentrate your studying on these.
    - The **ASB** has issued an ED examining its own **role**.
- Accounting policies may be adopted for the purpose of **manipulation.**
- **Changes in accounting standards** can have a significant impact on the financial statements.
- You will probably be asked to **advise the directors** on the implication of a change in accounting standards, or on the effect of using the correct accounting treatment.

Quick Quiz

1   What are the main current issues?

2   What is the most likely role for the ASB in the future?

3   Give an example of a proposed FRS which, if it becomes a full standard, will have a significant impact on the financial statements.

Answers to Quick Quiz

1   See Paragraph 2.1

2   Contributing to the development of global accounting standards.

3   FRED 36 *Business combinations*

Now try the questions below from the Exam Question Bank

Number	Level	Marks	Time
Q28	Examination	25	45 mins
Q29	Examination	25	45 mins
Q30	Examination	50	90 mins

Mathematical tables

Present value table

Present value of 1 = $(1+r)^{-n}$ where r = discount rate, n = number of periods until payment.

This table shows the present value of £1 per annum, receivable or payable at the end of *n* years.

Periods					Discount rates (r)					
(n)	1%	2%	3%	4%	5%	6%	7%	8%	9%	10%
1	0.990	0.980	0.971	0.962	0.952	0.943	0.935	0.926	0.917	0.909
2	0.980	0.961	0.943	0.925	0.907	0.890	0.873	0.857	0.842	0.826
3	0.971	0.942	0.915	0.889	0.864	0.840	0.816	0.794	0.772	0.751
4	0.961	0.924	0.888	0.855	0.823	0.792	0.763	0.735	0.708	0.683
5	0.951	0.906	0.863	0.822	0.784	0.747	0.713	0.681	0.650	0.621
6	0.942	0.888	0.837	0.790	0.746	0.705	0.666	0.630	0.596	0.564
7	0.933	0.871	0.813	0.760	0.711	0.665	0.623	0.583	0.547	0.513
8	0.923	0.853	0.789	0.731	0.677	0.627	0.582	0.540	0.502	0.467
9	0.914	0.837	0.766	0.703	0.645	0.592	0.544	0.500	0.460	0.424
10	0.905	0.820	0.744	0.676	0.614	0.558	0.508	0.463	0.422	0.386
11	0.896	0.804	0.722	0.650	0.585	0.527	0.475	0.429	0.388	0.350
12	0.887	0.788	0.701	0.625	0.557	0.497	0.444	0.397	0.356	0.319
13	0.879	0.773	0.681	0.601	0.530	0.469	0.415	0.368	0.326	0.290
14	0.870	0.758	0.661	0.577	0.505	0.442	0.388	0.340	0.299	0.263
15	0.861	0.743	0.642	0.555	0.481	0.417	0.362	0.315	0.275	0.239
16	0.853	0.728	0.623	0.534	0.458	0.394	0.339	0.292	0.252	0.218
17	0.844	0.714	0.605	0.513	0.436	0.371	0.317	0.270	0.231	0.198
18	0.836	0.700	0.587	0.494	0.416	0.350	0.296	0.250	0.212	0.180
19	0.828	0.686	0.570	0.475	0.396	0.331	0.277	0.232	0.194	0.164
20	0.820	0.673	0.554	0.456	0.377	0.312	0.258	0.215	0.178	0.149

Periods					Discount rates (r)					
(n)	11%	12%	13%	14%	15%	16%	17%	18%	19%	20%
1	0.901	0.893	0.885	0.877	0.870	0.862	0.855	0.847	0.840	0.833
2	0.812	0.797	0.783	0.769	0.756	0.743	0.731	0.718	0.706	0.694
3	0.731	0.712	0.693	0.675	0.658	0.641	0.624	0.609	0.593	0.579
4	0.659	0.636	0.613	0.592	0.572	0.552	0.534	0.516	0.499	0.482
5	0.593	0.567	0.543	0.519	0.497	0.476	0.456	0.437	0.419	0.402
6	0.535	0.507	0.480	0.456	0.432	0.410	0.390	0.370	0.352	0.335
7	0.482	0.452	0.425	0.400	0.376	0.354	0.333	0.314	0.296	0.279
8	0.434	0.404	0.376	0.351	0.327	0.305	0.285	0.266	0.249	0.233
9	0.391	0.361	0.333	0.308	0.284	0.263	0.243	0.225	0.209	0.194
10	0.352	0.322	0.295	0.270	0.247	0.227	0.208	0.191	0.176	0.162
11	0.317	0.287	0.261	0.237	0.215	0.195	0.178	0.162	0.148	0.135
12	0.286	0.257	0.231	0.208	0.187	0.168	0.152	0.137	0.124	0.112
13	0.258	0.229	0.204	0.182	0.163	0.145	0.130	0.116	0.104	0.093
14	0.232	0.205	0.181	0.160	0.141	0.125	0.111	0.099	0.088	0.078
15	0.209	0.183	0.160	0.140	0.123	0.108	0.095	0.084	0.074	0.065
16	0.188	0.163	0.141	0.123	0.107	0.093	0.081	0.071	0.062	0.054
17	0.170	0.146	0.125	0.108	0.093	0.080	0.069	0.060	0.052	0.045
18	0.153	0.130	0.111	0.095	0.081	0.069	0.059	0.051	0.044	0.038
19	0.138	0.116	0.098	0.083	0.070	0.060	0.051	0.043	0.037	0.031
20	0.124	0.104	0.087	0.073	0.061	0.051	0.043	0.037	0.031	0.026

Cumulative present value table

This table shows the present value of £1 per annum, receivable or payable at the end of each year for n years.

Periods (n)	Discount rates (r)									
	1%	2%	3%	4%	5%	6%	7%	8%	9%	10%
1	0.990	0.980	0.971	0.962	0.952	0.943	0.935	0.926	0.917	0.909
2	1.970	1.942	1.913	1.886	1.859	1.833	1.808	1.783	1.759	1.736
3	2.941	2.884	2.829	2.775	2.723	2.673	2.624	2.577	2.531	2.487
4	3.902	3.808	3.717	3.630	3.546	3.465	3.387	3.312	3.240	3.170
5	4.853	4.713	4.580	4.452	4.329	4.212	4.100	3.993	3.890	3.791
6	5.795	5.601	5.417	5.242	5.076	4.917	4.767	4.623	4.486	4.355
7	6.728	6.472	6.230	6.002	5.786	5.582	5.389	5.206	5.033	4.868
8	7.652	7.325	7.020	6.733	6.463	6.210	5.971	5.747	5.535	5.335
9	8.566	8.162	7.786	7.435	7.108	6.802	6.515	6.247	5.995	5.759
10	9.471	8.983	8.530	8.111	7.722	7.360	7.024	6.710	6.418	6.145
11	10.37	9.787	9.253	8.760	8.306	7.887	7.499	7.139	6.805	6.495
12	11.26	10.58	9.954	9.385	8.863	8.384	7.943	7.536	7.161	6.814
13	12.13	11.35	10.63	9.986	9.394	8.853	8.358	7.904	7.487	7.103
14	13.00	12.11	11.30	10.56	9.899	9.295	8.745	8.244	7.786	7.367
15	13.87	12.85	11.94	11.12	10.38	9.712	9.108	8.559	8.061	7.606
16	14.718	13.578	12.561	11.652	10.838	10.106	9.447	8.851	8.313	7.824
17	15.562	14.292	13.166	12.166	11.274	10.477	9.763	9.122	8.544	8.022
18	16.398	14.992	13.754	12.659	11.690	10.828	10.059	9.372	8.756	8.201
19	17.226	15.678	14.324	13.134	12.085	11.158	10.336	9.604	8.950	8.365
20	18.046	16.351	14.877	13.590	12.462	11.470	10.594	9.818	9.129	8.514

Periods (n)	Discount rates (r)									
	11%	12%	13%	14%	15%	16%	17%	18%	19%	20%
1	0.901	0.893	0.885	0.877	0.870	0.862	0.855	0.847	0.840	0.833
2	1.713	1.690	1.668	1.647	1.626	1.605	1.585	1.566	1.547	1.528
3	2.444	2.402	2.361	2.322	2.283	2.246	2.210	2.174	2.140	2.106
4	3.102	3.037	2.974	2.914	2.855	2.798	2.743	2.690	2.639	2.589
5	3.696	3.605	3.517	3.433	3.352	3.274	3.199	3.127	3.058	2.991
6	4.231	4.111	3.998	3.889	3.784	3.685	3.589	3.498	3.410	3.326
7	4.712	4.564	4.423	4.288	4.160	4.039	3.922	3.812	3.706	3.605
8	5.146	4.968	4.799	4.639	4.487	4.344	4.207	4.078	3.954	3.837
9	5.537	5.328	5.132	4.946	4.772	4.607	4.451	4.303	4.163	4.031
10	5.889	5.650	5.426	5.216	5.019	4.833	4.659	4.494	4.339	4.192
11	6.207	5.938	5.687	5.453	5.234	5.029	4.836	4.656	4.486	4.327
12	6.492	6.194	5.918	5.660	5.421	5.197	4.988	4.793	4.611	4.439
13	6.750	6.424	6.122	5.842	5.583	5.342	5.118	4.910	4.715	4.533
14	6.982	6.628	6.302	6.002	5.724	5.468	5.229	5.008	4.802	4.611
15	7.191	6.811	6.462	6.142	5.847	5.575	5.324	5.092	4.876	4.675
16	7.379	6.974	6.604	6.265	5.954	5.668	5.405	5.162	4.938	4.730
17	7.549	7.120	6.729	6.373	6.047	5.749	5.475	5.222	4.990	4.775
18	7.702	7.250	6.840	6.467	6.128	5.818	5.534	5.273	5.033	4.812
19	7.839	7.366	6.938	6.550	6.198	5.877	5.584	5.316	5.070	4.843
20	7.963	7.469	7.025	6.623	6.259	5.929	5.628	5.353	5.101	4.870

Exam question bank

1 Fundamental principles

Fundamental Principles require that a member of a professional accountancy body should behave with integrity in all professional, business and financial relationships and should strive for objectivity in all professional and business judgements. Objectivity can only be assured if the member is and is seen to be independent. Conflicts of interest have an important bearing on independence and hence also on the public's perception of the integrity, objectivity and independence of the accounting profession.

The following scenario is an example of press reports in recent years which deal with issues of objectivity and independence within a multinational firm of accountants:

'A partner in the firm was told by the regulatory body that he must resign because he was in breach of the regulatory body's independence rules, as his brother-in-law was financial controller of an audit client. He was told that the alternative was that he could move his home and place of work at least 400 miles from the offices of the client, even though he was not the reporting partner. This made his job untenable. The regulatory body was seen as 'taking its rules to absurd lengths' by the accounting firm. Shortly after this comment, the multinational firm announced proposals to split the firm into three areas between audit, tax and business advisory services; management consultancy; and investment advisory services.'

Required

Discuss the impact that the above events may have on the public perception of the integrity, objectivity and independence of the multinational firm of accountants.

2 Glowball   45 mins

The directors of Glowball, a public limited company, had discussed the study by the Institute of Environmental Management which indicated that over 35% of the world's 250 largest corporations are voluntarily releasing green reports to the public to promote corporate environmental performance and to attract customers and investors. They have heard that the main competitors are applying the *Global Reporting Initiative* (GRI) in an effort to develop worldwide format for corporate environmental reporting. However, the directors are unsure as to what this initiative actually means. Additionally they require advice as to the nature of any legislation or standards relating to environmental reporting as they are worried that any environmental report produced by the company may not be of sufficient quality and may detract from and not enhance their image if the report does not comply with recognised standards. Glowball has a reputation for ensuring the preservation of the environment in its business activities.

Further the directors have collected information in respect of a series of events which they consider to be important and worthy of note in the environmental report but are not sure as to how they would be incorporated in the environmental report or whether they should be included in the financial statements.

The events are as follows.

(a)   Glowball is a company that pipes gas from offshore gas installations to major consumers. The company purchased its main competitor during the year and found that there were environmental liabilities arising out of the restoration of many miles of farmland that had been affected by the laying of a pipeline. There was no legal obligation to carry out the work, but the company felt that there would be a cost of around £150 million if the farmland was to be restored.

(b)   Most of the offshore gas installations are governed by operating licences which specify limits to the substances which can be discharged to the air and water. These limits vary according to local legislation and tests are carried out by the regulatory authorities. During the year the company was prosecuted for infringements of an environmental law in the USA when toxic gas escaped into the atmosphere. In 20X9 the company was prosecuted five times and in 20X8 eleven times for infringement of the law. The final amount of the fine/costs to be imposed by the courts has not been determined but is expected to be around £5 million. The escape occurred over the sea and it was considered that there was little threat to human life.

(c)   The company produced statistics which measure their improvement in the handling of emissions of gases which may have an impact on the environment. The statistics deal with:

    (i)   Measurement of the release of gases with the potential to form acid rain. The emissions have been reduced by 84% over five years due to the closure of old plants.

    (ii)   Measurement of emissions of substances potentially hazardous to human health. The emissions are down by 51% on 20X5 levels.

    (iii)   Measurement of emissions to water which removes dissolved oxygen and substances that may have an adverse effect on aquatic life. Accurate measurement of these emissions is not possible but the company is planning to spend £70 million on research in this area.

(d)   The company tries to reduce the environmental impacts associated with the siting and construction of its gas installations. This is done in a way that minimises the impact on wildlife and human beings. Additionally when the installations are at the end of their life, they are dismantled and are not sunk into the sea. The current provision for the decommissioning of these installations is £215 million and there are still decommissioning costs of £407 million to be provided as the company's policy is to build up the required provision over the life of the installation.

Required

Prepare a report suitable for presentation to the directors of Glowball in which you discuss the following elements.

(a)   Current reporting requirements and guidelines relating to environmental reporting   **(10 marks)**

(b)   The nature of any disclosure which would be required in an environmental report and/or the financial statements for the evens (a) – (d) above   **(15 marks)**

(Total = 25 marks)

3 Large company

C & R plc is a large company which operates a number of retail stores throughout the United Kingdom. The company makes up financial statements to 30 September each year.

On 1 October 20X6 the company purchased two plots of land at two different locations, and commenced the construction of two retail stores. The construction was completed on 1 October 20X7.

Details of the costs incurred to construct the stores are as follows.

	Location A	Location B
	£'000	£'000
Cost of land	500	700
Cost of building materials	500	550
Direct labour	100	150
Site overheads	100	100
Fixture and fittings	200	200

The construction of the stores was financed out of the proceeds of issue of a £10 million zero coupon bond on 1 October 20X6. The bond is redeemable at a price of £25,937,000 on 30 September 20Y6. This represents the one and only payment to the holders of the bond.

Both stores were brought into use on 1 October 20X7. The store at Location A was used by C & R plc but, due to a change of plan, the store at Location B was let to another retailer at a commercial rent.

It is the policy of C & R plc to depreciate freehold properties over their anticipated useful life of 50 years, and to depreciate fixtures and fittings over 10 years. The cost of such properties (including fixtures and fittings) should include finance costs, where this is permitted by the regulatory framework in the United Kingdom.

Required

(a)   Compute the amounts which will be included in fixed assets in respect of the stores at Locations A and B on 30 September 20X7.

Give full explanations for the amounts you have included.

(b)   Compute the change to the profit and loss account for depreciation on the fixed assets at the two locations for the year to 30 September 20X8, stating clearly the reasons for your answers.

4 FRS 11

Under FRS 11 *Impairment of fixed assets and goodwill*, it may be necessary to calculate an asset's value in use to compare with its carrying value. Where the income stream of an asset cannot be identified separately, it can be grouped with other assets in an 'income-generating unit'. In relation to the allocation of assets to such units, consider the following two scenarios, and answer the related questions.

(a)   Suppose an entity has three independent streams, A, B and C, with net asset directly involved in the income streams with carrying amounts of £100m, £150m and £200m respectively. In addition there are head office net assets with a carrying amount totalling £150m. The relative amounts of the net assets are a reasonable indication of the proportion of head office resources devoted to each income stream. The income-generating units are defined as follows.

Income-generating unit	A	B	C	Total
	£m	£m	£m	£m
Net assets directly involved in income-generating unit	100	150	200	450
Head office net assets	33	50	67	150
Total	133	200	267	600

Required

Suppose that there is an indication that a fixed asset in Unit B is impaired and a value in use calculation was done. To which figure would the recoverable amount be compared?

(b)   Suppose an entity acquires a business comprising three income-generating units, X, Y and Z. After five years, the carrying amount of the net assets in the income-generating units and the purchased goodwill compares with the value in use as follows.

Income-generating unit	X	Y	Z	Goodwill	Total
	£m	£m	£m	£m	£m
Carrying amount	80	120	140	50	390
Value in use	100	140	120		360

Required

What should be recognised by way of an impairment loss?

5 Invest

(a) Invest plc has a number of subsidiaries. The accounting date of Invest plc and all its subsidiaries is 30 April. On 1 May 20X8, Invest plc purchased 80% of the issued equity shares of Target Ltd. This purchase made Target Ltd a subsidiary of Invest plc from 1 May 20X8. Invest plc made a cash payment of £31 million for the shares in Target Ltd. On 1 May 20X8, the net assets which were included in the balance sheet of Target Ltd had a fair value to Invest plc of £30 million. Target Ltd sells a well-known branded product and has taken some steps to protect itself legally against unauthorised use of a brand name. A reliable estimate of the value of this brand to the Invest group is £3 million. It is further considered that the value of this brand can be maintained or even increased for the foreseeable future. The value of the brand is *not* included in the balance sheet of Target Ltd.

For the purposes of preparing the consolidated financial statements, the directors of Invest plc wish to ensure that the charge to the profit and loss account for the amortisation of intangible fixed assets is kept to a minimum. They estimate that the useful economic life of the purchased goodwill (or premium on acquisition) of Target Ltd is 40 years.

Required

(i) Compute the charge to the consolidated profit and loss account in respect of the goodwill on acquisition of Target Ltd for its year ended 30 April 20X9, in accordance with FRS 10 *Goodwill and intangible assets*.

(ii) Explain the action which Invest plc must take in 20X8/X9 and in future years arising from the chosen accounting treatment of the goodwill on acquisition of Target Ltd.

(b) You are the management accountant of Investor plc, a listed company with a number of subsidiaries located throughout the United Kingdom. Investor plc currently appraises investment opportunities using a cost of capital of 10 per cent. Goodwill on consolidation is normally written off on a *pro rata* basis over twenty years.

On 1 April 20X9 Investor plc purchased 80 per cent of the equity share capital of Cornwall Ltd for a total cash price of £60m. Half the price was payable on 1 April 20X9; the balance was payable on 1 April 20Y1. The net identifiable assets that were actually included in the balance sheet of Cornwall Ltd had a carrying value totalling £55m at 1 April 20X9. With the exception of the pension provision (see below), you discover that the fair values of the net identifiable assets of Cornwall Ltd at 1 April 20X9 are the same as their carrying values. When performing the fair-value exercise at 1 April 20X9 you discover that Cornwall Ltd has a defined-benefit pension scheme that was actuarially valued three years ago and found to be in deficit. As a result of that valuation, a provision of £6m has been built up in the balance sheet. The fair-value exercise indicates that on 1 April 20X9, the pension scheme was in deficit by £11m. This information became available on 31 July 20X9.

Assume that today's date is 31 October 20X9. You are in the process of preparing the consolidated financial statements of the group for the year ended 30 September 20X9. Your financial director is concerned that profits for the year will be lower than originally anticipated. She is therefore wondering about extending to 40 years the period of the write-off of goodwill on acquisition of Cornwall Ltd.

Required

Calculate the write-off of goodwill on acquisition of Cornwall Ltd in the consolidated accounts of Investor plc for the year ended 30 September 20X9. You should fully explain and justify all parts of the calculation. Assume that the twenty year write-off policy is followed.

6 FRS 17

In November 2000, the ASB issued FRS 17 *Retirement benefits*. This covers the treatment of pensions and other retirement benefits in the employer's accounts, and replaces SSAP 24 *Accounting for pension costs*. The main changes are to defined benefit schemes.

(a)   What are the main provisions of FRS 17?
(b)   What are the main drawbacks of the Standard?

7 Taxable

The following information has been provided by the directors of Taxable plc as at 30 November 20X1:

(a)   At 30 November 20X1 there is an excess of capital allowances over depreciation of £90 million. It is anticipated that the timing differences will reverse according to the following schedule:

	30 Nov 20X2	30 Nov 20X3	30 Nov 20X4
	£m	£m	£m
Depreciation	550	550	550
Capital allowances	530	520	510
	20	30	40

(b)   The directors wish to revalue a property by £10 million as at 30 November 20X1.

(c)   The balance sheet as at 30 November 20X1 includes deferred development expenditure of £40 million. This relates to a new product which has just been launched and the directors believe it has a commercial life of only two years.

(d)   Corporation tax is 30% and the company wishes to discount any deferred tax liabilities at a rate of 4%

Required

Explain the deferred tax implications of the above and calculate the deferred tax provision as at 30 November 20X1 in accordance with FRS 19.

Note: Present Value Table (extract)

Present value of £1 ie $(1+r)^{-n}$ where r = interest rate, n = number of periods until payment or receipt.

Periods (n)	4%
1	0.962
2	0.925
3	0.889
4	0.855
5	0.822

8 PQR

PQR has the following financial instruments in its financial statements for the year ended 31 December 20X5:

(a)   An investment in the debentures of STU, nominal value £40,000, purchased on their issue on 1 January 20X5 at a discount of £6,000 and carrying a 4% coupon. PQR plans to hold these until their redemption on 31 December 20X8. The internal rate of return of the debentures is 8.6%.

(b)   A foreign currency forward contract purchased to hedge the commitment to purchase a machine in foreign currency 6 months after the year end.

(c)   100,000 redeemable preference shares issued in 20X0 at £1 per share with an annual dividend payment of £6 per share, redeemable in 20X8 at their nominal value.

Required

Advise the directors (insofar as the information permits) about the accounting for the financial instruments stating the effect of each on the gearing of the company. Your answer should be accompanied by calculations where appropriate.

9 Hedging

A company owns 100,000 barrels of crude oil which were purchased on 1 July 20X2 at a cost of £26.00 per barrel.

In order to hedge the fluctuation in the market value of the oil the company signs a futures contract on the same date to deliver 100,000 barrels of oil on 31 March 20X3 at a futures price of £27.50 per barrel.

Due to unexpected increased production by OPEC, the market price of oil on 31 December 20X2 slumped to £22.50 per barrel and the futures price for delivery on 31 March 20X3 was £23.25 per barrel at that date

Required

Explain the impact of the transactions on the financial statements of the company for the year ended 31 December 20X2.

10 Leased warehouse

A leased warehouse has been modified to include offices, mezzanines, etc and under the terms of the lease the company, when it moves out, is obliged to return the building to its original state. If the business continues to expand, the directors believe they will have to move out in the next two to three years. The lease does not expire until 2010. The company received a quote for the reinstatement costs of £200,000 and have started to build this up last year at £50,000 a year.

How does FRS 12 *Provisions, contingent liabilities and contingent assets* affect the accounting treatment the company adopts?

11 Elliot

The accountant of Elliot Ltd, a book wholesaler, decided that the time had come to computerise the company's accounting records. The difficulty was that, at that moment, Elliot did not have sufficient funds to meet the capital cost of the hardware. Instead, the company approached Better Leasing plc to finance the purchase through a lease. The agreed terms of the lease were as follows.

Start date:	1 July 20X2
Monthly payments:	£1,989.00
Number of payments:	20

The computer cost £30,600. Better Leasing plc pays tax at 35% and obtains capital allowances of 25% on a reducing balance basis on the cost of the computer.

The cash flow statement for the computer lease from the point of view of Better Leasing (actuarial methods after tax) for the year to 30 June 20X3 was as follows.

Quarter to	Net cash investment at beginning of period £	Cash outflow £	Cash inflow £	Average net cash investment £	Interest paid £	Profit after tax taken out of lease £	Net cash investment at end £
30.9.X2	–	(30,600)	1,989	(28,611)	(715)	(115)	(29,441)
31.12.X2	(29,441)	–	1,989	(27,452)	(686)	(110)	(28,248)
31.3.X3	(28,248)	–	1,989	(26,259)	(657)	(104)	(27,020)
30.6.X3	(27,020)	–	1,989	(25,031)	(626)	(99)	(25,756)

Required

(a) Demonstrate how the lease would be shown in the balance sheet of Better Leasing at 30 June 20X3, and in the profit and loss account for the year. Produce a note on accounting policy for leases.

(b) State the main assumptions underlying the net cash investment calculation.

(c) State how the profit is produced which is taken out of the lease. On what basis is this profit allocated to accounting periods?

(d) Assuming Better Leasing used the investment period method rather than the actuarial method after tax, state how the gross earnings should be allocated.

12 FRS 5 scenarios

Scenario I

Shakey plc enters into an agreement with Farout Factors plc with the following principal terms.

(a) Shakey plc will transfer (by assignment) to Farout Factors plc such trade debts as Shakey plc shall determine, subject only to credit approval by Farout Factors plc and a limit placed on the proportion of the total that may be due from any one debtor. Farout Factors plc levies a charge of 0.15% of turnover, payable monthly, for this facility.

(b) Shakey plc continues to administer the sales ledger and handle all aspects of collection of the debts.

(c) Shakey plc may draw up to 80% of the gross amount of debts assigned at any time, such drawings being debited in the books of Farout Factors plc to a factoring account operated by Farout Factors plc for Shakey plc.

(d) Weekly, Shakey plc assigns and sends copy invoices to Farout Factors plc as they are raised.

(e) Shakey plc is required to bank the gross amounts of all payments received from debts assigned to Farout Factors plc direct into an account in the name of Farout Factors plc. Credit transfers made by debtors direct into Shakey's own bank account must immediately be paid to Farout Factors plc.

(f) Farout Factors plc credits such collections from debtors to the factoring account, and debit the account monthly with interest calculated on the basis of the daily balances on the account using a rate of base rate plus 2.5%. Thus this interest charge varies with the amount of finance drawn by Shakey plc under the finance facility from Farout Factors plc, the speed of payment of the debtors and base rate.

(g) Farout Factors provides protection from bad debts. Any debts not recovered after 90 days are credited to the factoring account, and responsibility for their collection is passed to Farout Factors plc. A charge of 1% of the gross value of all debts factored is levied by Farout Factors plc for this service and debited to the factoring account.

(h)   Farout Factors plc pays for the debts, less any advances, interest charges and credit protection charges, 90 days after the date of purchase, and debits the payment to the factoring account.

(i)   On either party giving 90 days' notice to the other, the arrangement will be terminated. In such and event, Shakey plc will transfer no further debts to Farout Factors plc, and the balance remaining on the factoring account at the end of the notice period will be settled in cash in the normal way.

Required

Consider the nature of the above agreement and resulting transactions and state how these should be reflected in the accounts of Shakey plc.

Scenario II

You are the management accountant of D Ltd which has three principal activities. These are the sale of motor vehicles (both new and second-hand), the provision of spare parts for motor vehicles, and the servicing of motor vehicles.

During the financial year ended 31 August 20X6, the company has entered into a type of business transaction not previously undertaken. With effect from 1 January 20X6, D Ltd entered into an agreement whereby it received motor vehicles on a consignment basis from E plc, a large manufacturer. The terms of the arrangement were as follows.

(a)   On delivery, the stock of vehicles remains the legal property of E plc.

(b)   Legal title to a vehicle passes to D Ltd either when D Ltd enters into a binding arrangement to sell the vehicle to a third party or six months after the date of delivery by E plc to D Ltd.

(c)   At the date legal title passes, E plc invoices D Ltd for the sale of the vehicles. The price payable by D Ltd is the normal selling price of E plc *at the date of delivery*, increased by 1% for every complete month the vehicles are held on consignment by D Ltd. Any change in E plc's normal selling price between the date of delivery and the date legal title to the goods passes to D Ltd does not change the amount payable by D Ltd to E plc.

(d)   At any time between the date of delivery and the date legal title passes to D Ltd, the company (D Ltd) has the right to return the vehicles to E plc *provided they are not damaged or obsolete.* D Ltd does not have the right to return damaged or obsolete vehicles. If D Ltd exercises this right of return then a return penalty is payable by D Ltd as follows.

Time since date of delivery	*Penalty as a percentage of invoiced price ***
Three months or less	50%
Three to four months	75%
More than four months	100%

* ie, the price that would otherwise be payable by D Ltd if legal title to the vehicles had passed at the date of return.

(e)   E plc has *no right to demand* return of vehicles on consignment to D Ltd unless D Ltd becomes insolvent.

The managing director suggests that the vehicles should be shown as an asset of D Ltd only when title passes, and the purchase price becomes legally payable.

Required

Using the details of the agreement between D Ltd and E plc outline with reasons the appropriate accounting treatment in D Ltd's book.

13 Peter Holdings

Peter Holdings plc is a large investment conglomerate.

Required

Explain how divisional performance should be measured in the interest of the group's shareholders.

14 Andrews   **45 mins**

Andrews Ltd, a manufacturer and retailer of golf clubs, disposed of its retail outlets in January 20X5. Extracts from the company's draft financial statements show:

PROFIT AND LOSS ACCOUNT
FOR THE YEAR ENDED 31 OCTOBER 20X5

	20X5	20X4
	£'000	£'000
Turnover	3,900	4,300
Cost of sales	(2,652)	(2,795)
Gross profit	1,248	1,505
Distribution costs	(302)	(430)
Administrative costs	(107)	(210)
Operating profit	839	865
Exceptional item – sale of retail outlets	16	–
	855	865
Interest payable	(4)	(15)
	851	850
Taxation	(290)	(285)
Profit for the year	561	565
Dividends	(96)	(105)

BALANCE SHEET AS AT 31 OCTOBER 20X5

	20X5		20X4	
	£'000	£'000	£'000	£'000
Fixed assets		970		810
Current assets				
Stocks	470		340	
Debtors	420		360	
Investments	50			
Cash at bank and in hand	20		40	
	960		740	
Current liabilities	(590)		(725)	
Net current assets		370		15
Long term liabilities		–		(150)
		1,340		675
Capital and reserves				
Share capital		350		350
Revaluation reserve		200		
Profit and loss account		790		325
		1,340		675

Average ratios for the appropriate industrial sector for 20X5 and for Andrews Ltd are as follows.

	Industrial sector	Andrews Ltd	
	20X5	20X5	20X4
Gross margin	33%	32%	35%
Net margin (before taxation)	22%	21.5%	20.1%
Fixed asset turnover	4.5 times	4.0 times	5.3 times
Current ratio	1.5:1	1.63:1	1.02:1
Quick ratio	1.0:1	0.83:1	0.55:1
Return on shareholders' funds	48%	42.2%	85.9%

Required

Comment on the 20X5 profitability and liquidity of Andrews Ltd in the light of the available information.

(25 marks)

15 Angus

During the completion of the financial statements of Angus plc for the year ended 28 February 20X7, the following matters have been brought to your attention.

(a) On 1 March 20X6, the company revalued its freehold land and buildings (for the first time) to £20 million (land element £4 million) and the accounting records were adjusted to this value. The property originally cost £16 million on which annual depreciation of £280,000 had been charged. Accumulated depreciation to 29 February 20X6 was £2.8 million. Depreciation of £400,000 has been charged to the profit and loss account for the year ended 28 February 20X7.

(b) The company's accounting policy for research and development has been to capitalise the cost and amortise this over 10 years. On 1 March 20X6, when deferred development expenditure of £1.5 million was held as an intangible fixed asset, this policy was changed to immediate write off of development expenditure.

(c) The company announced the intended closure of its European operations on 31 January 20X7 when a formal closure plan was approved and adopted. On 10 March 20X7, the company contracted to terminate various operating leases and sell other fixed assets. The fixed assets had a net book value of £10.5 million and an agreed sale value of £9 million. The lessors of the assets held under operating leases agreed to terminate the contracts for a payment of £350,000. The European operations contributed 10% of turnover and profit.

(d) As a result of the closure in (c) above, the company will need to carry out a fundamental reorganisation of its other activities at a cost of £1.25 million.

(e) After accounting for the above items, the company's draft financial statements show turnover of £200 million, profit before taxation of £18 million and a tax charge of £6 million. The company has paid a dividend of £2 million. Shareholders' funds at 1 March 20X6 were £500 million.

Required

(a) Prepare the following statements, suitable for publication, for Angus plc for the year ended 28 February 20X7:

(i) Profit and loss account
(ii) Statement of total recognised gains and loses
(iii) Reconciliation of movements in shareholders' funds
(iv) Note of historical cost profits and losses

(b)   Explain briefly:

    (i)   The purpose of the statement of total recognised gains and losses

    (ii)   The extent to which a user of the accounts will be better able to make decisions by referring to a statement of total recognised gains and losses rather than the statement of movements on reserves that is produced to comply with the Companies Act 1985

16 Share-based payment
45 mins

(a)   J&B granted 200 options on its £1 ordinary shares to each of its 800 employees on 1 January 20X1. Each grant is conditional upon the employee being employed by J&B until 31 December 20X3.

J&B estimated at 1 January 20X1 that:

    (i)   The fair value of each option was £4.

    (ii)   The exercise price of the options was £1 and the market value of a J&B share on 1 January 20X1 was £3.

    (iii) Approximately 50 employees would leave during 20X1, 40 during 20X2 and 30 during 20X3 thereby forfeiting their rights to receive the options. The departures were expected to be evenly spread within each year.

    (iv)   In the event, only 40 employees left during 20X1, 20 during 20X2 and none during 20X3, spread evenly during each year.

Required

The directors of J&B have asked you to illustrate how such schemes will be accounted for under FRS 20.

    (i)   Show the double entries for the charge to the profit and loss account for employee services over the 3 years and for the share issue, assuming all employees entitled to benefit from the scheme exercised their rights and the shares were issued on 31 December 20X3.

    (ii)   Explain how your solution would differ had J&B offered its employees cash based on the share value rather than share options.   **(12 marks)**

(b)   At the beginning of year 1, Kingsley plc grants 100 shares each to 500 employees, conditional upon the employees' remaining in the entity's employ during the vesting period. The shares will vest at the end of year 1 if the entity's earnings increase by more than 18 per cent; at the end of year 2 if the entity's earnings increase by more than an average of 13 per cent per year over the two-year period; and at the end of year 3 if the entity's earnings increase by more than an average of 10 per cent per year over the three-year period. The shares have a fair value of £30 per share at the start of year 1, which equals the share price at grant date. No dividends are expected to be paid over the three-year period.

By the end of year 1, the entity's earnings have increased by 14 per cent, and 30 employees have left. The entity expects that earnings will continue to increase at a similar rate in year 2, and therefore expects that the shares will vest at the end of year 2. The entity expects, on the basis of a weighted average probability, that a further 30 employees will leave during year 2, and therefore expects that 440 employees will vest in 100 shares at the end of year 2.

By the end of year 2, the entity's earnings have increased by only 10 per cent and therefore the shares do not vest at the end of year 2. 28 employees have left during the year. The entity expects that a further 25 employees will leave during year 3, and that the entity's earnings will increase by at least 6 per cent, thereby achieving the average of 10 per cent per year.

583

By the end of year 3, 23 employees have left and the entity's earnings had increased by 8 per cent, resulting in an average increase of 10.67 per cent per year. Therefore 419 employees received 100 shares at the end of year 3.

Required

Show the expense and equity figures which will appear in the financial statements in each of the three years.

(13 marks
(Total marks = 25)

17 Exclusion of subsidiaries

In large and complex groups of companies, there are often difficulties in deciding how to treat certain companies when preparing the consolidated financial statements for the year.

Required

(a)   State the treatments, required by legislation and by UK accounting standards, of subsidiaries which are unsuitable for inclusion in the consolidated accounts.

(b)   Comment on the validity of each of the treatments so required.

18 Highland

Highland plc owns two subsidiaries acquired as follows:

1 July 20X1   80% of Aviemore Ltd for £5 million when the book value of the net assets of Aviemore Ltd was £4 million.

30 November 20X7   65% of Bachman Ltd for £2 million when the book value of the net assets of Buchan Ltd was £1.35 million.

The companies' profit and loss accounts for the year ended 31 March 20X8 were:

	Highland plc	Aviemore Ltd	Buchan Ltd
	£'000	£'000	£'000
Sales	5,000	3,000	2,910
Cost of sales	(3,000)	(2,300)	(2,820)
Gross profit	2,000	700	90
Net operating expenses	(1,000)	(500)	(150)
Other income	230	–	–
Interest payable and similar charges	–	(50)	(210)
Profit/(loss) before taxation	1,230	150	(270)
Taxation	(300)	(50)	–
Profit/(loss) after taxation	930	100	(270)
Dividends declared but not paid	200	50	–

Additional information

(a)   On 1 April 20X7, Buchan Ltd issued £2.1 million 10% loan stock to Highland plc. Interest is payable twice yearly on 1 October and 1 April. Highland plc has accounted for the interest received on 1 October 20X7 only.

(b)   On 1 July 20X7, Aviemore Ltd sold a freehold property to Highland plc for £800,000 (land element – £300,000). The property originally cost £900,000 (land element – £100,000) on 1 July 19W7. The property's total useful economic life was 50 years on 1 July 19W7 and there has been no change in the useful economic life since. Aviemore Ltd has credited the profit on disposal to 'Net operating expenses'.

(c)   The fixed assets of Buchan Ltd on 30 November 20X7 were valued at £500,000 (book value £350,000) and were acquired in April 20X7. The fixed assets have a total useful economic life of ten years. Buchan Ltd has not adjusted its accounting records to reflect fair values.

(d)   All companies use the straight-line method of depreciation and charge a full year's depreciation in the year of acquisition and none in the year of disposal.

(e)   Highland plc charges Aviemore Ltd an annual fee of £85,000 for management services and this has been included in 'Other income'.

(f)   Highland plc has accounted for its dividend receivable from Aviemore Ltd in 'Other income'.

(g)   It is group policy to amortise goodwill arising on acquisitions over ten years.

Required

Prepare the consolidated profit and loss account for Highland plc for the year ended 31 March 20X8.

19 Ullapool

Ullapool plc made the following investments in the year ended 31 October 20X7:

Kyle Ltd

1 May 20X7: 70% of the ordinary share capital acquired. The consideration comprised:

£1 million cash payable 1 May 20X7
3 million 25p ordinary shares issued 1 May 20X7 (market value 50p)

Share issue costs of £100,000 were incurred. Professional advisers' fees on the acquisition amounted to £150,000.

Portree Ltd (incorporated on 1 November 20X6)

31 August 20X7: 30% of the ordinary share capital acquired. The consideration comprised £590,000 cash.

The summarised draft balance sheets of the companies as on 31 October 20X7 showed:

	Ullapool Plc £'000	Kyle Ltd £'000	Portree Ltd £'000
Fixed assets	6,000	2,900	1,800
Investments – Kyle Ltd	2,750	–	–
– Portree Ltd	590	–	–
Current assets	1,660	1,300	700
Current liabilities	(2,800)	(650)	(500)
	8,200	3,550	2,000
Share capital			
– ordinary shares of £1 each	–	1,700	800
– ordinary shares of 25p each	4,750	–	–
Share premium	1,250	–	–
Profit and loss account	2,200	1,850	1,200
	8,200	3,550	2,000

Other information:

(a) The investment in Kyle Ltd of £2,750,000 represents the cash consideration, the issue of shares, share issue costs and professional advisers' fees.

(b) The company estimates that a further cost of the acquisition of Kyle Ltd was £50,000 for its own staff time. This has been charged to the profit and loss account in the year ended 31 October 20X7.

(c) The fixed assets of Kyle Ltd had a market value of £290,000 in excess of their net book value at 1 May 20X7. In all other respects, market values are not significantly different to net book values.

(d) Any goodwill arising is to be capitalised.

(e) At the dates of acquisition of Kyle Ltd and Portree Ltd, the balances on their profit and loss accounts were £1.25 million and £1 million respectively.

(f) The stock of Ullapool plc includes goods purchased from Portree Ltd for £51,000 on 10 October 20X7. Portree Ltd applies a mark up on the cost of its goods of 50%. Ullapool plc has paid for half of these goods purchased on 30 October 20X7 but Portree Ltd did not receive and account for the cheque until 3 November 20X7.

(g) On 17 July 20X7, Kyle Ltd sold a fixed asset to Ullapool plc for £150,000. The asset's original cost was £200,000 in the year ended 31 October 20X3 and accumulated depreciation to the date of sale was £100,000. It has a remaining useful life of 4 years at the date of sale. Ullapool has charged depreciation on the asset of £37,500 in the year ended 31 October 20X7.

Required

Prepare the consolidated balance sheet of Ullapool plc as on 31 October 20X7.

20 Dales

Dales plc acquired 80,000 shares in National plc on 1 May 20X2, when the latter company's profit and loss account stood at £350,000. On 1 December 20X2, National plc acquired 90,000 shares in Park Ltd, when the profit and loss account of Park stood at £50,000. None of the companies hold any other investments. Draft balance sheets for the three companies as at 31 December 20X6 are as follows:

	Dales plc £'000	National plc £'000	Park Ltd £'000
Tangible fixed assets	600	400	300
Investments	420	140	–
Stocks	380	215	170
Debtors	160	195	110
Cash	20	–	40
	1,580	950	620
less:			
Creditors (trade)	(90)	(80)	(90)
Overdraft	–	(25)	–
Debentures	(140)	–	(50)
	1,350	845	480
Share capital (£1 ordinary shares)	500	100	100
Profit and loss account	850	745	380
	1,350	845	480

The following points are also relevant:

(a)   Dividends have yet to be proposed as follows:

Dales	£50,000
National	£40,000
Park	£30,000

(b)   Goodwill is recognised as an asset in the balance sheet. Dales does not consider there has been any impairment in its value.

Required

Prepare the consolidated balance sheet of the Dales plc group as at 31 December 20X6.

21 Armoury   **45 mins**

Bayonet plc purchased 6,000 shares in Rifle Ltd on 1 January 20X3 for £10,000. Rifle Ltd had purchased 4,000 shares in Pistol Ltd for £9,000 on 31 December 20X2. The balances on the profit and loss accounts of the acquired companies were £8,000 and £6,500 respectively.

The balance sheets of the three companies as at 31 December 20X9 are as follows:

	Bayonet plc £	Rifle Ltd £	Pistol Ltd £
Fixed assets			
Investment in Rifle	10,000	–	–
Investment in Pistol	–	9,000	–
Other fixed assets	14,500	12,140	17,500
	24,500	21,140	17,500
Current assets			
Stocks	6,300	2,100	450
Debtors	4,900	2,000	2,320
Cash	500	1,440	515
	11,700	5,540	3,285
Creditors: amounts falling due within one year	5,700	2,280	1,985
Net current assets	6,000	3,260	1,300
	30,500	24,400	18,800
Share capital and reserves			
50p ordinary shares	5,000	4,000	2,500
Profit and loss account	25,500	20,400	16,300
	30,500	24,400	18,800

Required

Prepare the consolidated balance sheet of Bayonet plc as at 31 December 20X9.

Note: Goodwill is capitalised and amortised over a period of five years.

Assume there was no movement in the reserves of Pistol between 31 December 20X2 and 1 January 20X3.   **(25 marks)**

22 Murder, Mystery and Suspense

45 mins

On 1 January 20X3 Murder Limited acquired 60% of Mystery Limited.

On 30 July 20X1 Murder Limited acquired 10% of Suspense Limited and on the same day Mystery Limited acquired 80% of Suspense Limited.

The balance sheets of the three companies as at 31 December 20X7 are as follows:

	Murder Ltd £'000	Mystery Ltd £'000	Suspense Ltd £'000
Tangible fixed assets	2,430	1,410	870
Investment in Mystery Ltd	900	–	–
Investment in Suspense Ltd	55	240	–
	3,385	1,650	870
Current assets			
Stock	450	200	260
Debtors	610	365	139
Cash	240	95	116
	1,300	660	515
Current liabilities			
Trade creditors	1,130	410	384
Net current assets	170	250	131
	3,555	1,900	1,001
Capital and reserves			
Ordinary share capital	500	200	100
Share premium	250	120	50
Profit and loss account	2,805	1,580	851
	3,555	1,900	1,001

During the year, Mystery Ltd sold goods to Suspense Ltd for £260,000 at a mark-up of 25%. All of these goods remain in stock at the year end.

The reserves of the three companies may be summarised as follows:

	30.7.X1 £'000	1.1.X3 £'000	31.12.X7 £'000
Murder Ltd	1,610	1,860	2,805
Mystery Ltd	700	950	1,580
Suspense Ltd	46	261	851

Any goodwill arising has been fully amortised.

Required

Prepare the consolidated balance sheet of Murder Limited group as at 31 December 20X7. **(25 marks)**

23 Holmes and Deakin

Holmes Ltd has owned 85% of the ordinary share capital of Deakin Ltd for some years. The shares were bought for £255,000 and Deakin Ltd's profit and loss account at the time of purchase was £20,000. It is group policy to recognise goodwill as an asset. The goodwill was deemed to have an indefinite useful life and no impairments have been identified.

On 28.2.X3 Holmes Ltd sold 40,000 of the Deakin shares for £160,000. The only entry made in respect of this transaction has been the receipt of the cash, which was credited to the 'investment in subsidiary' account. Holmes has made no entries regarding the declared dividend from Deakin Ltd.

The following draft summarised accounts are available:

PROFIT AND LOSS ACCOUNT FOR THE YEAR TO 31.5.X3

	Holmes Ltd £'000	Deakin Ltd £'000
Profit before tax	200	110
Taxation	90	60
Profit after tax	110	50
Dividends declared	50	30
Retained for the year	60	20

BALANCE SHEET AS AT 31.5.X3

	Holmes Ltd	Deakin Ltd
Fixed assets:		
Tangible (NBV)	535	178
Investment in Deakin Ltd	95	–
Current assets:		
Stock	320	190
Debtors	250	175
Cash	80	89
Creditors: amounts falling due within one year		
Trade creditors	(295)	(171)
Taxation	(80)	(60)
Dividend declared but not paid	(50)	(30)
	855	371
Deferred taxation	(95)	(31)
	760	340

	£'000	£'000
Capital and reserves		
Share capital £1 ordinary shares	500	200
Profit and loss account	260	140
	760	340

Required

Prepare, in draft form:

(a)   The profit and loss account of Holmes Ltd for the year to 31.5.X3;
(b)   The consolidated profit and loss account of Holmes Ltd for the same period;
(c)   A consolidated balance sheet as at 31.5.X3; and
(d)   A statement of retained reserves at 31.5.X3.

Assume that the capital gain will be subject to taxation at 33%.

24 Harvard

65 mins

The draft financial statements of Harvard and its subsidiary, Krakow sp. z o.o. are set out below.

BALANCE SHEETS AT 31 DECEMBER 20X5

	Harvard £ '000	Krakow PLN '000
Fixed assets		
Property, plant and equipment	2,870	4,860
Investment in Krakow	840	–
	3,710	4,860
Current assets		
Stock	1,990	8,316
Trade debtors	1,630	4,572
Cash	240	2,016
	3,860	14,904
Non-current liabilities		
Loans	1,920	–
Current liabilities		
Trade creditors	5,030	4,356
	620	15,408
Shareholders' funds		
Share capital (£1/PLN1)	118	1,348
Retained earnings	502	14,060
	620	15,408

PROFIT AND LOSS ACCOUNTS FOR THE YEAR ENDED 31 DECEMBER 20X5

	£'000	PLN''000
Turnover	40,425	97,125
Cost of sales	35,500	77,550
Gross profit	4,925	19,575
Distribution and administrative expenses	4,400	5,850
Investment income	277	–
Profit before tax	802	13,725
Income tax expense	300	4,725
Profit for the period	502	9,000
Dividends declared during the period	700	3,752

The following additional information is given:

(a) Exchange rates

	Zloty (PLN) to £
31 December 20X2	4.40
31 December 20X3	4.16
31 December 20X4	4.00
15 May 20X5	3.92
31 December 20X5	3.60
Average for 20X5	3.75

(b) Harvard acquired 1,011,000 shares in Krakow for £840,000 on 31 December 20X2 when Krakow's retained earnings stood at PLN 2,876,000. Krakow operates as an autonomous subsidiary. Its functional currency is the Polish zloty.

(c)   Krakow paid an interim dividend of PLN 1,448,000 on 15 May 20X5 and declared a final dividend of PLN 2,304,000 just before the year end. Harvard has not yet accounted for the dividend receivable.

(d)   The translation differences (gross) in the consolidated financial statements at 31 December 20X4 relating to the translation of the financial statements of Krakow (excluding goodwill) was £208,000. Retained earnings of Krakow in Krakow's separate financial statements in the post-acquisition period to 31 December 20X4 as translated amounted to £1,372,000.

(e)   No impairment losses were necessary in the consolidated financial statements by 31 December 20X5.

Required

(a)   Prepare the consolidated balance sheet at 31 December 20X5.   **6 marks**

(b)   Prepare the consolidated profit and loss account and an extract from the statement of movements in reserves for retained earnings and translation reserve for the year ended 31 December 20X5.

12 marks

18 marks

(Total marks = 36)

25 Tastydesserts   45 mins

The following are extracts from the financial statements of Tastydesserts plc and one of its wholly owned subsidiaries, Custardpowders Limited, the shares in which were acquired in 31 October 20X2.

BALANCE SHEET

	Tastydesserts plc and subsidiaries 31 December		Custardpowders Limited 31 October
	20X2	20X1	20X2
	£'000	£'000	£'000
Goodwill	42	–	–
Tangible fixed assets	4,764	3,685	694
Associated undertakings	2,195	2,175	–
Stocks	1,735	1,388	306
Debtors	2,658	2,436	185
Bank balances and cash	43	77	7
Creditors	(1,915)	(1,546)	(148)
Bank overdrafts	(176)	(343)	–
Taxation	(235)	(200)	–
Dividend declared but not paid	(82)	(63)	–
Deferred taxation	(111)	(180)	–
	8,918	7,429	1,044
Share capital	4,896	4,776	400
Share premium	216	–	
Reserves	2,458	2,000	644
Loans	1,348	653	–
	8,918	7,429	1,044

PROFIT AND LOSS ACCOUNT

	Tastydesserts plc and subsidiaries 31 December 20X2 £'000
Net profit for year before taxation	546
Share of associated undertakings profits	190
	736
Taxation (incl. £70 from the associate)	196
	540

The following information is also given:

(a) The consolidated figures at 31 December 20X2 include Custardpowders Limited.

(b) The amount of depreciation on fixed assets during the year was £78,000. There were no disposals.

(c) The cost on 31 October 20X2 of the shares in Custardpowders Limited was £1,086,000 comprising the issue of £695,000 unsecured loan stock at par, 120,000 ordinary shares of £1 each at a value of 280p and £55,000 in cash.

(d) Goodwill is considered to have an indefinite useful life.

(e) Dividends paid by Tastydesserts (parent) during the period amounted to £63,000.

Required

Prepare a cash flow statement for Tastydesserts plc and subsidiaries for the year ended 31 December 20X2 using the indirect method. **(25 marks)**

26 Public sector organisations

The laws, regulations and guidelines relating to public sector accounts are rather different from those which apply to private sector organisations. As far as public sector organisations are concerned:

(a) State why these differences exist
(b) Explain the main differences
(c) Outline the consequences for public sector accounts

27 German competitor 45 mins

You are the chief accountant of Tone plc. The managing director has provided you with the financial statements of Tone plc's main competitor, Hilde GmbH, a German company. He finds difficulty in reviewing these statements in their non-UK format, presented below.

HILDE GmbH
BALANCE SHEET AS AT 31 MARCH 20X5 (in DM million)

	31.3.X5	31.3.X4		31.3.X5	31.3.X4
ASSETS			CAPITAL AND LIABILITIES		
Tangible fixed assets			Capital and reserves		
Land	1,000	750	Share capital	850	750
Buildings	750	500	Share premium	100	
Plant	200	150	Legal reserve	200	200
	1,950	1,400	Profit & loss b/fwd	590	300
			Profit & loss for year	185	290
Current assets			NET WORTH	1,925	1,540
Stock	150	120			
Trade debtors	180	100	Creditors		
Cash	20	200	Trade creditors	170	150
	350	420	Taxation	180	150
			Other creditors	75	50
Prepayments and				425	350
accrued income					
Prepayments	50	70			
	2,350	1,890		2,350	1,890

HILDE GmbH
INCOME STATEMENT FOR THE YEAR ENDED 31 MARCH 20X5 (in DM million)

	20X5	20X4		20X5	20X4
EXPENSES			INCOME		
Operating expenses:			Operating income:		
Purchase of raw			Sale of goods produced	1,890	1,270
materials	740	400	Variation in stock of		
Variation in stocks			finished goods and WIP	120	80
thereof	90	40	Other operating income	75	50
Taxation	190	125	Total operating income	2,085	1,400
Wages	500	285			
Valuation adjustment					
on fixed assets:					
depreciation	200	150			
Valuation adjustment					
on current assets:					
amounts written off	30	20			
Other operating					
expenses	50	40			
Total operating					
expenses	1,800	1,060			
Financial expenses					
Interest	100	50			
Total financial					
expenses	100	50			
TOTAL EXPENSES	1,900	1,110	TOTAL INCOME	2,085	1,400
Balance: PROFIT	185	290			
SUM TOTAL	2,085	1,400		2,085	1,400

Required

Prepare a report for the managing director:

(a) Analysing the performance of Hilde GmbH using the financial statements provided   **(18 marks)**

(b) Explaining why a direct comparison of the results of Tone plc and Hilde GmbH may be misleading

(7 marks)

(Total = 25 marks)

28 Badgo

45 mins

You are the management accountant of Badgo plc, a company with subsidiaries all over the world. The draft consolidated financial statements of the group for the year ended 31 December 20X9 are given below.

CONSOLIDATED PROFIT AND LOSS ACCOUNT FOR THE YEAR ENDED 31 DECEMBER

	20X9	20X8
	£m	£m
Turnover	2,000	1,900
Cost of sales	(1,400)	(1,330)
Gross profit	600	570
Other operating expenses	(400)	(300)
Share of operating profit of associate	35	–
Operating profit	235	270
Investment income		4
Interest payable	(65)	(50)
Profit before taxation	170	224
Taxation	(53)	(69)
Profit for the year	117	155
Declared dividends	60	80

CONSOLIDATED STATEMENT OF TOTAL RECOGNISED GAINS
AND LOSSES FOR THE YEAR ENDED 31 DECEMBER

	20X9	20X8
	£m	£m
Profit for the financial year	117	155
Currency translation difference on foreign currency net investments	5	(4)
Total gains and losses for the year	122	151

CONSOLIDATED BALANCE SHEET AT 31 DECEMBER

	20X9		20X8	
	£m	£m	£m	£m
Fixed assets				
Intangible assets	4		5	
Tangible assets	380		360	
Investments (*see note*)	400		–	
		784		365
Current assets				
Stocks	235		222	
Debtors	300		285	
Short-term investments			100	
Cash in hand and at bank	1		1	
	536		608	
Current liabilities				
Trade creditors	135		128	
Taxation	53		69	
Dividends payable	60		80	
Bank overdraft	170		80	
	418		357	
Net current assets		118		251
Long-term loans		(181)		(157)
		721		459
Capital and reserves:				
Called-up share capital		300		200
(£1 shares)				
Share premium account		100		
Profit and loss account		321		259
		721		459

Note: investment in associate

During the year the group invested in 35% of the equity share capital of Stateside Inc, a company incorporated in the United States of America. No other investments appear in the consolidated balance sheet.

A non-executive director has recently received a copy of the draft consolidated financial statements. His attendance at Board meetings has been irregular over the last year and he plays no part in the day-to-day running of the group. He has sent you a memorandum that contains a number of questions and asks you to draft a reply. The questions are as follows:

(a) We have raised more money from our shareholders this year and our turnover has gone up. Even so, profits and dividends have fallen. How do you explain this?

(b) I don't understand why the retained profit for the year is £57 million when the balance of retained profits shown in the balance sheet has increased by a different amount. Is this a mistake?

(c) I am pleased to see that we made an investment in Stateside this year. I was told we paid £380 million for it but it's in the consolidated balance sheet at £400 million. Why is this? Have we paid for it out of the money we raised from our shareholders this year?

(d) A few weeks ago I saw a set of accounts for Stateside Inc that had been sent over by their accountants. The accounts were drawn up in US$. They showed that the company had made a loss in the year ended 31 December 20X9. We have shown our share of Stateside's results in our accounts as a profit. I know the results have to be translated into before we can consolidate them but I don't see how this process can turn a loss into a profit. Have we made a mistake?

Required

Draft a report to the non-executive director that responds to the questions he has raised.

The non-executive director is not a financial expert. Therefore he is not interested in a reply that contains a mass of detailed figures. What he wants is a basic idea of the key issues that relate to each one of his questions. Therefore any supporting calculations that may be relevant should be included as an appendix to the report.

The allocation of marks to the answers to the four questions is:

Question (a)	**(8 marks)**
Question (b)	**(5 marks)**
Question (c)	**(6 marks)**
Question (d)	**(6 marks)**
	(Total = 25 marks)

29 Planet   45 mins

Planet plc has provided the following draft consolidated balance sheet as at 30 November 20X2.

PLANET PLC
GROUP BALANCE SHEET AS AT 30 NOVEMBER 20X2

	£'000
Fixed asset	
Intangible assets	10,360
Tangible assets	76,240
	86,600
Net current assets	55,800
Total assets less current liabilities	142,400
Creditors: amounts falling due after more than one year	(25,400)
Provisions for liabilities	(1,800)
	115,200
Minority interests	(18,200)
	97,000
Capital and reserves	
Called up share capital	32,200
Share premium account	10,000
Profit and loss account	54,800
Shareholders' funds	97,000

The group accountant has asked your advice on several matters. These issues are set out below and have not been dealt with in the draft group financial statements.

(i)   Planet purchased a wholly owned subsidiary company, Moon, on 1 December 20X0. The purchase consideration was based on the performance of the subsidiary. The vendors commenced a legal action on 31 March 20X2 over the amount of the purchase consideration. An amount had been paid to the vendors and included in the calculation of goodwill but the vendors disputed the amount of this payment. On 30 November 20X2 the court ruled that Planet should pay an additional £16 million to the vendors. The directors do not know how to treat the additional purchase consideration and have not accounted for the item. Goodwill is written off over five years and there is no time apportionment in the year of purchase.

Note. Ignore the effect of the time value of money.

(ii) Planet has corporate offices under an operating lease. A requirement of the operating lease for the buildings is that the asset is returned in good condition. The operating lease was signed in the current year and lasts for six years. Planet intends to refurbish the building in six years time at a cost of £12 million in order to meet the requirements of the lease. This amount includes the renovation of the exterior of the building and is based on current price levels. Currently there is evidence that due to exceptionally severe weather damage the company will have to spend £2.4 million in the next year on having the exterior of the building renovated. The company feels that this expenditure will reduce the refurbishment cost at the end of the lease by an equivalent amount. There is no provision for the above expenditure in the financial statements.

An 80% owned subsidiary company, Galaxy, has a leasehold property (depreciated historical cost £16 million). It has been modified to include a swimming pool for the employees. Under the terms of the lease, the property must be restored to its original state when the lease expires in ten years' time or earlier termination. The present value of the costs of reinstatement are likely to be £4 million and the directors wish to provide for £400,000 per annum for ten years. The lease was signed and operated from 1 December 20X1. The directors estimate that the lease has a recoverable value of £19 million at 30 November 20X2 and have not provided for any of the above amounts.

Additionally Planet owns buildings at a carrying value of £40 million which will require repair expenditure of approximately £12 million over the next five years. There is no provision for this amount in the financial statements. Depreciation is charged on owned buildings at 5% per annum and on leasehold buildings at 10% per annum on the straight line basis.

(iii) On 1 December 20X1, Planet entered into an agreement with a wholly owned overseas subsidiary, Dimanche, to purchase components at a value of 4.2 million krona on which Dimanche made a profit of 20% on selling price. The goods were to be delivered on 31 January 20X2 with the payment due on 31 March 20X2. Planet took out a foreign currency contract on 1 December 20X0 to buy 4.2 million krona on 31 March 20X1 at the forward rate of £1 = 1.4 krona.

At 30 November 20X2, Planet had two-thirds of the components in stock. The spot rates were as follows.

£1 equivalent

1 December 20X1	1.3 krona
31 January 20X2	1.46 krona
31 March 20X2	1.45 krona
30 November 20X2	1.35 krona

The initial purchase of the stock had been recorded on receipt at the forward rate and the forward rate had been used for the year end valuation of stock. The directors are unsure as to how to treat the items above both for accounting and disclosure purposes but they have heard that the simplest method is to translate the asset and liability at the forward rate and they wish to use this method.

(iv) Galaxy has developed a database during the year to 30 November 20X2 and it is included in intangible fixed assets at a cost of £6 million. The asset comprises the internal and external costs of developing the database. The cost of the database is being amortised over 10 years and one year's amortisation has been charged. The database is used to produce a technical computing manual which is used by the whole group and sold to other parties. It has quickly become a market leader in this field. Any costs of maintaining the database and the computing manual are written off as incurred. The computing manual requires substantial revision every four years.

Required

(a) Explain how the above four issues should be dealt with in the consolidated financial statements of Planet. Show the accounting entries that need to be made. **(19 marks)**

597

(b)   Prepare a revised group balance sheet at 30 November 20X2 taking into account the four issues discussed in part (a).   **(6 marks)**

(Total = 25 marks)

30 Wingit

90 mins

The following draft financial statements relate to the Wingit Group plc.

DRAFT GROUP PROFIT AND LOSS ACCOUNT
FOR THE YEAR ENDED 30 NOVEMBER 20X7

	£m	£m
Turnover		
Continuing operations	4,458	
Discontinued operations	1,263	
		5,721
Cost of sales		(4,560)
Gross profit		1,161
Distribution costs	309	
Administration expenses	285	
		(594)
		567
Income from interests in joint venture		75
Defence costs of take-over bid		(20)
Operating profit		
Continuing operations	438	
Discontinued operations	184	
		622
Loss on disposal of tangible fixed assets	(7)	
Loss on disposal of discontinued operations (note (a))	(25)	
		(32)
Interest receivable	27	
Interest payable	(19)	
		8
Profit on ordinary activities before taxation		598
Tax on profit on ordinary activities (note (c))		(191)
Profit on ordinary activities after taxation		407
Minority interests – equity		(75)
Profit attributable to members of the parent company		332

Dividends for the period amounted to £130m.

GROUP STATEMENT OF TOTAL RECOGNISED GAINS AND LOSSES
FOR THE YEAR ENDED 30 NOVEMBER 20X7

	£m
Profit attributable to members of the parent company	332
Deficit on revaluation of land and buildings	(30)
Deficit on revaluation of land and buildings in joint venture	(15)
Gain on revaluation of loan	28
Total recognised gains and losses relating to the year	315

BPP
LEARNING MEDIA

DRAFT GROUP BALANCE SHEET AS AT 30 NOVEMBER 20X7

	20X7 £m	20X6 £m
Fixed assets		
Intangible assets	60	144
Tangible fixed assets (note (d))	1,415	1,800
Investments (notes (b) and (e))	600	–
	2,075	1,944
Current assets		
Stocks	720	680
Short term investments (note (e))	152	44
Debtors (note (f))	680	540
Cash at bank and in hand	24	133
	1,576	1,397
Creditors: amounts falling due within one year (note (g))	(1,601)	(1,223)
Net current assets	(25)	174
Total assets less current liabilities	2,050	2,118
Creditors: amounts falling due after more than one year	(186)	(214)
Provision for liabilities – bid defence costs	(30)	(15)
Minority interests – equity	(330)	(570)
	1,504	1,319
Capital and reserves		
Called up share capital	440	440
Share premium account	101	101
Revaluation reserve	33	50
Profit and loss account	930	728
Total shareholders' funds – equity	1,504	1,319

The following information is relevant to the Wingit Group plc.

(a)   The group disposed of a major subsidiary Piece plc on 1 September 20X7. Wingit held an 80% interest in the subsidiary at the date of disposal. Piece plc's results are classified as discontinued in the profit and loss account.

The group required the subsidiary Piece plc to prepare an interim balance sheet at the date of the disposal and this is as follows.

	£m	£m
Tangible fixed assets (depreciation 30)		310
Current assets		
Stocks	60	
Debtors	50	
Cash at bank and in hand	130	
	240	
Creditors: amounts falling due within one year		
(including corporation tax – £25m)	(130)	
		110
		420
Called up share capital		100
Profit and loss account		320
		420

The consolidated carrying values of all the assets and liabilities at that date are as above. The depreciation charge in the profit and loss account for the period was £9 million. The carrying amount relating to goodwill in the group accounts arising on the acquisition of Piece plc was £64 million at 1 December 20X6. The loss on sale of discontinued operations in the group accounts comprises:

	£m
Sale proceeds	375
Net assets sold (80% × £420m)	(336)
Goodwill	(64)
	(25)

The consideration for the sale of Piece plc was 200 million ordinary shares of £1 in Meal plc, the acquiring company, at a value of £300 million and £75 million in cash. The group's policy is to amortise goodwill arising on acquisition but not in the year of sale of a subsidiary. The amortisation for the year was £20 million on other intangible assets.

(b) During the year, Wingit plc had transferred several of its tangible assets to a newly created company, Kevla Ltd, which is owned jointly by three parties. The total investment at the date of transfer in the joint venture by Wingit plc was £225 million at carrying value comprising £200 million in tangible fixed assets and £25 million in cash. The group has used equity accounting for the joint venture in Kevla Ltd. No dividends have been received from Kevla Ltd but the land and buildings transferred have been revalued at the year end.

(c) The taxation charge in the profit and loss account is made up of the following items.

	£m
Corporation tax	171
Tax attributable to joint venture	20
	191

(d) The movement on tangible fixed assets of the Wingit Group plc during the year was as follows.

	£m
Cost or valuation 1 December 20X6	2,100
Additions	380
Revaluation	(30)
Disposals and transfers	(680)
At 30 November 20X7	1,770
Depreciation	
1 December 20X6	300
Provided during year	150
Disposals and transfers	(95)
At 30 November 20X7	355
Carrying value at 30 November 20X7	1,415
Carrying value at 1 December 20X6	1,800

(e) The investments included under fixed assets comprised the joint venture in Kevla Ltd (£265 million), the shares in Meal plc (£300 million), and investments in corporate bonds (£35 million). The bonds had been purchased in November 20X7 and were deemed to be highly liquid, although Wingit plc intended to hold them for the longer term as their maturity date is 1 January 20X9.

The short term investments comprised the following items.

	20X7	20X6
	£m	£m
Government securities (Repayable 1 April 20X8)	51	23
Cash on seven day deposit	101	21
	152	44

(f) A prepayment of £20 million has been included in debtors against an exceptional pension liability which will fall due in the following financial year. Interest receivable included in debtors was £5 million at 30 November 20X7 (£4 million at 30 November 20X6).

(g) Creditors: amounts falling due within one year comprise the following items.

	20X7	20X6
	£m	£m
Trade creditors	1,300	973
Corporation tax	181	150
Dividends payable	80	70
Accrued interest	40	30
	1,601	1,223

Required

(a) Prepare a group cash flow statement using the 'indirect method' for the Wingit Group plc for the year ended 30 November 20X7 in accordance with the requirements of FRS 1 *Cash flow statements*. Your answer should include the following.

(i) Reconciliation of operating profit to operating cash flows
(ii) An analysis of cash flows for any headings netted in the cash flow statement

(Candidates should distinguish net cash flows from continuing and discontinued operations.) **(27 marks)**

The notes regarding the sale of the subsidiary and a reconciliation of net cash flow to movement in net debt are not required.

Wingit has a subsidiary, Springit. On 1 December 20X7, the chief executive of Springit, Mr Springer, retired from the company. The ordinary share capital at the time of his retirement was six million shares of £1. Mr Springer owns 52% of the ordinary shares of Springit and the remainder is owned by employees. As an incentive to the new management, Mr Springer agreed to a new executive compensation plan which commenced after his retirement. The plan provides cash bonuses to the board of directors when the company's earnings per share exceeds the 'normal' earnings per share which has been agreed at £0.50 per share. The cash bonuses are calculated as being 20% of the profit generated in excess of that required to give an earnings per share figure of £0.50.

The new board of directors has reported that the compensation to be paid is £360,000 based on earnings per share of £0.80 for the year ended 30 November 20X8. However, Mr Springer is surprised at the size of the compensation as other companies in the same industry were either breaking even or making losses in the period. He was anticipating that no bonus would be paid during the year as he felt that the company would not be able to earn the equivalent of the normal earnings per share figure of £0.50.

Mr Springer, who had taken no active part in management decisions, decided to take advantage of his role as non-executive director and demanded an explanation of how the earnings per share figure of £0.80 had been calculated. His investigations revealed the following information.

(i) The company received a grant from the government of £5 million towards the cost of purchasing a fixed asset of £15 million. The grant had been credited to the profit and loss account in total and the fixed asset had been recognised at £15 million in the balance sheet and depreciated at a rate of 10% per annum on the straight line basis. The directors explained that current thinking by the Accounting Standards Board was that the accounting standard on government grants in the UK was conceptually wrong because it misstates the assets and liabilities of the company and hence they were following the approach which has recently been advocated internationally.

(ii) Shortly after Mr Springer had retired from the company, Springit made an initial public offering of its shares. The sponsor of the issue charged a fee of £300,000. The fee on 1 February 20X8 was paid by issuing one hundred thousand £1 ordinary shares at a market value of £120,000 and by cash of £180,000. The directors had charged the cash paid as an expense in the profit and loss account. Further, they had credited the value of the shares issued to the sponsor in the profit and loss account for the year as they felt that the shares were issued for no consideration and that, therefore, they should offset the cash paid by the company. The public offering was made on 1 February 20X8 and involved vesting four million ordinary (exclusive of the sponsor's shares)

shares of £1 at a market price of £1.20. Mr Springer and other current shareholders decided to sell three million of their shares as part of the offer, leaving one million new shares to be issued.

(iii)   The directors sold on 1 December 20X7 a property under a twenty year lease to a company, Highball, which the bank had set up to act as a vehicle for investments and special projects. The consideration for the lease is £4.5 million. Springit has signed an unconditional agreement to repurchase the lease of the property after four years for a fixed amount of £5.5 million. The property has been taken off the balance sheet and the profit on the transaction, which has been included in the profit and loss account, is £500,000. The profit has been calculated by comparing the consideration for the lease with the carrying value of the property.

Depreciation on the property is charged at 5% per annum on the carrying value of the asset.

(iv)   Springit had made a 1 for 4 rights issue on 31 December 20X8. The cost of the shares was £1.60 per share and the market price was £2.00 per share before the rights issue. The directors had ignored this transaction because it occurred after the balance sheet date but they intend to capitalise the profit and loss reserve to reflect the bonus element of the rights issue in the financial statements for the year ending 30 November 20X9. The financial statements are not yet approved for the current year.

(v)   The directors had calculated earnings per share for the year ended 30 November 20X8 as follows.

Net profit	£4.8 million
Ordinary shares of £1	6,000,000
Earnings per share	£0.80

Mr Springer was concerned over the way that earnings per share had been calculated by the directors and also he felt that some of the above accounting practices were at best unethical and at worst fraudulent. He, therefore, has asked you for technical and ethical advice on the practices of the directors.

Required

(a)   Prepare a cash flow statement for Wingit group for the year ended 30 November 20X7. **(27 marks)**

(b)   Advise Mr Springer as to whether earnings per share has been accurately calculated by the directors showing a revised calculation of earnings per share. **(16 marks)**

(c)   Discuss whether the directors may have acted unethically in the way they have calculated earnings per share. **(7 marks)**

(Total = 50 marks)

Exam answer bank

1 Fundamental principles

Independence

It is important that auditors are, and are seen to be, independent. **Independence** is at the heart of the auditing profession as auditors claim to give an **impartial, objective** opinion on the truth and fairness of the financial statements.

Objectivity

A **family relationship** between an auditor and the client **can substantially affect the objectivity** of the audit, so auditors are advised not to build close personal relationships with audit clients and should not audit a company where family are employed in a capacity which is sensitive to the accounts, for example, in the finance department, although this is **not prohibited by law**.

In this instance, the **partner was not the reporting partner** for the audit client in which his brother-in-law was a financial controller. According to generally accepted ethical practice then, the firm appeared to be independent of the audit client if the related partner did not have anything to do with the audit.

Resolution?

The regulatory body required the audit partner to move 400 miles. This presumably implies that the partner was requested to change offices within the firm by which he was employed. Given current levels of computer networking and other **communications** common in business, this would appear to be an **arbitrary distinction**, as a partner in an office 400 miles away could have similar access and influence over a single audit carried out by the firm as a partner in the locality.

Independence in appearance

However, in this situation, the regulatory body appear to be concerned about the appearance of independence. They appear to be concerned that the public will not perceive the distinction between a partner and a partner who reports on a specific engagement. This may or may not be fair. Arguably, it is only in publicising the problem that the public are likely to have a perception at all.

Also, given the comments made about modern communications above, the public are unlikely to be convinced that moving a member of staff to a different office will solve this independence problem, if they perceive that there is one.

Split of audit firm

The decision of the firm to split into three divisions could **enhance the public perception of the independence of the audit department**. While there might be **underlying scepticism** relating to the reasons behind the split (which could merely be for marketing purposes or to enable non-audit divisions to raise capital more easily), the **underlying benefit for objectivity still exists**.

However, some audit clients will be unhappy with the move of the firm as it will entail their appointing several different service providers to gain the services they previously got from the one audit firm.

2 Glowball

> **Tutorial note**. A good test of report writing skills. To produce a good answer here you need to be able to explain the main issues in environmental reporting and to identify these in a scenario. Don't forget to think about FRSs, especially FRS 12 when reading the scenario. Your answer should read well as a report to the directors, as well as addressing all the technical issues.

REPORT

To: The Directors
        Glowball plc
From: A N Accountant
Date: 12 May 20X1

Environmental Reporting

Introduction

The purpose of this report is to provide information about current reporting requirements and guidelines on the subject of environmental reporting, and to give an indication of the required disclosure in relation to the specific events which you have brought to my attention. We hope that it will assist you in preparing your environmental report.

Current reporting requirements and guidelines

Most business, certainly those in the UK, have generally ignored environmental issues in the past. However, the use and misuse of natural resources all lead to environmental costs generated by business, both large and small.

There are very few rules, legal or otherwise, to ensure that companies disclose and report environmental matters. Any **disclosures tend to be voluntary**, unless environmental matters happen to fall under standard accounting principles. Environmental matters may be reported in the accounts of companies in the following areas.

- Contingent liabilities
- Exceptional charges
- Profit and capital expenditure focus

- Operating and financial review comments
- Profit and capital expenditure focus

The voluntary approach contrasts with the position in the United States, where the SEC/FASB accounting standards are obligatory.

While nothing is compulsory, there are a number of **published guidelines** and **codes of practice**, including:

- The *Valdez Principles*

- The Confederation of British Industry's guideline *Introducing Environmental Reporting*

- The ACCA's *Guide to Environment and Energy Reporting*

- The Coalition of Environmentally Responsible Economies (CERES) formats for environmental reports

- The Friends of the Earth *Environmental Charter for Local Government*

- The Eco Management and Audit Scheme Code of Practice

The question arises as to verification of the environmental information presented. Companies who adopt the Eco Management and Audit Scheme must have the report validated by an external verifier. In June 1999, BP Amoco commissioned KPMG to conduct an independent audit of its greenhouse gas emissions in the first ever **environmental audit**.

Comments on 'environmental events'

(a)   Of relevance to the farmland restoration is FRS 12 *Provisions, contingent liabilities and contingent assets*. Provisions for environmental liabilities should be recognised where there is a **legal or constructive obligation** to rectify environmental damage or perform restorative work. The mere existence of the restorative work does not give rise to an obligation and there is no legal obligation. However, it could be argued that there is a constructive obligation arising from the company's approach in previous years, which may have given rise to an **expectation** that the work would be carried out. If this is the case, a provision of £150m would be required in the financial statements. In addition, this provision and specific examples of restoration of land could be included in the environmental report.

(b) The treatment of the **fine** is straightforward: it is an obligation to transfer economic benefits. An estimate of the fine should be made and a **provision** set up in the financial statements for £5m. This should be mentioned in the environmental report. The report might also **put the fines in context** by stating how many tests have been carried out and how many times the company has passed the tests. The directors may feel that it would do the company's reputation no harm to point out the fact that the number of prosecutions has been falling from year to year.

(c) These statistics are good news and need to be covered in the environmental report. However, the emphasis should be on **accurate factual reporting** rather than boasting. It might be useful to provide target levels for comparison, or an industry average if available. The emissions statistics should be split into three categories:

- Acidity to air and water
- Hazardous substances
- Harmful emissions to water

As regards the aquatic emissions, the £70m planned expenditure on **research** should **be mentioned in the environmental report**. It shows a commitment to benefiting the environment. However, **FRS 12 would not permit a provision** to be made for this amount, since an obligation does not exist and the **expenditure is avoidable**. Nor does it qualify as development expenditure under SSAP 13.

(d) The environmental report should mention the steps the company is taking to minimise the harmful impact on the environment in the way it sites and constructs its gas installations. The report should also explain the policy of dismantling the installations rather than sinking them at the end of their useful life.

Currently the company builds up a provision for decommissioning costs over the life of the installation. However, FRS 12 does not allow this. Instead, the **full amount must be provided** as soon as the obligation to transfer economic benefits exists. The obligation exists right at the beginning of the installation's life, and so the full £407m must be provided for. A corresponding asset is created.

3 Large company

> **Tutorial note**. This question required candidates to compute the amounts which should be capitalised in respect of two retail stores' developments and also the subsequent depreciation.
>
> In part (a) notice that the requirement asked for 'full explanations' as well as the numbers. Make sure you do both. The calculation of the interest charge on the bond was potentially tricky. You could have worked it out from first principles, or used tables. Even if you couldn't work it out, you could guess (always guess 10% – you'll actually be right in a huge number of questions) or at least explain the treatment – no one detail will carry many marks. In part (b) again the key to a good pass mark here is to give sufficient effort to the 'reasons', not just the calculations.

(a) This is a zero coupon bond and FRS 4 requires the premium on redemption to be treated as an **interest cost**.

The effective rate is 0.38555 $\left(\dfrac{10,000,000}{25,937,000}\right)$ which from tables gives an interest rate of 10% pa over ten years.

Interest incurred whilst the assets are under construction can be capitalised, hence each building can include an interest cost of 10%.

Amounts to be included in fixed assets are as follows.

	A £'000	B £'000
Land	500	700
Building materials	500	550
Labour	100	150
Overheads	100	100
Fixtures and fittings	200	200
	1,400	1,700
10% interest	140	170
Capitalise	1,540	1,870

(b)   *Location A*

The store is retained for the **company's own use**. It should therefore be **depreciated** under the principles of FRS 15.

Depreciation to be charged (£'000s).

Land: nil
Buildings: (500 + 100 + 100+ 70)/50 = 15.4
Fixtures and fittings: (200 + 20)/10 = 22

Location B

This store meets the criteria of SSAP 19 *Accounting for investment properties* to be treated as an **investment property**. Hence only the fixtures and fittings will be depreciated with a charge of £22,000. The land and buildings will be **carried in the balance sheet at open market value**.

If this exceeds the cost of £1,700,000 (700 + 550 + 150 + 100 + 200) then any surplus will be credited to a revaluation reserve. If there is a deficit it will need to be charged to the profit and loss account. This is because there is no balance on the revaluation for reserve against which it can be charged.

4 FRS 11

Tutorial note. A quick introductory question. More detailed questions are found in the Kit.

(a)   If there were an indication that a fixed asset in income-generating unit B was impaired, the value in use of B would be compared with £200m, not £150m.

(b)   An impairment loss of £20m is recognised in respect of income-generating unit Z, reducing its carrying amount to £120m and the total carrying amount to £370m. A further impairment loss of £10m is then recognised in respect of the goodwill.

5 Invest

> **Tutorial note**. Review your answer carefully, as every paper this examiner writes tends to include goodwill in the main consolidation question and/or a stand-alone question like this.

(a)   (i)   The net assets of Target included in the calculation of goodwill have a fair value of £30m which excludes a brand valued at £3m.

The brand should only be included as an intangible asset if its value can be reliably measured on initial recognition, the question states the value is 'reliable'.

However, the ASB took the view under FRS 10 that internally developed intangible assets such as brands are very difficult to value and the recognition of internally generated brands is effectively prohibited.

Therefore it is assumed that **although the value of the brand can be reliably measured** by an estimate and that the value will increase or be maintained, the value of the brand is **subsumed within the valuation of goodwill.** Goodwill is thus calculated as follows.

	£m
Fair value of purchase price	31.0
Fair value of net assets acquired (30 × 80%)	(24.0)
Fair value of brand (3 × 80%)	(2.4)
Positive purchased goodwill	4.6

Amortisation of goodwill

1 May 20X8 to 30 April 20X9 = £4.6m/40 = £115,000

Note. there is no amortisation of the brand, as it is considered to have an indefinite useful life. However, there will need to be an annual impairment review of the brand.

(ii)   Under FRS 10, where goodwill and intangible assets have limited useful lives, they should be amortised to the profit and loss account over those lives. Normally the **rebuttable presumption** under FRS 10 is that the life is considered to be 20 years or less.

The useful economic life of goodwill may exceed 20 years provided that:

(1)   The asset justifies using a longer write off period (ie the goodwill is considered sufficiently durable)

(2)   The goodwill is capable of continued measurement

However, the directors of the Invest Group must subject the carrying value of goodwill to an **annual impairment review** at the end of each reporting period (beginning 31 March 20X9) and the carrying value revised if the value is impaired. The revised carrying value will then be written off over the remaining life (or the shorter life) and the resulting impairment loss charged to the P&L account. Impairment means that the carrying value of the goodwill is compared o the recoverable amount of the goodwill (the greater of net realisable value and economic value). FRS 11 deals with impairment reviews.

(b)   *Fair value of consideration*

	£'000
Fair value of consideration payable now	30,000
Fair value of consideration deferred £30m/1.10^2	24,793
	54,793

Note. Per FRS 7 *Fair values in acquisition accounting* deferred consideration should be valued at its present value. The consideration is payable in two years' time and is discounted accordingly.

Fair value of net assets

	£'000
Per balance sheet	55,000
Add back: provision	6,000
Deduct: deficit	(11,000)
	50,000

Note. FRS 7 requires that defined benefit pension schemes should be shown at their fair value. As the pension scheme was in deficit by £11m at the date of acquisition, this must be deducted in arriving at the net assets figure. The provision of £6m already in the balance sheet is no longer needed and must be added back.

Calculation of goodwill

	£'000
Cost of investment	54,793
Share of net assets acquired	
80% × 50m	40,000
Goodwill	14,793

Write off in the year to 30 September 20X9:

14,793/20 × 6/12 = £369,825

6 FRS 17

> **Tutorial note**. In an exam you should expect a numerical element as well as a discussion. Study the example in the chapter on retirement benefits carefully.

(a) **FRS 17** abandons the use of actuarial values for assets in a pension scheme in favour of a **market value approach**. They are to be measured at **fair value**. Likewise, pension **liabilities** must be measured on a **market basis**, using the **projected unit basis**. Liabilities will be discounted at the current rate of return on a high quality corporate bond of equivalent term and currency to the liability.

An asset will be recognised to the extent that an employer can recover a surplus through reduced contributions and refunds. A liability will be recognised to the extent that the deficit reflects the employer's legal or constructive obligation. The resulting asset or liability is presented separately on the face of the balance sheet after other net assets.

The use of market values at the balance sheet date introduces **volatility** into the measurement of the surplus or deficit in the pension scheme. Such volatility was largely absent from the actuarial values used under SSAP 24. Internationally the volatility stemming from market values is dealt with by averaging the market values over a number of years and/or spreading the gains and losses forward in the accounts over the service lives of the employees. There are problems with this approach.

(i) It gives rise to figures in the balance sheet that do not represent the current surplus or deficit in the scheme.

(ii) It creates charges in the profit and loss account that are contaminated by gains and losses that occurred up to fifteen years previously.

The ASB has developed an alternative approach to cope with the volatility. The **profit and loss account** shows the relatively stable ongoing **service cost, interest cost** and **expected return** on assets measured on a basis consistent with international standards. The effects of the **fluctuations in market values**, on the other hand, are not part of the operating results of the business and are treated in the same way as revaluations of fixed assets, ie are recognised immediately in the second performance statement, the **statement of total recognised gains and losses**. This has two advantages over the international approach.

(i) The balance sheet shows the deficit or recoverable surplus in the scheme.

(ii) The total profit and loss charge is more stable than it would be if the market value fluctuations were spread forward.

(b) There are possible disadvantages to the new approach.

(i) The new standard is very **complicated**.

(ii) It could be argued that the disclosure requirements are so extensive that preparers and users of accounts will get **lost in the detail**.

(iii) Concerns about the new accounting standard may cause more **employers to move to defined contribution schemes**, thereby putting the risk on the employee.

(iv) The standard aims to aid consistency by the use of market values. However, much depends on the 'expected return on assets' which the actuary will be free to choose. Using a high expected return will increase profits, but since variations in future years go through the STRGL and not the profit and loss account, profits will not suffer in future years if the expected return is not realised. In other words **there will still be room for manoeuvre**.

7 Taxable

Deferred tax implications

(a) Accelerated capital allowances: full provision should be made for the excess capital allowances. The provision should be discounted based on a calculation of the timing of its reversal.

(b) Revaluation: assuming there is no binding contract to sell the property, no provision is required.

(c) Deferred development expenditure: the amount capitalised (which will have been allowable for tax as incurred) is a timing difference. Full provision is again required, discounted based on the timing of reversals.

Provision:

	£m
Accelerated capital allowances (W1)	27
Deferred development expenditure (W2)	12
	39
Discount	(2.8)
Discounted provision for deferred tax	36.2

Workings

1 *Capital allowances*

Timing differences £90m
∴ undiscounted provision £90m × 30% = £27m

Years to come	Reversal of timing difference £m	Deferred tax liability (x 30%) £m	Discount factor	Discounted liability £m
02	20	6	.962	5.8
03	30	9	.925	8.3
04	40	12	.889	10.7
	90	27		24.8

2   *Deferred development expenditure*

Timing difference £40m

∴ undiscounted provision £40m × 30% = £12m

Years to come	Reversal of timing difference	Deferred tax liability (x 30%)	Discount factor	Discounted liability
	£m	£m		£m
02	20	6	.962	5.8
03	20	6	.925	5.6
	40	12		11.4

3   *Total discounted provision (24.8 + 11.4) = £36.2m*

8 PQR

General

Where an entity uses financial instruments FRS 29 *Financial Instruments: Disclosures* requires certain disclosures to be made about those financial instruments to allow the user of the financial statements to make assessments of risk vs return.

These include, for example:

- Financial risk management objectives, policies and processes, including hedging;
- For each class of financial instrument:

   - Accounting policies for classification and measurement;
   - Exposure to credit risk, liquidity risk and market risk (eg due to changes in interest rates);
   - Fair value at the balance sheet date.

(a)   Investment in debentures

Given that these debentures are planned to be held until redemption, they would be classed as a financial asset – investment held to maturity – held at amortised cost. This means that they are initially shown at their cost (including any transaction costs) and their value increased over time to the redemption value by applying a constant effective interest rate which takes into account not only the annual income due from the coupon, but also amortisation of the redemption premium. Their value is reduced by distributions received, ie the coupon.

Consequently the amortised cost valuation of these debentures at the year end would be:

	£	
Cost (40,000 – 6,000)	34,000	
Effective interest at 8.6%	2,924	shown as finance income
Coupon received (4% × 40,000)	(1,600)	debited to cash
	35,324	

The debentures are an asset belonging to the equity holders and so as the increase in value is recognised until redemption, the equity of the business will increase, marginally reducing gearing.

(b)   Forward contract

Providing the forward contract meets the following criteria it qualifies for hedge accounting:

- Designated as a hedge on entering into the contract (including documentation of company's strategy)
- Expected to be 'highly effective' during its whole life (ie gains/losses on the hedging instrument vs losses/gains on the hedged item or vice versa fall within the ratio 80% to

125% – this is likely to be the case with a foreign currency forward contract, FRS 26, para AG108)

- The hedge effectiveness can be reliably measured.

A foreign currency forward contract can be argued to be either a hedge of the future cash flow or a hedge of the fair value of the machine to be purchased. FRS 26 *Financial Instruments: Recognition and Measurement* therefore allows foreign currency hedges of firm commitments to be classed as either a cash flow hedge or a fair value hedge.

If the contract is classed as a cash flow hedge, given that the machine is not yet recognised in the books, any gain or loss on the hedging instrument is split into two components:

- The effective portion of the hedge (which matches the change in expected cash flow) is recognised initially in reserves. It is transferred out of reserves either when the asset is recognised (reducing the asset base and future depreciation) or when the cash flow is recognised in the profit and loss account (eg by depreciation). Both options therefore apply the accruals concept.

- The ineffective portion of the hedge is recognised in the profit and loss account immediately as it has not hedged anything.

If the contract is classed as a fair value hedge, all gains and losses on the hedging instrument must be recognised immediately in the profit and loss account. However, in order to match those against the asset hedged, the gain or loss on the fair value of the asset hedged is also recognised in the profit and loss account (and as an asset or liability in the balance sheet). This is arguably less transparent as it results in part of the asset value (the change in fair value) being recognised in the balance sheet until the purchase actually occurs – consequently, FRS 26 allows the option to treat foreign currency forward contracts as a cash flow hedge.

Gearing will be different depending on whether the forward contract is accounted for as a cash flow hedge or a fair value hedge (and whether a gain or loss on the hedging instrument occurs). Gearing will be less volatile if a fair value hedge is used as the change in fair value of the hedged asset is also recognised offsetting gains or losses on the hedging instrument, whereas this is not the case until the asset is purchased (and recognised) for the cash flow hedge.

(c) **Redeemable preference shares**

Redeemable preference shares, although called shares, are not, in substance, equity, they are a debt instrument, ie a loan made to the company which receives interest and is paid back at a later date.

Consequently, FRS 25 requires them to be classed as such, ie as a liability in the balance sheet. The 'dividends' paid will be shown in the profit and loss account as finance costs and accrued at the end of the year if outstanding, whether declared or not.

The shares are consequently a financial liability held at amortised cost. In this case, given that the shares are issued and redeemed at the same value, the effective interest rate and nominal coupon rate will be the same (6%) and each year £6,000 will be shown as a finance cost in the profit and loss account and the balance outstanding under creditors at each year end will be £100,000 as follows:

	£	
Cash received/ b/d value	100,000	
Effective interest at 6%	6,000	shown as finance cost
Coupon paid (6% × 100,000)	(6,000)	credited to cash
	100,000	

In the financial statements for the year ending 31 December 20X7, the shares will need to be reclassified as a creditor falling due within one year.

Given that these shares are classed as a financial liability, gearing will be higher (as they are treated as debt) than if they were ordinary shares (which would be treated as equity).

9 Hedging

The futures contract was entered into to protect the company from a fall in oil prices and hedge the value of the stocks. It is therefore a fair value hedge.

The stocks are recorded at their cost of £2,600,000 (100,000 barrels at £26.00) on 1 July 20X2.

The futures contract has a zero value at the date it is entered into and so no entry is made in the financial statements. However, the existence of the contract and associated risk would be disclosed from that date in accordance with FRS 29.

At the year end the stocks must be shown at the lower of cost and net realisable value. Hence they will be shown at £2,250,000 (100,000 barrels at £22.50) and a loss of £350,000 recognised in the profit and loss account.

However, a gain has been made on the futures contract:

	£
The company has a contract to sell on 31 March 20X3 at £27.50	2,750,000
A contract entered into at the year end would sell at £23.25 on 31 March 20X3	2,325,000
Gain (= the value the contract could be sold on for to a third party)	425,000

The gain on the futures contract is also recognised in the profit and loss account:

Dr Future contract asset	£425,000
Cr Profit and loss account	£425,000

The net effect on the profit and loss account is a gain of £75,000 (£425,000 less £350,000) whereas without the hedging contract the whole loss of £350,000 would have been the only impact on the profit and loss account.

Note

If the stocks had gained in value, this gain would also be recognised in the profit and loss account as hedge accounting is being applied (normally gains on stocks are not recognised until sale). A loss would have occurred on the futures contract, which would also be recognised in the profit and loss account.

10 Leased warehouse

Tutorial note. FRS 12 has generally come up as part of a multi-standard questions, a question type increasingly popular with this examiner. You may also get FRS 12 in the context of an environmental question.

In this situation, an obligation to restore the building to its original state arises at the time the alterations were made. If there is nothing the company can do to avoid the obligation, then full provision for the estimated reinstatement costs of £200,000 should be made by means of a prior year adjustment, assuming that discounting the provision is unlikely to have any material effect.

The company should also set up a corresponding asset in accordance with para 66 of FRS 12. This is because an obligation to return the property to its original state is incurred as a result of constructing the offices, which represent access to future economic benefits that are to be enjoyed over more than one period. Therefore, an asset is recognised at the same time as the provision. In practice, this would be added to the cost of the offices etc and depreciated over the shorter of the lease term and their useful life.

The prior year adjustment made should take account of the effect of any backlog depreciation. Care should also be taken to ensure that capitalising the provision does not result in stating the asset at above its recoverable amount. Therefore, it may be necessary to test the asset for impairment under FRS 11 *Impairment of fixed assets and goodwill*.

11 Elliot

> **Tutorial note**. This question looks at the methods of lessor accounting. The numbers are quite straightforward.

(a) PROFIT AND LOSS ACCOUNT
FOR THE YEAR ENDED 30 JUNE 20X3
(EXTRACT)

	£
Rental (£1,989 × 4)	7,956
Less capital repayment (balance)	4,614
	3,342
Less interest (£715 + £686 + £657 + £626)	2,684
Profit before tax (£428 × $^{100}/_{65}$)	658
Taxation (W)	832
	1,490
Deferred tax (balance)	1,062
Net profit (£115 + £110 + £104 + £99)	428

Working

	£
Rental	7,956
WDA (25% × £30,600)	(7,650)
	306
Interest payable	(2,684)
	(2,378)
Taxation @ 35%	832

BALANCE SHEET
AS AT 30 JUNE 20X3 (EXTRACT)

	£
Debtors	
Investment in finance leases (£30,600 − £4,614)	25,986

The balances relating to taxation and deferred tax will be included in the balance sheet.

The notes to the accounts will also disclose the rentals receivable under finance leases of £7,956 and the £30,600 cost of assets acquired to let under finance leases.

Accounting policy note

Income from finance leases is credited to the P&L account to give a constant periodic rate of return on the net cash investment. Assets under finance leases are stated in the balance sheet as debtors at the total value of rental receivable less finance charges relating to future periods.

(b) The major assumptions used in the calculation of net cash investment relate to the variables involved as follows.

  (i) Interest rates and taxation charges will occur as predicted in the future.

(ii)   The company will generate sufficient taxable profits to absorb the tax deductible expenses and capital allowances which have been predicted.

(iii)   Other costs, such as administrative costs, will be immaterial.

(iv)   The lease continues for its full term.

Any change in the above assumptions will require a new calculation as at the date when the change occurred.

(c)   The profit on the lease arises because there is a difference between:

(i)   The rental payments made

(ii)   The sum of the interest suffered on the average net cash investment (calculated at the cost of funds to the lessor) and taxation

The profit is allocated to individual accounting periods based on the proportion of the average net cash investment during the period to the total average net cash investment.

(d)   As opposed to the actuarial method after tax, the investment period method allocates gross earnings over that part of the lease in which the lessor has a net cash investment, in proportion to the net cash investment at each interval.

12 FRS 5 scenarios

Scenario I

> **Tutorial note**. This scenario is based on an illustration in FRS 5 and it demonstrates the thought processes required to determine how an item should be treated.

The commercial effect of this arrangement is that, although the debts have been legally transferred to Farout Factors plc, Shakey plc continues to bear significant benefits and risks relating to them. Shakey plc continues to bear slow payment risk as the interest charged by Farout Factors plc varies with the speed of collections of the debts. Hence, the gross amount of the debts should continue to be shown on its balance sheet until the earlier of collection and transfer of all risks to Farout Factors plc (ie 90 days.).

However, Shakey plc's maximum downside loss is limited since any debts not recovered after 90 days are in effect paid for by Farout Factors plc, which then assumes all slow payment and credit risk beyond this time. Thus, even for debts that prove to be bad, Shakey plc receives some proceeds. (For a debt of £100 that subsequently proves to be bad, the proceeds received would be £100, less the credit protection fee of £1, less an interest charge calculated for 90 days at base rate plus 2.5%.)

Hence, assuming the conditions given in FRS 5 for linked presentation for certain non-recourse finance arrangements are met, a linked presentation should be adopted. The amount deducted on the face of the balance sheet should be the lower of the proceeds received and the gross amount of the debts less all charges to the factor in respect of them. In the above example, for a debt of £100 this latter amount would be calculated at £100 less the credit protection fee of £1 and the maximum finance charge (calculated for 90 days at base rate plus 2.5%). Assuming the proceeds received of £80 are lower than this, and accrued interest charges at the year end are £2, the arrangement would be shown as follows.

	£	£
Current assets		
Stock		X
Debts factored without recourse		
Gross debts (after providing for credit protection fee and accrued interest	97	
Less non-returnable proceeds	(80)	
		17
Other debtors		X

In addition, the non-returnable proceeds of £80 would be included within cash and the P&L account would include both the credit protection expense of £1 and the accrued interest charges of £2.

Scenario II

REPORT

To: Managing Director
From: An Accountant
Date: 30 September 20X6
Re: *Reporting the substance of transactions*

D Ltd's transactions with E plc

The nature of these transactions can be assessed by looking at each aspect (a) to (e) in turn.

(a)   *Legal title on delivery*

The legal title is irrelevant under FRS 5 as it is the substance of the transaction which is important, not its legal form.

(b)   *Legal title when sold/after 6 months*

At either of these dates the entire risks and benefits associated with the cars have definitely transferred to D Ltd and they are therefore assets of the company. The question remains: how to account for the cars before this date.

(c)   *Price payable*

The date at which D Ltd is invoiced for the cars is also irrelevant. The monetary cost of the asset is known and this cannot be changed because of increases in the normal selling price (ie D Ltd is insulated from the risk of price rises – a benefit). If the cars are recognised as an asset, the corresponding liability owed to E plc can be recorded. The liability will then be increased by 1% per month. The 1% per month charge can also be included in the asset cost as a capitalised finance charge. The pricing situation indicates that the cars are an asset of D Ltd as the company bears the slow-movement risk.

(d)   *Obsolescence etc*

D Ltd bears the entire risk of obsolescence and damage to the cars, ie there is no right to return obsolete or damaged vehicles. D Ltd has the right to return vehicles but is prevented from doing so because of the harshness of the penalty payments. These points would imply that the vehicles are assets of D Ltd from delivery.

(e)   *Return to manufacturer*

E plc has no right to demand return of the stock and again this indicates that the cars are an asset of D Ltd. The right to claim the cars back if D Ltd becomes insolvent is merely a Romalpa-type clause which is fairly standard when any type of stock is sold on credit.

Summary and accounting treatment

In summary, the cars should be treated as assets from the date of delivery. The asset should be recognised *and* the corresponding liability to E plc, from the date of delivery.

13 Peter Holdings

> **Tutorial note**. It is not yet clear how the examiner will test this area.

Divisional performance should be measured, in the interests of the group's shareholders, in such a way as to indicate what sort of return each subsidiary is making on the **shareholder's investment**. Shareholders themselves are likely to be interested in the performance of the group as a whole, measured in terms of return on shareholders' capital, earnings per share, dividend yield, and growth in earnings and dividends. These performance ratios cannot be used for subsidiaries in the group, and so an alternative measure has to be selected, which compares the return from the subsidiary with the value of the investment in the subsidiary.

Two performance measures could be used. Both would provide a suitable indication of performance from the point of view of the group's shareholders.

(a)   Return on capital employed, which from the shareholders' point of view would be:

$$\frac{\text{Profit after interest}}{\text{Net assets at current valuation minus long - term liabilities (eg long - term borrowings)}}$$

(b)   Alternatively, residual income could be used. This might be:

Profit after debt interest

Minus   A notional interest charge on the value of assets financed by shareholders' capital
Equals   Residual income.

Residual income might be measured instead as:

Profit before interest (controllable by the subsidiary's management)
Minus   A notional interest charge on the controllable investments of the subsidiary
Equals   Residual income.

Each subsidiary would be able to increase its residual income if it earned an incremental profit in excess of the notional interest charges on its incremental investments – ie in effect, if it added to the value of the group's equity.

14 Andrews

The financial statements provided for Andrews Ltd in 20X4 and 20X5 represent two very different sectors. The 20X4 statements include retailing as well as manufacturing, whereas 20X5 statements represent manufacturing alone. We are not provided with a breakdown of how much turnover and profits or losses are associated with the discontinuation of the retail sector. Applying FRS 3 to the profit and loss account would therefore have given us more useful information to work from.

It must also be taken into consideration that the industrial sector ratios are more likely to be relevant to the 20X5 financial statements than to the 20X4 statements. Bearing these differences and incomplete information in mind it is not possible to comment fully on the 20X5 profitability and liquidity of Andrews Ltd, but using available information the following can be said.

Profitability

The gross margin fell 3% from 20X4 to 20X5 indicating that there was probably a higher gross return on retail sales than from manufacturing goods. The 32% achieved in 20X5 is very close to the industry average and hence acceptable. Net profit margin (excluding exceptional gain on sale of retail outlets) has risen to approach the industry norm following the sell-off of retail outlets. This would indicate that the shops were expensive to run which is probably one reason why they were sold.

Despite selling off all the retail outlets the fixed asset turnover appears to have fallen and is disappointingly below the industry average. However this is principally due to the effect of a revaluation in the year. If this revaluation was stripped out the fixed asset turnover in 20X5 would increase to 5.1 times which is much in line with the previous year and healthily above the average for the industry. The return on shareholders' funds appears to have halved from 20X4 to 20X5. This ratio, however, does not take into account the influencing factors, ie the revaluation in 20X5 and the long term liability in 20X4. However even if alternative ratios were used taking these factors into consideration it still appears that ordinary shareholders will be less happy in the short term with their investment.

Inc conclusion, as like is not being compared with like it is very difficult to make accurate comparisons. The sell-off of retail outlets appears to have depressed profitability and efficiency but it may be that the figures given in the financial statements are misleading.

Liquidity

In 20X4 Andrews Ltd appears to have a severe liquidity problem. Both its current and quick ratios were below the industry average. However the sale of its retail outlets appears to have boosted the cash flow to the company. As well as paying off its long term loan both the current and quick ratios have improved markedly. The current ratio is above the industry average whilst the quick ratio is close to it albeit slightly below average.

There is a worrying trend, however, in that stock has increased by more than a third in 20X5 compared to 20X4. As there are no further retail outlets this is clearly all stock from manufactured goods. It indicates that the company is having difficulty finding alternative outlets for its stock.

Another worrying indicator is that debtor collection period has increased from 31 days to 40 days. However, it is possible that this increase is entirely due to the fact that the retail outlets operated on a cash sales basis and now goods are being sold to other retailers all sales are credit sales.

Summary

From the limited information available it would appear that Andrews Ltd has improved its liquidity position due to selling off its retail outlets. Time will show whether or not this relief is temporary or longer term.

In the short term at least profitability is not so good, but once again the figures given are distorted due to year on year differences.

15 Angus

> **Tutorial note**. Aspects of FRS 3 could come up in all types of question – make sure you are familiar with all its statements and notes.

(a)   (i)   ANGUS PLC
PROFIT AND LOSS ACCOUNT FOR THE YEAR ENDED 28 FEBRUARY 20X7

	Continuing	Discontinued	Total
	£'m	£'m	£'m
Turnover	180.00	20.00	200.00
Operating profit (W1)	18.99	2.11	21.10
Loss on disposal of fixed asset (W2)		(1.50)	(1.50
Loss on disposal of discontinued operations		(0.35)	(0.35)
Cost of fundamental reorganisation	(1.25)	(0.35)	(1.25)
Profit on ordinary activities before taxation	17.74	0.26	18.00
Tax on profit on ordinary activities			(6.00)
Profit on ordinary activities after taxation			12.00

(ii)   STATEMENT OF TOTAL RECOGNISED GAINS AND LOSSES

	£m
Profit for the year	12.0
Surplus on revaluation of fixed assets (W3)	6.8
Total recognised gains and losses	18.8
Prior year adjustment	(1.5)
Total gains and losses recognised since last annual report	17.3

(iii)   RECONCILIATION OF MOVEMENTS IN SHAREHOLDERS' FUNDS

	£m
Profit for the financial year	12.0
Dividends	(2.0)
	10.0
Other recognised gains and losses	6.8
Net addition to shareholders funds	16.8
Opening shareholders' funds (originally £500m before deducting prior year adjustment of £1.5m)	498.5
Closing shareholders' funds	515.3

(iv)   NOTE OF HISTORICAL COST PROFITS AND LOSSES

	£m
Reported profit on ordinary activities before taxation	18.00
Difference between a historical cost depreciation charge and the actual depreciation charge for the year calculated on the revalued amount (400k – 280k)	0.12
Historical cost profit on ordinary activities before taxation	18.12
Historical cost profit for the year retained after taxation, minority interests, extraordinary items and dividends (18.12 – 6 – 2)	10.12

Workings

1   *Operating profit*

	£'m
Profit before tax	18.00
Add back losses	
Fixed assets	1.50
Termination	0.35
Reorganisation	1.25
	21.10

2   *Loss on sale of fixed assets*

	£'m
NBV	10.5
Proceeds	(9.0)
	(1.5)

3   *Surplus on revaluation*

	£'m
Revalued amounts	20
NBV at 28.2.X6 (16m – 2.8m)	(13.2)
Surplus	6.8

(b)   (i)   The purpose of the STRGL is to be an 'all inclusive' statement of gains and losses occurring in an entity during a period.

The P&L account excludes items deemed to be unrealised such as revaluations/forex differences that go directly to the reserves. These can, however, represent very material amounts. FRS 3 therefore requires companies to provide this extra statement to give increased prominence to these items.

(ii)   As illustrated in parts (a) and (b) the two statements differ as dividends are not shown in the gains and losses statements as it represents a distribution of gains made not a loss.

By only including true gains and losses, not anything which changes net assets, the statement has a clearer purpose than the reserve statement.

Reserve notes are usually included at the end of the financial statements. The STRGL is a primary statement and must therefore be given due prominence within the financial statements.

One explanation might be that the statement of movement on reserves has not a regulatory or mandatory format so that it is clear that the movements contained in the statement are not presented in a uniform format and are not well understood by the user.

The efforts to improve the presentation of information in the accounts is designed to produce decision useful information. By advocating additional primary statements the ASB might be setting the scene for further primary statements that could be used to accommodate future developments, eg value statements with a reconciliation to the historical cost profit.

16 Share-based payment

(a)   (i)

31.12.X1		£	£
DEBIT	P&L account	184,000	
	(690 (W3) × 200 × £4 × 1/3)		
CREDIT	Other reserves		184,000

31.12.X2			
DEBIT	P&L account (W1)	194,667	
CREDIT	Other reserves		194,667

31.12.X3			
DEBIT	P&L account (W2)	213,333	
CREDIT	Other reserves		213,333

Issue of shares:

DEBIT	Cash	148,000	
DEBIT	Other reserves	592,000	
CREDIT	Share capital (740 × 200 × £1)		148,000
CREDIT	Share premium		592,000

Workings

1   *At 31.12.X2*

(710 (W3) × 200 × £4 × 2/3)	378,667
Less: previously recognised	184,000
∴ charge	194,667

2   *At 31.12.X3*

(740 (W3) × 200 × £4)	592,000
Less: previously recognised (W1)	378,667
	213,333

3   *Estimated number of employees entitled to options*

End 20X1

Number remaining	760
Estimate of future leavers	(70)
	690

End 20X2

Number remaining	740
Estimate of future leavers	(30)
	710

End 20X3

Number entitled to options	740

(ii)   If J&B had offered cash payments based on the value of the shares at vesting date rather than options, in each of the three years an accrual would be shown in the balance sheet representing the expected amount payable based on the following:

BPP
LEARNING MEDIA

	x		x		x	
No of employees entitled to rights at the year end	x	Number of rights each	x	Fair value of right (adjusted for expected forfeiture)	x	Cumulative proportion of vesting period elapsed

The movement in the accrual would be charged to the profit and loss account representing further entitlements received during the year and adjustments to expectations accrued in previous years.

The accrual would continue to adjusted (resulting in a profit and loss account charge) for changes in the fair value of the right over the period between when the rights become fully vested and are subsequently exercised. It would then be reduced for cash payments as the rights are exercised.

(b)

	Expense	Equity (per balance sheet)
	£	£
Year 1	660,000	660,000
Year 2	174,000	834,000
Year 3	423,000	1,257,000

Workings

1	Year 1 $440 \times 100 \times £30 \times \frac{1}{2}$ (using original estimate of 2-year period)	£660,000

		£
2	Year 2 * $417 \times 100 \times £30 \times 2/3$ (using revised estimate of 3-year period)	834,000
	Previously recognised	(660,000)
	∴ expense	174,000
	* $(500 - 30 - 28 - 25)$	

3	Year 3 $419 \times 100 \times £30$	1,257,000
	Previously recognised	(834,000)
		423,000

17 Exclusion of subsidiaries

Tutorial note. The option of excluding subsidiaries had, in the past, led to off balance sheet finance transactions by companies. CA 1989 and FRS 2 tightened up the rules on exclusion.

(a) In certain circumstances and under certain conditions, UK accounting standards and UK company law allows subsidiaries to be accounted for other than by consolidation in group accounts. The relevant accounting standard is FRS 2 *Accounting for subsidiary undertakings* and s 229 of the Companies Act 2006 contains the statutory rules.

CA 2006 provides that a subsidiary may be omitted from the consolidated accounts of a group in one of the following cases.

(i) In the opinion of the directors, its inclusion 'is not material for the purpose of giving a true and fair view; but two or more undertakings may be excluded only if they are not material taken together'

(ii)   In the opinion of the directors, its inclusion is undesirable because the business of the holding company and subsidiary are so different that they cannot reasonably be treated as a single undertaking. 'This .... does not apply merely because some of the undertakings are industrial, some commercial and some provide services, or because they carry on industrial or commercial activities involving different products or provide different services'

(iii)   There are severe long-term restrictions in exercising the parent company's rights

(iv)   The holding is exclusively for resale

(v)   The information cannot be obtained 'without disproportionate expense or undue delay'

(b)   *Dissimilar activities*

The validity of excluding a subsidiary on the grounds of the dissimilarity of business activities is questionable. The proponents of this treatment argue that the combination of the financial statements of very different businesses produces consolidated accounts of limited meaning. They claim, for example, that the balance sheet ratios and profitability indicators produced by such accounts would be misleading.

This shortcoming is, moreover, largely overcome by appropriate segmental analysis which is a requirement of company law and of SSAP 25. The exclusion of subsidiaries from consolidated accounts has undoubtedly permitted considerable abuses in the area of 'off balance sheet finance' and the additional detail and disclosure that would follow from a requirement to consolidate such subsidiaries is warranted by the need to curb such practices. FRS 2 requires the subsidiary's accounts to be presented separately in the group accounts and the group holding to be accounted for on an equity basis.

Severe long term restrictions

Where control is impaired the use of 'frozen' equity accounting is probably preferable to reverting to a cost and dividend basis particularly where the activities of the subsidiary are material to the results or financial position of the group. The treatment is, however, potentially confusing where the holding company has investments in other associated companies and clear disclosure is required. Where this treatment is used there is a clear implication that it is expected that the impairment of control will be temporary and this assumption has to be reviewed periodically. On balance it is considered that this treatment is preferred to the cost and dividend basis so long as impairment of control does not become permanent.

Temporary control

Where control is temporary, it is appropriate that the investment should be treated as a current asset, since the intention that the investment is to be liquidated in the near future should be reflected in the accounts. The proviso is that the investment has never been consolidated as there was *always* an intention to sell.

Disproportionate expense/undue display

This argument is rejected entirely by FRS 2.

18 Highland

HIGHLAND PLC
CONSOLIDATED PROFIT AND LOSS ACCOUNT
FOR THE YEAR ENDED 31 MARCH 20X8

	£'000
Sales	
(5,000 + 3,000 + 4/12 × 2,910)	8,970.0
Cost of sales	
(3,000 + 2,300 + 4/12 × 2,820)	(6,240.0)
Gross profit	2,730.0
Net Operating Expenses (W6)	(1,747.5)
Profit before interest & tax	982.5
Interest Receivable (W2)	140.0
Interest Payable	(50.0)
	1,072.5
Taxation	
(300 + 50)	(350.0)
	722.5
Minority interest (W8)	26.0
Profit attributable to the members of Highland plc	748.5

Workings

1 *Group structure*

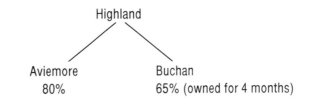

Highland

Aviemore
80%

Buchan
65% (owned for 4 months)

2 *Interest*

$2,100,000 \times 10\% =$

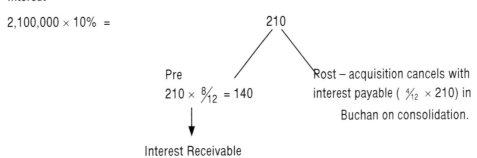

210

Pre
$210 \times {}^8\!/_{12} = 140$

↓

Interest Receivable

Post – acquisition cancels with
interest payable (${}^4\!/_{12} \times 210$) in
Buchan on consolidation.

3 *Unrealised profit on disposal of freehold property*

		£'000	£'000
Land	Proceeds	300	
	Net book value	(100)	
	Profit on disposal (in Aviemore)		200
Buildings	Proceeds (800 – 300)	500	
	Net book value (800 × ${}^{40}\!/_{50}$)	(640)	
	Loss on disposal (in Aviemore)		(140)
Proportion of loss depreciated (1/40)			3.5
			63.5

Fair Value depreciation

$$500 - 350 = {}^{150}/_{10} = 15 \times \frac{4}{12} = \text{£}5,000$$

5   *Goodwill*

		Highland £'000	Aviemore £'000
Cost		5,000	2,000
Net Assets Acquired			
4,000 × 80%	=	(3,200)	
(1,350 + 150) × 65%	=		(975)
		1,800	1,025
Amortisation: 1,800/10	=	180	
$1,025/10 \times \frac{4}{12}$	=	34	

6   *Net operating expenses*

	£'000
1,000 + 500 + (4/12 × 150)	1,550
Profit on disposal (W3)	63.5
Amortisation (180 + 34)	214
Less: management services	(85)
Fair value depreciation (W4)	5
	1,747.5

7   *Other income*

	£'000
Per P + L	230
Less: management services	(85)
Less: dividend from Aviemore	(40)
Less: interest from Buchan	(105)
	–

8   *Minority interest*

	£'000
Aviemore	
(100 – 63.5 profit on disposal) × 20%	7.3 dr
Buchan	
$[(270 \text{ loss} \times \frac{4}{12}) + 5 \text{ (W4)}] \times 35\%$	33.25 cr
	25.95 cr

Hence, rounding to nearest £'000, MI of £26,000 is *credited* to the P&L account.

19 Ullapool

ULLAPOOL PLC
CONSOLIDATED BALANCE SHEET AT 31 OCTOBER 20X7

	£
Intangible fixed assets (W9)	382,000
Other fixed assets (W5)	9,152,500
Investment in associate (W6)	644,900
Current assets (W7)	2,960,000
Current liabilities (2,800 +650)	(3,450,000)
	9,689,400
Share capital	
– 25p ordinary shares	4,750,000
Share premium account (W11)	1,150,000
Profit and loss reserves (W8)	2,648,650
	8,548,650
Minority interests (W10)	1,140,750
	9,689,400

Workings

1   *Group structure: Year end 31.10.X7*

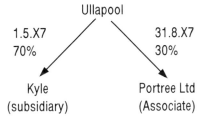

2   *Cost of Kyle*

	£
Cash	1,000,000
Shares @ fair value	1,500,000
(3m × 0.50)	
Advisers' fees	150,000
	2,650,000

Staff costs are correctly expensed rather than included within cost of investment in accordance with paragraph 85, FRS 7.

3   *Stock transfer*

150%	Transfer price	51,000
100%	Cost	34,000
50%	Mark-up	17,000
∴ PUP =		17,000
Cash in transit = (51,000 × ½) =		25,500

In Portree's books:

Dr Bank	25,500
Cr Debtor (Portree)	25,500

4   *Fixed asset transfer*

	£'000	£'000
Proceeds	150	
Net book value (200 – 100)	100	
Profit on disposal (in Kyle)		50
Proportion of profit depreciated (¼)		(12.5)
Unrealised profit		37.5

5   *Fixed assets*

	£'000
Ullapool	6,000
Kyle	2,900
Fair value adjustment *	290
Less: PUP on FA transfer (W4)	(37.5)
	9,152.5

* no data given re: depreciation rates. Depreciation on fair value uplift therefore ignored.

6   *Associate (Portree)*

	£'000
Net assets	2,000
(Receipt of cheque does not change P's net assets)	
Less: Unrealised profit on stock transfer	(17)
	1,983
× Group share @ 30% =	594.9
Add capitalised goodwill (W9)	50
	644.9

7   *Current assets*

	£'000
Ullapool	1,660
Kyle	1,300
	2,960

8   *P+L reserves (£'000's)*

	U	(70%) K	(30%) P
Reserves today – given	2,200	1,850	1,200
PUP on stock (W3)			(17)
PUP on fixed asset (W4)		(37.5)	
	2,200	1,812.5	1,183
Less: pre acquisition reserves of subsidiary and associate		(1,250)	(1,000)
		562.5	183

K	70% × 562.5	393.75
P	30% × 183	54.9
		2,648.65

9 *Goodwill*

	£'000	£'000 K	£'000	£'000 P
Fair value of consideration (W2)		2,650		590
Fair value of assets acquired:				
Capital	1,700		800	
Pre-acquisition reserves				
– P+L reserve	1,250		1,000	
– FV reserve	290			
	3,240		1,800	
	× 70% =	(2,268)	× 30% =	(540)
		382		50

10 *Minority interest in Kyle*

	£'000
Net assets per question	3,550
Fair value adjustment	290
PUP on fixed asset transfer (W4)	(37.5)
	3,802.5
Minority interests 30%	1,140.75

11 *Share premiums*

Share issue costs should be debited to share premium account, rather than added into the cost of investment. This is the recommended treatment according to CA85 and is required by FRS 4.

Journal to correct:

DEBIT	Share Premium Account	£100,000
CREDIT	Cost of investment	£100,000

∴ Share Premium = 1,250,000 – 100,000 = 1,150,000

20 Dales

DALES
CONSOLIDATED BALANCE SHEET AS AT 31 DECEMBER 20X6

	£'000	£'000
Intangible fixed assets (W2)		65
Tangible fixed assets		1,300
Current assets		
Stocks	765	
Debtors	465	
Cash	60	
	1,290	
Creditors: amounts falling due within one year:		
Trade creditors	260	
Overdraft	25	
Dividends payable	50	
Dividends payable to minority shareholders (W3)	11	
	346	
		944
		2,309
Creditors: amounts falling due after more than one year:		
Debentures		190

		2,119
Share capital		500
Profit and loss account (W5)		1,353.6
		1,853.6
Minority interests (W4)		265.4
		2,119

Workings

1 *Group structure*

D

↓ 80% effectively
∴ D owns 72% of Park

N

↓ 90%

P

2 *Goodwill*

(i) Dales acquired 80% of National:

	£'000	£'000
Cost:	420	
Net assets acquired:		
Share capital	100	
Profit and loss account	350	
	450	
× 80%		(360)
		60

(ii) Acquisition of Park by National:

	£'000	£'000
Cost of investment	140	
Net assets acquired:		
Share capital	100	
Profit and loss account	50	
	150	
× 90%		(135)
		5

3 *Dividends payable to minorities*

National:	20% × 40,000 =	8,000
Parks:	10% × 30,000 =	3,000
		11,000

BPP
LEARNING MEDIA

4   *Minority interests*

	£'000
National:	
Net assets at 31.12.X6	845
Less cost of investment	(140)
Goodwill (W2)	5
Dividends receivable	27
Dividends payable	(40)
Net assets at 31.12.X6 (as adjusted)	697
Minority 20% =	139.4
Parks:	
Net assets at 31.12.X6	480
Dividends payable	(30)
	450
Minority 28%	126

Total minority interests = 139.4 + 126 = £265,400 in net assets.

5   *Profit and loss account reserves*

	Dales £'000	*National* £'000	*Park* £'000
Per question	850	745	380
Dividends payable	(50)	(40)	(30)
Dividends receivable from National (80% × 40)	32		
from Park (90% × 30)		27	
	832	732	350
Less: pre acquisition reserves of subsidiaries		(350)	(50)
		382	300
Share of National (80% × 382)	305.6		
Share of Park (72% × 300)	216		
	1,353.6		

21 Armoury

BAYONET PLC

CONSOLIDATED BALANCE SHEET FOR THE YEAR ENDED 31 DECEMBER 20X9

	£	£
Fixed assets		
Other (14,500 + 12,140 + 17,500)		44,140
Current assets		
Stocks (6,300 + 2,100 + 450)	8,850	
Debtors (4,900 + 2,000 + 2,320)	9,220	
Cash (500 + 1,440 + 515)	2,455	
	20,525	
Creditors: amounts falling due within one year		
(5,700 + 2,280 + 1,985)	9,965	
Net current assets		10,560
		54,700
Capital and reserves		
Share capital – 50p ordinary shares		5,000
Profit and loss account (W4)		38,330
		43,330
Minority interests (W3)		11,370
		54,700

Workings

1 Group structure

```
                         B
                         │
                         ▼   6,000  = 75%      ∴ B effectively owns 75% × 80%
                             8,000                = 60% of Pistol

        M.I.    25%      R
                         │
                         ▼   4,000  = 80%      ∴ M.I. in Pistol = 40%
                             5,000                (20% direct and 25% × 80% = 20% indirect)

        M.I.    20%      P
```

2 Goodwill

	£
Cost of investment	10,000
Fair value of separable net assets acquired	
Rifle (4000 + 8000 − 9000) × 75%	(2,250)
Pistol (2500 + 6500) × 60%	(5,400)
	2,350

3 Minority interests

	£
Rifle Ltd	
(24,400 − 9,000) × 25%	3,850
Pistol Ltd	
Share of net assets at 31.12.X9	7,520
(40% × £18,800)	
Minority interests in group net assets	11,370

4   *Profit and loss account*

	Bayonet £	Rifle £	Pistol £
Per question	25,500	20,400	16,300
Less: pre acquisition reserves of subsidiaries		(8,000)	(6,500)
	25,500	12,400	9,800
Share of Rifle Ltd			
(75% × 12,400)	9,300		
Share of Pistol Ltd			
(60% × 9,800)	5,880		
	40,680		
Goodwill amortised to date (W1)	(2,350)		
	38,330		

22 Murder, Mystery and Suspense

MURDER LIMITED
CONSOLIDATED BALANCE SHEET AS AT
31 DECEMBER 20X7

	£'000	£'000
Tangible fixed assets (2,430 + 1,410 + 870)		4,710
Current assets		
Stocks (450 + 200 + 260 − 52) (W1)	858	
Debtors (610 + 365 + 139)	1,114	
Cash (240 + 95 + 116)	451	
	2,423	
Current liabilities		
Trade creditors (1,130 + 410 + 384)	1,924	
Net current assets		499
		5,209
Capital and reserves		
Ordinary share capital		500
Share premium		250
Profit and loss account (W4)		3,395.38
		4,145.38
Minority interests (W3)		1,063.62
		5,209.00

Group structure

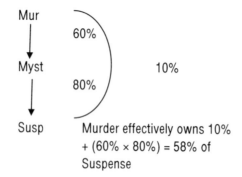

Murder effectively owns 10%
+ (60% × 80%) = 58% of
Suspense

Workings

1   *Unrealised profit on stock*

$$\text{Mark-up} = \frac{25}{125} \times 260{,}000 = \underline{£52{,}000}$$

2   *Goodwill*

	£'000
Goodwill	
Cost of investment	900.00
Fair value of separable net assets acquired	
M (200 + 120 + 950 − 240) × 60%	(618.00)
S (100 + 50 + 261) × 48%	(197.28)
	84.72

Alternative calculation

Murder in Mystery group

	£'000	£'000	£'000
Cost			900
Consolidated net assets acquired			
Share capital		200	
Share premium		120	
P&L a.c – Mystery	950		
– Suspense			
(261 − 46) × 80%	172		
– Goodwill			
(240 − 80%[100+50+46])	(83.2)		
		1,038.8	
		1,358.8	
		× 60%	815.28
			84.72

Murder in Suspense

	£'000	£'000
Cost		55
Net assets acquired		
Share capital	100	
Share premium	50	
P&L a/c	261	
	411	
× 10%		41.1
		13.9
Total goodwill		98.62

3   *Minority interests*

		£'000
Mystery Ltd – net assets		1,900
cost of investment		(240)
provision (W1)		(52)
consolidated net assets		1,608
M.I. = 40% × 1,608,000 =		£643,200
Suspense Ltd – consolidated net assets		£1,001,000
Minority interests = 42% × 1,001,000 =		£420,420
Total MI = 643.2 + 420.42 =		£1,063,620

4   *Profit and loss account*

	Murder £'000	*Mystery* £'000	*Suspense* £'000
Per question	2,805	1,580	851
Less: PUP (W1)		(52)	
Less: pre acquisition			
reserves of subsidiaries		(950)	(261)
	2,805	578	590
Share of Mystery			
(60% × 578)	346.8		
Share of Suspense			
(58% × 590)	342.2		
	3,494		
Goodwill amortised to date (W2)	(98.62)		
	3,395.38		

23 Holmes and Deakin

(a)   HOLMES LTD
       PROFIT AND LOSS ACCOUNT FOR THE YEAR TO 31.5.X3

	£'000
Operating profit	200.0
Profit on disposal on shares in subsidiary (W1)	100.0
Dividend receivable (65% × 30)	19.5
Profit on ordinary activities before taxation	319.5
Tax on profit on ordinary activities (90 + 33)	123.0
Profit on ordinary activities after taxation	196.5

	£'000
MOVEMENTS ON RESERVES	
As at 1.6.20X2 (260-60)	200
Profit for the year	196.5
Dividends payable	(50)
As at 31.5.20X3	346.5

(b) HOLMES LTD

CONSOLIDATED PROFIT AND LOSS ACCOUNT FOR THE YEAR TO 31.5.X3

	£'000	£'000
Operating profit		310
Profit on disposal of shares in subsidiary		72.5
Profit before tax		382.5
Taxation (90 + 60 + 33)		183.0
Profit after taxation		199.5
Minority interest:		
15% × 50	7.5	
20% × $\frac{3}{12}$ × 50	2.5	
		10.0
Profit for the financial year		189.5

(c) HOLMES LTD

CONSOLIDATED BALANCE SHEET AS AT 31.5.X3

	£'000	£'000
Fixed assets		
Intangible – goodwill (W4)		52
Tangible (NBV)		713
Current assets		
Stock	510	
Debtors	425	
Cash	169	
	1,104	
Creditors: amounts falling due within one year:		
Creditors (295 + 171 + 10.5)	(476.5)	
Tax (80 + 60 + 33)	(173)	
Dividend payable	(50)	
Net current assets		404.5
		1,169.5
Provision for liabilities and charges		
Deferred taxation		(126)
		1,043.5
Capital and reserves		
Share capital £1 ordinary shares		500
Profit and loss account (W3)		424.5
		924.5
Minority interest (340 × 35%)		119
		1,043.5

(d) Movements on Consolidated Reserves

	£'000
As at 1.6.20X2 (W2)	285
Retained profit for the year	139.5
As at 31.5.20X3 (W3)	424.5

Workings

1   *Exceptional item – profit on disposal*

	£'000	£'000
Sale proceeds		160
Less original cost of shares (40/170 × 255)		60
Holding company gain		100
Less tax on capital gain (33%)		33

	£'000	£'000
Sale proceeds		160
Net assets at disposal		
Share capital	200	
Reserves b/f	120	
To disposal ($50 \times \frac{9}{12}$)	37.5	
	137.5	
× 20%		71.5
Goodwill (W4)		16
		72.5

2   *Profit and loss account brought forward*

	£'000
Holmes (260 – 60)	200
Deakin (140 – 20 – 20) × 85%	85
	285

3   *Proof of retained reserves as at 31.5.X3*

	£'000
Holmes (per part (a))	346.5
Deakin (140 – 20) × 65%	78
	424.5

4   *Goodwill*

Cost of investment		255
Net assets acquired		
Share capital	200	
P&L	20	
	220	
85%		187
		68

Sold	Remaining
40/170	130/170
16	52
w/off on disposal (W1)	on B/S

24 Harvard

(a) CONSOLIDATED BALANCE SHEET AT 31 DECEMBER 20X5

	£'000
Fixed assets	
Property, plant and equipment (2,870 + 1,350 (W1))	4,220
Goodwill (W4)	147
	4,367
Current assets	
Inventories (1990 + 2,310 (W1))	4,300
Trade receivables (1630 + 1,270 (W1))	2,900
Cash at bank and in hand (240 + 560 (W1))	800
	8,000
Non-current liabilities	
Loans	1,920
Current liabilities	
Trade payables (5,030 + (1,210 (W1) − 480 (W3)))	5,760
	4,687
Share capital (£1)	118
Retained earnings (W5)	3,054
Translation reserve (W6)	445
	3,617
Minority interest (25% × 4,280 (W1))	1,070
	4,687

(b) CONSOLIDATED PROFIT AND LOSS ACCOUNT FOR YEAR ENDED 31 DECEMBER 20X5

	£'000
Turnover (40,425 + 25,900 (W2))	66,325
Cost of sales (35,500 + 20,680 (W2))	56,180
Gross profit	10,145
Distribution and administrative expenses (4,400 + 1,560 (W2))	5,960
Profit before tax	4,185
Income tax expense (300 + 1,260 (W2))	1,560
Profit for the period	2,625
Attributable to:	
Equity holders of the parent	2,025
Minority interest (25% × 2,400 (W2))	600
	2,625

STATEMENT OF MOVEMENTS IN RESERVES FOR THE YEAR ENDED 31 DECEMBER 20X5 (EXTRACT)

	Translation reserve £'000	Retained earnings £'000
Balance at 31 December 20X4 (W6)/ (W5)	168	1,729
Currency translation differences [(W7) (349 × 75%) + (W4) 15)]	277	–
Profit for the period		2,025
Dividends		(700)
Balance at 31 December 20X5 (W6)/ (W5)	445	3,054

Workings

1   *Translation of Krakow – balance sheet*

	PLN'000	Rate	£'000
Property, plant and equipment	4,860	3.6	1,350
Stock	8,316	3.6	2,310
Trade debtors	4,572	3.6	1,270
Cash	2,016	3.6	560
	19,764		5,490
Share capital	1,348	4.4	306
Retained earnings			
– pre-acquisition	2,876	4.4	654
– 20X3 – 20X4 (given)	5,936		1,372
– 20X5 Profit	9,000	3.75	2,400
– 20X5 Dividends	(3,752)	(W2)	(1,009)
	14,060		3,417
Translation reserve (100%, excludes goodwill)			
– brought forward (given)	–		208
– for year (W7)	–	β or (W7)	349
Trade creditors	4,356	3.6	1,210
	19,764		5,490

2   *Translation of Krakow – profit and loss account and dividends*

	PLN'000	Rate	£'000
Revenue	97,125	3.75	25,900
Cost of sales	77,550	3.75	20,680
Gross profit	19,575		5,220
Distribution and administrative expenses	5,850	3.75	1,560
Profit before tax	13,725		3,660
Tax expense	4,725	3.75	1,260
Profit for the period	9,000		2,400
Dividends			
– interim	1,448	3.92	369
– final	2,304	3.6	640
	3,752		1,009

3   *Dividend receivable from Krakow*

75% × 640 (W2) = 480

4   *Goodwill*

	PLN'000	PLN'000
Cost of combination (840 × 4.4)		3,696
Less: share of net assets acquired		
Share capital	1,348	
Retained earnings	2,876	
	4,224	
Group share (75%)		(3,168)
Goodwill at acquisition (PLN)		528
Goodwill at acquisition (£) (528,000/4.4)		120
Exchange gain 20X3 – 20X4 β		12
Goodwill at 31 December 20X4 (£) (528,000/4.0)		132
Exchange gain β		15
Goodwill at balance sheet date (£) (528,000/3.6)		147

5   *Proof of retained earnings*

(i)   At 31 December 20X5

	Harvard £'000	Krakow £'000
Per question/(W1)	502	3,417
Add: dividend receivable (W3)	480	
	982	
Less: retained earnings at acquisition (W1)		(654)
		2,763
Group share (75%)	2,072	
Goodwill impairment losses to date	(0)	
	3,054	

(ii)   At 31 December 20X4

	Harvard £'000	Krakow £'000
Harvard (502 – (−198))/Krakow (W1) (654 +1,372)	700	2,026
Less: retained earnings at acquisition (W1)		(654)
		1,372
Group share (75%)	1,029	
Goodwill impairment losses to 31.12.X4	(0)	
	1,729	

6   *Translation reserve*

(i)   At 31 December 20X5

	£'000
Translation of Krakow (75% × (208 + 349 (W7))	418
Translation of goodwill (12 + 15 (W4))	27
	445

(ii)   At 31 December 20X4

	£'000
Translation of Krakow (75% × 208)	156
Translation of goodwill (W4)	12
	168

7   Exchange differences

	£'000
Net assets of Krakow at 31 December 20X5	4,280
Less: net assets of Krakow at 31 December 20X4	
(15,408 – 9,000 + 3,752) @ 4.0	2,540
Increase over the year	1,740
Less: retained profit for the year (W2) (2,400 – 1,009)	1,391
Exchange differences	349
Group share (75%)	262

25 Tastydesserts

CASH FLOW STATEMENT FOR THE YEAR ENDED 31 DECEMBER 20X2

	£'000	£'000
Net cash inflow from operating activities (Note 1)		767
Dividends received from associated undertaking (W4)		100
Taxation		
Corporation tax (W3)	(160)	
Tax paid		(160)
Capital expenditure		
Purchase of fixed assets (W1)	(463)	
Net cash outflow from capital expenditure		(463)
Acquisitions and disposals		
Payments to acquire subsidiary	(55)	
Cash acquired	7	
Net cash outflow from acquisitions		(48)
Equity dividends paid		(63)
Increase in cash		133

Notes to the cash flow statement

1   Reconciliation of operating profit to net cash inflow from operating activities

	£'000
Operating profit	546
Depreciation	78
Increase in stocks (1,735 – 1,388 – 306)	(41)
Increase in debtors (2,658 – 2,436 – 185)	(37)
Increase in creditors (1,915 – 1,546 – 148)	221
	767

Workings

1   Purchase of tangible fixed assets

TANGIBLE FIXED ASSETS

	£'000		£'000
b/d	3,685		
Acquisition of Custardpowders	694	Depreciation	78
∴ Cash additions	463	c/d	4,764
	4,842		4,842

2   *Goodwill*

GOODWILL

	£'000		£'000
b/d	–		
Acquisition of Custardpowders $(1,086 - (1,044 \times 100\%))$	42	∴ Impairment losses	0
		c/d	42
	42		42

3   *Tax paid*

TAXATION PAID

	£'000		£'000
Therefore		Brought forward	
– Cash	160	– tax	200
		– deferred tax	180
			380
Carried forward		P & L a/c (196-70*)	126
– tax	235		
– deferred tax	111		
	506		506

* Associate's tax

4   *Dividend from associate*

INVESTMENT IN ASSOCIATE

	£'000		£'000
B/f	2,175		
P&L (190 – 70)	120	∴ dividend received	100
		C/f	2,195
	2,295		2,295

5   *Shares issued*

SHARE CAPITAL (INCLUDING PREMIUM)

	£'000		£'000
		B/f share capital	4,776
		B/f share premium	
C/f share capital	4,896	On acquisition	
C/f share premium	216	$(120,000 \times 280p)$	336
		∴ issued for cash	–
	5,112		5,112

26 Public sector organisations

(a)   The principal reason for the differences stem from the different way in which the organisations receive their funding and how they are controlled.

In the private sector capital funds are generally provided by means of the issue of shares or by the owners. From the point of view of the company, accounts are necessary initially to report to the shareholders or owners. Since shareholders will be interested in comparing investment prospects of different companies it is necessary that accounts are prepared using standard accounting principles.

Private sector accounts are also used by potential lenders and creditors to determine the credit worthiness of companies so the accounts need to be prepared in such a way that this can be determined.

In the private sector, revenue income is derived from the customers but this does not result in any accounting obligation because customers are free to use other suppliers if the service provided is unsatisfactory.

In the public sector, the sources of funds both capital and revenue are ultimately from the public in the form of taxation, council tax and charges for services. These are controlled by central government and local authorities. Since there is no choice on behalf of the providers of these funds the function of the accounts is rather different to those of the private sector and more rigorously controlled.

(b) The main differences between the laws regulations and guidelines are as follows.

(i) *Laws.* In the private sector the accounts are governed by the various Companies Acts. These specify the items which must be included in the accounts and the general format. The purpose of the provisions in these acts is to ensure the accounts give a 'true and fair' view of the financial position and performance of the company for the shareholders, lenders and creditors.

In the public sector there are separate laws for each service requiring them to produce accounts. Some of these services, such as the NHS, are funded by central government and in these cases the laws generally state simply that accounts must be prepared. The relevant government department is responsible for the format in which the accounts are to be prepared for the purpose of reporting to Parliament.

In the case of local authorities, funds come from central government in the form of the revenue support grant, from the local population in the form of council tax and from the users of services in the form of charges. The laws relating to the accounts of local authorities require the accounts to be prepared in such a way as to account to each of these groups.

(ii) *Regulations.* Although the laws indicate the general way in which accounts are to be prepared, not all eventualities can be covered and there is much room for variation in the way particular financial transactions can be accounted for. As a consequence of this, Financial Reporting Standards have been produced by the accounting profession specifying in more detail how items are to be treated in the accounts with a view to producing accounts which are more comparable and reliable.

All accounts in the public and the private sector are produced in accordance with the Financial Reporting Standards and, if these are not complied with, the auditor may qualify the accounts.

However, these standards are written primarily with the private sector in mind and under certain circumstances the requirements of central government regarding the accounts in some public sector organisations will override these.

(iii) *Guidelines.* In the public sector the purpose of the accounts is to report to central government, local tax payers and users of the services. As a consequence it is often necessary that the accounts be produced in a particular format to provide the necessary information, or to include details of particular aspects of the financial transactions. Consequently, Secretaries of State have considerable powers under the law to issue detailed guideline on how the accounts are to be prepared. An example of this is the Manual of Accounts produced by the Department of Health. This gives the precise format of the accounts together with great detail of accounting procedures to be adopted. In some cases these powers have been delegated to CIPFA, for example for local authority accounts.

(c)   The consequences for the public accounts in the public sector is that, although the accounts are produced using generally the same principles as the private sector, their details are often quite different depending on the bodies to be reported to.

In central government departments, such as the Health Service, the accounts are produced fundamentally to account to Parliament for the funds voted to the Health Service. Consequently they are produced in an absolutely prescribed form so that they can be easily consolidated. The reporting to the general public on the use of funds is a secondary consideration as it is assumed that parliament are responsible for the use of the funds on behalf of the taxpayers. However, the NHS Trusts are required to produce annual reports for general circulation. Although there is no similar requirement for District Health Authorities, guidelines have been introduced for them to produce an annual report on a voluntary basis.

In case of local government, the annual report which they are required to produce includes comparative statistics and information about the council's policies which are intended to inform the general public about the activities of the council. This is necessary because the council which is responsible for the expenditure is elected by the residents of the area.

27 German competitor

> **Tutorial note**. You do not need to know about German accounting practice to answer this question, just a basic knowledge of the differences between the European and UK models and your common sense! Think of this as an interpretation of accounts questions.

To: Managing Director
From: An Accountant
Date: xx.xx.xx
Re: *Hilde GmbH*

(a)   *Analysis of performance plus commentary (DM million)*

Profit and loss a/c			% Increase (decrease)
	20X4	*20X5*	
Sales	1,270	1,890	49
Cost of sales			
Material purchased	400	740	
De-stocking of materials	40	90	
Material cost	440	830	89
Labour cost	285	500	75
Depreciation	150	200	33
Current assets written off	20	30	50
Other operating expenses	40	50	25
Finished goods stock increase	(80)	(120)	50
	855	1,490	
Operating profit before other income	415	400	(4)
Profit rate on turnover	32%	21%	
Other operating income	50	75	50

Cash flows

	DM million
Share capital issued	200
Increased creditors	75
Increased accruals	20
Profit ploughed back (185 + 200)	385
	680

These flows were used to finance:

Purchases of plant (550 + 200)	750
Net stocks	30
More credit to customers	80
	860

Difference: reduction in cash reserves	180

Other relevant performance measures

	20X4	20X5
Debtors' turnover		
$= \dfrac{\text{Trade debtors}}{\text{Sales}} \times 365$	$\dfrac{100}{1{,}270} \times 365$	$\dfrac{180}{1{,}890} \times 365$
	= 29 days	= 35 days
Current ratio		
$= \dfrac{\text{Current assets}}{\text{Current liabilities}}$	$\dfrac{420 + 70}{350}$	$\dfrac{350 + 50}{425}$
	= 1.4	= 0.94
Quick ratio		
$= \dfrac{\text{Current assets} - \text{Stock}}{\text{Current liabilities}}$	$\dfrac{100 + 200 + 70}{350}$	$\dfrac{180 + 20 + 50}{425}$
	= 1.06	= 0.59

Commentary

(i)   Material costs and labour costs have risen at an alarming rate in 20X5 and to a certain extent other costs have also increased substantially. These increases are far greater than the increase in turnover. A lack of co-ordination of production to sales has created a substantial build up of finished goods in stock.

(ii)   Interest costs and other operating income have both increased substantially, but because debt and investments (respectively) are not shown on the balance sheet it is not possible to judge why these rises have taken place. One possibility is that the increases in the value of land and buildings represent additions which are being rented out.

(iii) Creditors have increased only slightly considering the increases in stock purchases during the year. This may indicate that the company's trade creditors are taking a very firm line with the company and thus the trade creditors balance is being held firm.

(iv)   Although shares were issued during the year, at a premium of 100%, the fact that appropriations are not disclosed in the P&L account makes it very difficult to determine what type of dividend policy the company is following, and hence what kind of return shareholders have received over the two years.

(v)   The length of credit period given to debtors has increased (if all sales are on credit). While trading conditions may make this slip in credit control a necessity, it is regrettable that the company cannot obtain the same more relaxed terms from its creditors; this would balance out working capital requirements, at least to some extent.

(vi)   The stock situation is what has changed most dramatically betw[...]. [...] rise in balance sheet stocks of DM 30m may appear moderate, but it represents a [...] DM 120m in finished goods and a fall of DM 90 m in raw materials. It may be the case that the company is manufacturing less and buying in more finished goods, but the increase in labour costs would tend to negate this. It seems more likely that the company has greatly over-estimated the level of sales for 20X5, and has therefore ended 20X5 with an anomalous stock position.

(vii)   The cash levels held by the business, while perhaps on the high side at the beginning of the year, now appear far too low. The company is verging on an overdraft situation, in spite of receiving cash from a share issue during the year. The working capital situation, and in particular the stock levels, must be resolved in order to recover the liquidity position of the business. If not, then there will be some difficulty in paying creditors and taxes in the near future.

(b)   A direct comparison of the results of Tone plc and Hilde GmbH may be misleading for the following reasons.

(i)   It is unlikely that the two companies follow the same, or even similar, accounting policies, for example on stock valuation, depreciation, valuation of land and buildings etc. Also, the general approach to debtor recoverability may be more or less prudent in the UK than under Tone's approach. These policies would have to be investigated to discover whether comparison is really feasible.

(ii)   Hilde GmbH's creditors are not split between short and long term, ie those due within one year and in more than one year (if any). Gearing ratios cannot be calculated, and the current and quick ratios calculated in (a) are of limited value.

(iii)   There may be local or country-specific types of relationships between debtors and creditors which are different from the UK methods of doing business.

(iv)   There is an interest charge shown in the P&L account but the balance sheet shows no separate disclosure of loans. The explanation may be that an interest charge is payable on the share capital in place of dividends.

(v)   A legal reserve is shown. There is no indication of what type of reserve this may be comparable with (if any) in UK financial statements.

(vi)   The P&L account does not show a figure of gross profit making it difficult to compare margins.

(vii)   The expenses include valuation adjustments for fixed asset depreciation and current assets. It is not clear how these arise. They may simply comprise the normal depreciation charge and, say, a provision against doubtful debts and obsolete stock. It is true of many of the P&L account figures, that a lack of knowledge about how, say, 'cost of sales' is computed, prevents comparison with UK accounts.

28 Badgo

> **Tutorial note.** Candidates were not expected to reconcile the cost of the investment in Stateside Inc of £380m with its carrying value at 31 December 20X9 of £400m in response to part (c).

20Y0 REPORT

To: Non-Executive Director
From: Management Accountant
Date: 24 May 20X0

Introduction

This report addresses your questions regarding the draft consolidated financial statements for the year ended 31 December 20X9. The group's results and position were affected to a large degree by our investment in Stateside Inc. This is reflected in my responses.

(a)   Fall in profits and dividend for the year (question (a))

As you correctly note, there has been a **modest increase in turnover** (5%). You should be aware that the 20X9 turnover figure does **not include any sales made by Stateside Inc** as this is accounted for under FRS 9 by the 'equity method' of accounting. As you will note, the consolidated profit and loss account for 20X9 takes credit for 35% of the associate's operating profit for the year and **no results of the associate before operating profit are included**.

The **gross profit margin** has remained constant at 30% (ratio 1). The underlying problem with regards to profitability, and hence the reason for the fall in the proposed dividend, is the significant **increase in operating expenses.** These have risen by one third during 20X9 (see also ratio 2).

In addition to the large increase in operating expenses, there has also been a **very large increase** (of 30%) in **interest charges** during 20X9. This arises mainly because we have **increased our bank overdraft and long-term loans in order** to finance our investment in Stateside Inc (see below). The group's liquidity, as well as profitability, is under pressure as a result of this acquisition.

Dividends have fallen by 1/4 , but this must be seen in the context of the 50% increase in share capital. In fact, the **proposed dividend per share has halved** from 40 pence per share to 20 pence per share. A reduction in the proposed dividend becomes inevitable if we are to ensure there is an **adequate level of retained profits** to help finance future developments, ie we maintain dividend cover at just under 2.0 times. There remains the problem of how to finance this dividend of £60m, given the current level of the bank overdraft.

(b)   Increase in retained profits of £62m (question (b))

As you rightly point out, retained profits for 20X9 is £57m while the profit and loss account (P&L) in the balance sheet has increased by £62m (£321m – £259m).

This difference can be explained if you look at the consolidated statement of total recognised gains and losses (**STRGL**) for 20X9. This statement shows any other gains or losses not recognised in the P&L, normally because they are not realised (and therefore are not distributable as dividends). In effect, the **investment in Stateside Inc has been 'revalued'** or restated from its original cost in US$ (during 20X9) to be translated into £ sterling at the exchange rate between the two currencies on 31 December 20X9.

In this case there was a **gain** of $5m on the translation (into £ sterling) of our foreign investment and we have recognised this in the STRGL. The translation of our short-term foreign currency investments at the end of 20X8 showed a loss of £4m and this was reported in the STRGL for that year.

In summary, the balance on the P&L at 31 December 20X8 (of £259m) had increased by **both the retained profit** for 20X9 (£57m) and the **favourable currency translation** difference (£5m) to give the reported figure of £321, at 31 December 20X9.

(c)   Carrying value and financing of investment in Stateside Inc at 31 December 20X9

As you correctly state, the group paid £380m for the investment in the associate during the year. However, as this is an investment in which the group has a **significant influence** (by virtue of the 35% shareholding), it has been accounted for in both the profit and loss account and the balance sheet under the *Associates and joint ventures* **'equity method'** of accounting in accordance with FRS 9.

FRS 9 requires the carrying value of the investment to be shown at **the group's 35% share** of Stateside Inc's equity at the balance sheet date. This carrying value will have increased by the group's 35% share of the retained profits of the associate earned since our acquisition earlier in 20X9.

In addition, the **translation of this investment** from US$ into £ sterling at the year end, compared to the translation of the investment at the exchange rate between the two currencies at the time of acquisition, has resulted in the **£5m gain** already referred to. This has also increased the investment's carrying value.

This investment of £380m was **financed**, in part, from the **funds raised from shareholders** during the year. This financed £200m (including the share premium), whilst the sale of our short-term investments (if liquidated at book value) raised a further £100m and long-term loans financed a further £24m. The remaining **£56m must have been financed from the bank overdraft**. This latter form of finance is a **matter for concern** as it is normally intended as a source of short-term funds and it is not appropriate to finance long-term investments. In this case, the overall effect has been to maintain capital gearing at around 1/3 (ratio 4).

(d)   Financial statements of Stateside Inc in US dollars (question (d))

I have assumed in the absence of the US accounts that you are correct in stating that the company reported a loss for 20X9. The move from a loss in US$ to a profit in £ sterling will not have been caused by the translation into £ sterling of the net investment as the company's operating profit/loss was translated at the **average exchange rate** for the post-acquisition period or at the closing rate at 31 December 20X9.

The discrepancy will be accounted for by the effect of **different accounting policies** used in America to comply with their accounting standards and generally accepted accounting practice (GAAP) which tend to adopt a **more prudent approach than** is usually adopted in **the UK**.

In accordance with UK practice, the financial statements of Stateside Inc will need to be **re-stated** to UK-based accounting standards and principles as a preliminary to preparing UK consolidated financial statements. This will ensure the shareholders are provided with a **true and fair view** of the group's financial performance and position, as **consistent accounting policies** will have been followed.

You will need to provide a **reconciliation** showing differences between US and UK practice (or GAAP) in order to explain the material differences in accounting practice and hence in the reported results of Stateside Inc.

Conclusion

I hope this report has been useful in explaining several aspects of the accounting effects of the acquisition of our significant interest in Stateside Inc and other issues affecting the group's performance and position for 20X9. If you have any further queries on these financial statements, please do not hesitate to contact me.

Signed: Management Accountant

APPENDIX: ACCOUNTING RATIOS

Year ended/at 31 December		20X9 £m	20X8 £m
(1)	Gross profit margin	$\frac{600}{2,000} = 30\%$	$\frac{570}{1,900} = 30\%$
(2)	Operating expenses/sales	$\frac{400}{2,000} = 20\%$	$\frac{300}{1,900} = 15.8\%$
(3)	Dividend cover	$\frac{117}{60} = 1.95$ times	$\frac{155}{80} = 1.94$ times

Year ended/at 31 December		20X9	20X8
(4)	Capital gearing		
	$\frac{\text{Long} - \text{term loans} + \text{bank overdraft}}{\text{Capital employed (inc bank o/d)}}$	$\frac{181+170}{1,072} = 33\%$	$\frac{157+80}{696} = 34\%$

29 Planet

(a) (i) **Additional purchase consideration**

The company should **recognise a liability of £16 million and additional goodwill of £16 million**. Although FRS 7 *Fair values in acquisition accounting* sets a time limit for recognition of fair value adjustments this applies only to the acquired assets and liabilities. There is **no time limit** for the recognition of **goodwill relating to contingent consideration** (FRS 7 paragraph 57).

The increase in goodwill is an adjustment to an accounting estimate made in a previous period. Therefore it should be amortised over four years (the remaining useful economic life of the goodwill).

The accounting entries required are:

		£'000	£'000
DEBIT	Profit and loss account (amortisation)	4,000	
DEBIT	Intangible assets (goodwill)	12,000	
CREDIT	Creditors: Amounts falling due within one year		16,000

(ii) **Buildings**

In each case the main issue is whether Planet should recognise a provision for future repair and refurbishment expenditure.

Operating lease

FRS 12 *Provisions, contingent liabilities and contingent assets* states that a provision should only be recognised if there is a **present obligation resulting from a past event**. The terms of the lease contract mean that Planet has an obligation to incur expenditure in order to return the buildings to the lessee in good condition. The past obligating event appears to be the signing of the lease.

However, **future repairs and maintenance costs** relate to the future operation of the business. They are **not present obligations** resulting from past events. If FRS 12 is interpreted strictly, no provision should be recognised. The repair costs should either be charged as operating expenses in the period in which they occur or capitalised as assets.

Despite this, there is a strong case for recognising a provision for at least some of the expenditure. An Appendix to FRS 12 explains that where a lessee is required to incur periodic charges to **make good dilapidations** or other damage occurring during the rental period, these liabilities **may be recognised**, **provided that the event** giving rise to the obligation under the lease **has occurred**. Damage to the building has occurred because of the severe weather and therefore a provision should be recognised for the £2.4 million needed to rectify this damage.

Whether any further amounts should be provided depends on the event that gives rise to the present obligation. It is possible to argue that the obligating event is the occurrence of specific damage to the building, but the cost of repairing actual dilapidation to the building during the year would be **difficult to estimate accurately**. It could also be argued that the obligating event is the passage of time, because some expenditure would be necessary if the lease were terminated immediately. Therefore a further £1,600,000 should be provided (£12 million less £2.4 million divided by six). The total provision is £4 million.

The accounting entries required are:

		£'000	£'000
DEBIT	Profit and loss account	4,000	
CREDIT	Provisions for liabilities		4,000

Leasehold property

In this case the company has a present obligation to incur expenditure as a result of a past event (the creation of the swimming pool). Under FRS 12 a **provision should be recognised for the full restoration cost** of £4 million. It is not possible to build up the provision over ten years as the directors propose.

Because the swimming pool represents access to future economic benefits, the future cost also represents an **asset** and this **should be recognised**. The asset will be depreciated at 10% per annum.

The carrying value of the leased building is £19.6 million (£16 million + £4 million − £400,000). This is above the recoverable amount of £19 million and therefore an impairment loss of £600,000 should be recognised.

The accounting entries required are:

		£'000	£'000
DEBIT	Tangible fixed assets	4,000	
CREDIT	Provisions for liabilities and charges		4,000
DEBIT	Profit and loss account (group retained profits)	320	
DEBIT	Minority interest	80	
CREDIT	Tangible fixed assets (depreciation)		400
	(4,000 × 10%)		
DEBIT	Profit and loss account (group retained profits)	480	
DEBIT	Minority interest	120	
CREDIT	Tangible fixed assets (impairment)		600

Owned buildings

Future repair expenditure does **not** represent a **present obligation** of the company because there has been **no past obligating event**. The repairs relate to the future operations of the company and in theory the expenditure **could be avoided** by selling the buildings. Under FRS 12 no provision can be recognised.

Any loss in service potential of the asset should be reflected in the depreciation charge. If the repairs are necessary to restore the service potential of the asset the expenditure should be capitalised.

(iii) **Agreement with subsidiary**

This has several implications for the financial statements. Because two thirds of the stock remains unsold, the **unrealised inter-company profit** of £400,000 ($^2/_3$ × 4.2 million dinars ÷ 1.4 × 20%) **must be eliminated**.

The accounting entries required are:

		£'000	£'000
DEBIT	Profit and loss account (group retained profit)	400	
CREDIT	Stock		400

In addition, because Planet is a listed company it must comply with the requirements of FRS 13 *Derivatives and other financial instruments: disclosures*. The **forward contract is a derivative** financial instrument. By entering into the contract the company has fixed the price of the stock and has avoided the effect of changes in the exchange rate. **No exchange gain or loss is recognised** on the transaction. The company is required to **disclose its accounting policy** in respect of hedge accounting, which is to translate its foreign currency assets and liabilities at the forward rate at the date of delivery (as permitted by SSAP 20 *Foreign currency translation*). It is also required to disclose certain information about the contract, including details of any gains and losses carried forward in the balance sheet at the balance sheet date and the extent to which these are expected to be recognised in the profit and loss account in the next accounting period.

Because Planet entered into the contract without incurring any costs, the **book value** and the **fair value** of the forward contract were **nil** at its inception date. The cost of the stock to the company was £3 million (4.2 million ÷ 1.4) but by 31 March 20X1 (the settlement date), exchange rates had moved so that the company would only have paid £2,896,552 for the stock at the spot rate of 1.45. Therefore the company has made a **loss** of £103,448. **One third** of this (£34,482) relates to the **stock sold** and has effectively been **recognised** in the **profit and loss account for the year**. The **remainder** (£68,966) is **carried forward in the value of stock** and will be recognised in the profit and loss account in the next accounting period. There is an argument for **reducing this figure by 20%** as this is the amount of the

inter-company profit which is eliminated on consolidation. The amount of the loss to be disclosed under FRS 13 is therefore £55,173.

(iv) **Database**

The issue here is whether the cost of developing the database can be capitalised as an intangible asset. FRS 10 *Goodwill and intangible assets* states that **internally generated** intangible assets may **only be capitalised** if they have a **readily ascertainable market value**. This means that the asset must belong to a **homogenous population** of assets that are equivalent in all material aspects and there must be an **active market**, evidenced by frequent transactions, for that population of assets. The database very clearly fails to meet these criteria.

However, the expenditure has resulted in a new product which is now generating income for the group. Under SSAP 13 *Accounting for research and development* the cost of using of scientific or technical knowledge in order to produce new or substantially improved products **may be capitalised as development expenditure** provided that the project meets certain **criteria**. There must be a clearly defined project, the expenditure must be separately identifiable, the outcome of the project must be capable of being assessed with reasonable certainty, future revenue must exceed costs and adequate resources must exist to enable the project to be completed. As the project has been completed and the manual has quickly become a market leader it appears that these conditions have been met.

Because the manual will require substantial **revision every four years** the development costs should be **amortised over this period** (rather than the ten years proposed by the directors).

The accounting entries required to record the additional depreciation are:

		£'000	£'000
DEBIT	Profit and loss account (group reserves)	720	
DEBIT	Minority interests	180	
CREDIT	Intangible fixed assets ((6,000 ÷ 4) − 600)		900

(b) PLANET PLC
REVISED GROUP BALANCE SHEET AT 30 NOVEMBER 20X2

	£'000
Fixed assets	
Intangible assets (10,360 + 12,000 − 900)	21,460
Tangible assets (76,240 + 4,000 − 400 − 600)	79,240
	100,700
Net current assets (55,800 − 16,000 − 400)	39,400
Total assets less current liabilities	140,100
Creditors: amounts falling due after more than one year	(25,400)
Provisions for liabilities (1,800 + 4,000 + 4,000)	(9,800)
	104,900

	£'000
Capital and reserves	
Called up share capital	32,200
Share premium	10,000
Profit and loss account (W)	44,880
	87,080
Minority interests (18,200 − 80 − 120 − 180)	17,820
	104,900

Working: profit and loss account

	£'000
Draft	54,800
Amortisation of additional goodwill (contingent consideration)	(4,000)
Provision for repairs (operating lease)	(4,000)
Additional depreciation (leased property)	(320)
Impairment loss (leased property)	(480)
Unrealised profit (inter-company sales)	(400)
Amortisation of development expenditure (database)	(720)
	44,880

30 Wingit

(a)   WINGIT GROUP
CASH FLOW STATEMENT FOR THE YEAR ENDED 30 NOVEMBER 20X7

	£m
Cash inflow from operating activities (note 1)	875
Returns on investments and servicing of finance (note 2)	(214)
Taxation (W7)	(115)
Capital expenditure (note 2)	(312)
Acquisitions and disposals (note 2)	(80)
Equity dividends paid (W6)	(120)
Cash inflow before use of liquid resources and financing	34
Management of liquid resources (note 2)	(143)
Decrease in cash	(109)

Notes

1   *Reconciliation of operating profit to operating cash flows*

	Continuing £m		Discontinued £m		Total £m
Operating profit (W1)	458		184		642
Depreciation	141	(150 – 9)	9	(note (a))	150
Goodwill amortisation	20	(note (a))			20
Share of joint venture profit	(75)				(75)
Increase in stocks (incl Piece)	(40)		(60)		(100)
Increase in debtors (incl Piece)	(119)	(W2)	(50)	(Piece)	(169)
Increase in creditors (incl Piece)	327	(note (g))	105	(Piece)	432
Operating activities continuing operations	712		188		900
Bid defence	(5)	(W3)			(5)
Pension prepayment	(20)				(20)
	687		188		875

2   *Gross cash flows*

Returns on investments and servicing of finance

	£m
Interest received (4 + 27 – 5)	26
Interest paid (30 + 19 – 40)	(9)
Minority interest dividend (W4)	(231)
	(214)

Capital expenditure

	£m
Purchase of tangible fixed assets (note (d))	(380)
Sale of tangible fixed assets (W5)	68
	(312)

Acquisitions and disposals

	£m
Cash paid to acquire interest in joint venture (note (b))	(25)
Cash disposed on sale of subsidiary (note (a))	(130)
Cash element of disposal proceeds (note (a))	75
	(80)

Management of liquid resources

	£m
Purchase of corporate bonds (see note (e))	(35)
Purchase of government securities (increase) (see note (e)) (51 – 23)	(28)
Cash on seven day deposit (increase) (see note (e)) (101 – 21)	(80)
	(143)

Note. None of the above are deemed to be 'cash' under the terms of FRS 1 revised.

Workings

1   *Operating profit*

	£m
Operating profit per P&L (continuing operations)	438
Add back bid defence costs	20
	458
Operating profit on discontinued operations	184
	642

2   *Debtors*

	£m
At 30.11.X7	680
Pension prepayment (note (f) in question)	(20)
Interest receivable (note (f) in question)	(5)
	655
At 30.11.X6	540
Interest receivable (note (f) in question)	(4)
	536
Increase (before allowing for disposal)	119

3   *Bid defence*

	£m
20X6 Provision b/f	15
20X7 P&L charge	20
	35
20X7 Provision c/f	30
Paid	5

4   *Dividend paid to minority interest*

MINORITY INTEREST MEMORANDUM WORKING ACCOUNT

	£m		£m
Disposal of MI in Piece			
(420 × 20%)	84	Balance b/f 1.12.X6	570
Balancing figure = cash paid	231	P&L: minority interest share	75
Balance c/f 30.11.X7	330		
	645		645

5   *Disposal of fixed assets*

	£m
Net book value of all disposals (note (d)) (680 – 95)	585
Assets of Piece sold (at NBV)	(310)
Assets transferred to joint venture (note (b))	(200)
NBV of fixed assets sold	75
Loss on disposal (per P&L account)	(7)
Sale proceeds	68

6   *Equity dividends paid*

	£m
Balance b/f 1.12.X6 (note (g))	70
Appropriation	130
Balance c/f 30.11.X7 (note (g))	(80)
Paid	120

7   *Taxation*

	£m
Balance b/f 1.12.X6	150
Taxation balance disposed on sale of subsidiary	(25)
Taxation attributable to joint venture	(20)
P&L tax charge for year	191
Balance c/f 30.11.X7	(181)
Tax paid	115

(b)   Earnings per share is a widely used measure of financial performance. Detailed guidance on its calculation and on presentation and disclosure issues is given in FRS 22 *Earnings per share.*

The directors may **manipulate the numerator** in the EPS calculation by **selecting accounting policies** designed generally to boost the earnings figure, and hence the earnings per share. The **denominator** in the calculation, that is the number of shares by which the earnings figure is divided, is **harder to manipulate**, although the directors may try, as explained below.

(i)   **Government grant**

SSAP 4 *Accounting for government grants* allows two methods of accounting for government grants.

(1)   Net the grant off against the cost of the asset and depreciate the net figure.

(2)   Carry the grant as a **deferred credit** and release it to income over the life of the asset to offset the depreciation charge.

Since netting off is illegal under the Companies Act 1985, most companies use the deferred credit approach.

The **directors** justify their treatment of the government grant by reference to an IASB Discussion Paper. This states that a grant should be **credited to income in the period in which it is made** rather than over several periods. Furthermore, the international thinking is that a **grant is not a liability**, and therefore should not be netted off against the asset to which it relates (SSAP 4, treatment (1)). It could also be argued that **deferred income** does

not constitute a liability according to the *Statement of Principles* definition (SSAP 4, treatment (2)).

Whatever the merits of the position taken in the discussion paper, **SSAP 4 is in force in the UK, and must be followed.** The grant should therefore be removed from the profit and loss account. Only £500,000 (£5m ÷ 10 years) should be credited to income; the balance of £4.5m should be shown as a deferred credit.

(ii) **Share issue**

In the calculation of EPS, the directors have used the number of shares in issue when Mr Springer retired from the company (6 million). They have **not taken into account the new issue of shares** made at the initial public offering. The number of new shares issued is one million plus the sponsor's shares of 100,000. This needs to be **time apportioned** (the shares were in issue for ten months) and added to the denominator of the EPS calculation.

The treatment of the **issue costs is also incorrect**. FRS 25 *Financial instruments: presentation* treats these as being **inseparable from the consideration received,** and requires that they be taken to reserves. Usually the profit and loss reserve is used, but if certain statutory requirements are met, they may be set off against the share premium account. It was therefore incorrect to credit the value of the shares to the profit and loss account and likewise incorrect to charge the cash paid to the profit and loss account.

The **accounting entries** should have been as follows.

DEBIT	Profit and loss reserve/share premium	£300,000	
CREDIT	Cash		£180,000
	Share capital		£100,000
	Share premium		£20,000

(iii) **Lease**

The lease arrangement includes an unconditional agreement to repurchase the lease. The substance of the transaction is therefore that of a loan secured on the property, rather than a genuine sale. Lease accounting is generally governed by SSAP 21, but FRS 5 *Reporting the substance of transactions* gives clearer guidance in the case of sale and repurchase transactions. The asset must be shown on the balance sheet and the 'sale proceeds' must be shown as a finance liability. The profit on the transaction (£500,000) needs to be eliminated from the profit and loss account. In addition, depreciation needs to be charged on the carrying value. The carrying value of the property is the lease consideration of £4.5m less the profit, ie £4m. Depreciation at 5% per annum is therefore £200,000.

Interest needs to be charged to the profit and loss account, since this is in substance a loan. Assuming this can be accrued on a straight line basis, this interest charge is (£5.5m − £4.5m) ÷ 4 years, ie £250,000.

(iv) **Rights issue**

The **rights issue** took place **after the company's year end.** The proceeds of the rights issue were not available for use during the accounting period. It would not therefore be appropriate to adjust EPS to reflect the part of the rights issue that was effected for fair value.

However, **an adjustment needs to be made for the bonus element** in the rights issue, since this is deemed to affect the number of shares, and hence EPS for all accounting periods.

The bonus element is $\dfrac{\text{fair value of share before rights issue}}{\text{theoretical ex rights price}}$

The theoretical ex right price is:

			p
Initial holding	4	× 200p	800
Rights issue	1	× 160p	160
	5		960

$$\therefore \text{TERP} = \frac{960}{5} = £1.92$$

The fair value of the share is £2.00, therefore the bonus element is:

$$\frac{2.00}{1.92} = \frac{25}{24}$$

The number of shares in the EPS calculation needs to be increased by $^1/_{24}$.

Revised EPS calculation

Revised earnings

		£'000
	Net profit per directors	4,800
(i)	Government grant taken to deferred income	(5,000)
	Credited to income in year	500
(ii)	Cash paid	180
	Shares issued to sponsor	(120)
(iii)	Profit on 'sale' eliminated	(500)
	Depreciation	(200)
	Interest charge	(250)
		(590)

Revised number of shares

	Per directors	6,000,000
(i)	Additional shares issued	
	$1,100,000 \times \dfrac{10}{12}$	916,667
		6,916,667
	Bonus element: $6,916,667 \times \dfrac{1}{24}$	288,194
		7,204,861

$$\therefore \text{Loss per share} \quad \frac{(590)}{7,204,861} = (8.2\text{p})$$

(c) **Ethical matters**

It is not always easy to determine whether creative accounting of this kind is **deliberate or whether it arises from ignorance or oversight**. One thing is clear: when the correct accounting treatment is used, an earnings per share of **80p is converted into a loss per share of 8.2p**. Since the directors are entitled to a cash bonus for an EPS of above 50p, there is certainly an **incentive** for them to select accounting policies designed to boost it.

The directors' explanation for their treatment of the **government grant** does **not stand up to scrutiny**. SSAP 4 is not a complicated accounting standard and has been in force for many years. The treatment proposed is only at the Discussion Paper stage, and the directors are probably more concerned with their bonus than with definitions of a liability.

The treatment of the **issue of shares** may simply reflect **lack of knowledge** on the part of directors, rather than unethical accounting. When corrected, the earnings figure is actually increased, although the number of shares is also increased. Furthermore, unlike SSAP 4, this is a complicated matter, and the treatment of issue costs can often be misunderstood. It is more likely, therefore, that the directors were confused about the appropriate treatment.

Regarding the **sale and repurchase agreement**, again it is difficult to say whether this off balance sheet scheme was deliberate. Whether it was or not, it is **clearly outlawed by FRS 5**, which has been in force for some time.

The **failure to include the bonus element** of the post balance sheet rights issue in the calculation of the number of shares may be deliberate, but it is more likely to be an **error** or oversight.

In conclusion, while unethical intent cannot be proved, it is clear that **accounting standards have not been followed**, and generally in a manner **likely to boost EPS**. Accusations of fraud should not be made without taking legal advice, but the **directors should be made aware** in no uncertain terms of their **responsibility** for the accuracy and fairness of the financial statements and their **obligation to apply accounting standards**.

ACCA
Pilot paper: questions and answers

SECTION A: This question is compulsory and MUST be attempted

Question 1

The following draft financial statements relate to Zambeze, a public limited company:

ZAMBEZE
DRAFT GROUP BALANCE SHEETS AT 30 JUNE

	20X6 £m	20X5 £m
Fixed assets		
Goodwill	30	25
Tangible assets	1,315	1,005
Investment in associate	270	290
	1,615	1,320
Current assets		
Stock	650	580
Debtors	610	530
Cash at bank and in hand	50	140
	1,310	1,250
Creditors: amounts falling due within one year	(1,581)	(1,430)
Net current liabilities	(271)	(180)
Total assets less current liabilities	1,344	1,140
Creditors: amounts falling due after more than one year	(850)	(600)
Net assets	494	540
Capital and reserves		
Called up share capital	100	85
Share premium account	30	15
Revaluation reserve	50	145
Profit and loss account	254	250
Minority interest – equity	60	45
Capital employed	494	540

ZAMBEZE
DRAFT GROUP PROFIT AND LOSS FOR THE YEAR ENDED 30 JUNE 20X6

	£m
Turnover	4,700
Cost of sales	(3,400)
Gross profit	1,300
Distribution and administrative expenses	(600)
Finance costs (interest payable)	(40)
Share of profit in associate	30
Profit before tax	690
Taxation (including tax on income from associate £10 million)	(210)
Profit after taxation	480
Minority interest	(25)
Profit attributable to members of parent company	455

ZAMBEZE
DRAFT GROUP STATEMENT OF TOTAL RECOGNISED GAINS AND LOSSES
FOR THE YEAR ENDED 30 JUNE 20X6

	£m
Profit for the financial year	455
Foreign exchange difference of associate	(5)
Impairment losses on tangible assets offset against revaluation surplus	(95)
Total recognised gains and losses for the period	355

ZAMBEZE
DRAFT RECONCILIATION OF GROUP SHAREHOLDERS' FUNDS
FOR THE YEAR ENDED 30 JUNE 20X6

	£m
Total recognised gains and losses for the period	355
Dividends paid	(446)
New shares issued	30
Total movement during the year	(61)
Shareholders' funds at 1 July 20X5	495
Shareholders' funds at 30 June 20X6	434

The following relates to Zambeze.

(i)   Zambeze acquired a seventy per cent holding in Damp, a public limited company, on 1 July 20X5. The fair values of the net assets acquired were as follows:

	£m
Tangible fixed assets	70
Stock and work in progress	90
	160

The purchase consideration was £100 million in cash and £25 million (discounted value) deferred consideration which is payable on 1 July 20X6. The difference between the discounted value of the deferred consideration (£25 million) and the amount payable (£29 million) is included in 'interest payable'. Zambeze wants to set up a provision for reconstruction costs of £10 million retrospectively on the acquisition of Damp. This provision has not yet been set up.

(ii)   There had been no disposals of tangible fixed assets during the year. Depreciation for the period charged in cost of sales was £60 million.

(iii)   Creditors: amounts falling due within one year comprised the following items:

	20X6	20X5
	£m	£m
Trade creditors	1,341	1,200
Interest payable	50	45
Taxation	190	185
	1,581	1,430

(iv)   Creditors: amounts falling due after more than one year comprised the following:

	20X6	20X5
	£m	£m
Deferred consideration – purchase of Damp	29	–
Liability for the purchase of tangible fixed assets	144	–
Loans repayable	621	555
Provision for deferred tax	30	25
Retirement benefit liability	26	20
	850	600

(v)   The retirement benefit liability comprised the following:

	£m
Movement in year	
Liability at 1 July 20X5	20
Current and past service costs charged to profit and loss	13
Contributions paid to retirement benefit scheme	(7)
Liability 30 June 20X6	26

There was no actuarial gain or loss in the year.

(vi)   Goodwill was impairment tested on 30 June 20X6 and any impairment was included in the financial statements for the year ended 30 June 20X6. Group policy is to amortise goodwill over five years but because goodwill was impairment tested on 30 June 20X6, no amortisation was charged in the year.

(vii) The Finance Director has set up a company, River, through which Zambeze conducts its investment activities. Zambeze has paid £400 million to River during the year and this has been included in dividends paid. The money was invested in a specified portfolio of investments. Ninety five per cent of the profits and one hundred per cent of the losses in the specified portfolio of investments are transferred to Zambeze. An investment manager has charge of the company's investments and owns all of the share capital of River. An agreement between the investment manager and Zambeze sets out the operating guidelines and prohibits the investment manager from obtaining access to the investments for the manager's benefit. An annual transfer of the profit/loss will occur on 30 June annually and the capital will be returned in four years time. The transfer of £400 million cash occurred on 1 January 20X6 but no transfer of profit/loss has yet occurred. The balance sheet of River at 30 June 20X6 is as follows:

RIVER: BALANCE SHEET AT 30 JUNE 20X6

	£m
Investment at fair value through profit or loss	390
	390
Share capital	400
Retained earnings	(10)
	390

Required

(a)   Prepare a group cash flow statement for the Zambeze Group for the year ended 30 June 20X6 using the indirect method.   **(35 marks)**

(b)   Discuss the issues which would determine whether River should be consolidated by Zambeze in the group financial statements.   **(9 marks)**

(c)   Discuss briefly the importance of ethical behaviour in the preparation of financial statements and whether the creation of River could constitute unethical practice by the finance director of Zambeze.   **(6 marks)**

(Total = 50 marks)

Two marks are available for the quality of the discussion of the issue regarding the consolidation of River and the importance of ethical behaviour.

663

Section B: TWO questions ONLY to be attempted

Question 2

Electron, a public limited company, operates in the energy sector. The company has grown significantly over the last few years and is currently preparing its financial statements for the year ended 30 June 20X6.

Electron buys and sells oil and currently has a number of oil trading contracts. The contracts to purchase oil are treated as fixed assets and amortised over the contracts' durations. On acceptance of a contract to sell oil, fifty per cent of the contract price is recognised immediately with the balance being recognised over the remaining life of the contract. The contracts always result in the delivery of the commodity.

(4 marks)

Electron has recently constructed an ecologically efficient power station. A condition of being granted the operating licence by the government is that the power station be dismantled at the end of its life which is estimated to be 20 years. The power station cost £100 million and began production on 1 July 20X5. Depreciation is charged on the power station using the straight line method. Electron has estimated at 30 June 20X6 that it will cost £15 million (net present value) to restore the site to its original condition using a discount rate of five per cent. Ninety-five per cent of these costs relate to the removal of the power station and five per cent relates to the damage caused through generating energy. **(7 marks)**

Electron has leased another power station, which was relatively inefficient, to a rival company on 30 June 20X6. The beneficial and legal ownership remains with Electron and in the event of one of Electron's power stations being unable to produce energy, Electron can terminate the agreement. The leased power station is being treated as an operating lease with the net present value of the income of £40 million being recognised in the profit and loss account. The fair value of the power station is £70 million at 30 June 20X6. A deposit of £10 million was received on 30 June 20X6 and it is included in the net present value calculation. **(5 marks)**

The company has a good relationship with its shareholders and employees. It has adopted a strategy of gradually increasing its dividend payments over the years. On 1 August 20X6, the board proposed a dividend of 5p per share for the year ended 30 June 20X6. The shareholders will approve the dividend along with the financial statements at the general meeting on 1 September 20X6 and the dividend will be paid on 14 September 20X6. The directors feel that the dividend should be accrued in the financial statements for the year ended 30 June 20X6 as a 'valid expectation' has been created. **(3 marks)**

The company granted share options to its employees on 1 July 20X5. The fair value of the options at that date was £3 million. The options vest on 30 June 20X8. The employees have to be employed at the end of the three year period for the options to vest and the following estimates have been made:

Estimated percentage of employees leaving during vesting period at:

Grant date 1 July 20X5	5%	
30 June 20X6	6%	**(4 marks)**
Effective communication to the directors		**(2 marks)**

Required

Draft a report suitable for presentation to the director of Electron which discusses the accounting treatment of the above transactions in the financial statements for the year ended 30 June 20X6, including relevant calculations.

(Total = 25 marks)

Question 3

The following balance sheet relates to Kesare Group, a public limited company at 30 June 20X6:

	£'000
Assets	
Fixed assets	
Tangible assets	10,000
Goodwill	6,000
Other intangible assets	5,000
Financial assets (cost)	9,000
	30,000
Debtors	7,000
Other receivables	4,600
Cash	6,700
Current assets	18,300
Trade creditors	(5,000)
Current tax liability	(3,070)
Creditors: amounts falling due within one year	(8,070)
Net current assets	10,230
Creditors: amounts falling due after more than one year	
Long term borrowings	(10,000)
Deferred tax liability	(3,600)
Employee benefit liability	(4,000)
	(17,600)
Net assets	22,630
Capital and reserves	
Share capital	9,000
Profit and loss account	9,130
Other reserves	4,500
Capital employed	22,630

The following information is relevant to the above balance sheet.

(i)   The financial assets are valued at fair value through profit or loss but are shown in the above balance sheet at their cost on 1 July 20X5. The market value of the assets is £10.5 million on 30 June 20X6.Taxation is payable on the sale of the assets.

(ii)   Other tangible assets comprise an asset which was purchased on 1 July 20X5 for £5 million and which qualifies for a government capital grant of £1 million. The asset has a useful life of five years. The grant has been credited to the profit and loss account and capital allowances are restricted by the amount of the grant. Assume a tax writing down allowance of 25% per annum.

(iii)   The defined benefit plan had a rule change on 1 July 20X5. Kesare estimate that of the past service costs of £1 million, 40 per cent relates to vested benefits and 60 per cent relates to benefits that will vest over the next five years from that date. The past service costs have not been accounted for and the actuarial gain before accounting for the past service costs was £600,000.

(iv)   The company had purchased an investment property on 1 July 20X5 at a cost of £3 million. This was included in tangible assets at this amount at 30 June 20X6. The value of the property at 30 June 20X6 was £5 million and the gain was included in the profit and loss account. The company had no intention of selling the property in the near future. The property qualifies for capital allowances at 4% per annum. No deferred taxation had been provided for on the investment property.

(v)   Assume taxation is payable at 30%.

Required

(a)   Discuss the main objectives of the recognition of deferred taxation and the conceptual principles upon which the timing difference approach to deferred taxation is based.   **(7 marks)**

(b)   Show, with suitable explanations, any adjustments that would be required to the deferred tax liabilities and balance sheet amounts as a result of items (i) – (iv) above.   **(18 marks)**

(Total = 25 marks)

Two marks will be awarded for the quality of the discussion of the objectives and conceptual principles in (a).

Question 4

A significant number of entities and countries around the world have adopted International Financial Reporting Standards (IFRS) as their basis for financial reporting, often regarding these as a means to improve the quality of information on corporate performance. However, while the advantages of a common set of global reporting standards are recognised, there are a number of implementation challenges at the international and national levels if the objective of an improved and harmonised reporting system is to be achieved.

Required

(a)   Discuss the implementation challenges faced by the International Accounting Standards Board (IASB) if there is to be a successful move to International Financial Reporting Standards.

(18 marks)

(b)   The Accounting Standards Board recently issued FRED 36 *Business combinations* (IFRS 3) and amendments to FRS 2 *Accounting for subsidiary undertakings*. The proposals radically change the basis of reporting business combinations and transactions with minority interests.

Discuss how the above exposure draft will fundamentally affect the existing accounting practices for business combinations   **(7 marks)**

(Total = 25 marks)

Two marks will be awarded for the quality of the discussion of the ideas and information.

Paper P2 Corporate Reporting (UK) Commentary

General

As will be the pattern, Question 1 is a case study. It starts off with a group cash flow statement, then draws on your knowledge of criteria for consolidation and finally goes into ethical matters. In Section B, you have three questions:

Question 2 is a multi-standard question dealing with environmental provisions, leasing, EABSD and share-based payment.

Question 3 is all about deferred tax. Nasty. Avoid this, unless you really like the topic.

Question 4 is a nice, practical question on implementing IFRS, with a current issues aspect thrown in.

Question 1

Top tips. Some students don't like group cash flow statements, but they really are a gift. You can simply ignore any complications – at least to start off with – and concentrate on getting the easy marks (see below). Set out your proforma, and, if you can, try to set out your workings in the order shown in our answer. This order has been designed so that the easy workings come first. Part (b) requires straightforward bookwork knowledge of the criteria for consolidation, but also application of this knowledge to the matter of River. Part (c) requires a general discussion of ethical behaviour, but also, more specifically, how these general principles may be applied in the case of River.

Easy marks. Look at the marking scheme for Part (a). There are six marks for operating activities – most of which you know from your non-group cash flow studies at earlier levels. The property plant and equipment working has a few complications, but the same complications come up regularly, so if you learn our working you can't go too far wrong. Tax, interest and dividends are all straightforward. Turning to parts (b) and (c), as indicated above, there are easy marks for a more general discussion, as well as trickier marks for specific application. And write clearly, so you earn those extra two marks for communication.

Question 2

Top tips. This is a multi-standard question on environmental provisions, leases, proposed dividend and a share option scheme. The good thing about this kind of question is that, even if you don't know all the standards tested, you can get marks for the ones you do know. The question on the power station is similar to one you will have already met in this kit, and you have come across longer, more complicated questions on share-based payment, a favourite topic with this examiner.

Easy marks. The proposed dividend is straightforward, as is the explanation (if not the calculations) for the provision. The treatment of share options provides 4 easy marks for nothing much in the way of complications.

Question 3

Top tips. To state the obvious, this is a question best avoided unless you like deferred tax. However, if you do, or if you dislike other topics more, the question may be broken down into components where you can get a foothold. Layout is important to avoid getting muddled.

Easy marks. For those not fond of high speed number-crunching, there are some fairly easy marks in Part (a) available for a general discussion about concepts and the framework. In addition there are some easy marks for adjustments to the financial statements, most of which do not relate to the deferred tax aspects. In general, however, this is not a question that lends itself to easy marks.

Question 4

Top tips. Part (a) of this question is topical and practical, and you should have been prepared for this topic to come up. If you weren't, learn our answer carefully – you may be able to apply it to some variant of the question in an exam. Part (b) is on current issues, specifically the changes proposed to accounting for business combinations in recent exposure drafts. The examiner has specifically stated that he will not set a whole question on an exposure draft, or test the detail. The focus will be on the main implications for the financial statements, as here.

Easy marks. As you can see from the marking scheme, much of the mark allocation is 'subjective'. Thus does not mean you can say anything you want or waffle, but it does mean that credit is given for any valid points, provided you can back them up with arguments. So keep writing and stay calm and logical. A quick answer plan will help.

P2 Pilot Paper (UK)   **Answers**
Corporate Reporting (United Kingdom)

1 (a) Zambeze Group
Group Statement of Cash Flows for the year ended 30 June 2006

	£m	£m
Net cash flows from operating activities (Note 1):		862
Cash contributions to pension scheme		(7)
Dividends received from associate (working 3)		35
Returns on investment and servicing of finance (Note 2)		(89)
Taxation (working 4)		(190)
Capital expenditure and financial investment (Note 2)		(651)
Acquisitions and disposals (Note 2)		(100)
Equity dividends paid (working 6)		(46)
Cash outflow before use of liquid resources and financing		(186)
Financing:		
issues of shares	30	
increase in debt	66	96
Decrease in cash in period		(90)

Note 1
Reconciliation of operating profit to net cash inflow from operating activities

		£m
Operating profit (690 + 40)		730
Depreciation		60
Impairment of goodwill (working 2)		8
Decrease in stock (650–580–90)	20	
Increase in debtors	(80)	
Increase in creditors	141	81
Associate's profit		(30)
Current and past service costs		13
		862

Note 2
Analysis of cash flows for headings netted in cash flow statement
Returns on investment and servicing of finance

	£m
Interest paid (working 5)	31
Minority interest – equity dividend	58
	89

Capital expenditure and financial investment

	£m
Purchase of tangible fixed assets (working 1)	(251)
Investment in River	(400)
	(651)

Acquisitions

	£m
Purchase of Damp	100
	100

Working 1

	£m
Tangible fixed assets	
Balance at 1 July 2005	1,005
Impairment losses	(95)
Depreciation	(60)
Purchases (by deduction)	395
Acquisition – Damp	70
Closing balance	1,315

Cash flow is £395 million minus the liability for tangible fixed assets of £144 million, ie £251 million.

Working 2

	£m
Purchase of subsidiary:	
Net assets acquired	160
Group's share of net assets (70%)	112
Goodwill	13
Purchase consideration (100+25)	125

	£m
Goodwill:	
Balance at 30 June 2005	25
Goodwill on subsidiary	13
Impairment	(8)
Balance at 30 June 2006	30

	£m
Minority interest:	
Balance at 1 July 2005	45
Acquisition of Damp (160 x 30%)	48
Profit for year	25
Dividend	(58)
Balance at 30 June 2006	60

Working 3

	£m
Dividend from associate:	
Balance at 1 July 2005	290
Income (net of tax) (30–10)	20
Foreign exchange loss	(5)
Dividends received (difference)	(35)
Balance at 30 June 2006	270

Working 4

		£m	£m
Taxation:			
Balance at 1 July 2005	Income tax		185
	Deferred tax		25
Income statements (210–10)			200
Tax paid (difference)			(190)
Balance at 30 June 2006	Income tax	190	
	Deferred tax	30	
			220

Working 5

	£m
Interest paid:	
Balance at 1 July 2005	45
Profit and loss	40
Unwinding of discount on purchase	(4)
Cash paid (difference)	(31)
Closing balance at 30 June 2006	50

Working 6

The cash payment to River should be shown as "financial investment" of £400 million and the dividend paid will then be £(446–400) million, ie £46 million.

(b) FRS 2 *Accounting for subsidiary undertakings* essentially adopts the definitions of parent undertaking introduced by the Companies Act 1985. An undertaking is deemed to be a parent of another undertaking where:

(i) over more than one half of the voting rights are owned by the parent; or

(ii) the parent has the right to exercise dominant influence over the undertaking or

(iii) the parent is a member and has the right to appoint or remove members of the board of directors who hold the majority of the voting rights at board meetings; or

(iv) the parent has a participating interest in the undertaking and exercises dominant influence.

Dominant influence is that which is exercised to achieve the operating and financial policies desired by the holder of the influence. The influence has to be exercised and is identified by its effect in practice.

FRS 2 *The definition* is based on the power of one entity to "control" another through the exercise of share holder control. FRS 5 *Reporting the substance of transactions* takes the view that the definitions above are not conclusive in determining what entities are to be consolidated. FRS 5 defines a quasi subsidiary and envisages situations where the need to give a true and fair view will require the consolidation of quasi subsidiaries. The key feature is control which means the ability to direct the financial and operating policies to gain economic benefit from its activities. Control is also indicated by the ability to prevent others from exercising those policies or enjoying the benefits of the subsidiary's net assets. Control can be derived from a variety of sources and exercised in a number of ways. If the 'owner' has accepted real and severe constraints on the normal powers of ownership, then the real benefits of ownership must lie elsewhere. The ability to control decision making alone is not sufficient to establish control for accounting purposes but must be accompanied by the objective of obtaining benefits from the entity's activities. If a company obtains the benefits of ownership, is exposed to the risks of ownership, and can exercise decision making powers to obtain those benefits, then the company must control the third party. The overall substance of the arrangement must be considered.

Zambeze should consolidate River as Zambeze controls it through the operating guidelines. Zambeze also receives 95% of the profits and suffers all the losses of River. The guidelines were set up when River was formed and, therefore, the company was set up as a vehicle with the objective of keeping certain transactions off the balance sheet of Zambeze. The investment manager manages the investments of River within the guidelines and incurs no risk and receives 5% of the profits for the management services.

(c) Ethics in accounting is of utmost importance to accounting professionals and those who rely on their services. Accounting professionals know that people who use their services, especially decision makers using financial statements, expect them to be highly competent, reliable, and objective. Those who work in the field of accounting must not only be well qualified but must also possess a high degree of professional integrity. A professional's good reputation is one of his or her most important assets.

There is a very fine line between acceptable accounting practice and management's deliberate misrepresentation in the financial statements. The financial statements must meet the following criteria:

(i) Technical compliance: A transaction must be recorded in accordance with generally accepted accounting principles (GAAP).

(ii) Economic substance: The resulting financial statements must represent the economic substance of the event that has occurred.

(iii) Full disclosure and transparency: Sufficient disclosure must be made so that the effects of transactions are transparent to the reader of the financial statements.

In the case of River, it could be argued that the first criterion may be met because the transaction is apparently recorded in technical compliance with FRS, but technical compliance alone is not sufficient. The second criterion is not met because the transaction as recorded does not reflect the economic substance of the event that has occurred.

Accounting plays a critical function in society. Accounting numbers affect human behaviour especially when it affects compensation, and to deliberately mask the nature of accounting transactions could be deemed to be unethical behaviour.

River was set up with the express purpose of keeping its activities off the balance sheet. The Finance Director has an ethical responsibility to the shareholders of Zambeze and society not to mask the true nature of the transactions with this entity. Further, if the transaction has been authorised by the Finance Director without the authority or knowledge of the Board of Directors, then a further ethical issue arises. Showing the transfer of funds as a dividend paid is unethical and possibly illegal in the jurisdiction. The transfer should not be hidden and River should be consolidated.

2   Oil Contracts

The accounting policy adopted for the agreements relating to the oil contracts raises a number of concerns. The revenue recognition policy currently used is inflating revenue in the first year of the contract with 50% of the revenue being recognised, but a smaller proportion of the costs are recognised in the form of depreciation. Over the life of the contract, costs and revenues are equally matched but in the short term there is a bias towards a more immediate recognition of revenue against a straight line cost deferral policy. Additionally oil sales result in revenue whilst purchases of oil result in a tangible fixed asset. Under FRS18 *Accounting Policies*, the question of whether revenue has arisen is judged independently from the matching concept according to whether an asset has been created. If it has, revenue is recognised. Similarly, if a liability has been created in the period, a related expense may have occurred and is recognised. The Statement of Principles adopts this "asset" and "liability" approach also. Similarly the Amendment to FRS5 *Reporting the substance of transactions – Revenue Recognition*, is based on the principles that a seller generates revenue by performing contractual obligations and in exchange obtains the right to consideration. Thus when performance of a contract takes place over time the revenue should be recognised as performance takes place. The current accounting practice seems out of line with the basic principles of revenue recognition.

However, the election of the company to use some form of deferral policy for its agreements is to be commended as it attempts to bring its revenue recognition policy in line with the length of the agreements. The main problem is the lack of a detailed accounting standard on revenue recognition. The result is the current lack of consistency in accounting for long-term agreements. However, it may be advisable to adopt a deferral policy in terms of this type of revenue. The contracts always result in the delivery of the oil in the normal course of business and are not, therefore, accounted for as financial instruments as they qualify as normal sale and purchase contracts.

Power Station

Under FRS12 *Provisions, Contingent Liabilities and Contingent Assets*, a provision should be made at the balance sheet date for the discounted cost of the removal of the power station because of the following reasons:

(i)   the installation of the power station creates an obligating event
(ii)   the operating licence creates a legal obligation which is likely to occur
(iii) the costs of removal will have to be incurred irrespective of the future operations of the company and cannot be avoided
(iv)   a transfer of economic benefits (ie the costs of removal) will be required to settle the obligation
(v)   a reasonable estimate of the obligation can be made although it is difficult to estimate a cost which will be incurred in twenty years time (FRS12 says that only in exceptional circumstances will it not be possible to make some estimate of the obligation)

The costs to be incurred will be treated as part of the cost of the facility to be depreciated over its production life. However, the costs relating to the damage caused by the generation of energy should not be included in the provision, until the power is generated which in this case would be 5% of the total discounted provision. The accounting for the provision is as follows:

	£m	£m
Present value of obligation at 1 July 2005 (15÷1.05)	14.3	
Provision for decommissioning (95% x 14.3)	13.6	
Provision for damage through extraction (5% x 14.3)		0.7

Balance Sheet at 30 June 2006

	£m	£m
Tangible fixed assets:		
Cost of power station	100	
Provision for decommissioning	13.6	
	113.6	
less depreciation (113.6÷20 years)	(5.7)	
Carrying value	107.9	
Other provisions:		
Provision for decommissioning 1 July 2005	13.6	
Unwinding of discount (13.6 x 5%)	0.7	
		14.3
Provision for damage (0.7÷20 years)		0.1
		14.4

Profit and Loss Account

	£m
Depreciation	5.7
Provision for damage	0.1
Unwinding of discount (finance cost)	0.7

A simple straight line basis has been used to calculate the required provision for damage. A more complex method could be used whereby the present value of the expected cost of the provision is provided for over 20 years and the discount thereon is unwound over its life.

Operating Leases

Under SSAP21 *Accounting for leases and hire purchase contracts* a lease is classified as a finance lease if it transfers substantially all the risks and rewards "incident" to ownership. All other leases are classified as operating leases. In this case, the beneficial and legal ownership remains with Electron and Electron can make use of the power station if it so wishes. Also for a lease asset to be a finance lease the present value of the minimum lease payments should be substantially all of the fair value of the leased asset (normally 90 per cent or more). In this case this amounts to 57.1% (£40 million ÷ £70 million) which does not constitute "substantially all". Thus there does not seem to be any issue over the classification of the lease as an operating lease. The immediate recognition as income of the future benefit at net present value is a little more problematical. SSAP21 says that lease income from operating leases should be recognised on a straight line basis over the lease term unless another systematic and rational basis is more representative. This applies even if the payments are not made on such a basis. If a fee is received as an "up front" cash payment then FRS18 and FRS5 should be applied. If there is future involvement required to earn the fee, or there are retained risks or risk of the repayment of the fee, or any restrictions on the lessor's use of the asset, then immediate recognition is inappropriate. The present policy of recognising the total lease income as if it were immediate income which it is not, would be difficult to justify. Similarly, as regards the deposit received, revenue should only be recognised when there is performance of the contract. Thus as there has been no performance under the contract, no revenue should be accrued in the period.

Proposed dividend

The dividend was proposed after the balance sheet date and the company, therefore, did not have a liability at the balance sheet date. No provision for the dividend should be recognised. The approval by the directors and the shareholders are enough to create a valid expectation that the payment will be made and give rise to an obligation. However, this occurred after the current year end and, therefore, will be charged against the profits for the year ending 30 June 2007.

The existence of a good record of dividend payments and an established dividend policy does not create a valid expectation or an obligation. However, the proposed dividend will be disclosed in the notes to the financial statements as the directors approved it prior to the authorisation of the financial statements.

Share options

Equity-settled transactions with employees would normally be expensed on the basis of their fair value at the grant date. Fair value should be based on market prices wherever possible. Many shares and share options will not be traded on an active market. In this case, valuation techniques, such as the option pricing model, would be used. FRS20's objective for equity-based transactions with employees is to determine and recognise compensation costs over the period in which the services are rendered. In this case, the company has granted to employees share options that vest in three years' time on the condition that they remain in the entity's employ for that period. These steps will be taken:

(i)   the fair value of the options will be determined at the date on which they were granted

(ii)   this fair value will be charged to the profit and loss account equally over the three year vesting period with adjustments made at each accounting date to reflect the best estimate of the number of options that eventually will vest

Shareholders' equity will be increased by an amount equal to the profit and loss account charge. The charge in the profit and loss account reflects the number of options that are likely to vest, not the number of options granted or the number of options exercised. If employees decide not to exercise their options because the share price is lower than the exercise price, then no adjustment is made to the profit and loss account. Many employee share option schemes contain conditions that must be met before the employee becomes entitled to the shares or options. These are called vesting conditions and could require, for example, an increase in profit or growth in the entity's share price before the shares vest. In this case the vesting condition is the employment condition. £940,000 (£3 million x 94% x 1/3) will be charged in the profit and loss account and to equity at 30 June 2006.

3   (a)   The objective of accounting for deferred tax is to ensure that the future tax consequences of past transactions and events are recognised as assets or liabilities in financial statements. The objective is based on the definition of a liability set out in the *Statement of Principles*. A liability for deferred tax should be recognised only for past transactions or events that give rise to an obligation to pay more tax in the future. Timing differences arise out of differences between an entity's taxable profits and its results as stated in the financial statements. Gains and losses are included in tax assessments in periods different from those in which they are recognised in the financial statements. Past transactions and events will have future tax consequences if they are recognised as timing differences that have originated but not reversed at the balance sheet date. An entity will have an obligation to pay more tax or a right to pay less tax where it has no discretion to avoid the future reversal of a timing difference. (An entity may originate a new timing difference which may postpone tax payable or recoverable.) This approach has been called the "incremental liability approach" and the Accounting Standards Board believes it is consistent with the *Statement of Principles*.

     (b)   (i)   Financial assets that are valued at fair value through profit and loss should be valued at fair value with any increase in value going to the profit and loss account. Thus the gain of £1.5 million should be included in the profit and loss account and the balance sheet value increased. Revaluation of non-monetary assets does not give rise to a timing difference because taxable profits are not affected and no future tax liability arises as a result of the revaluation (unless there is a binding sale agreement). However, FRS19 states that deferred tax should be recognised on timing differences arising when an asset is continuously revalued to fair value with changes being recognised in the profit and loss account. Thus deferred tax should be provided of (£10.5 million − £9 million) @ 30%, ie £450,000.

           (ii)   Government grant

                  Government grants are dealt with in SSAP4 *Accounting for government grants*. Grants should be credited to revenue over the useful life of the related asset and not credited fully in the year of receipt. Grants can be deducted from the cost of the asset or treated as a deferred credit of which a proportion would be credited to revenue annually. SSAP4 warns that Counsel's opinion is that a deduction from cost method is unlawful. The timing difference arising on this item would be:

BPP
LEARNING MEDIA

	£000
Cost of asset	5,000
Depreciation	(1,000)
Carrying value	4,000
Unamortised deferred income (1,000 – 200)	(800)
Net carrying value in financial statements	3,200
Cost of asset	5,000
less grant	(1,000)
	4,000
Capital allowance (25%)	(1,000)
Tax written down value	3,000
Timing difference	200
Deferred tax (3200–3000) @ 30%	60

(iii) Pension costs

The defined benefit plan should recognise (40% of £1 million + 60% of £1 million/5) ie £520,000 of the past service costs as an increase in the liability. Retained earnings will be charged with the same amount. This increase in the liability will reduce the actuarial gain to (£600–£520)K, £80,000. Therefore, deferred tax of £80,000 x 30%, ie £24,000 will be recognised in the STRGL as the actuarial gain will have been recognised there.

(iv) Investment property

Investment properties should not be depreciated (SSAP19) but should be included in the balance sheet at their open market value. Changes in the value of the investment properties should not be taken to the profit and loss account but should be taken to the investment revaluation reserve. Thus the gain on the investment property (£2 million) should be taken out of the profit and loss account and credited to investment revaluation reserve. Deferred tax is only provided on the gain arising on the revaluation if there was an intention to sell the investment property. As the company has no intention to sell, then no deferred taxation is provided on the gain. However, the company will have to provide deferred taxation on the difference between nil depreciation and the capital allowances £120,000 claimed at the tax rate of 30%, ie £36,000.

	Balance Sheet £000	Profit and Loss Account £000	Other reserves £000
Balance per balance sheet		9,130	4,500
(i) Financial assets	9,000		
Revaluation	1,500	1,500	
	10,500		
(ii) Grant	800	200	
Reversal of grant income		(1,000)	
Depreciation of fixed asset	(1,000)	(1,000)	
(iii) Pension costs – liability	(4,000)		
Past service costs	(520)	(520)	
	(4,520)		
(iv) Investment property		(2,000)	2,000
Increase in deferred tax (below)		(546)	(24)
		5,764	6,476
Deferred tax liability per balance sheet			3,600
Adjustment for			
Financial asset		450	
Government grant		60	
Pension costs (to STRGL)		24	
Investment property		36	570
Adjusted deferred tax liability			4,170

4 **(a)** International Financial Reporting Standards (IFRS) were initially developed for the preparation of group accounts of listed companies. The use of IFRS is growing such that in some countries that are building or improving their accounting regulatory framework, IFRS based corporate reports are deemed to be more reliable and relevant than local GAAP reports. In many of these countries IFRSs are the statutory requirement for legal entities and, therefore, an implementation issue that has arisen is that the national law has to be reconciled with the requirements of IFRS.

Another implementation issue relates to small and medium-sized enterprises (SMEs) in terms of whether a separate set of standards should be developed and what should be the underlying conceptual and methodological basis for such standards. Effective implementation requires continuous interaction between the International Accounting Standards Board (IASB) and national regulators. The IASB has issued a draft Memorandum of Understanding on the role of Accounting Standard Setters and their relationship with the IASB. It identifies responsibilities that the IASB and other standard setters should adopt to facilitate the ongoing adoption of or convergence with IFRS.

With the increase in the number of entities applying IFRS, the demand for implementation guidance is growing. The International Financial Reporting Interpretations Committee (IFRIC) has been given the task of meeting this demand but there may be a need for additional coping mechanisms as a limited number of interpretations have been issued since the inception of IFRIC.

Variations in translation of IFRS could introduce inconsistency. In some countries the capacity for highly technical translation is low and there may be a conflict with existing national terminology and legislation. Additionally, time lags in the local "endorsement" process and in translating new IFRS could mean that financial reports may not be consistent with the latest body of standards. Additionally the successful implementation of IFRS will depend upon the robustness of the local regulatory framework. Effective corporate governance practices, high quality auditing standards and practices, and effective enforcement or oversight mechanisms will be required to underpin the IFRS. Often endorsement of the standards is required as part of the implementation process. For example, in the European Union, after IFRSs have been issued by the IASB, they must go through an endorsement process before companies listed in the European Union are required to apply them. This process could create standards that differ from those of the IASB.

Implementation of IFRS can have implications for a number of legislative areas. The more complex the regulatory framework, the more problems will arise. There can be tax, price control and company law implications, and certain sectors, such as banking and insurance, may be subject to additional regulation that may require special reporting requirements. Entities may find that they are in breach of existing covenants with lenders where the provision of funding is based on national GAAP ratios. Similarly corporate law may set out the requirements on distribution of dividends and unless the necessary corporate law amendments are made then dividend distributions would be based on national GAAP which might create confusion.

An international mechanism for the co-ordination of enforcement of IFRS is required. IOSCO provides an infrastructure for enforcement with respect to publicly listed companies. IOSCO has put forward proposals for the regulatory interpretation and enforcement of IFRS. On a more local level, the European Union has established the Committee of European Securities Regulators whose role is to improve co-ordination among securities regulators and ensure implementation of legislation in the European Union.

The complex nature of IFRS and the sheer volume of standards make the task of implementation difficult. The standards are deemed to be "principles based" and this may lead to inconsistencies of application, particularly in countries without a critical mass of experienced accountants. Most accountants will have been trained to apply domestic accounting standards, and where there are options in IFRS, then it is likely that the accounting practice closest to their National GAAP will be chosen. Similarly IFRSs utilise fair value measurement extensively and market information is required to more accurately reflect the value. The nature of this market information will vary around the world. If market information is not available, an alternative source can be obtained by simulating a hypothetical market or by using mathematical modelling. Experience of such techniques will vary worldwide, and this experience will be variable in such areas as actuarial estimation, impairment testing, and valuing share based payments. The concepts set out in IFRS may be new to some accounting professionals and may be difficult to grasp.

(b) Under current accounting practice the objective of acquisition accounting is to reflect the cost of the acquisition. To the extent to which it is not represented by identifiable assets and liabilities (measured at their fair value), goodwill arises and is reported in the financial statements. These exposure drafts adopt a different perspective and require the financial statements to reflect the fair value of the acquired business. The recognition of the acquired business at fair value will mean that any existing interest owned by the acquirer before it gained control will be remeasured at fair value at the date of acquisition with any gain or loss recognised in the profit and loss account.

The proposals treat the group as a single economic entity and any outside equity interest in a subsidiary is treated as part of the overall ownership interest in the group. As a consequence, transactions with minority shareholders are to be treated as equity transactions. No gain or loss will be recognised in the profit and loss account. Accounting for business combinations has to date been based on the "parent entity" concept where the extent of non-controlling interests and transactions with non-controlling interests are separately identified in the primary financial statements.

It is also proposed that goodwill is to be recognised in full even if control is less than 100%. FRS2 currently requires that goodwill arising on acquisition should only be recognised with respect to the part of the subsidiary undertaking that is attributable to the interest held by the parent entity.

Goodwill, after initial recognition, is to be measured at cost less impairment losses, and amortisation is not to be permitted. The ASB concluded that more useful information would be provided if goodwill was not amortised but subjected to a rigorous and operational impairment test. FRS10 "Goodwill and Intangible Assets" seeks to charge goodwill to the profit and loss account only to the extent that the carrying value of goodwill is not supported by the current value of goodwill within the acquired business.

Costs incurred in connection with an acquisition are not to be accounted for as part of the cost of the investment but will be charged in the profit and loss account. There will also be changes to the way in which some assets and liabilities acquired in a business combination are recognised and measured. The FRED requires assets and liabilities acquired to be measured and recognised at fair value at the acquisition date. Currently estimated fair values are used and guidance is given as to how to measure 'fair value' in the current standard. This guidance often results in the measurement of assets and liabilities in a manner which is inconsistent with fair value objectives.

P2 Pilot Paper (UK)
Corporate Reporting (United Kingdom)

1	(a)	Operating activities	6
		Retirement benefit	3
		Associate	3
		Subsidiary treatment	4
		Tangible fixed assets	3
		Goodwill	2
		Minority interest	3
		Taxation	3
		Dividend paid	3
		Interest	2
		River	2
		Issue of shares	1
			35

	(b)	Issues	9

	(c)	Ethical discussion		3
		River		3
			AVAILABLE/MAXIMUM	**50**

2		Oil contracts	5
		Power station	8
		Operating leases	5
		Proposed dividend	3
		Share options	4
		AVAILABLE/MAXIMUM	**25**

3	(a)	Subjective		7

	(b)	Financial assets		4
		Grant		4
		Pension		4
		Investment property		4
		Adjustments		4
			AVAILABLE	**20**
			MAXIMUM	**18**
			AVAILABLE	**27**
			MAXIMUM	**25**

4	(a)	Subjective		18
	(b)	Subjective		7
			AVAILABLE/MAXIMUM	**25**

Index

Note: **Key Terms** and their page references are given in **bold**.

Review Form & Free Prize Draw – Paper 2 Corporate Reporting (UK) (6/07)

All original review forms from the entire BPP range, completed with genuine comments, will be entered into one of two draws on 31 January 2008 and 31 July 2008. The names on the first four forms picked out on each occasion will be sent a cheque for £50.

Name: _____   **Address:** _____

_____

_____

How have you used this Text?
(Tick one box only)

☐ Home study (book only)

☐ On a course: college _____

☐ With 'correspondence' package

☐ Other _____

Why did you decide to purchase this Text? *(Tick one box only)*

☐ Have used BPP Texts in the past

☐ Recommendation by friend/colleague

☐ Recommendation by a lecturer at college

☐ Saw advertising

☐ Saw information on BPP website

☐ Other _____

During the past six months do you recall seeing/receiving any of the following?
(Tick as many boxes as are relevant)

☐ Our advertisement in *ACCA Student Accountant*

☐ Our advertisement in *Pass*

☐ Our advertisement in *PQ*

☐ Our brochure with a letter through the post

☐ Our website www.bpp.com

Which (if any) aspects of our advertising do you find useful?
(Tick as many boxes as are relevant)

☐ Prices and publication dates of new editions

☐ Information on Text content

☐ Facility to order books off-the-page

☐ None of the above

Which BPP products have you used?

Text	☑	Success CD	☐	Learn Online	☐
Kit	☐	i-Learn	☐	Home Study Package	☐
Passcard	☐	i-Pass	☐	Home Study PLUS	☐

Your ratings, comments and suggestions would be appreciated on the following areas.

	Very useful	Useful	Not useful
Introductory section (Key study steps, personal study)	☐	☐	☐
Chapter introductions	☐	☐	☐
Key terms	☐	☐	☐
Quality of explanations	☐	☐	☐
Case studies and other examples	☐	☐	☐
Exam focus points	☐	☐	☐
Questions and answers in each chapter	☐	☐	☐
Fast forwards and chapter roundups	☐	☐	☐
Quick quizzes	☐	☐	☐
Question Bank	☐	☐	☐
Answer Bank	☐	☐	☐
Index	☐	☐	☐

Overall opinion of this Study Text   Excellent ☐   Good ☐   Adequate ☐   Poor ☐

Do you intend to continue using BPP products?   Yes ☐   No ☐

On the reverse of this page are noted particular areas of the text about which we would welcome your feedback. The BPP author of this edition can be e-mailed at: katyhibbert@bpp.com

Please return this form to: Nick Weller, ACCA Publishing Manager, BPP Learning Media Ltd, FREEPOST, London, W12 8BR

Review Form & Free Prize Draw (continued)

TELL US WHAT YOU THINK

Because the following specific areas of the Text contain new material and cover highly examinable topics etc, your comments on their usefulness are particularly welcome.

Please note any further comments and suggestions/errors below

Free Prize Draw Rules

1   Closing date for 31 January 2008 draw is 31 December 2007. Closing date for 31 July 2008 draw is 30 June 2008

2   Restricted to entries with UK and Eire addresses only. BPP employees, their families and business associates are excluded.

3   No purchase necessary. Entry forms are available upon request from BPP Learning Media Ltd. No more than one entry per title, per person. Draw restricted to persons aged 16 and over.

4   Winners will be notified by post and receive their cheques not later than 6 weeks after the relevant draw date.

5   The decision of the promoter in all matters is final and binding. No correspondence will be entered into.